# A NEW HISTORY OF SOCIAL WELFARE

Phyllis J. Day

*Purdue University*

PRENTICE HALL, Englewood Cliffs, New Jersey 07632

LIBRARY OF CONGRESS
Library of Congress Cataloging-in-Publication Data

Day, Phyllis J.
    A new history of social welfare / Phyllis J. Day.
        p.   cm.
    Bibliography
    Includes index.
    ISBN 0-13-613440-8
    1. United States--Social policy.   2. Social policy--History.
3. Public welfare--United States--History.   4. Public welfare-
-History.     I. Title.
HN57.D33  1988
361.6'1'0973--dc19                                           88-9617
                                                              CIP

Editorial/production supervision and
  interior design: *Marianne Peters*
Cover design: *Joel Mitnick Design, Inc.*
Manufacturing buyer: *Peter Havens*

*To*
*My Mother*
*Nora Isabel Seymour Phelps*
*1892—1957*
*who loved unconditionally and taught me unconditional love*

*And to All Women*
*for Their*
*Wisdom, Strength, Courage, and Endurance*

Printed in the United States of America

10  9  8  7  6  5  4  3  2  1

ISBN 0-13-613440-8

Prentice-Hall International (UK) Limited, *London*
Prentice-Hall of Australia Pty. Limited, *Sydney*
Prentice-Hall Canada Inc., *Toronto*
Prentice-Hall Hispanoamericana, S.A., *Mexico*
Prentice-Hall of India Private Limited, *New Delhi*
Prentice-Hall of Japan, Inc., *Tokyo*
Simon & Schuster Asia Pte. Ltd., *Singapore*
Editora Prentice-Hall do Brasil, Ltda., *Rio de Janeiro*

# CONTENTS

# PREFACE

Traditionally, a preface is the place where we thank those who have contributed to the accomplishment that is a book. Throughout my life, people have touched me with their feelings, thoughts, and knowledge, and this book is, in a very true sense, a part of the part of me that was part of them. My teachers, my colleagues, my students, my friends, my family of origin and of marriage—all who participated in my life have contributed to the book.

The book itself is an attempt at answering the "why" of social welfare. In great part, it is a history of those involved in the social welfare institution, not as its wielders, but as its subjects/victims/recipients/clients. It seeks to redress in part the loss of history for women, people of color, and other oppressed groups, and to relate intimately the place of the labor force and working people with the social welfare institution. The breadth of the book insures its failure to adequately cover its aspirations. I am well aware of much left undone, either through lack of space/time or knowledge. However, it is a beginning from which students and others can seek more deeply and, hopefully, fill in the blanks that I could not.

*A New History of Social Welfare* is exactly that—an attempt to look at the earliest forces for both aspects of social welfare—social treatment and social control. These themes are carried forward from a perspective that considers the synergistic relationships of economy, polity, religion, and social welfare and asks the "why" of treatment and/or control. To this end, attention is paid to anthropological and archeological evidence of the ways people related to each other from as early as 20,000 B.C. It is from that point that the book views the societal contexts of social welfare and the needs of society's members either to provide care for valued members or to ensure enough members for social tasks.

Because social welfare today is so deeply affected by institutional racism, sexism, classism, and "otherism," the historical and evolutionary sources of these "isms" is given a great deal of attention. One of the results of institutional discrimination has been an "elimination" of history, or a selective compilation as a series of achievements of men who are generally Caucasian or Aryan and of the elite and/or warrior classes. This reading of history ignores or in many ways belittles the contributions of women, of people of color, and of the poor laborers upon the backs of which history occurred. While *A New History* cannot hope to redress all these issues, it does provide much new or reinterpreted historical information to set events in a more unbiased social context.

Of particular import in this perspective is the analysis of humankind's "relationships with deity"—religions—both in providing charity and in elaborating upon or perpetuating social control. This dichotomy of religiously-legitimated charity or control underlies the development of social welfare in all its ramifications, the values that provide the "push" to helping or controlling "others," and the ways in which the profession of social work itself came into being and grew. Religions thus are synergistically related to other major institutions of society, whether we speak of European feudalism, the European invasions of the Western Hemisphere, colonial America, the Progressive movement of the early 1900s, or the conservative backlash of the Reagan era. This synergism, then, becomes the key to this book's historical analysis of social welfare and the social work profession.

And now to thank those who helped me with this project. The greatest influence on the book and on my life was my mother, Nora Seymour Phelps, dead these many years. She gave me, from the beginning of my life, the courage to follow my ideals and convictions and to search for reality no matter where the path might lead. Though her heart finally failed her, her spirit never did. Also, my sisters have contributed more than they know, with strength, endurance, and courage throughout their hard lives: Avah, who always knows that "things will be better tomorrow": Evah, with her gentle courage; and Lois—scrappy and determined to have what the world offers. Thanks also to my mentors: Rosemary C. Sarri, who serves as a model, however unattainable, for more women than she knows; and John E. Tropman, who always believed in me. My former husband, Jerald R. Day, and my children—Jerry II, Nora, Merry, Sean, and Joy—have helped and supported me in innumerable ways, as have my friends.

On the more prosaic level, my thanks go to the editors and personnel at Prentice Hall, especially Nancy Roberts, Sociology Editor and Marianne Peters, my Production Editor; to my reviewers: Albert Roberts, Indiana University; George Siefert, Jr., Daemen College; and Jack Otis, University of Texas-Austin; to my daughter Merry Rose, for her careful reading of the manuscript to insure its coherence; and to my daughter Joy Alyssa, for her help in manuscript preparation.

My thanks to you all.

Phyllis J. Day

# 1

# *VALUES IN SOCIAL WELFARE*

## AN INTRODUCTORY STATEMENT

Once upon a time . . .
  This is a book about love—a story of people helping others, of organizations set up to ease the way of people in trouble, and of people joining together to work for the benefit of others. Love—the idea of helping others—inspires each of us to enter the field of human services, to share our efforts, and to work for the well-being of humanity. Our first and best intentions are to care for others, to help the disadvantaged "live happily ever after." But love is not enough. Social welfare and the profession of social work are much more complex, and we must not let fairy tales blind us.
  Love's dark side is power, and society, through social welfare, uses that power to control. Both help and control are traditions of social work and social welfare, and through them we help to maintain society's structures of inequality. Despite society's investment in social welfare, our own commitment as social workers, or the willingness or ability of our clients, we will not be able to change those structures unless we understand both sides of social welfare. As it is, our targets for blame and change are misplaced. We will blame our clients when they fail despite our efforts; they blame themselves for failure; and society blames both clients and social workers for wasted money and lost effort when poverty continues, when deviant behaviors rise, and when clients remain ungrateful and unrepentant. To understand this, we must throw away our fairy tales and begin to question the "why" of social welfare and social work.

*Why* is a good question, and one we should ask more often. Why have our welfare rolls grown, and why is there hunger in America? Why is there more crime and delinquency? Why are so many people homeless? Why are mental health clinics doing a booming business? Why are there so many people with problems, and why are our prisons filled to overflowing? And why do the costs for all forms of social welfare continue to rise? The answers lie in understanding society's institutions, how social welfare evolves from their interactions, and what purposes social welfare really serves.

Our purpose in this book is to ask these questions. Our major theme is that synergistic evolution[1] of the institutions of *polity, religion,* and *economy* throughout time creates both social problems and their solutions, and that social welfare and social work—its action arm—are the results. Synergy is "cooperative action of discrete agencies so that the total effect is greater than the sum of the effects taken independently."[2] We cannot study any of the institutions of society alone, for they are interdependent. We must look at their dynamic interactions to understand the institution of social welfare. Another theme is that society has rigid structures that maintain inequality, and that social welfare, because of its synergistic evolution, is a context for social control.

In this chapter, we will lay a groundwork for answering questions by looking at the place of social work and social welfare in society. We will look first at American social values; second, at issues of poverty and classism; and finally, at institutional discrimination in American society. We will try to discover the synergistic sources and meanings of our values and their impact upon perceptions and practices of social welfare. To do this, we may need to place some of our own beliefs and values in abeyance, for much of what we "know" is value. This is not an easy task, but it is essential.

## VALUES IN SOCIAL WELFARE

Social welfare in any society has two major purposes: social treatment (helping) and social control. We easily agree with the helping purpose but are generally almost unaware of the social control function of social welfare because it is hidden in ideas about equality and what we think is our "right" to change our clients. Society needs certain social controls, for some behaviors must be regulated so that interdependent people can live and work together. However, not all such control is positive, and social welfare controls aim at our most vulnerable citizens. Because our clients need our help, they must meet our (and society's) demands. Seldom do they participate in social welfare decisions that affect their lives in social welfare, and the price they pay for our help is often their personal freedom.

Our personal, societal, and social work values are, therefore, perhaps the most important factors in the practice of social work. Naomi Brill points out that

> We hold that all people are equal, but that those who do not work are less equal. . . . We hold that individual life has worth, but that only the fit should

survive. We believe that we are responsible for each other, but that those who are dependent upon others for their living are of less worth.

She says further that human service workers are walking value systems, and that they need to become aware of those values, evaluate them rationally, and change the irrational ones.[3] Paternalism, or the idea that we know what is good for others, is another problem. Because we have succeeded we think we have the right to impose our values and decisions on those who have not. It implies that our clients lack something, that they are less than whole persons, and

> . . . need to be brought up to our . . . levels . . . [W]e, as experts and whole persons, have the ability, knowledge and the right to round out, remake, fulfill, or "pull [them] up" . . . there is a "right way" which the expert knows, and a "wrong way" which the client does that underlies and colors the whole intervention process.[4]

Values permeate social welfare no matter the perspective, culture, or period of history: what we "ought to" provide or how we "ought to" deal with deviants. Every perception or reaction is value-laden and value-based, and we can never be truly objective. Therefore, as social helpers, we have no "right" to impose what we believe on the lives of others. Our clients' life situations and life experiences are different from ours, and though we can empathize, we cannot understand their lives. To assume that we do, to make life decisions for them, is unethical. While society has a right to control dangerous or destructive behaviors, most of social work does not involve those problems. We should not, therefore, enforce conformity to norms that may not be relevant to the life situations of others. In fact, this often creates or perpetuates their problems.

Our attitudes and values are often couched in religious, moral, or patriotic terms, and these attitudes and values are so much a part of our lives that we think they are facts rather than beliefs. A fact is the quality of being actual or having objective reality,[5] while a value is something intrinsically desirable.[6] Or, in more practical terms, a fact is the way things are, while a value is how we wish they were.[7] We "know" both facts and values, but we may confuse them and base important judgments on what we wish rather than on what is. We should always test what we "know" by remembering that whether something is a value or a fact is whether it has existed throughout history and in every culture.

### What Are Values?

In addition to values being "the way we wish things were," they have four identifiable characteristics, according to Hunter and Saleeby.[8]

1.  Values are *conceptual abstractions* drawn from immediate experience—from what we ourselves have learned about the world. Our unique experiences make each value unique to each of us (and to our clients).
2.  Values are *affectively charged for emotional mobilization;* that is, they make us want to take action or make us feel emotionally positive or negative about a

situation. Racism, for example, makes us angry when we see it in others, and perhaps embarrassed or unhappy when we see it in ourselves, and we want to do something about the problem.

3.  Values are *criteria by which our goals are chosen.* For example, abortion is a tremendously charged value in our society. Almost every one of us takes a stand on abortion, based on whether we believe in the right of every fetus to survive or the right of every woman to control her own body. We set goals about abortion for ourselves and often work to set abortion standards for others.

4.  Values are of *important rather than trivial concern.* We may prefer the color blue, or to go to one university rather than another, but these issues do not stir us to emotionally charged action. Rather, issues which involve basic questions of life, death, freedom, our rights as citizens or as workers, the concern we have for others—these are concerns which move us to anger, pride, fear, hope, or love and to actions to attain or resolve these emotions.

Miringoff and Opdycke say about values that

> They are always in a state of change; sometimes they merge to form coherent systems, sometimes they have vague relationships, often they are in conflict. . . . [They] may be influenced by occupation, race, age, class position, or by external factors such as changing economic conditions and new norms of social behavior.[9]

## Foundations of Charity and Control

To find where our values come from, or the reasons for the "way we treat others," we must trace our way to two human characteristics so important that they are doctrines basic to Western society. The first is *mutual aid;* the second is *protection from others and "otherness."* These characteristics are, respectively, the bases of values concerning social treatment and social control. Often contradictory, they have caused major dilemmas in the way our social welfare institution works.

According to Webster, "a society is an enduring and cooperating social group whose members have developed organized patterns of relationships through interaction with one another."[10] For early humankind, these included actions against predators, animal or human, and care for dependents (at first probably a mother/child bond). The need for defense resulted in fears of "outsiders" and "otherness," while bonding was extrapolated into mutual aid in the wider society.

As families bonded together to share food and protection, mutual aid expanded to include other cooperative efforts such as building, hunting, or farming. Care of children came to include the caring for the helpless or valued members of the tribe—often the elders, who had been instrumental in leadership or religious activities. Even today we are likely to look first to the family of the person in need for help. In tandem with mutual aid, the abhorrence of "otherness" and defense against it meant protection of herds and homes from predators and, later, aggression to win more land and wealth from others. Eventually, fear and hatred of those outside the kin group were extended to ingroup persons who were "different" or posed a threat to tribal solidarity. A reluctance to share with "others" became firmly based, and today is a reluctance to help those who do not "fit."

## AMERICAN SOCIAL VALUES

In the United States, many basic values affect the human services, and all seem so positive that we rarely question them even when they contradict one another. However positive they may be for society in general, they can be intensely negative for certain groups in our society—women, children, the unemployed, or people of color, for example. Among the most basic are

1. Democratic egalitarianism and individualism.
2. Judaeo-Christian charity values.
3. The Protestant work ethic and capitalism.
4. Social Darwinism.
5. The new Puritanism.
6. Patriarchy.
7. Marriage and family values.
8. The "American Ideal."

### Democratic Egalitarianism and Individualism

Democratic egalitarianism originated with the founding of the United States. We believe that all citizens are equal before the law, and no one has privileges above the law based on class, heritage, wealth, or any factors irrelevant to citizenship. No citizen is "better" than any other. All citizens can share equally in societal decisionmaking, either through direct vote or representation. Although an equal share of resources is not guaranteed, the right to opportunities—education and employment to win that share, for example—is.

Despite the ideal, in practice we do not have equality in America. Originally, the Constitution gave citizenship only to male property-holders, denying it to women, the propertyless, white ethnic immigrants, and people of color, primarily Native Americans, people of African descent, Hispanics, and Orientals. Although all native-born men (except for Native Americans) became full citizens after the Civil War, women could not vote until 1918, and Native Americans gained citizenship even later. Even then, the rights of Afro-Americans were denied by fiat until the Civil Rights Acts of 1964, and women are still denied explicit equal rights under national law. Custom still restricts achievement opportunities from people of color, women, and other minority groups. Moreover, choice of candidates and policies often depends on wealth and power. The poor have little power to choose, and the middle class choose among those selected by the elite. Still, our persistent belief in American equal opportunity has major impact on our assessment of client motivations and capability.

Related closely to egalitarianism is individualism—the ideal of individual effort and personal motivation by which any American can achieve success. It is a frontier ideology, coming from early days in America when anyone could win success in the new world of free land. Today, the value persists in the idea that there are frontiers of the mind, and that education, technology, and hard work can win wealth and success if only we try hard enough. Everyone must be self-reliant—in control of and responsible for his or her own life—and sheer effort will bring success. To ask for help from others is an admission of weakness, and failure to achieve—money, happiness, status, whatever—is the fault of the individual rather than society.

From this comes our tendency to "blame the victim," that is, to place the burden of failure on personal lack of effort. People are poor because they will not work rather than because of high unemployment. A person who is robbed or raped should not have been where such crimes could happen, or in some way "asked for it." The aged poor should have planned better for retirement, and poor children are hungry because their parents fail rather than because society does not provide social insurance. Our "blanket value" of individual responsibility exonerates society and confirms personal failure for those who cannot or do not reach "success."

Success, of course, has many meanings, and social workers should help clients to achieve their own successes, not ours. Moreover, because American society is neither fully egalitarian nor democratic, structures such as institutional discrimination and class stratification keep some people from achieving as we might. Opportunities do not accrue automatically with citizenship, and "blaming the victim" will not overcome structural barriers to success.

### Judaeo-Christian Values

These values are based, first, on Judaic teachings of social justice and, second, on the teachings of Jesus as practiced in the early centuries of Christianity. They are nonsectarian and social rather than religious, and their major thrust is that those in need have a right to help and society has an obligation to provide for them. They are Western society's primary social ethics and are the basis for social altruism. Their prescriptions of love and charity are the reasons, probably, that people enter the human services.

Judaic prophets as early as Amos, in the eighth century B.C., enjoined people to charity as social justice and religious obligation. They believed that human relationships mirror those between deity and humanity, and that people must care for one another as God cares for them. Every person has intrinsic worth, and charity should be given without thought of self. Early Christian traditions reiterated and strengthened the prophetic Judaic teachings, adding ideas of equality for women. Jesus advocated for the poor and helpless, calling for justice for women, the poor, children, and other unfortunates. However, as time wore on, most of this advocacy position was lost.

If Judaeo-Christian values still underlaid the institution of social welfare, we would see a far different America. No one would be without enough to eat, clothing, or shelter. Every child would be assured of equal opportunity in the system, and society would take responsibility for all the disadvantaged. While work for self-support would still be encouraged, a person in need could seek help without stigma. Failure would not be blamed on the individual but on the social structures that prevented success. Oppression and exploitation would not exist, and success would be investing in the lives of others rather than in personal wealth for oneself.

Social work *ethics* reflect Judaeo-Christian values, but social work *practice* owes more to other, more individualistic, values. These distinctions help us to understand why our social programs are not always socially just, and why our clients cannot succeed despite our "good works." Although we may have decided on social work as our profession because of its ethical Judaeo-Christian values, society's goals for social welfare are more accurately based on other, more restrictive values.

### The Protestant Work Ethic

The Protestant work ethic is the moral basis for the American capitalistic economic system—the search for profit through business enterprises mostly uncontrolled by the government. A social rather than an economic creed, Americans regardless of religion accept the Protestant ethic as a part of American life. Its complex of values includes individualism, personal achievement and worth, the morality of wealth, and, for America, patriotism. In it, *work for economic gain* is the way to success, a sign of personal morality, and a moral obligation. Conversely, poverty and public dependency demonstrate immorality.

The work ethic springs from the mercantilist movement of the early Middle Ages, the many new technologies of the fourteenth century, and the Protestant Reformation. Martin Luther's belief in work as a "calling" and John Calvin's teachings on predestination were interpreted to mean that those predestined to salvation in this life could be identified by evidences of their wealth. If wealth, then, showed morality, surely poverty demonstrated immorality. With this line of reasoning, the wealthy could justify their wealth and their exploitation of workers to accumulate it. It also legitimated the idea that the rich had a moral obligation to save the poor by making them work. More goods than could be used could then be produced through new technologies and the exploitation of laborers, and the profits from their sale in the new international market could be reinvested to make more profits—the "just rewards" of the wealthy.

Our definitions of "worthy" and "unworthy" poor come from the Protestant work ethic. The worthy poor were those who could not work— the aged or disabled, for example. However, most poor people were thought just to be lazy; they could have worked if they wanted to, or could have supported their families if they worked hard enough. That their labor was purchased at the convenience of the owners rather than because of their need meant long periods of unemployment or underemployment, but the owners, and their religion, did not consider this important. The new doctrine of personal fault both relieved them of the economic burden of supporting the poor, and gave them "religious credit" for not furthering the immorality of pauperism.

Today, we still believe that poverty is the result of laziness or degeneracy, for the work ethic is so important a value in American society that we do not even see who the poor really are—young children, mothers who care for them, women, the aged, the disabled. Moreover, changing technologies and governmental programs mean new unemployment and underemployment, but we insist, because of the work ethic, that anyone who wants to work can earn enough to live on.

## Social Darwinism

The Protestant work ethic combined with nineteenth-century social and biological theories to produce a theory that said the poor, or economically unfit, had no inherent right to survive. Darwinism, a biological theory never intended to become an economic one, says that organisms that cannot survive in an ecological niche will die out. This theory was extrapolated by Malthus into a social and economic one: He looked at population trends and foresaw a future teeming with poor people supported by "worthy" hard workers. From these ideas arose Social Darwinism, which said that to support the poor was against the laws of "economic nature," and that the lives of people who were not "economically fit" should not be saved by giving them public assistance. Moreover, the economically unfit were poor by choice; that is, because of their moral degeneracy. If society continued to aid them, it too would be destroyed by their immorality. Since success is evident from wealth, those who fail economically are unfit for our society and *should* perish.

Although rarely espoused openly today, Social Darwinism exists covertly in many welfare policies and programs and in the public idiom. Along with the Protestant work ethic, it opposes Judaeo-Christian charity values and helps to explain our society's loathing of "reliefers." Programs of public assistance show these values clearly in low grants, stigmatization of recipients, insensitive and irrelevant eligibility testing, and attempts to put recipients to work regardless of wage or personal situations. We believe that supporting the needy contributes to their economic immorality, and we are blind to the support our work values give to the wealthy by maintaining a controlled low-wage work force.

## Puritan Morality

This value arose from the political, economic, and religious changes of the fourteenth century and now permeates American society. Puritan morality includes sexual morality, particularly for women; honesty in dealing with others; abstinence from things defined by religion and custom as immoral, such as promiscuity, gambling, or the use of alcohol or drugs to excess; and "proper" behavior—that is, behavior which will not offend others. Puritan morality also emphasizes the sanctity of marriage and family and patriarchal authority in the home and condemns life-styles such as communal living or homosexuality.

Today there is a new Puritanism spearheaded by the "Moral Majority" and adhered to by many, who call for a return to the patriarchal and Puritan morality of the past and campaign for legislation to enforce compliance with their beliefs. The movement uses modern technology in its battles: Television brings moral campaigns into our homes and promises a better world, and computer availability makes immediate contact on action issues possible. The effect is widespread. The new Puritanism has catapulted conservative people into office and removed more liberal incumbents, and its followers continue to sponsor laws restrictive to women's choices in reproduction, employment, and marriage and family roles. It is militant on the side of law and order, seeks limits on freedom of expression and of the press, and attacks the principle of separation of church in its school prayer support. On the international level, though today the world's nations are almost completely interdependent, it advocates national insularity and the need for military force to maintain it.

### Patriarchy

Patriarchy is a system in which power and authority are invested in men, and women and other powerless groups, such as children, workers, or slaves, are oppressed and often owned. In a patriarchal society, male authority permeates every institution: In the polity, men hold most appointed and elected offices and make laws, decisions, and policies; in the economy, men hold most positions of economic power and have primary control of capital, resources, and the production and distribution of goods and services; in religion, men hold the highest offices and decide on the moral standards of society; and in the family, men are the major decision makers and authority figures.

Patriarchy is more than the domination of women by men, though that is a major symptom. The system comes from early history when patriarchs—heads of families—took absolute power over their families and clans and conquered weaker tribes to confiscate their lands, wealth, and people. Their religions gave legitimation to conquest, and religion and patriarchy bonded together to produce a new kind of society. Patriarchy has now evolved into a worldwide system of exploitation by Western society: of women (sexism), the poor (classism), nonwhite persons (racism), and of persons and governments of Third World countries (colonialism or imperialism).

Women have suffered dual oppression: as women in male societies and as workers in patriarchal systems. They have been bought and sold or married for political liaisons; laws have controlled their sexuality; and their reproduction has been governed by law and religious custom to produce children as workers or to carry on men's inheritance. In marriage, in the labor force, or in systems of public assistance, they and their children are economically dependent, and ultimately their subsistance and their well-being depend on the largesse (or lack thereof) of men. Patriarchy also dictates sex role socialization: for men, support of the family is the major role; for women, all should be married and dependent on men for the greater share of their well-being.

According to sex role socialization, men and women have natural or God-given "spheres of competence." Men are stronger, more capable in politics and economics, more logical, and more independent and so should rule and control resources in households, in the workplace, and in positions of power throughout our social institutions. Their primary role is to support their families through paid employment. Women excel in caring for and loving others, in homemaking tasks, and in helping the dependent. They are more emotional, more intuitive and less logical, less able to deal with stress, more dependent, and more given to unruly or flighty reactions. In the home, women's proper role is wife, bearer and rearer of children, and homemaker for a nuclear family. Outside the home, they should be care-givers—social workers, nurses, housekeepers, secretaries, and teachers, especially on the elementary level.

Patriarchy is a primary issue for dependency, because its structures keep women dependent. Whether they will be employed, the kind of work they are hired for, and their income depend on the men in control of the job market. Women work in lower-paying stereotyped jobs, and their incomes for equal or comparable work are usually lower than those of men. Married women, whether they work or not, depend primarily on their husbands for economic support. Previously married women are ultimately responsible for dependent children, and must depend on the courts to ensure support from their husbands, on social insurance if their husbands die, on the employment market to give them jobs, or on public assistance to support them. In every case, women and their children are dependent on patriarchal systems—marriage, employment, legislative or judicial systems, and public assistance. Men also are dependent on patriarchal structures, but have more freedom since, after all, they are more legitimate in patriarchal systems. Nevertheless, most men are workers, and they are constrained to the single role of family support. To lose their jobs is devastating, for men usually base their self-concept on their work roles. Thus patriarchy can be brutal for men as well as for women.

## Marriage and the Nuclear Family

Marriage is one of the strongest American values. It is a social, sexual, and economic relationship in which a man and a woman are legally joined to found and maintain a family. In America, we believe that people should marry and raise families. Even with the explosive divorce rate since 1940 (now almost half of all marriages end in divorce) the goals and customs of courtship, marriage, and family persist, and "happily ever after" is still the ideal. The nuclear family is highly valued—husband, wife, and children living together and sharing emotional and economic resources.

Patriarchy underlies our society's expectations for marriage and family. While both men and women should be married, we stigmatize singleness for women, particularly after a certain age, while single men have a certain glamour. Young women, expecting to be married, seldom train for the reality of self-support, while young men do, knowing they will support families. Women who work after marriage are still considered by many to be "supplementing their husbands' income," even though in today's economy both marriage partners must work to support their families. Monogamy is both law and custom, and although serial monogamy is usual today (as people marry, divorce, and remarry), fidelity within any marriage is demanded for women and often overlooked for men. Sexuality outside the marriage bond is frowned upon unless it leads to marriage, and is considered promiscuity for women but "sowing wild oats" for men. If it leads to pregnancy, generally the woman is "blamed," and before marriage, within marriage, or after marriage custom demands that women take "life responsibility" for children. Married couples are expected to have children, and those who do not are often criticized. "A man's home is his castle," and men are authorities within their homes in their treatment of wife and children. In the outside world, men are the major liaisons, in gaining credit or for insurance or purchase agreements, for example.

If marriages fail, though the emotional consequences may be terrible for both men and women, the financial consequences are usually more severe for women. Even in the best cases, where men pay support conscientiously, there are now two families and two dwellings on a single income. If women work, their employment pays less than that of men even for most equal or comparable jobs, and women without professional training (because they did not expect to work) are generally hired only in sex-stereotyped, low-paying jobs. With children to support on a lower income, they are more likely than any other group to sink into poverty, and female-headed households—single mothers with children—are the fastest growing type of family.

There are equally strong negative values based on marriage. Anti-singleness is one, particularly for women; though in some situations, such as income tax, it works against both men and women. Divorced and never-married women, with a few exceptions, are also stigmatized, and even widows undergo some social ostracism. Heterosexuality is required, and the fear and hatred of homosexual people (homophobia or heterosexism) is one of our strongest prejudices. Also, although new family patterns are being tried, such as communes or extended families, homosexual couples, or nonmarried heterosexual couples living together without marriage, these are generally stigmatized by society. Female-headed families, for whatever reason there is no longer a man in them, are subject to many kinds of problems that indicate society's dislike both of women and non-conformity to marriage.

### The White Anglo-Saxon Ideal

Values about personal appearance, though they may at first seem trivial, interact with other attitudes in society and underlie our self-concepts. In a society which values the white, Anglo-Saxon Protestant ideal, to be or look different is no small thing. We are socialized early in life to admire the white middle-class "look": clothes we should wear and television-clean homes. Our early readers are of the "Dick and Jane" variety, and children's books and games favor pretty white children. Our history books tell us of intrepid Protestant white men who built a new world and their own fortunes; they tell us also of Native American *savages* and black *slaves*. Advertisements in books and on television show how we "ought to" look, and there are hundreds of books and health centers that promise to help us achieve that "look."

This "looksist" set of values includes individualism, racism (in that white people are preferred), and for men the Protestant ethic and for women dependency stereotypes. Generally speaking, men are supposed to be white, tall, dark (though sometimes blonde), and handsome. They are heroes—strong, young, virile, and independent. They are assertive and intelligent, and able to overcome all odds in the pursuit of excellence. The ideal woman is young, slender though buxom, blonde, blue-eyed, with delicate, beautiful features. She is dependent upon men and is loving, caring, and devoted to attaining a storybook home and family. Both men and women radiate health and activity.

There is an often not-so-subtle discrimination against those who look "different." It works against people who are not "handsome" or "pretty," against short men and tall women, obese people, older people, those who are not fair-skinned, and differently abled people who, defined by the wider society as "handicapped" or "disabled," do not reach our standards of physical perfection. We also see it in schools, where poor children may not be "clean enough," or their clothes may be shabby or unironed. It is particularly tied to racism: For example, Afro-American children prefer to play with white dolls but "discover" they themselves are not white when they come up against prejudice in schools.

Besides not liking others who are "different," we dislike ourselves if we are different. We are not thin enough, not tall enough, not short enough; too fat, too old, too dark, too clumsy, too ugly. Moreover, people prefer proximity to the American Ideal among those they work with, their love partners, their friends, and significant others, for it reflects well on people if they can attract beautiful others to their lives. While this kind of value should have no bearing on our attitudes to self or others, in fact it does, and we need to understand that part of our negative reaction comes not from what people are but how they look.

## ISSUES OF DISCRIMINATION

Our complex value systems legitimate social welfare as a helping process, but also set up expectations that can be negative and controlling. Two issues springing from these latter dominate economic life and social welfare services in the United States: classism and poverty, and institutional discrimination.

### Classism and Poverty

*Stratification and Wealth.*  Despite our belief in egalitarianism, the United States is basically a stratified society. *Social* stratification considers issues of position in society, education, employment, income, and even social aspirations as indicators of social position. *Class* stratification is the division of society into strata based on economic resources and assumes that other social indicators depend on income. *Classism* is prejudice against the presumed immorality of those in lower economic classes—beliefs that they are lazy, unmotivated, immoral, promiscuous, stupid, or incompetent.

All societies have some system of stratification, and some theorists argue that society needs to give rewards—money, prestige, and status—to ensure that necessary leadership positions are filled. People in the higher strata of society are motivated by such rewards to reach positions of power,[11] while the unmotivated take on the less pleasant tasks at lower positions. This sets up, then, "a theory of social position based on individual characteristics.[12] Studies that focus on lower social strata blame the poor personally for their lack of success, for their

> low motivation, alienation, pathology, low incentive, authoritarianism, inability to defer gratification, dependence, inferiority feelings, illegitimacy, fatalism, weak ego, matriarchal family structure, social organization, deep-seated distortion, marital instability, inability to interact with community institutions, superficial interpersonal relationships, suspicion of people outside the family structure, poorly developed voluntary associations, low levels of participation.[13]

Another set of theorists believes that society constructs barriers to achievement for some people. Tumin, for example, feels that class, race, religion, and sex are more important than are personal characteristics in lack of upward mobility, and that social stratification is repressive and limiting.[14] In our society, government and the economic elite maintain a political and economic status quo through legislative and administrative agreements on production. Among such agreements are unemployment levels, minimum wages, public assistance levels, training and education grants and opportunities, restricted housing and school systems, and so on. Within certain recent government constraints, employers have a constant pool of laborers seeking work at the lowest wage levels. They can pay these workers minimum wages, can hire and fire them more or less at will, and can deny them the benefits of longer-term employment. From this perspective, the market system itself creates the hardships of unemployment, underemployment, and life on public assistance. More obscure unwritten policies such as discrimination in unemployment or lack of access to birth control or abortions also keep the economy static in the larger sense. Politicians benefit with longer terms in office and the ability to control legislation, while the wealthy benefit through continued high profits.

The proportions of wealth and income for class strata in the United States have remained fairly stable for forty years despite programs intended to redistribute wealth. Although income has risen, the distribution of income is substantially without change (see Table l.l). The income of the wealthiest fifth of the population is at least seven times larger than the share of the bottom fifth, and while income has shrunk for the lower income levels, it has increased significantly for the top categories, especially increasing from 1981, the year President Reagan took office.

**TABLE 1.1**  **Distribution of Aggregate Income of American Families by Income Levels, Selected Years 1950–1985**

| YEAR | LOWEST FIFTH | NEXT LOWEST FIFTH | MIDDLE FIFTH | TOP-MIDDLE FIFTH | TOP FIFTH | TOP 5% |
|------|--------------|-------------------|--------------|------------------|-----------|--------|
| 1985 | 4.6% | 10.9% | 16.9% | 24.2% | 43.5% | 16.7% |
| 1981 | 5.0 | 11.3 | 17.4 | 24.4 | 41.9 | 15.4 |
| 1975 | 5.4 | 11.8 | 17.6 | 24.1 | 41.1 | 15.5 |
| 1970 | 5.4 | 12.2 | 17.6 | 23.8 | 40.9 | 15.6 |
| 1965 | 5.2 | 12.2 | 17.8 | 23.9 | 40.9 | 15.5 |
| 1960 | 4.8 | 12.2 | 17.8 | 24.0 | 41.3 | 15.9 |
| 1955 | 4.8 | 12.3 | 17.8 | 23.7 | 41.3 | 16.4 |
| 1950 | 4.5 | 12.0 | 17.4 | 23.4 | 42.7 | 17.3 |

*Source*: Winifred Bell, CONTEMPORARY SOCIAL WELFARE, New York: MacMillan Publishing Co., 1983, p. 57.

The percentage of income is substantially the same across the years, though the top 5 percent now has a greater share of the aggregate in income than at any time since 1955. The top fifth makes nearly ten times as much as the lowest fifth, and the top 40 percent makes about two-thirds of all income.[15]

Wealth is permanent property rather than income, and so is even more indicative of class stratification. It has not changed much over time: from 1910 until 1972, the richest 1 percent of adults has held about 21 percent of all wealth, though it rose to 36.3 percent in 1929 and was 29.2 percent in 1965. Bell says

> In 1972 more than three quarters of the wealth held by the top one percent was actually controlled by the top [one half of one percent] whose total net worth was . . . $721.7 billion . . . . [They held]
> *15.5 percent of real estate
> *56.5 percent of corporate stock
> *60.0 percent of bonds
> *13.5 percent of cash deposits
> *52.7 percent of debt instruments like notes and mortgages
> * 7.0 percent of life insurance (cash surrender value)
> *89.9 percent of all trusts
> * 9.8 percent of miscellaneous assets.[16]

All these assets are income producing and will earn even more money. Moreover, this top 1 percent of the population owns and controls the key economic corporations.[17] These data have not changed significantly over time.

*Poverty and Welfare.*    In our society, class stratification is the basis for poverty, not the other way around. While life for earliest humankind was surely hard and meager, subsistence depended on cooperation. Poverty, a social definition of relative differences in resources for groups in a society, was based on availability of food, prowess in gathering it, and ideals of mutual aid. Today's poverty depends on uneven distribution based on inegalitarian economic theories rather than on scarcity of resources. Social welfare is a partial response to need caused by these social theories, but is also based partly on the need to keep control of the poor and laborers available for production. Fortified by our value systems, poverty is, in our society,

1. An *economic* issue, both to keep people working and to provide them with subsistence.
2. A *political* issue based on the power to command production of resources.
3. A *class* issue entailing the division of society into economic strata.
4. A *religious* issue, for religion legitimates differential accumulation of wealth and defines charity as a religious duty.
5. A *women's* issue because of women's vulnerability to poverty, their life responsibility for children, and their caretaking of the needy.
6. An issue of *social control,* for since the fourteenth century the poor have been considered a social liability rather than a social obligation.

Two groups are traditionally most vulnerable to poverty: Women, along with their dependent children, and men and women laborers whose economic support depends on the desires of the privileged rather than their own needs. Women have been more continuously vulnerable because of the overlapping of sex and class discrimination: They share the economic status of the men on whom they depend, and without male support their economic options are limited. Moreover, most women are themselves workers. The poor are not a homogeneous group; they differ in as many ways as any segment of our population. However, they differ from the general population in ways stigmatized by society, and their differences are often compounded—first they are poor and/or unemployed, then many are women (often with dependent children) and/or people of color, and/or aged, and/or differently abled, and so forth. Multiple differences make for increasing social control.

Poverty and the poor have been continually redefined over time. Before medieval times, social and economic conditions were thought to cause poverty and there was no personal blame in being poor. With the beginning of mechanization and the end of feudalism, pauperism became first immoral and then criminal, and poor people were categorized into those whom society should or should not help. The state of the economy had little to do with opportunities for employment; thus blame fell on the poor for their own poverty. The concepts of worthy and unworthy poor arose, and by the beginning of the twentieth century, the worthy poor included people put out of work for social or systemic economic reasons, dependent children, the aged who had worked, and persons with physical or mental disability. By the middle of the twentieth century, the category of undeserving poor had changed again. While able-bodied men were still considered unworthy, women who were never married, divorced, separated, or deserted and had dependent children were also considered unworthy, and a note of sexual immorality was added to the idea of work immorality. The major stigmatization of poverty now falls on husbandless mothers and their children in the Aid to Families of Dependent Children (AFDC).

In 1974 all adult public assistance categories—Old Age Assistance, Aid to the Blind, and Aid to the Disabled—were moved to the Social Security Administration. This lessened the stigma of public assistance for most groups, and federal rather than local departments took over administration of the programs. Now only Aid to Families of Dependent Children, residual local programs of poor relief and general assistance, and Supplemental Security Income (SSI), which supplements Social Security benefits, are considered to be public assistance. AFDC is by far the largest of the three, and the AFDC program is administered at the local level, enabling welfare officials to monitor closely clients' moral and economic behavior. The Food Stamp Program of the Department of Agriculture is also administered at local levels, with the same kind of surveillance for its recipients, most often women and the families of the unemployed.

Poverty levels are set by the federal government on how much a short-term emergency diet would cost, and then multiplied by three, since people spend about a third of their income for food (see Table 1.2). States, however, set their own public assistance levels, which are generally lower than the federal poverty level. This, it is assumed, will provide a "work incentive" so that recipients will want to get off assistance. Experts estimate that only about a fourth of families living on such a budget get adequate nourishment, and special needs such as car repair or life insurance are not allowed for. Therefore, such a poverty line seriously underestimates the real needs of people, particularly since it lags behind inflation. In 1987, the poverty level for a family of four was a little more than $10,000.

By 1985, 33.1 million Americans, or about 14 percent of the population, lived below the official poverty level. Twenty-one percent of children under age 16, or about one of five, exists below the poverty level in the

**TABLE 1.2  Size of Family and Poverty Threshhold 1985[18]**

| SIZE OF FAMILY UNIT | POVERTY THRESHOLD |
| --- | --- |
| One person | $ 5,469 |
|   15 to 64 years | 5,593 |
|   65 years or older | 5,516 |
| Two persons | 6,998 |
|   householder 15 to 64 | 7,231 |
|   householder 65 and over | 6,503 |
| Three persons | 8,573 |
| Four persons | 10,989 |
| Five persons | 13,007 |
| Six persons | 14,696 |
| Seven persons | 16,656 |
| Eight persons | 18,512 |
| Nine or more persons | 22,083 |

United States (see Table 1.3). Approximately 75 percent of these poor are women and children, and two of every three poor adults are women.[19]

Of course, this is the official poverty line, but other means of determining poverty set the line much higher. By some estimates, 75 percent of all Afro-American and Hispanic children in the United States now live below the poverty level.[20]

The most vulnerable of the poor are children, and this group is increasing in number and in depth of poverty. Because of increasing divorce, their mothers usually bear the greatest burden of support, and women are increasingly shunted into poverty because of institutional sexism. This is called the "feminization of poverty."[21]

About 90 percent of AFDC recipients are women and their children, with an average grant of $120 per month.[23] Nearly half of all families in poverty are headed by women, and more than a third of all families headed by women live in poverty. To be a woman of color triples the jeopardy of poverty: While 9.1 percent of households headed by white women live in poverty, 27.1 percent of women-headed households in Afro-American and Hispanic families live in poverty. To be an aged woman without a husband nearly guarantees poverty: While the median annual Social Security grant for men is $5,479, for women it is $2,813, and 61 percent of all women over age 65 depend solely on Social Security for their income. Elderly widows had Social Security payments of $379 per month in 1982. However, divorced women of deceased men, if they had been married for ten years, had Social Security income of only $177 per month (1980).[24]

To quote statistics enables us to make comparisons among figures. To understand the despair of people who cannot feed their children, or scavenge in garbage cans for their food, or live over heat grates in the streets is more difficult. Most of us do not believe that poverty exists in the United States, or that if it does, it is the fault of the poor. These are easy rationalizations, ways out that permit us to maintain our own sense of well-being and to keep our values about hard work and individualism intact. However, poverty does not "just happen." It comes from our social values and the systems they maintain and is a result of a class-stratified society. The gap is maintained through economic practices enforced by legislation with deliberate intention to maintain the status quo.

With legislation and administrative decisions developed by persons who misunderstand social values for facts, our system protects the enterprises of the wealthy and causes them to grow. Although altruism exists, in such forms as grants and foundations, it exists within the context of the

**TABLE 1.3   Percentage Children Below the Poverty Line, 1985**[22]

|                | TOTAL | WHITE | AFRO-AMERICAN | HISPANIC |
|----------------|-------|-------|---------------|----------|
| Under age 18   | 20.7% | 16.2% | 43.6%         | 40.3%    |
| Under age 6    | 23.2  | 18.4  | 47.7          | 41.4     |

Source: U.S. Department of Commerce, Bureau of the Census, Current Population Reports Consumer Income 1987, Series P-60, No. 134 (Advance Report p. 31); and Statistical Abstracts 1987, Table A-L, "Weighted Average Poverty Thresholds in 1985" p. 33.

larger systems that perpetuate the problems of class stratification and poverty. As a society, we need major changes in social structures to end the disgrace of poverty. Such changes require values oriented to the comparative well-being of all citizens rather than to the maintenance of money privileges by a very few.

### Instititutional Discrimination

In America, institutional discrimination permeates our institutions and systems, so deeply embedded that it has become part of American societal structure. Based on irrational attitudes of hostility that have become reified in rules, regulations, and procedures, its forms—racism, sexism, homophobia or heterosexism, ageism, and "otherism"—deny equal rights and opportunities to groups of people even when no individual prejudice is involved. Moreover, the kinds of institutional discrimination interact with each other and with classism to enforce the status quo of our society: people discriminated against are more likely to be poor, and if more than one discrimination is present, the likelihood of poverty is even greater. For example, an aged Afro-American woman is in threefold jeopardy of being poor.

*Institutional Racism.*    Racism is prejudice against people of color: Afro-American, Hispanic, Oriental, and Native Americans. Our American values make us assume that race determines human traits and capacities and that white people are inherently superior to people of color. This is directly related to our hatred of "outsiders" or people who are different, and to the Protestant work ethic. The Protestant religion of our forebears legitimated their pursuit of wealth, and the idea that people of color were not as "human" as Caucasians allowed their exploitation. It was not simply their importation as slaves that has determined the continuing racism against Afro-Americans in this culture, nor their exploitation as workers.[25] Although many people have been exploited as they worked their way into the "American mainstream," people of color have been unable to move upward in American society regardless of their efforts, for they were not and could never be white. Over 80 percent of the American population is white. The rest of us are about 12 percent Afro-American, 5.5 percent Hispanic (about 12 million, with another 8 million illegal), and 2 percent other nonwhite groups, including Native Americans, Japanese Americans, and Chinese Americans.[26]

While estimates of Native American population at the time of conquest range upward from half a million, a more realistic figure is given by Dobyns: nearly 10 million in North America and tens of millions in Central and South America. By 1850, their population in North America, decimated by European weapons and disease, had fallen to approximately 200,000 to 300,000. In 1980, the Native American population was about 1.4 million.[27] More lived in cities than on reservations, and they are the most impoverished people in America. In 1980, their unemployment rate was more than double that of whites, and employment was heavily concentrated in lower-paying jobs—farm labor for men and service work for women. One-third lived in poverty. Housing and health care conditions are still worse for rural Native Americans than for any other group. Death rates are high, and people die young because of poor nutrition and lack of health care, which have worsened under the Reagan administration. Infant mortality is comparable to rates in poor Third World nations.[28]

Both Japanese and Chinese immigrants lived in the severest poverty when immigration began in the middle 1800s. However, Oriental Americans have managed to climb the economic ladder in America despite racism. Most are in white-collar jobs, though in larger cities women are likely to hold low-status, low-income service jobs. Oriental women have less income than do white women, but the 1980 median income for Japanese American families was slightly higher than that for whites.[29] Chinese Americans have not been quite so fortunate, nor have the most recent immigrants from Thailand or Korea. Still, their plight is not so desperate as that of other people of color in general.

Approximately 59 percent of our Hispanic Americans are of Mexican origin and 16 percent are of Puerto Rican heritage.[30] In 1979 one-fifth of Mexican Americans still fell below the official poverty line, and in 1980 median family income for Puerto Rican Americans was less than half that of white families.[31] Unemployment rates were 10.5 percent for Mexican Americans and approached 14 percent for Puerto Rican Americans in 1985. Most Hispanic workers are concentrated at lower job levels. Puerto Ricans are the poorest of American minorities, except for Native Americans.

The unemployment rate for Afro-Americans has consistently been about twice that of white people. In 1985, while the unemployment rate for white people was 6.2 percent, for Afro-Americans it was 15.1 percent (for Hispanics, 10.5 percent).[32] Even this is probably an underestimate: about half again that number are "discouraged workers"—those no longer seeking jobs. It is always higher among Afro-American youth, rising in the 1981-82 recession to 49.7 percent.[33] With underemployment—no jobs, part-time jobs, and jobs at poverty wages—their median income has remained at 55 to 60 percent of white income from the 1950s. This complicates marital stability: after two years of recession in 1981 the divorce rate for Afro-American families was two and a third times that of white families, and separation brought the rate almost four times as high. With unemployment held constant, the differences almost disappeared.[34]

Some individual Afro-Americans have succeeded: income in intact families rose from 62 to 77 percent of white families' income and, in northern and western regions, became equal.[35] Nevertheless, in the early 1980s, one-third of all Afro-American families were poor compared with one-tenth of white families.[36] Intact Afro-American families are two and a half times more likely to be poor, and such families headed by women are nine times more likely to be poor than are those headed by a white male.[37] Social programs do not help as much as we think: A National Urban League study in 1979 showed that 70 percent of Afro-American unemployed never get unemployment benefits, over half of poor Afro-American families get no welfare aid (such as AFDC), and half of all Afro-American families on welfare get no Medicaid.[38] Income is dictated by race, as shown in Table 1.4.

Institutional racism has a circular interconnection with poverty. For example, many Afro-Americans are poor and, therefore, must live in rental units owned by white people not living in the area. Their homes have a low property tax base, leading to poorly funded and equipped schools, and, given a choice, better or more experienced teachers will not work there. The lack of quality education and a high drop-out rate limit future employment and future income. Low income means they will remain in the ghettos. Even those who succeed may not be able to move because realtors and homeowners will not sell to them. If they can buy a home, they may be subjected to threats or bodily harm. Some theorists talk of a "culture of poverty,"[40] but we see rather a cycle of poverty based not on the values, beliefs, or desires of the poor but on institutional discrimination in housing, schools, and employment.

*Institutional Sexism.*    Sexism, probably our oldest prejudice, is gender privilege for men. It is based on patriarchal values and assumes the political, economic, intellectual, and spiritual inferiority of women solely on the fact of sex and without regard to individual capabilities. Institutional sexism has resulted in oppression and exploitation of women throughout history, and despite ongoing feminist movements, only since the 1960s have some of us recognized sexism as a national problem. Sexism is institutional in nature because it permeates not only home life, where the man is the authority, but economic, political, welfare, and religious structures.

In the economic arena, women's lack of power holds down their wages and makes them available at the need of the employer for temporary or seasonal work, and they have few job protections. They are subject to male rules for employment and are paid less than men for equal or comparable jobs. In the home, wife abuse has only recently come to our attention, and many women will not report it or act against it because of their fear of further abuse, stigmatization because they are unable to make their husbands happy, or poverty (among other problems). In the courts, male

**TABLE 1.4    Median Income by Race, 1985[39]**

|  | ALL FAMILIES | MARRIED COUPLES |
|---|---|---|
| Total | $26,433 | $27,735 |
| White | 27,686 | 29,152 |
| Afro-American | 15,432 | 16,786 |
| Hispanic | 18,833 | 19,027 |
| Mexican | 19,184 | xxx |
| Puerto | | |
| Rican | 12,371 | xxx |

*Source*: U.S. Department of Commerce, Bureau of the Census "Population Characteristics": *Statistical Abstracts of the U.S., 1987*, Table 19. "Selected Characteristics of Families—Poverty Status in 1985 of All Families and Families with Female Householder, No Husband Present," p. 29.

gender privilege is protected by low-support grants for dependent children, and in welfare low grants continue impoverishment. In law and in religion, women's right to control reproduction is continually challenged. In juvenile justice systems young women are incarcerated for "status offenses"—noncriminal morality charges. In mental health systems their assumed need for dependency or the needs of husband and children are often the telling factor in their treatment. They are seldom elected or appointed to high positions in the polity or religion. Finally, most religions still teach the "proper" roles for women as submissive and secondary, prolonging moral and emotional burdens for women who seek change in their personal situations.

Customs of education and training keep women "ghettoized" in low-paying sex-stereotyped jobs. They hold 80 percent of clerical jobs, 78 percent of service jobs, and 43 percent of professional jobs (mostly teachers and nurses). Even professional jobs, if they are "women's work," pay less than do men's lower skilled work, and often women are paid less for the same professional job. In April 1983, 69.5 percent of all women worked, but three out of five made less than $10,000 and one in three less than $7,000.[41] This means that nearly 60 percent of working women do not earn enough money to take them out of poverty. Married women make up 55 percent of working women yet earn less than do other working women, and women in general earn only 59 percent of what men earn. Increasingly women (and their children) are falling into poverty because of these skewed economic policies. In 1985,

*50.5 percent of all Afro-American woman-headed families were poor.
*53.2 percent of all Hispanic woman-headed families were poor.
*27.4 percent of all white women-headed families were poor.[42]

Today, divorce is on the upswing. Nationwide, women-headed families comprised 15 percent of all families in 1982, increasing between 1970 and 1980 by 24.1 percent. The number of these families has more than doubled since 1960, from 4.2 to 9.5 million families. Nearly one out of every four children lives with a single parent, usually the mother, and the poverty rate for this group is 36 percent. Among minority women-headed families, the rate is 53 percent. A family headed by a woman is four and a half times more likely to be poor than is a family that includes a married couple or one headed by a man (see Table 1.5).[43]

When families break up, usually the woman takes responsibility for the children, and more than half (52.3 percent) of the 12 million children who live in women-headed families are poor.[44] It has been said that a divorced man becomes single and a divorced woman becomes a single parent.[45] Support awards are low, and methods of collection are time-consuming, expensive, and ineffectual. In 1981, less than half of divorcing women (48.3 percent) were awarded child support, and less than half of these received the full amount.[46] Nearly 23 percent got less than what was ordered and 28.4 percent received nothing. The average support ordered in 1982 was $149.92 per month.[47] Public assistance (AFDC) gives an average grant (1986) of $351.45, with a low of $100.35 in Puerto Rico and $113.64 in Alabama and highs of $616.34 in Alaska and $552.84 in California.[48] This means that the lowest annual income on AFDC, in Puerto Rico, is $1,204, far below the poverty level. Even in Alaska, at $6,635, AFDC income is only a little more than one half the current poverty level. Low grants are said to provide a "work incentive," an encouragement to become employed. However, this "male pauper model" does not consider the lack of training of women for employment, their low wages, or child care needs. Moreover, seeking public assistance degrades women in terms of economic capability, sexual morality, and competence or fitness as mothers.

Aging is another complication for women. If they lose their husbands during their middle years, they are unlikely to find sufficient employment for family support because they lack current job training and experience. Social insurance payments end when their children reach age 17, and if they have no dependent children, they cannot receive AFDC. If they have dependent children, they may receive AFDC, but the grants are inadequate. About 52 percent of midlife women whose AFDC grants are terminated when their children reach age 18 remain in poverty.[50] Women's average earnings decrease compared to men's as they grow older. Because of lower overall wages during their employment years, they will receive lower social insurance and fewer pension benefits—in December 1986, the average male retiree received $6,580 in Social Security while the average older woman received $4,008.[51]

The myths of "Cinderella" and "the women's sphere" are so deeply engrained in our society that women themselves work to maintain them, by not training for better jobs, by accepting their secondary roles as natural, and by relieving men of responsibility for their impoverishment. Women will continue to be oppressed and exploited on all fronts of our society until we understand our patriarchal values, and changes in the sexist society are unlikely until our sexist myths are overcome.

*Institutional Ageism.*  *Ageism* is a preference for youth over older people and manifests itself not only in disrespect and the shunting aside of older people but in job discrimination against people after the age of about 40. Youth fits the American Ideal of active, assertive, future-oriented, and beautiful, and we see older people as ugly, doddering, unproductive, senile, or living in the past. Perhaps we fear our own aging, for we do not respect the wisdom and experience of our elders. Ageism is institutional in that, especially in economic issues but also in the family, older people are prevented from sharing in society. Many are poor, and despite our Social Security program, we do little to ensure that they will in fact be secure in

TABLE 1.5  Poverty Rates in Families, by Type and Race[49]

|  | INTACT FAMILIES | MALE | FEMALE |
| --- | --- | --- | --- |
| White | 6.9% | 12.2% | 27.9% |
| Black | 15.6 | 25.6 | 56.2 |
| Hispanic | 19.0 | 17.0 | 55.4 |

their old age. Also, our nuclear family system and our dedication to individualism move our elders out of the center of family life and into loneliness.

"Age" is a stereotype. Some people chronologically in their sixties may be as active, productive, and capable as much younger people. On the other hand, people as young as 30 often have stopped learning and become resigned and rigid in thought and deed. "Old" is an artificial designation that, in America, coincides with retirement age of about 65. We forget, however, that retiring people from work is relatively recent, from about the last half of the nineteenth century. It is an artifact of longer life and the demands that younger people be employed. When the Social Security acts of 1935 were passed, the United States was in the middle of its greatest depression. Giving pensions to older men not only gave them minimal support but took them out of the job market so that younger workers with growing families could be employed in what jobs there were. Women's retirement was not really an issue: they were discouraged from taking jobs away from men, but a great number were employed outside the home anyway. With labor demands and Social Security they were retired from the labor market along with men, but continued their usual jobs working in the home.

In 1985, there were 49,383,000 persons 55 years of age and older, with 27,322,000 persons 65 years and older.[52] Our elderly population above age 65 comprises 11.4 percent of the total. More than 80 percent of these Americans are retired even though they are "intellectually and physically capable of working."[53] Although we often think of older persons as less able to work, the slowdown that may occur is more than compensated for by experience, and older workers usually

> have lower turnover rates, produce at a steadier rate, make fewer mistakes, have a more positive attitude toward their work, and exceed younger employees in health and low-on-the-job-injury rates.[54]

Some pension plans make it attractive to retire as early as age 55. While some people may be ready to retire, because they are tired of working or have other things they want to do, enforced retirement may be a way of saying that society no longer has use for them. For many men, their work roles are their only roles, and retirement means for them a loss of identity. Moreover, the loss of income can be severe for many, particularly those working on the borderline of poverty. Approximately 12.6 percent of the elderly live in poverty (see Table 1.6), and their misfortune is compounded by racism and sexism. In 1981, 39 percent of elderly Afro-Amer-

**TABLE 1.6   Elderly Persons in Poverty, 1985[55]**

|  | TOTAL | WHITE | AFRO-AMERICAN | HISPANIC |
|---|---|---|---|---|
| Both Sexes | 12.6% | 11.0% | 31.5% | 23.9% |
| Male | 8.5 | 6.9 | 26.6 | 19.1 |
| Female | 20.8 | 16.2 | 43.8 | 39.0 |

icans lived below the poverty level. Women over 65 accounted for 70.9 percent of the aged poor in 1982.[56]

Across the board, a greater percentage of aged women are poorer than men, and the percentage soars among people of color. This reflects institutional sexism: Women throughout their lives earn lower wages, work only marginally during child-rearing years, receive inadequate child support and fringe benefits, and are therefore limited in the amounts of retirement pensions or OASDI payments they receive. It reflects also institutional racism, demonstrating that people of color often are not hired and, when they are, it is in marginal jobs primarily offering low pay and inadequate benefits such as retirement plans. Therefore, their old age is only minimally provided for.

Our societal emphasis on youth borders on geriatricide, in practice if not in intent. Our system of health care for the aged, Medicare, requires that they pay a monthly "premium," with another premium for extended care. The recession and recent budget cuts have increased these premiums, with the result that many of our elderly go without needed care. The poor elderly must exhaust most of their assets before they are eligible for Medicaid, a public assistance program. Life expectancy is about 71 years (for white women 77.7 years), and over three-fourths of the aged have at least one chronic condition. Moreover, the elderly face personal and emotional stress due to their time of life—loneliness, loss of loved ones, lack of purpose in life, retirement, and change of living arrangements—and these compound and often cause physical problems.

Institutional ageism, however, is not confined to the elderly. Rather, prejudice against *aging* begins around the age of 40. Businesses are unwilling to hire workers over this age, even though age discrimination is prohibited by law. Employers fear that older people will take too long to train and that their productivity will therefore be limited. Also, experienced workers must be paid more than new workers. Finally, medical insurance and fringe benefit costs paid by the company rise with the number of older workers. For these reasons, hiring at a later age and keeping productive people on after the age of 50 or so are discouraged.

This has been one of the most painful problems of the recent recession (1981–83), during which millions of blue-collar workers lost their jobs. This "new poor" group were middle-class workers who had worked for years with the same companies and believed they had security. However, the recession closed many industries, and employees young and old were laid off. Although they were promised that layoffs would be temporary, the deepening depression ensured their permanent unemployment. After their unemployment benefits were gone, they looked for new jobs but found that people between ages 50 and 65 would not be hired because of antiaging policies. Initially, this meant a lower standard of life, when they had been used to better. In the long run, lower or no income in the years when they expected their highest levels of earnings will mean lower Social Security and pension benefits in their retirement. For those whose identity revolved around support of their families, the toll in broken homes, mental illness, and even suicide has been high. Some have found work in marginal industries, but not before their accumulations of a lifetime were lost. Those still unable to find work are reduced to living on public assistance and food stamps.

*Homophobia or Heterosexism.*    This is a prejudice against or hatred of homosexuals—gay men and lesbian women. It is a product of Puritan morality and patriarchal values and is a form of institutional discrimination that permeates our social structures to deny a specific group equal rights and protections. It is estimated that about 15 percent of the nation's population is homosexual; that is, their love orientation is toward persons of the same sex. Because a heterosexual orientation is considered "normal," homosexuals fall outside the pale of major value systems—patriarchy, morality, marriage, nuclear family. Aside from sexual preference, the actions of homosexual people are no different from those of other members of the population, but stereotypes stigmatize and belittle them. Prejudice against them is usually religious in nature, based on heterosexist interpretations of Old Testament writings. However, homosexuality has existed throughout human history and was often considered preferable to heterosexuality.

Homophobia/heterosexism is blatant in our society despite the fact that some of our finest scholars, authors, and other highly productive people have been gay men and lesbians. Often they have been forced out of jobs. The profession of teaching is particularly forbidden because of the fear that children might be seduced into homosexuality. Some denominations of religions have only recently allowed homosexuals among their clergy; most will not acknowledge homosexual love relationships. Foster care or adoption is very difficult for even the most stable homosexual couple, and lesbian women and gay men divorcing heterosexuals have great difficulty in maintaining custody of their children. Defamation, blackmail against those who keep their sexual preference secret, and even physical injury are part of the expectations of homosexual people in our society. Discrimination forbids them the protection of many laws that most of us take for granted.

*Otherism.*    This is a catch-all category for people who, because of physical or social differences, do not fit the American Ideal. They may be differently abled, unsighted, obese, unattractive, or people "different" in innumerable ways. Discrimination against them varies: Those whom society calls "disabled," physically, emotionally, or mentally, are subject to more prejudice than are the obese or the unattractive. One estimate numbers handicapped persons in the United States at more than 40 million.

> There are 11.7 million physically disabled, 12.5 million temporarily injured, 2.4 million deaf, 11 million hearing-impaired, 1.3 million blind, 8.2 million visually impaired . . .[57]

There are also nearly 1 million mentally retarded people, and estimates of the seriously mentally ill range to about 2 million. While in 1843 Dorothea

Dix testified about the horrendous treatment accorded them, treatment today is, in some cases, as brutal: Foster care operators who abuse and sometimes even kill them; homeless people who must eat dog or cat food, or scavenge in garbage cans to eat; defenseless ones who are murdered on the streets; those who freeze to death when their covers of newspapers or cardboard homes cannot keep them warm enough. Of the 2 million seriously mentally ill in the United States, about 200,000 are in hospitals and treatment centers; 26,000 are in jails and prisons; 300,000 are in nursing homes; another 300,000 are in foster care or boarding homes; 200,000 live alone and 800,000 with their families; and 150,000 or so live in public shelters or on the streets.[58]

People with physical disabilities are probably the most discriminated against among the "different" in our society. Although they are guaranteed civil rights, such rights are often denied in ways as simple as access to buildings. Other rights are being eroded by the conservative trend of the 1980s; for example, the Education for All Handicapped Children Act of 1973 mandated school systems to identify and provide for the differently abled. Recent budget cuts have undermined such support systems for these children as social workers, psychologists, and special education teachers. Such wholesale cutting or elimination of programs for the disadvantaged demonstrates ever more clearly our underlying dislike for those who are "different" from the American Ideal.

This pervasive distaste toward "different" people in our culture adds an edge to those discriminated against in other ways. For example, people of color can never reach the examples set for American appearance because they are not white. Most women can never meet the American ideal of beauty, nor men of handsomeness. Obese people are constantly railed at, not only for health's sake but because fat is "ugly." These stereotypes of what people "should" look like may seem trivial in the face of more serious disadvantages. However, they are another part of a value system which honors certain people and demonstrates a social dislike of others.

Individual people may overcome the many barriers to success placed in their way by institutional discrimination, but as a group they cannot. This has little to do with their capabilities, will to succeed, or hard work but with the difficulty of overcoming social barriers. Whatever the situation, we need to look critically at why certain groups in our society are not succeeding so that we can develop compensatory plans and programs that will help make up for decades of institutional discrimination.

## CONCLUSION: VALUES AND POWER

When people seek our help, they admit they have lost control of part of their lives. However, they are *not* asking us to take over; rather, they need our help in regaining their own control. We must be very careful not to attempt to impose our own values upon them or to exercise our power over them. There are times, of course, when we must assert power—when people are a danger to themselves or to others—but this is the exception rather than the rule. In most cases, the use of power is an abuse of people, and our most precious values may encourage this abuse.

In general, social workers come from middle-class backgrounds, where hard work is the way to success. We believe in and reflect values of work, education, and perceptions of family life and define deviance by those lights. These values are not "wrong" or "bad" for us, and we can use them in our own lives as we please. However, now we know that values are not a reality common to all societies and cultures but derive from our own history and cultural belief systems. Most of our clients share these values, but because all people are unique so are their value interpretations, and some differences are sure to occur—reality is different to each of us. Too, the life situations of our clients require that they make different choices from those we might. We can never be in "the same situation" and must learn to respect their right to make the decisions best for them.

The provision of social services can be undermined by values in many ways. Although our primary mandate is to enable others, we may find ourselves placing unreasonable demands on their lives or seeking to control them. We become society's way of enforcing conformity to norms that may not be relevant to the problem at hand. Norman Goroff has called social workers "soft cops"[59] because our work often hides values that society, the agency, or we ourselves want to impose upon clients. They, however quickly, discover our hidden agendas and value biases and this discovery may hurt them deeply or cause them justifiable anger.

We began this chapter speaking about love, but we have discussed values that seem anything but loving. Probably some of your deepest beliefs have been touched in ways that you never expected. We may feel that since our work is inspired by love, it can only have good effects, but wisdom, not emotion, is the essence of the helping relationship. To help people to "fit in," if that is what they want, may be an appropriate task of social work. However, to aid them in understanding the institutions of society and to help them to use that knowledge in gaining their goals are probably the real gift of love to others.

## STUDY QUESTIONS

1. Name one universal morality issue that is a fact rather than a value.
2. What is the present-day impact of institutional discrimination on social welfare?
3. What are the positive and negative aspects of each American social value *vis-à-vis* social welfare?
4. Why is love not enough for social work practice? What else do we need?

## FOOTNOTES

[1]Peter A. Corning has posited a theory of human evolution which he calls "the synergistic hypothesis" in which biology and politics have interacted to create both modern humankind and its social structures. Carrying that idea further, we posit that all human social

structures, including that of social welfare, have evolved from the intimate and dynamic relationships among the polity, economics, and religion. The inclusion of religion is not a usual one, but we believe that humankind's relationship to spirituality and deity over time is primary in the consideration of both social treatment and social control aspects of social welfare. For further information on Corning's synergistic hypothesis, see Peter Corning, *The Synergistic Hypothesis: A Theory of Progressive Evolution* (New York: McGraw-Hill Book Company, 1983).

[2]Webster's *New Collegiate Dictionary* (Springfield, Mass.: G.& C. Merriam Company, 1980) p. 1174.

[3]Naomi Brill, *Teamwork: Working Together in the Human Services* (New York: J.B. Lippincott, 1976), pp. 12–15.

[4]Phyllis J. Day, "Social Welfare: Context for Social Control" *Journal of Sociology and Social Welfare* Vol.7 (March 1981, pp. 29– 44), p. 42.

[5]Webster's *Dictionary*, p. 406.

[6]Ibid., p. 1282.

[7]Beulah Compton, *Introduction to Social Welfare and Social Work: Structure, Function, and Process* The Dorsey Series in Social Welfare. (Homewood, Illinois: The Dorsey Press, 1980), p. 78.

[8]Mary Ski Hunter and Dennis Saleeby, "Spirit and Substance: Beginnings in the Education of Radical Social Workers." *Journal of Education for Social Work*, Vol. 13, no. 2, (Spring 1977), pp. 60–67.

[9]Marc L. Miringoff and Sandra Opdycke, *American Social Welfare: Reassessment and Reform* (Englewood Cliffs, N. J.: Prentice Hall, 1986), Ch. 1, p. 2.

[10]Webster's *Dictionary*, 1980, p. 1094.

[11]Kingsley Davis and Wilbert E. Moore, "Some Principles of Stratification," *American Sociological Review* Vol. 10 (1945), p. 246. Quoted in Miringoff and Opdycke, *American Social Welfare*, p. 8.

[12]Miringoff and Opdycke, *American Social Welfare*, pp. 9–11.

[13]Ibid.

[14]Melvin Tumin, "Some Principles of Stratification: A Critical Analysis," *American Sociological Review*, Vol. 10 No. 4, (1953), p. 380. Quoted in Miringoff and Opdycke, *American Social Welfare*, p. 11.

[15]Winifred Bell, *Contemporary Social Welfare* (New York: Macmillan Publishing Co., 1983), p. 57. Sources: U.S. Bureau of the Census *Population Reports, 1982*. Advance Report, Series P-60, no. 134, Table 4. (Washington, D.C.: U.S. Government Printing Office 1987).

[16]Ibid., p. 65; and U.S. Department of Commerce, Bureau of the Census, *Statistical Abstracts of the United States 1987*, Table C. "Comparison of 1985 Income and Poverty Measures," p. 5.

[17]Ibid., p. 99. Source: U.S. Bureau of the Census: *Current Population Reports, Consumer Income 1981*, Series P-60, No. 134 (Advance Report), p. 31).

[18]Ibid.; and *Statistical Abstracts 1987*, Table A-1, "Weighted Average Poverty Thresholds in 1985," p. 33.

[19]*Statistical Abstracts 1987* Table 19. "Selected Characteristics of Families . . . ," p. 30; and Table 18. "Poverty Status in 1985 of Persons by Race and Spanish Origin," p. 21; and Table 15. "Number, Poverty Rate . . . Persons . . . Below the Poverty Level in 1985 and 1984," p. 21.

[20]Conference on Women in Poverty, University of Michigan, Ann Arbor. October, 1985.

[21]A concept coined by Diana Pearce, 1977. It might better be called the pauperization of women, but the phrase has caught the public mind.

[22]U.S. Department of Commerce, Bureau of the Census, *Characteristics of the Population Below the Poverty Level: 1981*, CPR Series P-60, no. 138, Tables 1 and 37.

[23]U.S. Department of Health and Human Services, "Monthly Benefit Statistics" no. 12 (July 1986). Table 19, pp. 11 and 29.

24"Choices," Vol. III. (Forest Hills, New York), (Summer/Fall 1984), p. 8.

25Charles F. Marden and Gladys Meyer, 1962, quoted in Charles Zastrow, *Introduction to Social Welfare Institutions: Social Problems, Services, and Current Issues.* The Dorsey Series in Social Welfare (Homewood, Illinois: The Dorsey Press, revised edition 1982), p. 201.

26Derived from figures in U.S. Department of Commerce, Bureau of the Census: "U.S. Summary: General Social and Economic Characteristics, 1980 Census of Population," Table 75, pp. 1–13, December 1983.

27Joe R. Feagin, *Racial and Ethnic Relations,* 2nd ed., (Englewood Cliffs, N. J.: Prentice Hall, 1984), p. 177.

28Ibid., p. 198.

29Ibid., p. 341.

30Zastrow, *Social Welfare Institutions,* p. 204.

31U.S. Department of Commerce, Bureau of the Census, *Statistical Abstracts* Table 39, "Social and Economic Characteristics of the White, Black, and Spanish Origin Populations: 1985," p. 35.

32Ibid.

33Feagin, *Racial and Ethnic Relations,* p. 306.

34Bell, *Contemporary Social Welfare,* p. 119.

35Ibid.

36Feagin, *Racial and Ethnic Relations,* p. 233.

37Rosemary Sarri, Elizabeth Cramer, and Virginia duRivage, "Highlights: Socio-Economic Status of Women in Michigan and the United States," (Ann Arbor: The University of Michigan Institute for Social Work and the School of Social Work, 1983), p. 6.

38Feagin, *Racial and Ethnic Relations,* p. 233.

39U.S. Department of Commerce Bureau of Census. *Statistical Abstracts, 1987* Table 19, "Selected Characteristics of Families—Poverty Status in 1985 of All Families and Families with Female Householder, No Husband Present . . . ." (Washington, D.C.: U S. Government Printing Office, 1986), p. 29.

40Oscar Lewis, *La Vida* (New York: Random House, 1966).

41Sarri, Cramer, and duRivage, "Highlights."

42Ibid., p. 6.

43Ibid.

44Prudence Brown, *Women, Children, and Poverty in America* (New York: Ford Foundation, January, 1985) p. 41. Source: U.S. Department of Commerce, Bureau of the Census, *Money Income and Poverty Status of Families and Persons in the United States:1982,* CPR Series P-60, no. 140, Table 14.

45Diana Pearce, "Farewell to Alms," Center for National Policy Review, Catholic University Law School. Presented at the American Sociological Association Annual Meeting, San Francisco, September 1982.

46Sarri, Cramer, and du Rivage, "Highlights."

47Ibid.

48U.S. Department of Health and Human Services, Social Security Administration. "Monthly Benefit Statistics," Summary Program Data, no. 12. (July-October 1986), Table 13. "AFDC: Families, Recipients, and Payments by State, July 1986."

49Derived from U.S. Department of Commerce, Bureau of the Census *Current Population Reports,* Series P-60, no. 154. Table B. "Persons, Families, and Unrelated Individuals Below the Poverty Level in 1985 and 1984" (Washington, D.C.: U.S. Government Printing Office, 1986), p. 3.

50Sarri, Cramer, and duRivage, "Highlights," p. 8.

51U.S. Department of Health and Human Services, Social Security Administration "Social Security Bulletin," Vol. 46, no. 9 (September 1983), p. 12.

52U.S. Department of Commerce, Bureau of Census. *Statistical Abstracts of the United States, 1987,* Population Characteristics, Table 18, "Age, Type of Residence, Region and Work Experience—Poverty Status in 1985 of Persons by Race and Spanish Origin," p. 27.

[53]Zastrow, *Social Welfare Institutions*, p. 64.

[54]Ibid., p. 465.

[55]U.S. Department of Commerce, Bureau of the Census, *Statistical Abstracts 1987*, Table 18, "Age, Type of Residence, Region and Work Experience—Poverty Status in 1985 of Persons by Race and Spanish Origin." (Washington, D.C.: U.S. Government Printing Office, 1986), p. 27; and U.S. Department of Commerce, Bureau of the Census, *Current Population Reports* Series P-60, no. 154. "Money Income and Poverty Status of Families in the U.S. 1985." Advance Data from the March 1986 Current Population Survey. (Washington, D.C.: U.S. Government Printing Office, 1986), p. 17.

[56]Sarri, Cramer, and duRivage, "Highlights," p. 7.

[57]Ralph Dolgoff and Donald Feldstein, *Understanding Social Welfare* (New York: Longman Press, 1984), pp. 350–351.

[58]E. Fuller Torrey and Sidney M. Wolfe, *Care of the Seriously Mentally Ill: A Rating of State Programs,* (Washington, D.C.: Public Citizen Health Research Group, 1986), p. 1, pp. 5–8.

[59]Norman Goroff, "Humanism and Social Work: Paradoxes, Problems, and Promises," mimeographed. (West Hartford, Conn.: University of Connecticut School of Social Work, 1977.)

# 2

# THE INSTITUTION
# OF SOCIAL WELFARE

## THE MEANING OF SOCIAL INSTITUTION

A *social institution* is a set of interrelated and interlocking *concepts, structures,* and *activities,* enduring over time, that carry out the necessary functions of a society, for example, socialization, child-rearing, education, or commerce.[1] There are five major institutions of society (see Figure 2.1):

1. The *economy*
2. The *polity*
3. *Religion*
4. The *family*
5. *Social welfare* (which in our definition includes education)

The polity and the economy are the major underlying *macrosystems* by which our government is separated from other nations and by which people within our nation relate to society. Family, religion, and social welfare, though they also have wider applications, are usually more oriented to the *internal systems* (microsystems) of the society. Social welfare is an "interstitial institution," one that fills in the gaps left by other institutions.

Although the activities called social welfare have existed since the beginnings of human society, they became a social institution only when responsibility for particular groups of people became a function of the state or government. In early societies the extended family fulfilled all functions—economic and political needs, social control, and social integration. However, as families joined tribes and became communities and nations, and as work became divided and specialized, societal functions diversified into social institutions. Today, in most societies, they overlap one another, and social welfare overlaps them all.

The major functions of religion and the family are *socialization* and *social integration*. Socialization teaches us the norms, values, and ways of behaving in our society, and social integration helps us to "fit in" or be brought back into the fold after deviating in some way. Gilbert and Specht say that social integration

> has to do with the relationships among units in a social system. Members of a particular institution or of the system-as-a- whole must be loyal to one another and the system must achieve some level of solidarity and morale in order to function.[3]

Social integration makes us aware that we have stepped outside the bounds of the normal and points out how we can "change for the better." In addition, the idea of loyalty to one's family, group, and society is taught more formally than is the case in socialization.

*Economy.* The economy is all aspects of a society which relate to the production (making), distribution (meting out), and consumption (using) of goods and services. *Production* includes all outputs, from farm to manufactured goods, and capital—wealth accumulated in goods and profits and stored in stocks, bonds, sunk costs of manufacturing, savings, investments, and so on. *Distribution* is the marketing or meting out of products (goods and services). In America, we generally think that the market economy—what people buy and sell—is the major source of distribution. However, tax transfers are another major factor. They are monies taken from taxes and given directly, in cash, goods, and services, to select groups in society outside the labor market. For example, the poor receive money, food stamps, or subsidized housing; and the wealthy get tax breaks and subsidies such as farm price supports and land-bank monies or "bail-outs" for industries or corporations in trouble. *Consumption,* which keeps production and distribution moving, is the using up of consumer goods and services, whether through the market or through tax transfers.

The economy also includes the organization of the work force, employment, and planned unemployment to ensure the sufficient produc-

**FIGURE 2.1** Social Institutions[2]

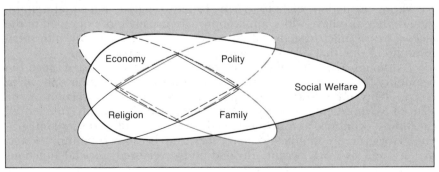

tion and consumption of consumer goods. In America, our Council of Economic Advisors suggests an unemployment rate of about 5 percent to ensure the availability of a work force to producers. The actual number of unemployed varies with the economy and with reporting, since discouraged workers and the underemployed are generally not counted in unemployment statistics. Discouraged workers are those who have never been able to find work, those whose unemployment benefits have run out, and others who have been unemployed for so long that they have stopped searching for work. Underemployed workers are those who work full-time but earn so little that their families may live in poverty, also skilled workers who cannot find skilled jobs.

Capital, wealth, and the tax system are also part of the economy. *Capital* is money (or economic resources) accumulated through profit and devoted to the further production of goods or to the accumulation of wealth. Profit is return on investment over costs of production, including labor, and surplus profit is that amount plus an excessive return for labor costs kept for private or corporate use. The American economy is capitalistic, that is, characterized by private or corporate accumulation of capital invested for private (or monopoly) gain. *Wealth* is the result of profit making and the retiring of resources from the market economy. Although wealth is generally less available for investment than is capital, if need arises, it can be sold and transformed into capital.

The *tax system* is the assessment of and levy upon income, production, and wealth by the government. Poor and middle-class people are taxed proportionately more than are corporations and the wealthy because of tax write-offs, loopholes, and the ability of the wealthy to influence tax legislation. This results in an increasing class stratification as the wealthy reinvest saved tax dollars in new profit making, while poorer classes have decreasing amounts to invest even in their own well-being. There are several direct taxes, including property, sales, and income. Property and sales taxes are "regressive," that is, taxed at a set rate regardless of the economic status of the taxpayer. Poorer classes, then, spend relatively more of their assets on these taxes than do the wealthy. Income tax is "progressive"; that is, those who earn more generally pay proportionately more. Taxes on corporate wealth depend both on the amount of wealth and its "form": wealth held in trusts or foundations may be virtually untaxable despite the benefit it brings to those who control such trusts and foundations. Indirect taxes are taxes placed on manufacturers that are then passed on in higher prices to consumers. Tax monies go to support the vast bureaucracies of the government; to provide for protection against other nations and negotiation with them; for public works such as roads, parks, bridges, and so on; and for public well-being in programs for the public good, such as education, health care, and welfare programs.

*Polity.* The polity is the *exercise of power* in a society. Any system—person, group, agency, organization, or wider system—that has *legal or normative* power, or in some instances *nonlegal* but *coercive or customary* power over other systems is a part of the polity.[4] Among systems constituting America's polity are national, state, and local governments based on national and state constitutions, laws, legislative and judicial decisions; the political system and political parties, including elections and appointments to office; the criminal and civil justice systems; and administrative rules, regulations, and customs at all levels of government and in all government bureaucracies.

Polities can enforce behaviors or impose or prevent change[5] whether or not people or systems agree with their actions. On the international level, polities engage in wars or other demonstrations of strength to the point of conquests of other nations or people, taking political prisoners or slaves, and enforcing their own laws and policies over unwilling countries by use of embargoes or occupation. Examples include the near-genocide of Native Americans and the slavery of African-born people and their descendants in our own country, and imperialism and colonialism in Third World countries today.

In the United States, the polity and the economy are so closely tied that it is difficult to see them as separate, for laws and regulations are based on the ideals of capitalism and the free market and much of the economy is politically supported. Higher socioeconomic classes often determine what legislation will be passed (through lobbying), what people will be elected to office (through financial contributions), and what contracts (such as for defense) will be developed and awarded.

*Family.*    The family is an economic and social unit in which people live within a society, and within which socially legitimated sexual relationships occur. In present-day America, the nuclear family—husband, wife, and children—is the normative ideal. In preindustrial times, the family was more clearly an economic unit, with members who worked at home farming, producing small craft items, marketing, giving child care, and educating and training family members in all aspects of life.

Now the meaning of "family" is markedly different from what it was even two decades ago because of new kinds of extended and nuclear families. Examples include the commune (several heterosexual couples, married or unmarried, living with their children as a social and economic unit); unmarried heterosexual or homosexual couples living together as a family unit, sometimes with children and often with a contract to specify the rights and obligations of each partner[6]; and, very common today, the single-parent household, often woman-headed and with dependent children. These and other families exist today with varying degrees of legitimacy.

*Religion.*    Religion is the complex of systems, organized or unorganized, by which individuals relate to deity and to their own existence. It entails spiritual and moral values concerning personal life, work, and other people. Because of the interrelationships of the Protestant work ethic and Puritan morality with polity and economy, the United States has been called a Christian nation. However, although Christian religions are numerically predominant, other religions such as Judaism, Islam, the Baha'i Faith, Buddhism, Unitarianism, and forms of paganism also exist. Atheism and agnosticism, which either deny deity or allow for the possibility of deity, are also ways in which people relate to existence. Humanism, centered on a philosophy of the dignity and worth of people aside from consideration of deity, is another legitimate spiritual focus of many. Freedom of belief and the doctrine of separation of church and state are protected by the Constitution. Nevertheless, present-day conservative trends threaten this freedom as religious groups attempt to insert sectarian beliefs into the American legal system.

*Social Welfare as an Institution.*    There are many definitions of social welfare in our own and other societies. Macarov tells us, for example, that in Poland social welfare is compensation for injuries suffered in great risks, such as war, which produce inability to work. In Australia it is a public right that benefits both individuals and society as a whole. Sweden's social welfare goal is to redistribute income more evenly, and in Iran goals include bettering the quality of the work force and encouraging people to save.[7] To most Americans, "social welfare" means giving money to the poor—to people who cannot or will not work to support themselves and their families.

However, that benefit, more properly called "public assistance," is not the whole of social welfare. Social welfare goes far beyond that, encompassing almost every kind of service provided to members of society. Walter A. Friedlander says it is

> [an organized] system of laws, programs, benefits, and services which strengthen or assure provisions for meeting social needs . . . basic for the welfare of the population and . . . the social order . . . to aid individuals and groups to attain satisfying standards of life and health, and personal and social relationships which permit them to develop their full capacities and to promote their well-being in harmony with the needs of their families and the community.[8]

The *Encyclopedia of Social Work* adds that social welfare is for the purpose of ensuring a basic standard of physical and mental well-being and to provide universal access to the mainstream of society.[9] Others add that it provides for those who cannot cope by themselves; creates social change and the modification of social institutions; strengthens society while it helps individuals; and provides services outside the market economy for those unable to succeed within it.[10] Compton gives us a comprehensive overview:

1. Social welfare is an *institution*
2. comprising *policies and laws* that are
3. operationalized by *organized activities of voluntary (private) and/or governmental (public) agencies*
4. by which a defined minimum of *social services, money, and other consumption rights* (medical care, education, and public housing, for example)
5. are *distributed to individuals, families, and groups* by criteria other than those of the marketplace or those prevailing in the family system
6. for the *purposes* of preventing, alleviating, or contributing to the solution of recognized social problems so as to improve the well-being of individuals, groups, and communities directly.[11]

Two additional areas should be included in the definition of social welfare. *First,* social welfare now includes some new areas: "for-profit" services, such as some nursing homes and day care centers; social services in business organizations, such as substance abuse counseling or day care for employees' children; and "natural" networks, the neighbors or parish priests who refer people to professional systems, for example.[12] *Second* is the "welfare model" of deviance, which Peter Day says presents welfare problems as

> public social problem[s] for which some remedial, correctional, or therapeutic intervention is required to alter, modify, or control the deviant and his behavior . . . [as] a public responsibility. . . . First, it sees deviant behavior as a public problem existing outside the framework of normal social life; second, it considers this behavior to be an expression of a deviant self different from that of the normal person; third, it promotes efforts to account for and correct this difference."[13]

This area of social welfare entails work with the delinquent, emotionally disturbed, or poor, among others. While such social control has been a legitimate part of American social welfare since its beginnings, some social work professionals have denied its existence as antithetical to individual freedom. However, more recent perspectives clearly indicate that social welfare is, in many ways, social control.

In this book, American social welfare is the *social institution* that provides society's sum total of all goods and services either

1.  *to enhance the social and economic well-being of society's members, and/or*
2.  *to ensure their conformity to current societal norms, standards, and ideologies.*

It is based on society's values, whether altruistic, economic, or political; is legitimated by legislation and/or custom; and is carried out by public agencies, private not-for-profit agencies, or agencies whose major goal is to enhance profit-making for its owner-investors. Social welfare has two kinds of functions:

1.  *Social treatment*—the provision of goods and services for the enhancement of human life
2.  *Social control*—generally, the provision of services to ensure the conformity of deviants. These functions determine the activities of human service professionals in carrying out society's mandates—laws and policies—regarding social services.

Most social welfare activities take place outside the market system—people do not individually purchase or pay for services that may or may not be altruistic. For example, criminal justice programs require control of those we fear; businesses provide counseling or child care services as much to ensure optimum productivity as to help their workers; and for-profit care homes, though they give care, are obviously run for money. Some services cross the line between social treatment and social control, for example, education or recreational programs such as Girl Scouts are aimed essentially at socialization and conformity but also are life-enhancing. In any case, social welfare goods and services are provided both for the benefit of individuals, families, and groups and to maintain order in society itself.

Social welfare's tremendously broad scope includes provision of sustenance—cash, food stamps, housing, medical care; parts of the legal system, as in juvenile and criminal justice; education and educational services aimed at counseling or rehabilitation; mental health care; child, family, and marital counseling; programs for special groups, such as the aged or those who are developmentally disabled; substance abuse programs; rehabilitative programs; and so on. Whenever other social institutions—family, church, economy—do not provide a service, social welfare fills in the gaps. For example, public programs such as Social Security pensions now care for aged people who were once supported by the extended family.

Gilbert and Specht give us a useful typology based on reasons for allocating services. The allocative principles are

1.  *Attributed need*—the unmet need is considered normal, and is attributed to systematic inadequacies (such as day care for children of working mothers).
2.  *Compensation*—a systematic failure resulting in a "debt" owed citizens for service (for example, veterans).
3.  *Diagnostic differentiation*—this implies individual deficiencies that must be assessed by professionals, such as physical or mental handicaps requiring special services.
4.  *Means-tested need*—services are provided but the individuals are considered somehow personally deficient.

Programs can be plotted from this typology. In a general way, they range from institutional to residual perspectives (see Figure 2.2).

## PERSPECTIVES ON SOCIAL WELFARE

A *perspective* is a viewpoint based on values from which to look at a phenomenon. Our perspectives on social welfare come from diverse values that determine what we think social welfare *should* do and what its causes, purposes, functions, and results *ought to be*. The *causes* of social welfare and its programs are, generally, the reasons they developed over time. Although we traditionally believe them to be altruistic, they are in fact interplay between altruism, the needs of the disadvantaged, and the desires of those in control. The *purposes* of social welfare are both to aid those in need and to maintain other structures and institutions of society, and these dual purposes reflect ambivalent goals and, hence, ambivalent *programs*, *effects*, and *results*. Thus their outcomes must be dually assessed on how well they serve clients and how effective they are for society's control purposes. If assessed only on client benefit, most would be considered failures, for the lives of clients are not changed much by most social welfare programs. Looked at from society's control viewpoint, however, they may be very effective.

| Attributed Need | Compensation | Diagnostic Differentiation | Means-tested Need |
|---|---|---|---|
| Social Security | Veterans' benefits | Special education | Public Assistance |
| Medicare | VA hospitals | Vocational rehabilitation | Medicaid |
| Home-delivered meals | College quota systems | Mental health | Food stamps |
| Head Start | Workers' Compensation | Half-way houses | Poor relief |

< --------------<--------------< --------------> --------------> --------------> -------------->

Institutional -------------------------------------------------------------------------Residual

Perspective

**FIGURE 2.2**   Sample Programs according to Social Allocation Typology.[14]

Our key to understanding this is "functionalism," which means the usefulness of social welfare in maintaining certain of society's structures. For example, public assistance programs are functional in a number of ways. The low levels of support do give subsistence, but they also save tax money and provide a "work incentive" to get people off welfare. This relieves society of the burden of adequate support and ensures employers of sufficient workers at low wages and minimum benefits. Public assistance programs also control sex-role behaviors by requiring that men work at almost any job and that women maintain "moral" sexual, economic, and child-rearing behaviors (upon threat of losing their grants and sometimes their children). Other programs have other functions: for example, mental hospitals warehouse the unwanted, emotionally ill, or aged; low assistance grants maintain markets for substandard or used goods; and social welfare programs provide jobs in social work and human service fields. If programs are not functional, they will cease to exist, and the fact that they continue despite public outcry and lack of service effectiveness indicates their functionalism for society.

A program may have both manifest and latent functions. A *manifest* function is one that is evident, usually written into the laws, mandates, or organizational constitutions and bylaws of a program. *Latent* functions are unstated and either assumed or hidden. Because a function is latent does not necessarily mean it is bad but that workers, clients, and relevant others may be unaware of its real purposes. For example, socialization to conformity in Girl or Boy Scouts is not written into the bylaws, nor is it particularly a "bad" thing, but it is a latent, or unadvertised, function. Another example, more insidious in nature, is the control of women through public assistance programs or in mental health systems that function to maintain a patriarchal society.

### The Residual Perspective

The traditional perspective of social welfare is that, while society should help in emergencies, people in need are responsible for their own problems and should solve them with a minimum of societal intervention. This is called the "residual perspective"[15] and prescribes short-term, stopgap social welfare measures that last only until the social institutions normally providing help can resume their functions (the family or employment in the economy, for example). The major criterion for service is whether people are above a set level of money and assets, determined by *means testing* to ensure that applicants get no more help than they "should." Organizations and agencies have different eligibility levels, but they are usually set somewhere near the state "poverty level." Residual programs may also involve severe restriction of personal freedom (jail, long-term commitment to mental hospitals); short-term emergency care such as that offered by hospital emergency rooms; or 24-hour holds for people with acute and/or life-threatening psychiatric disturbances. In emergency or personal detainment cases, danger to self or others rather than amount of assets is the general criterion for eligibility.

To discourage the use of social welfare programs, services are often the least or smallest possible, aid is given grudgingly, and people who seek help are stigmatized by society. Control rather than treatment is often the goal. Means testing is used particularly in subsistence programs—those offering food, shelter, and clothing—but also in such programs as mental health or family planning/health facilities to determine a "sliding fee," namely, how much clients can afford. Closely related to means testing is "less eligibility," a concept arising with the Elizabethan Poor Laws of 1601. In this concept, no person receiving public aid should get a grant higher than the lowest wage in the locality. Even today "less eligibility" may be considered when setting maximum amounts for public assistance grants.

The residual perspective is the basis for the "medical model" of social work treatment, in which social services are intended to "treat and cure" people who deviate from the "healthy society." This complex of ideas leads to "blaming the victim"[16] as responsible for her or his own problems and does not consider structural problems—lack of employment opportunities or special problems—as relevant. The most common example of a program in which the residual perspective dominates is that of public assistance. This perspective has kept public assistance limited both in eligibility and in amount of grants that are often too little to maintain health and welfare. Few programs are so residual in nature, but many have residual elements.

To recapitulate, a residual perspective mandates that social welfare programs should give aid to people

1.  In emergency situations, when other social institutions fail
2.  On a short-term basis
3.  As a stopgap measure, until the "normal" social institution once more comes into play
4.  With eligibility usually determined by means testing
5.  In a way which encourages recipients to find other means of help, usually by stigmatizing them
6.  Begrudgingly, especially in assistance programs, where the minimal is given

Let us consider a concrete example—a mother applying for AFDC.

1.  *Emergency.* She will only be considered if her husband or other relevant man no longer supports her (failure of family support). It is assumed that as soon as possible she will become employed or find some other means of support (such as marriage or other family resources) and will leave the program.
2.  *Short term.* Although there is no specified time limit to the AFDC program in theory, the woman's income and assets, along with her personal life, will be scrutinized often to ensure that she leaves AFDC as soon as possible.
3.  *Stopgap.* She will be allowed to receive AFDC payments only so long as she has no other means of support. A major program goal is to move people off the rolls as soon as possible.
4.  *Means testing.* Her income and assets are assessed to ensure that they fall below the already low eligibility limits of the AFDC program.
5.  *Stigmatizing.* Applying for AFDC is demeaning because our American value system is so strongly opposed to public assistance. Also, the application process often entails speaking of intimate and personal details of one's life to a stranger, and permanent public records, though confidential, are made of the application.
6.  *Grudging and minimal.* Not only will she be subjected to the embarrassment of asking for public money, the dollar amounts given are so minimal that they are known to be insufficient to maintain healthy subsistence on a longer than emergency basis.[17]

### The Institutional Perspective

This perspective is at the opposite end of the continuum from the residual perspective. Its major criterion is membership in the society— every person in a society has a right to its services, without means testing or stigma. Programs are *universal,* that is, they cover every person within their designated mandate, whereas residual programs are *selective* in nature and apply only to a selected few or selected groups. The institutional perspective leads to the "structural" or "social" model of social work—social problems are believed to come from oppressive or inegalitarian structures in society. Social problems are not based on personal fault, and therefore solutions do not lie in controlling, punishing, or stigmatizing the individual. Rather, they lie in search for root problems—such as classism, racism, or sexism—and their elimination.

Many programs of social welfare approach this end of the residual-institutional continuum. Public education, for example, is the right of all American children, and Social Security ensures a retirement income for almost every person in the United States and supports surviving children of deceased workers. An area in process of becoming institutional is mental health. Prior to the 1960s, the term used for people with emotional difficulties was "mentally ill," and they were usually stigmatized for and ashamed of their problems. Now mental health is a social right. Although there is a sliding fee scale, private or public funds pick up costs for service for those unable to pay, and no one is denied treatment because of being poor.

To recapitulate, then, the institutional perspective is a belief that

1. Social welfare services should be available to all members of society who fit a program's mandates.
2. There is no time limit for services, though there may be a time at which services can begin (such as school attendance or eligibility for Social Security pensions).
3. If there is any means testing, it is to determine the amount people can pay rather than to deny services.
4. There is no stigma either for applying for or receiving services.
5. There is no societal pressure to leave the program.

We have been discussing *perspectives* of social welfare, not the programs presented as examples. However, we can place programs along a continuum from residual to institutional as long as we remember that few programs are either wholly residual or wholly institutional (see Figure 2.3).

Some programs demonstrate both residual and institutional elements. For example, juvenile probation has residual elements because of the emergency nature of problems of children in trouble. However, institutional elements make protection under the system available to all children, including those who have suffered neglect and abuse. On the other hand, even though education is one of our most institutional programs, services

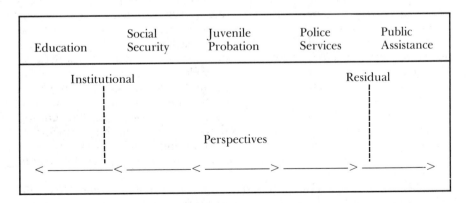

**FIGURE 2.3**  Continuum of Perspectives

of truant officers and some administrators in schools deal with emergency problems which are residual in nature.

### Conflict Perspectives in Social Welfare

While the foregoing perspectives provide some prescriptions for social work practice, they are basically static and descriptive, dealing only minimally with policy analysis or problem causation. Newer perspectives based on sociological, economic, and feminist theories are now being applied to social welfare that assess its social history and suggest proactive and often radical models for human service work. More or less related to the institutional perspective and to structural models of practice, they see recalcitrant societal structures rather than individual fault as causes of social problems. They criticize these structures and prescribe social action and social change to a much greater degree than do present structural models.

Generally, the newer perspectives are based on "conflict theory": they posit a conflict between those who control society's structures and those who are controlled and exploited by them. Piven and Cloward were among the first to develop these theories, noting in their book, *Regulating the Poor*, that throughout history, whenever the disadvantaged rebelled against exploitation, welfare programs and benefits were expanded until the rebellion ceased. Then, though benefits shrank, it was seldom to pre-rebellion levels and was enough to keep people quiet for a time. Thus expansion of welfare programs was not altruistic but political and economic: it quelled rebellions, and, because benefits were always meager, it kept a quiescent work force eager to take jobs with low wages and few benefits. This made labor costs cheap and profitable to producers.[18]

James Rule says that redefining *social conflicts* as *social problems* changes their nature and enables people to believe that solutions can be found.[19] Moreover, the redefinition places the burden for change on "deviants" and those hired to change them—social workers—and relieves society of the burden of changing its status quo. For example, if poverty is class conflict, the higher class must fight to keep its privileged position from those who would take away its benefits. Redefined as a social problem, now powerless social workers "own" and must solve it. The upper class is satisfied because society remains stratified, the poor believe that solutions will be found, and social workers strive to find solutions that most often will not work because they are powerless to change the conflict elements of the system. In the same way, if high unemployment is defined as a problem in motivation peculiar to Afro-American people, the solution is for social workers to teach motivation and job skills. That is a much easier task than ending racism, even though it cannot work because the definition is in error. Defined as racism, action to end exploitation is implied. The risks are great and the rewards few to social workers, so benefits of institutional racism to white society continue.

Seeing racism, sexism, or classism as social problems implies that solutions can be found in changing the victims rather than in changing society's exploitative structures. This "blaming the victim" stance is ineffectual, since victims of society are not generally to blame for their victimization. Although limited remedial or Band-Aid work can be done to ameliorate the damage, the damage-causing structures remain. On the other hand, seeing the "isms" as conflicts implies action against society, but this does not mean that action will occur. In the first place, most Americans believe our society is egalitarian and democratic, and action against it means action against those principles. Second, while seeing "isms" as conflict issues might provide the right "mind-set" to work for change, restructuring of the system is too much for most of us to undertake. Therefore, from either perspective little meaningful change is possible.

Among the perspectives deriving from conflict theory are Marxian, socialist, socialist feminist, radical feminist, and feminist welfarist models. *Marxian* and *socialist* perspectives look at class stratification and exploitative behavior and perceive social welfare as helping to maintain inegalitarian structures. Rather than remedial treatment for the disadvantaged, eradication of the oppressive economic and political structures is advocated. Class advantages would be eliminated and profit sharing and a government based on worker control would redistribute wealth. Disadvantaged people would receive sufficient resources from the government to satisfy their needs. To a great extent, these perspectives ignore gender issues, except to note that a different economic structure would eliminate gender stratification since it is based on worker oppression.

*Socialist feminism's* primary concern is the economic oppression of women, which began with the onset of private property and the loss of women's economic value to the family. In this view, women are doubly oppressed: first, as workers in a capitalist economy and, second, as wives dependent on husbands who are in turn exploited workers. Women are involved directly in production at work, and at home in two kinds of reproduction that serve the capitalist economy: biological reproduction to supply a new generation of workers and maintenance of a home that offers surcease to the weary laborer and renews him for more productive work. A restructuring of class stratification and a redefinition of marriage and family roles—perhaps their elimination—would prevent both primary and secondary oppression. An altered economic system would provide new access for all kinds of social care, and social welfare's concerns should be social action and social change to give economic and political empowerment to women.

*Radical feminism* is concerned with political exploitation of women under a patriarchal system enforcing gender privilege throughout history. In this view, both class and gender exploitation began with the onset of private property and the loss of women's co-equal status. Patriarchal sex-role socialization keeps women in subordinate and powerless roles and increases their dependency on men and male systems (such as public assistance or mental health systems). Women therefore believe in the "rightness" of male control and cooperate in their own subordination. Models for action include consciousness raising; values awareness; a reassessment of female roles in marriage, family, and society; and social action for empowerment even to the point of separatism, as in women's communities.

The *feminist welfarist* perspective is a critical analysis of social history that incorporates conflict theory, socialist and radical feminist perspectives, and the synergistic evolution of social welfare. It pays particular attention to economy, polity, and spiritual motivations concerning social treatment and social control. According to this perspective, value systems create a morally legitimate oppression for women and for the poor, and race privilege is superimposed on these. The perspective analyzes problems specific to women throughout history that have been, if not neglected, almost an aside in most studies of social welfare. Its arguments are predicated on sex-role socialization to a patriarchal society's expectations, that is, women as dependent, incompetent in money management, less mature, given to emotionality. Men are also considered to be victims of patriarchal sex-role stereotyping and exploitation. Although they have more power than women, their most important sex-role identification is as worker, making them very exploitable in a capitalistic society.

A major issue from this perspective is the povertization of women. Public dependency for women arises from different causes than for men, yet public assistance programs are based on male models of need, that is, the idea that adults who are able-bodied should work. However, women are not simply able-bodied workers, though they may be. They are socialized *to* family roles and *away from* lucrative employment by school and family systems; they have primary emotional and economic responsibility for dependent children; and the structures of society that deal with their dependence—courts and public assistance systems—do not provide adequate grants to lift them above poverty levels. Work itself is marginal and low-paying for most women, and few receive equal pay for equal or comparable work. To insist that work is their way out of poverty is a denial of the differential treatment accorded them throughout society's institutions.[20]

In addition, *needs of women* as well as *care by women* create special problems for social welfare. Women are the majority of workers as well as the majority of clients in social welfare systems. They have little power or recognition, they cannot command resources because they are inadequately represented in welfare policy bodies, and their charity work is derogated by society's antipoverty values. Men in social welfare, on the other hand, have more legitimation because they traditionally have worked with employment programs (unions, job training, social insurance). From this differential association with "undeserving" and "deserving" groups, neither women, social work, nor clients gain society's respect. Finally, social welfare itself contributes to the patriarchal control of women, the poor, and people of color. Established, financed, and directed by a white male political system, though women do much of its work, it is in general a male system, and it is oriented to maintaining the status quo of society.

To reiterate, conflict theory says that social problems

1. Lie in the structures of society rather than the fault of the disadvantaged.

2. Are the result of attempts of an elite group to maintain the privileges they have accumulated through exploitation of other classes.

3. Will endure until the structures themselves are changed.

The feminist welfarist perspective is a critical historical analysis that

1. Incorporates conflict theory and socialist and radical feminist perspectives.

2. Reconstructs social history to include perspectives of the poor, women, and races (and religions) other than the dominant white male system.

3. Sees social problems as the results of historical convergences of class privilege, race privilege, and patriarchal power.

4. Traces most social problems to structured inequalities primarily based on class, race, and gender.

5. Indicts social welfare as causative in great part to the maintenance of structured inequalities.

## THE SCOPE OF SOCIAL WELFARE

Social welfare ranges across all aspects of life, from birth to death, providing social services where other institutions fail or are inadequate.[21] *Social services* are helping or controlling activities performed by persons in the public (governmental) or private sectors, usually within *social agencies* formed around a particular social need, such as hunger, delinquency, or substance abuse. People who provide social services may be professional social workers with masters' or bachelors' degrees; paraprofessionals, specifically people indigenous to the client population who are trained by professional social workers but do not have professional degrees; laypersons, such as church volunteers; or people having little or no professional social work training but working in social agencies such as departments of public welfare, the juvenile division of the court system, or Social Security offices. Also, nonsocial work professionals provide counseling services—psychologists, psychiatrists, or members of the clergy, for example. Finally, self-help groups with or without professional association and staffing provide emotional support and help to members: examples include Alcoholics Anonymous or women's consciousness-raising groups.

*Public agencies* are established by law, on local (city or county), state, or federal levels, and are administered by public officials according to legal mandates. Some have local representative boards, but power resides in the legislation. *Private agencies* are nongovernmental, though they may have government charters and often receive some funding from governmental bodies. They are often called "voluntary" agencies, because they were established by voluntary groups, usually around a local need, and are funded substantially through private contributions. Some were developed by religious groups to provide social services specific to a religion's beliefs. Members of the community, on volunteer boards, make agency policy decisions, but staff and administration are often paid professionals. While some still have individual fund drives, many are now part of United Way agencies, which run annual fund drives and apportion out contributions by locally established criteria to member agencies.

Some organizations offering social services are not social agencies but provide help to enhance their primary goals. For example, schools may provide counseling for children and their parents around the issues of absenteeism or lack of motivation; hospitals give social services to the families of dying patients or arrange extended care for aged patients; and churches carry out their religious mandates to care for the poor with food baskets and soup kitchens. Some social agencies provide a wide variety of services, some target only a few, and often services or clientele overlap.

There are certain generally identifiable fields of social services. They include

1. Life necessity services
2. Educational, recreational, or rehabilitative services
3. Protective and/or custodial services
4. Personal social services.

*Life necessity services.*    These services supply food, clothing, shelter, and medical assistance. Public agencies provide the bulk of such services, though churches and/or such private agencies as Salvation Army, Goodwill Industries, Volunteers of America, or Catholic Charities supplement with grants or donations, or give temporary shelter. Food programs—lunch and breakfast or home-delivered meals—may be publicly or privately funded, and are carried out in schools, churches, and senior citizen centers.

By far the largest public programs are those of the federal Social Security acts of 1935 and their amendments. There are three major areas: Social Insurance, Public Assistance, and Maternal and Child Health. The largest program of *social insurance* is Old Age, Survivors, Disability and Health Insurance (OASDHI). (Other social insurances include Unemployment Insurance and Workers' Compensation, both state programs with varying degrees of federal input.) *Public assistance* programs include Aid to Families of Dependent Children (AFDC), Supplemental Security Income (SSI), and Medicaid (see Figure 2.4). State public assistance not connected with the Social Security Act of 1935 include General Assistance and Poor Relief. The Food Stamp program is also considered public assistance, although it is in fact a program of the Department of Agriculture. Among Maternal and Child Health programs are the Crippled Children's program, school lunches, family planning programs, and Women's, Infants', and Children's Nutrition (WIC).

Social insurance programs are generally work-related. Originally the Social Security Act established retirement pensions for aged workers and their spouses and pensions for the children of deceased workers (OASI). Health insurance (Medicare) was added in 1964, and in 1972 were added the public assistance programs (nonwork-related) of Old Age Assistance, Aid to the Blind, and Aid to the Permanently and Totally Disabled. OASDHI is primarily funded through the F.I.C.A. tax. Workers' Compen-

| Social Insurance | Public Assistance | Maternal and Child Health |
|---|---|---|
| OASDHI | AFDC | Family Planning |
| Medicare (the "H" in ASDHI) | Medicaid | WIC |
| Unemployment Insurance | SSI | Crippled Children |
| Workers' Compensation | General Assistance | Child Nutrition |
| | Poor Relief | |
| | Food Stamps | |

**FIGURE 2.4**   Selected Government Programs for the Poor

sation pays pensions or settlements for disabilities or death suffered by workers, and Unemployment Compensation provides benefits to workers laid off from regular employment for a time-limited period. Both the latter programs are federally mandated but financed by employers (through taxes or private carriers) and administered by the state.

While social insurance is not means-tested, public assistance applicants are not eligible if they have income and assets over a level set by each state. The AFDC program is federally mandated but administered according to state laws. Financing is 75 percent federal, 25 percent state. It is generally for poor children in single-parent families, although states may agree to support certain intact families: those whose wage-earner is incapacitated (AFDC-I) or remains unemployed after having exhausted all unemployment compensation (AFDC-UP). The federally mandated SSI program is financed by the federal government with state supplementation; is administered by county departments of public welfare; and supplements the income of people receiving OASDI whose grants are below state poverty levels (though states may limit recipients to only those receiving public welfare).

Medicaid is a federal health insurance program for all people below state poverty levels. States decide these levels, and county welfare departments administer the programs. While *Medicare* pays for hospitalization and some extended care in nursing facilities (along with a few other benefits) for the aged or permanently and totally disabled, *Medicaid* pays most costs for medical services, including hospitalization, surgery, physicians' house and office calls, and prescription drugs. Depending on the state it may also pay for hearing aids, prosthetics, eyeglasses, and the like. Public health departments may (depending on the state) provide tubercular testing, immunization clinics, well-baby clinics, family planning programs, venereal disease testing and treatment, and school health nurses; and control of communicable diseases, public health hazards, and epidemics.

Other federal public assistance programs include Food Stamps (a function of the Department of Agriculture); subsidized housing, in the form of loans, grants, or partial rent subsidies; railroad workers' and federal employee pensions; and medical costs for veterans (Veterans Administration). Food stamps are available to all persons under federal poverty levels, but states decide what groups will actually receive them. On the county and state levels, general assistance (GA) or poor relief programs aid people who are not eligible for federal programs. Counties decide on the level of aid and administer the programs, with state matching funds (usually 60 percent state). Counties often have medical assistance programs for hospital care and burial for county indigents who are not covered by other programs.

There are a variety of private organizations and brotherhoods (Elks, Lions) that work for cure or control of particular diseases or problems. Among them are the American Cancer Society, Crippled Children's Association, Muscular Dystrophy Association, March of Dimes Foundation, Epilepsy Foundation, Planned Parenthood clinics, and myriad others. They provide money for services, information, and education to the public; research; and prosthetics, eyeglasses, wheelchairs, and so forth. The American Red Cross maintains a blood bank and provides a variety of health services both to veterans and to citizens in times of emergency.

*Educational, Recreational, or Rehabilitative Services.* These services include job training; remedial education services; day care for children, whether custodial or educational; recreational programs and facilities; disability rehabilitation services; and educational and rehabilitative services for people in custodial care in, for example, prisons, mental hospitals, and juvenile detention facilities.

In addition to basic education, school districts often provide technical job training such as auto mechanics or typing. For young people who have dropped out or who have been pushed out of regular school, they may provide "alternative schools" offering basic education, training, personal or employment counseling, or remedial programs for literacy. General education degrees (GEDs) can be awarded there or in night schools. School social workers ("visiting teachers") counsel students, visit their homes to solve nonacademic problems, or undertake individual or group therapy with students or their families. Some may be "truant officers" or juvenile probation officers making sure that children attend school, stay out of trouble with the law, and are protected from neglect or abuse.

Several public programs offer job training and educational services for adults. The nationwide Work Incentive Program (WIN), which was a joint program requiring all AFDC recipients with no children under age 6 to register for job training, was dismantled and has been replaced in some states by state AFDC work training programs. Requirements vary depending on the state, but in general the programs require that women with no children under age 6 register for training, and many place recipients in jobs. Some states offer long-term educational help and training, including college (Massachusetts, for example, and Pennsylvania to a lesser extent).

These programs are intended to lower public assistance costs in the long run, and some are innovative and effective. However, many are little more than work relief programs with degrees of restriction for men and women, ages of children, job status of breadwinner, and so on. For example, one plan requires that recipients spend 10 hours a week looking for work and 30 hours working in "voluntary" community projects.

The War on Poverty job programs included the Manpower Development and Training Act of 1962 and Economic Opportunity Act in 1964; the Job Corps for youth no longer in school; and the Neighborhood Youth Corps, which provided summer employment for young people still in school. In 1974 the Comprehensive Education and Training Act (CETA) was established to train disadvantaged people for future employment. The Reagan administration replaced CETA with the Job Training Partnership Act (1981) and the Emergency Job Bill (1982), which give money directly to employers to develop jobs partnerships of business with local governments (Private Industry Councils), though need-based stipends can be awarded. Finally, State Employment Commissions provide registration, testing, and counseling for jobs in addition to administering the unemployment compensation program.

Vocational Rehabilitation is a Department of Education program administered by state education departments (amendments of 1954 and 1973). It provides a full range of services to disabled people to train them for employment: medical testing to assess the extent of disability; medical and surgical services to lessen the extent of impairment; personal and rehabilitation counseling; education including college, depending on ability; vocational training in private or public schools; such special equipment as hearing aids, guide dogs, wheelchairs, canes, or prosthetics; special training in sign language or social adjustment; sheltered workshops; money for transportation and living expenses while training; and assistance in finding a job and essential equipment, such as licenses, tools, or stock.[22]

Prisons, mental hospitals, and other such custodial care facilities also have rehabilitation and educational programs intended to provide released persons with job skills which will enable them to earn a living once out of custody. Private agencies such as Goodwill Industries and Volunteers of America also give training and rehabilitation in sheltered workshops, where people unable to work in the general marketplace receive minimal pay for the work they are able to do.

Day care facilities for children may be financed privately or by the AFDC program (to encourage mothers to enter the job force). Public welfare departments license and monitor private (approved) homes and private or public day care centers. Head Start, a War on Poverty program, provides educational care for children and other services to parents. Nursery schools offer early education and socialization skills to children in addition to day care. For adults with emotional, physical, or developmental problems, departments of education, mental health clinics, and private entrepreneurs provide day care, nursing home care, "half-way houses," or extended care. These may also give social opportunities, counseling, or a variety of other services, as do programs and centers for senior citizens.

Recreational agencies give opportunities for recreation, training, education, social experiences, and socialization to normative beliefs and standards in America. They include day camps, summer camps, programs of the Young Women's and Young Men's Christian Association or Hebrew Association (YWCA, YMCA, YWHA, YMHA), Boy Scouts, Girl Scouts, and their counterparts. Kahn says that

> In a major sense, social services exist to protect, to change, or to innovate with respect to many of the educational, child- rearing, value-imparting, and social induction activities once assumed by the extended family, the neighborhood, and relatives. The goal is socialization into communal values, transmittal of goals and motivation, and enhancement of personal development. Cognitive and emotional aspects of learning are encompassed.[23]

*Protective or Custodial Care.*    This type of care includes group homes and institutions for disturbed or delinquent children; programs for neglected or abused children and their parents; child guidance programs and school social work for troubled or troublesome children; foster care and adoption; homes for unwed mothers; mental hospitals or short-term group or custodial homes for emotionally disturbed persons; and protective services and nursing homes for the aged or developmentally disabled. Rehabilitative work in prisons and juvenile institutions is included in this category, as are juvenile and adult parole and probation work. Public agencies offering such care are usually connected with either departments of public welfare or the juvenile or adult justice systems, but may include private for-profit institutions, such as nursing homes, or not-for-profit organizations such as Crittenton Services or Salvation Army homes.

Protection for abused and neglected children and adults (particularly aged or developmentally disabled adults) is authorized under the Social Service Amendments to the Social Security Acts of 1935 (Title XX). Under this act, social workers from public welfare departments license nursing homes, foster homes, and private care homes; and deal with complaints of abuse by parents or other caretakers, including public or private institutions. At the local level, governments offer help for family violence through police department social workers, and private organizations are opening shelters for battered women and exploited children and runaways.

*Personal Social Services.*    This service offers

> brief, or intensive, personal help with environmental, situational, interpersonal, or intrapsychic programs. Frequently the goal is restoration of as much normal functioning as possible . . . [assuming control over] . . . dangerous or unacceptable deviance while help is rendered.[24]

They include therapy for individuals or groups in such areas as child or marriage problems, substance abuse, or emotional difficulties related to divorce, death, and so on; psychological testing and psychiatric services;

counseling on budgeting, credit, family planning, or employment; and access and advocacy services.

Although therapy and counseling are offered in some public settings—mental hospitals, for example—this has generally been the province of private social agencies. People intensively trained in clinical skills practice intervention techniques based on work by a number of theorists, among them Freud, Adler, Jung, Rogers, Perls, Ellis, or Glasser. The techniques range across psychosocial casework, problem solving, task-centered therapy, psychoanalysis, client-centered therapy, Gestalt therapy, or behavior modification. Mental health clinics or Family Service agencies are among the primary providers of such care, but other organizations offer it as part of their services—Planned Parenthood, shelters for battered women, schools, group homes, probation offices, or juvenile and adult detention centers, for example. Relationship with the counselor and client motivation are essential elements in the counseling process.

Access services enable clients to find, understand, and use social services. Through information giving, referral, and follow-up, they help clients through the maze of bureaucracies and regulations that might preclude help. In addition, access services may help to locate gaps in service and coordinate agencies or develop new services to fill them. Advocacy services enable and/or empower clients to gain rights and services to which they are eligible or entitled before the law. Legal action and lobbying and influence secure needed services, and clients are encouraged to social action in their own behalf. Community action agencies, developed during the War on Poverty, were the forerunners in advocacy, but now most social agencies offer limited advocacy. Legal Service Organizations are in the forefront of social action and social change.

## THE PROFESSION OF SOCIAL WORK

### What Is a Profession?

A profession, according to Greenwood, has the following elements:

1. A cognitive or intellectual component—expertise grounded in a relatively abstract, systematic, and communicable body of theory constantly replenished by discussion and research—transmitted by professional training and higher education;
2. Authority in society to speak for the needs of the recipient group and members of the profession;
3. Ethical codes—a normative "collectivity and service orientation" that places client needs above worker interests;
4. A monopoly to exclusively recruit and educate members, regulate, evaluate, and censure the professional behavior of colleagues; and
5. A professional culture—an organized group performing social functions within the matrix of society which requires socialization to its norms and ethics.[25]

Some would argue that social work is not a profession. Although it is theoretically based, other professions share both theory and skills used in social work, and those skills are neither exclusive nor (in many areas) highly technical. Its professional culture includes undergraduate and graduate schools, apprenticeship, and professional associations (National Association of Social Workers and Council for Social Work Education). However, other schools and programs teach human services, especially on the interpersonal level. Society recognizes its expertise in the field, but its ethical stance is often in conflict with major American values, undermining that authority. Another problem is that of respect; most of its practitioners are women and its clients are "deviants." Therefore, it is a "socially contaminated" occupation, with little credibility. Finally, because its scope is broad and its targets many, it has no exclusive "domain" for practice.

Nevertheless, on the continuum of occupations, social work falls near the professional end. Its general definition as a profession is

the professional activity of helping individuals, groups, or communities enhance or restore their capacity for social functioning and creating societal conditions favorable to this goal . . . the professional application of social work values, principles, and techniques to one or more of the following ends: helping people obtain tangible services; counseling and psychotherapy with individuals, families, and groups; helping communities or groups provide or improve social and health services; and participating in relevant legislative processes.[26]

Social work is different from other helping professions in specific ways. Included in these are the *overarching mission;* the *client system;* the focus on *"client-in-situation";* the *target of practice*; and the complex of values, knowledge, and skills that makes up the *ethical stance* of social work practice. First, social work intervention, though it includes intrapsychic therapy as do some other professions, goes far beyond personal problems of emotional or mental health. Social work's original mission was not personal but *social* intervention—reform of poverty and its causes. Although this has changed in many ways, the mission is still *social* in nature, dealing with elements beyond the person or client. These elements include not only mental health but financial security, employment satisfaction, marital health, elimination of inequality, and the attainment of civil and human rights for clients. Optimal social functioning in problematic areas of life is the goal of practice.

Unlike clients in other helping professions, the social work client may be an individual, a group, a family, an organization, a neighborhood group, or a political body. Moreover, the focus of practice is the "client-in-situation" (see Figure 2.5). The importance of the social environment in the helping process is a stated and formal criterion unique to social work, though other helping professionals surely deal with these relationships less formally. Social work considers the complex of systems that impact on clients, have influence on their behavior, and may create and maintain their problems. Unlike such disciplines as medicine or psychology, which generally separate clients from the contexts of their lives, social work recognizes that individual change is based on the context of lives.

In addition, the target of social work practice, rather than being the client, is the relationships and reciprocal interactions that instigate or perpetuate the problem situation (see Figure 2.6). The task of practice is to bring positive coherence to the interactions. To elaborate, the target of intervention for a depressed individual would be problematic relationships with spouse, children, employment, or other system. At a community level, it might be interactions among neighborhood groups and police, slum landlords, or public health officials. On the policy level, the target against which action might be taken would not be a legislator but the systems that kept a poor legislation in place or refused to institute a better law.

A final unique characteristic of social work as a profession is its carefully elaborated combination of values, knowledge, and skills. Vigilante says that the attitudes, behavior, and commitment of its members are the defining elements of social work as a profession,[27] and these derive from social work's ethical stance. In our first chapter, we discussed American social values. At this point we should note their professional interpretation in the Code of Ethics of the National Association of Social Workers. The following are excerpts the Code's major principles.[28]

I.   Conduct and Comportment
     A.   Maintain high standards of conduct and comportment in identity as social worker;

**FIGURE 2.5**   Client-in-Situation

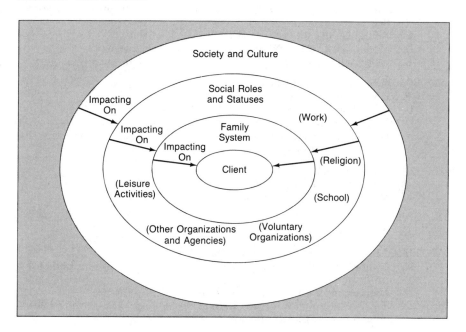

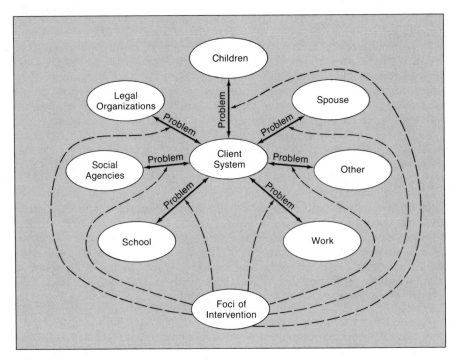

**FIGURE 2.6**  Targets of Practice

    B.  Sustain efforts to become and remain proficient in professional practice;

    C.  Recognize the service obligation of the profession;

    D.  Maintain highest standards of integrity and impartiality;

    E.  Guide scholarship and research by conventions of scholarly inquiry.

 II.  Ethical Responsibility to Clients

    F.  Give primary responsibility to client's interests;

    G.  Allow maximum self-determination for clients;

    H.  Respect the privacy of clients and their right to confidentiality;

    I.  Charge fair, reasonable, and considerate fees, with due regard for the clients' ability to pay.

III.  Ethical Responsibility to Colleagues

    J.  Give respect, fairness, and courtesy;

    K.  Maintain professional consideration for clients of colleagues.

IV.  Ethical Responsibility to Employers

    L.  Adhere to commitments made to employers.

 V.  Ethical Responsibility to the Profession

    M.  Uphold and advance the values, ethics, knowledge, and mission of the profession;

    N.  Help to make services available to the general public;

    O.  Take responsibility for identifying, developing, and utilizing knowledge for professional practice.

VI.  Ethical Responsibility to Society

    P.  Promote the general welfare of society.

## The Emergence of the Profession

According to Peter Day,

> Social work was an evolutionary phenomenon with roots in social philoso-
> phies and ethical values . . . a spontaneous development, a manifestation of
> awareness of the need to create a means of protecting and helping those
> individuals adversely affected by changes which are reshaping society.[29]

It emerged in the United States during the Industrial Revolution in the late
1800s, in great part a response to the needs of a rapidly expanding and
poverty-stricken immigrant population. Also, it reflected changing family
roles that freed middle- and upper-class single women from family responsibilities. No longer needed for teaching and child care in their families,
these women became "friendly visitors" to the poor. Their "mission," and
that of the budding profession, was the elimination of poverty.

Social work derived from two movements with very different ideological bases: charity organization societies and settlement houses. Charity
organization societies were developed by philanthropists to regulate the
use of charitable agencies by the poor. Immorality rather than unresponsive social structures was to blame for poverty, and "friendly visitors" could
"save" the poor by teaching them morality and good work habits. Settlement houses, often developed by women, were based on the ideal that
people could work together for a common goal and change society to make
it more relevant to the needs of the poor. In this view, the cause of poverty
was not personal fault or immorality but unresponsive social structures,
such as the economy and the polity. Grass-roots organization, education,
and training, provided in supportive group settings and without moral
stigma, were the means to success. New immigrants were the targeted
clientele, but other people needing help were also welcome.

Early social workers from either base soon realized that social structures were responsible for poverty, and they gathered data used to create
social reforms. However, "blaming the victim" and the "medical model"
remained in the public idiom. The casework model of practice, emphasizing personal attention and individual work with clients, is a direct result of
the charity organization societies' friendly visiting. On the other hand,
group work, community action, and social action methods of social work
developed from the settlement house movement.

By the end of the century, social work was no longer voluntary but
paid employment, and was given public recognition as an occupation. Still a
women's job, the public looked upon it as an extension of "women's
sphere"—home and family roles moved into the community. Formal training began in the early 1900s as the first step in professionalization, and
social workers began to be acknowledged authorities on the needs of disadvantaged and/or deviant people. However, the fight for professionalization
had not been completely positive. Greenwood notes that there is a preva-
lent apprehension that social work might have to scuttle its social action
heritage to achieve public acceptance as a profession.[30] Many practitioners
have in fact turned away from the mission of equality so that they might
accrue some of the benefits of a profession—status, better pay, and more

authority in the community. A majority now enter middle class, more status-laden mental health fields. Therefore, work with the poor and/or stigmatized disadvantaged is often left to people untrained in the knowledge, skills, and values of social work. Concern with social action and social change has, in great part, fallen by the wayside of professionalization, which often undercuts the historic mission of the profession itself.

## THE PRACTICE OF SOCIAL WORK

Professional social workers are trained and educated in baccalaureate or graduate programs of social work in colleges or universities. Basically, there are two approaches to professional practice: generalist and specialist (see Figure 2.7). *Generalist* workers are trained for a wide range of problems: information gathering, referral, basic assessment of the problem, contact with other agencies and relevant systems, and case and cause advocacy. They often have baccalaureate-level training and at this level do not have so much autonomy as specialist workers. Masters-level programs also give generalist training, at more depth and in greater detail than in baccalaureate programs.

   *Specialist* social workers are trained more intensively in special fields of social work. That might include clinical therapy, work with people with special needs (aging, developmental disablement, physical disabilities), or administration or policy. They are more likely to have graduate training and, on the job, more autonomy, often in supervisory or administrative

**FIGURE 2.7**  Generalist and Specialist Training

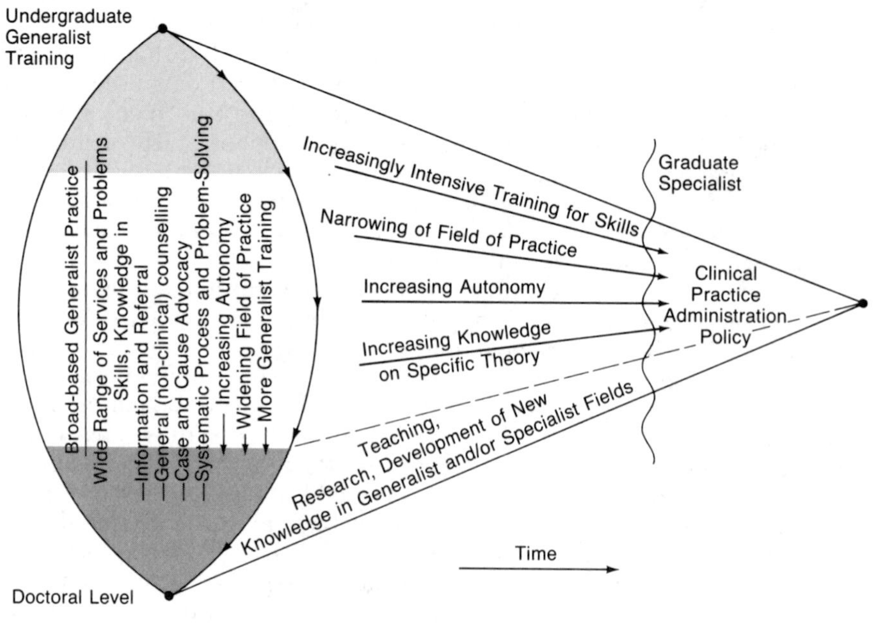

positions. At the doctoral level, social work training is given for research and/or the teaching of social work.

According to Gilbert and Specht, baccalaureate education includes an orientation on social work and social welfare, with knowledge of direct and indirect practice and knowledge of social welfare policies and programs. Masters-level work builds on that, adding development of in-depth knowledge on human growth and development, and skills in direct (counseling) and indirect (planning, administration) service methods. In addition, people at this level understand the application of research for counseling and for program evaluation, needs assessment, and policy analysis. Doctoral-level education includes knowledge and skills for research, consultation, and teaching and helps to build new knowledge on social work and social welfare.[31]

Traditionally, types of social work practice are divided into direct practice, or service on a personal level; and indirect practice, where the worker does not see clients but works on an organizational or institutional level. Gilbert and Specht say that

> Direct services are the specific and concrete activities in which professionals engage to help those who are experiencing social problems . . . therapy, counseling, education, advocacy, information gathering, referral, and [some] . . . aspects of community organization. . . . Indirect services [are] . . . planning, program development, administration, and program evaluation. The social worker . . . usually does not deal directly with people in need but, rather focuses on the institutional structure through which services are provided.[32]

Direct practice includes casework, group work, and some areas of community practice, while indirect practice takes the less direct areas of community practice, administration, and policy. Another way of dichotomizing practice is to divide it into "micro-level" and "macro-level" practice. These are generally analogous to direct and indirect practice, though system levels rather than type of client services is the determining factor.

1. *Casework* is work with individuals—counseling or intervention on the personal level to help overcome personal, intrapsychic, or systemic problems which prevent individuals from fulfilling their potentials. Mental health or child guidance counseling exemplify this kind of social work.

2. *Group work* is interventive work in interrelationships among members of a group or family, where the goal is group process as well as helping the members. Working with groups in a residential treatment center, with voluntary help groups such as Alcoholics Anonymous, or with consciousness-raising groups for women are examples of this kind of practice.

3. *Community practice* is work with indigenous groups in neighborhoods, areas, or communities to bring about changes in the social systems. Those changes are needed either because certain systems are oppressive (as would be slum housing) or to further the aims of the group in creating better systems (as in getting more police protection). Community practice may be directly with client groups, as resource person or facilitator of group action, or may be in indirect work, with other systems to insure clients their rights.

4. *Administration* and *policy* are professional practice to plan programs, work for legislation, or administer organizations. In these areas, social workers direct or become planners in organizations, or they may be legislative advisors or lobbyists, among other work.

5. *Research* investigates social problems to find new ways of service or add to the knowledge base of social work, and *teaching* prepares social workers for their professions.

The practice of social work seems at first to be divided into as many kinds of practice as there are practitioners. However, there are unifying principles that can be detailed, though there is much overlap. They include

1. The practice bases—values, knowledge, and skills
2. A systems framework
3. Levels of practice
4. Simultaneity in relational and cognitive skills

The idea of *combination* of skills, values, and knowledge is the underlying theme of practice at any level or in any style. We have already discussed the value base of social work; the *knowledge base* derives from many disciplines. Here are some examples: from psychology we obtain information on human development, mental health, and primary and secondary relationships; from sociology we learn of behavior in groups, societal values and norms, the place of person in organization and the uses of power, status, class, race, and sex; from learning theory comes information on how people assimilate new ideas and their stages of mental development; and from history we become aware of the broad sweeps of economics, the polity, and religion in creating and changing the institution of social welfare.

Types of *interventive techniques* depend first on the purpose of the intervention—whether social treatment or social control—and are related to the needs both of the client system and those of society. Second, they depend on the client system type—individual, group, organization, or other. Third, the kind of technique depends on the theoretical base the worker is using. Therapists may use any of a variety of techniques: Freudian psychoanalysis, Gestalt therapy, confrontative techniques, principles of learning theory, problem-solving models, and so on.

The *systems framework* looks at the "client-in-situation" and its interactive elements. The systems framework is, briefly, a perception that situation and interacting units form a perceived unity subject to cohesion and with identifiable characteristics and reactions. Each system has units, and each is embedded in a larger system. At any level, whether intrapersonal, interpersonal, or intersystem, actions will cause reactions. To picture this, imagine a box with Ping-Pong balls in it. Drop another Ping-Pong ball in, and every other one reacts. The system boundary is the box; the units are the Ping-Pong balls; the presenting situation is the position of Ping-Pong balls reacting with one another in the confines of the box (see Figure 2.8).

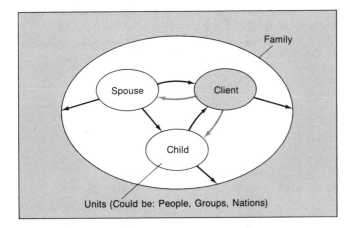

**FIGURE 2.8**  Interactions in a System

In social work, the client and the worker together form a dyadic system. However, that interaction is influenced both by the client's and the worker's other systems. Moreover, both are embedded in the societal system that establishes norms, rules, and the ways of behavior expected from its members (see Figure 2.9).

Because the trend toward professionalization has required specific identification of roles, tasks, skills, and other concepts of social work, we have in many ways lost track of the *holistic nature* of practice. Regardless of the system involved or the level of practice, the basic structure of social work relies both on cognitive skills (requiring analytic process tasks or information—data—tasks) and relational skills (requiring interpersonal or "people" tasks).

The simultaneous exercise of both these skills in all areas of practice provides social work with a unified base (see Figure 2.10).

This concludes our brief discussion of the profession and practice of social work for now. As we proceed through the book, however, we will note in more detail the development of the profession and its confluence with the major institutions of society. In particular, we will begin to see that our traditional beliefs about the purpose of social work as a helping profession may not be entirely accurate.

**FIGURE 2.9**  Embeddedness of Systems.[33]  *Source*: From Phyllis J. Day, Harry J. Macy, and Eugene C. Jackson, *Social Working: Exercises in Generalist Practice*, © 1984 ch. 5, fig. 5.1, p. 74. Reprinted by permission of Prentice Hall, Inc., Englewood Cliffs, N.J.

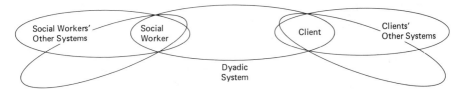

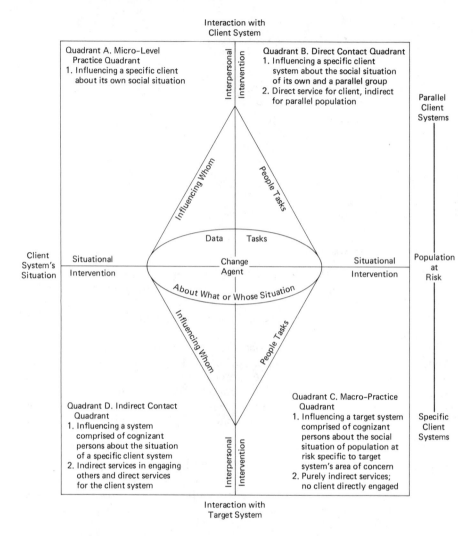

**FIGURE 2.10**   Simultaneity Model[34]   *Source*: Phyllis J. Day, Harry J. Macy, and Eugene C. Jackson, *Social Working*: *Exercises in Generalist Practice*. Englewood Cliffs, N.J.: Prentice Hall, 1984, p. 8.

## CONCLUSION: MODELS OF PRACTICE
## AND THE PROFESSION

In this chapter we have overviewed social welfare and social work. Of particular importance were the definitions of social institution, social welfare, and social work, for they provide us with common concepts. The perspective of social welfare as both social treatment and social control gives us new insights into the political and economic purposes that maintain social problems and prevent disadvantaged people from attaining equality in our society. Social work is more than concern and care. It is also a political activity aimed at control. Peter Day says that

> social work acts have political implications . . . about the way that an organization or group is run, and therefore about who has the power to get things done.[35]

and

> Care and control can be seen as complementary aspects of public policy towards the poor and deviant . . . these two elements, originally separately institutionalized, have converged in the role of . . . social workers.[36]

Our discussion of perspectives demonstrates that social conflict may be the basis for social problems, and that so defining them is functional for continuing inequality and the status quo in our society. Newer perspectives arising from the conflict model give us useful ways to understand this. Finally, the feminist welfarist perspective further illuminates the social welfare institution and the status of social workers as often unaware tools of forces not at all oriented to benevolence.

## STUDY QUESTIONS

1. What is the relationship of social welfare to the other institutions of society?
2. For your choice of social problems, what would constitute
   a. a residual perspective?
   b. an institutional perspective?
   c. a socialist or conflict perspective?
   d. a feminist welfarist perspective?
3. What are the elements of social work practice?
4. What is the definition of social welfare? Why does it include both social treatment and social control?
5. How do the polity, economy, and religion impact upon social treatment and social control?

## FOOTNOTES

[1]Compton quotes W.G. Sumner on the definition of an institution: "An institution consists of a concept (idea, notion, doctrine, interest) and a structure . . . .The structure is a framework or apparatus, or perhaps only a number of functionaries, . . . [which] holds the concept and furnishes instrumentalities for bringing it into the world of facts and action" (Gould and Kolb, 1964, p. 338). In Beulah Compton, *Introduction to Social Welfare and Social Work: Structure, Function, and Process*, (Homewood, Ill.: The Dorsey Press, 1980), p. 31. Neil Gilbert and Harry Specht say that an institution is a network " . . . of relationships that are generally accepted as the way of carrying out these essential social functions . . . human activities such as child-rearing and the production, consumption, and distribution of goods . . . raising and training the young . . . ." In *Dimensions of Social Welfare Policy*, (Englewood Cliffs, N.J.: Prentice Hall, 1974), p. 4.

[2]See charts on page 8, Gilbert and Specht, *Dimensions of Social Welfare Policy*, (Englewood Cliffs, N.J.: Prentice Hall, 1974).

[3]Ibid., p. 5.

[4]As the Ku Klux Klan or in situations of conquest over other polities.

[5]Compton, *Introduction to Social Welfare*, p. 46.

[6]The Internal Revenue Service now has a special listing for "Persons of Opposite Sex Sharing Living Quarters" (POSSLQ's).

[7]David Macarov, *The Design of Social Welfare*, (New York: Holt, Rinehart and Winston, 1978,) p. 23.

[8]Walter A. Friedlander, *Introduction to Social Welfare*, (Englewood Cliffs, N.J.: Prentice Hall, 1961), p. 4.

[9]National Association of Social Workers. *Encyclopedia of Social Work*, New York: NASW 1977), Vol. II, p. 1503.

[10]Klein, (1968), Romansky, (1971), Martin Wolins, (1976), discussed in Compton, *Introduction to Social Welfare*, pp. 28–29.

[11]Ibid., p. 34.

[12]Ralph Dolgoff and Donald Feldstein, *Understanding Social Welfare*, (New York: Longman Press, second edition 1984), p. 95.

[13]Peter R. Day, *Social Work and Social Control*, (London and (New York: Tavistock Publications, 1981), p. 12.

[14]Gilbert and Specht, *Dimensions*, pp. 68–74.

[15]Both the concepts of "residual" and "institutional" social welfare are taken from Harold L. Wilensky and C.N. Lebeaux, *Industrial Society and Social Welfare* (New York: Free Press, 1965).

[16]The phrase is taken from William O. Ryan, *Blaming the Victim* (New York: Pantheon Books, 1971).

[17]The idea of minimal subsistence level for public assistance is based on the concept of "poverty level." The first national "poverty level" was developed by Mollie Orshansky in the 1960s. It was derived from the idea that people spend one-third of their income for food. The poverty level became the cost for an emergency short-term food budget based on size of family and multiplied by three. With inflation, poverty levels have risen, but since they were intended only for short-term emergency care anyway they always fall far below the needs of poor persons.

[18]Frances Fox Piven and Richard Cloward, *Regulating the Poor*, (New York: Random House, 1971).

[19]James B. Rule, *Insight and Social Betterment: Applied Social Science* (New York: Oxford Press, 1978).

[20]Diana Pearce, "Farewell to Alms: Women and Welfare Policy in the Eighties." Paper presented at the American Sociological Association Annual Meeting, San Francisco, September 1982.

[21]Although education and health services are part of the institution of social welfare, each has developed its own professional mandates and functions. For this reason, we will discuss them only in terms of the social services each provides rather than with their primary focuses of education and health care.

[22]Charles Zastrow, *The Practice of Social Work*, (Homewood, Ill.: The Dorsey Press, 1985), p. 375.

[23]Alfred J. Kahn, *Social Policy and Social Services*, (New York: Random House, 1973), p. 29.

[24]Ibid., p. 30.

[25]Ernest Greenwood, "Attributes of a Profession" and "Attributes of a Profession Revisited," in Neil Gilbert and Harry Specht, *The Emergence of Social Welfare and Social Work*, 2nd ed., (Itasca, Ill.: F. E. Peacock Publishers, 1981), pp. 231–240 and 241–254, respectively.

[26]Dolgoff and Feldstein, *Understanding Social Welfare*, p. 285.

[27]Discussed by Greenwood, "Attributes," in Gilbert and Specht, *Emergence of Social Welfare,* p. 273.

[28]Taken from the NASW Code of Ethics as presented in Zastrow, *Practice of Social Work,* pp. 516–517.

[29]Peter Day, *Social Work and Social Control,* from discussion paper #3, (British Association of Social Workers, 1973), p. 3.

[30]In Greenwood, "Attributes of a Profession," p. 251.

[31]Gilbert and Specht, "Current Models of Social Work Practice," in Gilbert and Specht, *Emergence of Social Welfare,* p. 363.

[32]Ibid., p. 361.

[33]Phyllis J. Day, Harry J. Macy, and Eugene Jackson, *Social Working: Exercises in Generalist Practice* (Englewood Cliffs, N.J.: Prentice Hall, 1983), p. 75.

[34]Phyllis J. Day, Harry J. Macy, and Eugene C. Jackson. *Social Working: Exercises in Generalist Practice.* Englewood Cliffs, N.J.: Prentice Hall, 1984, p. 8.

[35]Peter Day, *Social Work and Social Control,* p. 4.

[36]Ibid. p. 16.

# 3

# THE BEGINNINGS
# OF SOCIAL WELFARE

## Political Economy
## and Early Societies

**PREHISTORY AND SOCIAL WELFARE TO 6000 B.C.**

The political economy of any society is the way in which decisions are made (or power is wielded) to ensure the society's economic sustenance and survival. In our earliest history, it was tied inextricably to religion and sharing, for provision of food *was* the economy and the way food was shared involved power. Obtaining food was the major task of early humankind, and was intimately related to petitions to deities of harvest and hunt to ensure an adequate food supply. Among our earliest archeological evidences, from about 25,000 B.C., are shrines and burial sites that show a communal life where all worked together to support the tribe. In prehistoric gathering and hunting societies,

> [s]ocial life is egalitarian. There is . . . no state, no organized government. Apart from religious shamans or magicians, the division of labor is based only on sex and age. Resources are owned communally, tools and personal possessions are freely exchanged . . .[1]

Men and women were co-equal, though a division of labor existed based on women's child bearing and food gathering to support their children.

Until recently, we assumed that men's hunting provided most food for their wives and families. However, newer interpretations of archeological data and studies of present-day nonmodern societies and primate groups show that gathering and scavenging by women was the most stable source of food supply.

> The techniques of hunting were probably much later developments . . .
> When . . . adult males brought back food to share, the most likely recipients
> would be first their mothers, and second their siblings . . . a hunter would
> share food *not* with a wife or sexual partner, but with those who had shared
> food with him: his mother and siblings.[2]

The numerically greater number of female than male deity figures
indicates that women had sacred status, probably because of their
seemingly magical ability to bear children and because they were the primary gatherers of food. Women served as priestesses of shrines, the centers of tribal life dedicated to goddesses of fertility and the harvest.
Moreover, because of their child-bearing and food-gathering functions,
they probably invented the first tools—containers to hold gathered food,
slings to hold babies, and cultural inventions such as social organization
and communication,[3] and food sharing between mother and children
developed into a rudimentary social welfare—mutual aid and caring for
designated powerless persons (children, the disabled) and those who had
benefited the tribe (the aged and sacred).

> [T]he act of sharing is so frequently a matter of polity as well as etiquette that
> even when food is scarce and hunger is acute generosity is more likely to
> prevail over hoarding simply because the maintenance or strengthening of
> social bonds is so important in rudimentary societies.[4]

During the Neolithic period, from 25,000 B.C. to about 6000 B.C.,
pastoral societies flourished all around the Mediterranean Sea and in the
valleys across North Africa and Asia. Where mild climates, fertile soil,
access to water, and a reasonable growing season occurred naturally,
societies retained their sex- and class-egalitarian nature for millenia. Communal life existed even after the Ice Ages from 15,000 to 10,000 B.C.
However, a new political economy evolved when, to ensure a more stable
food supply, women developed their food gathering into the science of
horticulture, and men turned from hunting to the domestication and herding of animals. No longer nomadic, their tribal life evolved to the crucial
social invention of private property. Now men began to "own" herds and,
later, their grazing lands. Thereafter, since men "owned" the land they
owned its products and the communal nature of food production changed
to private production under the ownership of men.

A change in religion legitimated both the secondary status of women
and the accumulation of private property. Around the fifth to second
millenium B.C., men became aware of the connection between coitus and
childbirth. Women's creative functions ceased to be magical, and women
lost much of their sacred status and they became dependent on the goodwill of the men who supported them. If male support ended—through
death, desertion, or divorce—women had few choices. They could become
public dependents, bond themselves to a new master through marriage or
agreement, enter prostitution, or eke out a living or starve. In all but the

last, they remained under the ownership of a man or men. Gender oppression began with women's double loss of economic input and sacred status, until eventually women too became the property of the male landowners. Coward says

> the explanations of the emergence of the paternal . . . [procreative] family were explanations for the emergence of individual property rights. . . . First, individual interests were conflated with . . . transmission from father to genetic offspring. Second, because of the theory of the origin of work as private property, it became possible to "sex" property, assuming a natural division of labour between the sexes. Men created it, therefore property was masculine. Finally, there is an assumption of an essential male psychology which seeks power through genetic self-perpetuation . . . the motor for the breakup of former collective society into individual units.[5]

As female power declined, male power grew. Although both male and female deities were worshipped well into the Bronze Age (1200 B.C.), men took power and men's religions became preeminent. In turn, these religions legitimated men's accumulation of wealth and power and their "god-directed" aggression against other tribes and peoples. They conquered societies and confiscated lands, herds, wealth, and often the people themselves, as slaves, becoming a new class elite with class stratification and division of labor. The poor, free or enslaved, worked to accumulate more for their masters. As religion legitimated the accumulation of wealth and personal power, the elite's allegiance to religion brought religion more power.

## THE BEGINNINGS OF HISTORY: 6000 TO 3000 B.C.

During the centuries between 6000 and 3000 B.C., wave after wave of migration—some peaceful and some based on conquest—surged across the world. Freedom from constant nomadism brought permanent settlements in areas most conducive to agriculture—around the Mediterranean, in the fertile basins of the Tigris and Euphrates Rivers, in the high plateaus of India, and along the valleys of the Nile in Egypt and the Yellow and Yangtse rivers of China. To the north, in the colder mountainous regions of the Caucasus, settlements were later in coming and northern nomadic and warlike tribes presented a constant threat to the established societies of the warmer south.

The new political economy meant that sharing was no longer the only means of personal and tribal survival. As some people sank into poverty, new forms of social care were established. Altruism played a part in such care, but a more pressing purpose was to ensure the availability of workers. Flooding and irrigation, adequate pasturing for herds, and control of marauding nomads meant that society now required political systems to coordinate work and protection. Patriarchs—heads of families and clans— assumed political power, and patriarchal religions evolved based on needs to control workers and women (to ensure heir legitimacy). Massive efforts to assure an orderly system of flood control, irrigation, and crop distribution were undertaken in the monolithic dynasties of China and Egypt, where the general population owed their labor to leaders and leaders owed basic necessities to the people. Dynasties also arose in pastoral areas around the Mediterranean and in the valleys of the Tigris and Euphrates rivers. The patterns of patriarchal classist societies developed among all the peoples of the known world.

### Africa and Egypt

There is a curious hiatus in our thinking and in our knowledge about Africa which is based on our pervasive Western racism. Long before the Egyptian dynasties, black Africans led the world in civilization. Africans used iron tools, employed mathematics, cultivated grain, painted pictures and created pottery of great beauty, and worshipped gods. Egypt owes much of its civilization to the influence of people from the interior of Africa. Though we usually think of Egyptians as white or Semitic, they were black-, brown-, and yellow-skinned people. At least one-third of the people in ancient Egypt were black Africans. Many of her soldiers were black, and "Black peoples toiled on the pyramids, offered prayers to the sun-god, and served with distinction in the state bureaucracy."[6]

Throughout the ancient world, Africans were honored for their intelligence, their beauty, and the extent of their civilization. Ethiopians were described as "the most powerful, the most just, and the most beautiful of the human race."[7] For more than fifty centuries, Africans fought, traded, and intermarried with Egyptians, and Egypt's history is theirs also. Many of her pharaohs were of African descent, including the beautiful and venerated Queen Nefertari. In the middle of the eighth century B.C., the Ethiopian kings Kashta and Piankhy conquered Egypt, and Ethiopians ruled benevolently for more than a century, rebuilding her fortunes, abolishing capital punishment, and renewing her religions.

In ancient Egypt before 5500 B.C., there was a strongly matriarchal system, and the royal successor was probably female. As patriarchy began to gain power, this provided a strong inducement for sister-brother marriage, and the ruler of the first dynasty was expressly said to be male.[8] From then on, the ruling houses called "pharaohs" slowly shifted to male rule until even the word "pharaoh" came to mean "male ruler." Poor laws developed to provide for a reasonably healthy and constant work force, with channels for the poor to take their complaints directly to the pharaoh. It was believed that God gave the poor the power to curse their oppressors throughout eternity. Since the Egyptians believed in life after death, this was no small threat, and those in power feared the curse. Therefore, Egyptian social welfare was based both on the economic need for workers and the religious need for salvation.[9]

The need to maintain a work force to build dikes against the ever-threatening floods caused the development of the "corvée." This meant that every adult man owed the pharaoh one year's work out of every seven. While this was not slavery (though there were slaves in Egypt), for that year the person belonged to the pharaoh and could be used to the death in his service. After systems of irrigation and flood control were well established, during the later dynasties, corvée labor built tombs and shrines. A bureaucratic system, directed by the grand vizir, was responsible for labor projects; for harvesting, storing, and distribution of grain; and for charity oriented to maintaining the strength of laborers for work.

During the fourth through sixth dynasties (2700–2200 B.C.), peasants became owned by midlevel lords. Dutiful work was among the strongest ethics, as was the accumulation of personal wealth through trade. Supplies were centrally controlled, and when uprisings occurred or when food was limited, frontiers were closed so that

> the available harvest and supplies would suffice for the local population . . . .
> Thus centralized planning and coordination are not inventions of the modern age and, specifically, careful provision of food supplies was a fundamental social welfare effort directly tied to national intentions and needs.[10]

### Mesopotamia in the Bronze Age: 3000 to 1200 B.C.

In the fertile valleys of the Tigris and Euphrates rivers, a more pastoral, more diverse, and more egalitarian set of societies evolved. Not dependent on mass labor as in Egypt, they were smaller and less monolithic. Wave after wave of migrants settled with and assimilated into the Semitic tribes of the region. By about 3000 B.C., most cities were walled against aggression and came under the protection of individual warlords, and private ownership in herds of sheep and goats had begun. Shrines still provided for the needy, and those especially designated for care were widows, orphans, disabled peoples, and "strangers at the gate," or foreigners.

The creation of accounting methods and the rudiments of written languages developed among the Sumerians who moved into Mesopotamia in about 3000 B.C. Driven from their homes in central Asia by drought, they settled peacefully among the indigenous Semites in the area that is now Iraq and some parts of Turkey and Syria. At first Sumerian leaders were elected by vote based on strength and popularity, as occurred in most prehistoric tribes, and this evolved into a system of rulers and ruled. Gradually the Sumerians took over the land until their families and clans collectively owned about seven-eighths of it, the rest belonging to shrines where, as early as 2000 B.C., widows, orphans, and the poor were protected by the goddess Nanshe.[11] Land could be sold only if all the prominent members of the family or clan agreed, and the new individual owners became the ruling class or nobility. The land was worked for them by poor landless freemen.

Three principal classes developed: the nobility (*awilum*), or full citizen; the ordinary freeman or second class citizen (*mushkenum*); and the dependent freemen, generally called "clients." Slaves were a fourth class, mainly prisoners of war, and were not citizens but chattel. Only the wealthy were given education, possibly daughters as well as sons. Aside from officials, about one-fifth of the population were craftsmen, and the remainder were laborers. Men, women, and children worked at herding and irrigating, and they were paid in corn, wool, clothing, wine, or oil, or they might be paid in part or in full in silver.[12]

By this time, most cities were walled, and Semitic tribes began conquests resulting in a series of short-lived dynasties: The Akkadian dynasty, established in 2750 B.C., ruled for five hundred years; the Dynasty of Ur, characterized as an efficient bureaucracy, lasted from 2100 B.C. to 2000 B.C. Amorite warriors formed a third dynasty, and then Babylon ruled. Her sixth ruler, from 1792 to 1750 B.C., was Hammurabi, a benign ruler noted for his concern for social justice. He codified current laws and practices in the "Stele of Hammurabi," developed several centuries before Moses, whose laws were identical.[13] It demonstrated the general way of life from two thousand years before Christ until Babylon fell to Persia in 539 B.C., and particularly set down laws to protect widows, orphans, and the weak against the strong. Kingdoms or dynasties in Mesopotamia depended mostly on agricultural production and flocks of sheep and goats. For a time their kings dealt peaceably with one another to pasture their herds or to irrigate their lands. When conditions were particularly bad, arrangements might be made with a neighboring ruler to allow the flocks to cross into better-provided territory. At times, kings joined together in armies to prevent raids on their cultivated lands by the nomadic people of the desert.[14]

Until about 2000 B.C., shrines continued to serve the poor, distributing food in times of need. However, as societies evolved, the shrines began to loan at interest rather than give aid. Free peasants who had no resources in hard times gave themselves and their children into ownership of the temples, and by 1000 B.C. the shrines owned many prisoners of war, slaves donated or bequeathed, and formerly free persons. However, they remained an important source of care. Dolgoff and Feldstein say that

> There are three noteworthy points to observe about this ancient culture: temples were important economic forces; governmental action was taken to relieve economic burdens and pressures, probably to avoid serious conflicts; and temples served as "social welfare" agencies, anticipating major religious institutional functions to follow in later centuries.[15]

### Invasion, Conquest, and Patriarchal Religion

Pomeroy says

> Patriarchal religion . . . appeared in recognizable form in about 3000 B.C. and is clearly associated with invasion—the Cretes by the Greeks, the Mediterranean by people from beyond the Caucasus, and so on. This . . . show[s] the connection of a powerful male deity with invasion and war. There does not seem to be this connection with female goddesses and war . . .[16]

The association of patriarchal religion with aggression brought new beliefs about economic stratification and the accumulation of private property. Where once strangers and foreigners had been treated benevolently and aided, they were now "outgroups," people who worshipped other gods. It became a religious obligation to conquer or destroy them.

In about 2000 B.C., warlike tribes swarmed across the Caucasus and Transoceana and invaded the Persian highlands south of the Caspian Sea. Of greater size and strength than the indigenous people, they mowed through them from Greece to India with a deadly new war technology: horse-drawn war chariots with sickles on their wheels. So devastating were these invasions that, after more than twelve centuries of written records, a complete interruption occurs.

> Egyptian inscriptions virtually disappear between 1730 B.C. and 1580 B.C.; after the fall of Babylon around 1530 B.C. inscriptions in Babylonia also disappear . . . and are not resumed until 1400 B.C. Assyrian records vanish between 1720 B.C. and 1400 B.C. Hittite inscriptions suffer the same fate for more than a century. In short, a catastrophic hiatus occurred throughout the Middle East, a sort of Dark Ages brought about by multiple invasions of iron-bearing, horse-drawn chariot-riding barbarians . . . these great invasions . . . wrecked countless states, kingdoms, and even empires, and destroyed more than one rudimentary civilization.[17]

The invaders settled, intermarried, and assimilated into the indigenous Semitic tribes of the areas. Their male war gods became predominant, and tribal warfare became a way of life. Communally oriented societies became class and gender stratified.

In the fourteenth century B.C., Semitic barbarians formed a confederation called the Twelve Tribes of Israel. Inspired by a male war god and teaching a new monotheism, they ravaged Assyria and much of the Middle East for three centuries. More deadly than their enemies because they believed that worshippers of other gods should be killed, the Israelites often slew every living creature and burned every field in the kingdoms they conquered. Since their enemies were polytheistic and did not worship the Israelite god, their deaths were inconsequential. These holy wars aimed at spreading monotheism and the Israelite god. Conquest and assumption of the land, wealth, and persons of "outgroups" were a religious obligation. That the warriors gained wealth and power demonstrates once more the synergistic relationships of human history.

The Israelites laid the religious bases of Western Judaeo-Christian society, influencing social welfare in many unrecognized ways. Both the positive elements of dealing with the poor and the negative reasons for their dependency are clearly documented in the Old Testament of the Bible, which demonstrates that, like all other tribes emerging from the Bronze Age, our Israelite forebears were warriors. Although there are many prescriptions for care of widows, orphans, strangers, and the poor, these occurred three centuries after the period of conquest and may have been necessary reactions to aggression and restrictive patriarchy as the society matured. By this time the oppression of women, the poor, and "outsiders from the faith" had been set into society as religious precepts.

The outstanding characteristics of the ancient Israelite tribes included aggressive and warlike behaviors; differentiation into classes of ruling elite and dependent vassals; and male-dominant or patriarchal authoritarianism. Caring for others, as such care had arisen from an interdepen-

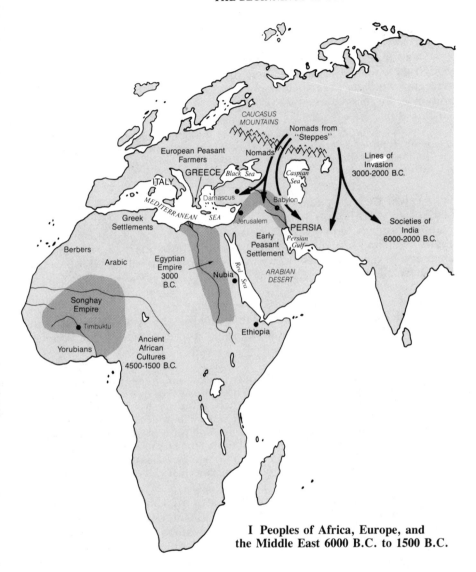

**I Peoples of Africa, Europe, and the Middle East 6000 B.C. to 1500 B.C.**

dent desert existence, no longer existed *as part of the natural order* except within the tribes. Rather, aid became a necessary addition to a stratified society, to maintain allegiance and a work force. Warlords and priests became the elite upper classes. The lower classes were artisans and laborers (*gerim*, who belonged to the tribe) and *metics*, or foreigners. Gerim were personally free but ritually impure, had no political rights, and could not own property, though they were given shelter and grazing rights. After the Exile, they were allowed intermarriage and conversion to Judaism, yet the effects continued to be class stratification and, often, debt slavery. Metics had no protection or personal rights under law unless they bonded themselves to a warlord.[18]

In addition, allegiance to a male deity reified the secondary status of even Israelite women. Pagan women, of course, could be killed out of hand or forcibly "married" to their conquerors. However, the social and legal position of Israelite women also suffered.

> The Decalogue ranked a wife among her husband's possessions, and while he could repudiate her she could not ask for divorce, and she remained legally a minor all her life. Wives and daughters did not inherit, except in the absence of male heirs.[19]

Wives called their husbands *ba'al* (master) or "lord," as slaves addressed their masters. Although wives in Egypt and Babylon at that time were heads of families, could acquire property, take legal action, and could inherit, Israelite women had no legal status. If husbands died, women were remarried to the husbands' brothers or put under guardianship of a male relative. While this protected them in the society, the society itself made the protection necessary.

Matrilineal inheritance was still the pattern in surrounding polytheistic religions, but as patriarchy took hold in the Israelite tribes, male line inheritance required sexual morality and monogamy for women. Stone says

> the lack of concern for the paternity of children among people of the Old Religion, which allowed matrilineal descent patterns to continue . . . was the crux of the persecution of ancient beliefs. It was surely apparent . . . that if a religion existed alongside their own, a religion in which women owned property, were endowed with a legal identity, and were allowed to relate sexually to various men, it would be difficult for the Israelites to convince their women that they must be property. . . . Each woman must be retained as possession of one man for the purposes of legitimizing their children.[20]

The admonitions against women written into the Deuteronomic revisions of the Jewish Book of Law clearly delineate the fate of Israelite women who disobeyed sexual prohibitions. Unmarried women had to remain virgin and were stoned or burned if they did not.[21] Unmarried women, if raped, were married to the rapist. After marriage, women had to be monogamous, although men might acquire any number of wives and concubines. Adultery was an offense against the husband's property, so both men and women could be put to death.[22] Women could be divorced at will by their husbands,[23] and daughters, like slaves, could be sold by fathers. Non-Israelite women could be killed outright or, if virgins, could be taken as wives or slaves.

Although later Judaic teachings redressed ancient Israel's aggressive behavior, three particular groups became vulnerable to poverty through the influence of this religion. One group is the poor, arising from class stratification; the second group is women, whose fate became dependent on the goodwill of men; and the third is "outgroup people"—those who, because they served other gods, were considered expendable and exploitable.

## MOVING INTO THE IRON AGE:
## 1200–400 B.C.

A thousand years before Christ, the legendary black Queen of Sheba made her visit to Solomon, and the riches of the earth seemed assured to Israel. It was the era of Zoroaster's revelation and the Magi of Persia,

> the age of Confucius, Lao-Tzu, and the great Chinese schools of philosophy, the age of the Upanisads and the Buddha in India, of Socrates, Plato, and Periclean Athens; of the great Hebrew prophets in Palestine—Elijah, Isaiah, and Jeremiah . . .[24]

The skill of writing became common, and oral traditions fell to disuse. In Greece, Homer began to write his epic poetry. Rome was founded, and the civilizations of both grew to prominence during the Archaic period from 700 to 400 B.C., when city-states began to develop. In Africa, the Ethiopian pharaoh Taharka steadfastly resisted the attacks of Assyrians, became a hero in Greek poetry, and assured Ethiopia's sovereignty for centuries.[25]

### Judaic Social Welfare

After Israel's period of conquest, her powers began to decline from about the eleventh century B.C. Eventually, her people were captured and enslaved in Babylon, and her prophets began to exhort the Jewish people to altruism. New laws began to address the grievances of the poor and the problems of women. Judaic charity rested on a priestly influenced community of free peasants and herdsmen[26] and was based on humankind's relationship with God and a God-ordered responsibility for self and others. Since all belonged to God, charity and giving without thought of self or salvation were one's responsibility to God.[27] Need was the only requirement for aid, and help was a duty and a human right. Responsibility for self meant to work for one's own support but, when necessary, to receive help without shame (Jeremiah). Charity, prayer, and repentence were the three pillars of the world.[28]

Dolgoff and Feldstein say that "Judaism bases its requirements for altruism on essentially two concepts: *Tzedakah* (or *tzaddakah*), a mixture of charity and justice; and *Chesed*, loving kindness.[29] The word for charity means righteousness or justice, and so giving charity meant simply being just or righteous, or as God required one to be. There was no special effort or conscious behavior denoted as being charitable: Honor to the poor was honor to God, and oppression was blasphemy. These concepts became law around the eleventh century B.C. and were codified in the Talmud after the Persian king Cyrus freed Israel from Babylonian captivity (600 B.C.). The Talmud is a collection of laws and traditions based on an intermingling of Persian and Jewish creeds. It was completed between 500 and 400 B.C. when, with imperial Persian approval, it became law for the Israelite people. Even today it constitutes authority on social welfare among Jews.

The Talmud and the Old Testament lay out laws for the treatment of the poor, widows, children, the sick, the old, and strangers. The hungry were to be fed, the naked clothed, and the stranger sheltered.[30] Farmers were forbidden to glean the corners of their fields or to pick up fallen fruit, so that those in need might have them.[31] The hungry were allowed to eat from the crops of others, though they could not carry food away with them.[32] Harvests every seventh year were dedicated to the poor, and in every fiftieth year—the Jubilee—slaves were emancipated and property outside the walled cities was returned to its original owners. (This last has been seen as an attempt to lessen the importance of private property but might have continued class stratification because of the earlier unequal distribution of land.) In fact, there was no record of starvation in peaceful times in Judaic culture.

The universal and institutional perspectives of Judaic social welfare are among its most notable characteristics, for there is no stigma to receiving charity. For example, in early times people could reach into a community charity box either to deposit money or take it out without others knowing which they did. Dolgoff and Feldstein say charity was institutionalized in two important respects: expected behavior of the donor and nonstigmatization and entitlement of the poor.

> Essentially, a culture developed that valued enterprise but without categorizing the poor as evil or idle . . . the society and individuals in it would be judged on the degree to which they provided for the poor without demeaning them.[33]

In later centuries, the Hebrew philosopher Maimonides refined charity into eight degrees, ranging from giving grudgingly to preventing poverty. These refinements and earlier Judaic laws concerning social welfare have been carried out for centuries in the daily lives of the Jewish people. They constitute a major basis for the institutional perspective on social welfare in society today: that members of society have a right to help.

In the theory and practice of present-day Jewish religion, many of the problems of class stratification legitimated by the religion of their early forebears have been redressed by what Miringoff and Opdycke call "temporizing values"—those that place humanistic charity before such overriding values as individualism or the work ethic.[34] However, in early societies, *all* Western tribal societies, including the Judaic, were warrior societies in which male deities legitimated oppression. This was coincidental to the era but is a fact of Western history, and those religious values that legitimate oppression still underlie our society.

### The Dynasties of China

China's history parallels that of Egypt, though at a later date. In early years, leaders were elected, but by about 1500 B.C., short-lived dynasties had developed. By 1000 A.D., the patriarchal Chou dynasty had overthrown the matriarchal Shangs,[35] and male rule became hereditary. Although clans and families owned property in common, the patriarch's decisions were absolute. Development of a feudal society coincided with patriarchy, and in about 800 B.C. monarchy developed. Serfs were taxed as property; therefore, many were emancipated because of major tax assessments between 600 and 400 B.C. Left to fend for themselves, many turned to the state for help.[36] Buddhism, founded in 500 B.C., inspired its priests, such as Mencius in the fourth century B.C., to exhort China's rulers to care for the poor, and poverty was redefined as a holy state. A meager system of welfare developed providing only food and shelter.

As feudalism collapsed, the ruling elite instituted the first unified Chinese empire in 221 B.C.[37] The emperor, as Son of Heaven, was owed obedience and loyalty but obligated by God to provide for his subjects.[38] Local patriarchs became an intermediary level of privileged bureaucrats over common people, who had few rights and were conscripted for armies and the government work force on coordinated systems of irrigation and flood control. The bureaucracy was hierarchical, with two senior officials, roughly corresponding to prime minister and head of civil service. Below them were offices of astrology, records, court and imperial household superintendent, security, crime and punishment, foreign affairs, treasury, and taxes and work projects. Next were forty-two civil service posts. The officials had their own social welfare system: one day of rest in five, sick leave, education for their children (the next generation of civil servants), and often retirement pensions of money or textiles.[39]

The bulk of the population were working class commoners. In return for service to the emperor, they received a subsistence level of support. Each adult man served one month per year on state building projects, and each spent two years in the army.[40] By the first century B.C., in times of natural disaster, the government's relief policy enabled the poor to buy food from its granaries or, if they could not pay, to receive free grain. In addition, the poor were taken from ravaged areas and resettled on new lands. We know little about poor women, but the patriarchal ideals of Confucius, teaching the traditional roles of wife and mother for women, came to prevail completely during the Han Dynasty (200 B.C.–200 A.D.).[41] We can assume few benefits for women apart from those of their men.

There were also noncitizens or substandard people, without rights to citizenship or social welfare. Slaves, less than 1 percent of the population, had been prisoners of war or children sold into slavery by their parents in times of hardship. Their masters had rights to their labor but not power of life and death. Those owned by the wealthy fared far better than did free peasants, who were subject to drought, famine, and pestilence. Concubines of the wealthy—sisters or female servants of wives of the wealthy—were another group of the substandard, and were usually released from concubinage into marriage. Convicts in the well-developed system of criminal justice were also substandard people. Punishment was designed to fit the crime and included head shaving (signifying loss of life after death); a maximum sentence of five years at hard labor; beheading; or cutting in two at the waist. Relatives of convicts also became noncitizens and were confiscated along with other goods. In extreme cases, family members were exterminated also.[42]

### India and the Caste System

Great civilizations developed in India well before 2000 B.C., but they collapsed during the great patriarchal invasions. Indian society rebuilt, reifying the Hindu caste system and immutably setting inequalities in social position. The caste system had different effects for social welfare than did Western class systems. Poverty was not a condition for personal blame, nor was it traceable to unjust structures of society. Rather, it was the effect of *karma*, a spiritual belief in reincarnation that placed persons in life positions so that they might atone for past lives or prepare for future ones. Because one's position in the next life (reincarnation) was determined by actions in the present life, an obligation must have prevailed to care even for the lowest caste, the "untouchables," along with a fatalism about the inevitability of poverty.

Rulers were enjoined to care for the poor by religious beliefs, but as in all societies, social aid was modified by economic and political elements. Nevertheless, as early as 300 B.C., hospitals and shelters for both people and animals were endowed by Prince Asoka of India. Much interpersonal helping must have been carried out by clans and kin within castes. For women, the caste system produced a rigid structure of inequalities within inequality. Women seemed to have far greater freedom in early Vedic times, when female deities held sway and before social and political patriarchy triumphed.[43] However, although in both China and India Tantric Buddhism emphasized the basic metaphysical equality between the sexes, neither granted women real equality. The freedom of Indian women was increasingly curtailed. They were not allowed education, and widows could not remarry, thus forcing them into poverty or prostitution if no male guardian would protect them. In fact, the problem of widows was solved by the practice of *suttee*, where widows were burned with their deceased husbands, along with his other possessions. Although it is commonly believed that they went willingly to death because of their sorrow, if they refused they were bound and thrown on the pyre anyway.[44] Islamic invasions dating from about 700 A.D. exacerbated the position of Indian women, and until only recently, historically speaking, India lay under the severely antifeminist rule of Turco-Afghan and Moghul.[45]

### Greece and the City-States

At about the time that ancient Judaism triumphed in the Middle East, the societies of Greece and Rome began to develop. In Greece,

> [w]hat happened in the Semitic Middle East found its echo. . . . [T]he pre-Homeric outlook on life was . . . an organic, unheroic view of human destiny. . . . The iron-bearing [patriarchal] invaders . . . despised this . . . [and] in Greece as in Palestine, all [was] taken over and turned upside down.[46]

In the Bronze Age, warrior societies conducted raids and forays to gain slaves and booty. Military preparedness was vital, and men served as warriors while women served as bearers of future warriors. Still, since upper-class wives maintained homes and businesses for husbands away at war, they acquired some wealth and power and had higher status at the close of this period (about 700 B.C.) than at any other time until the Hellenic period, about the time of Christ.

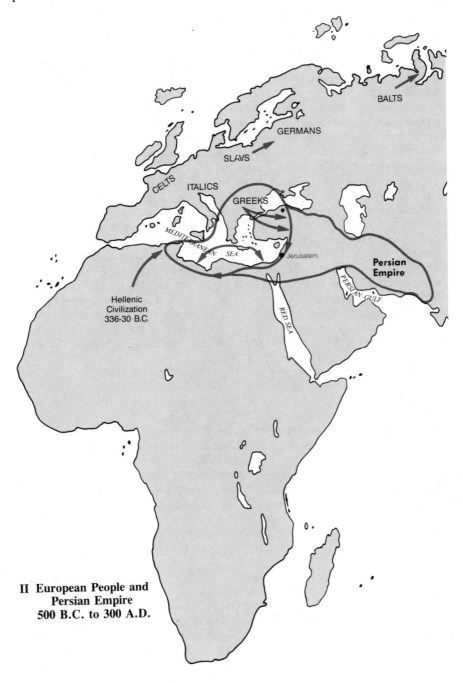

**II European People and
Persian Empire
500 B.C. to 300 A.D.**

From 700 B.C. until about 400 B.C., colonization became the goal of conquest. Population pressure was one reason: there was a rise in fecundity and a decrease in infant and juvenile mortality. There were twice as many men as women because of female infanticide. The Greek city-states were established by about 500 B.C., and urbanization meant city walls that afforded safety. Many farmers left the land to become a new poor working class, exacerbating the already present class stratification. To the early Greeks, work was a curse that brutalized the mind and made it unfit for thinking about truth or practicing virtue, and since work was despised so was the worker. The wealthy became an elite class based on the labor of slaves and poor citizens. Slaves, whether men or women, did much of the work of ancient Greece. However, their status could actually be higher than that of freed persons, depending on the wealth of their owners, and many when freed stayed with their old masters rather than become part of the poverty-stricken underclass.

Upper-class women in Athens were confined to the home, and as their activities became visible, they became less valued, particularly as they included tasks deemed appropriate to slaves. With a steady erosion of their legal status and matrilineal inheritance, they could not inherit their husband's property or incur debt, and their legal actions were not binding. Although they were citizens, they were under the guardianship of men—fathers, husbands, or male next of kin. Fathers arranged marriages to secure political liaisons and material bonds among families, retaining the right to revoke marriages. Girls were first married at about age 14 to men twice that age, and many died young in childbirth. Dying or divorcing husbands arranged new marriages for their wives. A wife's rape or adultery required divorce, and such women became outcasts, although the only penalty for rapists was a monetary fine.[47]

Women in the city-states of Sparta and Gortyn, though under the same general laws, had more status than did women in Athens because they could inherit from their husbands, too often killed at war. In time, women owned half the wealth of the cities. In Sparta, both men and women belonged to the state, and marriages were arranged eugenically. Children could be killed at birth because of physical weakness or deformity, for the goal was to produce superior people. However, once breeding obligations were fulfilled, sexual freedom—heterosexual or homosexual—was permitted. Homosexuality flourished in Greece, for the love of men for men was considered sacred. Women were equated with earthiness and men with mind and spirituality. However, the women of Sparta and Lesbos were particularly valued among both men and women, and both homoerotic and heterosexual relationships were formed with them and not disapproved by society.[48]

For poor women in all the city-states, life was more difficult though their status as virtual possessions of men by 500 B.C. gave them some protection. Pomeroy says that the lives of women lacking such protection were truly pitiful, especially if they had children, for most work they could do was done by slaves. Their work was essentially an extension of women's work in the home, for example, as washerwomen, workers in the clothing industry, vendors in the market, midwives, or nurses for children. Some became prostitutes, and some of these, the *hetarai*, even acquired transitory wealth and influence (though denied civil rights). Few Greek women became rich although some foreign women, engaged in large-scale financial transactions, did.[49]

The ideals of philanthropy and democracy, both important to western social welfare, arose with the Greek city-states. Democracy was only for the free citizen—man or woman—individualistic, endowed with reason by which to make free choice, and autonomous. Slaves and foreigners were excluded from citizenship in the Greek city-states. The concept of democracy, though limited to the unowned person of property, "enter[ed] into the western framework of political thought and influences our ideals about human rights in the modern world."[50] It is evident in our values of individualism, in ideas of equality, and in the representative structure of our government in America.

Philanthropy, another social welfare term, originally meant the benevolence of gods toward mankind, but by the fourth century B.C. its meaning had evolved to refer to the obligation of the powerful to help their subjects or dependents. Honor was the commodity sought by Greek citizens, and to gain it they gave donations of food, money, or oil to the city treasury for emergencies and food shortages; to citizen mutual aid societies; or to people of elite status in financial difficulty. Service in public office without pay was another means of gaining honor. The criterion for receiving largesse was citizenship or organization membership rather than need.

Philanthropy was intended only for the "worthy poor"—generally nobles or merchants—who were well reared and educated but had fallen on hard times. Reciprocity was expected in the form of honor, and donors earned status in the city and among the populace. The "unworthy poor" were persons at the bottom of society—workers and the unemployed—and philanthropic gifts were not given to them, for they were not "worth" the giving of help and could not reciprocate with honor. The unemployed were considered lazy and were expected to get along any way they could. Slaves were not eligible for citizenship and could not receive help. Needy foreigners were expected to return to their homelands. Beggars were rounded up and sent away, for aiding them was thought to encourage their pauperism. Poor, landless, or unemployed citizens were recruited as mercenary soldiers or given shares of land to colonize in far-off lands.

Caring for the poor had far different meanings in Greece than in older cultures, for it was self-seeking in terms of honor. Still, hostels and medical centers, the remnants of older religious shrines, were scattered throughout the country, and the Athenian state distributed grain to citizens during food shortages. There were also allowances and pensions for the crippled, public distribution of grain in bad times, and institutions for the custodial care of various unfortunates.[51] Orphanages and pensions were provided for children of fathers killed in war, and other orphans were supported until their eighteenth birthdays. However, attitudes toward the poor were harsh. The use of contraception, abortion, and infanticide was encouraged, and Plato urged euthanasia for the disabled or aged. Slavery, concubinage, and enforced colonization were also considered welfare, for the well-being of the state rather than the individual was the primary goal.

Macarov believes that, despite the fact that the concept of philanthropy originated in Greece, the *spirit* of philanthropy never existed there, for

> the nature of the society was such that the citizens *were* the state. . . . [This] may have arisen from a lack of religious commandments concerning charity. A concept of gods who competed with people, manipulated people, and behaved like people did not lend itself to divine commandments concerning people's actions. Thus, Socrates, Plato, and Aristotle did not include charity in their lists of the "natural virtues": prudence, temperance, fortitude, and justice. Indeed, according to Plato's *Republic*, the aged and the handicapped were to be done away with.[52]

In 359 B.C., Macedonian conquerors under Alexander the Great brought an end to the Greek city-states. This gradually ushered in new laws for women in all social classes. Earlier antifeminist legislation was rejected, and women were no longer confined to their houses. Polygamy, especially in royal families, became common, and divorce was often anticipated in marriage contracts. Queens ruled jointly with kings, and though women in Greece might need a male guardian, those in Hellenized areas away from the Greek mainland and in Egypt did not. The birthrate declined drastically, exacerbated by the practice of putting unwanted children out to die and the lack of interest in maintaining family lineage.

More people were needed, and in response to the decline new doctrines glorifying wife and mother roles for women arose, promulgated by the Stoics. Marriage and the rearing of children were elevated to the level of moral, religious, and patriotic duty. The straight-line, rational thinking and logic so loved by the Greeks were carried over into Roman society, and the dualistic reasoning of "man as mind/woman as body" was reemphasized, particularly in the period of Christianization.

### Early Roman Society and the Beginning of Christianity

Social welfare in Roman society was political. While in Judaism it was given from kinship and caring and in Greece for honor, in Rome in the early republic it was given in the form of doles—irregular gifts, especially to free men and boys—to gain votes. Therefore, only minimal help (if any) was given women and girls. Even wealthy women gave to men, for men held the power.

> The doles were motivated not so much by humanitarian reasons as by political desires to keep men pacified and curry favor with the crowds. . . . Since women, although citizens, could not vote, and their hunger was not likely to drive them to revolution, there was little point in including them in the largesse. Moreover, including women would have meant reducing the portions of men, and the benefactor would not have won the good will of those he courted.[53]

The dole was only enough for one, so wives and children of poor men might starve. However, eligibility depended not on need but on voting power, so even if they received a dole men could work to support their families.

In the late Republic (450–150 B.C.), there were a number of assistance programs in addition to the dole: occasional distributions of food by rich Roman citizens; private food programs; and public feasts established by private benefactors. In addition, trade and craft groups organized as "collegia," giving monthly contributions to a common fund for mutual aid.[54] Patronage by the wealthy supported their dependent workers with food, clothing, shelter, and other necessities. Some children's assistance programs were set up in the early Empire (100 B.C. to 100 A.D.) specifically for future recruitment of soldiers. Boys received more money than girls and were supported until ages 17 or 18. Girls were not as often supported—in one town, of 300 recipients, only 36 were girls—and their doles were at a lower level and stopped at age 14, when they were expected to marry. Female infanticide and neglect meant a higher death rate for girls, and if they lived, their life span was shorter by five to ten years than that of males because of poor health resulting from malnutrition and child-bearing at an early age.[55] Life expectancy in general was short, about 40 or 50 years for the elite class. Over half the wives of the poor died before age 30, most between 20 and 25.

Patriarchy was a major characteristic of both the late republic and the early empire. The *paterfamilias,* or father of the family, had absolute authority (*manus*) over women and children, even to slavery and death. Only men had legal rights—women could not appear in court, buy or sell property, or inherit their husbands' estates. Husbands judged their wives for crimes and could sentence them to death even for misdemeanors— certainly for infidelity. Priestesses and wealthy courtesans had some autonomy, as did freed women of guilds and crafts, who were not supervised by their husbands and seemed really to be free.[56] Most poor freed women, however, were working-class shopkeepers, artisans, domestics, woolworkers, or clothes makers. Slaves, men or women, could buy their freedom or be manumitted, but many stayed with their former owners rather than being released into the ranks of the poor to starve.

At the turn of the millenium, Greek, Roman, Jewish, Egyptian, and Eastern societies converged and blended, and Rome moved fully into Empire to become ruler of the Western world (see Map 3). Its territories expanded as far as the British Isles, and conquests amassed riches for the ruling class. Great wealth led to increasing corruption and even wider disparities between the rich and poor. The need for defense garrisons in far-flung lands and profligate spending by those in power led to huge tax assessments. Unbelievable poverty existed: by the second century A.D., despite dole and patronage systems,

> of 1.2 million people, all but 150,000 heads of families in Rome needed to draw on public foods, and in Constantinople another 80,000 were receiving free food.[57]

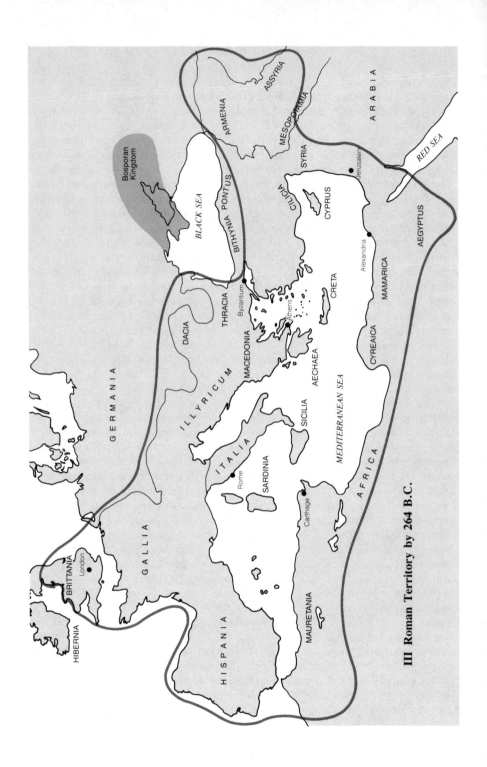

III Roman Territory by 264 B.C.

The financial structure was based on a tax system in which the poor were assessed proportionately more, significantly increasing poverty and bringing even less money into the central treasury as former workers fell into bankruptcy. For centuries Rome had hired mercenaries to man her troops, but now her wealth was concentrated in individual estates rather than in the central government, and mercenaries could no longer be paid.

This destructive economic stratification was only one of the internal problems besetting the Roman Empire. Internal revolt arose on all fronts—slaves under Spartacus, for example, or the revolt of Palestine in 66 A.D., where, in retaliation four years later, Titus razed Jerusalem. Jews, whose laws and customs differed from Roman laws, sought new political power and the radical Jewish zealots agitated for religious freedom. Among non-Jews, the religion of Isis, spreading from Egypt, brought new hope to the poor and enslaved and inspired them to revolt. Its primary converts were the disenfranchised—women and the poor—who gained little from the male-dominant and class-stratified state religion of Rome (under the war god Mithras). Roman religion denied religious office to most women and all slaves and freed persons, but the cult of Isis allowed women as well as men, slave as well as freed person, and poor as well as rich into its hierarchy. Each insurrection increased demands on the empire's strained economy.

From the time of the late Republic, women were increasingly emancipated. New marriage laws took away the rights of the *paterfamilias* and set limits on the legal subjection of wives. Common law marriages were usual, and a wife could retain her legal position by bearing three children or spending three nights a year away from her husband's home. After 195 B.C., women could administer their own dowries and divorce their husbands at will. By the end of the Republic, upper-class women were equal with men and owned much of Rome's wealth. In 18 B.C. Augustus brought marriage under control of the state because, since upper-class women refused to have children, Rome had increasingly fewer men to become controllers, officers, and bureaucrats in Rome's far-flung Empire. The lower-class birthrate, however, remained stable, producing ever more children born into poverty and more fuel for rebellion. At the same time, Teutonic barbarians began a series of increasingly successful border wars and raids against the Empire. Rome was beset from both within and without.

### Jesus and the New Religion

Into this time Jesus was born, a revolutionary who opposed both class and gender oppression. He reminded Jewish society of its prophetic past and spiritual teachings regarding the poor and oppressed, and decried the personal accumulation of wealth, emphasizing that unless their bounty was shared, rich men could not attain salvation.[58] Though Jesus and many of his associates were of the middle class, his appeal to the poor was immense. For a time, egalitarianism and communal sharing of resources and work were attempted, and leaders of the new religion encouraged the wealthy to take responsibility for the poor.

Jesus, of course, came from a patriarchal society (Judaism) that was very aware of class stratification but blind to the oppression of women. His awareness of gender oppression probably came from ideals of gender equality in Greek society and from the religion of Isis. Both women and men became his disciples, and his closest disciple was Mary Magdalene.[59] He overturned punishment for sexual offenses;[60] revised marriage laws to give women protection against divorce[61] and enforced monogamy on men as well as women, and recognized women's spiritual status.[62] Although patriarchy reasserted itself in the new religion within three centuries after his death, Jesus's teachings on women's spirituality and equality were clear.

Two perspectives on women fought for leadership in Christianity in the following centuries. The Byzantine church and movements such as Gnosticism and Montanism regarded both men and women as spiritual beings. Gregory of Nyssa, for example, postulated that both sexes have a spiritual and a bodily nature[63] and all have access to God through redemption. Rome's Paulist doctrines, advocated by Augustine (354–430 A.D.) and Tertullian (c. 130 A.D.), posited that men were beings of spirit and intellect while women represented earthliness and sin. Their ideas were based on women's (Eve's) original sin and on Paulist letters about women's proper place in home and church, that is, as secondary to husband in all matters sacred and secular.[64] Such teachings reconfirmed the patriarchy of Jewish and early Roman and Greek societies. By 300 A.D. the Roman Church had decreed Gnosticism heresy and disallowed teachings of the spiritual equality of women. In the fourth century A.D. Rome decreed that women, because of their deficient natures, could be redeemed only by their husbands or by renouncing their womanness to enter convents. These doctrines became dominant in Western society and are transmuted today into societal sex roles, including women's dependency.

The ideals of Christianity were a blending of Greek thought, Jewish teachings, and the resurgence of ideas on class and gender equality from the religion of Isis. Although we generally think of its center as Rome, in the early days the Roman church was basically a small illegal enclave of Hellenized Jews and Greeks. Jesus was a Jew from Semitic Asia Minor, and his teachings were first and more enduringly accepted there. Until the fourth century A.D., when Christianity became Rome's state religion, most of the Roman clergy were recruited from the East. The Latin church did not have time to grow, for all Rome's energies, including those of the church, went to protect the city, the greatest prize of the empire for invading barbarians.

> the Latin Church was soon engulfed by the barbarian invasions and, with little time for pointless theological disputations, had to take over the main burden of preserving what was left of civilization during the Dark Ages.[65]

In the Eastern church, an extensive system of poor relief developed. Christians pooled their possessions to provide a daily distribution of food. Both men and women were teachers and leaders, and women of wealth were instrumental in financing Christianity's growth and activities, establishing hospitals and monasteries and working with the poor.

the Byzantines [were] a nation . . . characterized by . . . many works of practical philanthropy . . . a virtue not only of the rich and prominent, but of all organizations and classes of people.[66]

In both Eastern and Roman churches, care for the needy became a major activity. In a sense, poverty was sanctified by Jesus, and early Christians based an "ethic of poverty" on his teachings.[67] To aid the poor was like having aided Jesus himself. Poverty, not wealth, was the way to salvation. The poor, slaves, widows, orphans, and those imprisoned, exiled, or working in mines as punishment for their Christian beliefs were aided. Women from the first were actively engaged in charitable works, opening the first hospitals and even the first monastic communities. Because Christians met in each other's homes, the concept of hospitality was elevated to religion.[68]

Ideas of work, private property, and wealth changed. Work was no longer degrading as Christians worked to support themselves, to demonstrate their worth to nonbelievers, and to serve the needy. Private wealth was considered immoral by early Christians because it created class disparities, but the religion's leaders soon realized it was a permanent characteristic of society and developed a new doctrine on wealth. Now the wealthy "owed" the needy the excess products of their wealth. By the fourth century, the good that wealth could do and the salvation that it would provide for the rich were major tenets of the religion. Salvation depended upon how one treated the needy—the hungry, thirsty, strangers, those needing clothes, the sick, or prisoners.[69] New systems of social welfare grew throughout the empire. Macarov notes that one of the earliest agencies for help of the poor was opened in Rome for sick slaves.[70]

By the middle of the second century, Christian charity was organized, with each church member expected to give a regular donation, often weekly, to the poor box. In addition, contributions of bread and wine were collected at the Eucharist, and a chosen officer, often a bishop, distributed the excess among the poor of the congregation.[71] Although at first this care was restricted to Christians, it was later extended to poor regardless of religion. The bishops of each diocese had supervisory control over all the churches in the district in distributing to the poor.[72]

Christianity became legal in 313 A.D. and was declared the state religion of the Empire under Constantine in 361 A.D., with his personal conversion. He believed that religion should be responsible for the needy, and Christianity became the state agency for charity. State, church, and voluntary social welfare functions thereafter overlapped, and the state was relieved of some of its burden regarding the poor. Privately endowed foundations, especially in Italy, invested capital in real estate mortgages, and interest was given to towns or state administrators for charitable uses. In Byzantium clergy distributed assistance, and in Rome a private voluntary group administered a state-supported social welfare system.[73]

## State and Church in Rome

Chastising the rich in the third century, St. Cyprian said "[They] add properties to properties and chase the poor from their borders. Their lands extend without limit or measure."[74] Although feudalism—in which serfs are hereditarily bound to the land and service to its lord—was not to develop for centuries elsewhere in Europe, it began in Rome even before the fall of the Empire (about 476 A.D.) as Rome disintegrated under internal forces and repeated Teutonic barbarian attacks. Many of the poor traded their freedom to wealthy landowners for protection in walled "manors." Small freeholders placed their land under the lord's control and became tenant farmers. The urban poor, competing with slaves for scarce jobs, also bonded themselves into serfdom, along with runaway slaves, army deserters, vagabonds, tax-ruined farmers, and peaceful immigrants from barbarian tribes. Used to hereditary service, by the fourth century these serfs were officially tied to the land.[75] Large Roman estates expanded considerably, and the lords were relieved of labor worries while their wealth was ensured.

Rome's ability to support herself and her empire was dealt a fatal blow in 410 A.D. when Visigoths, under Alaric the Great, destroyed the city and pillaged nearly its entire wealth.[76] In such a weakened state, the empire was easy prey for waves of Teutonic invaders eager for its fabled opulence. The whole central ruling structure collapsed and Western Europe was left in disarray, reverting to localized tribes. Cities shrank, and trade and communications diminished. Though several kingdoms followed the Roman Empire, none were able to hold the vast area together. Intermarriage between the invaders and the Roman senatorial and landowning classes took place in Gaul, Spain, and Italy, and from this sprang the feudal nobility that was to rule Europe. Angles and Saxons invaded Britain to be overthrown in turn by Danes and Normans. The process of barbarization became irreversible, plunging Western Europe into the Dark Ages.

As the Roman Empire fell, the power of the Holy Roman Church rose. It attracted the best administrative and political talents that the Western classical world had to offer and substituted its own bureaucracy for that of the collapsing imperial machinery. Roman civilization and culture now rested in the hands of the Church. The invading kings, respecting that culture, converted to Christianity. This legitimized the new royalty with the Catholic people of the conquered regions and demonstrated the power of the Church at king making. Where the Church had been a creature of the state, now many states owed it fealty, and its spiritual bond held the Western world together.

A synergistic spiral of power occurred: The conversion of conquerors to Christianity gave them power over the local populaces, while the right to crown kings bestowed political power upon the Roman church. Now political rulers could claim they ruled by divine right, and since Rome conferred this right on the many kings, uniting them in spirit, the Holy Roman Empire became the center of power throughout Europe. For example, in the fifth century, Clovis, the victorious king of the Salic Franks in Gaul, was baptized a Christian along with three thousand Frankish warriors. He then allied with other Christians and defeated his Visigoth and Burgundian enemies. With his Christian wife Clothilde, he subsequently turned Roman Gaul into what would become France.[77]

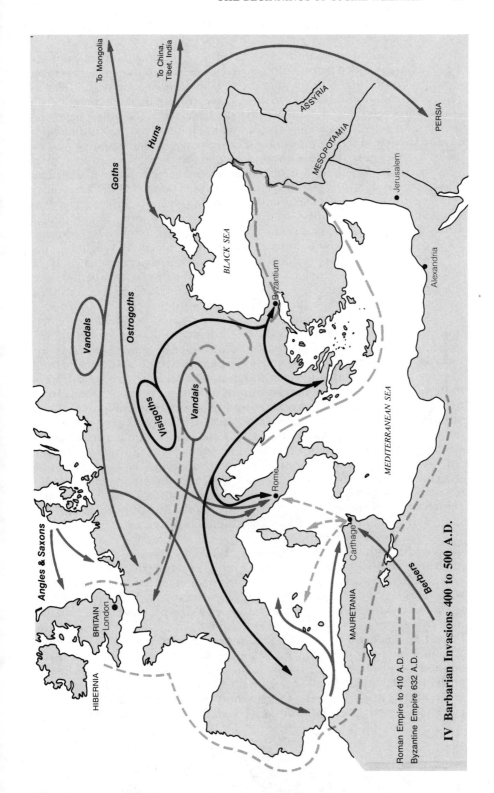

**IV  Barbarian Invasions 400 to 500 A.D.**

Roman Empire to 410 A.D. ----
Byzantine Empire 632 A.D. ---

## CONCLUSION: BEGINNINGS OF CHARITY AND CONTROL

In this chapter, we have considered the history of humankind and mutual aid. We have traveled across cultures, from western to eastern; across time, from prehistory to the beginning of the Holy Roman Empire; and across religions, from prehistoric, polytheistic deity worship through monotheism and to the beginnings of Christianity. We have noted the synergistic relationships of religion, economics, and politics that evolved class and gender stratification, and have seen social welfare change from communal mutual aid to a complex system that not only helped the poor but controlled their work behavior. Women's loss of economic and sacred power made them possessions of men, and class differentiation put the mass of workers under the control of a small male-dominated ruling elite. In every society, as humankind moved toward patriarchy and private property, a new political economy based on class stratification and gender oppression evolved. Exploitation became commonplace and was legitimated by religion.

The history of social welfare is also a history of societies and cannot be considered apart from them. The societies of our forebears, whether Jewish, Greek, Roman, barbarian, or Christian, have reified gender and class stratification even though their religions have ostensibly relieved oppression. Within each, social welfare has taken on new meanings with new times. In Judaism, social justice and human need were the keynotes, providing an institutional perspective that underlies some aspects of our social welfare today. Greek society developed ideals both of democracy and of philanthropy, although the meanings of those ideals were far different in those times than today. Roman society, a blending of many trends from the past, gave us political structures and processes that continue to affect our legal and social systems. Christianity as taught by Jesus gave new meaning to altruism, for it was a return to social justice, still a part of social welfare today. On the other hand, in the following centuries, patriarchal church leaders continued patterns of oppression as well as of aid. The Holy Roman Empire became a religiopolitical system of diverse kingdoms under the spiritual leadership of Rome, and a spiral of power between kings and church ensured the success of Christianity in the Western world and the success of royal lineages in the many kingdoms of feudal Europe.

Social welfare came full circle, for again religion was responsible for the poor, though its tenor had changed. While it still considered poverty to be the result of social and economic conditions rather than personal fault, now poverty was assumed to be both a proper state for many and a holy state. This legitimated good works and, in others ways, the right of an elite to control the poor. Although the church worked ceaselessly to alleviate the misery of the poor, through its benisons to kings and the ruling elite, it also helped to maintain structures that perpetuated oppression. The poor remained subject to the whims and desires of ruling elites in their pursuit of wealth and power, and social welfare became a means by which such goals were achieved. In all, synergistic relationships created forces that, a few centuries after the birth of Christianity, would set the economic, political, and religious overtones for social welfare in the world today.

## STUDY QUESTIONS

1. What were the reasons for the earliest social treatment? Social control?
2. What is meant by patriarchal religion? What was its effect on women, outsiders, and the poor?
3. Explain the similarities among such disparate dynasties as those in China, India, and Egypt. How did they differ from dynasties in the Near East?
4. What did today's institution of social welfare receive from Greece and the city-states? The Roman Empire? The Macedonian Greeks? The early Israelites?
5. What is the interrelationship among polity, economy, and religion in the Holy Roman Empire?

## FOOTNOTES

[1] Kathleen Gough, "The Origin of the Family," Rayna Reiter, ed., *Toward an Anthropology of Women* (New York: Monthly Review Press, 1975), pp. 62–63.

[2] Sally Slocum, "Woman the Gatherer: Male Bias in Anthropology," in Reiter, *Anthropology of Women* (New York: Monthly Review Press, 1975), pp. 45–46.

[3] Ibid.

[4] Ralph Dolgoff and Donald Feldstein, *Understanding Social Welfare* 2nd ed. (New York: Longman Press, 1984), p. 26.

[5] Rosalind Coward, *Patriarchal Precedents: Sexuality and Social Relations* (London: Routledge and Kegan Paul, 1983). p. 67.

[6] Lerone Bennett, Jr., *Before the Mayflower: a History of the Negro in America 1619-1964* (Chicago: Johnson Publishing Co., 1966), p. 7.

[7] Quoting Lady Flora Louisa Lugard, *Tropical Dependency*, (London, 1911). In Bennett, *Before the Mayflower*, p. 5.

[8] W. Flinders Petrie, *Social Life in Ancient Egypt*, (London: Constable and Co., Ltd., 1923), p. 110.

[9] Max Weber, *Ancient Judaism*, (New York: MacMillan Co., The Free Press, 1952). p. 252; and Noel Timms, *Social Work*, (London: Routledge and Kegan Paul, 1973), pp. 17–18.

[10] H.W.F. Saggs, *Everyday Life in Babylonia and Assyria*, 2nd ed. (New York: G.P. Putnam's Sons, 1967), p. 29.

[11] Taken from Samuel N. Kramer, quoted in Dolgoff and Feldstein, *Understanding Social Welfare*, p. 30.

[12] Saggs, *Everyday Life*, pp. 66–68.

[13] Ibid., p. 138.

[14] Ibid.

[15] Dolgoff and Feldstein, *Understanding Social Welfare*, p. 30.

[16] Sarah B. Pomeroy, *Goddesses, Whores, Wives, and Slaves: Women in Classical Antiquity* (New York: Schocken Books, 1975), pp. 12–13.

[17] Amaury De Riencourt, *Sex and Power in History* (New York: Dell Publishing Co.), p. 76.

[18] Weber, *Ancient Judaism*, pp. 32–33.

[19] De Riencourt, *Sex and Power*, p. 87.

[20] Merlin Stone, *When God Was a Woman* (New York: Harcourt, Brace, Jovanovich, 1976).

[21] Deuteronomy 22:23–25; Leviticus 21:19.

[22]Deuteronomy 22:23–25.

[23]Deuteronomy 24.

[24]De Riencourt, *Sex and Power,* p. 79.

[25]Bennett, *Before the Mayflower,* pp. 10–11.

[26]Weber, *Ancient Judaism,* p. 258.

[27]Isaiah 58:5–7.

[28]Walter Trattner, "The Background," in Neil Gilbert and Harry Specht, *The Emergence of Social Welfare and Social Work,* 2nd ed. (Itasca, Illinois: F. E. Peacock Publishers, 1981), p. 22.

[29]Pirke Avit 3:8 and 1:2. In Dolgoff and Feldstein, *Understanding Social Welfare,* p. 32.

[30]Deuteronomy 15:8.

[31]Leviticus 19:9; Deuteronomy 24:19–22.

[32]Deuteronomy 23:24–25.

[33]Dolgoff and Feldstein, *Understanding Social Welfare,* p. 32.

[34]Marc Miringoff and Sandra Opdycke, *American Social Welfare: Reassessment and Reform* (Englewood Cliffs, N.J.: Prentice Hall, 1986).

[35]De Riencourt, *Sex and Power,* pp. 170–174.

[36]Dolgoff and Feldstein, *Understanding Social Welfare,* pp. 28–29.

[37]De Riencourt, *Sex and Power,* p. 182.

[38]Michael Loewe, *Everyday Life in Early Imperial China* (New York: Harper & Row Perennial Library, 1968), p. 30.

[39]Ibid., p. 31.

[40]Ibid., pp. 70–75.

[41]Dolgoff and Feldstein, *Understanding Social Welfare,* p. 29.

[42]Loewe, *Early Imperial China,* pp. 61, 68.

[43]De Riencourt, *Sex and Power,* pp. 161–177.

[44]Mary Daly, *Gyn/Ecology: The MetaEthics of Feminism* (Boston: Beacon Press, 1978), pp. 145–146.

[45]De Riencourt, *Sex and Power,* pp. 77–78.

[46]Ibid., pp. 170–174.

[47]Ibid., p. 132.

[48]Ibid., p. 156.

[49]Pomeroy, *Goddesses,* p. 202.

[50]Dolgoff and Feldstein, *Understanding Social Welfare,* p. 36.

[51]Pomeroy, *Goddesses,* p. 228.

[52]David Macarov, *Design of Social Welfare* (New York: Holt, Rinehart, and Winston, 1978), p. 76.

[53]Pomeroy, *Goddesses,* p. 202.

[54]Gerald Handel, *Social Welfare in Western Society* (New York: Random House, 1982), p. 225.

[55]Pomeroy, *Goddesses,* p. 228.

[56]Ibid., p. 198.

[57]Quoted in Handel, *Western Society,* p. 31, from Marc Bloch, *Feudal Society: The Growth of Ties of Independence,* Vol 1, translated by L. A. Maryont (Chicago: University of Chicago Press. A Phoenix Edition, 1964), p. 61.

[58]Matthew 7:30 and 9:24.

[59]This is discussed in the *Gnostic Gospels* and also in De Riencourt, *Sex and Power;* and Michael Baigent, Richard Leigh, and Henry Lincoln, *Holy Blood, Holy Grail* (New York: A Dell Book, 1982).

[60]John 8:3–11.

[61]Matthew 19:8–9.

[62]Luke 8:254; Acts 9:17.

[63]Galatians 3:28.

[64]Timothy 2:915; Ephesians 5:22–24.

[65]De Riencourt, *Sex and Power*, p. 154.

[66]D. Constantalelos, *Byzantine Philanthropy and Social Welfare*, (New Brunswick, N.J.: Rutgers University Press, 1969), p. 11, in Macarov, *Design of Social Welfare*, p. 76.

[67]Mark 10:25; Luke 6:20.

[68]Dolgoff and Feldstein, *Understanding Social Welfare*, p. 36.

[69]Handel, *Western Society*, p. 49.

[70]Macarov, *Design of Social Welfare*, p. 76.

[71]Handel, *Social Welfare in Western Society*, p. 48.

[72]Dolgoff and Feldstein, *Understanding Social Welfare*, p. 37.

[73]Ibid., p. 34.

[74]Ibid., p. 35.

[75]De Riencourt, *Sex and Power*, p. 41.

[76]Ibid., p. 154.

[77]Ibid.

# 4

# FEUDALISM
# AND THE
# WELFARE STATE

## BEFORE HISTORY

Many forces changed Western society first to a feudal society and then to states in which laws regulated the treatment of laborers and the poor. Religion was one such force: The Roman Church completed the conversion of all barbarian peoples in Europe around 1000 A.D., legitimating kings and legitimated in turn by the new European rulers who appointed priests, bishops, and even popes. The Scientific Revolution and its growing agricultural technology were another, moving humankind from its organic relationship with nature and placing the power of production in the hands of an elite. Feudalism and church power changed as the Commercial Revolution brought the onset of capitalism and the Protestant Reformation. Social welfare became control rather than aid for the poor.

## THE DARK AND MIDDLE AGES

### Historical Context

Between the fall of the Roman Empire and the creation of the Magna Carta in 1215, the Dark Ages descended on Europe. Without a unifying government, cities shrank and communication and travel were disrupted. But the world was far from "dark" in the sense of stagnant. New forms of polity, economy, and religion were fermenting to create the framework for Western society. Throughout Europe would-be kings fought to maintain new territories, and the common people suffered as wars raged across their lands. The Christian religion continued its rise in both Byzantine and Holy

Roman Empires, and Islam rose and conquered great swaths of the Middle East, Africa, and Europe, bringing with it new concepts of government and scholarship.

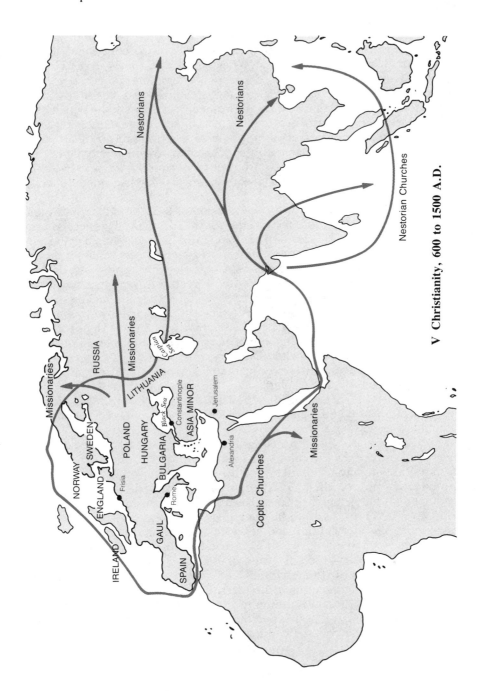

V Christianity, 600 to 1500 A.D.

In the Byzantine world, Constantinople remained the center of civilization until the thirteenth century. More influenced than Rome by egalitarian philosophies and traditions, the Eastern church discouraged both class and gender stratification. In Asia Minor, Syria, and Egypt, peasants settled into small farms and villages as free farmers. Taxes were reasonable, enabling them to remain free and keep their land, and in hard times the government and church collaborated to buy products and ensure employment in the monasteries.[1] While women in the Western church remained under the hard hand of patriarchy, Byzantine women were free under the famed Justinian Code of Laws (Justinian and Theodora, 527–565). In the East, inheritance through women was retained, the penalty for adultery was reduced from death to life in a convent (though men were still subject to capital punishment), and rape became punishable by death, with the rapist's property given to the injured woman.[2] Women and men often reigned together, and by the seventh century, a church-supported welfare state had developed in Alexandria, with maternity hospitals, medical facilities, and food rationing.[3]

In the seventh century, the new religion of Islam swept across Arabia and the Middle East, into Africa to the south, and to the Pyrenees Mountains in Europe. By the eleventh century, it had seized Hungary, Poland, and Prussia from the Byzantine empire. An aggressive and militant monotheism, it followed earlier monotheistic traditions by wiping out the old religions and eradicating the rights of women.[4] Although a few royal women retained power, most were totally subjugated, and veiling, once a mark of honor, became required as women were isolated in homes and harems. At the core of Islamic belief were moral living and right conduct, and it promoted an ethic of individual work and commercialism not unlike later Calvinist and Puritan beliefs. New sciences, including architecture and engineering, and new concepts of mathematics with new Arabic numerals, were developed by its scholars, and the concept of nation-state was instituted. By the twelfth century, Islamic hospitals were magnificently built and equipped and Islamic universities were the centers of scholarship and culture.

In Africa, the Sudanese kingdoms of Ghana, Mali, and Songhay, newly influenced by Islam, rivaled those of Rome. The University of Sankore in Songhay's Timbuktu was the world center of learning for law, surgery, and history. Ghana reached its peak early in the eleventh century, and Songhay apexed in the fifteenth century under the brilliant King Askia (1493–1512). He was said to be the equal of and superior to many European monarchs of the time,[5] and his realm, larger than all Europe, encompassed most of West Africa. The great Sudan empires ended in the seventeenth century, though states in East and South Africa, the East Coast, and Southern Rhodesia and Zimbabwe were centers of trade and culture into the eighteenth and nineteenth centuries.

In Europe, a hectic transition to a new kind of civilization began with the fall of the Roman Empire. Teutons, Franks, Visigoths, Angles, Saxons, and Celts warred across the continent, and near the time Justinian ruled the Byzantine Empire (518 A.D.), feudalism began its rise in France and Italy. Saxon kingdoms were established in England in the years 490–530, and in the eighth century the Viking Danes invaded England, to be

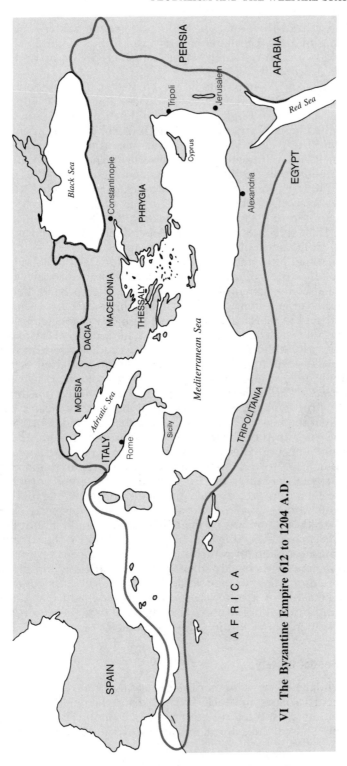

VI  The Byzantine Empire 612 to 1204 A.D.

defeated by Alfred the Great. In 800 Charlemagne was crowned by the pope as king of Italy, Germany, and France, founding the new Western empire, and two centuries later Macbeth murdered Duncan and usurped the throne of Scotland.

Normans and Saxons fought for control of England until, at the Battle of Hastings, William the Conqueror became king (1066). A short-lived feudalism came to England, ending in the thirteenth century with the signing of the Magna Carta by King John in 1215. The document granted civil rights to the people of England, but since it challenged the "divine right of kings," it was immediately annulled by the pope. Thereafter, it was reissued three times in modified form by Henry III (1216–1264). Toward the end of the Dark Ages, Huns and Poles repeatedly invaded Russia, and Genghis Khan subdued the north of China in 1216. By 1236 Mongolians and Tartars under Batu Khan were invading Russia and Europe, burning Moscow in 1236 and ending Russian independence. By 1259, Kublai Khan had united China and built Peking as his capital.

Women had little status in Europe except under the liberal Visigoth laws under which they jointly administered community property with their husbands and could claim a share of the land if the husband died first. In general, however, women were perpetual minors and possessions, to be bought and sold in marriage. Rape was a property crime against the husband, polygamy was common, divorce or renunciation of wives and concubines was easy. Although there were queens and warriors, most women were adjuncts to the male household, and under feudalism belonged as well to the liege-lord and the estate. As an example, marriage of feudal serfs involved a "bride price" to be paid to the lord. If the bride were comely, the price could be increased beyond the groom's means. By *droit de seigneur*, when the new price was defaulted, the husband could be thrown out and the wife raped by the lord, his knights, squires, pages, and possibly the chaplain. This was considered an honor for a mere peasant woman.[6]

Christianity enforced monogamy and decried divorce, and in this way brought a somewhat better life for women. By the eighth century, adult Frankish women were free of male guardianship, and by the tenth century Anglo-Saxon women had considerable power over property. Upon the husband's death, if there was no male heir, widows could inherit lands and title even if remarried, for the land belonged to family rather than individual. Also, in the rapidly growing cities, working women were freed from male domination of their earned property. Toward the end of the Dark Ages, married or single women could hold land, sell it, give it away, own goods, make a will or a contract, sue and be sued, and plead in the law courts in England and in Europe.[7] However, not until the eleventh century was a law written to forbid the selling of women.

### The Feudal Society

Prefeudal Europe was a rural free-peasant economy counterpointed by great medieval cities, in which the church and the rich held sway. Family and community constituted the fundamental economic units, though each farm family shared the natural resources of the territorial commons—

forests, pastures, and water. Communal resources were regulated by elected or appointed officers. Women and men worked their freeholds and resisted the would-be kings warring across their lands.

In the best of times the lives of peasants were in constant jeopardy and life expectancy for all people was no more than 40 years or so. Living conditions, poor health care, and poor nutrition made people weak, small in stature, prone to illness, and decimated by the plagues that periodically swept across Europe. Death by war was common for men, and childbirth a mortal hazard for women, rich or poor. Strayer and Munro say

> While . . . there was much inequality in normal times . . . all [were] equally helpless in periods of misfortune. They all lived in unsanitary conditions; they had no doctors, and at times pestilence swept away whole communities. Few families could store grain; a year of flood or drought created terrible famines. The peasants could not defend themselves against heavy-armed feudal cavalry, and if their lord became involved in a war they were almost sure to see their fields ravaged and their houses burned.[8]

Feudalism did not come easily to Europe, for peasants dreaded the near slavery of serfdom, which was

> a degrading thing. . . . What men feared and resented . . . was not its subordination but its arbitrariness. The hatred of that which was governed not by rule, but by will, went very deep in the Middle Ages.[9]

Finally, however, force and the need for military security made peasants give up their lands and freedom and swear allegiance to local strongmen. They bonded themselves to a lord in return for protection and rights to land use (as tenants or in "commons"). Every person had an ascribed status: Roles were predetermined, inherited, and immutable (as opposed to being achieved through work or effort). According to Handel

> Feudal society was the quintessence of hereditary aristocracy, privilege by birth instead of proved merit. A virtually impassable gulf separated the ruling class of lords and their fief-holders from the masses of peasants. Whatever their virtues or their vices, the rulers monopolized wealth, power, and prestige.[10]

Feudalism tied landhold with military service, and there was an "embeddedness" in the relationships among serfs, lords, and sovereigns. Unfree peasants owed their lives and work to the lord, and he owed them protection and good management of the community so that, in hard times, they might survive. Lords had land, power, a stable work force, the right to military conscription for their own battles and those of their sovereigns, and taxing power without redress. In time, the care of serfs by liege-lords became a kind of trust, a *noblesse oblige* or obligation of honor, and in theory all were provided for. However, the lord's right took precedence over every right, need, facet of life, or desire of the serfs. Every man and woman was bound to the lord, and brutal treatment, up to and including rape and murder, was not uncommon.

As the centuries passed, the serfs won some concessions. Many "owned" their property and their heirs could "inherit" if each swore fealty to the lord. As population increased and agricultural technology changed, serfdom became economically infeasible for lords. They began to charge rents and fees for use of the land and a new money economy emerged. Ascribed status obligations vanished and poverty became rampant under "contract labor." A new era of individualism and alienation began as lords were no longer obligated to support their serfs.

### The Scientific Revolution

During the thousand or so years of the Dark and Middle Ages, new technologies changed industry, architecture, and agriculture, alleviated hardships, and enhanced life. Inventions included the spinning wheel, water mill, windmill, wheelbarrow, crank, cam, flywheel, rudder, compass, stirrup, gunpowder, lateen sail, padded horse collar, and the nailed horseshoe.[11] As mechanization changed the way of life, the Church developed a religious doctrine that intermingled religion and science and mandated stewardship of the earth by men. Nature, already equated with the female, now took on characteristics assigned to women—passive, submissive, and controllable. This gynomorphic relationship was exacerbated as such church scholars as Thomas Aquinas posited a dual spirit/body approach to religion, in which mind and spirit were equated with men and women (and the earth) with body, "earthiness," and evil. Both persecution of women during the time of the Inquisition and Europe's ecological devastation during the Middle Ages were results of this equation.[12]

Until early feudal times, handhoeing and the three-field system, where land was allowed to lie fallow to increase its productivity, were the basic agricultural technologies. The invention of the oxen-drawn plow, though it put more land into production, kept an ecological relationship in which number of acres needing manure and number of animals supported on the manor were integrated. In times of good harvests, more oxen could be purchased to keep the land rich and to raise the subsistence level. However, as feudalism encroached, the new technologies and the demands of the lords altered the economy in significant ways. When the horse collar was invented, an ecologically unsound production began. More land was brought under cultivation in a shorter time (including that left fallow), and fewer animals meant less manuring. The commandeering of horses and oxen for war and taxes exacerbated this and prevented reinvestment in animals to keep the ground fertile. Another catastrophe, especially for the poor, was the "enclosure movement," where common lands for small gardens, domestic animals, and community water supply were taken over for pasturing sheep for wool export on the growing international market. By the late Middle Ages, enclosuring was nearly complete, and regulations for the use of meadows, pastures, and woodlands tightened, with hunting in the forest or the cutting of wood punishable by death.

The Roman water wheel and handmills slowly spread northward from Italy, reaching the British Isles by the eighth century and Scandinavia by the twelfth. Lords took a monopoly on them, requiring payment for grinding grain, making cloth and paper, and sawing timber. Although people kept illegal mills, retribution in the form of higher taxes, higher mill costs, or destruction of property was the price paid.[13] The draining of swamps, fens, and waterways for agriculture ruined local water and forest ecologies. By the thirteenth century, common use of woodlands was outlawed so that the elite could use wood as fuel in their homes and factories and for the building of the great sailing ships of the new international trade.[14]

### The Church and Social Welfare

The Roman Church was immersed in the politics of feudalism, a law unto itself, with governance, taxes, courts, and punishments. At its highest levels, corruption—the use of power for economic gain—was rampant. Any dissatisfaction or uprising to gain better treatment—such as the Magna Carta—was considered heresy. During the later Dark Ages, the Church established its own army, the monastic order Knights Templar, and its judicial arm, the Inquisition, to enforce its power both on foreign fronts (during the Crusades) and in Europe. Moslems and Jews were persecuted, as were non-Catholic Christians. For example, in 1209 a forty-year Crusade began against the Albigensian Christians in southern France. The whole of Languedoc was ravaged, crops destroyed, towns and cities razed, and a whole population put to death. In Bezier, at least fifteen thousand people were killed, many in the church sanctuary.

> When an officer inquired of the Pope's representative how he might distinguish heretics from true believers, the reply was "Kill them all. God will recognize his own."[15]

Lack of salvation and damnation to hell were overriding fears in the general populace, and to think or behave outside church mandates was nearly inconceivable. Coulton says

> [Medieval thought] is characterized . . . by the convictions that each man has a soul to save, and that therefore, salvation is the main end of every human being, not a distant ideal but the most practical duty that is set before all. . . . the last moment of life marked the man for an eternity of unspeakable bliss or of torment beyond all conception.[16]

Since both body and soul were charges of the Church, rulers did not need to give charity to control the populace. What little was given was, generally, either from whim or for salvation, often occurring on the ruler's deathbed. Usually, it was given to relatives, immediate retainers, military leaders, or the Church.

Many manor lords were also Church bishops, and they received taxes as well as tithes, donations, and legacies. Many used these for their own purposes rather than to help their parishioners. While Rome had central authority in the distribution of charity, local Church authorities established their own regulations, and the lower levels of the Church remained dedicated to serving the poor. Priests collected money and distributed food and help throughout their parishes. Need was still considered the result of social, political, and economic forces rather than personal fault, though some Church fathers believed that indiscriminate giving was morally harmful to recipients. Generally, though, help was given anyone seeking it, even Moslems and Jews. The able-bodied were expected to work for their keep after a few days.

By the sixth century, both women and men had established religious orders whose primary duty was to care for the unfortunate. Their monasteries and abbies evolved into the medieval hospital, which provided medical assistance but also housed and cared for travelers, widows, orphans, the aged, and the destitute.[17] By the eighth century, all church members were required to tithe, at first to support diocese and bishop. In time, Church revenues supported four areas equally: the bishop; the parish clergy; church upkeep; and the poor, widowed, disabled, orphaned, and aged. In England in the tenth century, support of the poor became a state law rather than a religious custom under King Ethelred. As early as 800 A.D., Charlemagne's laws prohibited begging and fined those who gave alms to the able-bodied.[18]

Women were increasingly involved in services to the poor under Church auspices, and some conventual orders pioneered in nursing elderly and indigent patients.[19] Abbeys and convents also served as refuges to unmarried women, nonconformists, and women intellectuals, and most learned women of the Middle Ages were nuns (though the majority were barely literate).[20] Nuns came primarily from the nobility, though some were from gentry and merchant classes. Peasant girls, craftsmen's daughters, and serfs almost never became nuns, for the Church required dowries of lands, rents, or cash, and sometimes even clothes and furniture. The Church's view of the spiritual inadequacy of women limited nuns' activities and restricted them to convents, though some, under the direction of a few powerful and wealthy abbesses, served in communities. Semiconventual orders, such as the twelfth-century Beguines, took temporary vows and served the poor, ill, disabled, aged, and prisoners in both cities and rural areas.

Church provision for able-bodied beggars and travelers, however, caused friction between church and state. Lords wanted to keep their serfs on their land, but the Church's policies allowed them to look for better work by supporting them as they traveled. This threatened the lords' labor supply and increased the numbers of "rogues and vagabonds" on the roads. Increasingly, these rogues began to prey on other travelers and on townsfolk, and to poach on lords' lands and forests, creating a crime problem.

In about 1140, the Italian monk Gratian compiled the *Decretum*, a set of laws regarding treatment of the poor made up of papal decrees, canons of church councils, and commentaries of church lawyers. It eliminated inconsistencies in canon law regarding treatment of the poor and distinguished between "voluntary poverty," that is, poverty for clerics, monks, or nuns, and the involuntary poverty of the oppressed and widows and orphans. It decreed that poverty was not a crime and that need alone obligated the Church to help the poor. Social justice was, again, the key-note, and the Church became increasingly critical of private wealth. By the beginning of the thirteenth century, the rich had to support the poor by law. These two interpretations of canon law—social justice and the obligations of the wealthy to the poor—set the institutional perspective on social welfare into Christian doctrine.

### Forms of Private Welfare

Besides the overall responsibility of church and feudal manor for the poor, private welfare continued throughout this era. Care for fathers who turned over their trades to their sons in return for support in their older years was court-enforceable, as were deceased husbands' provisions for widows. Although in most places such women were encouraged to re-marry, they also could continue to work their husbands' lands or receive a portion of the land until their deaths, when it reverted to eldest son. Sons might also take their mothers into their households or purchase "cor-rodies" from local monasteries. A *corrody* was a daily ration of bread and ale and a dish of pottage from the monastery kitchen; a room, a servant, and firewood; and a new robe, shoes, and underlinen once a year. Candles and fodder and stalling for horses, or sometimes a house and garden, might also be included.[21]

In the cities, crafts and guilds—voluntary societies for the protection and mutual aid of their members—aided disabled workers or those unable to earn a living and gave pensions to survivors of deceased workers. Dowries for craftsmen's daughters might also be a part of the benefits. Guilds

> maintained hospitals, fed the needy on feast days, distributed corn and barley annually, provided free lodgings for poor travelers, and gave other incidental help.[22]

Women could become guild members, but often not as equals. Usually craftsmen could employ only their own wives or daughters, and women were paid less for the same work. Many eked out their income with pros-titution or thievery, for which they were duly punished in stocks and pil-lory.

Finally, some kings, dukes, merchants, and lords provided alms or established hospitals or almshouses. Every major city in Europe and many of the smaller ones had hospitals, and between the twelfth and sixteenth centuries more than eight hundred were built in England alone (including those built by towns and craft and religious guilds). Private benefactors also underwrote almshouses for particular groups of people, for example, retired and disabled soldiers and sailors, old merchants, fishmongers.[23] Funeral feasts or doles were given, often specifically to the working poor, at donors' funerals and on anniversaries of their deaths. Amount of donation was not as important as wide disbursement, for the purpose was to ensure the deceased's salvation. Charity demonstrated to all that the pursuit of wealth was justified and pleasing to God. Although they misrepresented their wares, gave short measure, or charged high interest, by giving charity they could "achieve" the best of both worlds: maximum financial gain on earth and salvation in the afterlife.[24]

## THE DISSOLUTION OF FEUDALISM

Agricultural production increased phenomenally with new technologies but, though many peasants became small landholders, the majority were pushed out of the agrarian economy. Increasing numbers of vagrants roamed the land, some looking for work, some on religious pilgrimage (during the Crusades), some as itinerant peddlers. For the first time, as begging became a problem, laws were established to control the poor. Increasingly, voluntary charity and the Church were held responsible for supporting beggary and undercutting profits.

As crafts such as clothmaking moved from home industry to organized production, people of all ages, including children, were hired as piece-workers in their homes. The entrepreneur, a profit-making businessman,

> purchased wool in England, shipped it home, parceled it out to a family to clean, spin, card, and weave, took it back and gave it to another to full, then to another to dye, and to another to stretch, tease . . . and shear. Retrieving it for the last time, he gave it to an agent to sell.[25]

Work was from dawn to dusk, six days a week, and though it gave the appearance of "private enterprise" for the workers, in fact the entrepreneurs controlled their lives. They owned the houses in which workers lived and the stores where they bought goods, and sat on the city council to make their laws. Workers could work only for their own entrepreneurs, and this protected entrepreneurs from market fluctuations, war, or other calamity, for they could simply leave workers with unsellable cloth. Often workers bankrupted themselves to avoid debtor's prison. Conflict often resulted—the first strike in the industry occurred in 1245, among the weavers of Douai—but strikes were put down with the force of law. Punishments ranged from cutting out the tongues and banishing especially vocal protesters to the seizing of goods.[26]

Population increased slowly, held down by infant mortality, late marriages, early adult deaths, and abortion, infanticide, and available contraception. By the fourteenth century, the growth rate halted and began to decline. In 1315, because of the massive displacement of people from agriculture, food shortages became acute and waves of famine swept over Europe. Prices skyrocketed and many died of starvation.

### The Black Death and the Witchcraze

An already weakened population was then subjected to recurring waves of the Black Death, bubonic plague, carried from India on flea-infested rats riding the great sailing ships of the new international trade. In 1348, plagues swept over Europe and England and 90 percent of those infected died. In some places half the population succumbed.[27] A frantic populace demanded scapegoats for God's curse upon the land, and they were found in "socially indigestible" people—those unwanted by society. Among these were Jews, Moslems, lepers, the disabled, homosexuals, and women.

In the late 1200s, hatred of "different" people began to rise, partly because of the change from feudalism, the massive economic upheavals, and the religiocentrism and reification of Christian Church doctrine. Jews, for example, had to wear yellow stars or other distinctive dress, and there was missionary fervor against them, Muslims, and Christian heretics such as the Albigensians. Homosexuality, which was apparently widely accepted and practiced in twelfth-century Europe, was condemned by the Church by 1200 A.D. Laws grouped gay people with arsonists, sorcerers, and Jews as criminals deserving execution. Women, always under the surveillance of the Church because of their sexuality, exceeded the population of men by the 1300s, and they became another persecuted group. In the witchcraze, accused witches were often described as homosexual or women practicing aberrant sexuality.[28]

Jews were accused of poisoning public wells, and in the hysteria that followed some estimate that 90 percent were massacred[29] and their wealth confiscated by Christians. Often, they were herded into wooden buildings that were set to the torch or walled up in houses and left to suffocate or starve. The massacres waned with the plague, ending by 1351.[30] Moslems were expelled in growing numbers, and their culture in Europe began to fall into ruin. In France, King Philip ordered every leper burned to death, and throughout Europe people who were "different"—diseased and mentally or physically disabled, for example—were accused of witchcraft and burned. These killings, along with the massive plague mortality, caused a great shift in wealth as survivors usurped the resources of the dead to become a macabre *nouveau riche*.

Beginning around the time of the first bubonic plague, women became more vulnerable to charges of witchcraft, and their treatment as witches became much more horrifying. Until this time, "malifice," or the belief that some people could cause sickness or kill cattle by curses, had been dealt with by local vendettas or vigilantes. Clergy were urged to counsel women out of the belief that they could curse. However, the belief in witches, often women who were healers or midwives, became conflated with fear of Satanism and became a virulent misogyny.[31] Over the next three hundred years, hundreds of thousands of women were accused of witchcraft and killed. Of the total of accused witches, about 20 percent were men, but they do not seem to have been accused of deviant sexual relationships with the devil as were women.[32]

At first the poor and old were accused of witchcraft, tried, and burned. However, as the witchcraze rose, women of every age, status, and class, and some men, were killed. The first description of sorcery appeared in 1337, when a woman was sentenced to burn by the famous legal authority Judge Bartolo.[33] Soon ordinary conjurer's tricks and women's work at healing were metamorphosed into witchcraft. A papal bull by Innocent VIII put the Inquisition in charge of witch-hunting, and new and marvelous tests were created to try witches. If they died, they were innocent, but if they survived they were witches and had to be burned in the cleansing fire to save their souls.[34]

Accused women were often stripped, raped, and tortured before their trials, and estimates of the numbers killed range as high as nine million.[35] Some towns were completely depopulated of women, and many women committed suicide rather than undergo the Inquisition. Women were burned before their children's eyes as examples, and often the children were then thrown in the fire as well. No woman was safe: Even the saintly Jeanne d'Arc, warrior woman and leader of the king's forces in France, was accused and burned at the stake in 1431, at the age of 19.

In most cases, women accused of witchcraft were single beggar women, between the ages of 55 and 65, who had asked their neighbors for charity and had been denied. Klaits says

> To exist by the charity of their neighbors was the only recourse of the propertyless and enfeebled. Giving alms to the poor was an everyday reality, not simply an abstract religious injunction. The beggar was the typical welfare case. . . . Her knock on the door to ask for a bit of bread, butter, or beer was entirely ordinary in a society that relied heavily on individual acts of charity to assist the needy.[36]

However, this does not explain why these women were accused of witchcraft. According to Keith Thomas and Alan Macfarlane,

> saying no to a request for neighborly charity may have inspired a considerable sense of guilt . . . the emerging ethic of individualism may have been powerful enough to cause the denial of charity . . . but the old medieval ideal of communal responsibility could still provoke guilt feelings over the refusal. A justified curse was thought always to work, and . . . the ambivalent householder, later regretting his failure to give charity and thereby to forestall the domestic disaster that had subsequently occurred, suffered under a heavy burden of guilt. . . . Instead of blaming himself, the householder could project his guilt onto the charity seeker: she was the wrongdoer.[37]

Many witch accusations originated in charges against a quarrelsome neighbor, and midwives were often accused, since in this era, mothers and/or infants frequently died at childbirth. Poor widows lived on the margin of society; outsiders and newcomers aroused suspicion; and prostitutes, procurers, and tavern keepers, all of whom threaten family and community stability, were also among the extremely vulnerable groups.[38]

Politically, economically, and religiously this paranoia was reasonable. According to religious thought of the time, women without husbands were unqualified for salvation, were potential temptresses to sin, and often were consorts of Satan. By the fourteenth century, women's life span had increased so that they outnumbered men. Therefore, many could not marry, and widows often outlived their husbands. Poor women became economic burdens to families and society, though there was some meager support for widows and children. Many became prostitutes to survive, reaffirming the Church's condemnation of women's sexuality. Those who supported themselves by healing—typical women's work in this era—were in growing danger as healing was redefined as a science. Since scientific education was primarily available to men through the Church, the skills of women who practiced it were believed to have come from Satan. There was often an economic incentive to an accusation of witchcraft: Canon law divided a witch's property between accuser and judge.

There were independently wealthy women in that era—those who had worked in guilds, for example, or had developed their own businesses. Dowry law also returned women's marriage dowries to them on the deaths of their husbands, and this money could not be touched by others. Some used the money to begin commercial enterprises: money changing, loans, surety in commercial activities for others, and speculations. Many gifted their daughters and other women so that they might be independent. This threatened patriarchal control of the economy, and where no other legal means could gain control of their wealth, the accusation of witchcraft immediately forfeited it into the hands of men.[39]

The religious legitimation for gynocide allowed men to take both religious and political power over women. In a social sense, the witchcraze rid society of an unwanted, perhaps threatening population—independent women. In the economic sphere, society no longer had to support excess women and their never-to-be-born children who might have added to unemployment and dependency.

## LEGAL CONTROLS FOR WORKERS: POVERTY AS A CRIME

After the Black Death, a new "little Dark Age" descended on Europe. The devastation was so great that society seemed to stop, take a breath, and refocus on emerging needs and practices. The still agrarian-based economy was shattered by the phenomenal loss of labor and in the cities the developing mercantile economy faltered without a needy and exploitable work force. The diminished population created severe labor shortages, and, as peasants' work became scarce and valued, their status increased. In places like Germany, some reclaimed control of the land.

Until the fourteenth century, rulers had not been required to deal with issues of employment. Now, however, both nobility and the middle class (bourgeoisie) began to clamor for laws to control labor and vagrancy. Laws governing the right of people to come into cities, restrictive guild regulations, and city wage ordinances were enacted; in Paris, for example, wage raises could not exceed one-third of former level, prices were fixed, and profits of merchants were regulated. Workers were forbidden to organize for their own benefit.[40]

### The Statute of Laborers

England under Edward III gave Western society's most important response to the labor problem: the Statute of Laborers in 1349, revised within two years for harsher enforcement and to ensure the availability of migrant laborers in August's harvest season. Its intent was to bring employment under government control, and it was the *first significant law on a national level* aimed at the poor, not for their benefit but to protect the interests of a commercially oriented government. The statute regulated the movement of laborers to keep them where they were needed for production. Those found away from their own parishes were whipped, branded, sent to toil in the royal galleys, put into stocks, or given to anyone who claimed them. Able-bodied men and women under age 60 with no means of support were forced to work for any employer in need of their services, at no more than the prevailing wage, or be jailed. People who gave alms to the able-bodied, or hired them away from their own parishes, could themselves be fined and punished. During the 1350s and 1360s, fugitive laborers were declared outlaws and branded on the forehead with "F." Compton says that

> essential notions . . . were that begging, movement, vagrancy, and the labor shortage . . . were essentially the same problem . . . begging was not a problem in destitution but a threat to the labor supply . . . [and could be solved] by fixing a maximum wage, by forcing any unattached person to work for anyone who needed labor, by forbidding alms, and by limiting the right of workers to movement.[41]

Treating the poor as criminals meant that poverty had become a crime in society's eyes.

The Statute of Laborers reified Charlemagne's seventh-century legal codes, classifying the poor as "worthy" and "unworthy," and ushered in a personal rather than societal fault for poverty. It also began a gradual shift from church care for the poor to state control of labor by welding the nobility into an interest group in a *national* effort—for the first time—to dictate the future of labor. State and the elite classes would, from this time on, collaborate for their mutual good, while labor was at the mercy of both. The state would control the movements, wages, and subsistence of workers and the unemployed. The statute did not completely reject the idea of charity: Those unable to work—the impotent poor—might still receive alms in their own communities. However, not until the end of the 1400s were such groups as pregnant women, the severely ill, or people over age 60 allowed charity.

As government control became more repressive, social unrest increased. Riots occurred throughout Europe—in France in 1358 and 1382, in Italy in 1378, and in England in 1381. To stem the tide in England, in 1388 Parliament enacted the Statute of Artificers. It required all persons leaving their place of birth to have a "letter patent" telling their reasons for traveling, destinations, and date of return. Travelers without letters of patent might be returned home and indentured. Sturdy beggars—the able-bodied unemployed—transients, and those seeking higher wages were all treated the same, but the disabled or incapacitated were licensed to beg in their original homeplaces.

Over the next century, the European population increased—by 60 percent during the 1500s and another 30 percent between 1600 and 1640—causing a massive glut in labor.[42] Small farms were enclosed by the nobility, pushing farmers from the land and causing vast unemployment and poverty. Because of fluctuating markets, an intermittent supply of raw materials, seasonal demands, rising prices and inflation, and the failure of wages to keep up with needs, about a third of England's population could not find work. The number of rogues and vagabonds in the 1500s was larger in proportion to the population than ever before or since, and fear of crime and disorder was rampant.[43]

### The Commercial Revolution

Mercantilism, or a trade economy, became the predominant political economy of Western society during the Middle Ages. This meant that laborers were pressed into service to produce trade goods for the new international markets. This, in turn, took them away from the production of their own food, especially with the enclosure movement, and turned them into a work force dependent on the largesse of the mercantile class. Third, it ended the organic interrelationships of the old feudal society and moved people into cities and under labor contracts that could be broken at will by the upper classes. Fourth, it began a new money economy where wealth was no longer in land and goods but in cash, a fluid asset enabling the accumulation of profits beyond the reasonable costs of materials, labor, and investment. Finally, this created interest-gathering investments where wealth could be stored rather than distributed, opening the era of capitalism.

In the early days of mercantilism, a paternalistic elite provided for the poor much as had feudalism. Over time, however, mercantilist and national labor policies were influenced by the dominant interest in foreign trade, in which cheap labor played the critical role. This created a new ideology about the poor: Low wages would make them work longer and harder, and low wages would also keep them from buying foreign products, thus keeping money within the nation and aiding the favorable balance of trade. Following this ideology, social welfare developed as an adjunct to labor policy rather than to protect the poor. Its purpose was to keep a viable labor force for mercantilists and the state. Increasingly, new ideas of "work morality" placed responsibility for the livelihood of the poor solely on their own shoulders, in a political and economic climate over which they had no control. By state policy, they were now merely units of production in the great national economy—dispensable commodities to be bought and sold or warehoused according to the economic decisions of others. Unemployment became a problem for employers only if workers became so debilitated by starvation that they could not work, and for the state only if poverty created social unrest which lowered production and upset the international balance of trade.

## THE PROTESTANT REFORMATION: NEW MEANINGS FOR WORK AND WELFARE

Under mercantilism, both Church and state became supported by the moneyed middle class and began to redefine the unemployed poor as "unworthy." New religions were beginning: In Germany Martin Luther began his Protestant Reformation in the 1517, and England's Henry VIII instituted the Church of England in 1536. Klaits says

> Traditional Christian ethics taught that charity was a virtue and mutual responsibility was a religious obligation. In medieval times, the Catholic church . . . encouraged . . . the giving of alms for the support of the poor and disabled. With the Reformation came the dissolution of the Catholic welfare organization . . . and the state assumed the burden of welfare. . . . As for the poor, in this capitalistic world they were losers, to whom winners need no longer feel any special obligation.[44]

Now landowners and merchants paid taxes to support welfare, making charity less incumbent on Christians and placing it into a governmental bureaucracy.

### Lutheranism, Calvinism, and the Work Ethic

By far the most important event for the growth of mercantilism, capitalism, and ultimately social welfare was Martin Luther's break with the Catholic Church in 1517. Luther (1485–1546), a priest, protested Church corruption and deplored the selling of "indulgences" to ensure salvation after death. He taught that salvation could only be attained through the grace of God and that "right living" was the only means to salvation. One's vocation or work was a "calling" from God. Although Luther did not end poor relief and called for community chests to aid the needy, the implications of nonwork were clear. Those who accepted their "calling" through hard work obviously were more acceptable to God.

John Calvin, one of Luther's followers, made these implications even clearer with new definitions of work and wealth. He taught that salvation was predestined—decided by God before one's birth—and that wealth in this life was the evidence of the grace of God. Therefore, the purpose of all human activity was not to attain salvation but to glorify God. Industry, thrift, frugality, and asceticism were the marks of true Christians, and frivolity, sentiment, and interest in comfort and luxury were deplored. Work was more than a requirement imposed by nature or as punishment; it was a spiritual discipline. Calvin's influence gave Protestantism an international appeal from which both capitalism and modern Western society developed. Its creed was essentially hard, stoical, and uncompromising in its demands on followers.

A small ideological leap by his followers gave mercantilists religious affirmation both for their new wealth and for the exploitation of their workers to produce it. If wealth demonstrated morality, then surely poverty demonstrated immorality. Work as the means to wealth became the standard of the Protestant Reformation. Weber says

> The pursuit of riches, which once had been feared as the enemy of religion, was now welcomed as its ally. The habits and institutions in which that philosophy found expression survived long after the creed which was their parent had expired . . . it ends as an orgy of materialism.[45]

More than that, the encouragement of work in others was considered a holy task and the financial benefit to those who reaped the profits a just reward for ensuring morality. Meanwhile, the poor were doubly damned by the necessity of making a living in an exploitative economy and their newly defined immorality. The Protestant ethic became the keynote of Western society's policies in social welfare. Its psychological impact was phenomenal, for it fostered alienation from family and community, justified social stratification by income, became the model for self-concept, and made work the definition of spirituality. Poverty became moral degeneracy, and fault became centered in the self rather than in the structures of society.

Until this time, work had been considered, at worst, a punishment from God and, at best, a responsibility toward God and others. Before new technologies of storage and shipment, to produce more than could be used was only wasteful. Ancient Jews had considered work a necessity by which, in partnership with God, they would advance civilization. For early Greeks and Romans, work was a degrading activity that took the mind away from its essential tasks of thinking and spirituality. Early Christians considered work a penance for original sin and admired the nobility of poverty, encouraging work not for its own sake but to support self and the needy and gain salvation. However, the needs of the mercantile society and the Protestant Reformation changed our attitudes completely. Weber says

> this philosophy of avarice appears to be . . . the idea of the duty of the individual toward the increase of his capital, which is assumed as an end in itself. Truly what is here preached is not simply a means of making one's way in the world but a peculiar ethic. The infraction of its rules is treated not as foolishness but as forgetfulness of duty.[46]

Puritans joined businessmen in emphasizing the danger of pampering poverty, and giving charity was to abet the immorality of the poor.

### Women under Protestantism

Protestantism also reified religion's harsh patriarchy. Luther did not believe in celibacy for the religious and closed down monasteries and convents, putting an end to their widespread charitable work. Although he married a former nun, his attitudes toward women were oppressive. Women's calling, and their proper role, was "church, kitchen, and children." He said

> Take women from their housewifery and they are good for nothing. . . . If women get tired and die of bearing, there is no harm in that; let them die as long as they bear; they are made for that.[47]

Under Luther, marriage lost its status as a sacrament, for he agreed with some of his wealthy supporters that polygyny was not forbidden by the Old Testament. In fact, he recommended it to Henry VIII as a way out of his marriage difficulties. When Philip of Hesse requested a second wife,

Luther married them secretly in 1540, in the presence of two eminent Protestant theologians. The scandal leaked out, and Luther, though he withdrew from the position of bigamy, would not condemn it.[48] The early Anabaptists, following this lead, set up a system of "companion wives."

No less misogynistic were Calvin and the Scottish minister John Knox. The latter was eloquent in his condemnation of women rulers: Mary Tudor, Mary Stuart, Elizabeth I, Catherine de Medici. In 1558 he said their rule was

> contumely to God. . . . For who can deny that it is repugnant to Nature that the blind shall be appointed to lead and conduct such as do see . . . that the foolish, mad, and phrenetic shall govern the discreet and give counsel to such as be of sober mind. . . . Woman in her greatest perfection was made to serve and obey man.[49]

### Social Welfare and Work Morality

Protestantism and the work ethic swept over the world, and as the new standard of an emerging society it was reflected in all society's institutions including social welfare. Mencher says

> modern social welfare policy may be conceived of as commencing with the shift in the sixteenth century from the economic assistance programs of a declining feudal society to those of a rising commercial and secular world.[50]

Poverty as a crime was inextricable from vagrancy and begging, and work relief became a major innovation, setting people to work off their "criminal dependency" by such tasks as building roads or farming.

In 1525, Juan Luis Vives developed a prototype of present-day social welfare. A noted scientist, teacher of the daughters of Catherine of Aragon (a wife of Henry VIII), and a philosopher, he stressed individual and local investigation of the morality of the poor, dividing cities into parish quarters for a census of poverty. He advocated vocational training, employment, and rehabilitation for the able-bodied poor, and that children be indentured for work training. Those incapable of work or the genteel poor were given piecework in return either for outdoor relief—support in their homes—or care in almshouses, for although outdoor relief was far less expensive he believed it supported immorality. Parallel programs arose in Germany, Venice, France, Spain, and the Netherlands within the next twenty years. All centralized the distribution of voluntary charity in neighborhoods or communities and encouraged community chests and community responsibility.

Another prototype of service began with the Ladies of Charity, founded in 1617 by Vincent de Paul in France. A Catholic priest, he had been captured and sold as a galley slave. Upon his escape, he devoted his life to care for the poor and for prisoners, founding the Lazarites in 1618, an "association of priests organized to work among the outcasts of society and in the aid of prisoners."[51] The royal court of France helped to support his efforts, and the ladies of the court were initially interested in serving the poor. However, they were not dedicated to the work, and in 1663 the Sisters of Charity, a holy order with temporary vows, was founded. They did not wear habits or live in cloisters and tended to the aged, poor, sick, wounded, dying, and prisoners in the community. Following St. Vincent de Paul's ideals, the Conference of St. Vincent de Paul was organized in the 1700s by students Frederick Ozanam and Sylvain Bailly. They lived among the poor, visited them, and collected necessities for distribution. The pattern of anonymous giving, as well as the Society of St. Vincent de Paul, still exists.

Throughout Europe, social welfare activities of Church and state were merging and the governmentalization of social welfare began. Early in the 1700s, Syndic Sillen devised a plan for Hamburg, Germany, in which public officials (burgomasters) were appointed to investigate personally the poor in city districts, that "the deserving might be discovered and the undeserving rebuked." All charitable institutions were placed under a central bureau for supervision, and to prevent anyone from receiving unearned money the able-bodied were compelled to work and the unemployed were given public work.[52] People were placed in "work training"— given flax and yarn and taught to spin, and released after three months with a spinning wheel and a pound of flax.

Public health was a major concern of the Hamburg plan because ill health caused unemployment and poverty. To combat illness and increase capability for employment, Hamburg built a hospital for incurables, free schools for children ages 6 to 16, and free day care centers for children of working parents. The programs were financed from a combination of public taxes, one-half of Church poorbox collections, and weekly or annual citizen collections. Even children and servants had their own poorboxes at home, in which they put their pennies for the poor. Such programs became common in all of the European nations: In Bavaria, Count Rumford, a native Bostonian, recommended food and employment for every man, woman, and child and established a House of Industry which provided piecework and dinner. In Glasgow Reverend Thomas Chalmers encouraged the formation of charity societies by districts and proclaimed that every boy be taught to read and every girl to sew.

However, it was soon apparent that normal channels of employment, private training, or state-created jobs could not solve the massive problems of poverty. Neither state nor employer took personal interest in laborers except to ensure that they would work, and employment and its converse, poverty, depended on the needs of the employer rather than the worker. According to Handel, idleness became a triple threat: to the order of the state, the productivity of capitalism, and the carrying out of God's will.[53]

## SOCIAL WELFARE IN ENGLAND: THE TUDOR PERIOD

When Columbus voyaged into the New World, his first trip was delayed for a day by ships carrying Jews amd Moslems away from Spain in their final exile. At the same time, in England, the Tudors began their reign under

Henry VII (1485). A contemporary of Luther and Calvin, his response to the problems of the poor was to put beggars and idlers in the stocks, flog them, and return them to their place of origin. By the time of Henry VIII (1509–1547), social unrest, labor problems, and vagrancy were rampant, and he required in 1531 that all beggars be licensed. In 1536, angered by the pope's refusal to let him divorce, he founded the Church of England and confiscated most Catholic Church and monastery property. As had happened in Germany, the back of the Church's care for the poor was broken in England, and great numbers of monks, nuns, and monastery workers were released to unemployment. Thereafter, major responsibility for poor relief fell on the state, and though private foundations, guilds, and donors continued to support some charities, state welfare was the new rule.

Also in 1536, the "Act for Punishment of Sturdy Vagabonds and Beggars" prohibited begging and casual almsgiving, with such severe penalties as branding, enslavement, and execution. Idle children from ages 5 to 14 were taken from their parents and indentured. The State charged churchwardens and mayors to collect funds on Sundays, holidays, and festivals, for the first time paying them for their relief work and requiring accurate accounting. Although giving was still voluntary, the government was now involved in securing contributions. Funds from rich parishes were redistributed to poorer ones, instituting a kind of equity in poor relief throughout the kingdom, but poverty was so great that large-scale riots continued to occur.

In succeeding legislation under Henry VIII and Elizabeth I, the government moved from encouraged voluntarism to the imposition of taxes (called compulsory giving) based on property and income. Refusal to pay, or to serve as overseer of the poor if appointed by justices of the peace (for one-year terms), could mean imprisonment. The hoax of "voluntary giving" ended in 1572 with a general tax to provide poor relief. A community registration of the poor who had lived in the parish for three years was taken, and justices of the peace assigned them to private homes, paying their upkeep with the general tax. Over the next five years, a national system of welfare emerged in which, in one way or another, all persons could have been provided for.

A new Statute of Artificers that regulated wages and hours was passed in 1583. Intended to control and stabilize the labor market, it forced vagrants, vagabonds, and beggars between ages 12 and 60 to work at hard labor or be indentured. Indenture lasted a minimum of one year, and release required approval of local justices of the peace. Both employer and employee had to give three months' notice, and workers could not leave without a certificate of lawful departure. Apprenticeship lasted seven years, with the minimum age at completion 21 or 24. This served other functions besides learning a trade: It gave the master skilled labor; prevented young men from setting up competitive businesses; delayed marriage; and ensured control of the young and support of the old.

## THE POLITICAL ECONOMY OF CHARITY:
## THE ELIZABETHAN POOR LAWS OF 1601

In the 1590s, between one-fourth and one-third of the populations of most English towns could not find work, and many starved or froze to death. Bread riots broke out in some parts of the country, and rioting, thievery, and social disorder were common. To maintain civil order, the English poor laws were recodified in 1597, authorizing every county to build civil (rather than religious) almshouses for the impotent poor and workhouses for the able-bodied poor. Responsibility for relatives became law: parents were required to support their own parents and their children, grandparents their children and grandchildren, and capable children their parents and grandparents. Handel says

> requiring family members to support one another involves a recognition of social change on the part of the Parliament . . . an awareness that the traditional feudal relationships, which assured the aged or disabled serf a livelihood, had substantially passed out of existence. The traditional manorial village was being replaced by . . . independent household units . . . a concept of the family as distinct and separable from the community.[54]

The famous Elizabethan Poor Laws of 1601, a recodification whose power existed for more than two more centuries, legalized and formalized England's state responsibility for the poor. The importance of these laws lies not in the amount spent for care of the poor, for Coll estimates that public relief accounted for not more than 7 percent of the total in any one year for two generations after they were passed.[55] Rather, their importance is in defining social welfare as part of the national labor policy, placing it under the authority of the Privy Council. Never has the connection of social welfare to labor maintenance been so clear, setting the patterns of public assistance not only for England but for the United States today. They include local investigation and administration of relief, work as a component of all assistance, and categorization of the poor into three groups: the able-bodied poor, or "sturdy beggars"; the impotent poor, those incapable of self-support; and dependent children (a new category). That same Parliament passed a "law of charitable trusts" to keep trusts and endowments under government surveillance to control how much they helped workers. Private donors, churches, monasteries, foundations, and guilds continued to support the charities of their choice under this umbrella, but they were restricted from giving so indiscriminately that the poor could leave local employment. The law resulted in a great outpouring of private money for education, outdoor relief, and the building of almshouses,[56] functions to abet rather than contradict national policies toward the poor.

The Privy Council's labor policy discouraged the mobility of laborers and encouraged permanent employment. Employers were exhorted to create new jobs, to employ workers even in hard times, and to purchase raw materials and produce goods for sale even when no market existed (much like Reagan economic policy in the 1980s). Rents, prices, and wages were controlled, labor competition restricted, and marriage and the establishment of new households among the poor discouraged by the burning of available housing. Finally, the "normal" heavy punishments were given the unemployed or those who would not work for the common wage"—whipping and returning to place of residence, commitment to prison (or houses of correction), and in extreme cases banishment and death.[57]

At the local level, under the jurisdiction of the Privy Council, justices of the peace authorized the building of almshouses and workhouses, assessed taxes, and appointed tax collectors. They also appointed public overseers of the poor to ensure accountability for expenditures and to place more emphasis on labor than was common with church charities and to be more efficient in the use of tax money. (Service was compulsory and refusal meant fines or imprisonment.) They set the amount of poor relief; made disposition of the poor to private homes, almshouses, or workhouses; and decided on removal of children from parents judged unable to care for them (for economic or moral reasons). Imprisonment was the punishment for both those who would not work and those who would not pay poor taxes.

New mechanisms for the differential treatment of categories of the poor were also clarified under the Elizabethan Poor Laws. Institutionalization was preferred, because people believed that levels of support could be set better; costs for food, clothing, and shelter clearly determined; and "immoral" work behavior monitored. All institutional arrangements—orphanages, almshouses, workhouses, and prisons—had conditions in common. Many were little more than sheds divided into warrens of rooms with little heat or insulation. There were few if any sanitation facilities, and food was inadequate and often little more than watery gruel. Health and medical care were virtually nonexistent, and in most cases, well people were expected to care for those who could not care for themselves. Disease and infection ran rampant, and the bedridden or those chained in their places because of their behavior (the insane, perhaps), were often left to live or die in their own excrement. House overseers or managers were usually given a flat fee for the support of their inmates and to buy materials for work, and they were allowed to keep what was not spent. If they could skimp on the amount of food, heat, clothing, and shelter allowed the inmates, they could make profits for themselves, and this was the common practice. Work done by the inmates was sold to private entrepreneurs or contractors, and the profits went to the overseer or the state rather than to the workers. While some institutions were well run, most were not, and most became, after a time, undifferentiated dumping grounds for the unwanted.

### Almshouses for the Impotent Poor

The impotent poor were those unable to support themselves—the aged, ill, disabled, the genteel poor—those unequipped to work because of their upbringing, and sometimes pregnant women. Some outdoor relief was authorized for people able to stay in their homes, but this was always controversial because of the belief that it encouraged laziness and beggary. People were also assigned to live in private homes, and homeowners were paid at the "lowest bid" for their keep. All the poor had to do piecework to the extent of their capabilities. It is this group, perhaps, in which Christian ideas of charity were used more freely than was labor policy, for even though they had to work, to keep up their almshouses, and to take care of each other, there was still the belief that they were "deserving" of help. For women illegitimately pregnant, however, brutal treatment was the lot not only because of their sexual "immorality" but because their families, their communities, and the state feared the future dependency of their children.

Almshouses were usually mean buildings with little heat or insulation. Disease, lack of food, the cold of English winters, and lack of health care led to a high mortality rate, particularly among the aged and the sickly. The houses were usually out of the way, and state supervision was rare. Brutal treatment and inadequate provisions meant that being sent to an almshouse was often a sentence of death—again, an easy way for society to get rid of those who were no longer productive in the labor market.

### Dependent Children

As social welfare became labor policy, all its beneficiaries were considered past, potential, or present labor force. Social welfare efforts were bent on ensuring that each category of the poor would fit into its proper "work niche." Therefore, dependent children—orphans, foundlings, unwanted children, or those removed from their parents—were considered either to be future laborers or, more often, future dependents, and their assigned treatment was often so uncaring as to be murderous. Often they were simply left by their mothers on the roadside to die. When the government assumed responsibility, their treatment was little better. They could be placed in foster homes, sold to the lowest bidder—the family that would require the least public support for them—placed into indenture, or put in state orphanages, where social reformer Jonas Hathaway estimated that 82 percent died in their first year.[58] Infants were also placed with paid "wet-nurses," but, since nobody really wanted these children, few follow-up checks were made. Killing them or allowing their deaths was not uncommon and was, in a way, a service to the state, since they would not grow up dependent. Pay for their keep would continue until the officials discovered they were dead, often several months later. Fostering of older children, or indenturing them to families, was usually a means of getting work from them, and they were often worked to death. Those who survived were indentured to learn a trade (girls until 18 or married and boys until 24).

With the rise of the factory system, dependent children were contracted out to work in textile mills as early as the age of 3 or 4, for their small fingers were nimble at looms and spinning jennies. They worked from daybreak till dusk, with a half hour for breakfast and an hour for lunch. If they fell asleep during their 14- to 16-hour workday, or if they had to relieve themselves, they were slapped or whipped back to work. A great number died before they reached their teen years, but neither their deaths nor their lives were important in the scheme of labor policy. Not until 1802 did the law limit children's working hours to 12 a day, also forbidding night work. This did not, however, apply to children hired directly from their parents, for they could be worked without limitation. Under the Factory Act of 1833 children under age 9 were prevented from work, and by 1847, women and children under 18 could work only 10 hours a day in England.

### Sturdy Beggars or the Able-Bodied Poor

Workhouses were another major aspect of the labor policy. The forerunners of the later factory system, they were modeled on the combination almshouse, workhouse, and penal institution of Amsterdam (1596), where inmates worked in fine textiles and lace. Going into the 1600s, England was in fierce competition with the Dutch in the textile business, and by 1650 workhouses were widespread. The goal was to make a profit for the state, and work was often contracted out to private merchants and entrepreneurs. Some were fairly run, with artisans in charge of production and fair wages paid to the inmates, but most were forced labor prisons. The Workhouse Act of 1696 put inmates to work at spinning, knitting, linen weaving, lacework, and the manufacture of nets and sails, but they could not compete with trained workers, and workhouses continued to lose money.

Any able-bodied person seeking public aid was required to leave his family and live in the workhouse. This was called the "workhouse test," for it was believed that only the "truly needy" would agree to it. Work tests were devised to demonstrate willingness to work—chopping wood or moving rocks, for example (and later, sewing tests for women)—even if the work itself was unnecessary, unimportant, or inefficient. Workhouses were considered essential both to maintain work behavior and to punish those who did not want to work. They were tied to morality and were therefore maintained despite their high costs.

Although workhouses were first designed only for men, a revised Workhouse Act in 1722 put both men and women in workhouses, along with their children, adding a new category of the poor, able-bodied women, to the poor laws. Relief could be refused those who would not enter. Women were allowed to care for their children only at specified times during the day, and of the children forced to enter workhouses with their parents, only seven of one hundred survived the first three years.[59] Relief was refused to those who would not enter workhouses. Reformers Jonas Hathaway and Thomas Gilbert bitterly opposed workhouses, and Hathaway was able to push through a bill in 1767 that ruled that foster homes must be found for children under age 6, rather than have them in workhouses. In 1782, Gilbert introduced a statute directing overseers either to find work for the poor in the community (rather than contracting them out to private entrepreneurs) or to maintain them on poor relief. This began a revival of outdoor relief, made national policy in 1795 as the poor were given the right to receive relief in their own homes.[60]

### Prisons

Prisons were the final solution to the problem of unwanted people, a part of social welfare because of the crimes for which people could be sentenced and the categories of people incarcerated. Poverty, nonwork, and even the inability to pay small debts might mean imprisonment. People were as likely to be imprisoned or hanged for stealing bread as for murder or highway robbery. Prisoners were forced to pay fees to their jailers for their upkeep, and if they did not pay they would not be released until they could. Money was also extorted from their families, but little of this got to the prisoners.

Men and women of all ages, criminals, debtors, the poor, the insane, people with such diseases as epilepsy, prostitutes, pregnant women—were all thrown, willy-nilly, without segregation, into prisons. Conditions were worse than any other kind of institution, for the only law was that of the jailer. People suffered from filth, cold, disease, attacks by other inmates, or the brutality of the jailers. Feeding, clothing, and caring for the ill were farmed out to the lowest bidder, and liquor was always available. Clubs and whipping were used freely, and excrement was left to accumulate in the sleeping cells.

Prison reform began in 1681, when philanthropist Thomas Firmin began to pay debtors' costs and fees to free prisoners of good character. (He also put the greater part of his fortune into building a model self-supporting workhouse.) Reformer John Howard, who had been himself imprisoned by a privateer and later became the sheriff of Bedford (1733), demanded that jailers guilty of distortion be dismissed. However, real reform did not begin until the Prison Act of 1877 transferred prison administration to a central authority.

### Overview of Social Welfare in England

During the 1600s and 1700s, social welfare in England wavered from harsh enforcement of work and settlement laws to supporting workers in hard times. "Softer" poor laws, however, were never wholly altruistic and never threatened the labor hegemony of the wealthy. Police measures to control labor and prevent riots and revolutions were social welfare functions, and they favored employers and the entrepreneurial middle class. A new Settlement Act in 1662 kept laborers from seeking better jobs and could fine both worker and employer if higher wages than those set by the central authority were paid. Class interests continued to influence legislation, often in the guise of charitable intent. For example, in 1675, Parliament enacted a law providing poor relief from the public treasury

> to eke out the wages of the poor who received it—thus acting as a bounty upon the oppression of their employers . . . in weekly installments proportional to the number of children in the families . . . this acting directly as a bounty upon the increase of population.[61]

This enabled employers to pay low wages and refer their workers to poor relief for supplement and paid a bounty for increasing the labor force. The 1675 act also gave authorities the ability to predict the future: It allowed them to eject people and families from the locality if they *might* become dependent. This was never well enforced because poor relief was cheaper than was the ejection process, but it did give poor relief agents the power to declare certain people unwanted in advance. Those who could pay advance rent or put up a bond could stay, but by 1691 newcomers had to acquire a "certificate" to guarantee that they would not become dependent.

Policies in England continued to seesaw between restrictiveness and charity. One major revision was called the Speenhamland Act, a wage supplementation program based on the cost of living. Justices of the peace paid subsidies to poor employed families and relief to dependent families in their homes, according to family size, when the cost of bread rose to 1 shilling, a kind of early "consumer price index." As with the earlier law, however, the government thereby subsidized low wages. On the other hand, it allowed the poor to work in sheltered workshops rather than being incarcerated in workhouses. Speenhamland also urged employers to raise wages and requested counties to set aside land upon which the poor could grow food.

## THE INDUSTRIAL REVOLUTION AND THE EMERGENCE OF CAPITALISM

The Industrial Revolution is tied to the beginnings of cotton textile production, about 1760, and capitalism had emerged in embryo form with the Protestant work ethic, international trade, and the new money economy. Capitalism, legitimated by the Protestant work ethic, became the standard of Western society's political economy. Governmental laissez-faire policies offered legal protection to employers in their exploitation of workers, a collaboration that benefited both employers and government. A new middle class of artisans, professionals, and managers arose from the undifferentiated laboring class, and social reformers addressed themselves to altruism in the sense of supporting the poor so that they might better labor and in the new ideals of socialism—the right of workers to share in the decisions and the profits of their labor. Capitalism was an outgrowth of political and economic mercantilist policies.

### The Emergence of Capitalism

Keeping wages low increased the margin of profit, and so low wages were necessary to the nation's political economy. So was poverty. The mercantilist society that had overrun feudalism was transmuted, at least by the 1700s, into a capitalist society where

> the primary motivation which underlies economic decision making and patterns of economic development is the drive for profit. Each capitalist enterprise must try to grow and to expand its profits. If it does not do so, then another, more aggressive capitalist enterprise will take that company's share of the market . . . [It is] an economic system organized on the basis of competitiveness and competition . . . a value system and human behaviors which define a meaningful and successful life in the same terms.[62]

This had certain direct results for the poor. First, low wages were the most appropriate means, it was believed, to ensure a ready work force and maintain profits, so they were purposely kept low. Second, poverty increased, for either wages were kept too low for survival or, in times of economic depression, were nonexistent. Third, poverty's result for society was starvation, criminal activity, or social unrest. To control this and to maintain the economy, the government needed to take action, resulting in a collaboration of state and elite in the control of the poor. Fourth, though the government ostensibly maintained an attitude of "laissez-faire"—noninterference in business affairs—in reality it kept the work force available through restrictive social welfare policies that took police action against workers and/or subsidized low wages. Thus, government actually "rewarded" its successful businesses with protection for such rapacious business practices as underselling, monopolization, and worker exploitation. Finally, capitalism led to a society highly stratified by economics: a wealthy elite primarily interested in maintaining wealth; an emerging middle class of artisans, professionals, and managers; and a vast majority of "the poor"—those in and out of unemployment whose labor was perceived as a commodity for the good of business and the nation.

This did not mean that wealthy people were not concerned with human problems. Galper says that

> the reason . . . is not found in the absence of social- mindedness . . . or even in the absence of a socially concerned dimension to business as a whole . . . . if capitalists fail to maximize their profits, they will go out of business. If enough of them fail . . . the system as a whole will fail. As a result . . . productive capacity is not directed toward creating socially useful goods and services . . . [but] toward producing whatever will make a profit, and in any way possible. . . . They do what they must do, which tends to become what they believe in doing.[63]

A great many theorists appeared out of this Age of Enlightenment to analyze and rationalize the movement toward capitalism and industrialization. The first to address the principle of "laissez-faire" precisely was Adam Smith, whose treatise, *The Wealth of Nations*, was published in 1776. He said

> it is in vain . . . to expect . . . benevolence only. [Men] will be more likely to prevail if [they] can interest their self-love . . . and shew them that it is for their own advantage . . . Give me that which I want, and you shall have this which you want, is the meaning of every such offer . . . We address ourselves, not to their humanity but to their self-love, and never talk to them of their own necessities but of their advantages.[64]

Describing men's relationships in competition, he further said

> men . . . feel so little for another with whom they have no particular connection, in comparison of what they feel for themselves; the misery of one . . . is of so little importance to them in comparison even of a small convenience of their own . . . they would, like wild beasts, be at all times ready to fly upon him; and a man would enter an assembly of men as he enters a den of lions.[65]

The philosopher John Locke supported capitalism and held that the most important human right was the right to hold property. Utilitarians Jeremy Bentham, John Stuart Mill, and Joseph Townsend supported the idea of laissez-faire, since they believed that wealth was the primary source of happiness. The Utilitarian philosophy propounded the greatest good for the greatest number and espoused the equality of all members of society and their right to compete for their happiness. Education of the poor would help them safeguard their own interests rather than having the government do it for them. Although they believed that the unhappiness of some diminished the happiness of all, they felt that the government's efforts to redistribute wealth through poor relief would threaten the national economy. Therefore, they suggested a gradual elimination of poor relief.

Thomas Malthus's theories on population (1798) gave scientific support to the elimination of poor relief and the protection of wealth. He believed that population would outrun the world's ability to produce food, and that poor relief encouraged paupers to have more children, thus prolonging the misery of their ultimate starvation. Moreover, since poverty and immorality were equated, Malthus and later Social Darwinists believed that helping the poor would eventuate in a population of moronic and immoral persons, since the poor reproduced more rapidly than did the wealthy "moral" and intellectual elite. Malthus and David Ricardo, an economist (1772–1823), believed that unfettered self-interest was the only way that society could progress. Direct concern for the welfare of others, then, defeated the progress of society and was sure to result in failure.[66]

Karl Marx, Friedrich Engels, and their followers took the opposite view, criticizing capitalism for its exploitation of the poor and warning of the coming revolution of workers. Marx formulated the ideas of a class society or political economy in which the government was economically allied with and supported the elite, resulting in the constant oppression of the working force. This posited an ongoing class struggle which in time would cause the workers to overthrow the oppressive government. Then all would give according to their ability and be helped according to their need. Neither Marx nor Engels dealt in any depth with the problems of women in a capitalist society, though recognizing their double exploitation both as workers and as "reproducers of labor."

Although economic history has not demonstrated Marxist theories to be correct in all areas, the ideas illuminated both social reform and social welfare activism in that age and into the next century. Among such reformers was Robert Owen, a textile mill owner, who set up an ideal self-supporting industrial community and devised plans for cooperative agrarian organizations. His work became the model for English Socialism.

### The Industrial Revolution and the New Poor Law

In England and on the Continent, agricultural and industrial production revolutionized the social and economic bases of Western society as it moved into the 1800s. An extraordinary dislocation of people from their homes and employment occurred. People had moved to the cities for jobs, but now one machine could do the job of ten men at less cost. The trend away from home industry was complete, and the family as an integrated economic unit ceased to exist. Now each wage-earner—man, woman, or child—went out of the home to hard work in distant factories. The home became divorced from the workplace, for producing, selling, and consuming were relocated in different areas. Men could not support their families on such meager wages, so wives had to work at any kind of wage labor or in weeding and hoeing gangs on farms. Their competition with men for work kept wages for both sexes low. In the higher classes, women became "work useless," consumers of the goods others produced. It became "unladylike" to work, and idle wives were a badge of social success.

Contract labor removed workers from the production of their own food and necessities, and they became parts of the work machine itself, often replaceable parts, and their wages had little or no relationship either to quality or quantity of the product. The owners, who had little to do with the actual work of production, became the beneficiaries of their work. Money became the only goal of both workers and owners: For workers it meant basic survival; for owners, excessive luxury.

Hundreds of new five- and six-story factories were built to use new labor-saving technologies, putting vast numbers of workers out of jobs. In many towns, workers destroyed and burned hundreds of machines and factories, for example, the Luddite movement of 1811. The state's police power put down all such conspiracies, protecting the employers' interests. Fear of revolution, spurred by the American and French revolts, inspired antiworker legislation such as the Combination Acts of 1799 and 1800, which considered trade unionism to be conspiracy and treason.

Among the rich, altruism toward the poor continued under new social philosophies whose leaders included Thomas Bernard, Hannah More, and John Wesley, the founder of Methodism. Bernard established a society for "bettering the conditions and increasing the comfort of the poor" in 1796, in which the rich were enjoined to serve the poor. More established charity schools (1801) so that poor children could be educated; and Wesley spoke out for just wages and fair prices based on social justice rather than the free market. During the period between 1760 and 1820 real wages decreased by one-third[67] because of wars, rapid industrial change, poor agricultural years, and heavy taxes. Rents rose precipitously, and governments destroyed homes to limit the increase in new families. By now, the enclosure movement begun so long before was complete, and poor people had no rights to common lands, pastures, or water. By 1830, widespread revolt had created a demand for new, harsher, poor laws on the one hand and a cry for social reform for the poor on the other. Middle-class professionals and artisans began to organize to provide mutual aid benefits, but poor workers had little protection. Capitalism, industrialization, and the restrictive social welfare that supported them were the clear victors in the battle for workers' rights.

In 1832, every county in England underwent a study by the Royal Commission on Poor Relief. Its conclusions, on completion in 1834, were that poor relief was responsible for "permanent paupery" and that poor taxes were used as subsidies for profit making by employers. The study resulted in the New Poor Law of 1834, which added a new category—able-bodied females—to the list of the unworthy poor. According to the new law, public assistance was no longer a right, and to expect it was antisocial. Moreover, it specifically accused the poor of being at fault for their poverty and caused Benjamin Disraeli, one of the most eminent of Britain's prime ministers (1868, 1874–1880), to say that it announced to the world that "in England poverty is a crime."[68]

According to the New Poor Law, the government would no longer take the responsibility for providing work. There would be no more out-door relief except for the impotent poor and widows with small children. Two hundred new workhouses were built to house pauper families, where conditions were purposely so terrible that people went into them as an alternative only to starvation—these were the "truly needy." Poor relief expenses were reduced in the beginning, but workhouse care remained expensive. Counties were coordinated into "poor relief regions" under a central board appointed by the king, and the principle of "less eligibility"—that no person can receive more money from poor relief that is earned by the lowest-paid worker in the area—would be the guiding factor in meting out poor relief. From a work ethic and labor control point of view this makes good sense, for it provides an incentive to work. However, it enforces work at any wage, it punishes those who cannot work or cannot find employment (and their dependents), and does not consider special needs such as illness or other emergencies that arise. Nevertheless, the idea of "less eligibility" is so popular that it is still the standard of public assistance in the United States today.

In 1852, some outdoor relief was granted, and by 1854, 84 percent of paupers were on poor relief. By 1898, in England, 216,000 people were in workhouses.[69] Reform in England continued, resulting in a more socialistic system than in the United States. Studies to determine the causes of poverty revealed that widespread illness and disease were a major problem among the poor. Malnutrition and unsanitary living conditions were to blame:

> people lived in overcrowded quarters, and often adolescents and children of both sexes slept in one bed. This led to promiscuity, quarrels, delinquency, immorality, and rapid spread of contagious diseases. Many workingmen-boarders lived with families in the same room. Often seven to ten used one sleeping room, or lived in damp, dark cellars, without any ventilation. All over England the poorer quarters were without water supply and drainage; drinking water was often polluted in rivers or deficient pipelines. There were usually no outside toilets and no sewers . . . Refuse was thrown into the public gutter, and the dead were left unburied.[70]

In the late 1800s, Edwin Chadwick, a Poor Law Board commissioner, appalled by the living conditions of the poor, developed plans for water systems, sewage, drainage, and free public vaccination for cholera, typhus, and smallpox. However, he was bitterly opposed and lost his position. Within a decade, and with better results, Florence Nightingale (1820–1910), a nurse in the Crimean Wars, began reforms of nursing, hospitals, and medical practice that would revolutionize England's public health system. Also influential in the fight for the poor was Octavia Hill, who with the help of philanthropist John Ruskin, started rebuilding slums in London in 1864:

> She rented sanitary decent living quarters at low prices to working families who could not afford to pay higher rents . . . enlisted . . . volunteers who collected the monthly rents . . . and advised the families in economical home management.[71]

She was also one of the founders of the Commons Society, which built parks, gardens, and recreational facilities for the poor in London.

Among the most influential groups of this time was the Fabian Society, an English Socialist group among whose leading members were Sidney and Beatrice Webb. They were primarily interested in practical reforms such as women's suffrage, wage and working hours' legislation, housing projects, and education. Charity organization societies and the settlement house movements began in England about the same time. Edward Denison, a philanthropist, moved into a slum district to teach the Bible, history, and economics. He counseled the poor and became an advocate for them. Canon Samuel Barnett, a teacher, brought his students to his home in the slums at Whitechapel to serve the poor. Among his students was Arnold Toynbee, a man dedicated to the poor. Upon his death, Toynbee's friends built the first settlement house in the world, Toynbee Hall, in his honor. Its basic purpose was to bring educated men and women into contact with the poor, so that by common work and studies, they might both learn.

Following that period, care for the poor took a different turn in England than in the United States. Our purpose in discussing English social welfare is that welfare in the United States was modeled on that of England, particularly in terms of the Elizabethan poor laws of 1601 and the New Poor Law of 1834. However, while English social welfare was softened by its exposure to the ideas of Socialism and the activities of Socialist reformers, welfare in the United States remained uninfluenced by and perhaps adamantly opposed to Socialist influence. Without historical traditions of care for the poor, cut off from pre-Protestant Christian traditions, and influenced at a vulnerable state of development by a strict capitalist political economy, social welfare in the United States became "stuck" in its harsh antipoor, worker-exploitative past.

## CONCLUSION: REIFYING THE VALUES OF THE PAST

From the fall of the Roman Empire until the Industrial Revolution, the very basis of human existence was altered. Politically, small warring tribes became feudal estates and then nations, and social relationships changed from organic interconnections with family and community to alienated individuals whose primary concern had to be survival. Economically, a wealthy elite grew to control governments and to deal with the poor as cost units in production. According to Mencher

> Ownership no longer indicated merely the privilege of stewardship but signified free use of possessions unencumbered by any sense of mutual dependency or communal responsiblity . . . the laboring classes were . . . transformed into a wage-earning group, and although the worker continued to hold the employer responsible for his subsistence, the employer began to interpret wages as the price paid for a commodity of labor.[72]

Vast changes in technology created the beginnings of mercantilism, and such ecological catastrophes as the Black Death or the destruction of balances of nature increased the difficulties of survival for the poor. Religion reified the secondary status of women and certain "outgroups"—Jews, homosexuals, handicapped persons—even to the point of killing them, and mutated in response to both polity and economy from supporting the poor in difficult times to justifying their exploitation.

Social welfare changed with the other institutions from ideals of social justice and charity as a right to the redefinition of poverty as a crime. Mencher says

> The attitudes of the dominant elements in society toward the lower classes underwent some fundamental changes between the sixteenth and the eighteenth centuries . . . the paternalistic attitudes of the upper classes and the policies of the government were more sympathetic and placed less stress on the shortcomings of laborers as the cause of their conditions. By the close of the seventeenth century the laziness and immorality of the lower class were constantly referred to and alleged to account for their inferior standard of living.[73]

Social welfare became a civil rather than a religious concern and served the manifest function of controlling labor for the purposes of governmental and personal profit making by the new moneyed class.

While kind hearts and good deeds continued, even that changed as the poor were redefined as immoral or criminal. The Protestant work ethic became the moral basis underlying capitalism and social stratification, and people of all religions picked up its secular ideas of work and wealth. With government justification for exploitation based on the laissez-faire philosophy, capitalism became the major economic tenet of both Old and New Worlds. While England and Europe progressed into new beliefs about social welfare despite primarily capitalist philosophies, the ideals of Protestantism and Puritanism as civil or state religion and capitalism as the morally appropriate economic system became a basic tenet of the United States.

## STUDY QUESTIONS

1. What is feudalism, and what kinds of help for the poor did it produce?
2. What was the impact of religion on the feudal serfs and lords?

3. What was the impact of the scientific revolution on feudalism? On social welfare?
4. How did poverty become a crime?
5. What did mercantilism do to social welfare? The Protestant Reformation?
6. What impact did the Protestant Reformation have on women?
7. What did the Elizabethan Poor Laws do? What did they say?
8. Why are mercantilism, the Protestant Reformation, the Industrial Revolution, and capitalism so intimately related?

## FOOTNOTES

[1] Ralph Dolgoff and Donald Feldstein, *Understanding Social Welfare*, 2nd ed., (New York: Longman Press, 1984), p. 39.

[2] Amaury de Riencourt, *Sex and Power in History*, (New York: Dell Publishing, 1974), p. 156.

[3] David Macarov, *The Design of Social Welfare*, (New York: Holt, Rinehart, and Winston, 1978), p. 97.

[4] de Riencourt, *Sex and Power*, p. 194.

[5] Lerone Bennett, Jr., *Before the Mayflower: A History of the Negro in America* (Chicago: Johnson Publishing Company, Penguin edition, 1966), p. 18, quoting Alexander Chamberlain.

[6] Justine Glass, *Witchcraft: The Sixth Sense* (North Hollywood: Wilshire Book Co., 1973), p. 108.

[7] Frances Gies and Joseph Gies, *Women in the Middle Ages* (New York: Barnes and Noble Books, 1978), pp. 27–31.

[8] In Dolgoff and Feldstein, *Understanding Social Welfare*, p. 41, quoting Joseph R. Strayer and Dana C. Munro, *The Middle Ages 395–1500* (New York: Appleton-Century Crofts, 1970), p. 130.

[9] In Dolgoff and Feldstein, *Understanding Social Welfare*, p. 42, quoting Richard W. Southern, *The Making of the Middle Ages* (New York: A Dell Book, 1982), p. 50.

[10] Gerald Handel, *Social Welfare in Western Society* (New York: Random House, 1982), p. 32, taken from Herbert J. Muller, *Freedom in the Western World: From the Dark Ages to the Rise of Democracy* (New York: Harper and Row, 1963), p. 67.

[11] Gies and Gies, *Women in the Middle Ages.*

[12] Carolyn Merchant, *The Death of Nature* (San Francisco: Harper and Row, Publishers, 1980), ch. 1, "Nature as Female," pp.1–3.

[13] Ibid., p. 46.

[14] Ibid., pp. 46–47.

[15] Michael Baigent, Richard Leigh, and Henry Lincoln, *Holy Blood, Holy Grail* (New York: A Dell Book, 1982), p. 49.

[16] G. G. Coulton, *The Medieval Scene* (Cambridge: Cambridge University Press, 1930), p. 1, quoted in Handel, *Social Welfare*, p. 32.

[17] Walter Trattner, "The Background," in Neil Gilbert and Harry Specht, *Emergence of Social Welfare and Social Work*, 2nd ed., (Itasca, Ill.: F. E. Peacock Publishers, 1981). p. 25.

[18] Walter A. Friedlander and Robert Z. Apte, *Introduction to Social Welfare*, 4th ed., (Englewood Cliffs, N.J.: Prentice Hall, 1955), pp. 9–10.

[19] Gies and Gies, *Women in the Middle Ages*, p. 65.

[20] Ibid., p. 64.

[21] Ibid.

[22] Dolgoff and Feldstein, *Understanding Social Welfare*, p. 43.

[23]Merchant, *Death of Nature*, pp. 47–48.

[24]Gies and Gies, *Women in the Middle Ages*, pp. 168–169, 181.

[25]Ibid., pp. 157–161.

[26]Ibid.

[27]Merchant, *Death of Nature*, p. 48.

[28]Joseph Klaits, *Servants of Satan: The Age of the Witch Hunts* (Bloomington, Indiana: Indiana University Press, 1985), p. 21.

[29]Ibid., p. 21.

[30]Ibid., p. 37.

[31]Ibid., p. 77.

[32]Ibid., p. 52.

[33]Nider's *Formicarium*, in de Riencourt, *Sex and Power*, pp. 252–263.

[34]*Malleus Malleficarum*, discussed in de Riencourt, *Sex and Power*, pp. 249 ff. Jacob Sprenger's rationale for this state of affairs is interesting and ingenious. After stating the exceptional vulnerability of the "fragile sex" and the eagerness of women for explanations on this topic, he elaborates:

> Now the wickedness of women is spoken of in Ecclesiasticus XXV: All wickedness is but little to the wickedness of a woman . . . What else is a woman but a foe to friendship, an unescapable punishment, a necessary evil, a natural temptation, a desirable calamity, a domestic danger, a delectable detriment, an evil of nature, painted with fair colors! Therefore if it be a sin to divorce her when she ought to be kept, it is indeed a necessary torture . . . since they are feebler both in mind and body, it is not surprising that they should come more under the spell of witchcraft . . . they have slippery tongues, and are unable to conceal from their fellow-women those things which by evil arts they know; and since the natural reason is that she is more carnal than a man . . . she is an imperfect animal, she always deceives . . . a woman is beautiful to look upon, contaminating to the touch and deadly to keep." J. Sprenger, *Malleus Maleficarum* (New York: B. Blom, 1970), pp. 112–121, translated by M. Summers.

It is significant that in England, where judicial torture was not allowed, witch-hunting started much later. In 1487 the University of Cologne gave its official seal of approval to the *Malleus Malleficarium* and stated that

> "whosoever denied the reality of witches and witchcraft should be prosecuted for raising obstacles to the Inquisition's labors . . . it had the full support of public opinion, and on numerous occasions, the crowds, frightened by natural catastrophes, took matters in their own hands without waiting for official sanction and killed scores of unfortunate women . . . the Reformers themselves, Luther and Calvin at their head, entertained exactly the same beliefs regarding witchcraft as did Roman Catholics, and persecuted witches with as much fanaticism as their Catholic antagonists. Persecution started in earnest, however, to reach its climax, not under the relatively lenient Church of England, but under the fanatical Puritans; the number of Englishwomen who were burned without ever having been brought to trial will never be known but must have been considerable. King James VI was not far behind Pope Innocent VIII and Sprenger in his persecuting zeal." In de Riencourt, *Sex and Power*, p. 254.

[35]Mary Daly. *Gyn/Ecology: The MetaEthics of Feminism*, (Boston: Beacon Press, 1978).

[36]Klaits, *Servants*, p. 89.

[37]Keith Thomas, *Religion and the Decline of Magic* (London: Weidenfeld and Nicolson, 1971), p. 554; and Alan Macfarlane, *Witchcraft in Tudor and Stuart England* (New York: Harper & Row, 1970), esp. pp. 92–99, in Klaits, *Servants of Satan*, p. 89.

[38]Klaits, *Servants of Satan*, pp. 94–95.

[39]Eleanor S. Riemer, "Women, Dowries, and Capital Investment in Thirteenth Century Siena," in Marion A. Kaplan, ed. *The Marriage Bargain* (New York: Haworth Press, 1985), pp. 59–79.

[40]Dolgoff and Feldstein, *Understanding Social Welfare*, p. 46.

[41]Beulah Compton, *Introduction to Social Welfare and Social Work: Structure, Function, and Process* (Homewood, Ill.: The Dorsey Press, 1980), p. 153.

[42]Dolgoff and Feldstein, *Understanding Social Welfare*, p. 46.

[43]Gerald N. Grob, *State and Public Welfare in Nineteenth Century America*, (New York: Arno Press, 1976), p. 7.

[44]Klaits, *Servants of Satan*, pp. 90–91.

[45]Max Weber, *Protestant Ethic and the Spirit of Capitalism* (New York: Scribner, 1976), p. 3.

[46]Ibid., p. 54.

[47]de Riencourt, *Sex and Power*, p. 261.

[48]Ibid., p. 259, quoting from E. Lamy, *La Femme de Demain*, (Paris, n.d.), p. 100.

[49]John Knox, ed., *Works*, "First Blast of the Trumpet against the Monstrous Regiment of Women," in Merchant, *Death of Nature*, pp. 146–147.

[50]Samuel Mencher, *From Poor Law to Poverty Programs* (Pittsburgh: University of Pittsburgh Press, 1967), p. xvi.

[51]Frank Dekker Watson, *The Charity Organization Movement in the United States* (New York: Arno Press and the New York Times, 1971), p. 15, originally printed by Macmillan Publishing Co., 1922.

[52]Ibid., p. 23.

[53]Handel, *Western Society*, p. 63.

[54]Ibid., p. 96.

[55]Blanche Coll, *Perspectives in Public Welfare: A History*, U.S. Department of Health, Education, and Welfare, SRS 1969, (Washington, D.C.: U. S. Government Printing Office, 1971), p. 7.

[56]Ibid.

[57]Mencher, *Poor Law to Poverty Programs*, p. 30.

[58]Ibid., p. 27.

[59]De Schweinitz, *England's Road to Social Welfare*, (1943, p. 65–66), in Compton, *Introduction to Social Welfare*, p. 58.

[60]Ibid., p. 73.

[61]Grob, *State and Public Welfare*, p. 8.

[62]Jeffrey Galper, *Social Work Practice: A Radical Perspective* (Englewood Cliffs, N.J.: Prentice Hall, 1980), p. 25.

[63]Ibid., pp. 22–25.

[64]Adam Smith, *The Wealth of Nations* (New York: Modern Library, 1937), p. 14.

[65]Herbert W. Schneider, ed., *Adam Smith's Moral and Political Philosophy* (New York: Hafner, 1948), p. 25.

[66]Mencher, *Poor Law to Poverty Programs*, pp. 67–68.

[67]Ibid., p. 60.

[68]De Schweinitz, *England's Road*, p. 24.

[69]Handel, *Western Society*, p. 121.

[70]Friedlander and Apte, *Introduction to Social Welfare*, p. 94.

[71]Watson, *Charity Organization*, pp. 13–14.

[72]Mencher, *From Poor Law to Poverty Programs*, pp. 12–13.

[73]Ibid, pp. 9–10.

# 5

# *WELFARE MOVES TO THE AMERICAS*

## NEW WORLD—OLD WAYS

The conquest of the Americas demonstrates decisively Western society's obsession with wealth. While some early explorers were priests who came to convert Native Americans, most came for fortunes for themselves and the governments that supported them. Their religions, moreover, legitimated conquest and exploitation of others in the name of the now moral quest for wealth. Protestantism with its dour philosophies of labor and profit changed the social, spiritual, and economic consciousness of the world, and Catholicism, responding to the economic imperatives of emergent mercantilism, did not seriously object. Persecution of women, Jews, and non-Christian people was common, for example, and a papal bull issued in 1455 authorized Portugal to enslave all infidel people,[1] legitimating slavery even before the discovery of the New World. Such attitudes and behaviors in the colonization centuries (1500 to 1800) provided the basis for the political economy of the United States, including social welfare and the uses of the laboring poor.

Life in this era was bitter, exploitable, and cheap, and labor was a profit-making commodity. In Europe the great mass of people lived in desperate poverty, employed or unemployed, fed or starved at the will of their masters. Plagues and disease were common to all classes, and famine killed thousands. Cities swamped with people looking for work meted out severe punishments for large or small transgressions as the poor eked out their meager living with crime and prostitution. They lived in hovels, under bridges, or in the streets or were confined in almshouses or jails. Concern for the poor was almost always directed to their availability for work or to keep them from rebelling, and their treatment depended not on humanitarianism but on the business decisions of others.

Europeans who came to the Americas found a new land ripe for economic plunder. Whether in the high cultures of MesoAmerica or the democratic societies of North America, gold, silver, land, and the greater commodity, human labor, were available for the taking. At first contact, there were more than two hundred distinctive Native American groups, with a population estimated at ten million in North America and tens of millions in the rest of the hemisphere.[2] In North America, they included

1. Hunting, fishing, and farming societies of the East
2. Great Plains hunters and agriculturists
3. Fishing societies of the Northwest
4. Seed gatherers of California and the Southwest
5. Navaho shepherds and Pueblo farmers in Arizona and New Mexico
6. Desert societies in Arizona and New Mexico
7. The Alaskan groups

These many societies were at greatly differing stages of development, some with highly diversified social and economic systems. In North America, most of those along the Eastern Coast and in the Midwest were agrarian, and most had national boundaries within which they farmed, fished, and hunted. Some Southwestern societies were nomadic, while others were farming and herding societies. In MesoAmerica the Inca, Maya, and Aztec peoples had hierarchical priest-king societies that rivaled those of Egypt, Greece, or Rome. These existed alongside slash and burn agricultural societies in the lowlands.

Although every society was different, they were unilaterally treated as one by the invaders; that is, they were forced to submit or die. Through disease, forced labor, and the technologies of gunpowder, muskets, and cannon, of the millions in the Americas at first contact, by about 1850 only about 200,000 Native Americans remained in North America, and the high cultures of MesoAmerica had been wiped from the earth.

## THE INDIGENOUS PEOPLES OF AMERICA

As early as 25,000 B.C., immigrants from the Far East crossed the Siberian land bridge to range downward and outward through the Americas. By about 9000 B.C., Paleo-Indian big game hunting societies stretched from the grasslands of the Pacific coast to the Rockies in the east. Archaic cultures flourished, and after several millenia Woodland societies, with their invention of horticulture, emerged in the Ohio and Illinois valleys. Their stages of social development closely paralleled those of early Europe. They lived in dispersed villages, built huge burial mounds and earthworks, and demonstrated a highly developed religion and a system of social stratification with their grave goods. The Hopewell Culture began about 300

B.C. and reached its peak in the early centuries after Christ, enduring until about 850 A.D. An extensive trading network developed among societies from the Rockies to the Great Lake regions.

The democratic societies of North America counterpointed the hierarchical systems of the Incas, Mayans, and Aztecs in South and Central America. Here priests and kings, with their bureaucracies, ruled peasants and artisans through labor conscription, tribute, and taxation. Regular corvées (*mit'a*) farmed; worked in the royal mines; herded royal alpaca and llama; built roads, monuments, and temples; and warred and colonized— whole populations were moved to new territories to ensure common language and ethnic groups. Intensive agricultural systems, in which two-thirds of the population labored to provide food for the national granaries from which the people were fed, included both permanent and floodwater irrigation, permanent crop rotation, and fertilization. Great pyramids, statuary, and colonnaded temples graced cities that spread over hundreds of

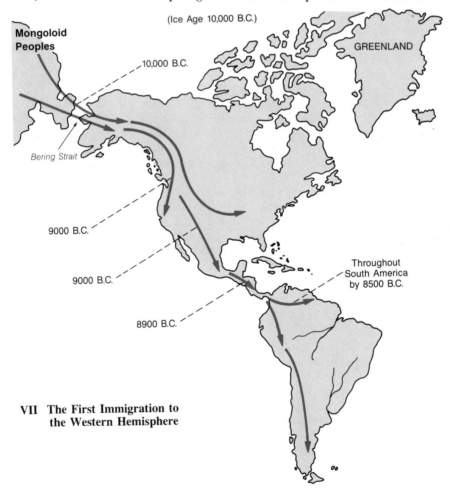

**VII  The First Immigration to the Western Hemisphere**

acres,[3] and vast engineering projects as early as 500 A.D. brought water to Peru's coastal valleys. Ceramic crafts and textile manufacturing compared in excellence with those of Europe, and metallurgical techniques for bronze, silver, and gold were widespread.[4] The Mayan calendar was more accurate than that employed in contemporary Europe, and long before the concept of the zero had become part of European mathematics, the ancient Maya used it in their calculations.

In architecture, metallurgy, astronomy, and statecraft, the most highly developed of the native American states were fully comparable with Old World civilizations. For example, the supreme Inca controlled the lives of as many as six million people. Teotihuacan, the largest city in the New World, covered an area of some 2000 acres by 800 A.D. Ten thousand people labored over a period of ten years to build its Pyramid of the Sun, and probably as many as 30,000 constructed the Inca's Sacsahuaman fortress, where three-hundred-ton megaliths were fitted together to form thirty-foot-high walls. A vast network of roads and suspension bridges across ravines and rivers connected the Incan empire.[5]

## THE EUROPEAN INVASION

Although Norse explorers had been in the New World centuries before Columbus found the Caribbean Isles in 1492, the impetus for colonization awaited the social and technological innovations of the Middle Ages and the push for international markets. Within a few decades after Columbus's first voyage, Dutch, English, French, Spanish, and Portuguese had begun the expansion that would create European-controlled nations on the bones of indigenous New World societies.

The French in early America were, perhaps, the least exploitative of the European invaders, for they assimilated with rather than tried to change Native American cultures. Voyageurs and priests, looking for adventure, trade, and souls to convert, sailed the Atlantic Coast and the St. Lawrence Seaway and traveled the Great Lakes and the Mississippi River in the early 1500s. France's Verrazano explored the Atlantic shores to Nova Scotia in 1524, and Cartier, in 1534, found the Iroquois in the St. Lawrence Valley. The French first settled unsuccessfully in Canada in 1541 and did not attempt settlement again until the founding of Quebec in 1608. France's occupation of Florida and part of the Gulf Coast began in 1562, and Jesuit missions were on the Great Lakes by 1633, ministering to the Five Nations—Mohawk, Oneida, Onondaga, Cayuga, and Seneca—who inhabited the area north of Lake Ontario.

### The Spanish in the New World

Spanish conquistadores came to America for riches to fill the coffers of their rulers, while Catholic priests joined them to convert the Native Americans to Christianity. They mapped the Caribbean, the Gulf of Mexico, MesoAmerica and much of South America, and the Southwest from

**VIII  The People of the Western Hemisphere
at the Time of Columbus**

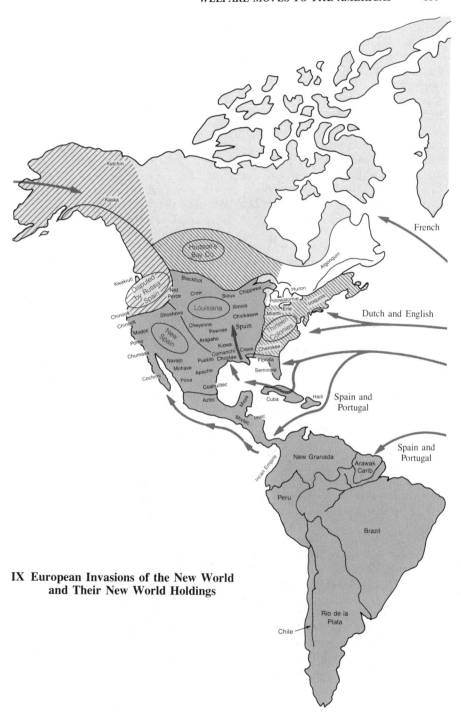

**IX  European Invasions of the New World
and Their New World Holdings**

the Rio Grande to California and Oregon. The first nonindigenous permanent settlers in what would become the United States were a group of African slaves abandoned by their Spanish owners in the area of South Carolina, in 1526.[6] The first permanent city in the New World was settled not at Plymouth Rock but by the Spanish at St. Augustine, Florida, in 1565. Slaving expeditions and disease stripped the Greater Antilles and the Bahamas of inhabitants by 1513, when Ponce de Leon raided Florida. Many who were enslaved committed suicide, others ran away, a great number were simply worked to death. The decimation of New World societies was abetted by the native peoples' lack of resistance to European diseases—smallpox, measles, bubonic plague, even respiratory infections. Epidemics of monstrous proportions occurred all through the first centuries of contact: a third of the population of the Tupinanba in Brazil was wiped out by smallpox in 1562, and Borinquen (Puerto Rico), which had a native population of 50,000 in 1493, was so reduced by 1530 that newly imported African slaves were the majority.[7] By the end of the 1600s, when West Indies sugar became the major import to Europe, most of the Caribbean's native populations had vanished.

The Spanish also plundered MesoAmerica, beginning with the Aztec nation's subjugation in 1519 by Hernando Cortes. Reigning rulers and bureaucracies were reduced to puppet governments, and the people were enslaved to work in gold and silver mines. By 1550, the fabulous silver mines of New Mexico had been discovered, giving Spain wealth untold in the European world of the time. However, the Spanish were not intent on building a culture but on raping it. Within a century, therefore, the population of the area had been so drastically reduced that society could not be sustained, and blooming cultures rivaling those of Europe ceased to exist. Recent demographic studies of central Mexico during the sixteenth-century reveal an astonishing decline in population, from some twenty millions to one million in less than one hundred years.[8]

Coronado's expedition up the Rio Grande (1540–1542) found villages of whitewashed and frescoed three- to five-story buildings with thousands of hospitable Pueblo Indian inhabitants. They had cultivated fields of maize, beans, squash, and cotton; had domesticated turkeys and dogs;[9] and had stores of grain for the winter and seeds for future plantings. Within a few years, tributes demanded by the Spanish had wiped out their stores and mass starvation began. Although they fled, the Spanish pursued and persecuted them mercilessly. A particularly despotic crown-appointed governor—Oñate—ravaged the tribes to such an extent that his removal was demanded by Franciscan missionaries, who were then given control. By the 1600s there were three thousand missionaries in the area, and with convents, churches, and hospitals, they managed the pueblos for the benefit of the natives. New systems of irrigation and the cultivation of new European plants began, and a European Catholic system of welfare was instituted for people who, before the invasion, had fully supported themselves and their own.

The Apache nations of the Great Plains, whose societies surrounded the Pueblos, were conquered by 1650. Spanish farms began to enclose their land, and disease and crop failures added to the distress already caused by massive tributes, leading to mass starvation and, finally, rebellion by both

Apache and Pueblo Indians. Apache raids were common all during the 1600s and more frequent after 1650. A 1680 revolt by the Hopis in the Rio Grande Valley, the Jemez Valley, and the Zuni Basin was begun as a response to the repression of native religion and killed most of the resident Spanish, including missionaries. A massive retaliation ensued, in which the Hopis, disheartened, surrendered without a fight, leaving the Spanish once more in control.

The Spanish Church maintained an essentially hands-off policy on slavery, since it was profitable for both Church and monarchy. Even priests owned both Native American and African slaves. However, Native Americans were considered subjects of Crown and Church, and one of the express purposes of sending priests and missionaries to the Americas was to save their souls. This moral paradox resulted in Spanish laws to protect Native Americans (1542) from exploitation. The Church maintained that slaves had human and spiritual rights, and slavery in South America was looked upon as a contract in which masters owned the slaves' labor but not their humanity.[10] The sanctity of marriage and family was assured by the Church, and spouses and children were unlikely to be sold away from each other; they could earn money for themselves after their work for masters was done; and they could buy their own freedom and that of their families. The possibility of freedom meant the development of a class of workers and artisans, which over time became a stable and free middle class. Moreover, the invading Spanish took wives both among the Native Americans and the African slaves, beginning a unique Hispanic heritage in which priests and missionaries took an important leading role.[11] In the northern colonies, where not only the work but the lives of slaves belonged to the master, these possibilities did not exist.

### Protestants in North America

Northern Europeans came to America from about 1522 to find Native Americans in permanent homes in palisaded villages, cultivating fields of corn, squash, and cucurbits. Eager for furs and for the fish abounding in the Atlantic waters, both Dutch and English set up joint-stock businesses, partly financed by merchants in Europe, and by 1632 the indigenous peoples had iron kettles, axes, arrowheads, and knives, though few had firearms.

The Dutch East India Company sought to expand its profitable international trade with resources from the New World by giving colonists "patroonships"—absolute ownership of huge tracts of land—in return for establishing a colony of fifty adults. Although Dutch settlers were at first scrupulous in their dealings with the Native Americans, land had a different meaning for Dutch and Native Americans, and before long the Dutch were taking advantage of this. According to Native Americans, Mother Earth could not be sold, and therefore, in return for insignificant amounts, the Dutch "bought" their lands from them. When Native Americans refused to move, the Dutch began to kill them, often wiping out whole villages. Early in the 1600s a Dutch governor offered bounties for Native American scalps as proof of their deaths.

From 1623 to 1626, New York, New Jersey, and part of Delaware were settled by Dutch Protestants. Their charter required that each settlement provide preachers, schoolmasters, and comforters of the sick and required pastors' assistants to give help and solace to the unhappy, ill, or disabled. These systems of welfare were undertaken from both religious and business perspectives. Vagabonds and beggars were "bonded" to patroons in return for their board and clothing, often for life. Deacons supervised by clergy gave outdoor relief gleaned from church collections and fines to the impotent, ill, and disabled. The church was the community conscience, encouraging neighborhoods to care for their own poor and to establish mutual aid associations. By 1664, ten of the twelve Dutch settlements had established schools controlled by church and court and supported by taxation, tuition, the Dutch East India Company, and the church. When the Dutch lost New Amsterdam to the English, English poor laws were substituted for Dutch community care.

### The English in New England

English colonists came for many reasons—to escape the poverty of peasant life in Europe, to find fortunes, for adventure, or, in the case of Pilgrims and Puritans, to escape retaliation by the newly restored monarchy—under Oliver Cromwell they had beheaded King Charles I in 1649. The depletion of England's own natural resources, especially its forests, made the New World a bonanza for materials increasingly scarce in England—potash, timber, pitch, tar, resin, iron, and copper. In addition, production of New World goods, particularly sugar, tobacco, coffee, and chocolate, made new fortunes. Adventurers, many of them second (or later) sons who could not inherit because of laws of primogeniture, came seeking legal or illegal fortunes and became pirates, lawbreakers, highwaymen, businessmen, and a new mercantilist elite. Some came not so freely, transported to America as an alternative to prison, kidnapped by ship captains or "Newlanders" who received a bonus for every man, woman, and child arriving alive in the New World, or enslaved by traders seeking free labor in the sugar plantations of the Caribbean or the cotton plantations of the South.

The first English colony was established at Roanoke, Virginia, in 1564, by Sir Walter Raleigh. It survived only three years, and the next colony, at Jamestown in 1607, was a commercial venture financed by the joint-stock Virginia Company and expected to produce a profit. The Massachusetts Bay Colony was settled in 1629 by Puritan businessmen. Pennsylvania was settled by Quakers who followed William Penn into exile from England. Georgia was the only New England colony not established as a religious haven or a business: England transported free people and gave them land and tools in return for a promise of military service should it be needed. Georgia also was the only colony to accept Jews as equals, and slavery was not permitted under its earliest charter.

At first the companies and colonists followed the Dutch lead in land purchase and relied on friendly natives to help them through severe winters. Soon, however, colonists simply took the land they wanted, killing or enslaving its inhabitants: during the mid-1700s, 5 to 10 percent of slaves were Native Americans, and as late as 1790, two hundred of the six thousand slaves in Massachusetts were Native Americans.[12] The colonists' brutality precipitated such wars as that war against the Wampanoag in 1675, where the leader, King Philip, was drawn and quartered and his skull displayed on a pole until the 1700s. There were heavy losses on both sides, but the English won and, after massacring many, sold the survivors as slaves. Quakers were the major exception to such genocide, continuing to deal scrupulously with the Native Americans, although they too had both Native American and African slaves.

While resources were plentiful in the New World, labor was scarce, and a concerted effort to populate the colonies began. By 1640, there were thousands of English colonists in New England. Spanish immigration to the entire New World between 1509 and 1790 was only about 150,000 people, but between 1600 and 1700, half a million English moved to the North American continent[13] to begin the hard life of subsistence farming.

In the early days, caves or houses covered with bark served as homes since colonists had no tools for turning logs into lumber. All members of the family worked: both in domestics—cleaning house, making yarn, grinding and milling flour, sewing, and spinning—and in the fields as they were needed. Men, when their labor in the fields was completed, worked with their wives at spinning and weaving. Religion as well as necessity prompted the work, for idleness was, according to religion, a sign that Satan was at work. In Massachusetts, wives who refused to serve their husbands by laboring obediently and frugally gave them grounds for divorce. Both boys and girls were taught household work, and both spent as much time in the workshop as in home or field. Many colonists, wealthy or poor, bound out their children as domestic help to others, so that they might learn the value of work.

While New England and Pennsylvania were settled by immigrant family groups, setting the stage for community democracies, the south was settled by people who transported the English manor system to the New World. They accepted the burden of *noblesse oblige*, taking on government and public responsibility, becoming justices of the peace and overseers of the poor. The ideal of "lord" and "serfs" was also transferred, making the concept of slavery easy.

Tobacco was the staple crop, and while for some time small farmers remained in the tobacco industry, large plantations soon took over. In the 1600s, in Virginia, small farmers were about one-twentieth of the population, but by 1730 one quarter of them had been squeezed out.[14]

### The Practice of Indenture

Because labor was scarce and the cost of passage high, the practice of indenture arose, whereby the price of passage was advanced to settlers who agreed to work it off, usually in five to eight years. The first indentured servants to arrive in the New World were probably a group of twenty Africans, brought to Jamestown a year before the *Mayflower*.[15] Following them, a quarter of a million people—probably one-half of all white immigrants, a third of them women—came as indentured servants.[16] For almost one hundred years, white indentured servants were the principle source of manpower in the New England colonies. In 1683 white servants represented one-sixth of Virginia's population. Two-thirds of the immigrants to Pennsylvania during the 1700s were indentured, and in four years, twenty-five thousand came to Philadelphia alone. In 1624 there were only 22 persons of African descent in Virginia, at a time when several thousand a year were being brought into South America. After 1680, slaves began to arrive in increasing numbers, but not until the 1750s did they exceed 25 percent of the population.

A regular and profitable traffic developed in indentured servants, and between 1654 and 1685, ten thousand sailed from Bristol alone, chiefly for the West Indies and Virginia. To control this traffic, a Colonial Board was created in 1661. People of all statuses were involved in the trade, and kidnapping and "recruitment" by "Newlanders" was common, with a commission gained on each person delivered live to the New World. The punishment for "man selling" was the pillory, a mild punishment considering the profit gained. In 1654, burgomasters of Amsterdam sent a cargo of nearly thirty poor children to Peter Stuyvesant at New Amsterdam, and under English laws, any dependent children could be deported to the colonies. London took from its almshouses three to four hundred boys and girls ages 10 to 15 to ship to the colonies.[17]

Convicts provided another steady source of white indentured labor. Three hundred capital crimes were recognized for which choice of punishment was hanging or indenture; for example, pickpocketing more than a shilling or shoplifting 5 shillings; stealing a horse or sheep; or poaching rabbits on a gentleman's estate. In 1717, a law gave indenture of fourteen years to those sentenced to death. Lesser offenses meant seven years of indenture: stealing clothing; burning corn; maiming or killing cattle; being a vagrant, rogue, idler, petty thief, gypsy, or a frequenter of brothels; or engaging in trade union activity.[18]

Ship captains also bought indentures for the danger-fraught three-month trip across the Atlantic, giving each person a space of 6 feet by 2 feet. Food was very scarce, since captains overbooked by double, and people fought with each other for the dead bodies of mice and rats. No one could leave the ships until their indenture was bought, and those without a buyer were put on the auction block. Parents were forced to sell their children, and husbands and wives were separated. Children under 5 could not be sold but were given away to serve until the age of 21.[19] Male indentured servants were more valuable, so ships' masters were paid twice as much for men as for women.

Bonds were usually for five to seven years, though often lasted longer because of debts to the master. Wages were room and board plus fare to America and "freedom dues"—a little extra to start off—at the end of indenture. These included clothing, food, a gun, and sometimes fifty acres. Lucky servants might get an additional wage—perhaps 3 pounds a year—or a suit of clothing at the end of service. Cash payments were rare—payment was often given in tobacco or other produce. Although the master controlled all personal affairs, indentured servants had legal rights and could sue. Usually marriage was forbidden, and child-bearing was considered an interruption in work and an impairment of health and stamina. Nevertheless, about one in five women did have children, and both mother and father had to pay a fine to reimburse the master for loss of services during pregnancy or submit to two years more indenture.

Political dissent was another cause for indenture. For example, when Ireland was conquered by England early in the 1600s and Irish peasants were pushed off their lands, they began to be shipped to the colonies to work for English colonials. About half were indentured at double the passage rate of others and for double the time—about twenty years, with extra years for debts to the master. Before the massive trade in Africans began, many Irish indentured servants were shipped to Caribbean plantations to replace Native Americans in the burgeoning sugar industry. In Barbados, they were used for

> grinding at the mills and attending the furnaces, or digging . . . having nothing to feed on . . . but potatoe roots, nor to drink, but water with such roots washed in it, besides the bread and tears of their own afflictions; being bought and sold still from one planter to another, or attached as horses and beasts for the debts of their masters, being whipt at the whipping post . . . for their masters' pleasure, and sleeping in sties worse than hogs in England.[20]

White servants and black slaves worked together in the West Indies for some time. Indentured servants, because they were not long-term property investments, were often more cruelly treated than were African slaves.[21] Africans were the better bargain, since the same money that could buy a white laborer for ten years could buy an African for life.[22] Also, indentured servants had some right to personal property, and their children were free, while children of slaves became the slavemaster's property.

By the 1700s, English migration had slowed considerably because overpopulation was no longer a problem and political dissent had lessened. Although indenture continued for some time, the vast numbers of migrants coming in by this means also declined, and no longer were kidnapping and illegal recruitment so likely. Some say that colonization of America was the largest and most successful welfare program in history.[23] Certainly for England this was true. It removed from the country its overpopulation, the poor, criminals, and undesirables, and at the same time returned a vast profit to the mother country. According to Handel,

> The colonizing efforts . . . combined philanthropic motives with political motives. . . . James Oglethorpe, an activist in the English movement to free debtors from prison, had the idea of helping such men get a new start in a New World. The project was financed with money raised by Oglethorpe and a large contribution from the English government, which hoped that [the] project would help solve the problems of vagrancy in England.[24]

### Women in the Colonies

Women constituted a third of the early immigrants to North America. Many were kidnapped to provide the new country with wives and laborers, and men colonists paid for wives from Europe; for example, the settlers at

Jamestown ordered two boatloads of women in 1619, paying 120 pounds each for their passage.

Once in the colonies, regardless of their status, women's scarcity made their lot better than that of their European counterparts (six men for every woman in seventeenth century Virginia, for example). Most could marry if they wanted or had the leverage to refuse an unsuitable proposal.[25] To increase the population, young people had much freedom in choice of mate. Women married and died young in the colonies. Jacobs says

> perhaps as many as four of every five of the first groups of women [died] . . . within five years. . . . [W]omen married early, sometimes at twelve or thirteen. . . . [There was] the common phenomenon of a man's outliving three or four of his wives.[26]

Childbirth was one of the most common causes of death, and women feared pregnancy because they knew they might have less than nine months to live. The average number of children was nine, but it was not uncommon for a woman to have twelve or fifteen, not many of whom lived to adulthood.

Marriage was considered the natural and desirable life for women who, though they contributed equally to the economy, were secondary to men both politically and religiously. Most sexual behavior was not disapproved if the couple were planning to marry, but if not, sexual immorality was taken very seriously. Women who bore children outside marriage could be taken to court and sentenced to public whipping, branding, and fines. Their children, if they could not support them or could not or would not name the father, could be taken and apprenticed to a tradesperson.[27] Moreover, ministers cautioned women to remain under husbands' control, and those who objected could be punished both by the husband and by the town. Adultery was the worst crime a woman could commit, for it was an offense against men's property rights. Divorce and legal separation were possible for women, but grounds were very difficult, and there were no laws forcing a man to support a wife from whom he was separated. In a separation the woman usually lost everything, even her children. A 1748 law allowed husbands to appoint guardians for their children and to apprentice them out to learn a trade, specifying that mothers were entitled only to their love and respect.[28] For most women, legal and religious ties could not be broken by men's adultery, abuse, or even desertion—only by death—and women alone seldom could find work that would free them from economic dependence, either on husbands or on the government.

Early in colonization, women had more rights than in later times, especially on the frontier where their labor was so desperately needed. There even married women could own property and sue in courts, and they were always favored by judges who defended them against personal abuse, enforced conjugal rights, and recalled runaway husbands.[29] They could also receive land grants as heads of families. For example, Pennsylvania offered 75 acres to women settlers, and if they brought servants and children, the grants were larger. Women also could develop their own lands: Margaret Brent, the colonies' first female lawyer, arrived in Maryland in 1638 and built a fortune in real estate. However, since land enabled women to remain single, most colonies soon refused to grant them land and denied them the right to inherit it.

Women and their daughters spun cotton, flax, and wool; looked after livestock; made butter and cheese; baked bread; cleaned and cooked; and bore and raised children. They doctored and nursed their families and prepared their own medicines—salves, balms, ointments, potions, and cordials.[30] Some women operated sawmills, distilleries, and slaughterhouses and were newspaper publishers or printers and teachers. They opened schools for women and achieved status as midwives, physicians, and apothecaries at least until the middle 1700s, when men entered the field of obstetrics. Women with a little capital opened small shops, selling anything from pastries and dry goods to hardware and liquor. Women could more easily take on unconventional roles in the South than in Puritan areas, for Puritans attached particular importance to regulating female behavior.[31]

Under common law, never-married women had the same rights as men and could buy and sell property, own businesses, sue in court, and so on (the *femme sole*). Once married, however, women entered the state of *femme couverte*, that is, their rights "covered" by those of their husbands. Husband and wife were one person, and that person was the husband.[32] Married women had no property and no money of their own. Even their clothing, jewels, household goods, livestock, and furniture belonged to their husbands, along with dowries and inheritances. In most instances husbands could sell wives' property without consent or take all their wives' earnings and allow them to starve.[33] Speth says

> The husband's absolute authority over his wife included the legal privilege of beating her [to be interfered with] . . . only if the husband was unduly brutal. At the beginning of the eighteenth century Elizabeth Wildy complained . . . that her husband not only whipped and maimed her but also held her in the fire until her clothes burned. The justices felt that in this case the husband had exceeded his right of "reasonable chastisement" and ordered him to appear in court and explain.[34]

Most American colonies granted three exceptions to these practices of common law. They upheld the wife's right to share her husband's home and bed, the right to be supported by him even if he abandoned her, and the right to be protected from his violence. However, if these happened there was not much recourse, since married women could not sue in court.

Widows had the same status as *femmes soles* in business affairs, though eldest sons got the bulk of deceased fathers' real estate, and personal property was divided among all the children. In common law, when men died without a will, widows inherited one-third of their husbands' real estate and a third interest in slaves and personal property, though the real estate reverted to eldest sons at their deaths. If men left less than their "thirds" to women, the women could sue; courts upheld the "thirds" custom because this reduced the chances that widows could become public dependents. Custom was more generous than law, and often husbands left more to widows than their "thirds," especially if there were minor children. Also, they rarely deprived their widows of minor children by appointing a legal guardian. Poor widows, however, had to depend on poor relief or hiring out, often to churches, and many took on the jobs of their husbands—farming, running shops, smithing—to support themselves and their children.

Because of their secondary spiritual status, women were generally forbidden to speak out on such important topics as religion. The dozens of Quaker women who came to the colonies seeking religious freedom in the 1600s were considered heretics, and were fined, whipped, jailed, and pilloried, and in a few instances, hanged.[35] Because government and religion were so closely related, especially in the Puritan colonies, those who argued religion might be considered traitors. An example was Anne Hutchinson, charismatic and intellectual wife of a prosperous businessman, who came to Massachusetts Bay Colony in 1634. She taught that people could approach God through prayer rather than solely through the mediation of a minister (Antinomianism). Brought to trial as a heretic before Governor John Winthrop, who was both judge and prosecutor, she was declared guilty before the trial and exiled from the colony. She then helped found Portsmouth, Rhode Island, on the basis of religious freedom. When her husband died in 1642, leaving her without protection, she fled to the wilderness and was killed, along with several of her children, in an Indian raid.

As in Europe, the colonies had a morbid preoccupation with women's devilish powers. Accusations of "witch" were used to eliminate bothersome individuals, and leaders popularized the idea that intellectual women were influenced by Satan. A clear example was Mary Dyer, one of Anne Hutchinson's followers. Accused of being in league with the devil, she was hanged in Boston Commons.[36] In another instance, in 1640 Ann Hibbens was excommunicated for complaining about poor work done in her home by carpenters. The magistrates believed her complaints were really against godly authority, and sixteen years later, after her respected husband died, she was executed as a witch.[37] In Salem, of two hundred persons accused in 1692, one hundred fifty, mostly women, were imprisoned. Fifty confessed and twenty-eight were condemned to die. Fourteen women and six men, one an ordained minister, were actually executed.[38]

Although in early colonial times women were recruited to come to the New World and marry, by the early 1700s there was a surplus of unwed and widowed women in New England. Inability to marry or find work meant that many were homeless and near starvation. "Warned out" of towns, along with their children, they wandered the country seeking work, and many disappeared into the forests forever.

By the late 1600s, there was an increasing market for textiles, and town councils saw home piecework for women and their children as a way to reduce public relief.[39] Merchants paid high prices for yarn, and by 1675 towns were providing the capital to set up woolen mills where poor women and their children were put to work at spinning. In Boston, where dependent women were very numerous, the town collected 900 pounds to build a workhouse. This was the first attempt to organize female labor under one roof.

The widows for whom it was designed refused to go there, objecting to the indignity, to the rigidity of its rules, and to being cut off from friends and community.[40]

The town fathers finally opened it as a factory in 1750.

Home manufacture waned as factories were built in response to the cotton revolution. Soon there were hundreds of cotton mills throughout New England, and factory owners, citing philanthropy as well as economics, petitioned towns to send them poor women and children to work in their mills. By the late 1700s many towns required overseers of the poor to bind out indigent women and children to the factories.

## SOCIAL WELFARE IN THE COLONIES

Although the colonists adopted England's poor laws almost whole cloth, there were fundamental differences in their ideologies of poor relief practice. First, in England, there was an overabundance of workers in cities, the result of people being pushed off the land. Vast unemployment, pools of workers waiting to be hired, poverty, vagrancy, and crime were the issues social welfare addressed. In the early days of colonial America, on the other hand, labor was scarce and everyone could, theoretically, work. In fact, wages in New England were 30 to 100 percent higher than in England. In a subsistence economy of extreme scarcity, money was not available for the poor, even those obviously dependent because of disability.

Second, while in New England upward mobility was limited only by effort, at least in theory, class stratification was firmly set in England and *noblesse oblige* provided a system of private charity—legacies, endowments, and bequests to provide substantial funds for hospitals, asylums, and orphanages. In the colonies, private charities played an insignificant role until the end of the eighteenth century.[41] Finally, religion, historically the bastion of last resort for the poor, now insisted upon individual effort and decried poor relief as contributing to the spiritual degradation of the poor. People who did not abide by the idea of the work ethic were punished, driven out, or deported, or even hanged.

### Early American Poor Laws

As in European Protestant countries, there was a belief that wealth and condition were divinely ordained. Paupers were treated as morally deficient, and were required to take paupers' oaths and have their names exhibited in the city hall or marketplace or published in newspapers. In some places they were required to wear the letter "P" on their sleeves. The numbers of "worthy poor" were very slim; since everyone started with an "equal chance," few were considered worthy of governmental help. One group considered worthy from the first were veterans, along with their families or survivors, because of their service to the colonies in the Indian wars. They received pensions—outdoor relief—as a right, as early as

1636.[42] By 1777, all states except Connecticut had special provisions for veterans. People injured in Indian raids were also worthy, at least of short-term help, as disaster victims.

Keynotes in care of the poor were local responsibility, relative and community responsibility, and categorization. Even in earliest colonial times, there were many public dependents. Essentially, they were the unemployable: the aged, disabled, orphans, unwanted children, and widows with children. Another group needing public relief were children of mixed races and old slaves freed so their masters would not have to support them when they could no longer work. More public dependents came from the frequent wars with Native Americans; recurring epidemics of smallpox, dysentery, measles, yellow fever; poor harvests or bad weather in times when production of food depended on nature and natural disasters could mean starvation; uncontrollable fires; high childbirth mortality; and the hazards of life in a new country.

### Local Responsibility

By 1642, colonial towns had given township or parish supervisors authority to collect poor taxes, investigate applicants for poor relief to determine their worthiness for aid, and dispense poor relief. In addition to poor taxes, monies for relief came from fines for refusal to work at harvest time, for selling at short weight, for not attending church, and for illegally bringing a pauper into town. If a town would not collect poor taxes, local county courts were empowered to assess and dispense funds. By 1636 Plymouth and Massachusetts courts were placing out the poor, and in 1642 Plymouth's first official poor law directed that every case of poor relief be discussed at a town meeting. By 1662 colonies had adopted the English Law of Settlement and Removal, and all colonial towns had to supply food, firewood, clothing, and household essentials for their own poor.

To qualify for poor relief, people had to own property or have lived in a town for a prescribed time—by 1700 for one year. While in England the unemployed had to stay in their home areas, in the colonies the unemployed and undesirables had to move on. As early as 1639, eight years after Boston was settled, the courts there had the power to send the poor to towns where they could be employed or to deport them from the country.[43] Strangers were not welcome: Newcomers or "foreigners," even if they came from other colonies, were given three years probation in some communities. If they could not support themselves and their families within that time, they were sent back to their former places of residence or banished. By 1725, strangers could stay no more than twenty days in many towns without the council being officially informed, and by 1767 no one could move into a town without the council's permission. In 1789, residency laws required that people be in a town for two years or be age 21 and have paid taxes for five years. They could also become residents by town vote. By 1793, five years without being "warned out" was required for residency.[44] "Warning out" had two meanings. First, it warned outsiders that they were not welcome in the towns, were not eligible for poor relief, and might be subject to punishments that ranged from stocks and pillory, flogging, tarring and feathering, to hanging. Second, residents themselves could be warned out, serving notice that if they stayed, they could not expect poor relief and might be indentured if they were in danger of becoming public dependents.

### Family Responsibility

Families had a unique importance in colonial poor laws because they provided social control for the religiopolitical governments. Their role was to ensure that their members would not become dependent on the government. Every person under age 21 had to live with a family, and county courts or administrators had the power to place any child or dependent person with a family. Families that could not maintain independence for their members were considered dangerous to the community both economically and morally. Axinn and Levin say

> Despite the family's usefulness, the impetus to maximize individual and family well-being did not center on the individual as family member or on the individual family as a unit. When a family was in trouble, the concern was to save its potentially productive members.[45]

By 1675, relative responsibility was established by law: Persons had to be bonded by their families to move in, and diseased or poor persons had to be cared for by relatives.

People were expected to care for their own as a matter of course, but when this was not possible the needy were placed with families with the understanding that they would work to pay their keep. The aged, disabled, ill, and infants were placed with the town paying the family to tend to them. The poor—unemployed men and women, widows and their dependent children, and children who were orphaned, illegitimate, unwanted, or removed from their parents by order of the court—were auctioned off to the person who would charge the town the least for their care; indentured, so that their bonds were held by the family where they were placed; or apprenticed. Apprenticeship was usually for children of the better class, so that they might learn a trade.

Some outdoor relief was given to those who were more or less worthy, so that they could stay in their own homes—the aged and ill, for example. Guardians might be appointed for them to make sure they were properly cared for. However, the general rule was to place them. Some families made it a business to provide places for the needy, and set up what today would be called private care homes to take in several people in return for pay from the town. These differed from the town poorhouses, which were built, supported, and administered by the courts or towns. Although almshouses and workhouses were growing in popularity in larger towns, most small towns could not support them.

### Classification of the Poor

Most people who were poor, regardless of their situations, were assumed morally unworthy and were classified as

*Impotent poor*, who were aged or disabled long-term residents who could no longer work or people with severe physical or mental handicaps.

*Able-bodied poor*—both men and women—who were employable in some capacity but solicited aid from the community.

*Dependent children*, for whom the goal of towns and courts was to ensure that they did not follow in the degenerate footsteps of their pauper parents.

*The Impotent Poor.*   The impotent poor were considered burdens on family and community and were expected to work to their limits. If not, the family had control of their lives up to though not including murder, and care ranged from that provided by loving relatives to being chained or locked in unheated sheds, at the mercy of the elements, until they died. Dependent children were under the care of local governments rather than parents from the time they were born and could be taken from parents considered unworthy. In addition to these children, dependent children included orphans and abandoned, unwanted, and illegitimate children. Widows were unlikely to be considered worthy poor and were urged to remarry, but a significant number—those whose husbands had been poor or indentured—were left destitute and could not find new husbands. Single women were seen as a threat to morality and the economic security of the town. Both they and widows were often banished from the community if they could not eke out a living as a servant or by sewing and family or neighbors would not provide bond.[46]

*The Able-bodied Poor.*   The able-bodied poor—both men and women who could be employable in some capacity—were considered to be going against God's law when they asked for relief rather than working. People believed that America was a land where personal gain was unlimited, and laziness was the primary reason for poverty. Punishments for poverty were the same as those for offenses against the community—bonding, warning out, selling to the lowest bidder (auctioning off), flogging, branding, or jailing. The poor were often put to work on public projects. Most towns auctioned them off, but because this led to brutal treatment, inadequate care, hunger, and exploitation, reformers demanded they be placed in almshouses, workhouses, or houses of correction.

In 1660, Boston built a house of correction in which all indigents were herded together; in 1739, a workhouse that was a combination penal institution and poorhouse for vagabonds, rogues, idle persons, criminals, the poor, and the insane. Grob gives us a description of almshouses:

In most of these places cleanliness is an unknown luxury, all is filth and misery and the most degrading, unrelieved suffering. The inmates, sane and insane, were found in many instances huddled together without discrimination of age, sex, or condition; conmingling in unrestrained licentiousness and with results shocking to all sense of decency and humanity.[47]

In most almshouses and in some jails were children ranging in age from 1 month to 14 years.

Idlers and vagabonds were particular threats to colonial self-sufficiency and safety, but any objectionable people—for reasons religious, political, or moral—could be brought before the local courts and judged "rogues." Punishment for both men and women was public whipping and deportation to their former residences or confinement in jail. Demented and maimed persons were deported or sold and criminals and delinquents were driven from town: For lesser crimes they could be flogged or mutilated, and for more severe crimes they could be executed. Debtors were imprisoned for owing as little as 2 cents, and they had to provide their own necessities while in prison or go without.

*Dependent Children.* Colonial laws were particularly concerned that children should not follow the road into idleness and poverty. Poor families were requested to bind out their children to service, and as early as 1641 the courts had the right to take the children of the poor and indenture them to guard against the "contagion of parental failure."[48] A statute in Virginia in 1646 accused the poor of obstinacy in not binding out their children and ordered county commissioners to take two children from every poor family and bind them out to flax houses. The county also placed orphans, illegitimate children, and unwanted children. Illegitimate white children "belonged" to the parish if fathers failed to support them, and they were bound out by church wardens until fathers reimbursed the parish. Children of slaves and indentured servants were also bound out.

According to parish records, one-third of all those bound out were orphans. The remainder were children whose parents apprenticed them to learn a trade. They then lived with the master and rarely saw their families, and masters were responsible by law not only for material welfare but for spiritual guidance. Apprentice masters, along with guardians of wealthy orphans and orphanage matrons, were required to teach boys reading and writing and give all children Christian training. Most boys were apprenticed to carpenters, shoemakers, blacksmiths, or planters, while girls became domestics, though some learned to knit, spin, and sew. Apprenticeship contracts were registered by the courts, and the practice assured the colonies of an ongoing supply of artisans and craftspeople.

Child labor was viewed as beneficial to both child and society, teaching the sanctity of work and the evils of idleness. Boston spinning schools opened in 1656, and children and other poor were placed in them and paid by the piece. This gave the town income at minimum expense and provided employment for society's potentially rebellious elements. Unlike apprentice masters, employers were not responsible for children's well-being or education even though often they had contracts supposedly to protect them. To promote the work ethic among the poor, the Society for Encouraging Industry and Employing the Poor was established in 1751 to promote the manufacture of woolen cloth and to employ indigent women and children, and in 1759 Boston opened a spinning school for female children.

The importance of education in America led to both public and private school systems. In 1647 Massachusetts required towns of over fifty households to have a teacher for elementary school, and if there were more than a hundred families in a town, high school was mandated. This system, paid for by fees and taxes, was not compulsory; however, town selectmen could investigate any home to see that children were adequately taught there. In both New York and New Jersey, Dutch Reformed parochial schools began, with poor children attending free and fees charged those who could afford them.[49] New Jersey had the first land grant schools, in which certain lands were set aside for support of schools, and New York and New Jersey in 1704 established private catechism schools for people of African descent. In 1787, New York City created the first free school for such children, and a New Jersey law in 1788 required that they be taught to read. In the South, education lagged because farms and plantations were scattered. While white families had tutors for children or educated them in England, children of African descent were, on the whole, denied education because it was thought to make them unruly.

### Private Philanthropy

Despite the lack of money available for social welfare in the early colonies, there was some private philanthropy. It was, in general, based either on mutual aid or the ideal of providing work as a solution to pauperism. Quakers, for example, asked the needy—even non-Quakers— to present their problems to the group, and the meeting voted food, clothing, shelter, coal. Friendly visitors called on those needing help, and such help was not confined to members of their religion. Voluntary giving rather than taxes supplied necessities, which often included employment or materials for home handicrafts.[50] Quakers also established almshouses, workhouses, and later penitentiaries where the immoral could reflect on their misdeeds.

Many societies were related to religion or crafts: For example, the Friends Almshouse in Philadelphia for poor Quakers was established in 1713, and the Boston Episcopal Society in 1724. In New York, the Society of the House of Carpenters was established in 1767. As did many ethnic groups, free Afro-Americans founded mutual aid societies to help both free and slave. For example, in Boston, a Masonic Lodge was founded by free Afro-Americans in 1784, and in 1787 the Philadelphia Free African Society was founded to provide mutual aid in sickness and for widows and orphans. This society also provided schooling and apprenticeship for children of African descent.[51]

Benjamin Franklin was a strong proponent of both voluntary associations and self-help. He preached the gospel of industry, frugality, and sobriety as the way to individual freedom, and he believed in personal, social, and civic responsibility. To these ends, he established a library and a volunteer fire company, worked to ensure the paving of roads and the cleaning and lighting of Philadelphia, worked to establish a police force, and founded a hospital and an academy that became the University of Pennsylvania. As a founding father of our country, he epitomized the meaning of social welfare of the time.[52]

Religion, particularly the Evangelical movement, brought new concerns for the poor along with ethics of individual responsibility and social order. It claimed that the rich had a responsibility toward the poor, and that the poor owed gratitude and work to them.

The Great Awakening, another religious movement, brought two great preachers, George Whitefield and Jonathan Edwards, who led a series of religious revivals between 1730 and 1750. They preached a humanitarian ethic that transformed philanthropy from the province of the upper classes to a shared activity of all classes, appealing both to conscience and to altruism.

In the century before the Revolution, great depressions created a need for social welfare that neither public nor private funding alone could handle. Joint funding, therefore, became the pattern—one that continued until 1935. Rather than giving money for explicit causes, private donors gave money to the government for charitable purposes, and government officials, such as overseers of the poor, asked churches to take up collections to be given for support of public dependents.

## SLAVERY IN THE AMERICAS

There were many Africans in the New World before the onset of slavery. They were explorers, servants, and slaves who accompanied French, Spanish, and Portuguese in expeditions in both North and South America, including Pedro Alonso Niño, who piloted one of Columbus's ships. Free African immigrants were not considered racially inferior in early days. They could accumulate property and testify in court, and they toiled in the fields and fraternized with white indentured servants.[53] However, with slavery came racism. Virginia led the way in enslavement of people of African heritage when in 1660 it made them servants for life, forbade intermarriage with whites, and gave children born of African-descended women the status of their mothers. Although there were some religious qualms about making Christians slaves, in 1667 it was decreed that conversion to Christianity would have no bearing on slave status.

Slavery as practiced in North America was a response to the Protestant religioeconomic dictum that wealth demonstrates morality and to the even older dictum of fear and hatred of "outsiders." Because Africans did not worship the Christian God, their lives were insignificant compared to the mandate of wealth for their masters. While South American slaves had human rights because of the intercession of the Catholic Church, North American slaves were considered less than human—reduced to work or breeding animals. Masters owned not only their work but their lives, and Protestantism did not forbid their use (or that of white workers) even to death. Wealth-producing work was an end in itself, dictated by God to the faithful and therefore religiously legitimate. Although certainly some people detested slavery, the protests of the few were drowned in the approval of the many. Slavery was not, for the most part, seen as evil at all but almost a morality, since it "protected" slaves from destitution, put them to work, and led to wealth for God's chosen. These beliefs created a system of slavery unequaled in brutality and gave rise to the American brand of racism.

### The Golden Triangle and the Triangular Trade

The slave trade was called the "triangular trade." The triangle began in Europe, with ships and exports supplied by the English and French sent to Africa to purchase slaves. From Africa it went to the West Indies, where slaves were sold to the New World to supply raw materials. The triangle was completed when the raw materials were shipped to England (with a stopoff in New England) for manufacture.

In the the early 1600s, many small farmers in the Caribbean produced sugar, for the cost of passage for slaves from Africa was too high to be expedient. However, as coffee and chocolate became popular in Europe, sugar consumption skyrocketed so that by 1700 it had become the most valuable agricultural commodity in international trade. This had two results. The first was an economic dispossession of small farmers in the Caribbean as the wealthy plantation owners took over:

> Barbados in 1645 had 11,200 small white farmers and 5,680 Negro slaves. In 1667, there were 745 large plantation owners and 82,023 slaves. . . . The price of land skyrocketed. A plantation of 500 acres which sold for 400 pounds in 1640 fetched 700 pounds for a half share in 1648.[54]

Because of the sugar trade, Barbados, with its 166 square miles, was worth more to England in the 1700s and 1800s than the whole of New England, New York, and Pennsylvania combined.

Second, African slavery became economically profitable.[55] White indenture to the Caribbean was dying down and Native American workers were dying out. One African was said to be worth five Native Americans because of resistance to European diseases and experience as a slave in Africa. African slavery became the way of the future for, first, the sugar plantations and, then, for the cotton plantations of the South.

Most African slaves came from an area bordering the West Coast of Africa—they were Hausas, Mindinagos, Yorubas, Ibos, Efiks, Krus, Fontins, Ashantis, Dahomeans, Binis, and Sengalies.[56] First the Portuguese, then the Dutch, French, and English (under the auspices of Elizabeth I) seized leadership in the slave trade. Slave raids throughout Africa, especially the West Coast, decimated the continent of as many as forty million people, most in the prime of their lives.[57] The strongest and healthiest men and women survived the passage to the Americas. Many of the rest died in Africa during and after their capture, walking the hundreds of miles to the coast to be picked over, branded, and chained, or on the slave ships themselves. During the Middle Passage, they were packed into holds and chained at the neck and feet, often with no more than eighteen inches of head room each for the six to ten weeks of the passage. They died of suffocation, starvation, and epidemics of smallpox and dysentery. Some committed suicide, or killed those they loved or those who had food. Those who died were thrown overboard, and sharks followed slave ships regularly. Some gave birth to children while still in chains. Young women and girls were often taken for the pleasure of the crew.

Occasionally, when a ship was seriously damaged or disease ran rampant, slaves were thrown overboard to make the ship lighter, or ships were deserted in midocean, their cargo of men and women chained helplessly together below the decks,[58] for they were considered "animal cargo." In 1783, short of water, the captain of the *Zong* threw 132 slaves overboard (they often did this with livestock, such as horses). Damages were awarded the owners for property, and the idea of mass murder never occurred.[59] One African says

> I was soon put down under the decks and . . . with the loathesomeness of the stench and crying together, I became so sick and low that I was not able to eat. . . . On my refusal to eat, one of them held me fast by the hands and laid me across, I think the windlass, and tied my feet, while the other flogged me severely. . . . One day, when we had a smooth sea and a moderate wind, two of my wearied countrymen who were chained together . . . preferring death to such a life of misery, somehow made through the nettings and jumped into the sea.[60]

There were 155 recorded uprisings on shipboard by slaves between 1699 and 1845. When they reached America, diseased slaves were left to die and the remaining sold either to dealers or directly to plantation owners. The price of slaves fluctuated with the market: George Washington bought a man in 1754 for $250 but ten years later had to pay $285. Slaves were available either for cash or for a small down payment with small monthly payments.

Over the period of the slave trade, from 1502 to 1860, 9.6 million Africans were brought to the New World, most to the Indies and South America and only 5 to 6 percent to North America. Prior to 1790, an estimated 275,000 Africans were brought to the North American colonies, with another 70,000 in the next decade. Over 6 million were brought to the Americas in the 1700s, at 50,000 to 100,000 every year. Altogether, approximately half a million Africans were brought as slaves to North America.[61] Aside from the disruption of cultures of those brought to the Americas, the societies of Africa, large and small, advanced or more primitive, were ruined as these millions of the strongest and youngest were taken from their homes. Undoubtedly, this mass deportation of native Africans led to the ease by which colonialism was soon enforced upon Africa itself.

In England after the 1700s, slaveowners dominated Parliament, and the founding of banks based on the triangular trade began in the late 1700s and early 1800s. England and Scotland also developed insurance houses—such as Lloyds of London, originally a coffee house that listed runaway slaves—to insure both slaves and slave ships and thus began the property insurance system of the world.[62] The slave trade, of course, was not looked upon as inhumane. In a time when life was so cheap, and poverty was so much looked upon as personal sin, slavery was merely another—very lucrative—business. Indeed, many English humanitarians were included in those who ran the slave trade. Edmund Burke was one such, as was John Cary, who in England founded a society for the Incorporation of the Poor. Bryan Blundell, a noted slave trader, was trustee, treasurer, chief patron, and most active supporter of a charity school; and slave traders, because of their wealth from the trade, often held high offices in the government of England.

By the time George Washington became president in 1789 there were four million people in America. Approximately one of every four of them was a slave, of which about one-third were women.


## TOWARD THE REVOLUTION

Economics was at the base of the rebellion against King George and England. English law forbade the colonies to manufacture goods from the raw materials they produced, and only English-built ships could be used to transport raw materials to England and the finished products colonists were required to buy back from England. To aid England's wool business, laws required that all slaves and servants wear wool, even in the Caribbean, and that the dead be buried in suits of wool. Colonists were required to eat fish caught from English ships on Fridays and Saturdays, and as early as 1615 England had a monopoly on refining sugar produced in the West Indies. Such laws galled the colonists, many of whom had come to America to find freedom and financial success, and they began to fight against forced purchase of goods more efficiently produced in America. In addition, English treaties with Native Americans kept them from legally exploring and settling the land beyond the Appalachians.

The northern colonies produced food for sugar workers because planters did not want to take the land out of sugar production. By supplying food, however, they were taking trade from England in return for sugar supplies. England therefore imposed the Stamp Act, which required a tax on sugar imports to the northern colonies, and Americans refused to pay or to ship food to the sugar islands. Because of this, fifteen thousand Jamaican slaves died of famine between 1780 and 1787.[63] Moreover, colonials began to manufacture and process the raw materials of America despite English bans. They especially began to trade in rum from Caribbean sugar, textiles from southern cotton, and iron from northern mines. American rum production competed with English spirits made from corn and gave Americans an edge in the slave trading industry. In 1770, New England exports of rum to Africa represented over four-fifths of the total colonial exports of the time. Metallurgy also became important—fetters and chains and padlocks, irons for branding, axes for clearing the colonial land, and guns.

### Women in the Revolution

Because of the general status of women at the time of the Revolution, their participation in developing the new country was limited. For example, although in North Carolina fifty-one women proclaimed their right to participate in political activities, no women attended the Continental or state congresses convened to argue the question of Revolution. Abigail Adams, wife of John, was nearly alone in her outspoken insistence that men misused their political power when they denied women equal rights. She continually tried to encourage the inclusion of women's legal and civil rights in the new government, writing to her husband to

> remember the ladies . . . if particular care and attention is not paid to [us] we are determined to foment a rebellion, and will not hold ourselves bound by any laws in which we have no voice or representation.[64]

Mercy Otis Warren, sister of patriot James Otis, was among the major intellectual writers of the Revolution. An antifederalist, she wrote plays and published under a male name, corresponding on public questions with both Samuel and John Adams, John Hancock, and George Washington. John Adams and many other men were concerned with women's rights, for a spirit of equality permeated liberal thought. Thomas Paine wrote an impassioned plea for their inclusion in the Constitution, and Benjamin Franklin said the women were unequal only because of the limits placed on them by education and tradition.[65]

As many as twenty thousand women went to war in the Revolution, on both the British and American sides. They were cooks, nurses, doctors, laundresses, guides, seamstresses, and porters. More were with the British as paid staff, because American soldiers could rely on volunteer patriots to care for their needs. Women were not simply observers, as this following account of the British entering Cambridge illustrates:

> Poor dirty emaciated men, great numbers of women, who seemed to be the beasts of burden having a bushel basket on their back by which they were bent double, the contents seemed to be pots and kettles, various sorts of furniture, children peeping through gridirons and other utensils, some very young infants who were born on the road, the women bare feet, clothed in dirty rags.[66]

Hundreds of women participated in Benedict Arnold's disastrous assault on Montreal, which began in late fall. Led by ill-informed guides, ill-equipped for the bitter winter, and unaware that game would not be available, many starved, died of pneumonia and typhoid, or became lost and froze to death.

The Daughters of Liberty formed to boycott British products, especially tea, and many women supplied the Revolutionary Army with clothes, food, and other provisions. Some women fought as soldiers and were rewarded with army pensions for themselves and their families. For example, Deborah Sampson Gannett dressed as a man and became an infantry soldier at age 18. After the war she married, and when she died at age 67, her husband applied for and received a pension based on her military service. (Not again until the 1970s was there a ruling by Social Security that the spouse of a working woman was entitled to her pension.) Other well-known women heroes were Mary Ludwig Hayes, who went with her husband and replaced him at the cannon when he was wounded, and Molly Pitcher, who carried water to the wounded men.

## THE NEW NATION AND ITS CONSTITUTION

It is ironic that one goal for which the Revolutionary War was fought was equality when in America women still had the status of children and idiots and the slave trade was still active, with half a million slaves in the nation. Both free and slave persons of African descent fought during the Revolution, many for the English, for they were not welcomed in the Revolutionary Army. However, after the winter at Valley Forge, Washington was willing to accept any fighting man, and approximately 100,000 runaway slaves joined the Revolutionary Army and were freed.

In 1773 slaves in Massachusetts petitioned the legislature for freedom, and this petition was followed by eight others during the Revolutionary War. Slavery was effectively terminated in the North by 1777. Five of the original thirteen states emancipated their slaves before the federal Constitutional Convention met in New York in 1788. Partial antislavery measures were enacted by New York in 1788, with total emancipation in 1799, while New Jersey began to pass antislavery legislation in 1786.[67] Vermont was first to abolish slavery in 1777, followed by Massachusetts and New Hampshire in 1783 and Connecticut and Rhode Island in 1784.

Despite the new freedoms the Constitution guaranteed, it was a creation of its time. As such, it was an elitist document; that is, it was written by white male property owners and assures their rights without due consideration of the rights of others—women, people without property, or people of nonwhite ethnicity. Although there was some agitation before its writing to ensure the abolition of slavery, this was dropped to gain support from southern slaveholders for ratification, and slavery itself was given formal recognition—in the determination that slaves were three-fifths of a white man for purposes of determining voter representation; in the fugitive slave section, which assured that slaves would be returned to their masters; and in the permission to continue the slave trade until 1808. In addition, the Constitution gave the vote only to property owners and men with certain levels of education, ensuring an elitist and mercantilist bent. For example, James Madison believed that the establishment of a national government was the most important protection for the elites against mass movements that might threaten property. Dye and Zeigler say

> Men like Patrick Henry and Richard Henry Lee of Virginia vigorously attacked the Constitution as a "counter-revolutionary document" . . . the new government would be "aristocratic," "all-powerful," and a threat to the "spirit of republicanism" and the "genius of democracy." . . . [It sets up] . . . an aristocratic upper house and an almost monarchial presidency.[68]

In fact, the leaders of the Revolution had asked George Washington to be permanent president, and had even prepared for him a throne, but he refused. To counteract accusations of aristocracy, Congress provided the Bill of Rights at its first meeting.

Although four decision-making bodies were established by the Constitution, only one, the House of Representatives, was to be elected by the people. The Senate was to be elected by state legislators and the president by an Electoral College. The powers of government were almost unilaterally based on the protection of property rights. Congress was given power to tax, to regulate interstate commerce, to protect money and property, to regulate communication and transportation, to conduct military affairs, and to protect the rights of slaveowners to their slaves.

The Constitution did not deal with the problems of the poor, although popular workingmen's movements demanded a federally controlled monetary system (rather than factory scrip), the abolition of debts, and an equal distribution of property. Congress was given the authority to provide for the common welfare, but common welfare was not social welfare. The theme of individual responsibility and individual achievement permeated the new government, and the upsurge of liberalism did not change the nation's perspective on the causes of poverty or the needs of the poor. Because the political economy of the times was elitist, so was the Constitution: Those who wrote it were involved in profitmaking through the labor of the poor. Factions seeking equality were either ignored or defeated in the battle, and the class stratification that had been custom in the New World became a legal part of American government. Those who had no voice before the Revolution were denied voice in the new nation.

## CONCLUSION: REVOLUTION TO STATUS QUO

The Constitution does provide citizens with assured freedoms and civil rights whether its authors intended that or not. Many such rights have been fought through the customs and courts of the land, and the Constitution and its amendments, particularly as interpreted by the Supreme Court, have made it possible for these fights to be won. Over the two hundred years of the existence of the new nation, though the basic protection of property rights has been maintained, civil rights probably not conceived of as possible at the Revolution have come to pass. The abolition of slavery was the first of many civil rights to be assured, with women's suffrage and equal opportunity in employment, education, and other areas of life to come later. Despite its elitist beginning, and despite the roadblocks put in the way of equality, the basic underpinnings of the Constitution and the democratic orientation of the people of the United States have slowly made inroads on our racist, sexist, and classist society. Some of us are impatient that the promises of equality have not been fulfilled, and the impatience is well taken. However, patterns of equality are set in law, traditions, and customs, and as we continue, the promises will be kept.

## STUDY QUESTIONS

1. What kinds of social welfare existed in the early colonies? On what were they based?
2. What were the differences between slavery in North America and slavery in South America?
3. How did indenture and slavery differ, and how did those differences set patterns for racism based on color?
4. What impact did the Revolution have on treatment and/or control of the poor?
5. How did religion influence the provision of social welfare for the poor? For children?

## FOOTNOTES

[1] Eric Williams, *Capitalism and Slavery*, (New York: G.P. Putnam's Sons, Capricorn Book Edition, 1966).

[2] Henry F. Dobyns, "Estimating Aboriginal American Population." *Current Anthropology*, (October 1966), pp. 395–416.

[3] Marvin Harris, *Patterns of Race in the Americas*, (New York: W. W. Norton and Company, 1964), p. 3.

[4] Ibid., pp. 7-10.

[5] Harris, *Patterns of Race*, pp. 8–10.

[6] Lerone Bennett, Jr., *Before the Mayflower: A History of the Negro in America, 1619–1964*, rev.ed., (Chicago: Johnson Publishing Company, Penguin Edition, 1966), p. 101.

[7] Joe R. Feagin, *Racial and Ethnic Relations*, 2nd ed., (Englewood Cliffs, N.J.: Prentice Hall, 1984), p. 298.

[8] Harris, *Patterns of Race*, p. 15.

[9] Carl A. Sauer, *Seventeenth Century in North America*, (Berkeley: Turtle Island Foundation, 1980).

[10] Ibid., p. 60.

[11] Stanley Elkins, *Slavery*, 2nd ed. (Chicago: University of Chicago Press, 1968), p. 61.

[12] Feagin, *Racial Relations*, p. 179.

[13] Harris, *Patterns of Race*, pp. 80–82.

[14] Williams, *Capitalism and Slavery*, p. 26.

[15] Bennett, *Before the Mayflower*.

[16] Carole Hymowitz and Michaele Weissman, *A History of Women in America*, (New York: Bantam Books, 1980), p. 8.

[17] Beulan Compton, *Introduction to Social Welfare and Social Work*, (Homewood, Ill.: The Dorsey Press, 1980), 199.

[18] Williams, *Capitalism and Slavery*, pp. 11–12.

[19] Compton, *Introduction to Social Welfare*, p. 188

[20] In Williams, *Capitalism and Slavery*, p. 17, quoting L.F. Strock, ed., *Proceedings and Debates in the British Parliament Respecting North America*, (Washington, D.C., 1924–41), I. 249.

[21] From the *Calendar of State Papers*, Colonial Series, v. 229. Report of the Council for Foreign Plantations (August, 1664), in Williams, *Capitalism and Slavery*, p. 18.

[22] Williams, *Capitalism and Slavery*, p. 18.

[23] Compton, *Introduction to Social Welfare*, among others.

[24] Gerald Handel, *Social Welfare in Western Society*, (New York: Random House, 1982), p. 67.

25William Jay Jacobs, *Women in American History*, (Encino, Calif.: Glencoe Publishing, 1976), p. 7.

26Ibid., p. 3.

27Hymowitz and Weissman, *History of Women*, p. 11.

28Linda E. Speth, "More Than Her Thirds: Wives and Widows in Colonial Virgina," in Linda Speth and Alison Duncan Hirsch, eds. *Women, Family, and Community in Colonial America: Two Perspectives*, (New York: Haworth Press, 1983), p .11.

29Amaury De Riencourt, *Sex and Power in History*, (New York: Dell Publishing, 1974), p. 308.

30Julia Cherry Sprull, "Housewives and Their Helpers," in Linda K. Kerber and Jane de Hart Mathews, eds., *Women's America*, (New York: Oxford University Press, 1982), p. 26.

31Alice Kessler-Harris, *Out to Work: A History of Wage-Earning Women in the United States*, (New York: Oxford University Press, 1982), p. 13.

32Hymowitz and Weissman, *History of Women*, p. 22.

33Ibid., p. 23.

34Speth, "More Than Her Thirds," p. 11.

35Hymowitz and Weissman, *History of Women*, p. 21.

36Jacobs, *Women in History*, p. 14.

37Kessler-Harris, *Out To Work*, p. 16.

38Hymowitz and Weissman, *History of Women*, p. 128.

39Kessler-Harris, *Out To Work*, p. 17.

40Ibid.

41Walter A. Friedlander and Robert Z. Apte, *Introduction to Social Welfare*, (Englewood Cliffs, N.J.: Prentice-Hall, 1974), p. 62.

42Compton, *Introduction to Social Welfare*, p. 198.

43Gerald N. Grob, advisory editor, "Maryland Report on Almshouses," in *The State and Public Welfare in Nineteenth Century America*, (New York: Arno Press, 1976), pp. 6–7.

44Ibid., a note in Senate Document 2, January 1859 historical references taken from the New Colony of Plymouth and Massachusetts Colonial Acts, p. 38.

45June Axinn and Herman Levin, *Social Welfare: A History of the American Response to Need*, (New York: Harper and Row, 1982), p. 19.

46Kessler-Harris, *Out to Work*, p. 5, quoting Walter Bremner, ed., *Children and Youth in America: A Documentary History*, (New York: Arno Press, 1969). Originally published in 1914, p. 12.

47Grob, *The State and Public Welfare*, p. 16.

48Axinn and Levin, *Social Welfare*, p. 20.

49Compton, *Introduction to Social Welfare*, pp. 201–202.

50Ibid., p. 198.

51Ralph Dolgoff and Donald Feldstein, *Understanding Social Welfare*, 2nd ed., (New York: Longman Press, 1984), p. 65.

52Compton, *Introduction to Social Welfare*, p. 176.

53Bennett, *Before the Mayflower*, p. 36.

54Williams, *Capitalism and Slavery*, pp. 23 and 25.

55Harris, *Patterns of Race*, pp. 13–14.

56Bennett, *Before the Mayflower*, p. 38.

57Ibid., p. 30.

58Jacobs, *Women in History*, p. 11.

59Williams, *Capitalism and Slavery*, p. 46.

60Oloudah Equiano, "The Interesting narrative of Oloudah Equiano," in Thomas R. Frazier, *Afro-American History: Primary Sources*, (New York: Harcourt, Brace, and World, 1970), pp. 18–20.

61Feagin, *Racial Relations*, p. 213.

[62]Williams, *Capitalism and Slavery*, p. 108.

[63]Ibid.

[64]Jacobs, *Women in History*, p. 19.

[65]Ibid., p. 16.

[66]Hymowitz and Weissman, *History of Women*, quoting Sally Smith Booth, *The Women of '76*, (New York: Hastings House, 1973), p. 144.

[67]Thomas R. Dye and L. Harmon Zeigler, *The Irony of Democracy*, (Belmont, Calif.: Wadsworth Publishing Co.). p. 42.

[68]Ibid., p. 51.

# 6

# AMERICA TO THE CIVIL WAR

## THE FIRST CIVIL RIGHTS MOVEMENT

After the Revolution, egalitarian ideals took second place to laissez-faire capitalism, industrialization, and expansionism. The Constitution and new state governments assured elitist control: only white male Christians had suffrage in most states, and in some to vote or run for office required ownership of property up to $5,000. Not until 1856 could all white men vote in the New England states if they did not hold property, though frontier states usually gave suffrage to all white men.[1] Some territories came into the union with suffrage for women; for example, Wyoming would not enter the Union unless it was allowed to continue women's suffrage, and Utah insisted on women's suffrage to maintain polygamy for the Mormon Church against the voting power of newcomers.

According to Jacksonian democracy, every (white male) person could succeed with individual hard work. This was, according to Dye and Zeigler,

> by no means a philosophy of leveling egalitarianism. The ideal of the frontier [was] wealth and power won by competitive skill . . . [creating] a *natural aristocracy*.[2]

Mencher says that

> The conservatives . . . had little faith in the lower classes and saw in them a constant threat to the well-being of society.[3]

Laissez-faire capitalism expanded into all areas of business, bringing a new Western elite. Money was federalized: Rather than state or company scrip, federal money was put in state banks, thus breaking the Eastern monopoly of economic and political power.[4] Uncontrolled industrialization moved work from agrarian households to the cities.

The proportion of wage laborers increased—in New York City, for example, from 5.5 percent in 1796 to 27.4 percent in 1855—enabling employers to lower wages and increase their profits. Men were hired from the crowds of unemployed on the streets for day or seasonal work, and irregular employment, vast unemployment, labor uprisings, and the growth of labor movements resulted.[5] The powerful Protestant orientation to work remained. Macarov says

> Factories needed workers, and workers need jobs, not just to make money but also to be moral, religious, law-abiding people. Factory owners thus did people a favor by allowing them to work, and workers were expected to be grateful to the point of not . . . asking for higher wages or better working conditions. This was not only ingratitude but almost blasphemy.[6]

Mobility and industrialization weakened family structure and community ties. Churches, neighbors, friends, and relatives could no longer be depended on for help in need. As the family and the economy changed, surplus unmarried women became teachers and social reformers. The idle wife became a mark of status for wealthier men, who hired (or bought) lower-class women to do household chores. The latter, considered sexually available and usable by upper-class men, were thought of as the "sexual sewer" of the rich.

The 1800s brought massive social experimentation, with money, time, and energy available to indulge in such issues as the franchise for women, ending exploitation of children, emancipation of slaves, temperance, and moral reform of the poor. The altruism of the times was based on the ideals of the immorality of the poor, work as the only moral source of income, and almsgiving as the path to immorality. *Social* responsibility for poverty was rejected even though social data convinced such eminent philosophers as John Stuart Mill and John Marshall that poverty was the result of social exploitation.[7]

Slave labor and the cotton gin, invented in 1791, made cotton easy and cheap to produce. By the 1820s, more than half of American exports were in cotton textiles, and southern plantation owners refused to relinquish their new near-aristocracy by ending slavery. In the North, the new industrial elite made fortunes from the labor of immigrants—men, women, and children as young as 5—who produced textiles, made clothes, mined iron and coal, and built transportation and communication links across the nation and around the world.

## THE BURGEONING CITIES

### Immigration and Migration

Shortly before the Revolution, America had some two and a quarter million white settlers, and only five cities had populations of eight thousand or more. Within fifty years, the population had reached ten million,[8] a quarter of which by 1820 was settled beyond the Alleghenies, on Native American lands. Coll says the tide of immigrants

> rose steadily from only 129,000 in the 1820s to 540,000 in the following decade . . . to a pre-Civil War peak of more than 1.75 million in the 1850s. Altogether, about 6 million immigrants crossed to the "land of opportunity" between 1820 and 1860—roughly half of them from Great Britain and Ireland, about 2 million from Germany, and about 50,000 from the Scandinavian countries.[9]

For a short time, the move West averted a labor flood and maintained reasonable wages in the Eastern cities. Soon, however, destitute immigrants "were like an army encamped in the midst of New York,"[10] stranded, with little help either to move inland or to establish new lives.

Almshouses, which cared for the poor and ill, were often the first stop of immigrants sick from infections and the deprivations of the Atlantic crossing. By 1796 almshouse commissioners were complaining of the enormous expense from foreign-born immigrants and not until 1847 did immigration authorities decide that immigrants were entitled to aid based on their payment for passage. The Board of Commissioners of Immigration collected taxes and imposed indemnity bonds on immigrants, crews, and ships arriving at New York ports. These funds supported arriving immigrants or reimbursed local communities for outdoor relief, medical help, education, transportation, and job placements. Ward's Island in New York City's East River became a hospital and refuge for unemployable persons, and a nursery and school for illegitimate children and orphans. By 1855 there was a central landing for immigrant processing.[11]

While immigration exploded, migration from rural areas increased dramatically as people moved to the cities for work. The urban population grew at the rate of about 40 to 50 percent per decade, and cities became squalid warrens of people living in acute poverty, beset by plagues and death-dealing illnesses, unemployment, disease, and starvation. Even minimal sanitation and safety was lacking—garbage and refuse flowed through the streets in open drains. There were no bathing facilities and almost no indoor plumbing, and water was drawn from street pumps or hydrants.

> sewage disposal and police and fire protection were often left to chance. . . . Water supplies became polluted, and epidemics, gang wars, and street crime raged unchecked. Saloons, brothels, and gambling houses flourished in ethnic neighborhoods, confined there by authorities who would not tolerate their existence in "better" neighborhoods, and patronized by people from all over the city.[12]

The slums were breeding grounds for tuberculosis, pneumonia, and diphtheria, and frequently children died of "some unknown disease"—starvation.

> Periodically . . . the United States was ravaged by deadly plagues—yellow fever, cholera, typhoid, to name the most virulent—caused by filth, impure

water, and other unsanitary conditions. The plagues struck with most force in the cities . . . and here sickness and death claimed first—and in greatest numbers—the poor.[13]

The supply of housing and services never caught up with the need, and people lived in sheds, garrets, and dark and poorly ventilated tenements. One row of tenements could house five hundred people, with up to two hundred in a single building—almost a thousand an acre.[14] Rooms were divided and redivided, and when there were no more rooms people lived in cellars. In 1843 in Boston there were nearly eight thousand people in cellars, and in 1846, just three years later, there were twenty-nine thousand. By 1850 one of every twenty lived in a cellar, the average number per room was six and the maximum twenty. Begging was widespread, and children roamed the streets—an estimated ten thousand abandoned, orphaned, or runaway children in 1852. Life expectancy after moving into the Boston slums was 14 years.[15] Hymowitz says

> Though most immigrants were in the prime of life, between the ages of fourteen and forty-five, they died more readily than the native-born. Their children, and especially their babies, died even more frequently. . . . In Chicago, before 1900, three of every five babies died before age five.[16]

### Employment and Unionization

For a short while after the Revolution, most people did not depend solely on wages; they were artisans, small landowners, tenants, traders, and urban mechanics. Even in New England, where large textile mills had developed by the beginning of the 1800s, factories were considered temporary places of employment for the poor or for young women putting away savings for marriage.[17] Men found farm work and the ownership of land more profitable than factory labor, so women and children became the logical source for factory work. By the end of the War of 1812, approximately two thirds of all factory workers were women[18] and children, who got about a fourth of the wages earned by men for the same work. Their average week's pay was $1.50, the same as for women who did piece work at home. The factory day began at 4:30 A.M., even for small children, and ended at sundown,[19] a day of hard physical labor in dangerous settings. Children were "sold" out to labor, with parents and employers colluding about their ages so they could work.

> Here is a little child, not more than five years old . . . .She has on one garment, if a tattered sacking dress can be so termed! Her bones are nearly through her skin, but her stomach is an unhealthy pouch, abnormal. She has dropsy.

> It is eight o'clock when children reach their homes—later if the mill work is behind and they are kept over hours. They are usually beyond speech. They fall asleep at the table, on the stairs.[20]

Before the Revolution, mill work for women was socially acceptable and often closely supervised. Some mills, such as that established by Francis Cabot Lowell in Massachusetts, were model communities with limited hours, schools, and chaperoned dormitories. However, conditions deteriorated even here, and in both 1834 and 1845 women struck for the 10-hour workday and higher pay. In response, the state legislature upheld the employer, conducting hearings and then visiting

> for an on-the-scene investigation. The committee report rejected the workers' demands for a ten-hour day, noting the special responsibilities that laborers owed to their employers.[21]

By 1810 millworkers were the cheapest labor available—children, older married immigrant women and immigrant men, and those who otherwise would have been on poor relief. By 1831, mills employed nearly nineteen thousand men and thirty-nine thousand women; by 1850 women were 24 percent of the total number of workers, and by 1900 19 percent.[22] Hymowitz describes millwork:

> The ten- to twelve-hour work day of women and children was spent in factories and mills that were dirty, noisy, dark, smelly, and dangerous. Hundreds of workers were jammed together in dimly lit rooms that were stifling hot in summer, cold and drafty in winter. The moist, lint-filled air in the cotton mills bred tuberculosis. In other industries women breathed dangerous fumes of paint and naptha, tobacco, and glass and brass dust. Materials were flammable, and factory buildings were firetraps. Machines were cleaned and adjusted while they were running . . . workers often lost fingers and even hands in accidents.[23]

Families were often paid in liquor, tobacco, or company scrip, usable only in company stores or for company-owned housing. Company credit, necessary in layoffs, increased their indebtedness and dependency on the company and limited their job mobility. This was common in mines, construction, factories of all sorts, and handwork industries such as sewing. There were

> almost no pensions; few men left much in the way of savings when they died; and life insurance spread slowly, especially among the working class. . . . factory production replaced the putting out system, and . . . contrary to popular stereotypes (which are based on the minority of young women who worked in mills), there was very little industrial work open to any women in towns and cities before the late 19th century and almost none to married women.[24]

Wars with France (1807-1809) and England (War of 1812) depleted the economy and caused a severe depression (1815 to 1821). By 1819, 500,000 people were unemployed, and at times a third of the labor force was idle.

In Philadelphia alone, of 9700 employed in thirty businesses, 7500 were fired. Properties of farmers and small businesses were taken over by creditors.[25]

Wages fell 30 to 50 percent, most New England factories closed, and whole families starved or froze to death.[26] The unemployed formed citizens' committees and marched on the government, and fighting, looting, violence, and employment riots were common. Few social programs could cope with the mass distress, and soup kitchens opened and newspapers ran ads calling for food, money, clothing, and shelter for the poor.[27]

Trade unions formed as early as 1790, demanding: a family wage for men, that is, enough pay to support a family; free education for children and the curbing of child labor and apprenticeship abuses (both to help children and to keep them out of the labor market); free public lands for settlement; restriction on private use of prison labor, as when prisoners were contracted out for work, undercutting wages; the establishment of a 10-hour day; control of currency by the government (rather than scrip issued by employers); the right to organize; and public work programs to protect the unemployed.

By 1837 there were at least five national unions—cordwainers, comb-makers, carpenters, weavers, and printers—and two-thirds of New York's workers were organized, women taking the lead in organizing the mills. Strikes became common, even though the police were brought in and workers were brutalized and killed. However, by the beginning of the Civil War the labor movement had collapsed. In part this was because of the adamant opposition of businesses and the courts, in part because the Civil War made soldiers out of unemployed, and finally because the Homestead Act of 1862 made free lands available for Western settlement.

## PRIVATE PHILANTHROPY

Despite the mass unemployment, and wages so low that saving was impossible and illness or accident devastating, the rich continued their diatribe against the laziness and intemperance of workers,

> unable to understand why the poor could not save for a rainy day . . . . even while conceding that times were hard in 1820–21, the New York Society for the Prevention of Pauperism insisted that this was an unusual occurrence.[28]

There was little separation of public and private interests: private groups formed associations and worked for legislation, often later inspecting or administering agencies set up and funded by government.

### Religious Answers to Poverty

Protestant religious groups led the way in social reform with dual goals: to help the unfortunate and to win newly arrived, supposedly un-Christian immigrants to Protestantism. Such organizations as the New York City Mission Society and the New York Female Moral Reform Society distributed food and clothing along with religious tracts and advocated better housing and sanitation along with moral improvement.[29] The Protestant reform movement led to

> reform schools, mental hospitals, and new kinds of prisons. In cities, experiments with mass education began under private auspices . . . and by the middle decades of the century public educational systems had started to appear . . . private philanthropists created YMCAs for young rural migrants to cities, other reformers founded specialized institutions for the deaf and dumb, blind, feeble-minded, and idiots . . . [and began] campaigns to alter the treatment of criminals, delinquents, the mentally ill, and school children.[30]

Jewish immigrants brought with them their heritage of charity and mutual aid. Although Sephardic Jews came to America as early as the 1600s, by 1800 there were still only five thousand Jews in the United States. They contributed substantial monies to the Revolution but were still denied voting rights except in South Carolina. By 1790 they could vote in five states but as late as 1869 (North Carolina) and 1876 (New Hampshire) restrictions remained. Excluded, by and large, from American social welfare, they shared their resources with new immigrants through mutual aid societies, especially for education and work.

Catholicism supplied its traditional forms of charity both in the Hispanic Southwest and with the new immigrants from Ireland and Italy in the East. Despite the poverty of Eastern immigrants in the 1850s and 1860s, Catholics began a most effective program of outdoor relief. Catholic Charities, St. Vincent de Paul Societies (1850), and Little Sisters of the Poor groups (1840) sprang up and, on the model set by Sisters of Charity as early as 1809, began to build orphanages, schools, hospitals, and other facilities for those in need. Katz says

> Catholic spokesmen distrusted the [Protestant] . . . often militantly anti-Catholic bias. They viewed [for example] the Children's Aid Society . . . as an agency designed to place Catholic children in Protestant homes. . . . The unwillingness of Protestant reformers and officials to honor Catholic sensibilities cannot be missed.[31]

Especially after 1860, the Catholic Church made heroic efforts to alleviate urban suffering, dependence, and sickness. For example, Catholics probably provided half the money for children's institutions in Buffalo near the end of the 1800s and probably spent more of their incomes on charity than did Protestants.[32] The Catholic Church also gave more attention to needs of Afro- and Native Americans, particularly those of children, than did Protestant charity.

### Social Reform Ideals

Coinciding with the great depressions of the 1800s, eminent philanthropists began to issue reports on poverty, blaming it on the poor: their idleness, ignorance, spendthriftiness, hasty marriages; their use of pawnbrokers, lotteries, houses of prostitution; and gambling.[33] The most intense criticism was aimed at intemperance (despite the fact that the poor were often paid in liquor): A report in 1817 estimated that of the fifteen thousand people on charity, seven-eighths were pauperized by liquor[34]; and John V. N. Yates, New York's secretary of state, stated in his famous report in 1824 that intemperance was the cause of two-thirds of permanent dependency.

Yates also found that poor laws were inadequate, ripe for misuse, and inhumane, and that a ninth of poor relief funds were used in court suits to deny clients' eligibility rather than for the benefit of the poor. He noted the barbarity of farming out or selling the poor, particularly children, but also deplored their treatment and lack of education in the local almshouses. Idiots and lunatics, also put in almshouses, had no adequate care and were often brutally mistreated. Along with other philanthropists, Yates called for poor relief to be turned over to private charities, both to provide more humane treatment and to save money. He also claimed that present laws encouraged beggary and vagrancy, and called for provision of employment for the able-bodied poor in almshouses, where they could both support themselves and provide for other inmates unable to do so.[35]

The Yates report concluded that only 27 percent of the poor could actually work. The rest were aged, blind, ill, or had mental or physical handicaps (35 percent) or were under the age of 14 (38 percent). He recommended that every county have a poorhouse with education for children, farms for producing food, and facilities for hard labor for able-bodied inmates. In addition, he asked that no healthy male age 18 to 50 be given outdoor relief and that street begging be punished, that attempts to return paupers to earlier places of residence be abolished as too costly, and that an excise tax be levied on distilleries to combat drunkenness.[36]

Plans for rehabilitation of the poor and for poor relief administration were similar to those in Europe in the 1500s. The 1818 Report by the Society for the Prevention of Pauperism recommended the prevention of beggary and the restriction of saloons; the establishment of employment bureaus and savings banks; mutual aid and life insurance to deal with employment hazards; supplies for home industry; and cooperation among charitable agencies. It also recommended division of cities into districts, with poor relief administered by friendly visitors to give moral support on living without temptation to drink and other vices.[37]

Reform advocate Matthew Carey summed up the prevailing reform viewpoint, saying that

> Every man, woman, and grown child able and willing to work should be given employment.
>
> The poor should be able to support themselves by industry, prudence, and economy, without depending on aid.
>
> Their sufferings arise from their idleness, dissipation, and extravagance.
>
> To support the poor through taxes, charitable individuals, or benevolent societies leads to the fostering of their idleness and improvidences, producing or increasing the distress it is intended to relieve.[38]

Unitarian minister Joseph Tuckerman was among the most socially aware reformists. He argued against wages too low to supply even the bare necessities of life, and the frequent occurrence of periods, even of months together, during which numbers . . . find it impossible to procure any employment whatever by which to keep themselves from destitution and suffering.[39]

In 1832 he began a "ministry at large" that anticipated almost every aspect of the later charity organization societies and the profession of social work. He found inadequate housing and urban problems instrumental in other problems and noted the radical importance of the "child problem" as a special form of charity. Watson says that

> his most detailed report, written as agent of a State Commission . . . advocates . . . tests of work for the able-bodied, houses of industry worthy of the name for the more capable, and the refer[ral] of all temporary poverty [relief] to private relief. . . . [He] was the first American not only to distinguish between pauperism and poverty but to advocate consistently the abolition of outdoor relief, the cooperation of all forces working on charitable problems, the principle of the registration bureau, and personal visitation or friendly visitation.[40]

### The Association for Improving the Condition of the Poor

A bitter winter in 1837–38, in the middle of a massive depression, broke the back of private charity, and starvation and death by freezing were once more common. By 1840, there were over thirty relief-giving agencies, and in 1843 the most notable was developed—the Association for Improving the Condition of the Poor (AICP). It was founded by philanthropist Robert Hartley in New York, who claimed that before the poor could be moral they must eat. Still, his plan was the European model: division of cities into wards with local residents as advisory committees; planned rather than haphazard giving; trained friendly visitors to investigate poverty, distribute relief, and give counsel, encouragement, and advice; and the cooperation of all charities, including reciprocal referral. Casework—personal attention—was believed helpful in itself even without providing relief, and paid staff and volunteers should both be used.

The AICP's friendly visitors—usually women—were told:

> You become an important instrument of good to your suffering fellow-creatures when you aid them to attain this good from resources within themselves . . . when [their] sufferings are the result of improvidence, extravagance, idleness, intemperance, or other moral causes which are within their own control; and endeavor . . . to awaken their self-respect, to direct their exertions, and to strengthen their capacities for self-support. . . . Avoid all appearance of harshness, and every manifestation of an obtrusive and censorious spirit.[41]

The principle of less eligibility—that no reliefer get as much money as the lowest paid worker—was primary, and the AICP would not, at first, distribute alms, giving only a little money and small quantities of food and clothing.[42] Recipients were required to abstain from alcohol, send young children to school, and apprentice children of a suitable age for vocational training. Although based on Protestant ideals, the AICP did not limit its help to Protestants.

Soon the AICP became involved in social reform, acting against lotteries, Sabbath desecration, gambling dens, and intemperance. As it accumulated data on social conditions, its leaders became convinced that alcoholism, promiscuity, and child neglect came from the filth and overcrowding of the slums rather than personal fault. On this basis, it opened a model tenement and petitioned for the appointment of the first state legislative commission to investigate tenements. Concern for public health and personal hygiene led it to open two dispensaries for the indigent sick (1846), establish a hospital for crippled children, open a public bathhouse, and campaign for a law forbidding the adulteration of milk. For children, it demanded compulsory school attendance laws and was instrumental in passing legislation to provide for the care and instruction of idle truants and for the arrest and detention of vagrant children. In 1851, under AICP auspices, New York opened a juvenile asylum for such children.[43]

AICPs spread throughout the country, and by 1877 they had reversed their stand on almsgiving, which then became their major function. While the AICP movement provided innumerable services to the poor, perhaps in the long run its most valuable contribution was in the compilation of data: the beginnings of social research about poverty and deviance and the framework for the profession of social work.

### Special Interest Charities

A number of other charities based on special needs or particular populations developed over the decades before and around the Civil War. Among them were the American Female Guardian Society, Homes for the Friendless, the Mission to Children of the Destitute, the Society for the Relief of the Ruptured and Crippled, the Association for the Relief of Respectable Aged and Indigent Females, the Home for Little Wanderers, and the American Temperance Society. Youth agencies and missions became common, the most noted of which was probably the Young Men's Christian Association, established in America in 1851 to protect young men coming to the city from the dangers of irreligion, intemperance, and immorality. It provided living quarters with sanitary facilities at a low price and also gave relief to poor families in the neighborhood, coordinated local welfare services, and made surveys of needs. Jewish centers for both boys and girls were established in the 1840s. The first YWCA was established in Boston in 1866 and in New York in 1867. Boys' Clubs began to be formed about 1860 to give boys an opportunity to participate in sports and activities in a Christian atmosphere. The Salvation Army, known for its charitable work with the urban poor, was organized by William Booth in 1865; and Volunteers of America, providing shelter and some work for indigent men vagrants, was founded later by his son and daughter-in-law.[44]

Particular ethnic groups also formed mutual aid societies. One of the earliest was the Philadelphia Free African Society, established in 1787. By the 1830s there were more than a hundred benevolent societies for people of African descent. Chinese immigrants brought mutual aid societies based on family, territories in China, trade and guild associations, and mutual political groups. Immigrant women organized local and national mutual aid clubs, for example, the Finnish Cooperative Home and the Polish Women's Alliance. The latter was one of the largest of women's groups to develop in the late 1800s, with ties both to Polish nationalism and the international feminist movement. Such groups raised money for ethnic churches and lodges; built orphanages, hospitals, and other such institutions; formed health insurance and death benefit companies; and gave outdoor relief. Their leaders championed the rights of workers, especially of women and children employed in the mines and mills, and supported women's strikes with food and money. The Polish Women's Alliance gave health insurance to women workers' families and death benefits to husbands and orphaned children.[45]

## GOVERNMENTAL RESPONSES

The American Revolution scarcely changed government poor laws. Categorization into worthy and unworthy poor, local and relative responsibility, harsh treatment, and the work component remained virtually the same as in colonial times. The four basic treatment methods continued to be

1. Workhouses or poorhouses (almshouses)
2. Outdoor relief
3. Auctioning off the able-bodied
4. "Selling" those unable to work to the lowest bidder

However, two new trends began to influence social welfare. First was a gradual shift from local to state power, with states demanding that every county build a poorhouse. While local authority and responsibility had been the keynote of care in colonial times, increasingly the states set policy and standards for poor relief in the 1800s. Second, both private and public charities came to believe that poorhouses were less expensive, more efficient, and more humane than outdoor relief, and institutionalization became a major goal in social welfare.

### The All-Purpose Almshouse

Institutionalization gathered momentum during the 1820s as increasing restrictions were placed on outdoor relief. In 1821 the general court of Massachusetts ordered Josiah Quincy (later governor) to investigate poverty. The committee concluded that

1. Outdoor relief was wasteful, expensive, and destructive to morals.
2. Almshouses were most economical because the poor could be forced to work in them.
3. The poor should be employed in agricultural work.
4. A citizen's board should supervise the almshouses rather than leaving them to local contractors.
5. Intemperance was the most powerful cause of pauperism.

Quincy said

> That of all modes of providing for the poor, the most wasteful, the most injurious to their morals and destructive to their industrious habits is that of supply in their own families . . . . the most economical mode is that of Alms Houses; having the character of Work Houses or Houses of Industry, in which work is provided for every degree of ability in the pauper; and thus the able poor made to provide, partially, at least, for their own support; and also to the support, or at least the comfort of the impotent poor.[46]

Such men as Yates, Quincy, Hartley, and others remarked on the inhumanity of auctioning off workers or selling the dependent poor, saying that those auctioned off were often literally worked to death, tortured, and forced to live in filth, ignorance, and disease. Children, the aged, or the ill were taken in only for the pittance paid by poor relief officials, and the money was used not for their support but as income for the care-givers. Infants given out for care (baby farming) died early from starvation and neglect. Coll says that

> Whatever their shortcomings, almshouses were humanitarian as compared with the irresponsible, cruel systems of auctioning the poor or contracting for their care with persons who were often on the edge of dependency themselves.[47]

Despite the professed morality of placing people in almshouses, the real purpose was to save taxpayers money. Katz says

> Stripped of rhetoric, the goals of much nineteenth century reform can be reduced to a desire to lower property taxes and to keep the streets safe. Although some reform advocates claimed lofty social goals, by and large prosaic fears of crime and rising expenses for poor relief fueled the moral-social control tradition.[48]

Poorhouses were the forerunners of penitentiaries, and poverty was considered petty criminality except in times of epidemics or severe depressions.

By 1832, fifty-one of New York's fifty-five counties had poorhouses, and they were soon everywhere. Supervisors were political appointees whose pay came from inmates' work, either on the workfarm or contracted out to private businesses. "Savings" were accrued by holding down costs— food, clothing, and heat. Supplies for poorhouses were also contracted out privately. A report on county poorhouses says

> In two counties, the committee found that the poorhouses were supplied by contract, the contractor being allowed to profit by all the labor which he could extract from the paupers. In both counties, the contractor was a *superintendent of the poor*; in one, he was also *keeper of the poor house*. In one, the keeper received his compensation from the contractor; and in this case the food supplied was not only insufficient in quantity but consisted partly of tainted

meat and fish. The inmates were consequently almost starved. They were also deprived of a sufficiency of fuel and bedding, and suffered severely from the cold. So gross and inhuman was the conduct of the contractor for this poor house that two female inmates (lunatics) were frozen in their cells (or rather sheds) during the last winter, and are now cripples for life.[49]

The committee spoke out against almshouses and for outdoor relief, saying that "half the sum requisite for their maintenance in the poor house would often save them from destitution" and that

> Common domestic animals are usually more humanely provided for than the paupers in some of these institutions; where the misfortune of poverty is visited with greater deprivations of comfortable food, lodging, clothing, warmth and ventilation than constitute the usual penalty of crime. The evidence taken by the committee exhibits such a record of filth, nakedness, licentiousness, general bad morals, and disregard of religion . . . as well as of gross neglect of the most ordinary comforts and decencies of life, as if published in detail would disgrace the State and shock humanity.[50]

With each year poorhouse conditions deteriorated as overcrowding waxed and supervision waned. People with all kinds of problems were put in them together, without sanitation or privacy—orphans, foundlings, unmarried mothers, prostitutes, and criminals. Even the deserving poor—the aged, ill, or disabled—were confined in poorhouses,

> the lunatic suffering . . . in a dark and suffocating cell in summer, and almost freezing in the winter . . . a score of children . . . poorly fed, poorly clothed, and quite untaught . . . the poor idiot . . . half-starved and beaten with rods because he is too dull to do his master's bidding . . . the aged mother . . . lying in perhaps her last sickness, unattended by a physician, and with no one to minister to her wants . . . a woman [lunatic] is made to feel the lash in the hands of a brutal underkeeper.[51]

The Massachusetts State Charities Board, in 1858, appointed a special committee to investigate public charitable institutions. Its report found that

> In the month of May, 1858, there were in the State almshouses . . . a total of 2425; and of these 1176 were little boys and girls, 483 were on the sick list, 200 were insane or demented, and only 70 were able to do any kind of outdoor labor. . . . The entire proceeds for the labor is only $1.50 per head. . . . [and] the average weekly support is 83 cents per person.[52]

People in poorhouses had little medical care and died quickly, often from malnutrition. According to that same report, in a poorhouse that accommodated eight hundred people, from May through October, thirty-nine adults and twenty-one children died, and in the previous six months, in the winter, forty-eight adults and forty-six children died. No more than 3 percent of children under the age of 1 lived.[53] The deaths were of "natural" causes rather than contagion. The committee recommended that

1. A permanent State Board of Charities be created.
2. The board be given powers of examination, power to transfer inmates from one institution to another, and power to pardon.
3. The local trustee/investigator system be maintained.
4. Trustees be appointed by the State Board to hold office for five years.
5. Harmless lunatics be transferred to almshouses where they can be kept more cheaply.

The committee also recommended that children placed in reform schools be given work or education; be placed in foster homes where feasible; be given privileges for good behavior; and that their parents be forced to pay for their keep. Finally, they spoke out against the administration of almshouses, saying

> in fact, it has seemed to us . . . that the great problem to be resolved in regard to these institutions was, not how the unhappy inmates can be made to pay their way, but how the swarms of officials we found in them could be made to earn their own salaries . . . . the salaries of the overseers and officials absorb so much that no kind of labor, agricultural or mechanical, can be made profitable to the State when carried on in governmental institutions.[54]

One result of such studies was that churches or benevolent associations began to found institutions for specific problem groups. Another was that states rather than local counties began to take responsibility for certain classes of the distressed or deviant, for example, the insane and feeble-minded.

In the early 1800s, the proportion of women in poorhouses was about 30 percent, rising to 40 percent by the Civil War and 47 percent during the Civil War. Short-term residency for all persons was high: In the period between 1853 and 1886, 29 percent were there less than a week and 44 percent less than three weeks. About 20 to 25 percent remained about fifteen months, and the elderly and children remained for years. In the early poorhouse days, whole families were incarcerated, but after 1850 fewer whole families entered. Poorhouses were used more heavily during depressions, especially by young men who remained only till they found work. After 1875, laws removed children from poorhouses and they became homes for the aged poor and for single mothers with infants. By 1900, 85 percent of the inmates were aged.[55]

Various institutions and organizations grew out of the poorhouse experience—penitentiaries, the juvenile justice system, schools for the deaf and blind, general hospitals, and mental hospitals among them.

### Outdoor Relief

Although institutionalization was intellectually a more popular solution for caring for the distressed and deviant, outdoor relief was more manageable. Poor relief administrators saw it as both less expensive than poorhouses and less likely to cause labor rebellions or the breakup of families. In the South, where *noblesse oblige* still existed, outdoor relief was both common and acceptable.[56] In the North, it was increasingly discouraged but only Baltimore prevented it entirely. In New York, for example, between 1830 and 1860 temporary outdoor relief accounted for 34 to 50 percent of all expenditures for relief; and in Boston in 1832, while forty-five hundred persons were in almshouses, there were more than fifteen hundred families and nearly four hundred individuals on outdoor relief.[57] Philadelphia blamed inadequate almshouses for the growing need for outdoor relief and over ten years (ending in 1824) spent $621,000 for outdoor relief and $470,000 for almshouses.[58] By 1857, Philadelphia preferred outdoor relief, with investigation and supervision by paid staff, as less expensive and more humane than almshouse care.

As politicians took firmer hold of the reins of poor relief, graft and corruption became rampant. Administration was careless, extravagant, and corrupt; for example, in 1826, when suffrage was extended to all white male citizens without reference to property holdings, politicians began to disburse money to buy the support of the new voters (as in New York's Tammany Hall scandal). To combat this, stricter rules of eligibility were instituted, and paid personnel were hired to administer aid. Private charity began to demand that poor relief be returned to them, arguing that public charity was degrading to its recipients and that politicians could not be trusted with it.[59]

## SOCIAL TREATMENT IN THE 1800s

### Medical Care and General Hospitals

The first general hospital, for both mentally and physically ill, was begun in 1755 by Thomas Bond and Benjamin Franklin, who solicited public monies matched by private funding. In Philadelphia a decade later, Dr. John Morgan established the first medical school at King's College (Columbia University). Marine Hospitals Service, the first federal program in public health, was set up in 1789 to care for seamen. However, the first public hospitals were really the county poorhouses, for every county was required to care for the medically indigent. In rural poorhouses, care, if given at all, depended on the other inmates—one reason so many died. However, by the end of the 1700s, larger almshouses set aside special medical wards where the poor occasionally saw a doctor. Urban poorhouses became teaching hospitals, where treatment was a combination of old remedies, guesses, and experimental treatment or surgery, for little was really known about the human body. Few healing medicines existed, and smallpox, yellow fever, diphtheria, malaria, and dysentery resulted in high death rates and incapacitation for those who survived medical treatment or illnesses contracted at the hospitals.

Mortality rates from tuberculosis were very high in the 1800s, and were twice as high for women as men, at about 8 percent.[60] The dangers of child-bearing had changed little over history, except that now the use of forceps presented dangers from infection and injury. For poor women, without adequate nutrition and forced to work during their pregnancies, the dangers were worse. Employers gave no time off for pregnancy or recovery from childbirth, and a day's absence from work could mean loss of the job.[61] For the poor,

> only those too far gone to protest would make the trip to a public hospital where inadequate nursing and unsanitary conditions actually diminished one's chance of survival.[62]

Those who could not avoid hospitals often paid for it in the coin of experimentation. This was especially true for women as male doctors developed an interest in gynecology and reproduction after the discovery of the ovum in 1824. While poor women (and slaves) rarely had the kind of "women's problems" that incapacitated upper-class women, their organs could be explored to determine why. If the experiments were successful, the treatment was extended to middle-class clients. By 1830, thirteen states had laws establishing that only "regular" doctors could practice, and in 1848 the American Medical Association was established.

During this era, women were increasingly being constrained to idleness or invalidism. An upper-class wife

> was the social ornament that proved a man's success: her idleness, her delicacy, her childlike ignorance of "reality" gave a man the "class" that money alone could not provide.[63]

A host of mysterious ailments rose, among them sick headaches, nerves, and hysteria, and doctors related them all to women's reproductive organs. Women were seen as sickly and sickly was seen as feminine: Normal female processes were considered pathological—puberty, menstruation, pregnancy, childbirth, and menopause—the "death of the woman in the woman." Possibly the remuneration given by wealthy female patients increased the diagnoses of ill health. Perceptions of beauty for "ladies" also caused such illnesses:

> The fainting and swooning attributed to many nineteenth century ladies was often caused not by an innate delicacy but by their constrictive underwear. The corset caused more than discomfort, when laced too tightly it could actually dislocate a woman's kidneys, liver, and other organs.[64]

The new gynecological specialists controlled women in many ways. Often female castration—ovariotomy—was prescribed for "taming" unruly women; education was discouraged, and women were told to cultivate their maternal feelings because "good" women had no sexual feelings.

Medical treatments were often worse than the problem. According to the earliest available records (circa 1912) patients had a fifty-fifty chance of coming away from treatment worse than when it began. Standard therapeutic approaches were bleeding, violent purges, heavy doses of mercury-based drugs, and use of opium. Treatments for "women's ailments" could be bizarre indeed: bleeding by leeches applied to the genitals or breasts to provoke menstruation, and

> in some cases leeches were even applied to the cervix despite the danger of their occasional loss in the uterus.[65]

While men generally controlled the medical field during the decades of the 1800s, a few women were able to make inroads on their monopoly through alternative medical schools, which graduated women as well as men. Harriet Hunt, denied admission to Harvard twice, went to such a school and practiced medicine and her own brand of psychiatry with mostly women as clientele. Traditional schools seldom admitted women, but Elizabeth Blackwell (1821–1910) was finally admitted to Geneva Medical College where, despite being ostracized and harassed, she graduated first in her class in 1849. Denied employment by hospitals, she opened a small dispensary in a slum district. Her patients were mostly women and children.

She was joined in 1858 by her sister Emily (1826–1910), who had graduated from the medical college at Western Reserve in 1854, and Dr. Marie Zakrzewska (1829–1902), a Polish immigrant who had received her medical training in Europe, in 1856. The younger Blackwell began medical social work for patients in their homes, and she and Zakrzewska raised funds for the dispensary, which was incorporated in May 1857 as the New York Infirmary for Women and Children.

> Perhaps nobody, nowadays, can understand the willingness and devotion of the women who assisted me in . . . this primitive little hospital: who were willing to work hard, in and out of hours; who fared extremely plainly and lodged almost to uncomfortableness, yet who felt that a good work was being accomplished for all womankind. And this was true of all—students, nurses, and domestic help. . . . We had constant applications from students to share in the experience of practice.[66]

Elizabeth Blackwell worked during the Civil War in organizing the Women's Central Association of Relief and the United States Sanitary Commission, selecting and training nurses. She later consulted with Florence Nightingale and opened the Woman's Medical College within her infirmary. Emily Blackwell took over operation of both medical college and infirmary when her sister retired, and Zakrzewska, after having accepted a professorship of obstetrics in Boston, went on to found the New England Hospital for Women and Children in July 1862.

### Mental Hospitals and Psychiatry

The first law for the treatment of the insane was passed in Massachusetts in 1676, ordering selectmen to provide care and protect the community from the insane. In North Carolina, in the early 1700s, church-wardens were ordered to confine the insane in almshouses. Generally, however, the mentally ill and retarded were left with their families. Those who were violent were thought possessed by the devil, and they were often whipped, shackled in the marketplace, or kept in outside pens despite the weather. Many were locked in basements, attics, or outhouses; put in strait-jackets; chained to walls; or jailed. The first colonywide mental hospital was built in 1769 in Virginia, but most communities simply sectioned off rooms from other institutions; for example, in 1791 New York General Hospital appropriated its cellar for the insane. In 1821 Bloomingdale Asylum was created in the New York General Hospital. Not until 1870 did Willard, the first state hospital for the insane, open.

Benjamin Rush—statesman, physician, and educator—is considered to be the father of American psychiatry. Physician-general for Washington's forces in the Revolution, he opened the first free medical clinic in America during the early 1800s. Becoming interested in the treatment of the insane, he studied under Phillippe Pinel of France, who advocated "moral treatment": paternal kindness, guidance, occupational therapy, and humaneness. Rush introduced moral treatment in a Pennsylvania hospital in 1783. His methods included cold and hot baths, heated and ventilated rooms, simple tasks for the patients, and training the staff for kindness. He also separated the sexes and the violent from quiet patients.

In the early 1800s, private asylums were established on Rush's model. The mentally ill were often treated in their own communities, where they could be visited by friends and family. These asylums became training centers for the new science of psychiatry. Until this time, inmates had been subject to public torment, but the new asylums charged fees to see them, and they were exhibited only once or twice a week. People were committed easily and informally, with an application from a relevant other signed by a physician. It was particularly easy for husbands to commit troublesome wives.

While private care progressed, public care was still terrible. A report from Maryland says

> As you enter, the crash of bolts and clank of chains are scarcely distinguish-able amid the wild chorus of shrieks and sobs which issue from every depart-ment. The passages are narrow, dark, damp, and exude a noxious effluvia. The first common room you examine . . . is perhaps for females. Ten of these, with no other clothing than a rag around their waists, are chained to a wall, loathsome and hideous, but when addressed evidently retaining some of the intelligence and much of the feeling which in other days ennobled their nature. In shame or in sorrow one of them perhaps utters a cry; a blow which brings blood to temple and a tear from the eye, an additional chain, a gag, an indecent or contemptuous expression compels silence. If you ask where these unfortunate creatures sleep, you are led to a kennel eight feet square with an unglazed airhole eight inches in diameter [where] . . . five persons sleep. The floor is covered and walls bedaubed with filth and excrement; no bedding but wet decayed straw, and the stench so insupportable that you turn away and hasten from the scene.[67]

The push toward state care of the mentally ill began with the forma-tion of the Boston Prison Discipline Society, and its study of conditions in public jails led to other investigations, including that of Dorothea Dix (1802–1887), the most famous psychiatric reformer of the 1800s. Born to a moderately wealthy family, Dix became interested in the mentally ill when she volunteered to teach Sunday School to women in an East Cambridge jail in 1841. There she found a group of insane women locked in unheated cells and suffering from gross neglect. Bettering the treatment of the retarded and insane became her goal in life. She visited every almshouse, workhouse, prison, and jail in Massachusetts, finding inmates in bare, filthy, and often unheated cells. Often the straw and chaff from their beds, cemented with their own excrement, was their only covering. Men and women were kept together, nude, with only male attendants. Whippings and beatings were common.

Dix maintained that the state had moral and legal obligations to the insane and called upon influential friends Horace Mann and Samuel Gridley Howe to help her mobilize the press and the public. Together they secured passage of a bill to enlarge Worcester Asylum (1843). Following this success, Dix investigated other states, where conditions were as terrible. Most states, however, were either unwilling or unable to fund adequate care for the mentally ill. She concluded the federal government must take the responsibility and in 1848 submitted a proposal to Congress to reserve five million acres of land, its income to be used for the care of the indigent insane. The bill noted that precedents existed in land grants for public schools, schools for the deaf, and support for the private railroad industry. It was passed with more than she had hoped for: 10 million acres for the indigent mentally ill and 2.5 million for facilities for the indigent deaf and mute.

However, President Franklin Pierce vetoed the bill, saying that to support the indigent insane would open the doors to federal care for any indigent, and the veto was upheld by a wide margin. Pierce was probably accurate in his assessment of the power of the bill to open doors to the poor at the federal level. For the first time, aside from a few veterans' benefits, comprehensive federal legislation would have provided the beginnings of a welfare state nearly a century before it became a *fait accompli* with the Social Security Act of 1935. While Pierce has been portrayed as the villain who delayed social welfare for eighty years, he was merely operating under the assumptions and requirements of his time. He believed in strict adherence to precedent and fought the myriad schemes to set aside federal lands for the use of big business and special interest groups, one of which Dix represented. Additionally, her request was tied into the controversial issue of disbursement of federal land. Finally, public support for the poor would have counteracted the maintenance of a low-wage work force and the religious dicta of work morality. In all, Pierce's conservative action was merely a part of the political economy of the times.

Pierce was president for only four years, yet the bill was not readmitted despite the fact that after his tenure federal land was disbursed for other worthy causes. The Morrill Act, for example, gave each state income from thirty thousand acres of land for every member of Congress, to be used for agricultural and technical colleges, and the same session, under Lincoln, passed the Homestead Act. Although Dix could not mobilize enough public support to resubmit the bill,[68] she continued her work for the insane until the end of her life, forty years later.

### Education

Education as a way to individual achievement has been a persistent ideal in America. After the Revolution, and particularly when industrialization produced a glut of workers on the market, it grew from a desirable goal to one that became mandatory. The agrarian life no longer needed as many children to work, and cities were flooded with them—unwanted, orphaned, abandoned, and neglected. Their education would serve a multitude of purposes: It would help them to get ahead, keep them from public dependency and crime, and preserve jobs for men whose wages they undercut in the job market.

Education was a concern even earlier than the Revolution: Among the first educators in America was Anthony Benizet, who came to Pennsylvania in 1731 as a schoolmaster. He taught both black and white children and worked for the rights of Native Americans and against racism and slavery. Benjamin Franklin, because of his opposition to public relief, also called for public education early in the nation's history. However, women were most instrumental in establishing schools, both for children and for themselves. High school teaching required men educators with college degrees, but women with high school educations were allowed to teach in elementary schools. They were paid two or three dollars a week while men were paid ten or fifteen.[69]

By 1802 overseers of the poor were required to provide education in Pennsylvania, and Washington, D.C., had schools for poor children by 1804. In 1812, New York required schools to stay open three months of the year to qualify for state funds. Although by 1831 education for children of African descent—even those who were free—was outlawed, the push for white education went on. Massachusetts was the first state to require school attendance in 1852, for children ages 8 to 14, for nine months each year.

Frances Wright (1795–1852), a Scottish immigrant, traveled the country to speak in favor of free public schools and opened an interracial school at Nashoba, Tennessee that failed. Prudence Crandall also tried in 1833–34 to operate a school for girls of African descent in Canterbury, Connecticut, but after pupils and teachers were stoned, the well poisoned with excrement, the school doors and windows smashed, and the building set afire, she admitted defeat.[70]

Among the leaders in education for women were Emma Hart Willard (1787–1870), Elizabeth and Emily Blackwell, Catharine Beecher, and Lucretia Mott (1793–1880). Their problems were many. For example, Willard was refused admission to Vermont's Middlebury College but later established the Academy for Female Education and, in 1821, the Troy Female Seminary, which offered a full high school education to girls: solid geometry, philosophy, science, and history. She wrote her own history and geography textbooks and became wealthy from their sale. In 1823, Catharine Beecher, sister of Harriet Beecher Stowe, set up a teachers' seminary and unsuccessfully tried to establish a chain of teachers' colleges.

Oberlin College in Ohio, founded in 1833, was the first to set up a rigorous educational program for both women and men. Its original goal for women was to train them to become ministers' wives or intelligent mothers and homemakers. Over time, Oberlin became an important center for the antislavery movement and for feminism.

Elizabeth Ann Bayley Seton (Mother Seton) (1774-1821) began parochial education in the United States. A convert to Catholicism after her husband died, she opened a Catholic free school in 1809 at Emmetsburg, Maryland, and later founded St. Joseph's College for Women.[71] In addition to her work in education, she established the American congregation of the Sisters of Charity and what would become the Gray Ladies in hospitals and orphanages. By the time of her death, the Sisters of Charity of St. Vincent de Paul had twenty communities of volunteers. Seton was beatified in 1963 and in 1975 became the first native-born American to be canonized.

### Care of the Blind, Deaf, and Retarded

Blind, deaf, and otherwise handicapped children were usually placed in almshouses. In 1810, Dr. John Stanford, a minister, went to such an almshouse and became interested in their plight. Later, Dr. Thomas H. Gallaudet from Hartford went to Europe to learn how to teach the deaf. He returned with a teacher, Laurent Clerc, to found America's first institute for the deaf in 1817. More private asylums were built as subsidies from states were obtained: Massachusetts and Connecticut in 1819, New Hampshire in 1821, Vermont and Maine in 1825, and Kentucky in 1826. Essentially, the treatment was for the children to develop internal controls by a system of rewards and punishments.

Drs. John D. Fisher and Samuel G. Howe traveled to France and Switzerland to observe how the blind and the retarded were taught. Returning to the United States, they established a facility for the blind in a mansion donated by Thomas H. Perkins, later called the Perkins Institute and the Massachusetts School for the Blind. In 1846, Dr. Howe was given state funds to establish the Massachusetts School for Idiotic and Feeble-Minded Youth on the base of the Perkins Institute.[72] By the time of the Civil War, there were schools for the retarded in New York, Pennsylvania, Ohio, and Connecticut, all established under state rather than local auspices.

### Early Juvenile Systems and Penitentiaries

In the cities, children were becoming a massive problem. Thousands of abandoned, orphaned, or "latch-key" children whose parents had to leave them all day committed petty crimes, but were judged as adults—sentenced to adult jails and prisons without hope for probation or pardon, and whipped, mutilated, or hung for stealing bread or shoes. Their age was not grounds for mercy, for there was no concept of "childhood"—children were simply small adults.

However, the growing sciences of sociology and psychology, the lessened need for their labor because of new factory technologies, and the growing altruism of the times led to new concern for children. In 1823, philanthropists Thomas Eddy and John Griscom established the Society for Reformation of Juvenile Delinquents and, with an initial subscription of $418,000 from private donors, the New York City House of Refuge in 1825. It was a prison, manufactory, and school until 1932, when it merged with the New York State Vocational Institution. Boston opened a House of Reformation in 1836 and Philadelphia in 1828. In 1847 a public state reform school for boys opened in Westboro, Massachusetts, and one in Lancaster for girls in 1854. The latter had small group cottages, no fences, and no barred windows. From the beginning of this separate system for juveniles, children were assigned for indeterminate sentences, with their release left to the discretion of the school managers. Courts had the right to commit children over the objections of parents on charges of vagrancy or incorrigibility. Not until 1869 were children given legal representation, and the first Juvenile Court was not established until 1911, in Illinois.

The reformatory movement was part of the growing child-saving concern, and it went hand in hand with the development of new forms of penology.

Reformatories were based on indeterminate sentencing—at the discretion of either the judge or the reformatory administrator—and "organized persuasion" rather than "coercive restraint." The idea was to give the inmate control over his or her progress toward freedom through "industry and good conduct" and to keep delinquents safe from exposure to temptation. Zebulon Brockway recommended a series of "graduated reformatory institutions." The first would be a House of Reception where the prison authorities took information on prisoners' ancestry, constitutional "propensities" (toward crime or poverty—part of Social Darwinism), and early socialization so that a plan of treatment could be formulated. The second was an Industrial Reformatory to train inmates for work; and the last was an Intermediate Reformatory where they worked and learned to live in society.[73]

Frederick Wines was appointed a special commissioner to the Second International Penitentiary Congress in Stockholm in 1878, and returned to advise Congress on child legislation. Among his proposals were that children should not be punished but educated for work through moral training, religion, and labor, that reformatories be segregated according to religious preferences, and that the number in each should be small enough for personal attention. The lives of the inmates were to include primary education and be characterized by simplicity in diet, dress, and surroundings. Reformatories were built away from the cities so children would not be distracted from their moral education. Manual labor was favored over intellectual education, keeping a class bias, and racist bias trained children of African descent to cook, wait on tables, and launder while white children were taught agriculture and factory work.

The Elmira, New York Reformatory, for male first offenders ages 16 to 30, was founded in 1870 and opened six years later. Intended as a model system to rehabilitate young people through education and training, it was soon so overcrowded that reform took second place to control. With only five hundred cells, by 1899 it held fifteen hundred inmates. Discipline was an integral part of the "treatment" program: Military drill, "training of the will," and long hours of tedious labor were the essence of the plan.[74] Zebulon Brockway, its director, required inmates to

> observe regular army tactics, drill, and daily dress parade. . . . By means of the military organization . . . the general tone . . . changed from that of a convict prison to the tone of a conscript fortress . . . a convict community under martial law.[75]

In the 1890s, charges of brutality prompted investigation, but Brockway's political influence cleared him and within a year divested the accusing Board of Charities of its authority to monitor prisons.[76]

Beginning with Elmira, reformatories were built across the nation. Despite the enlightened ideas of the reformers, the reality was often repressive: steel cages for inmates, maximum security cell blocks, inmate feuds, and corporal punishment—often violent and vicious. Many child-savers and reformers, including Homer Folks, began to advocate instead the "cottage system." Here inmates were placed in small group homes on the reformatory grounds, presided over by a "Christian gentleman and lady who . . . hold the relation of father and mother toward the youth."[77] These medium-security cottage reformatories gradually replaced the jail-like large reformatories.

The adult criminal justice system rose from almshouses, jails, and prisons. In 1776 Quakers established the Philadelphia Society for Alleviating the Miseries of Public Prisons. They believed that the best treatment was isolation and meditation and instituted the first penitentiary in 1823, for the able-bodied poor. Prisoners—including debtors and vagrants—were confined only at night, and worked in silence during the day in prison workshops. Older inmates were put in solitary cells and deprived of communication, while younger offenders were placed in dormitories. All were expected to meditate on their deviance and to pray for forgiveness in institutions in country settings, away from the temptations of city life. Inmates worked at simple tasks such as farming, with the expectation that such a return to a life of quiet would teach them the error of their ways. Penitentiaries were the beginning of the idea that criminals could be rehabilitated by treatment rather than punishment.

Other prisons not based on the penitent model but using some of their ideas were built: at Auburn, New York in 1816, followed by Sing Sing in 1825 and San Quentin, in California, in 1852. The two major systems of the reform era were the "Auburn, or silent," system, characterized by enforced silence and group activities, and the "Pennsylvania, or Eastern," system of solitary confinement. This latter "star model" had a central rotunda and seven cell blocks starring out like the spokes of a wheel, enabling guards at the center to observe inmate activities in all the cell blocks.[78] Although methods were more humane than had been the former floggings, physical abuse, and incarceration with no work or recreation, rehabilitation was rare. The inmate power system—a hierarchy among the prisoners based on force—taught criminality with much more effectiveness than prison officials taught rehabilitation. Prisoners were neither penitent nor rehabilitated when released, and yet the innovations remained because of the political power of the reformists. Officials also liked the rehabilitative methods for they gave them more power over inmates.[79]

The use of probation began with Isaac Hopper, a man who informally helped discharged prisoners find homes and jobs. Then, in Boston in 1841, John Augustus agreed to supervise people who had committed minor offenses, to post their bail, and to report back to the court rather than have them put in prison. He used his own money for their rehabilitation, and his method was both more conducive to rehabilitation and much less expensive than was prison. Thereafter, the practice grew throughout the criminal and juvenile justice systems. From early times, social workers have been involved in probation work, surveilling probationers and attempting to help them remain apart from criminal activity.

## NON-WHITE MINORITIES:
## EXPENDABLE COMMODITIES IN THE NEW NATION

Galper says,

> The genesis of racism in the United States is deeply rooted in capitalism. . . . Racial oppression, as the basis for generating an unpaid labor force, enabled this country to move from a relatively primitive agricultural state of economic development to a more mature, heavily industrialized state. It provided a speedy way to accumulate the surplus that industrialization requires.[80]

Although white workers also were exploited, the effects were greater for people of color—genocide for Native Americans, the destruction of cultures and societies of Africans brought to America, and imperialism in the lands of Hispanics.

### Native Americans:
### A Case of Genocide

Under English rule, Native Americans had the rights of independent sovereign nations, and this ideal continued after the Revolution. In 1778, Washington declared a policy of peaceful adjustment, and Supreme Court decisions and the Northwest Ordinance of 1787 upheld the rights of Native Americans to hold their lands. Quoting from the ordinance,

> The utmost good faith shall always be observed towards the Indians; their land and property shall never be taken from them without their consent; and in their property, rights, and liberty, they shall never be invaded or disturbed, unless in justified and lawful wars authorized by Congress; but laws founded in justice and humanity shall from time to time be made, for preventing wrongs being done to them, and for preserving peace and friendship with them.[81]

In 1790 Indian traders were licensed, and in 1796 government stores opened to give supplies on credit to Native Americans. However, "manifest destiny"—the belief that white people should own all of North America—was given tacit approval by all presidents after Adams, and so white people began to intrude on Native American lands. As they defended their territories, Americans retaliated with murders, planned raids, and action by state and federal militias.

The diversity of the Native American nations generally prevented organized resistance against the invaders. Even so, Shawnee Chief Tecumseh, along with his prophet brother Tenskwatawa, began to organize to fight. While Tecumseh was recruiting nations in the south to join the Shawnee Confederacy, Indiana Territory Governor William Henry Harrison marched against Tecumseh's encampment at Tippecanoe with eight hundred militiamen. The Prophet led the defending Shawnee forces, promising that bullets would not hurt them, and most were slaughtered. That defeat, while Tecumseh was only days from bringing fifty thousand men against the United States, ended organized resistance by the Shawnee Confederacy. Tecumseh joined the British in the War of 1812 and was killed in 1813.[82]

In 1824, under Presidents Monroe and Adams, the Bureau of Indian Affairs was organized in the War Department (moving to the Department of Interior in 1849). Pressures to remove Native Americans beyond the Alleghenies increased, as between 1816 and 1848, twelve states gained enough white population to be admitted to the Union. Treaties were negotiated, honored, and broken as Native Americans agreed or were forced to give up their lands east of the Mississippi to white settlers.[83] Andrew Jackson, inaugurated in 1828, encouraged states to defy Supreme Court rulings that protected Native American rights. States' militias wiped out Native American protest or retaliation. Jackson's Indian Removal Act of 1830, which authorized $500,000 to aid Native Americans in their adjustment to new territories, moved all but a handful of Eastern Native Americans west of the Mississippi. This removal is the infamous Trail of Tears.

About half the Creek nation died during the migration and the first years in the West. Oklahoma, where most nations were moved, was already the home of the Five Nations of the Southeast, and became "a vast concentration camp."[84] During the next ten years, more than seventy thousand people were moved. Among them were the Sauk and the Fox, who made a desperate but doomed stand in Illinois; the Ottawas, Potawatomies, Wyandots, and Shawnees; the Kickapoos, Winnebagos, Delawares, Peories, and the Miamis. Only a few remnant groups were left, in New York, Florida, Maine, and Virginia, along with a large group of Cherokees in the Great Smoky Mountains who had resisted so strongly they were allowed to remain.

> Forced migration at gunpoint was the lot of some native groups after they had been defeated. Among the famous forced marches was the one imposed on thousands of Cherokees, Creeks, Chicasaws, Choctaws, and Seminoles, who . . . were forced to move to the Oklahoma Territory. . . . Other tribes in

the West, such as the Navahos, were rounded up after military engagements and forced to migrate to barren reservations.[85]

The Indian Trade and Intercourse Act (1834) was intended to strengthen the federal government's aid to Native Americans. However, white intrusion continued, ranging from honest treaty making to genocidal forays aimed at exterminating the "Indian menace." The discovery of gold in California in 1849 sent thousands of whites westward, and the Kansas-Nebraska Act of 1854 and the Homestead Act in 1862, which gave 160 acres of unoccupied government land to anyone who lived on it for five years, authorized white settlement of Iowa, Kansas, and Nebraska. Between 1840 and 1860, an estimated 250,000 white settlers migrated across the plains to the West Coast.[86] In 1869 the transcontinental railroad brought white hunters who destroyed the bison-based economy of the Plains tribes.

Despite the media glamorization of the battles of white settlers against "savage" Native Americans,

> a total of only 362 white settlers and 426 Native Americans died in all the recorded battles between the two groups along wagon train routes. There is only one documented attack by Native Americans on a wagon train, in which there were two dozen casualties for the white settlers.[87]

White settlers, often looked upon as victims of the Native Americans and glorified as pioneers of the new nation, in fact engaged and succeeded in massive territorial aggression. This conquest refuted most religious and political doctrines of equality and personal freedom. Ironically, some of the democratic traditions of the United States probably arose from Native American cultures; for example, the statement that "all men are created equal, that they are endowed by their creator with certain inalienable rights" comes from Native American law. Possibly the model for state-federal relationships also came from the League of the Iroquois, brought back by Benjamin Franklin from tribal councils he attended, where the sovereignty of each nation balanced with that of the league. The Iroquois Constitution provided for initiative, referendum, and recall as well as suffrage for both men and women.

Two major doctrines were reinforced by the conquest: the doctrine of profit and the concept that "outsiders," or those who are "different" in beliefs and actions, are less than "human." This legitimated conquest in the names of progress and Christianization. It was nothing less than genocide: the trickery and deceit with which the conquest began; the murder and enslavement of Native American peoples; their removal person by person and nation by nation until the continent "belonged" to the white government; the attempts to wipe out Native American culture by taking away their children, placing them on reservations, and denying them such essentials as food, clothing, and shelter; and the savage decimation of their remaining population by war and murder after European diseases had taken their toll. It is a tribute to the persistence of their cultures and religious beliefs that they still survive.

## Chinese in America

Chinese were among the first immigrants to the North American coast after its rediscovery in 1492. Spanish explorers moving up the coast toward Oregon hired them to build their ships before the 1600s and continuing into the middle 1700s. However, few came from China to settle permanently because of their strong family ties and their religious needs to tend the spirits of their ancestors in their homelands. In fact, emigration from China was a capital offense.

China had remained a self-sufficient feudal economy from the onset of the dynasties in 221 B.C. and did not become involved in world trade until invasions by Europeans in the middle 1800s. European demands for trade caught China in its last dynasty (though it lasted until 1917), when the emperor was more interested in building monuments than in defense. In 1840 Europeans, including the British, Spanish, and Portuguese, carried out the first Opium War against China, breaking open the country for trade. The second Opium War, from 1856 to 1860, ended China's unity and self-sufficiency, for all practical purposes.

Although Americans did not participate in these wars against China, they took advantage of the new kinds of trade the Europeans brought before and after the wars. One of these was the trade in men. While "shanghai'ing" became common, perhaps the most active in kidnapping of Chinese were the Portuguese, based in Macao. This was called the "pig trade," where the kidnapped Chinese were "sold" to Americans for their passage and put to work in mines and on the railroads. While they were nominally free persons, they began life in America in debt slavery to those who bought their passage and their lives were little better than that of slaves. The Chinese were shipped to America in conditions similar to those of Africans: chained, in 18-inch spaces, with minimal food, water, and health care, and a high death rate during passage was common.[88]

## The Contributions of People of African Descent

As the demand for cotton became insatiable throughout the world, the price of slaves increased until it became cheaper to breed than to buy them. There were premiums on the good breeder, and female slaves, because they could reproduce, were more profitable than were male slaves. A breeding woman was worth from one-sixth to one-fourth more than one who did not breed.[89] Infants could be sold away like calves from cows, and white men, who had free access to slave women, sold their own children. Virginia, which did not depend on the cotton industry, became a primary "slave-raising" state, while Washington, D.C., was among the top slave markets until the 1850s.

The price of a good slave for the fields increased from $300 in 1820 to over $1000 in 1860, in spite of the fact that the slave population grew from about a million and a half to nearly four million during this period.[90]

The Constitution authorized slavery by determining that, for representation purposes, a person of African descent was three-fifths of a white, requiring the return of fugitive slaves to their masters, and delaying the ban on slave trading until 1808 (although it continued into the 1850s). Even free Afro-Americans in the North were nonpersons: They were not allowed voting rights, except in a very few cases where they owned property; their children could not be educated in schools with white children; and they were segregated in housing, employment, transportation, and medical services. Employment was mostly limited to domestic service at extremely low pay for women, and little work was available for men of African descent.

*Slave owner and cotton culture.*    Fewer than one in four southern families owned slaves, and nearly half the slaves lived on small farms worked by twenty or fewer. However, about seven thousand families owned fifty or more slaves, and these were the families who set the goals of the South. Slaves on small farms were less frequently sold away than were those of larger plantations, and those in the coastal South—Virginia, Maryland, Georgia, the Carolinas—worked under better conditions than did those in Alabama, Mississippi, Arkansas, Texas, or Louisiana.[91]

The "cotton culture" existed from the Carolinas and Georgia into the Mississippi Valley. Every state had its own "slave code." Slaves could not assemble in groups of more than five or so when away from their plantations and could not leave plantations without passes. Even free Afro-Americans had to carry passports to prove their status. At first, religion was not allowed, but after a time, slaves were allowed to believe in those parts of the Christian religion that taught unquestioning obedience to their masters in return for happiness in heaven. Preachers could only preach what they were told, and religious meetings had to be witnessed by white people. Every white person had police power over every person of African descent, free or slave

> the slave, if slavery were to be successful, had to believe he was a slave. . . . Each slave was taught . . . that he was totally helpless and that his master was absolutely powerful . . . that he was inferior to the meanest white man and that he had to obey every white man without thinking, without questioning. Finally, if these lessons were learned, the slave looked at himself through the eyes of his master and accepted the values of the master.[92]

Plantation owners' wives were an integral part of slave life. They supervised work within the home, sewed clothes for slaves, and doctored them. The black/white woman relationship often resulted in vicious cruelty to slaves and their children, deriving, perhaps, from the evidences of the white husbands' sexual involvement with slaves. The census of 1860 testified to the frequency that masters exercised their sexual "privileges" on slave women. By that year there were nearly 600,000 children of mixed racial background.[93] Husbands were warned to take no action against white rapists on pain of death.

The rape of black women was an attack on black men as well as on black women, who were warned not to call on their men for protection unless they wanted to see them lynched and raped. Rape was used to reinforce a sense of powerlessness in black men.[94]

Although some slaveowners earned a reputation for kindness and others for cruelty, most fell in between, taking some care for their property but willing to resort to cruel punishments.

> Masters who were psychotic [or] sadistic . . . devised ingenious methods of punishment. And "kind" masters whipped the skin off slaves' backs and washed them down with brine.[95]

*Slave families.*   Slaves were encouraged to marry and have families, and could often pick their own mates, for their owners felt that families and love relationships stabilized the slaves and kept them from running away. Monogamy was enforced, and adultery was a major offense. If slaves married outside their plantations, the man was generally given a pass to visit on Wednesday and Saturday nights and all day Sunday. Children took their fathers' names and adoptions were permitted. However, family life depended on the grace of the master, and there was the constant threat of selling away children or spouses. In fact, rebellions often occurred because of this, and often whole families escaped together to avoid it.

Children were usually cared for in a communal arrangement, mothered and fathered by anyone who was near, because of the constant labor demanded of both men and women. Old women tended them in "children's houses," with older children helping until the age of 8 or so, when they were given shoes and clothing other than gunny sacks and were set to work.

> Feeding slave children out of a common pot as though they were animals and ignoring their desire for modesty . . . was part of the attempt to condition slave children to view themselves as less human than whites and perhaps not human at all.[96]

There was sexual equality among men and women slaves, with both taking over the chores of the family after their work for the master was completed. Food was issued once a week, clothes twice a year.

Although slaveowners often lightened the work of pregnant women, the cumulative effect of malnutrition, hard work, and many babies was devastating. There were many miscarriages, babies were often sickly, and infant mortality was high. While some say that mothers often smothered their children to keep them from slavery, more recent evidence indicates that the term "smothering" was used to record unexplained deaths. The incidence and timing of the deaths indicates a striking resemblance to Sudden Infant Death Syndrome—a reflection of extreme poverty, low birth rates, and poor post- and prenatal care. After emancipation, when women resisted gang labor and took lighter tasks through their pregnancies, the rate of "smothered infants" was only one-fifth of that before the Civil War.[97]

*The work of slavery.* The plantation was a combination factory, village, and police precinct, complete with totalitarian regimentation. On large farms, work was organized either by "tasks" or by "gangs." On the task system when a job was done the slaves had free time for themselves—for gardens and the like. In the gang systems, field hands were worked by overseers paid by immediate production and "drivers" with whips given rewards for fast pace.[98] There was also a system of rewards for hard work—a good worker was given bonuses, prizes, and the opportunity for occupational mobility into skilled trades or manager positions. This was effective to the extent that, at the end of the Civil War, 83 percent of mechanics and artisans in the South were people of African descent.[99]

Seven out of eight slaves were field workers. Women were expected to work as hard as men in the fields, and then do women's work in the slave quarters. Their third job was to reproduce. Davis says

> Where work was concerned, strength and productivity under threat of the whip outweighed considerations of sex. In this sense, the oppression of women was identical to the oppression of men. . . . Expediency governed the slaveholder's posture toward female slaves. When it was profitable to exploit them as if they were men, they were regarded, in effect, as genderless, but when they could be exploited, punished, and repressed in ways suited only for women, they were locked into their exclusively female roles.[100]

Slave women were also used for hauling ore in southern mines. House slaves in the South were treated as nonexistent, often sleeping in the same rooms as their masters. Urban slaves could be hired out a year at a time and had more freedom than did plantation slaves.

*Slave rebellions.* Slavery did not continue without resistance: non-violent resistance, slowed working pace, feigned illness, and strikes. Violent resistance and rebellion were constant fears among plantation families, and at least 250 slave revolts are recorded. Southern families feared their slaves would copy the revolt in Haiti, in 1791, where more than 100,000 of its half-million slaves joined with a voodoo priest named Boukman and for three weeks ravaged the white plantations.

> In an instant . . . twelve hundred coffee and two hundred sugar plantations were in flames; the buildings, the machinery, the farmhouses, were reduced to ashes; and the unfortunate proprietors were hunted down, murdered, or thrown into the flames.[101]

Toussaint L'Ouverture took over leadership as governor of Haiti in 1801, but betrayed by Napoleon on a state visit to France, he died in prison. His successor, Jean-Jacques Dessalines, continued to fight so persistently that in 1803 Napoleon gave up his dream of making Haiti the foothold of his western empire and ceded the Louisiana Territory to America for 4 cents an acre.

Rebellion in the South was not long to follow. In the early 1800s Gabriel Prosser gathered weapons and a force of a thousand slaves to march on Richmond. When heavy rains cut them off from the city, they were captured and at least thirty-five, including Prosser, were hanged. Another rebellion occurred in 1811 near New Orleans, where several hundred slaves attacked whites on plantations. Dozens were killed and the leaders executed—their heads displayed along the route to New Orleans. An 1822 conspiracy of several thousand armed slaves was led by Denmark Vesey against Charleston, South Carolina, but again they were betrayed and Vesey and thirty-six others were hanged.[102] The most famous rebellion was led by Nat Turner in 1831. It spread throughout Virginia and North Carolina, and whole white families died in their plantations. The Turner rebellion ended when the militia was called out, and though Turner escaped, he was executed several months later.

Harriet Tubman (1820?–1913) was also a leader in the resistance. Called the "Moses of Her People," she escaped slavery in 1849, then returned time after time to lead others—more than three hundred—to freedom. Rewards for her capture reached $40,000. After emancipation, she served as scout, spy, and nurse for the Union forces in South Carolina. After the war, she settled in Auburn, New York, taking orphans and old people into her home. The Harriet Tubman Home for Indigent Aged Negroes was supported by former abolitionists and the citizens of Auburn. When she applied for a federal pension for her war service, she was awarded $20.00 per month (half that of white pensioners).

*Free persons of African descent.* From the time of the Revolution, abolitionists of both races worked together. One such movement was the American Colonization Society (1817), which sought to settle freed slaves in Liberia. The American Anti-Slavery Society, formed in 1833 under the leadership of William Lloyd Garrison and Arthur Lewis Tappan, tried to educate free Afro-Americans to gain U.S. citizenship. The most famous abolitionist was Frederick Douglass, a powerful orator and ex-slave, who spoke out both for abolition and for women's rights.

In 1826 John Russwurm became the first man of African descent in America to graduate from college, at Bowdoin. He joined with Samuel E. Cornish to found the first newspaper for Afro-Americans, *Freedom's Journal*, in 1827. The first national convention of Afro-Americans, chaired by Richard Allen, was held in 1830. In 1838 David Ruggles founded the first magazine for people of African descent, the *Mirror of Liberty*. Two colleges for Afro-Americans opened, Lincoln University in Pennsylvania and Wilberforce University in Ohio, founded by the African Methodist Episcopal Church. In 1855 John Mercer Langston became the first elected Afro-American public official, a township clerk in Ohio.

The Missouri Compromise, in 1829, divided the Louisiana Purchase along the Mason-Dixon line and admitted Maine as a free state and Missouri as a slave state. In 1850 a new compromise admitted California free, created two new territories of New Mexico, and added a drastic fugitive slave law to soothe Southern plantation owners. It also prohibited slave trade in Washington, D.C. The last slave ship landed at Mobile Bay, Alabama, in 1859—the same year that John Brown attacked Harper's Ferry, in which raid the thirteen white and five Afro-American men were captured and hanged by Robert E. Lee. The Compromises began to give way, and in 1857 a Southern-dominated Supreme Court handed down the *Dred Scott* decision claiming that slaves were personal property, to be protected for their owners. It also declared the Missouri Compromise unconstitutional because the federal government did not have the power to forbid slavery in any territory (the states rights issue).

Before the Civil War, there were half a million free persons of African descent in the United States—11 percent of the population—half in the South. Many were well-to-do. They had churches, literary debating societies, fraternal organizations, and societies for mutual aid. Among the freed slaves, indigent or helpless people were supported by relatives, friends, neighbors, and relief associations; and free Afro-Americans established schools and orphanages to aid children of African descent.[103]

### Hispanic Americans

Hispanic Americans have a history divergent from that of Native Americans because, having been conquered by Spain, they became Spanish citizens. Their settlement of the Southwest dates from about 1530, when land grants were given them by the Spanish crown. Mexico won independence from Spain in 1821, and Anglo-Americans almost immediately began infiltrating, at first by trying to purchase Mexico's northern border along the Rio Grande. There, several thousand Hispanics had a self-sufficient economy, with almost no poverty because of the Church and land-owners who found work for the indigent.

An estimated four thousand white settlers were in the Texas area in 1821, but by the 1830s there were twenty thousand new Anglo immigrants.[104] In a thinly disguised rationalization for imperialism, they rebelled against the Mexican government and called for help against oppression. In 1845 Texas simply was annexed by the United States, precipitating the Mexican War of 1846, and in 1848, the Mexican government was forced to cede Texas for $15 million under the Treaty of Guadalupe Hidalgo. The United States took most of Mexico's northwest borders, including California where, before the Gold Rush, there were seventy-five hundred Hispanic settlers.

The Treaty guaranteed that the land rights of Mexican people now in the United States would be protected, along with personal property rights and religious freedom. However, as white settlers moved into the Southwest, these guarantees were ignored. Anglo settlers sued against Spanish land grants and typically won in Anglo courts, for many Hispanics had lost evidences of title and had little money to fight the court decrees. The Gadsden Purchase, in 1853, took even more land under white control. Taxes were also used to disinherit the Hispanics, for Americans levied property tax rates at levels only the largest of Spanish landholders could afford, thereby forcing small Hispanic entrepreneurs off their land and into low-wage labor for Anglos.[105] Violence was common: In the 1850s, two thousand white miners attacked Mexicans in Sonora, killing dozens and wiping out a community. By 1870 Hispanics in New Mexico were disenfranchised.

As with Native American resistance stereotypes, there are persistent myths about heroic battles of white settlers against Hispanics. The most popular is that of the Alamo, where 180 principled, presumably native-born Texans fought against Mexican bandits. However, Santa Ana's Mexican troops were a legal army and most of the "defenders" of the Alamo were ne'er-do-well newcomers and adventurers, brawlers such as James Bowie, William Travis, and Davy Crockett. The Alamo, in addition, was one of the best fortified sites in the West, with twice as many cannons, better rifles, and better training than the Mexican forces had. Many whites at the Alamo surrendered rather than be killed, and the Hispanics were winning until General Sam Houston made a surprise attack from the north, wiping out most of the Mexican army.

The same myths persist about Mexican bandits attacking white settlers. However, these fighters were actually guerillas resisting the takeover of Mexican land and wealth. There were numerous raids during the 1830s and 1840s, and Juan Cortina, a Mexican hero, fought for the poor in the Texas borderlands, clashing with local militia and Texas rangers in the 1850s and 1860s. Far from being an uneducated and uncouth criminal, he issued formal statements of grievances detailing the stealing of lands and setting up of biased legal systems. Colonel Robert E. Lee was sent to Texas to put down Cortina, but only succeeded in limiting his activities.

The lawlessness against Mexicans had a semiofficial status with the Texas rangers, a kind of vigilante force to terrorize and subordinate Mexicans. Numerous lynchings were recorded, and white settlers often became rich with the help of the Texas rangers. An estimated 2.0 million acres of private land and 1.7 million of communal land were lost between 1854 and 1930 in New Mexico alone. A study in Texas found that in 1850–1860 one-third of Hispanic Americans were ranch- and farmowners, one-third skilled artisans or professionals, and one-third Hispanic laborers. However, by 1900 the number of ranch- and farmowners had dropped to 16 percent, while two-thirds of the Mexican population had become manual labor.[106]

By the 1880s, Hispanic labor was being used extensively on the railroad, and by 1900, American capital—railroads, agribusiness, and the federal government—owned the Southwest. In 1902, the National Reclamation Act brought irrigation to Southwest farms, and the Homestead Act was extended into that area. White farming population was insufficient to meet labor demands, and Mexican workers became an agrarian labor class.

## THE WOMEN'S MOVEMENT IN THE 1800s

The two major issues of this era were abolition and suffrage. Suffragists realized the economic ties among slavery in the South, economic exploitation of workers in the North, and the suppression of women. Although women were not "owned" in the sense that slaves were, they were

> almost treated like Negro slaves, inside and outside the home. Both were expected to behave with deference and obedience towards owner or husband; both did not exist officially under the law; both had few rights and little education; both found it difficult to run away; both worked for their masters without pay; both had to breed on command and to nurse the results.[107]

Women could not vote; could not practice law, theology, or medicine; could not sign wills or contracts without husband's consent; and could not serve on juries. All wages they earned belonged to their husbands as did real estate and other property; laws of divorce favored the husband, and husbands were awarded custody of children.

Although the image of the strong and hardy pioneer woman persisted into the 1800s, new theories of human behavior placed women in a "sphere" that limited them to home, family, and economic control by husbands. "Feminine traits" became desirable and necessary for middle-class women. Poor women, of course, were not included in this image—they continued to labor in domestic and factory work and often took in sewing or laundry or kept boarders in their homes for extra money.

Among the first to note the connections between abolition and women's rights were Sarah and Angelina Grimke. The daughters of an aristocratic slave-holding family in the South, Sarah joined the Quakers and moved to Philadelphia in 1822, where Angelina joined her seven years later. They became active abolitionists, and Angelina became the first "respectable" American woman to speak in public, presenting the Massachusetts legislature with a petition signed by twenty thousand women demanding an end to slavery. Her pamphlets were burned in the South, and both sisters were condemned by the clergy, who saw their public lobbying as an un-Christian assault upon the social order and the sanctity of home and family.[108] (The 1837 pastoral letter of the Congregationalist churches, using the New Testament as base, implied that feminists were antiscripturalists whom God would punish with the loss of ability to have children, degeneracy, and ruin for "taking the place of men.")

Other women also were active in the movement. Lucy Stone was an ardent feminist who worked with William Lloyd Garrison against slavery. She married Henry Blackwell (brother of Drs. Emily and Elizabeth), and both she and her husband agreed that she would be called by her maiden name. (Others who adopted the style were called "Lucy Stoners.") Ernestine Potowski Rose (1810–1892), a Polish immigrant in 1836, was a fearless abolitionist, speaking against slavery even in the South. She campaigned for property rights for women, women's suffrage, and easier divorce laws.[109] Lucretia Mott (1793–1880), a teacher and social reformer, helped to organize the Philadelphia Anti-Slavery Society. She and her husband James gave up a profitable cotton business because it was the product of slavery. In 1840, she attended the World Anti-Slavery Convention but was refused seating as a delegate because she was a woman. At the convention, she met Elizabeth Cady Stanton, and the Motts and Stantons became close friends.

Elizabeth Cady Stanton married abolitionist Henry B. Stanton over her father's objections and became an ardent worker for women's suffrage. Along with Susan B. Anthony and others, including Frederick Douglass, she organized the Seneca Convention on women's issues in 1848, where the audience of three hundred included forty men (but no persons of color). The convention called for equal educational rights; fairer laws for marriage, divorce, and property ownership; the end of a double moral standard; the right to write, speak, and teach on a basis equal with men; and equal participation in the trades, professions, and commerce. All the resolutions passed immediately except Cady Stanton's demand for women's suffrage. Even her husband opposed it, but Frederick Douglass lectured in its favor, and the resolution survived a close vote on the floor.[110]

Well before the Seneca Falls Convention, Susan B. Anthony (1820–1900) had joined Cady Stanton in working for women's suffrage. Cady Stanton did the theoretical work, including the ideals and language of the campaign for women's rights, and Anthony built the organizational machinery. The daughter of a prosperous mill owner, Stanton took a job teaching when her father suffered reverses in his business. Astonished at the low pay, she became a radical feminist. She arranged state and regional women's conventions, organized a petition campaign for women's property laws that passed in 1860, and became a leader for Garrison's American Anti-Slavery Society.

Sojourner Truth, born as a slave about 1797, was as concerned about women's rights as with abolition. All twelve of her brothers and sisters and two of her own children were sold before her eyes. One of her first acts when freed by New York's emancipation law (1827) was to sue, successfully, for the return of a son who had been sold away from her. She felt she had been touched by God to work for abolition and women's rights and became an evangelist and an abolitionist, walking and preaching throughout New York and Connecticut and later Ohio, Indiana, Missouri, and Kansas. She became known as a moving speaker on both topics, rivaling in eloquence Frederick Douglass, with whom she frequently shared the speaker's platform.

Between the Seneca Falls convention and the beginning of the Civil War, there were some changes in the status of women. In 1848 New York enacted a law guaranteeing that women could keep the property they had before marriage, along with new bequests and gifts. Pennsylvania, California, and Wisconsin soon followed suit. (However, the intention was not completely altruistic—it protected the land of wealthy property owners who resented seeing land and riches pass out of the family through marriage.) In 1860 another bill in New York granted married women rights to wages, allowed wives to make contracts without the husband's approval if he were incompetent, and guaranteed inheritance rights after a husband's death. In addition, the Homestead Acts of 1860 and 1890 gave free land to both men and women—husbands and wives together were given 640 acres, while single persons received only half that amount.

The common interests between women and slaves bound them together until after the Civil War, when the Fourteenth Amendment specifically gave the right to vote to men, including men of African descent, but not to women. Even faithful supporters of women's rights such as Horace Greeley and Wendell Phillips would not support women's protests against the amendments. Frederick Douglass told women to be patient, for this was the Negro's hour, and race, not sex, was the issue because people of African descent were still being killed. The women's movement split bitterly: Lucy Stone and Julia Ward Howe led the American Women Suffrage Association, supporting freed men's suffrage and seeking to work within the system and avoid "peripheral" women's issues. Cady Stanton and Anthony formed the more radical National Women's Suffrage Association and aligned themselves with all kinds of women's causes: the double standard in marriage, free love, labor unions, and the civil rights of prostitutes.[111] They suggested a racist trade-off: educational but not sexual qualifications for voting. "Educated suffrage" meant gaining the votes of middle-class educated white women and writing off those of lower-class people of African descent and immigrants.

The national suffrage movement probably had no more than ten thousand members at any one time and faced its greatest opposition in the South, whose people remembered suffragists as abolitionists. Western states very often offered state suffrage to women, for women were a scarce commodity, often outnumbered by men by twenty to one. Wyoming, Utah, Colorado, and Idaho all granted women's suffrage.

## CONCLUSION: WORKING TOWARD FREEDOM

Between the Revolutionary and Civil wars, the United States fermented with social reform and social change. The economy went from a colonial agrarian one to massive industrialization, and because of the demand for cotton America took her place in international trade. On both international and continental fronts, the United States became a power to reckon with: Both France and Spain gave up their rights to American territories and England ceded rights to the sea while America sprawled and brawled across the continent, taking by force what it could not buy or gain by trickery. The structure of families changed, from extended to nuclear—isolated and alienated. Fortunes were made in both North and South on the exploitation of workers—immigrants, freed persons, or slaves—who were helpless against the political, economic, and social control of the wealthy elite.

In social welfare, Protestant ideas of poverty and the morality of work continued to direct the treatment of distressed and deviant. Both private charity and public agencies called for institutionalization of those who could not care for themselves. This created almshouse/poorhouse conditions so horrendous that, with the growing social awareness of the century, new treatment was devised for special groups—the mentally ill; children; the blind, deaf, retarded, or disabled; juvenile and adult offenders; and so on. New methods of treatment and rehabilitation grew, some succeeding while others failed.

Finally, in the major social movements of the century, white women of all economic classes and all persons of the laboring classes (slave or free) were the driving forces for change. Pitted against a white male elite bolstered by church and government and determined to maintain the status quo of power and profit, the battle was slow. Incremental changes were inevitable, but even such a revolutionary change as the Civil War brought few increments in practice. The equality won for slaves, if only in the abstract, was not mirrored in new rights for women, Native Americans, Hispanics, or Orientals. Those freedoms, and true freedom for Afro-Americans, were to be delayed for decades more.

## STUDY QUESTIONS

1. What was the first Civil Rights movement in the United States?
2. What was the impact of urbanization and immigration on social welfare?
3. What were private and public responses to need before the Civil War?
4. What political influences surrounding the Dix bill prevented its passage? What might it have accomplished if passed?
5. Compare the treatment of Native Americans, Hispanic Americans, and people of African descent in terms of colonialism, genocide, and their status as human beings.
6. How did the Women's Movement contribute to social welfare?

## FOOTNOTES

[1]For example, Massachusetts and New York required male voters to have $300, up to $1,000 to run for Congress, $1,500 to $3,000 to run for Senate, and $5,000 to run for governor. Pennsylvania allowed any man who paid taxes to vote or run for office and in 1812 New York allowed the same, even extending voting rights to some free property-owning Afro-Americans. See Thomas R. Dye and L. Harmon Zeigler, *The Irony of Democracy*, (Belmont, Calif.: Wadsworth Publishing Co., 1970), pp. 6–14; and Beulah Compton, *Introduction to Social Welfare and Social Work: Structure, Function, and Process*, (Homewood, Ill.: The Dorsey Press, 1980), p. 218.

[2]Dye and Zeigler, *Irony of Democracy*, p. 65.

[3]Samuel Mencher, *From Poor Law to Poverty Programs*, (Pittsburgh: University of Pittsburgh Press, 1967), p. 141.

[4]Dye and Zeigler, *Irony of Democracy*, p. 67.

[5]Michael B. Katz, *Poverty and Policy in American History*, (New York: Academic Press, 1983), p. 10.

[6]David Macarov, *Work and Welfare: the Unholy Alliance*, (Beverly Hills, Calif.: Sage Publications, 1980), pp. 234–235.

[7]Mencher, *Poor Law to Poverty*, p. 167.

[8]Ibid., p. 136.

[9]Blanche Coll, *Perspectives in Public Welfare: A History*, U.S. Department of Health, Education, and Welfare, SRS 1969, (Washington, D.C.: U.S. Government Printing Office, 1971), pp. 22–23.

[10]Mencher, *From Poor Law to Poverty Programs*, p. 77.

[11]Compton, *Introduction to Social Welfare*, p. 226.

[12] Maxine Seller, *Immigrant Women*, (Philadelphia: Temple University Press, 1984), p. 50.

[13]Coll, *Perspectives in Public Welfare*, p. 24.

[14]Carole Hymowitz and Michaele Weissman, *A History of Women in America*, (New York: Bantam Books, 1980), p. 195.

[15]Ibid.

[16]Ibid., p. 198.

[17]Mencher, *From Poor Law to Poverty Programs*, pp. 133–134, from John A. Drout and Dixon R. Fox, *The Completion of Independence*, (New York: Macmillan Publishing Co., 1944), pp. 373-374.

[18]Compton, *Introduction to Social Welfare*, p. 228. Referenced from Edith Abbott, *Women in Industry: A Study of American Economic History*, (New York: Arno Press, 1910, pp. 48–62, first published by *The New York Times*, 1909).

[19]William Jay Jacobs, *Women in American History*, (Encino, Calif.: Glencoe Publishing, 1976), p. 31.

[20]Hymowitz and Weissman, *History of Women*, p. 238, quoting Marie Van Vorst, a wealthy woman who took a job posing as a poor woman in a South Carolina mill to investigate working conditions of women and children.

[21]Jacobs, *Women in History*, p. 32.

[22]Compton, *Introduction to Social Welfare*, p. 228.

[23]Hymowitz and Weissman, *History of Women*, p. 236.

[24]Katz, *Poverty and Policy*, p. 12.

[25]Mencher, *From Poor Law to Poverty Programs*, p. 137.

[26]Compton, *Introduction to Social Welfare*, p. 227.

[27]Coll, *Perspectives in Public Welfare*, p. 34.

[28]Ibid.

[29]Seller, *Immigrant Women*, p. 162.

[30]Katz, *Poverty and Policy*, p. 202.

[31]Ibid., p. 115.

[32]Ibid., p. 194.

[33]1818 Report of the Society for the Prevention of Pauperism, founded in 1817 by Thomas Eddy and John Griscom, and reported in Mencher, *From Poor Laws to Poverty Programs*, pp. 145–146, quoting John B. McMaster, *A History of the People of the United States*, (New York: D. Appleton, 1895), pp. 527–528; and John V. N. Yates, Secretary of the State of New York, 1824.

[34]David Scheider and Albert Deutsch, *The History of Public Welfare in New York State*, (Chicago: University of Chicago Press, 1938), p. 212.

[35]J. V. N. Yates, "Report of the Secretary of State in 1824 on the Relief and Settlement of the Poor," reprinted in the *34th Annual Report of the State Board of Charities of the State of New York, 1900*. Vol. 1, pp. 939–963.

[36]Frank Dekker Watson, *The Charity Organization Movement in the United States*, (New York: Arno Press and *The New York Times*, 1971), p. 690.

[37]Compton, *Introduction to Social Welfare*, p. 236.

[38]Quoted in Philip S. Foner, *History of the Labor Movement in the United States*, (New York: International Publishers, 1947), p. 98, reported in Mencher, *From Poor Law to Poverty Programs*, p. 144.

[39]Watson, *Charity Organization*, p. 73.

[40]Ibid., pp. 75–76.

[41]Coll, *Perspectives in Public Welfare*, p. 36.

[42]Ibid., p. 37.

[43]Mencher, *From Poor Law to Poverty Programs*, p. 83.

[44]Compton, *Introduction to Social Welfare*, p. 287.

[45]Seller, *Immigrant Women*, p. 179.

[46]Coll, *Perspectives in Public Welfare*, p. 30.

[47]Ibid., p. 22.

[48]Katz, *Poverty and Policy*, p. 196.

[49]Gerald N. Grob, advisory editor, *The State and Public Welfare in Nineteenth Century America*, (New York: Arno Press, 1976), p. 3 of Senate Document D.

[50]Ibid., pp. 6–7.

[51]Coll, *Perspectives in Public Welfare*, p. 25.

[52]Grob, *State and Public Welfare*, p. 9 of Senate Document D.

[53]Ibid., p. 53 of Senate Document 2: "Massachusetts State Charities Report of the Special Joint Committee Appointed to Investigate Charitable Institutions of the Commonwealth of Massachusetts, 1858," (Boston: William White, printer to the State, 1859).

[54]Grob, *State and Public Welfare*, p. 50 of Senate Document 2.

[55]Katz, *Poverty and Policy*, discussing the Erie County, New York, poorhouse, pp. 66 and 217.

[56]Coll, *Perspectives*, p. 22.

[57]Ibid., p. 31.

[58]Ibid., p. 29.

[59]Watson, *The Charity Organization Movement*, p. 79, referenced from Robert W. Bruere, "The Good Samaritan, Inc.," *Harper's Monthly Magazine*, 1910, Vol. CXX, p. 834.

[60]Barbara Ehrenreich and Dierdre English, *Complaints and Disorders: The Sexual Politics of Sickness*, (New York: The Feminist Press, Glass Mountain Pamphlet #2, 1973), p. 19.

[61]Ibid., p. 47.

[62]Ibid., p. 48.

[63]Ibid., p. 16

[64]Hymowitz and Weissman, *History of Women*, p. 68.

[65]Ehrenreich and English, *Complaints and Disorders*, p. 33.

[66]Seller, *Immigrant Women*, pp. 97–98.

[67]Grob, *State and Public Welfare*, p. 13: "A Report on the Public Charities, Reformatories, Prisons, and Almshouses of the State of Maryland," by C. W. Chancellor, Maryland Secretary of the State Board of Health, July 1877.

[68]See Seaton W. Manning, "The Tragedy of the Ten-Million-Acre Bill," *Social Service Review*, Vol. 36 (March 1962), pp. 44– 50; and Roy Franklin Nichols, *Franklin Pierce*, (Philadelphia: University of Pennsylvania Press, 1958), p. 289.

[69]Jacobs, *Women in History*, p. 17.

[70]Ibid., p. 25.

[71]Ibid, p. 22.

[72]Compton, *Introduction to Social Welfare*, p. 285.

[73]From Zebulon Brockway, *Fifty Years of Prison Service*, pp. 397–398, discussed in Anthony M. Platt, *The Child Savers: The Invention of Delinquency*, 2nd ed., (Chicago: University of Chicago Press, 1977), p. 48.

[74]Platt, *Child Savers*, p. 73.

[75]Ibid., pp. 67–68.

[76]Compton, *Introduction to Social Welfare*, p. 289.

[77]Platt, *Child Savers*, p. 63.

[78]Albert Roberts, in a preliminary review of Day, *A New History of Social Welfare*.

[79]Grob, *State and Public Welfare*, p. 100.

[80]Jeffrey Galper, *Social Work Practice: A Radical Perspective*, (Englewood Cliffs, N. J.: Prentice Hall, 1974), p. 51.

[81]Joe R. Feagin, *Racial and Ethnic Relations*, 3rd ed., (Englewood Cliffs, N.J.: Prentice Hall, 1986), p. 179.

[82]Carolyn Merchant, *The Death of Nature: Women, Ecology, and the Scientific Revolution*, (San Francisco: Harper and Row, 1980), p. 28.

[83]Compton, *Introduction to Social Welfare*, p. 221.

[84]Feagin, *Racial Relations*, p. 178.

[85]Joseph Hraba, *American Ethnicity*, (Itasca, Ill.: F. E. Peacock Publishers, 1979), p. 222.

[86]Feagin, *Racial Relations*, p. 178.

[87]Ibid., p. 181.

[88]Jack Chen, *The Chinese of America*, (San Francisco: Harper & Row, 1980), pp. 1–30.

[89]Lerone Bennett, Jr. *Before the Mayflower: A History of the Negro in America, 1619–1964*, (Chicago: Johnson Publishing Company, Penguin Edition, 1966), p. 84.

[90]Dye and Zeigler, *Irony of Democracy*, p. 57.

[91]Ibid., p. 57.

[92]Bennett, *Before the Mayflower*, p. 93.

[93]Hymowitz and Weissman, *History of Women*, p. 62.

[94]Jacobs, *Women in History*, p. 12.

[95]Bennett, *Before the Mayflower*, p. 75.

[96]Hymowitz amd Weissman, *History of Women*, p. 48.

[97]Michael P. Johnson, "Smothered Slave Infants: Were Slave Mothers at Fault?" in Linda K. Kerber and Jane DeHart Mathews, eds., *Women's America*, (New York: Oxford University Press, 1982), pp. 102–105.

[98]Hymowitz and Weissman, *History of Women*, p. 43.

[99]Hraba, *American Ethnicity*, p. 43.

[100]Angela Davis, *Women, Race, and Class*, (New York: Vintage Press, 1983), p. 6.

[101]Bennett, *Before the Mayflower*, p. 99.

[102]Feagin, *Racial Relations*, p. 218.

[103]Dye and Zeigler, *Irony of Democracy*, p. 71.

[104]Feagin, *Racial Relations*, p. 270.

[105]Ibid.

[106]Ibid., p. 272.

[107]A. Sinclair, *The Emancipation of the American Woman*, (New York: 1966), p. 4.

[108]Hymowitz and Weissman, *History of Women*, p. 823.

[109]Sellers, *Immigrant Women*, p. 256.

[110]Jacobs, *Women in History*, p. 43.

[111]Hymowitz and Weissman, *History of Women*, p. 173.

# 7

# THE AMERICAN WELFARE
# STATE BEGINS

The Civil War affirmed federal responsibility over states' rights and laid the groundwork for the United States to become a welfare state. The first evidence came in the Freedmen's Bureau, a federally legislated program that cut across state lines to care for people displaced by the Civil War. Massive economic problems, including major depressions, pushed responsibility for social welfare upward from local overseers of the poor, first to city or county welfare departments, then to states, and finally, with the Social Security Acts of 1935, to the federal government.

Three social welfare movements attained importance during the period from 1865 to 1900: the Charity Organization Society (COS) movement, the settlement house movement, and the child-saving movement. The first two led the developing profession of social work down two different paths, the COS toward individual casework, and settlements toward grass-roots organizing for social action and social reform. Child-saving overlapped the others: It took children from their parents and placed them where they might learn the values of hard work, following COSs' beliefs in overcoming the genetic elements of pauperism, while settlement house movements worked on child labor laws, grass-roots aid, and education for children. The labor movement also became a social welfare issue, as COS workers tried to hold down social unrest and settlement house workers fought for reforms.

Both COS and settlement house movements were based on socioreligious ideals: the morality of work and wealth, the personal fault of the poor, and ideas of social justice. In addition, burgeoning new sciences—genetics, sociology, and psychology—had growing influence in both. While COSs sought to contain change brought by immigrants from Southern and Eastern Europe, settlement work was a part of those wider reform movements that included Socialism, Populism, and the Social Gospel movement.

Although history looks upon the emerging social work profession as a caring society's response to need, this was not wholly true.

> Welfare reform and the bureaucratic style of relief that it sponsored served the purposes of industrial capitalism in three ways: . . . made relief increasingly humiliating and unpleasant and so provided an incentive to labor; . . . emphasized the parasitic and degraded qualities of the very poor, thereby reducing popular sympathy and justifying retrenchment and repression; and . . . divided the working class against itself at the very moment when labor militancy was growing.[1]

The class backgrounds of social welfarists and the political dynamics of the times demonstrated the presence of elite ideals in the developing profession. They quite intended

> to pacify an unruly, exploited urban proletariat through encouraging them to accept their class position as morally just.[2]

According to Saville,

> the Welfare State . . . [is] a result of the interaction of three main factors:
>
> 1. the struggle of the working class against their exploitation,
> 2. the requirements of industrial capitalism . . . for a more efficient environment in which to operate and . . . the need for a highly productive labor force, and
> 3. recognition . . . of the price that has to be paid for political security.[3]

Piven and Cloward state the case more succinctly, saying that the provision of welfare arises from the need to quell rebellion among the poorer classes and through provision of some but not all their demands to maintain a low-wage work force.[4]

## THE CIVIL WAR: A NEW NATION EMERGES

More than any other reason, the Civil War erupted because the Southern states tried to maintain economic control over their own production. The North, in international competition with England, sought high tariffs against foreign goods, but the South insisted on lower tariffs and adopted a "doctrine of nullification" that simply would not charge taxes they opposed. To fight this, Northerners and Westerners created the Republican party, and in the four-way presidential race in 1860, their conservative candidate, Lincoln, won 40 percent of the vote (98.6 percent of the northern vote).[5]

Lincoln was not an abolitionist. In fact, he opposed civil and social equality for slaves, saying in 1858

I am not, nor ever have been, in favor of bringing about . . . the social and political equality of the white and black races . . . of making voters or jurors of Negroes, nor qualifying them to hold office nor to intermarry with white people . . . there must be a position of superior and inferior; and I as much as any other man am in favor of having the superior position assigned to the white race.[6]

However, he was a pragmatist who did not want to destroy the Southern elite on whom the manufacturing North depended. His goals were to restore orderly government, establish federal over states' rights, and prevent the disruption of the northern manufacturing monopoly.

His election moved the nation toward secession and conflict. Within a year, South Carolina seceded from the United States, followed by ten other states within six months. Unable to tolerate the loss of economic control secession threatened, and pressured by liberals to abolish slavery, Lincoln declared war. Southern politicans left the government and Northern industrial capitalists took their place, changing the political emphasis of the nation from agrarian to industrial and plunging the South into economic depression. The North's economic diversification enabled it to profit immensely in the sale of armaments and provisions for soldiers and to continue its profitable international trade. Meanwhile, the South faced devastation and famine as it sought to turn cotton plantations into food production and to buy arms for the war. Working people in the North feared a new influx of freed slaves would take their jobs, and after the Draft Law of 1863, rioted in the streets of New York. This left hundreds of people of African descent dead and caused a million dollars' worth of damage.[7] At the onset of the Civil War, there were more than 500,000 free Afro-Americans in the United States, half in the South.

For the North, the Civil War was a poor man's war. The Draft Law gave upper-class men the legal right to buy their way out of the Army for $300 or hire others to take their places. Poor men had no such escape and their families became destitute, for soldiers' pay was about $13.00 per month, with no allotments provided for the families they left behind. Although in 1862 the government established a pension fund for disabled veterans and for the dependents of those killed in the war, along with orphanages and homes for the disabled, dependents of living soldiers went without help. They took jobs in textile mills and munitions factories in greater numbers than ever but were paid a fraction of what men had earned.

Most Civil War battles were fought in the South. There, formerly pampered white wives tried desperately to produce food for themselves, their families, and the Confederate troops and to supervise now unruly and rebellious slaves. Union soldiers, storming through the country, burned the fields and killed stock so that Confederate soldiers could not be provisioned, and the meager supplies grown or hoarded by Southern women were destroyed. To survive, they looted stores and stole, and some few—Rose O'Neal Greenhow and Belle Boyd, for example—joined the Confederate forces as spies and saboteurs, blowing up bridges and communication lines used by Union forces.

The many slaves who sought to enlist in the Union forces were an embarrassment to Lincoln, who maintained that the war was a disagreement among white gentlemen that had nothing to do with slavery. When Northern freedmen tried to volunteer, he thanked them and sent them home, though liberals, abolitionists, and Afro-American leaders asked Lincoln to "hit the South where it would hurt the most: free the slaves and give them guns."[8] He insisted that his policy on slaves was to have no policy and for almost two years appeased the slaveholding border states by allowing Union commanders to return fugitive slaves to their owners. Although the Emancipation Proclamation went into effect January 1, 1863, it did not apply to slaves in loyal border states or in sections under Union control in the South. Finally, Congress emancipated the District of Columbia and declared that escaped slaves were contraband rather than property and generals stopped returning them.

Afro-American soldiers were paid only half the salary of white soldiers, and many fought without pay. Over all, there were at least 186,017 Afro-American troopers in the Union Army, with losses of 68,178.[9] Their rallying cry was forty acres and a mule—the same chances given white settlers. Captured by Southern forces, they were almost routinely killed. When Fort Pillow, Tennessee, was captured by southern Major General Nathan Forrest, 300 persons of African descent, including women and children, were slaughtered—shot, nailed to logs and burned, and buried alive.[10]

### Charity in the Civil War

Of the 300,000 Union soldiers who died in the Civil War, two-thirds died from infections—typhoid, malaria, and dysentery—rather than battle wounds. The casualty rate on both sides was about 50 percent. The Army Medical Corps was unprepared for such carnage and had fewer that 150 surgeons, some of whom joined the Confederacy. Women stepped into the breech, at first with an interest in "moral regeneration" or "medical charity." Soon, however, at least 3,200 women were tending the wounded alongside doctors. Early in the war, such women, who actually handled men's bodies, were considered little more than prostitutes, but this changed because of the value of their work to the armies. Dr. Elizabeth Blackwell began to train women for combat work, and later Dorothea Dix supervised them as the superintendent of nurses of the Army Medical Corps.[11] Clara Barton, who founded the American Red Cross after the Civil War (1881), organized a facility that secured medicine and supplies, searched for the missing, and nursed the wounded. In 1864 she was formally appointed the superintendent of nurses for the Army of the James.

Middle-class northern women were most concerned about the destitute dependents of soldiers, and they established more than twenty thousand female aid societies to relieve the poor and sew clothes for soldiers. Then, looking at conditions on the battlefield, a group of women from the best families in New York—Blackwell, Schuyler/Hamilton, Roosevelt, Astor, Stuyvestant—formed the Women's Central Association of Relief to improve conditions on the battlefield. The group gained official Union recognition and evolved into the U.S. Sanitary Commission, a private agency. Schools, newspapers, theaters, private donors, and a series of "sanitary fairs" contributed $50 million to support it. The commission inspected camps and hospitals, transported the wounded, provided food and clothing on the battlefront, and arranged special relief for dependents. It constructed new buildings to provide accommodations for bathing, washing, and the sanitary disposal of wastes, and developed new techniques to evacuate the wounded, including railroad cars with swinging bunks, operating rooms, and quarters for nurses and surgeons.[12] It also set up an entire fleet of floating hospitals for coastal and river work, and developed a massive campaign against scurvy by asking women to collect lemons, potatoes, dried fruit, onions, and pickled vegetables. Special projects helped the "walking wounded" by distributing paper and envelopes to write home; collecting vital statistics; obtaining back pay and removing false charges of desertion from records; and establishing soldiers' homes in leading cities where transient soldiers could find food and lodging. Over the period of the war, the commission served more than 4.5 million meals and furnished more than 1 million men with places to sleep.[13] It aided both Union and Southern soldiers in prison camps.

## AFTER THE CIVIL WAR

### The Freedmen's Bureau

In 1862, ten thousand slaves were left to fend for themselves when the Union defeated Confederate forces at Port Royal. To aid them, Lincoln authorized two volunteer organizations—the National Freedman's Relief Association of New York and the Boston Education Commission—to distribute food and clothing, rehabilitate abandoned and pillaged homes, establish schools for black children, and use free labor in cotton cultivation. The Freedmen's Bureau was established on the Port Royal model. Located in the War Department from which it drew food, clothing, and medical supplies, it was the first *federal* welfare agency in the United States. In 1866 it was renewed for two years over President Johnson's veto, with an allotment of $6.9 million. Extended until 1872, it helped repair the damages of the Civil War for all the needy in the South regardless of race or wartime loyalties.

Thousands of white southerners as well as freed slaves relied on the Freedmen's Bureau for relief, for need was the only criterion for eligibility. There were no residence requirements because of the great displacement caused by the war. A comprehensive family agency, it provided food, shelter, and clothing; counseling to restore family relationships; advocacy for children; and free medical care and employment services, including training. It also distributed land and building materials at minimal amounts; established institutions for the orphaned and elderly and opened more than four thousand schools for children of both races. Further, it became an agency for civil rights advice and advocacy.

In its first three years, the bureau distributed 18.3 million rations, of which about 5.2 went to white people. By the end of its fourth year, 21 million rations had been distributed, with 6 million going to white people. The bureau either helped found or supported Howard, Atlanta, and Fisk universities, Hampton Institute, and Talladega College.[14] Its most important impacts for social welfare, aside from its overarching federal nature, were that it was a model for private and public cooperation, and that it required high standards of accountability from its cooperating agencies.

### Services for Veterans

Over 2 million men served in the Union forces, with a casualty rate of 43 percent. For them, but not for survivors of the Confederate army of 781,000 men (casualty rate 52 percent), the government undertook a wide range of services. In March 1865 Lincoln nationalized military and naval asylums for totally disabled officers and voluntary servicemen. Later, the government built and operated a group of national homes for veterans in economic distress because of wartime disabilities. Veterans' homes in the South served only Union veterans, while Southern states provided pensions, outdoor relief, and institutions for the disabled and orphaned children of Confederate veterans.

Over the next 25 years, the federal government liberalized eligibility for veterans' services and increased the level of benefits. In 1866, it spent $15 million for veterans' pensions, increasing in 1882 to $30 million and in 1889 to $86 million. In 1890, Congress passed the Dependent Pension Act to keep Union veterans who had served at least ninety days (and their wives) from going to poorhouses or becoming public dependents. By 1898, expenditures for veterans had tripled, covering over 745,000 persons, with federal and state governments providing cash payments, medical services, and homes.[15]

## POSTWAR POLITICAL ECONOMY

Before the war states were almost independent "nations," but the Civil War made each a unit of the Union. The victory reinforced economic domination by the industrial North, which now dictated its terms of production and blocked industrialization in the South. The loyal were rewarded: Union veterans got pensions, Northern manufacturers got tariffs, and the people of both West and North got free lands in the West (under the Homestead Act of 1864). Railroad promoters received land grants that tied West and North together and ensured that the flow of commerce would bypass the South.[16] Finally, although local laws continued to block equality for people of color, slavery ended, and federal civil rights for Afro-American men were instituted.

The war brought wealth and power to Northern industrialists. New markets opened in the expanding West and the rebuilding South, and Eastern banks and stock markets established credit to aid in the accumulation of capital. Corporate pools, trusts, holding companies, and monopolies appeared, and free market competition declined. Dye and Zeigler say that

> as business became increasingly national in scope, only the strongest or the most unscrupulous survived. Total output and total capital investment increased while ownership became concentrated and small competitors disappeared. Monopolies emerged, and great family fortunes developed.[17]

Capital investment in manufacturing nearly quadrupled in the twenty years following 1879 (at $2.5 billion) and reached $11.5 billion in 1904.[18] While in 1860 there were 140,000 factories and 1 million laborers in the work force; by 1900 factories increased to 208,000 with a work force of 4.7 million laborers. Manufactured products increased in value from $1.8 billion to $11 billion, and the gross national product nearly tripled ($6.7 billion in 1869 to $17.0 billion in 1900).[19] Taxes and tariffs protected the small wealthy elite of the nation.

The federal government tried to limit monopoly building by passing the Interstate Commerce Act (1887) in an effort to control railroad barons. By 1890 fourteen states and territories had antimonopoly laws, and thirteen states had antitrust laws. However, these and the Sherman Anti-Trust Act of 1890 were mostly ineffective. In 1884 the Bureau of Labor Statistics was formed to collect information on the subject of labor, its relation to capital, and earnings, and in 1889 problems of farmers led to the Department of Agriculture being upgraded to cabinet status.

The large low-wage labor force—immigrants, Afro-Americans, women, widows, and children—aided national growth, though these population groups profited little from it. Industrial workers, including women and children, worked a six-day week, 12 to 14 hours a day, for one or two dollars per week. Periods of unemployment were frequent in cities, and agricultural workers faced floods, blizzards, and droughts. Two major depressions, in 1873–78 and 1893–98, threw hundreds of thousands of people out of work.[20] In 1893–94, 40 percent of the factories in the country shut down. Fifty to 66 percent of working families were poor and 33 percent lived in abject poverty. Labor armies, such as Kelly's and Coxey's (1894), marched on Washington to demand jobs.

## LABOR AND UNIONIZATION

*Women.* During the war, women had entered the labor market in great numbers—almost 300,000 of them, earning about one-third the wages of men. The government hired many in post office and clerk jobs, where they earned an average of $300 a year less than men for the same jobs. They also sewed for the government, obtaining cut fabric from government warehouses and returning finished clothes for a fixed price.[21] By 1879, 70 percent of all women workers were domestics, and one-fourth of all nonfarm workers were women. By 1890, 4 million women ages 14 and up were employed—18 percent of the female population and 17 percent of the labor force. A decade later, 5 million were working, especially women of color and the foreign born. Many were married. When the typewriter came into general use in the 1890s, women who before had refused to work alongside immigrant women or in factories took jobs in offices, earning as much as $7.00 a week.[22]

Women were subject to many kinds of exploitation but seldom complained for fear of losing their jobs. In the garment industry, for example, bosses made "mistakes" in computing piecework; fined them for singing, talking, laughing, or washing; and charged for everything they used—machinery, electricity, needles, thread, drinking water, washrooms. The price for needles was 25 percent more than bosses paid, and for electricity 20 percent more. They were charged 325 to 400 percent above the cost of materials, and often had to give sexual favors in return for the job, a raise, or a better position.[23]

*Tramps.*    One of the most problematic issues of the time was that of "tramps." Men out of work began traveling the country looking for jobs, asking for handouts, and staying temporarily in poorhouses. The Civil War had taught them that tramping was no worse than bivouac duty, where they had camped out and lived off the land. Although American generosity dictated that to refuse food to a wanderer was the worst form of meanness, a massive fear of tramps began to shake the nation.

> It was the context as well as the quantity of population movement—increased labor, militancy, and the unmistakable emergence of an industrial proletariat—that prompted respectable citizens to transform unemployed, wandering, hungry, and perhaps often angry men into a new and menacing class called tramps.[24]

Professor Francis Wayland of Yale helped to legitimate public hatred of tramps by writing that tramping was not the inability to find employment but the unwillingness to work, and that tramps were labor agitators who stirred up discontent, preached revolution, and threatened the political and social stability of America. He called tramps "a disease, a virus of demoralization infecting the will of the working class."[25] In fact, working people were joining together in what might have become a revolution against the great corporations and monopolies. The abolition of outdoor relief and the call for imprisonment of tramps was related to the control of this union.

> Nineteenth century discussions of pauperism either omitted or rejected the impact of depressions, economic cycles, seasonal unemployment, and technological change on the ability of men to find work . . . [and] refused to acknowledge that most tramps were men on the road only a short time seeking work, not a permanent and dangerous class.[26]

*Labor Unions.*    While labor unions had been agitating for labor reform from the early 1820s, the war and free land in the West had all but ended their activity. After the war, American unions began once more to gain strength. The first National Labor Council was called by craft unions in 1866, and in 1878 the International Labor Union was formed (it ended in 1882). Farmers organized to prevent railroad robber barons from taking their lands, and by 1875 there were 30,000 local granges with a membership of 2.5 million. More than 1 million Afro-American farmers organized the Colored Farmer's Alliance in union with the populist grange movement.

The Knights of Labor formed in 1869, gaining 50,000 members by 1883 and 700,000 by 1886.[27] It demanded an 8-hour day, equal pay for equal work, an end to child labor, and cooperation among workers. Teachers, farmers, and even housewives formed their own locals and sent delegates to the general assembly. Women were welcomed in the Knights of Labor, which accepted everyone but bankers, lawyers, gamblers, and owners of stock. In 1886, women constituted 10 percent of its 500,000 members, with 200 separate locals ranging from housewives and washwomen to farmers and factory workers. However, the Knights of Labor became identified with radicalism and, beset by internal turmoil, its membership dropped to 100,000 by 1890.

One of the most important unions for women was the Working Women's Protective Union, formed by women of all classes. Until 1894 it provided legal services for victimized women, built boarding houses and protective shelters for women, placed nearly two thousand women in jobs each year, and collected unpaid wages for them.[28] Afro-American women formed their own unions, which were welcomed into the National Colored Labor Union at its founding in 1869.

The American Federation of Labor, created in 1881, was a federation of craftsmen and artisans and welcomed neither laborers nor women. Although its national policy admitted women, locals generally did not, and the few that did would not seek equal pay. In fact, the AFL sought to get women out of the labor force through protective legislation, proposed in both 1892 and 1894. While the AFL claimed that the 8-hour workday and the prohibition of female employment on foot-powered machinery were aimed at "protecting" weak women, these rules actually were aimed at taking women out of better-paying jobs. Berch says

> The leading figure in AFL's anti-women worker campaign was . . . president Samuel Gompers . . . [who contended] that the wife as a wage-earner is a disadvantage economically considered, and socially is unnecessary.[29]

## POPULATION, IMMIGRATION, AND THE PEOPLE

### White Immigration and Black Migration

During the war, immigration was encouraged and immigrants were excused from military service to staff the factories or secure the West. From 1870 to 1900, the U.S. population more than doubled, from 31.5 million to 76 million. Nearly 14 million of this increase—a third of population growth—was from immigration.[30] Migration to the cities increased: In

1860, 20 percent of the population was in the cities, but forty years later, 40 percent was urban. By 1900 nonfarm employment was substantially in excess of farm employment: In a labor force of 29 million workers, 18 million were nonfarm workers.[31] The percentage of Afro-Americans in the population remained stable: 13 percent in 1865 and 12 percent in 1900. Their in-migration to the north was limited during this period: In 1860, there were 156,000 in the East, 184,000 in the North Central states, and 4 million in the South. By 1900, there were only 385,000 in the East and 175,000 in the North Central states, while the southern Afro-American population had reached 8 million.[32]

The presence of new ethnic and religious groups, along with freed slaves, brought new dilemmas of racism, religious discrimination, and ethnocentrism or nativism. Immigrant Italian Catholics refused to adopt the new (Protestant) ways of America, keeping their language, religion, and native customs intact. Often, immigrants saved enough money to bring kin and even entire villages to America, where they developed their own churches and schools. Political exiles, such as Jews, forced from their German, Russian, and Austro-Hungarian homelands, brought new and disturbing ideas of political freedom with them—socialism and the right of workers to share in profits.

### Oriental Immigrants

Chinese men began to immigrate to America in 1820, but women were rarely allowed in. Nearly all these immigrants came from seven districts in southern China, in the province of Kwangtung near Canton. The Chinese knew little about current wages and so were easy to exploit, but they were unwilling to return to China because poverty there was so desperate. Their immigration continued to be encouraged for a short time after the Civil War when the Central Pacific Railroad, finding itself behind the Union Pacific, began to hire them from Western mines and directly from China. During the 1870s Chinese men were almost one quarter of the wage laborers in California.[33]

However, the United States was in the midst of a great economic depression in these decades, and the Chinese were perceived as taking jobs that otherwise white men might have. They were forced out of mining by whites and, after the intercontinental railroad was completed, lost construction jobs also. In a time of unionization, "anticoolie" unions were formed: the United Brothers of California and the Anti-Chinese Union of San Francisco in 1876; the California Workingmen's Party in 1877. Samuel Gompers of the AFL declared that the Chinese worked for depressed wages and were beyond the pale of labor organization, and the International Workingmen's Association and the Knights of Labor advocated an end to their immigration. Republican candidate Rutherford B. Hayes put an anti-Chinese plank in his platform.

Violence marked anti-Chinese activities throughout the Civil War decade, but after 1870 it became sustained and coordinated. Laws were passed regulating Chinese shrimp catches, prohibiting the hiring of Chinese by corporations and municipal works, authorizing the removal of

Chinese residents from city boundaries, prohibiting them from engaging in fishing, denying them licenses for businesses or occupations, prohibiting attendance at public schools, and finally stopping all Chinese immigration via the Exclusion Acts of 1880. In 1871 a massacre took place in Los Angeles in which twenty-two Chinese were killed and hundreds were driven from their homes. "Riot Night" in San Francisco, on July 23, 1877, began when a crowd listening to labor organizers erupted into violence against the Chinese, and over the next three days burned Chinese laundries and homes, attacked a steamship company that brought Chinese to America, and did half a million dollars' worth of damage before police, army troops, the navy, and about five thousand citizens ended the riot.[34]

Between 1879 and 1882, Congress passed two bills suspending Chinese immigration, but both were vetoed because they violated international treaties with China. In 1882 the first Chinese Exclusion Act was passed, suspending immigration for ten years and barring Chinese aliens from citizenship. Renewed in 1892 and made permanent in 1904, it was not repealed until 1943, when the Chinese were America's allies in World War II. The Geary Act of 1892 and the McCreary Amendment of 1893 required all Chinese to carry certificates of residence with identifying photographs or be subject to arrest and deportation.[35] The Immigration Acts of 1924 virtually ended Chinese and other Oriental immigration until 1968.

Social Darwinism, racism, and economic motivation made Chinese the targets of discrimination and violence from their first immigration. Local ordinances prohibited them from working in some areas, taxed them discriminately, and controlled them with mob violence—they were beaten, burned, shot, and lynched. By 1900, 57 percent of Orientals in the United States, primarily Chinese, were in domestic service.[36] They became a middleman minority in the West, in trade and commerce, as agents, labor contractors, rent collectors, money lenders, and brokers—people with easily liquidated assets. Many invested in laundries, for there they owned businesses rather than having to sell their labor. Few white protectors or social reformers took their part, probably because reformers, if they cared, were in the East, and the frontier West had few laws to control violence.

The Chinese brought with them traditions of mutual aid: trade guilds that were both work and birthright associations giving fraternal welfare; Hui Kuans, or linguistic divisions; class or lineage clubs and organizations; and "tongs," voluntary associations based on mutual interests, primarily protection and the provision of illegal goods such as drugs and prostitutes. In great part the welfare efforts were aimed at financing education for the young. Another Chinese welfare device was the Rotating Credit Association, where a core of participants each made a contribution and then each contributor got all or a part of the amount.

### Native Americans after the War

Railroads were at the heart of American expansionism and created new elites of robber barons who took land from farmers and decimated the resources of Native Americans. By 1865 there were 35,000 miles of railroads, four years later the transcontinental railroad was completed, and by 1900 there were 175,000 miles of railroad across the United States. For Native Americans, the railroads meant, often, starvation as the great herds of bison were killed off for sport.

In 1871, the federal government in effect eliminated the political rights of Native Americans by declaring them wards of the federal government and refusing to recognize them as independent nations. It was cheaper to feed them than to kill them—a study in 1870 estimated the cost per dead Native American was about $1 million. The Allotment Act of 1887, called the Dawes Act, further destroyed their cultures by dividing the land—approximately 140 million acres—among individual freehold farmers. Many quickly sold or were cheated out of their allotments, and some 90 million acres of the best land was transferred to whites while 90,000 Native Americans were left landless. The Bureau of Indian Affairs was responsible, through Indian Agents, for supplies, education, instruction in farming, and supervision of lands. They were also to distribute food when times were hard. However, by the 1880s, Indian agents were notoriously corrupt and incompetent, withholding supplies to sell for profit. In some agency towns, agents were near-dictators, helping white settlers to take over Native American land. A member of the Assiniboine testified before a congressional committee that

> They gave us rations once a week, just enough to last one day, and the Indians they started to eat their pet dogs. After they ate all their dogs up they started to eat their ponies. All this time the Indian Bureau had a warehouse full of grub. . . . Early that spring in 1884 I saw the dead bodies of the Indians wrapped in blankets and piled up like cordwood . . . the other Indians were so weak they could not bury their dead; what were left were nothing but skeletons.[37]

Well-wishing reformers won government support to open boarding schools for Native American children, taking them from their parents and interrupting the child-rearing process to "Americanize" them. In 1887 the government appropriated $1.2 million to the Bureau of Indian Affairs and to missionary groups for 227 boarding schools to enroll 14,300 children.[38] Placed there for four to eight years, the children were subjected to strict "moral" discipline, their hair was cut to end their "heathen" ways, and they were not allowed to see their parents for months.

One result of the oppression and decimation of Native American societies was the rise of a new religion—the Ghost Dance. It was developed by a Paiute Messiah named Wovoka but also called Jack Wilson, possibly a descendant of Tecumseh's brother, the Prophet. It taught that white men would disappear and that living and dead Native Americans would be reunited. In 1889 there was a resurgence of the Ghost Dance, and it became more militant as the injustices of the white man were counted: the extermination of the bison, the removal West of the many Eastern societies, confinement on reservations where the people were at the mercy of Indian agents, and the stealing of their land. Some Ghost Dance followers began to preach active resistance to the whites, and apprehensive white authorities alerted the military to stop their assemblies.[39]

In 1890, the U.S. Cavalry mistook a gathering of Sioux Ghost Dancers at Wounded Knee, South Dakota, for an Indian uprising. Nearly three hundred Sioux, including women and children, were massacred. The soldiers continued to kill until almost everyone was murdered. A survivor, Black Elk, said

> Men and women and children were heaped and scattered all over the flat at the bottom of the little hill where the soldiers had their wagon-guns, and westward up the dry gulch all the way to the high ridge, the dead women and children and babies were scattered. . . . The snow drifted deep in the crooked gulch, and it was one long grave of butchered women and children and babies, who were only trying to run away.[40]

This was only one massacre. Abetted by the new technology of the Gatling gun, federal soldiers, vigilantes, and settlers set about genocide. Not until after World War I was any real thought given to the rights of Native Americans, and by this time, their lives, societies, and cultures were all but lost.

### Emancipation and the Plight of the Freedmen

In the South, cities were in ruin, transportation lines destroyed, and fields barren. There was no money for seeds, machinery, or livestock, and near famine occurred because of drought and the lack of organized workers. The first concern of Southern states was to get artificial limbs and cash payments to veterans so they could work, and the second was to provide for war orphans. States established central public welfare offices to distribute food and clothes to poor whites but gave nothing to the impoverished freedmen. As in fourteenth-century Europe as feudalism fell, so now former slaves were left without even the small protections of food and shelter in the winter.

Poor white laborers returned to the South to find themselves in competition for work with four million freedmen. Cotton mills came to the South, and a Populist alliance of freed slaves and white laborers was in the making. However, because this threatened white elite political and economic control, southern capitalists encouraged race hatred and pitted white worker against black. Many white laborers believed that emancipation itself was a plot of northern capital to lower wages and enlarge its labor pool.[41] Entrepreneurs—carpetbaggers—coming from the North either to help the freed slaves or to cheat them aggravated the situation.

For Afro-Americans, the change from slavery to wage-earning status meant that tens of thousands of people died from starvation, disease, and privation. For example, in the years immediately following the war, one-fourth of all infants in some communities died in their first year and life expectancy declined by 10 percent.[42] Before the war, the plantation had assured stability; after the war, tenant farming, sharecropping, and the independent ownership of small farms became a tenuous way of life. Afro-Americans from 1860 to 1900 never owned more than 6 percent of the land of the rural south.[43]

During Reconstruction (1867–1877) in the South, Senator Charles Sumner and House Representative Thaddeus Stevens were the strongest supporters of freedmen. Bennett says, in fact, that slaves owed their freedom more to these two than to Lincoln.[44] Lincoln's plan for Reconstruction included giving free land to freed persons, but his assassination left Reconstruction in the hands of easily influenced Andrew Johnson. Johnson set out to appease plantation owners, first by pardoning them and then demanding that former slaves turn over their land to the former owners. He refused to break up plantations and turned ex-slaves over to former masters with no protections against reprisals. Appalled, Stevens gained the support of Congress to put the South under military control until free elections could be held. Since Afro-Americans outnumbered whites in Mississippi, South Carolina, Louisiana, and Florida, they were elected as governors and lieutenant governors, secretaries of state, supreme court judges, and state treasurers. In their new positions they helped to formulate new state constitutions for the southern states.

Congress enacted the Fourteenth and Fifteenth amendments, which assured citizenship and the right to vote to Afro-Americans and guaranteed their rights to life, liberty, and the pursuit of happiness. Before long, however, their leaders were accused of corruption and of being led by Northern carpetbaggers and scalawags. At least five thousand leaders were killed, and many of those elected were refused seats. Bennett maintains that their greatest crime was the violation of the American caste system

> If there was anything Southern whites feared more than a bad Negro government, it was a good Negro government.[45]

Revenge became the keynote of the South. Retaliation against Afro-American Union veterans was common: In Memphis in 1866, forty-six veterans were killed and seventy-five were wounded in a Memphis raid, five women were raped, and twelve schools and four churches were burned. In New Orleans, thirty-five veterans were killed and over one hundred wounded. The Ku Klux Klan held its first national meeting in Nashville in April 1867, under the leadership of Nathan Bedford Forrest, of the Fort Pillow massacre. Soon the South was honeycombed with chapters: the Knights of the White Camelia, Red Shirts, White League, Mother's Little Helpers, and the Baseball Club of the First Baptist Church.[46] Many Ku Klux Klan members were well-known politicians and landowners in the community. Any atrocity against Afro-Americans was permitted, from raiding their holdings to raping the women, from castrating men to lynching and burning them. There was no protection from the Ku Klux Klan except submission, and often that was not enough. Members of the Klan legitimated their actions by swearing devotion to the flag, to "racial purity" (particularly of white women), and to Christianity. One lynching took place every two days or so, approximately one hundred per year in the 1880s and 1890s.[47] Newspapers advertised lynchings in advance, and crowds came on chartered trains to see them. People also were roasted alive over slow fires and otherwise mutilated. Although there was some opposition to lynching, the violence and horror of this reign of terror left most people in too much fear to protest or even to flee.

The presidential race between Rutherford B. Hayes and Democrat Samuel J. Tilden was crucial in the treatment of freed persons. Elections were disputed in South Carolina, Florida, and Louisiana. Though the Electoral Commission upheld Hayes's claim to the states, Democrats threatened to hold up election results past the day of inauguration, leaving the country presidentless unless Hayes agreed to the South's demands for "home rule"—the right to deal with Afro-Americans as they chose. Upon this agreement, he was elected. Federal troops were withdrawn from the South in 1877, and the racial caste system was established, including the exclusion of Afro-Americans from nearly all trades except agrarian labor and domestic service, from education (*Plessy* v. *Ferguson*, 1896), and from the political process.

Soon new laws—"Black Codes"—were passed in all former Confederate states except Tennessee. They denied Afro-Americans property rights, specified the work they could do, and forbade work as artisans and mechanics. Orphans or children whose parents were judged unable to care for them were apprenticed, often to their former masters, with no guarantees of food, clothing, or shelter such as white apprenticed children had. Every Afro-American needed a written labor contract or a license from the police to carry with them. While white unemployed workers were "unemployed," unemployed Afro-Americans were "vagrants" who could be tried and sent to prison. Other charges for which they could be imprisoned were idleness, quitting a job or making too much money, insulting gestures, or "disrespect" —women who resisted sexual attacks by white men were "disrespectful." Although victims of these laws could appeal, in white courts they seldom won. Black codes were ignored by a federal government eager to pacify the Southern gentry.

Once convicted, Afro-American men or women were likely to be sentenced to chain gangs, their labor sold to employers or factories or given for local governmental projects for leases of ten to twenty years. The convict lease system—first established in Georgia—was profitable to both employers and state, and there came to be a "compelling economic reason for increasing the prison population."[48] Chain gangs were often used as "schools" for "undisciplined" young Afro-Americans who had grown up since slavery. Chains welded to their bodies, men and women together— there was no sex discrimination in prison—they lived in unbelievable conditions, and 30 percent of those given over to state overseers died. Davis says

Whereas the slaveholders had recognized limits to the cruelty with which they exploited their "valuable" human property, no such cautions were necessary for the postwar planters who rented black convicts for relatively short terms. In many cases sick convicts are made to toil until they drop dead in their tracks.[49]

Bennett adds

> After a study of Southern chain gangs, Fletcher Green, a modern scholar, concluded that they had no parallel except in the persecutions of the Middle Ages and the concentration camps of Nazi Germany.[50]

Those who learned to live under the black codes were, in a short time, once more subservient tenant farmers on land they had briefly owned. Seventy-five percent of Afro-American farmers became tenant farmers, and though they were paid for the food or cotton they produced, the cost of seed, equipment, housing, and food purchased from the landowner kept them in debt, often for life. This indebtedness produced a new form of quasi-slavery.

Seeing the continued retribution against freed persons and hoping to lessen it, Booker T. Washington, president of Tuskegee Institute (which he built), declared there must be some kinds of segregation. He used the parable of the open hand with separate but equal fingers, one that could close in a fist for common causes, and said that questions of social equality were extremist folly. This speech, called the Atlanta Compromise, asked for support for education, an end to killing, and economic opportunity for Afro-Americans. Although his hoped-for benefits did not appear, his "separate but equal" appeal helped to justify enactment of Jim Crow laws throughout the South.[51] Upheld by the Supreme Court in 1875, such laws asserted that individuals, though not states, could legally discriminate against Afro-Americans.

Jim Crow laws limited areas in which Afro-Americans could live, and Jim Crow sections appeared in both northern and southern towns. In addition, housing, facilities, education, medical treatment, and burial became segregated. Literacy, property, and poll tax tests kept Afro-Americans from voting, as did the "grandfather clause," which denied the vote to people whose grandfathers had not voted. This ended Afro-American political power—for example, in 1896 there were 130,344 Afro-American voters in Louisiana, but in 1900, two years after the grandfather clause was passed, only 5,320 voted.

## "TRUE WOMANHOOD"

After the Civil War, white middle- and upper-class career women formed a new generation of educated women. Seventy-five percent of college women who graduated before 1900 remained single, many moving into settlement work or casework. Freed by new homemaking technologies—washing machines, nonfire cookers, vacuum cleaners—and new amenities that freed them from food preparation—canned food, bread cheaper to buy than to bake—middle-class women aspired to paid work, social reform, and college. Married women began to enter the labor force in great numbers, and by 1890 women comprised 18 percent of the labor force.[52]

Puritan upbringings and Protestant beliefs still dominated American thought, and a moral outcry was raised against women who, by working outside the home, flaunted the "natural order." Part of this was economic, for women now controlled their own money and undercut men's wages in the marketplace. However, a great deal had to do with the new definitions of the "virtuous" woman. The result was the *Cult of True Womanhood*, which taught that women were more highly evolved spiritually than were men, as evidenced by their obvious lack of sexual desire,[53] and that their unique attributes—compassion, nurturance, and morality—"unfitted them for competitive economic struggle."[54] Therefore, although their natural place was in the home, women—especially unmarried women—could move into the outside world, making it purer and more moral by attacking uncleanness and immorality. Moral issues—prohibition, prostitution, criminality, prison improvement, pure food and drug laws, child labor, public sewers, corruption in government, and peace, for example—were the new province of "true womanhood."[55]

Across the nation, professional women, ethnic women, Afro-American women, and working women began to form thousands of clubs, and by the late 1880s coalesced into national organizations such as the National Council of Clubs and the General Federation of Women's Clubs. By 1920 the latter had nearly a million members active in improving the social environment, investigating sanitation and government corruption; raising money for worthy causes such as hospitals, schools, or homes for the aged; or becoming involved in the labor struggles of wage-earning women. Wealthy women, free to use their money as they wished, often sponsored meetings and speeches and donated their money profusely to good causes, especially those involved in health care. (For example, between 1885 and 1889, five new nursing schools were created in Chicago, founded and funded by women donors.)

Afro-American women's clubs supported the new class of working women by giving them places to live, a community of safety, and emotional and spiritual help. Of the 2.7 million Afro-American women over the age of 10, a million worked for wages: nearly 39 percent in agriculture, 30.8 in domestic service, 15.6 percent as laundresses, and 2.8 percent in manufacturing.[56] Despite discrimination, they still managed to enter some professions. Charlotte E. Ray (1850–1911) became the first Afro-American woman lawyer to practice in the United States, receiving her law degree from Howard University. When prejudice forced her from the practice, she turned to teaching. Caroline V. Still became a doctor, and Anna J. Cooper became a teacher in Washington, D.C. Fannie Barrier Williams founded the first school for Afro-American nurses.

In 1874 the first truly national women's organization was born—the Women's Christian Temperance Union (WCTU). In it, alcohol was considered not only as the downfall of families but the support of powerful political machines, since saloons were the meeting places of political bosses. Its major purposes were to protect women from drunken husbands and fathers and protect the sanctity of the home. In twenty years the WCTU gained more than 200,000 members.

The organization rose to prominence under the leadership of chief organizer Frances Willard (1839–1898), its president for twenty years (beginning in 1879). Called from the presidency of the Women's College of Northwestern University, Willard challenged WCTU's conservative leadership and linked suffrage and temperance, saying that women could stop the liquor traffic if they had the vote. She also fought the national drug trade from 1883 on, and any reform that would help women and children interested her. She lobbied for women's suffrage, recovery homes for alcoholic women, and reform schools for juvenile offenders. She helped to organize the General Federation of Women's Clubs in 1889 and laid the groundwork for the National Council of Women. By her death in 1898, WCTU had a membership of nearly a quarter million adults and almost as many in youth groups.[57] At that time, a serious split developed between suffrage forces and antiliquor forces and WCTU divorced itself from the suffrage issue.

Most women's issues were in some way connected with women's sexuality and men's attempt to control it. The Cult of True Womanhood, the arguments against women's suffrage, the extension of women's "sphere" into public service, and the fight against immorality—particularly sexual immorality—were both sexist and sexual in nature. Important influences at issue were Freud's interpretation of women's psychology, the moral outrage against contraception, and the spread of venereal disease throughout the middle-class population.

Freud's studies of the psychology of women were influenced by current stereotypes about women. His research, thus biased, gave "scientific" reasons for the "place of women" at the turn of the century. Among his most influential beliefs were that women could overcome their basic biological inferiority to men by bearing children (especially male children), and that competitive women or those who sought careers had "masculinity complexes" that could be cured by a return to domesticity. Also, wives—of the upper classes—were "pure women," sexually passionless and dependent. They were proper wives, mothers, and moral social reformers. Even obvious signs of their sexuality— pregnancy and childbirth—were finessed away as "duty." If they had to have careers, only those that spread their "womanliness" into society—charity work, teaching, nursing—were acceptable. On the other hand, lower-class women were passionate and sexual, and therefore immoral. Their sexual or economic exploitation was, therefore, legitimate.[58]

Although research by Dr. Clelia Duel Mosher (1863–1940), a pioneer in the study of women's sexuality, indicates that the perception of women as passionless was a male fantasy,[59] this belief was common and strong. For example, Dr. Theophilus Parvin said in 1883,

> I do not believe one bride in a hundred . . . accepts matrimony from any desire for sexual gratification . . . it is with shrinking or even with horror, rather than with desire.[60]

Nathan Hale, Jr., summed up his review of the sexual advice literature at the turn of the century with a similar conclusion:

Many women came to regard marriage as little better than legalized prostitution. Sexual passion became associated almost exclusively with the male, with prostitutes, and women of the lower classes.[61]

Male doctors in that era were so convinced that the "normal" women had no sexual interest that if it occurred they took drastic measures against it, for example, cliterodectomy, ovariectomy, or incarceration in insane asylums. Gynecologists sought to alleviate all kinds of physical and mental conditions through ovariectomies—incurable or obscure pelvic pains, hysteria, weakness, and "temperamentalism." Wives who did not "behave" or submit to the control of their husbands were often subjected to such operations and, given that little anesthesia was available, became docile even at the threat of ovariectomy. When antisepsis and anesthesia made abdominal operations safer and surgeons became more skillful at their tasks, operations to rid women of their "hysteria" became even more common.

Before the discovery of the ovum in 1824, abortion was considered contraception, and there were few restrictions. By 1840 there was an upsurge of abortions, and until the Civil War one-third of the states had no abortion laws. In states where abortion was against the law, doctors rather than women were punished. At the end of the Civil War, when the population of men was decimated, physicians instigated and carried out a campaign against abortion. Forty statutes passed in the period 1860–1890, declaring any interruption of gestation a crime, with the woman considered at fault and acting against God and nature.[62] The severely declining birthrate among white upper classes was another reason for the campaign: Between 1860 and 1910, live births decreased by nearly one-third. The birthrate among Afro-Americans remained high but still declined, while it decreased by 26 percent among immigrant women. This latter inspired more outcries based on Social Darwinism and the duty of white women to produce children so that the United States would not be taken over by the "degenerate classes."

Contraception was also condemned, and women who practiced it were called immoral. As early as 1821 Dr. Charles Knowlton of Boston was prosecuted for writing a book on mechanical and chemical means of contraception,[63] but it did not really become a legal issue until after the Civil War. There was, in fact, a great deal of contraceptive information available—the rhythm method, use of condoms or sponges soaked in antiseptic solutions, intrauterine stem pessaries—but doctors generally refused to discuss it with women. The advice to women who wanted to avoid having children without a good reason was

Get a divorce and vacate the position for some other woman, who is able and willing to fulfill all a wife's duties as well as to enjoy her privileges.[64]

The Comstock Act in 1873 made it illegal to give contraceptive advice, and some physicians were prosecuted under the new law.

The declining birthrate was not solely because of contraception. Rather, much of the decline, as well as infant mortality and blindness and maternal morbidity and mortality, was caused by venereal disease. Barren marriages and "one-child sterility" were often the results of gonorrheal infection, most often in the wife (since doctors colluded with husbands in hiding the infection). One physician, writing in 1910, argued that

> prior to 1850, just 2 percent of our native-born white women were sterile, whereas by 1900 the ratio had increased to one in five. Venereal disease . . . was behind this. . . . Other physicians presented figures purporting to show that from 20 to 75 percent of childless marriages were the result of venereal disease-induced sterility.[65]

The German physician Emil Noeggerath stated in 1879 that most reproductive diseases were caused by gonorrhea. Others estimated that up to 75 percent of all major gynecological surgery was because of gonorrhea.[66]

Unfortunately, the attack against venereal disease became an attack against prostitutes. Prostitution was one way women could survive: It paid better than most low-wage jobs they could find, even though a prostitute's life expectancy was only four years. Many immigrant women, unable to find jobs, engaged in "casual prostitution" until they could find work. Many other women became unwilling prostitutes under the hard hands of their former lovers or white slavers who sold them in cities around the world. Seldom if ever were the men who frequented prostitutes blamed for carrying disease back to their wives; in fact, men were encouraged to take sexual satisfaction elsewhere rather than to "bother" their "pure" wives. In 1874 Dr. Marion Sims, president of the American Medical Association, recommended national regulation and licensure of prostitution to control venereal disease. However, this was opposed by people who believed regulation would legitimate prostitution and open up legal "red light" districts and by feminists, who argued that women would be prosecuted for proliferation of disease rather than the men who used them.

## EMERGING PHILOSOPHIES AND SOCIAL WELFARE

Two ideals influenced the development of social welfare after the Civil War. The first was Social Darwinism, which defined the worthy and moral as those who succeeded economically. Charity organization societies followed this "scientific" ideal, relying also on the emerging sciences of genetics, sociology, administrative management, and psychology. The second ideal was the populist democratic/socialist movement influenced by the economic philosophy of Karl Marx and Friedrich Engels, the British Fabian Socialist movement, and the Social Gospel movement. Marxism posited that the government was a tool of the economic elite in exploiting workers while the Fabians sought collective ownership of the means of production. The Social Gospel movement, led by Protestants, wanted social reform through a return to the basics of Christianity. From 1870 on, populism challenged capitalism, calling it "the science of extortion, the gentle art of grinding the faces of the poor."[67] Populism was one inspiration for labor unions, the grange movement, women's clubs, and, in social welfare, the settlement house movement.

## Social Darwinism and the Charity Organization Society

Throughout the 1800s, some social reformers argued that poverty was caused not by personal deviance but by social and economic structures arising from industrialization. However, conservativism and work morality continued to have a greater impact than did social reform on employment practices and social welfare. New scientific knowledge about genetics and psychology provided "proofs" that, indeed, the causes of deviance (including poverty) lay within the individual. Social Darwinism taught that white Anglo-Saxons (preferably Protestants from northern Europe) were genetically better than people of other ethnicities. Moreover, a better world could be created by "containing" people afflicted with problems such as poverty; mental, emotional, or physical disabilities; or not being white. Nature should be allowed to take its course in ridding society of such defective people and to help them was against God's law. Therefore, science and religion joined in legitimating institutionalization, inadequate poor relief, taking children from families, and in the case of people of color, murder.

Herbert Spencer, an English philosopher with great influence in America between 1870 and 1890, became the spokesman for Social Darwinism, saying

> If they are not sufficiently complete to live, they die, and it is best they should die. . . . The whole effort of nature is to get rid of such, to clear the world of them, and make room for better.[68]

He argued that poor laws provided for the

> artificial preservation of those least able to take care of themselves. The poverty of the incapable, the distresses that come from the imprudent, the starvation of the idle, and those shoulderings aside of the weak by the strong were "the decrees of a large far-seeing benevolence."[69]

The class bias is clear: Social aid takes people out of the labor market, makes them unavailable for work, and thereby undermines the God-given reward—wealth—of nature's fittest. The poor and needy,

> [u]nfit to survive . . . were nevertheless kept alive by humanitarian charity. Far from contributing to the development of mankind and society, they were dead weight—a drag on the movement to ultimate perfection. Consequently, pity for those afflicted with problems was replaced with blame, leading to the creation of an outcast class viewed and treated not with indifference but with contempt.[70]

Helping the poor or deviant went against the efficient operation of the "invisible hand" of the market. Not only the poor were to blame: so were those who helped them. This "guilt by association" works against the social work profession even today.

Social Darwinism became a major creed of the charity organization societies (COSs), which began in London in 1869 and in Boston in 1877 under the leadership of the Reverend S. Humphreys Gurteen. By 1894 there were 92 COSs in the United States, and at the close of 1904, approximately 150. The vast majority were in large cities in the East and North—over 50 were in cities with populations of more than 60,000.[71]

The purpose of COSs was to organize all charities in an area so that needy people could be served but would not be able to get help from more than one charity. To do this, they developed central case registries and forums in which all agencies, including the police, could work closely together on "cases." Paid staff investigated applications for charity, and volunteer "friendly visitors" personally interviewed applicants in what would become casework practice. Volunteer boards determined eligibility and set grants on a case-by-case basis. Systems of accountability were bureaucratized and COSs kept case records to collect social statistics on poverty, unemployment, wages, family expenditures, disease, and working conditions. Wealthy volunteers became difficult to find, and soon paid workers administered COSs in all major cities. By 1892 women workers far outnumbered men and thereafter dominated the leadership and development of the emerging profession of social work.

An explicit goal of the charity organization society movement was to restore the "natural order" of class stratification. It was no coincidence that the movement began at a time of economic turmoil, with massive unemployment, low wages, and people displaced by the war. The burgeoning wealth of the upper classes was salt in the wounds of those without enough to eat, and social disruption was everywhere. The end of the Civil War brought war production layoffs at the same time the labor market was flooded with returning soldiers, new immigrants, war widows, and freed slaves. For the first time in history, unemployment was a national problem. Charity organization societies, developed and maintained by the elite classes, had more than altruism at stake.

Although heredity could not be changed, "moral" environments and treatment could alleviate some of the results of bad heredity. Casework consisted primarily of moral advice, although workers were told not to make moral judgments. Outdoor relief was given only as a last resort because it was material rather than spiritual and "demoralized the poor." Josephine Shaw Lowell (1843–1905), founder of the Charity Organization Society of New York and of many custodial institutions for the retarded, said

> relief-giving . . . seeks material ends by material means, and therefore must fail. . . . For man is a spiritual being, and, if he is to be helped, it must be by spiritual means.[72]

People were encouraged to work even when no work could be found, and severe work tests were given the able-bodied, though at a fair wage. Gambling, intemperance, and vice were attacked as the routes to the disease of pauperism.

COSs helped women and children only if the breadwinner died, and then only if the friendly visitor felt it better to keep the family together. Institutionalization was preferred—mothers to poorhouses and children to orphanages, to "train them away" from the heritage of pauperism. Drunkards' families were not helped unless the drunkard left: Their wives were then considered widows. Deserted families, however, got no help for fear that it would encourage other men to desert. The aged were helped only if they were not to blame for their own destitution. If families were eligible for support, the COS first asked relatives, friends, churches, former employers, and fraternal societies. If that did not work, private donors and charities were approached.

COSs also cooperated with police, often directing their actions toward beggars, vagrants, and wayward husbands. Plain clothes officers often reported daily to the COS. On COS advice, vagrants were sent to houses of correction for two to six months, and then to state farms on indeterminate sentences with a maximum of two years.[73] In addition, COSs worked with public relief agencies, investigating applicants and at times handling the entire public outdoor relief system. Early COSs lobbied for housing reform and worked to bring disease preventative techniques such as vaccinations into the community. They built tuberculosis sanitoriums and fresh air camps for slum children; provided day nurseries and sewing rooms; taught mothers thrift, better health care, and home economics; found employment for men; and lobbied for legislation to discourage vagrancy and vice.[74]

Josephine Shaw Lowell was a major force in the COS movement. During the Civil War, she had worked in the U.S. Sanitary Commission, later becoming chief fund raiser for the National Freedmen's Relief Association of New York. A member of the New York Charities Aid Association, she did research in 1875 on able-bodied beggars, and in 1876 became the first woman member of the New York State Board of Charities. There she reported on the conditions in and administration of jails, almshouses, hospitals, orphanages, and other public institutions. Her call for reform led to the nation's first custodial asylum for mentally retarded women (Newark, New Jersey, in 1885), and a state training school for girls in 1886. She led in founding the New York Charity Organization Society in 1882 and in organizing the Consumers' League of New York in 1890. She also founded the Woman's Municipal League to mobilize politically conscious women behind reform legislation, and, in later days, became a strong supporter of organized labor and a frequent organizer for striker relief. Lowell set the standards for the COS movement. She believed the almshouse or workhouse would become the agency for moral regeneration and training and was instrumental in setting up COS eligibility guidelines.[75]

The most advanced thinking of the time on charity came from Amos G. Warner, a political economist who in 1894 wrote the book *American Charities*. Warner had headed the Baltimore Charity Organization Society and the Public Charities of Washington, D.C. According to his analysis, poverty came not from personal willfulness but from the complex interrelationships of personal and economic factors. The most common causes for relief applications were bad health, illness, industrial accidents, and industrial diseases. Most dependents, he found, were not capable of work. Although unemployment and illness caused almost half the poverty in cases he studied, he still concluded with a list of objective causes of poverty which included "evil associations and unwise philanthropy—which caused indolence and a variety of unhealthy appetites."[76]

By 1900, COS goals and delivery of services had changed significantly. Although in 1895 a majority in principle had no general fund for material relief, by 1901, of seventy-five societies, all but six provided outdoor relief in urgent cases from either emergency or general funds. By 1904, about half the charity organization societies maintained funds for relief.[77] The careful data workers had collected demonstrated clearly that poverty's causes were societal rather than personal in nature. Social work was becoming a profession, with casework practice and both personal and social diagnoses—the beginning of the "person-in-situation" focus of today's profession. Both United Funds and the Family Service Association came directly from the Charity Organization Society.

### Private Interest Agencies

A multitude of other private agencies aimed at moral regeneration of the poor got their start or grew during the decades after the Civil War. By 1880 there were at least thirty nondenominational missions in city slums, along with orphanages, hospitals, homes for the aged, and homes or institutions to take in mothers or immigrants. Some aimed at religious conversion and/or help for tramps—among them the Salvation Army and Volunteers of America. Others, such as Crittenton Services, focused on the problems of women, unwanted pregnancy, prostitution, or temperance.

William Booth founded the Salvation Army in London shortly after the Civil War. His daughter, Evangeline Cory Booth (1865–1950) grew up in Salvation Army work and in England became known as the White Angel of the Slums. In 1889, at the age of 23, she took command of all Salvation Army forces in London and surrounding areas. Her older brother Ballington and his wife Maud commanded the Salvation Army in the United States. When they broke away to found the Volunteers of America, Evangeline took temporary leadership until her sister (Emma Booth-Tucker) and brother-in-law took charge. Evangeline took over the organization in Canada until Emma died (1904) and then returned to lead the U.S. forces, where she proved herself a fine administrator and efficient money raiser. She set up a disaster relief service following the San Francisco earthquake and later instituted hospitals for unwed mothers, a chain of residences for working women, and homes for the aged. During World War I she set up canteens for soldiers, earning the Distinguished Service Medal for her work.[78]

Evangeline's sister-in-law Maud Ballington Booth joined the Salvation Army in 1882. After pioneering work in the London slums, she and her husband, Ballington Booth, moved to the United States and successfully established the U.S. Salvation Army. After being ordered by William Booth to another post, they resigned and organized the Volunteers of America (1896). While Ballington concentrated on the Volunteers of America, Maud organized the Volunteer Prison League to establish rehabilitation missions in prisons throughout the nation. In addition, she established welfare programs for prisoners' families, postrelease employment counseling, and half-way houses, all supported by contributions from her lecture tours.[79]

Crittenton Services began when Charles Crittenton opened four missionary homes for "fallen women" in California. Kate Harwood Waller Barrett (1857–1925), who had been educated in the Florence Nightingale Training School in nursing and attained her medical degree from the Women's Medical College of Georgia in 1892, contacted him because of her interest in the plight of prostitutes and unwed mothers. She opened Crittenton homes for unwed mothers, moving them in the direction of vocational training and skills for motherhood rather than moral proselytizing. In 1895 she established the National Florence Crittenton Mission as vice president in charge of more than fifty semiautonomous homes. Invited to the 1909 White House Conference for Children, she later became a special representative of the Labor Department on a commission investigating moral grounds for the deportation of women aliens.[80]

### Populism and The Settlement House Movement

While COSs sought to differentiate between the classes, using Social Darwinism as a basis, settlement houses sought to reconcile class differences and were opposed to Social Darwinism. The basic settlement house ideal was to have wealthy people move into areas where the poor and disadvantaged lived so that both groups could learn from each other. Canon Samuel Barnett, pastor of the worst parish in London, established the first settlement house there in 1884. Toynbee Hall was based on the Social Gospel movement and attracted middle-class people to emulate Jesus in living among the poor. The first American settlement house was the Neighborhood Guild, established by Dr. Stanton Coit and Charles B. Stover on the Lower East Side of New York with the help of Dr. Jane E. Robers and Jean Fined. In 1889, Jane Addams founded Hull House in Chicago, and Vida Scudder founded the College Settlement, a club for girls, in New York City. Soon Lillian Wald established the Henry Street Settlement, where she taught nursing to immigrant women. From the Henry Street experience a great number of public health services arose, including, in 1893, the Visiting Nurses Association. By 1910, there were more than four hundred settlement houses in the United States, mostly in eastern and midwestern cities.[81]

Settlement houses were run in part by groups that used them, and they emphasized social reform rather than relief or assistance. Three-fourths of settlement workers were women, and most were well educated and dedicated to working on problems of urban poverty.[82] Early sources of funding were wealthy individuals or clubs such as the Junior League, and at first their founders tried to provide "culture" to members—art, music, and lectures, for example. When they found a need, they added new features such as playgrounds, day care, kindergartens, baths, and classes in English literacy. Other services included art exhibits, lectures, and classes in homemaking, cooking, sewing, and shopping, especially for immigrant women who were not used to the facilities available in the United States such as grocery stores and the products they offered—fresh bread, milk, and canned goods. Settlement workers tried to improve housing conditions, organized protests, offered job training and labor searches, supported organized labor, worked against child labor, and fought against corrupt politicians. Over time settlement houses became centers of social reform, and clubs, societies, and political groups such as the Socialist party used them as bases of operation.

The most famous settlement house was Hull House in Chicago, established by Jane Addams and her friend Ellen Gates Starr in 1889 on the pattern of London's Toynbee Hall. It attracted many powerful women in its work. Among them, Jane Addams stands out. In her early years, after graduation from college, she was plagued by ill health. Unable to work, she traveled with her friend Ellen Starr to England in 1887 and there became interested in Toynbee Hall. Returning to Chicago, she established Hull House and began her work in social reform. She became the most famous woman in America, a model of feminine virtue. She was

> a gifted scholar, a brilliant administrator, a shrewd tactician, and a marvel of a businesswoman, who handled an annual budget of several hundreds of thousands of dollars. But people kept insisting she was a saint.[83]

She influenced Theodore Roosevelt to mount a progressive reform platform in his presidential campaign in 1912, and became a leader in the Progressive party, although she considered resigning when it exhibited racist tendencies. With her founding of the International Society for World Peace, she became a "serious threat to national security."[84] Although she won the Nobel Peace Prize in 1931, when she died in 1935 she was considered by the FBI to be the most dangerous woman in America.

Addams was greatly influenced in her work by Florence Kelley (1859–1932), who changed her from a philanthropist to a reformer. Kelley, a Cornell graduate who became a socialist, was divorced in 1891 and moved to Hull House. There she worked for labor and political reform, particularly for children and immigrants. In 1892 reform Governor John Altgeld appointed her to the State Bureau of Labor Statistics, and she began to investigate factories and sweatshops in Chicago, involving Hull House women in her work. She became head of the National Consumers League and lobbied for fair labor practices, maximum and minimum hours, and minimum wages for women.[85]

Mary O'Sullivan (1864–1943) also came to Hull House, where she interested Addams in the problems of working women. A labor leader and reformer, she organized the Chicago Women's Bindery Union in 1889. She and Addams organized a cooperative apartment house for working women, and women bindery workers held their union meetings at Hull House. O'Sullivan became one of Florence Kelley's twelve investigators into conditions in tenements and factory "sweat boxes" in 1892. In the same year, she became the American Federation of Labor's first woman organizer.[86]

Julia Lathrop (1858–1932) was appointed by Illinois Governor John

Altgeld to the Illinois Board of Charities in 1893. During her tenure, she personally inspected all 102 county almshouses and farms in the state, along with all Cook County's charity institutions. A strong advocate of community care for mental patients, she became a charter member of Clifford W. Beers's National Committee for Mental Hygiene. Concerned with children, she helped Lucy Flower, Addams, and others in their fight for the first juvenile court system in the world, and Lathrop was the first woman to head a federal bureau—the Children's Bureau. There she instituted studies on child labor, mothers' pensions, illegitimacy, juvenile delinquency, nutrition, and the mentally retarded.[87]

Lucy Flower (1837–1921), with Dr. Sarah Stevenson and others, helped found the Illinois Training School for Nurses in 1868. In 1886 she drafted legislation for a state industrial school for dependent boys, and though her bill was defeated, a private agency for that purpose was organized in 1889. She helped organize the Chicago Bureau of Charities, the Cook County Juvenile Court, the Protective Agency for Women and Children, and the Lake Geneva Fresh Air Association for poor urban children. Appointed to the Chicago Board of Education in 1891, she introduced kindergartens and manual and domestic training classes. She was the first woman to hold a statewide elective office in Illinois, as trustee to the University of Illinois.[88]

Grace Abbott came from work at Hull House to become director of the Immigrants' Protective League. With her sister Edith Abbott, she joined the faculty of the Chicago School of Civics and Philanthropy, one of the first schools of social work in the nation.[89] Appointed to the staff of the federal Children's Bureau, she succeeded in having clauses prohibiting child labor written into all government war contracts during World War I. In 1921 she was named its head, succeeding its first director Julia Lathrop.[90]

Dr. Alice Hamilton studied medicine at the University of Michigan, specializing in bacteriology and pathology. At Hull House she developed a well-baby clinic, and then went to the New England Hospital for Women and Children in Boston. There her interests in bacteriology led her to study medical problems of women in tenements and houses of prostitution. Later, she became a pioneer in industrial diseases.[91]

Hannah Greenbaum Solomon (1858–1942) became the first Jewish member of the Chicago Women's Club in 1877 and helped to establish the National Council of Jewish Women and the Illinois Federation of Women's Clubs (1896). In 1899 she was elected treasurer of the National Council of Women, and with Susan B. Anthony and May Wright Sewall represented it at the International Council of Women in Berlin in 1904. Working with Jane Addams and other social reformers on child welfare concerns, she helped to rehabilitate the Illinois Industrial School for Girls.[92]

Hull House and the many settlement houses throughout the nation provided forums and centers for women reformers. The movement led the way to community organization and group work practice within the profession of social work.

## CHILD-SAVING

Child-saving took impetus from both COS and settlement house movements. COSs believed that poverty was inherited but that by taking children out of bad environments adult pauperism could be prevented, while the settlement house movement worked diligently for child protective labor laws.

Before the 1870s, children were regarded as small adults, and childhood did not exist. From this perspective, their work was not exploitation but their duty to family, society, and God. As a result, children were required to work as soon as they were able—often in the mills by the age of 3. They were also charged with adult crimes and tried as adults; for example, children could be hanged for stealing a loaf of bread. They were generally expected to maintain themselves. Even laws that required poor and dependent children to be taken from their parents and placed in foster homes or indentured were not for the benefit of the child's happiness—indeed, many would have probably preferred to remain with their families regardless of poverty—but to ensure good and moral work behavior throughout their lives.

Several trends changed this common perspective toward children. First, after industrialization child labor was not so necessary. Indeed, much of the concern of labor unions about child labor was not that the children were being exploited but that, hired in place of men, their wages held down those of adults.

Second, with the decline in birthrate children became more valued, especially among the upper classes, whose concern for their own children led to concern for all children. Also, this coincided with their growing interest in "saving" the lower classes.

Third, the social reform movements of the 1800s began to redefine children as different from adults and protect them from abuse, neglect, and dependency. New knowledge available in psychology, sociology, and learning theories also contributed to new perspective on the rights of children, and child welfare became a field in itself and juvenile justice systems came into being.

While many would date the onset of the idea of *parens patriae* (the government taking the place of parents) from this time, in fact the state had continuously intervened in child care, though usually to put children to work or keep them from becoming state dependents. Child protection became a new standard for social reformers, though the first action to protect a child came when the Society for Prevention of Cruelty to Animals sued to have an abused child taken from her foster parents (*Mary Ellen* case, 1875). Embarrassed that there was no such protection for children, both public and private agencies moved to organize. Adequate food, shelter, clothing, and medical care—part of the growing reform movements for all people—were more easily justified on altruistic grounds for children.

Benevolent societies formed to provide nurseries and day care for children of poor and working women, where before the only recourse for these women had been to put their children in orphanages. The earliest day care center in the United States opened in New York City in 1854, and enough more opened in the next three decades to found the National Federation of Day Nurseries in 1898. Private philanthropies also opened orphan asylums, such as the Benevolent Ladies Association Home, a facility for children whose mothers had died during birth or poor children whose mothers worked. Mothers of good character without homes could also be sheltered there. The idea was to isolate children from outsiders, including parents, to rehabilitate them through discipline and obedience to authority.

Children of African descent presented a special problem, for few people really cared about them. However, some tried to care for them. In Philadelphia, in 1822, the Quakers founded an orphanage for the Care of Colored Children, followed by orphanages in 1835 in Providence and in 1836 in New York. White mobs burned Philadelphia's orphanage in 1838, and, during the Draft Riot of 1863, five hundred white men burned the New York asylum. An orphanage at Albany indentured such children at the age of 12. Here, a trust fund was established in payments of $100 per year by the indenturer and given to the child at age 21.[93]

"Contamination" by poverty was a major concern of both public and private child-savers. Therefore, taking children away from poor mothers was common practice, and outdoor relief and mothers' pensions were discouraged.

> Reformers . . . argued that it was better to break up a poor family than to risk accustoming children to life on the dole, which was so inherently demoralizing that it would transform them into lifelong paupers.[94]

Ironically, public agencies were more willing to give outdoor relief to mothers than were social workers, who argued that such aid should be given only if the mothers were closely supervised.

Still, placements left much to be desired. Until the 1870s, most children were placed in catch-all almshouses, where, child-savers believed, their potential to poverty only increased. The numbers of children placed in almshouses doubled between 1856 and 1868, and the New York Board of Charities reported in 1875 that 9 percent of all inmates were children (593) and nearly 300 over the age of 2 were "intelligent and in need of training." Following this report, New York passed a law prohibiting children's placement in poorhouses unless they were defective, diseased, deformed, idiots, epileptics, or paralytics, that is, unfit for reform because they could never become self-supporting. In 1883 Pennsylvania passed a similar law.

The orphanage movement was underway. Some states started statewide orphanage and placement systems; others required counties to provide them. The orphanages, however, were run on the almshouse model, with overseers earning their wages by saving on supplies. Mortality rates were about 20 percent.[95] Work morality was the major emphasis: rigid discipline, work schedules, and harsh punishments for rule infractions.

Perhaps the best known child-saver was Charles Loring Brace, who began the Children's Aid Society in 1853 (a national private agency that merged with Family Services in the 1960s). Brace believed that pauper families should be prevented from getting any kind of relief that would keep them together. His solution was to relocate children with families in the West, where they might learn the benefits of hard work in an untouched environment. For twenty years, haphazardly and without follow-up, agents loaded children on trains and shipped them to cities in the West, where they were "picked over" and chosen by families. Unfortunately, many families just wanted the extra help and badly mistreated the children. Many simply disappeared, either running away, getting lost, or dying. More than fifty thousand children over a twenty-five-year period were shipped to the West, from four thousand a year in the 1870s to about five hundred in 1892.

The first Children's Aid Society was established in New York, with Boston in 1864 and most major cities following. They became adoption agencies with high standards for placement, requiring extensive knowledge of the child and his or her needs, a comprehensive study of available homes, and consistent supervision by the agency. Counseling and rehabilitation of parents were intended to keep families together, and this had priority over foster home placement. Adoption, which had been a simple agreement by the parties, began to require legal evidence of transfer of children similar to a registration of deeds. However, as early as 1851 Massachusetts required a judge to determine if adoption was in the best interests of the child, along with consent of the natural parents.[96] By the late 1800s, orphanages, foster homes, and adoption were common.

Child-saving cut across all fields of reform, from public dependency to the establishment of juvenile justice systems. The first juvenile court law in the nation, in Illinois in 1899, was drafted by the Illinois State Conference of Charities and strongly influenced by such women as Jane Addams, Florence Kelley, and other Hull House workers. It was called "An Act to Regulate the Treatment and Control of Dependent, Neglected, and Delinquent Children," and dealt with children under age 16. The law provided a special juvenile court room and a separate record-keeping system and allowed for the appointment of juvenile probation officers. Within ten years, there were similar laws in twenty-two states, and by 1919 all states except Connecticut, Maine, and Wyoming had juvenile court laws.[97]

Undoubtedly much child-saving sprang from altruism, but other motives included the fear of pauperism, children's wages that lowered men's salaries, and the need to get children off the streets and out of criminal activity. For whatever reason, the public good required that children be "rescued," and as the movement progressed toward the twentieth century, there was a tacit acknowledgment, perhaps spurred by the new science of psychology, that children had special needs.

## PUBLIC WELFARE EFFORTS

Although social welfare history usually stresses private philanthropy, in the late 1800s public welfare actually touched more people. Asylums, orphanages, workhouses, and almshouses gave more shelter and care, and these along with outdoor relief provided more necessities of life to the poverty-stricken. While private and public charities had cooperated, with private philanthropy setting standards for service, the Civil War brought greater centralization and more coordination to bear on the massive needs of the nation. In the 1880s, governments slowly withdrew from subsidizing private organizations and built their own service systems, especially in income maintenance, corrections, and institutional care for the insane, retarded, or physically handicapped. Private charity interests continued with special groups of the deviant or distressed—unwed mothers, prisoners, immigrants, and children—but turned to professionalized casework rather than maintenance. Gradually, their services were offered as additions to public services rather than in place of such services, and two systems of welfare developed.

While private charities insisted that outdoor relief was more costly to society and more degrading to recipients, public bureaucracies, through their studies and statistics, were noting that institutions cost society more in money, shattered families, longer-term care, and unhappiness. Almshouses were not only more expensive but more difficult to supervise humanely, and the public sector moved toward outdoor relief. County supervisors of the poor urged that institutionalization in poorhouses be used very selectively. Public monies continued to subsidize some private agencies, particularly those serving women and children, but increasingly demanded accountability for the funds. By the 1890s, few agencies but those serving the aged were publicly subsidized, and public monies were given to county boards of supervisors for outdoor relief. Cash grants ranged from $5 to $30 per month, but the more common kind of support was in food, clothing, or shelter.

During that period, poverty was severe even for the working. For example, in Lawrence, Massachusetts, the average salary was $500 a year in 1875, but a small family needed more than $600 simply to pay for essentials. After 1876, wages there fell in response to economic depression, but prices fell too slowly to compensate. Tenement rents in 1893, when wages dropped below $300, were often $200 a year. With depressions, or when people were injured or killed on the job, or when employers decided to lay off workers for any reason, disaster struck the common family. Add to this the massive immigration and the large "army of unemployed" tramps roaming the country, and only the centralized and coordinated government systems could possibly be adequate—although adequacy was seldom achieved.

By the end of the century, the average wage in the United States was between $400 and $500 per year for a 10-hour day, 6-day week, while the poverty line was $460 for a family of five. There were no employment benefits, and unemployment was frequent. Women and children were a necessary part of the labor force, for a man could not support his family alone. Almost 40 percent of the population lived in cities, and women comprised 20 percent of the work force.[98] Ten million people, or 12 percent of the total population, lived in poverty, and four million people received public assistance.[99] In New York State, state institutions supported 8,494 people, and there were 73,117 in almshouses. Almshouses also gave outdoor relief to 209,092 people compared with the 30,560 people aided in 1900 by private societies.[100]

Because the poor were so often ill, public health became an issue. The discovery of germs made public officials realize that some highly infectious diseases could be prevented through vaccination, aseptic treatment conditions, and better health conditions among the poor—nutrition, sewers, and so on. Although only a start was made in this era, the federal government moved toward national action. In 1878 foreign quarantine was made a responsibility of the Marine Hospitals Service (forerunner of the Public Health Service). Emergency funds to prevent epidemics were appropriated in 1883 and a hygienic laboratory added in 1887. The service took over foreign and interstate quarantine in 1893.

Public welfare monies were often used by politicians to buy votes. Immigrants used to the *padrone* system of their native countries were easily persuaded by money, food, and help in finding jobs. Officials gave special services to voters, while nonvoters, regardless of need—women and children, for example—went unaided. Friends and relatives of politicians were often financed from the public coffers. For example, during the 1873–78 depression, Boss Tweed stole $100 million from the New York City treasury. Serious irregularities in the Department of Public Charities and Corrections led to the complete suspension of outdoor relief from July 1874 to January 1875, and private agencies were flooded with desperate people seeking aid. Public relief was only partially resumed, primarily in distributing coal and giving aid to the blind. In 1876 and 1877, funds were allotted to be distributed through voluntary agencies.[101] In graft-infested Brooklyn, a municipal reform movement cut all outdoor relief in the winter of 1878, a period of depression and labor conflict, and citizens rioted.[102]

The separation of private and public welfare continued as control moved from local overseers to state governments. This centralization brought the creation of state boards of charities and corrections, later to become state departments of public welfare. The first was in Massachusetts, in 1863, under the directorship of Dr. Samuel Gridley Howe (president for ten years), who emphasized the importance of keeping families together whenever possible, and recommended humane treatment for those within institutions. The boards' primary goal was to control and coordinate private and public agencies, which would in turn assure legal standards of care.

Howe instituted a study of lunatic asylums, state hospitals, almshouses, industrial schools, and charitable institutions to which the state gave aid. Board members inspected state institutions and private ones receiving state monies, including local almshouses and jails. From the survey, Howe developed a plan of inmate classification and regulations for administration. Because of concern for children, in 1869 a "state visiting agent" was appointed to attend the court trials of juvenile delinquents and to assume care for the children not committed to reform schools—a forerunner of the juvenile probation officer.[103] In 1885, the Massachusetts' state board became the first to supervise charitable, medical, and penal institutions. Other states soon followed: Boards formed in Connecticut, New York, Wisconsin, Rhode Island, Pennsylvania, Michigan, Kansas, and Illinois. By 1897, sixteen states had state boards of charity.

The major results of such boards were better care and protection of dependent children, since they were removed from poorhouses and placed in licensed children's asylums or foster care homes; more uniform and efficient administration of local public relief; a decrease in urban pauperism through the protection of immigrants; and improved care for the mentally ill. The state boards also gave a nationwide voice to social welfare by establishing, in 1865, the American Social Science Association, which later became the National Conference on Social Welfare.[104]

National organization was next, and Massachusetts, Connecticut, New York, and Wisconsin met in 1874 to form the Conference of Boards and Public Charities, a national network of private and public charities. In 1879 voluntary agencies were invited to participate in the conference's annual meetings. The 1874 conference officially condemned outdoor relief, in the middle of the 1873–78 depression, for demoralizing the work force. Within ten years COSs dominated the conference, though it remained a forum for current thought and new policy. For example, in 1886 Frederick H. Wines questioned the pseudoscientific statistics that showed individuals to be the cause of poverty and crime, urging that the conference look at

1. The invention of labor-saving machinery
2. Aggregation of capital in large and wealthy corporations
3. Aggregation of population in urban centers
4. Emancipation of women[105]

At the seventeenth conference in 1890, Josephine Shaw Lowell argued that people should be given aid only "when starvation is imminent." Poverty or nonwork, in the majority's view, was a threat to a sound and moral economic system. She mentioned the obvious failure of public relief: the rising populations of poorhouses and mental hospitals, and the growing number of unemployed vagrants, or tramps. In rejoinder, Franklin B. Sanborn, secretary of the Massachusetts State Board, made a plea for outdoor relief or "family aid," saying that outdoor relief statistics often included medical care and burials and so were overstated; that except in hard times few able-bodied people were in poorhouses; that there would never be enough institutions for all the poor; and deploring the idea that separating families was the best way to prevent dependency. As the century waned, private charities began to support government relief efforts. Many recommended mothers' pensions to keep families together, and most supported the move by the court system to create a juvenile justice system. By the end of the century, these trends had solidified. Public and private charities were clearly separated, and centralization of public welfare and outdoor relief had been accomplished.

## PROFESSIONALIZATION OF SOCIAL WORK

Another postwar trend was the professionalization of social work. In 1882 the newly formed Children's Aid Society of Pennsylvania began a training program, and in 1894 the New York Society conducted a course of twelve

lectures on practical social problems. By the later 1890s, the Boston Associated Charities were paying workers to learn COS techniques and giving
lectures on social and philanthropic topics. Instrumental in the profession's
development was Mary E. Richmond (1861–1928), who in over forty years
of practice defined casework and the importance of "person-in-situation."

Richmond began her social work career as an assistant treasurer in
the Baltimore Charity Organization Society and rose through the ranks to
become its general secretary. She developed a consistent and coherent
social work philosophy based on professional training and social research,
and maintained that both personal casework and social action were necessary to practice. In 1893 she began a series of educational conferences for
friendly visitors, using social histories as case material; in 1897 she
developed a plan and curriculum for a "school of philanthropic training."
Both Edward T. Devine, executive secretary of the New York Charity
Organization Society, and Robert de Forest, its president, supported her
efforts, and in 1898 sponsored a course in applied philanthropy based on
her ideas. This developed into the New York School of Philanthropy in
1901, offering a full academic year of classes for beginners in social services. The school, which depended on community agencies for field training, changed its name to the New York School of Social Work in 1919.

In 1899 Richmond published *Friendly Visiting Among the Poor,* and,
after numerous articles and lectures expounding her method, she published *Social Diagnosis* in 1919. This became the basic casework text for
social work education. It taught the importance of social investigation prior
to diagnosis and that treatment be based both on insight and on social
action.[106] In 1909 Richmond was named director of the Charity Organization Department of the new Russell Sage Foundation in New York City,
where she directed social research and developed further the methodology
of social work. As the rift between tax-supported relief and private casework efforts developed, Richmond took the latter view, arguing that outdoor relief, especially mothers' pensions, could not give the caring supervision that private social work practice provided. In addition, she noted the
possibility of graft and unaccountability in public welfare and believed that
private agencies would be more careful of how money was spent.[107]

In the same period of time, the Chicago School of Civics and Phi-
lanthropy was instituted under the direction of Hull House worker Julia
Lathrop and Graham Taylor of the Chicago Commons Settlement. It
became the Institute of Social Sciences in 1903–04, under the Extension
Division of the University of Chicago and later the Graduate School of
Social Service Administration. It emphasized research and social planning.
Both it and the New York School were tied to city agencies for field place-
ment instruction, a practice considered essential in the budding profession.

The profession of social work continued on its two courses: that
begun by the COS movement, which looked to individual casework to
"cure" the distressed and deviant, using the "medical model," and that
following the settlement house movement, namely, community action,
group work, and social action and reform against structural problems of
society (structural model).

## CONCLUSION: MOVING TOWARD REFORM

As society and social welfare entered the 1900s, vast changes had been accomplished in the United States, yet the underlying motivations for aiding others remained the same or became strengthened by new pseudo-scientific reasoning. The upheaval of the Civil War had assured federal supremacy over states' rights, but where it suited the purposes of the elite, states continued to act as they had—oppression of Afro-Americans, for example, or child labor for the profits of the rich. Social welfare had moved from the direction and influence of private philanthropists to centralization and bureaucratization, in both public and private sectors, and the two had become finally separated. Yet the philosophies of blaming the victim, the morality of work, and the control of the poor by state, alone or under the direction of an economic elite, remained.

Social work moved from volunteer friendly visiting to become a professional career, with goals and training and with an elaborate methodology of social diagnosis and social casework. Split into two philosophies—the charity organization society and the settlement house movements—it lost its elitist character. Social reform movements still tried to control the poor and to teach Puritan and work ethic morality. Philanthropy, though it still existed, had distanced itself from social problems and was involved in "higher" issues—the provision of public libraries, the endowment of colleges, or funding new social research, for example.

The underlying issues of sexism, racism, and classism continued to direct the economic and political system of the nation. Social Darwinism, new scientific theories and information about diseases and medical practice, Freudian ideas about psychology, the new discipline of sociology, and the Cult of True Womanhood all gave legitimation to the exploitation of people of color and white immigrants, to women, and to working people. Although labor unions were gaining power, they were also becoming exploitative, especially of women and people of color. Women's work became degraded in status and in salary—office work or social work, for example. The Gilded Age, a period of immense accumulation of wealth for a very few, provides a showcase for exploitation. Although it freed some people so that they could begin social reform, that freedom—in suffrage, in labor reform, in social welfare, and in political reform—came on the backs of others. Katz says

> Welfare reform and the bureaucratic style of relief that it sponsored served the purposes of industrial capitalism in three ways; . . . [by making] relief increasingly humiliating and unpleasant [to provide] . . . an incentive to labor; . . . [by emphasizing] the parasitic and degraded qualities of the very poor, thereby reducing popular sympathy and justifying retrenchment and repression; and [by dividing] . . . the working class against itself at the very moment when labor militancy was growing.[108]

Social treatment progressed in new government and private agencies as the developing social work profession provided new methods and careful research on the causation and remedy for many social ills. Yet social control was an inextricable part of social welfare, just as advanced by the new technologies as was social treatment. It was visible, and explicitly stated, in new regulations and procedures, in the exploitation of workers, in its inattention to the needs of people of color, and in the repression, once more, of women—the prostitute, blamed for venereal disease; the woman worker, subject to low pay and terrible working conditions; the married woman, at the economic mercy of husband and society; the widow, threatened with removal of her children; and the professional woman who, under the guise of nurturing society, participated unknowingly in the control and exploitation of other women.

## STUDY QUESTIONS

1. How did the Civil War affect social welfare for women? For people of color? For the poor?

2. What were the major contributions of the Freedmen's Bureau to American social welfare?

3. What were the major social welfare movements during the late 1800s? How were they similar and different in their treatment of the poor?

4. What is Social Darwinism? How did it apply to new immigrant groups? What was its effect on social welfare?

5. What was the status of women before, during, and after the Civil War? Why?

6. What was the status of people of African descent after the Civil War? How was their freedom blocked?

7. What happened to Native Americans and Hispanic Americans during this period?

8. How did the economy, polity, and religion relate to the treatment of people of color leading up to and after the Civil War?

## FOOTNOTES

[1]Michael B. Katz, *Poverty and Policy in American History*, (New York: Academic Press, 1983), p. 130.

[2]Marvin B. Gettelman, "Charity and Social Classes in the U.S., 1874–1900," *American Journal of Economics and Sociology*, Vol. 22 (April-July 1963), 313–29, reported in Jeffrey Galper, *Social Work Practice: A Radical Perspective*, (Englewood Cliffs, N.J.: Prentice Hall, 1974), pp. 427 ff.

[3]J. Saville, "The Welfare State: An Historical Approach," in E. Butterworth and R. Hobman, *Social Welfare in Modern Britain*, (Glasgow: Fontana-Collins, 1975), referenced in Peter Day, *Social Work and Social Control*, (London and New York: Tavistock Publications, 1981), p. 14.

[4]Frances Fox Piven and Richard Cloward, *Regulating the Poor*, (New York: Random House, 1971).

[5]Thomas R. Dye and L. Harmon Zeigler, *The Irony of Democracy*, (Belmont, Calif.: Wadsworth Publishing Co., 1970), pp. 69–70.

[6]Ibid., p. 79.

[7]Carole Hymowitz and Michaele Weissman, *A History of Women in America*, (New York: Bantam Books, 1980), pp. 148–149.

[8]Lerone Bennett, Jr., *Before the Mayflower: A History of the Negro in America*, (Chicago: Johnson Publishing Co., 1969), p. 67.

[9]Joseph Hraba, *American Ethnicity*, (Itasca, Ill.: F. E. Peacock Publishers, 1979), p. 266.

[10]Bennett, *Before the Mayflower*, p. 168.

[11]William Jay Jacobs, *Women in American History*, (Encino, Calif.: Glencoe Publishing, 1976), pp. 96–97.

[12]Ibid., p. 98.

[13]Ibid.

[14]June Axinn and Herman Levin, *Social Welfare: A History of the American Response to Need*, 2nd ed., (New York: Harper & Row, 1983), p. 94.

[15]Ibid., p. 92.

[16]Ibid.

[17]Quoted from V. O. Key, in Dye and Zeigler, *Irony*, pp. 79–80.

[18]Katz, *Poverty and Policy*, p. 130.

[19]Blanche Coll, *Perspectives in Public Welfare: A History*. U.S. Department of Health, Education, and Welfare, Social Rehabilitation Service 1969 (Washington, D.C.: U.S. Government Printing Office, 1971), p. 40.

[20]Ibid., p. 41.

[21]Axinn and Levin, *Social Welfare*, p. 97.

[22]Alice Kessler-Harris, *Out to Work: A History of Wage-Earning Women in the United States*, (New York: Oxford University Press, 1982), p. 146.

[23]Angela Davis, *Women, Race, and Class*, (New York: Vintage Press, 1983), p. 137.

[24]Kessler-Harris, *Out to Work*, p. 91.

[25]Hymowitz and Weissman, *History of Women in America*, (New York: Bantam Books, 1980), p. 240.

[26]A nineteenth century discussion of pauperism.

[27]Jacobs, *Women in American History*, p. 107.

[28]Kessler-Harris, *Out to Work*, p. 91.

[29]Bettina Berch, *The Endless Day: The Political Economy of Women and Work*, New York: Harcourt Brace Jovanovich, 1982), pp. 40–41.

[30]Axinn and Levin, *Social Welfare*, p. 131.

[31]Coll, *Perspectives in Public Welfare*, p. 40.

[32]Ibid.

[33]Hraba, *American Ethnicity*, p. 305.

[34]Jack Chen, *The Chinese in America*, (San Francisco: Harper & Row, 1980), pp. 136–142.

[35]Ibid., pp. 162–164.

[36]Hraba, *American Ethnicity*, p. 302.

[37]Joe R. Feagin, *Racial and Ethnic Relations*, 2nd ed., (Englewood Cliffs, N. J.: Prentice Hall, 1984), pp. 194–195.

[38]Ibid., p. 199.

[39]Ibid., p. 201.

[40]Ibid.

[41]Hraba, *American Ethnicity*, p. 216.

[42]Bennett, *Before the Mayflower*, pp. 92–93.

[43]Ibid., p. 202.

[44]Ibid.

[45]Ibid., p. 217.

[46] Ibid., p. 197.

[47] Hraba, *American Ethnicity*, p. 278.

[48] Bennett, *Before the Mayflower*, p. 197.

[49] Davis, *Women, Race, and Class*, p. 89.

[50] Bennett, *Before the Mayflower*, p. 239.

[51] "Jim Crow" was a name made famous in a comedy in the early 1700s. It became synonymous with Afro-Americans.

[52] Kessler-Harris, *Out to Work*, p. 185.

[53] Hymowitz and Weissman, *History of Women*, p. 205.

[54] Kessler-Harris, *Out to Work*, p. 185.

[55] Hymowitz and Weissman, *History of Women*, p. 220.

[56] Davis, *Women, Race, and Class*, pp. 87–88.

[57] Jacobs, *Women in American History*, p. 144.

[58] Hymowitz and Weissman, *History of Women*, p. 299.

[59] Dr. Clelia Duel Mosher studied the sexual habits of married women as a student at the University of Wisconsin prior to 1892. The project spanned twenty years, 70 percent born before 1870. Most were more highly educated than poor, with twenty-seven teachers. They were upper-middle or middle-class women rather than members of a leisure class. "Despite the high level of education . . . they confessed to having a pretty poor knowledge . . . of sexual physiology before marriage . . . The great majority (of 45 women) said that they had experienced orgasms.

[60] Carl N. Degler, "What Ought to Be and What Was: Women's Sexuality in the 19th Century," in Judith Walzer Leavitt, ed., *Women and Health in America*, (Madison, Wisconsin: University of Wisconsin Press, 1984), pp. 40 ff.

[61] Ibid.

[62] Pamela Johnson Conover and Virginia Gray, *Feminism and the New Right: Conflict over the American Family*, (New York: Praeger Publishing, 1983), pp. 4–8.

[63] Beulah Compton, *Introduction to Social Welfare and Social Work*, (Homewood, Ill.: Dorsey Press, 1980), p. 298.

[64] James Reed, "Doctors, Birth Control, and Social Values, 1830–1970," in Leavitt, ed., *Women and Health*, p. 127.

[65] Ibid., p. 201.

[66] Mark Thomas Connelly, "Prostitution, Venereal Disease, and American Medicine," in Leavitt, ed., *Women and Health*, p. 201.

[67] Referenced from Sidney Fine, *Laissez-Faire and the General Welfare State*, (Ann Arbor: University of Michigan Press, 1964), p. 173, in Gerald Handel, *Social Welfare in Western Society*, (New York: Random House, 1982), p. 213.

[68] Dye and Zeigler, *Irony of Democracy*, p. 73.

[69] Coll, *Perspectives in Public Welfare*, p. 42.

[70] Macarov, *Design of Social Welfare*, p. 197, paraphrased from Piven and Cloward, *Regulating the Poor*, pp. 165–166.

[71] Frank Dekker Watson, *The Charity Organization Movement in the United States*, (New York: Arno Press and *The New York Times*, 1971), p. 281. Originally published by Macmillan, 1921.

[72] Coll, *Perspectives in Public Welfare*, pp. 44–45, quoted from Mrs. Charles Russell Lowell, "The Economic and Moral Effects of Public Outdoor Relief," *National Conference of Charities and Corrections Proceedings, 1879*, p. 203.

[73] Watson, *The Charity Organization Movement*.

[74] Compton, *Introduction to Social Welfare*, p. 286.

[75] Coll, *Perspectives in Public Welfare*, p. 61.

[76] Watson, *The Charity Organization Movement*, p. 324.

[77] Ibid.

[78]Robert McHenry, ed., *Famous American Women: A Biographical Dictionary from Colonial Times to the Present*, (New York: Dover Publications, 1980), p. 44.

[79]Ibid., p. 45.

[80]Ibid.

[81]Handel, *Social Welfare in Western Society*, p. 70.

[82]Hymowitz and Weissman, *History of Women*, p. 224.

[83]Ibid., p. 232.

[84]Ibid., p. 233.

[85]Ibid., p. 228.

[86]McHenry, *Famous American Women*, p. 234.

[87]Ray Ginger, "Women at Hull House," in Linda K. Kerber and Jane DeHart Mathews, eds., *Women's America*, p. 272.

[88]McHenry, *Famous American Women*, p. 135.

[89]Ibid., p. 1.

[90]Ibid.

[91]Ginger, "Women at Hull House," in Kerber and Mathews, eds., *Women's America*, p. 272.

[92]McHenry, *Famous American Women*, p. 387.

[93]Bennett, *Before the Mayflower*.

[94]Katz, *Poverty and Policy*, p. 193.

[95]Compton, *Introduction to Social Welfare*, p. 298.

[96]Gerald N. Grob, *The State and Public Welfare in Nineteenth Century America*, (New York: Arno Press, 1976), p. 137, quoting from Senate Bill 2, (Boston: William White, printer to the State, 1859).

[97]Axinn and Levin, *Social Welfare*, p. 146.

[98]Dye and Zeigler, *Irony of Democracy*, p. 79.

[99]Coll, *Perspectives in Public Welfare*, p. 64.

[100]Katz, *Poverty and Policy*, p. 190.

[101]Coll, *Perspectives in Public Welfare*, pp. 43–44.

[102]Katz, *Poverty and Policy*, p. 233.

[103]Walter A. Friedlander and Robert Apte, *Introduction To Social Welfare*, (Englewood Cliffs, N.J.: Prentice Hall, 1974), p. 80.

[104]Ralph Dolgoff and Donald Feldstein, *Understanding Social Welfare*, (New York: Longman Press, 1984).

[105]Axinn and Levin, *Social Welfare History*, p. 102.

[106]McHenry, *Famous American Women*, pp. 346–347.

[107]Ibid.

[108]Katz, *Poverty and Policy*, p. 130.

# 8

# THE PROGRESSIVE ERA, WAR, AND RECOVERY

## THE PROGRESSIVE ERA

The Progressive Era—between 1900 and World War I—was a time of prosperity for the United States. For the general population, the basic conditions of life improved as technologies changed the way of life—better roads and communication systems; electrification; better housing, water supply and waste disposal systems; more amenities in terms of food, clothing, and other goods; and better hospitals and medical technology. The "democratic" thrust of the Progressive Era meant more citizen participation and an increase in government responsiveness and honesty; and this led to secret ballots, direct primaries, and direct election of senators (the Seventeenth Amendment in 1914); civil service reform; regulation of campaign expenditures; accountability in government; the initiative, referendum, and recall; and local rule under city commission and city manager forms of government. New social legislation included antitrust laws, the Children's Bureau, child labor laws, and health and safety laws. The progressive income tax gave the federal government the means with which to govern on a national basis.

To question the government and the control of the economy by the elite became possible; for example, Louis Brandeis pointed out that low-paying industries and those who controlled them were subsidized by employees, families of employees, and society as a whole.[1] The radical voice of reform became strident as "muckraking" newspapers exposed big business, city bossism, graft, and corruption. Progressive reform was sought by a many-sided coalition—small businessmen, writers, settlement house workers, social workers, lawyers, clergymen, farmers, labor reform movements, unions, women reformers and suffragists, middle class club-women, black men and women, and politicians. Many of the nation's intellectuals were members: John Dewey, Paul Douglas, Jack London, Walter Lippman,[2] and Charlotte Perkins Gilman. The growth of the Socialist party became one indication of the movement: It had fewer than 5,000 members in 1900 but nearly 120,000 by 1912. Eugene V. Debs, its chair, ran for president in 1912, winning 6 percent of the popular vote—900,000 of 15 million votes cast—on a platform calling for government takeover and regulation of private industry.[3] In that election, more than 1,000 socialists were elected to public office.

The progressive movement was also a reaction against big business and corporate profits, and under pressure the government tried to intervene in big business. The Sherman Anti-Trust Act had been more or less ineffective until 1902, when the Supreme Court ruled against further incorporation of railroads by the Northern Securities Company. In 1906 the Interstate Commerce Commission was given power to fix rates for railroad storage, refrigeration, and terminal facilities; and for sleeping car, express, and pipeline companies. Telegraph and telephone companies were brought under ICC regulation in 1910.[4] In 1909 a 1 percent tax on corporate incomes over $5,000 was imposed; in 1913 the states ratified the sixteenth amendment, imposing progressive taxes on personal income.

Great trusts and monopolies formed or became stable: Standard Oil, Consolidated Tobacco, U.S. Steel. By 1914, supercorporations dominated coal, agrimachinery, sugar, telephone and telegraph, public utilities, iron and steel, railroads, oil, tobacco, and copper.[5] Between 1899 and 1929, total output of manufacturing increased by 273 percent,[6] and the gross national product had increased sixfold (see Table 8.1).

By 1910, 5 percent of the population owned nearly half the nation's property,[7] and in 1919 not quite 4 percent of the industrial organizations

**TABLE 8.1 Gross National Product (in billions)**

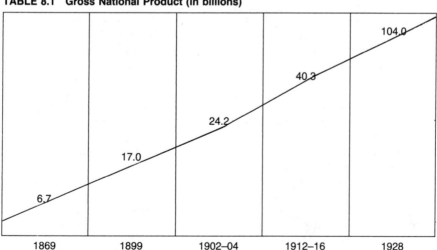

| 1869 | 1899 | 1902–04 | 1912–16 | 1928 |
|------|------|---------|---------|------|

(Values on graph: 6.7, 17.0, 24.2, 40.3, 104.0)

employed half the nation's workers and contributed more than two-thirds of the gross national product.

Poor laborers, whether men or women, were kept "in their places" by interlocking mechanisms of business, courts, social work, and government. "Protective legislation" based partly on social values that women were incapable of heavy work kept them in low-paying marginal jobs and gave employment to men who could work when and where women could not. At no other time in history did the nation demonstrate so clearly its racist, sexist, and classist biases. Social Darwinism legitimated the eugenics movement, which advocated that all inferior people be sterilized so that their children would not "infect" society—immigrants not of Anglo-Saxon or Germanic stock, who were often English-illiterate; people of color; criminals and prostitutes; and the physically, mentally, or emotionally impaired. By 1915 twelve states had adopted sterilization laws based on the eugenics movement.[8] Dr. Harry Laughlin, a geneticist in the Eugenics Record Office, said in 1922

> We in this country have been so imbued with the idea of democracy, or the equality of all men, that we have left out of consideration the matter of blood or natural inborn hereditary mental and moral differences. No man who breeds pedigreed plants and animals can afford to neglect this thing.[9]

By 1932 the Eugenics Society could boast that at least twenty-six states had passed compulsory sterilization laws and that thousands of "unfit" persons had been prevented from reproducing.[10] In 1939 the Birth Control Federation planned a "Negro project," which, though not formally carried out, can still be observed in the "voluntary" sterilization of poor women—particularly Afro-Americans and Hispanics—that occurred during the 1960s and 1970s.

By the early 1900s, the United States had fulfilled its "manifest destiny" to control much of the continent. Now, in an era of worldwide imperialism, it began small imperialisms: Hawaii, Puerto Rico, Guam, and the Philippines were annexed in 1898, Cuba was made a protectorate in 1901, the Panama Canal Zone was in effect annexed by treaty in 1903, and the Virgin Islands were purchased from Denmark in 1917. Internally consolidated by railroads, the telegraph, and the telephone, northern European nations were engaged in wider imperialism: England and France peacefully divided up the African continent, and Russia, looking eastward, fought its losing battle with Japan. Landlocked Germany, surrounded by other nations eager to expand, began plans as early as 1903 to prevent the encirclement it feared from surrounding nations.

The new activities, new technologies, expansionism, and reforms that burgeoned after the Civil War burst into the twentieth century fueled by the Industrial Revolution. Speed became the new master of societies—gone were the leisurely agrarian settings that fostered extended families, time for local reforms, and even world diplomacy. The technologies of communication and transportation made local emergencies national and even international; for example, the San Francisco earthquake in 1906 mobilized help from agencies all over the nation and brought scientists from

Japan to help with the crisis. The quake and its fire destroyed nearly 30,000 buildings and ravaged the downtown area. About 200,000 persons were left homeless and damage was estimated at $500 million. Yet within a year the city was back on its feet.

On June 28, 1914, Archduke Ferdinand, heir to the Austro-Hungarian throne, was assassinated. This brought a flurry of telegrams, telephone calls, threats, and pleas, and in the critical period between July 23 and August 4

> there were five ultimatums with short time limits, all implying or explicitly threatening war. . . . In the final days the pressing requirements of mobilization timetables frayed the last shreds of patience. And even before mobilizations were formally announced, armies prepared for war, making a shambles of the efforts of diplomats . . . as time and the peace slipped away.[11]

Suddenly the world was at war, and neither time nor distance protected countries: Some people predicted that enemy air forces would bomb New York City. The country quickly adjusted to war conditions: Work in the munitions and supply business, in transportation, and in the production of steel led to such high profits that unemployment almost disappeared. Afro-Americans from the South were recruited to work in northern factories, and the immigration of Mexicans was encouraged: More than 2 million Afro-Americans came north, and more than 70,000 Mexicans entered the United States. In 1918, the same year that Czar Nicholas and his family were executed in Russia, Woodrow Wilson proposed the Fourteen Points on which the League of Nations was founded. For his work, he won the Nobel Peace Prize in 1919. However, in its new isolationism, the United States refused to join the League when it was formed in 1920.

In the period after World War I, peace and prosperity returned for many. The average family could now earn enough to live comfortably, particularly with credit now being offered for consumer purchases. Although the recession in 1921 brought widespread strikes, especially among dockworkers and steelworkers, standards of living continued to increase, and with higher profits and sales came high employment and a rise in real wages. A new belief in the "invisible hand" of the marketplace once more brought harsh reaction against public dependency.

Those who continued to help the poor or to work for social reform were considered un-American, and a "Red Scare" occurred because of fear that the people's revolution in Russia might spread to the United States. It brought accusations of Bolshevism against socialists, suffragists, labor reformers, pacifists, settlement house workers, and social workers and encouraged many to get out of poor relief and into casework practice. Criminal syndicalism laws made it a felony to advocate violence for political change, and twenty-four states passed laws threatening jail for anyone displaying a red flag (350 persons were jailed). Vigilantes attacked unionists and "reds," and loyalty oaths were instituted for teachers and other public employees. U.S. Attorney General Mitchell Palmer, on one night in 1920, arrested four thousand people in thirty-three states for being radical aliens, and great numbers were deported.[12] People advocating political positions different from those in power were persecuted. For example, in 1918 Eugene Debs was sentenced to ten years (commuted in 1921) under the espionage and sedition laws, and Marcus Garvey, a Black Nationalist leader, was deported on trumped-up charges of mail fraud.

## POPULATION MOVEMENTS AND IMMIGRATION

During the first two decades of the twentieth century, population rose from 46.8 million to more than 100 million, with more than half living in the cities. Between 1920 and 1930, 6 million people moved from farms to the cities.[13] Reasons for urbanization included immigration, a general migration to the cities, and an increase in migration of Mexicans and southern Afro-Americans into unskilled nonfarm jobs. Urban industrial growth and incorporation made possible the undercutting of small businesses by large corporations, and in rural areas the new agribusiness put tenant farmers and small owners off the land because they were unable to afford new high-production technology.

From 1900 until the Immigration Acts of 1921 and 1924, more than nineteen million immigrants came to the United States,[14] more than 75 percent from Southern and Eastern Europe. By 1910, less than 20 percent of the population of New York City was native born.[15] Nearly two-thirds of the population was poor, and a third lived in desperate poverty. Women and children worked at lower wages than men, and men working full time averaged between $400 and $500 per year, though it was estimated that the average family needed at least $600 to $800 to survive.[16] Wages were about 60 percent short of basic subsistence.

Spurred both by the labor glut and by Social Darwinism, Congress passed the Immigration Act of 1907. Amended in 1910, it charged a head tax of $4.00 on each immigrant and listed those to be excluded: idiots, imbeciles, the feeble-minded, insane, paupers, those likely to become paupers, people with contagious diseases, criminals, anarchists, children under 16 unless accompanied by an adult, and laborers under short-term work contracts.[17] Quota restrictions passed in 1924 (in effect until 1965) were first based on national origin and the numbers of nationals in the United States according to the 1880 census, and then, in 1929, to the 1920 census data. This effectively limited all Far Eastern immigration and greatly limited immigration from any Southern or Eastern European country.

Although the Oriental Exclusion Act of 1880 had been written primarily against the Chinese, it applied also to Japanese. They came despite its restrictions and prospered. Their mutual benefit societies offered jobs to newcomers and education for children, and with their greater skills in horticulture they were able to compete with white farmers despite the high cost of the barren land they bought. To control this, Congress passed an alien land bill in 1913 forbidding Japanese aliens to own land. They circumvented it by incorporating with white partners or deeding it to their American-born children until 1920, when another amendment forbade this practice.

Japanese immigrants faced a rabidly racist American population. By 1905 newspapers, unions, the American Legion, and the California Farm Bureau were campaigning against the "Yellow Peril." Attacks on Japanese people and businesses became common: even the Japanese scientists coming to help after the San Francisco earthquake were beaten. However, as a world power fresh from its victory over Russia, Japan could offer some protection to its nationals. Therefore, rather than banning Japanese immigration, President Theodore Roosevelt signed the infamous "Gentlemen's Agreement" with Japan, "voluntarily" limiting immigration to former resident aliens and their immediate families (1907–08).

Because Japanese women could not immigrate unless they had relatives in the United States, Japanese men simply arranged marriages by proxy with women in Japan, but in the 1920 immigration amendment Congress also forbade importation of "mail-order brides." By 1922 the Japanese had been declared "aliens ineligible for citizenship" (*Ozawa* v. *U.S.*, 1922), and the Oriental Exclusion Act of 1924 almost completely stopped their immigration until 1968. They remained a small group prospering in agriculture and service occupations: By 1919 they ran 47 percent of all hotels and 25 percent of all grocery stores in Seattle, for example.[18] By 1941 they raised 42 percent of California's truck crops. However, at the onset of World War II, much of their wealth was seized, and they were incarcerated in concentration camps.

Hispanic immigration, legal or illegal, has always been encouraged by U.S. business interests, despite the overt public outcry against it. In 1902, when the federal government passed the National Reclamation Act that watered the Southwestern deserts, white farmers could not meet the growing labor demands in truck and cotton farming, railroad construction, mining, and maintenance. They recruited Mexicans, who soon comprised about two-thirds of the labor force there. Soon, however, new agricultural technologies pushed out Hispanic workers, and they moved up the California coast and into the Midwest as migrant workers. Another major recruitment era was World War I, and after the war agribusiness encouraged their immigration—in the 1920s, 500,000 workers and their families immigrated. Mexicans were specifically exempted from the Immigration Acts of 1921 and 1924.

When the Depression came, Mexicans were no longer wanted and the Immigration and Naturalization service created a border patrol to stop their illegal entry, making it a felony in 1929. Still, in the crop season, businessmen openly recruited them to the United States. After crops were in, neither their employers nor the law felt any obligation to return them to their homes. The company store system kept them in debt to their employers, and thousands were stranded without food, shelter, or clothing, and with no claim on schools, hospitals, or welfare. Their own mutual aid societies provided very limited help at times, and often the Mexican government itself appropriated funds to help its nationals stranded in the United States.

Between 1931 and 1940 only 22,000 Mexicans immigrated. Often they moved to cities, where they became strike-breakers in the great labor movements of the era and were subject to violence from other workers.

Even those legally in the country had little legal protection from such attacks, and a movement to "repatriate" them began. Approximately half a million Hispanics unable to prove citizenship were deported, though the majority were in fact American citizens. Texas and California deported the largest numbers, but in Illinois and Indiana fully half of all Hispanics were "repatriated."

After World War II another Hispanic group, the Puerto Ricans, began to move slowly into the United States along the Eastern Seaboard They, however, were American citizens, for Puerto Rico had been ceded to the United States at the end of the Spanish American War and its people given citizenship in 1917 (Jones Act). As their island was slowly taken over by white landowners, they began to move to mainland cities. Although in 1899 they had owned 93 percent of their land, by 1930 absentee companies owned 60 percent.

## OPPRESSION OF AFRO- AND NATIVE AMERICANS

Although social reformers took on nearly every other cause in the Progressive Era, the civil rights of people of color remained almost untouched. Over the history of the National Conference of Social Welfare, for example, only two programs were held on racial minorities.[19] Some settlement houses recognized their problems as they began to migrate to cities, but the few that actively tried to recruit Afro-Americans found that their other clients refused to come. There were a few moderately successful black settlement houses, especially in the large cities, but on the whole Afro-Americans were subject to rigid segregation or were blocked from even the meager social services that were provided other poor people. They were successfully excluded from unions and from employment, though women found it easier to work, as domestics, than did men.

In 1900, nine-tenths of all Afro-Americans lived in the rural South, but a new "enclosure movement" of their lands began after the Civil War, making them tenant farmers of their former owners or pushing them to Northern cities. Two million migrated: The largest number—87,000—came to Washington, D.C. Baltimore, New Orleans, Philadelphia, and New York each had more than 60,000 Afro-American citizens.[20] In 1913, they owned 550,000 homes, operated 937,000 farms, managed 40,000 businesses, held $700 million in funds, and more than 70 percent were literate. They had 40,000 churches, 34 colleges in the South, 35,000 teachers, and 1.7 million students in public schools,[21] although rigid segregation was still maintained in all facilities.

World War I brought thousands of Afro-Americans to Northern factories. Thousands more entered the Army—370,000 soldiers and 1,400 officers went into race-segregated units. More than half fought in France, often assigned to the French Army. Among them, Henry Johnson and Needham Roberts were the first Americans cited for bravery, although Afro-Americans were usually assigned to menial chores. An official order from General Pershing in 1918 reinforced segregation: the prevention of contact between French and Afro-American officers was ordered so that white soldiers would not be offended, and contact between French women and Afro-American soldiers was forbidden. White officers could not eat, shake hands, initiate conversations with them, nor commend them.[22]

A great outpouring of hatred against Afro-Americans took place during and after the War, related to the fear that they would take "white" jobs. In 1916 there were 54 lynchings, and despite a "silent march" of 20,000 protesters in Washington organized by the NAACP (National Association for the Advancement of Colored People), violence escalated. In East St. Louis on July 12, 1917, white workers drove nearly 6,000 Afro-Americans from their homes and killed between 40 and 200. In 1918, there were 64 lynchings and in 1919, with returning veterans seeking jobs, 83 Afro-Americans were lynched and 11 burned alive. The Ku Klux Klan was revitalized: A rally at Kokomo drew 200,000 people. One of every 8 white men belonged to the Klan at its height, and their terror was directed not only at Afro-Americans but at Hispanics, Jews, and Catholics. Klan membership included senators, representatives, judges, sheriffs, and other government officials.

No Afro-American could escape persecution, as the following account demonstrates (1918). Mary Turner, a pregnant woman, was hanged, doused with gasoline and motor oil, and burned.

> As she dangled from the rope, a man stepped forward with a pocketknife and ripped open her abdomen in a crude caesarean operation. Out tumbled the prematurely born child. . . . Two feeble cries it gave—and received for answer the heel of a stalwart man, as life was ground out of its tiny form.[23]

The following summer, 1919, was called the Red Summer because of its violence. Over twenty-six riots broke out across the country: In Washington, Chicago, Omaha, and Knoxville, 170 Afro-Americans were killed and 537 injured. They defended themselves and some whites died, as did whites who tried to help Afro-Americans. For example, in Omaha, a mob lynched and burned an Afro-American and hanged the mayor who tried to prevent his lynching.

### Afro-American Leaders

Booker T. Washington was considered the "quintessential black" to white leaders: For example, Andrew Carnegie donated $600,000 in U.S. Steel bonds to Tuskegee with the stipulation that $150,000 be used to support Washington and his family so that he could continue his great work. He was invited to dine at the White House by Theodore Roosevelt, and some say that Roosevelt's defeat in 1912 had to do with his friendship with Washington, which alienated the solid South. Bennett says that Washington practically ruled "Black America" from 1895 to 1915.[24] He sent annual messages to "his people" and had the final word on their political appointments. A strong advocate of vocational education, he urged them to seek economic rather than political advantage.

Among the more radical leaders was William Edward Burkhardt

DuBois, a Harvard graduate. He returned to America in 1894, having studied at the University of Berlin, but was appalled at the submissive attitudes of his Afro-American students. He and another Harvard graduate, William Monroe Trotter, organized a strategy planning meeting in 1905 at Niagara Falls to demand civil, political, and social rights. This meeting, attended by Jane Addams, laid the groundwork for the National Association for the Advancement of Colored People, of which DuBois became the only Afro-American officer as director of research and publicity. In 1909 the First National Committee on the Negro met officially to form the NAACP. (Florence Kelley and Lillian Wald were present.) Trotter went on to form the more militant leftist National Equal Rights League. It consistently opposed such segregated facilities as YMCAs and settlement houses, and established the Afro-American press as a dominant force in the protest movement.

Marcus Moziah Garvey was the first radical nationalist of African descent of the twentieth century. His Negro Improvement Association advocated nationalism and a separate nation in Africa. The association's platform of racial separation, racial pride, and worldwide political liberation attracted millions of followers, mainly urban working-class Afro-Americans. Garvey's goal was a united Africa under Africans, and in 1921 he declared himself provisional president of the new Republic of Africa. Raising more than $10 million, he organized cooperatives, factories, a commercial steamship venture, and a private army. In 1925, accused of mail fraud, he was deported to his native Jamaica and died in London in 1940.[25] Amy Jacques Garvey, his second wife, played an active role as secretary, colleague, and leader in her own right in the organization.

Other Afro-American women were leaders in the Progressive Era. Mary McLeod Bethune (1856–1913), the daughter of slaves, was perhaps the most influential woman of her time. Educated by missionaries, she started a girls' school in 1904, in Daytona Beach, Florida. Her class of 5 paid 50 cents each for tuition, and in two years she had 250 students. She paid her regular teachers $15 to $20 a week and relied heavily on volunteers. Later, she organized Bethune College, buying a former dumpsite for $250, and in 1922 amalgamated her girls' college with Cookman College, the first higher education institution for Afro-American men in Florida. Bethune-Cookman College had on its campus a fully equipped twenty-bed hospital, for its students were served unwillingly and inadequately in white hospitals.[26]

Ida B. Wells Barnett (1862–1931), also a daughter of slaves, was a journalist and activist. Educated at Rust and Fisk Universities, she began her teaching career in 1884 at age 14. However, when she criticized the quality of education she lost her job. Later, she bought an interest in the *Memphis Free Speech* newspaper and began an antilynching campaign. A protester against segregation, she sued the Chesapeake and Ohio Railroad for forcibly removing her from an all-white railroad car. Moving to Chicago, she organized local women in various causes and served as secretary of the National Afro-American Council. In 1910 she founded and became president of the Negro Fellowship League. From 1913 to 1916, she served as a probation officer in the Chicago municipal court. While she took part in the 1909 meeting of the Niagara group, she refused to become involved in the NAACP because of its conservatism.[27]

Clubs such as those formed by Wells Barnett became the backbone of help for Afro-American women and families in the cities of the North. Darenkamp et al. say

> the formation of black women's clubs represents a notable historical movement of this time. Along with fighting for equality for blacks and providing companionship, the black reform societies helped black women find employment, set up day nurseries and kindergartens, and established homes to protect young black women from sexual abuse. Like most middle-class white women of the era, black club women were middle class and educated but unlike many of their white counterparts the vast majority worked outside the home.[28]

Although Afro-Americans were still subject to such social welfare/social control efforts as juvenile and criminal justice, for all practical purposes these women's clubs and mutual aid societies took over the functions that social work provided for white people.

The National Urban League, formed in 1910, had as its goals economic opportunity and civil equality through persuasion and conciliation. Its first executive officers were George Edmund Haynes, the first Afro-American to receive a degree from the New York School of Social Work, and Eugene K. Jones. The league's welfare component served as a channel for contributions from white benefactors to Afro-Americans in need.

### Native Americans

Native American activism, though repressed by the government and the Bureau of Indian Affairs, still existed in the Progressive Era. The pan-Indian Society of American Indians was founded in the early 1900s to develop pride and a national leadership and to encourage educational and job opportunities—only a fourth of Native American children were being educated. A new religion also rose and was incorporated in 1919 as the Native American Church. Its sacrament of peyote was thus protected from attacks by Christian missionaries.

Those Native Americans who fought in World War I were rewarded with citizenship, and in 1924 all Native Americans became citizens, though they remained wards of the government. In 1928 appropriations for education were increased, and by the mid-1930s some boarding schools were replaced by day schools under the Johnson-O'Malley Act, which gave aid to states that would provide public education to Native Americans.

## LABOR AND THE UNIONS

The economy of the Progressive Era did not rise smoothly. There were depressions in 1907, 1910, 1919, and 1920 before the major crash in 1929. Each depression was accompanied by labor riots, strikes, and counteractions by police and courts. The depression of 1907–08 paralyzed the country, but led to the formation of such unions as the International Ladies' Garment Workers Union (ILGWU). Major strikes, often led by women, broke out in 1909 when charities reported double the number of applicants in winter and quadruple the number in the spring.[29] In the depression of 1914–15, a conservative estimate of two million were jobless. In New York City, relief recipients increased by 23 percent in 1913 and 57 percent in 1914,[30] though charity expenditures increased only 14 and 17 percent, respectively. The New York AICP paid men $2.00 a day for a maximum of three days for working for the city because the city could not afford to give them relief. In 1919, a vast wave of strikes broke out across the nation, and on Memorial Day in south Chicago police fired on a peaceful demonstration of workers, supporters, wives, and children, killing about thirty people, most of whom were shot in the back.[31]

Trade union membership declined throughout the early 1900s, from 3.3 percent in 1900 to a low of 1.5 percent in 1910. By 1920 it had surged upward to 6.6 percent.[32] Women were among the most active organizers, for the highly touted "protective legislation" proposed by unions and reformers benefited women far less than it did men. It stressed their inability to do hard labor or work long hours and cut back work hours, night work, heavy work, and overtime hours and reserved those jobs for men. If women won equal pay through their union activities, jobs went to men who were preferred as workers for the same price. Protective legislation was first tested in 1908 in Oregon, where it set a national precedent for government intervention for women and children in the labor market. It also set a precedent for legal discrimination against women in terms of the jobs they could hold and the wages they would be paid, and contributed to channeling women into the rapidly expanding white collar sector.[33]

In 1900, the average workweek for organized laborers was 57 hours in general, while those in the building trades worked a 48-hour week.[34] Unorganized laborers, such as steelworkers, worked a 12-hour day and an 84-hour workweek. Women and children often worked more than 15 hours a day, at wages of about $1.50; for example, in 1905 a group of laundry workers in Illinois were hospitalized from exhaustion after working 16 to 20 hours a day in the heat and dampness of steam-filled plants. Women were told that if they did not work on Sundays they need not come in at all.[35]

### Women and Unions

Over 5 million women were employed in 1900, making up one-fifth of the nation's total work force. By 1910, women comprised 25 percent of the labor force. A Women's Bureau survey during that period showed that 90 percent worked for economic reasons, and that 25 percent were the principal wage-earners. By 1920, 25.6 percent of working women were in white-collar jobs; 23.8 percent in manufacturing; 8.2 percent in domestic service; and 12.9 percent in agriculture. A typical commercial laundry worker worked more than 40 hours a week and took home less than $15.00 a month. In the same year, 75 percent of Afro-American women worked in agricultural labor, domestic service, and laundry work. In factories, they were paid less than were white women and up to a third less than men. The work force was rigidly segregated, and amenities were given only to white women—lunchrooms, cloakrooms, fresh drinking water, clean toilets.[36] In the 1920s, less than two million of the eight million wage-earning women were married, but by 1930 more than three million were married. Employers often refused to hire married women and frequently fired them when they married. Twenty-six states had laws prohibiting the hiring of married women.

Women were among the most active unionists because of the low pay and terrible conditions under which they worked. Industry-bred diseases were common, and women workers had a mortality rate more than double that of nonworking women and a third more than working men. In 1903 women founded the National Women's Trade Union League, which sought equal pay, an 8-hour workday, minimum wages, and full citizenship rights for women. The NWTUL was part of the American Federation of Labor, which tolerated but did not wholly support it, and AFL president Samuel Gompers vehemently fought both women's labor and "socialist movements."

Partly in response to AFL's refusal to help women and partly because of the socialist reforms taking place at the time, in 1905 radicals formed the Industrial Workers of the World (IWW), which advocated complete abolition of the wage system and the employing class. In the first five years of the century, it waged 13,964 strikes and 541 lockouts.[37] One such strike was against the mills in Lawrence, Massachusetts, where the governor sent in fourteen hundred militiamen to back up police and state troopers. They were directed to "strike the women on the arms and breasts and the men on the head."[38] Strikers sent their starving children to strike supporters in other cities rather than end the strike, and the children aroused such sympathy that Lawrence mill owners refused to let any more leave.

> [T]roopers surrounded the railway station, clubbed the children and their mothers, and then arrested them. The mothers were charged with "neglect" and "improper guardianship."[39]

In 1909, when general strikes shook the nation, the NWTUL called a strike among garment workers against Leiserman and Company's Triangle Shirt Waist Factory. At the time, 80 percent of the garment workers were women; 70 percent were between the ages of 16 and 25; 65 percent were Jewish; and 26 percent were Italian. Twenty thousand struck the company. The police beat and clubbed them and threw them in jail. According to one judge who tried a young woman striker, "You're not striking against your employer . . . you're striking against God."[40] Yet every day up to fifteen hundred women joined the union. Middle-class women who had never before considered the plight of working women contributed money for bail and for relief.

This strike led to the founding of the International Ladies' Garment Workers Union, which by 1914 was the third largest unit in the AFL. In 1913 the ILGWU signed the famous "protocol" contract, limiting work by gender. Only men could be hired as cutters and pressers, and the lowest-paid men had to earn more than the highest-paid woman, even for the same work. Cutters were paid $27.50 a week, while finishers, examiners, and sample makers—jobs reserved for women—were paid $9.50, $11.50, and $13.00 respectively.[41] Modest gains of the strike included a 52-hour workweek and limited overtime. However, some of the most important demands for health and safety were ignored, and two years later the Triangle Shirt Waist factory caught fire. The factory, which had 500 workers, was on the top three floors of a ten-story building. Fire exits were kept locked to make sure employees did not steal from the company, and fire hoses were left unconnected. There was little chance for escape. Some women burned to death, others jumped from the windows, falling like "bundles of burning cloth" to their deaths. In all, 146 workers died. The judge fined the owners $75.00 for negligence.[42]

Among women important in the union movements were Bessie Abramovitz; Harriet Stanton Blatch, daughter of Elizabeth Cady Stanton; Elizabeth Gurley Flynn; Rose Schneiderman; Agnes Nestor of the glovemakers; Mary Kenney O'Sullivan of the bookbinders, and Leonora O'Reilly. Abramovitz helped organize the Amalgamated Clothing Workers of America, one of the first unions to provide health care, housing, adult education, scholarships, and day care centers. Blatch organized the Equality League of Self-Supporting Women in factories, laundries, and garment shops. At its height it had nineteen thousand members. Flynn, a socialist, participated in twenty strikes and was arrested fifteen times between 1906 and 1926. Schneiderman organized for both the NWTUL and the ILGWU, becoming president of the latter. She also organized summer schools for working women; served as chairperson of the industrial section of the Women's Suffrage party; became secretary of the New York State Department of Labor; and was an unsuccessful candidate for the U.S. Senate. Franklin D. Roosevelt named her a member of the Labor Advisory Board in his administration.[43] Despite women's activities in the labor movement, they did not achieve top positions even in occupations they dominated.

## SOCIAL WELFARE IN THE PROGRESSIVE ERA

Several important changes took place in social work in the early 1900s. First, settlement house workers were progressively excluded from the profession of social work. Second, professionalization took the form of Mary Richmond's social diagnosis and casework method, which, though it considered the impact of environment on distress, remained oriented to personal rather than structural change. Third, bureaucratization and the use of scientific management techniques created new organizational structures and processes for accountability in the profession. Fourth, social workers, though they still protested that private charities could provide better psychic care to the distressed, formed new coalitions with public agencies who provided the funds for relief. For example, in 1914 they developed the

Association of Public Welfare Officials in New York. Finally, though business interests were not altruistic, welfare became increasingly a business issue, and businesses encouraged welfare as a part of municipal reform to defuse political agitation and bypass political machines.[44]

In 1910 Kansas City organized the first Board of Public Welfare, followed in 1913 by Cook County in Chicago. In 1917 Illinois instituted a State Department of Public Welfare and other states followed suit, with governors appointing heads of welfare. This innovation from traditional political appointments took public welfare out of politics except through the governor. Coll says

> The reform spirit in which many social workers interpreted their role in the early 20th century marked a departure from concern about pauperism to concern about poverty and a corresponding turnabout from the doctrine of personal fault to stress social and economic conditions as prime causes of hunger and squalor.[45]

After World War I, social reform was overwhelmed by the sense of prosperity and the belief that work would provide the final triumph over poverty. Spiraling prices and freely available credit increased profits and led the economy upward. The United States was the richest country in the world: by 1925 it was producing 55 percent of the world's iron; 66 percent of its steel; 62 percent of its petroleum; 52 percent of its lumber; 60 percent of the cotton; 80 percent of the sulfur; and 95 percent of the automobiles.[46] Demands for social insurance and public relief were considered a betrayal of the American way and public dependents and social workers parasites or subversives. Settlement houses were believed to be hotbeds of radicalism, and gradually they became traditional social agencies, losing their autonomy as they took money from the newly developing community chests. Professional casework, with its emphases on individual blame and middle-class morality, became the byline of the profession.

A new split in services for the needy emerged: the first cohort comprised of professional social workers disassociating themselves from the "unworthy" poor through casework practice; the second public welfare bureaucrats, often political appointees without training. These latter were the "moral descendants" of overseers of the poor and were often chosen precisely for their antiwelfare stances. Poor relief remained extremely discretionary, based on personal values and beliefs relegitimated by the booming economy. Only the "morally deserving" were aided—often the aged, sometimes the handicapped, and white widows who could subject themselves to moral investigation.

Religious, ethnic, and class differences continued to influence the provision of welfare. Protestant mission societies demanded church or Sunday school attendance as the price of assistance, and many new immigrants, particularly Catholics and Jews, avoided all church-related agencies, even nonevangelistic ones such as the YMCA. Language was also a barrier, and immigrants were stereotyped as ignorant, slovenly, stubborn, and "inert" if they did not want, or could not afford, a middle-class life-style. Middle-class workers in both ethnic and mainstream agencies considered themselves better than those they helped, who often paid in the coin of humiliation for food, shelter, and clothing.

An enormous expansion of public education coincided with the great immigrations at the turn of the century. Kindergartens, vacation schools, extracurricular activities, and vocational education and counseling were offered by the schools, with such organizations as corporations, unions, churches, YMCAs, YWCAs, and settlement houses co-sponsoring Americanization classes for immigrants.[47] Some states experimented with home teachers who took women to clinics, instructed them, and advised them on personal problems, housekeeping, and child care—the beginning of school social work. Visiting teachers paid little attention to girls, who were expected to stay home to help with housekeeping and younger children, but encouraged boys to stay in vocational education programs. Less money was spent for girls' education than for boys, and girls dropped out much more often.

Home economics classes were considered particularly important for immigrant women; however, few attended classes because they had little time or their husbands forbade it. For example, the immigrant population in Chicago in 1920 was over 300,000, but only 400 women attended "mothers' classes," and of these only 240 were regular students. Vocational education was highly supported for men. The Smith-Hughes Act of 1917 allotted 42 percent of its grants to schools of agriculture and 28 percent to trade or industrial schools. Seven percent went for general education and 23 percent for home economics courses for women. By 1920, most states had compulsory education to age 14, with a greatly lengthened school year. By 1923, there were 68 land grant colleges, with 24 state universities and 17 colleges for Afro-Americans.

### Reforms for Children

At the turn of the century, one out of six children were gainfully employed—7 million children between the ages of 10 and 15. No one knows how many under the age of 10 worked, especially Afro-American children on southern farms. Sixty percent of the children who worked on farms were employed by people other than their parents. Others worked in cotton, woolen, and silk mills; in clothing and tobacco sweatshops; in coal mines and iron mills; and up to 2.5 million in street trades.[48] Underage children working illegally were taught to hide when inspectors came. In 1900 Pennsylvania employed 120,000 children in mines and mills, and New York reported some 92,000 employed who were under 15 years old.[49] As textile mills moved south, employment of children increased until they comprised 30 percent of all textile millworkers.[50] New labor laws and compulsory education began to make inroads on child labor: By 1910, only 2 million were working; by 1920, 1 million; and by 1930 about 667,000.

One of the most outspoken advocates against child labor was Irish immigrant Mary Harris Jones (Mother Jones) (1830–1930). She fought for labor all her life—the 1877 Pittsburgh railroad strike, the Haymarket riot of 1886, the Pennsylvania coal miners strike in 1900, and the garment and streetcar workers' strikes in 1909. First an organizer for the Knights of

Labor, she also organized for the United Mine Workers and the IWW. While supporting a textile mill strike in Pennsylvania in 1903, she found that 10,000 of the 75,000 mill workers were children, many of them maimed by machinery. She publicized the plight, speaking of

> Eddie Dunphy, a little fellow of twelve, whose job it was to sit all day . . . handing in the right thread to another worker. . . . Eleven hours a day . . . with dangerous machinery all about him . . . for three dollars a week. And . . . Gussie Ragnew, a little girl from whom all the childhood had gone. Her face was like an old woman's . . . little boys with their fingers off and hands crushed and maimed. . . . Philadelphia's mansions were built on the broken bones, the quivering hearts, and drooping heads of these children.[51]

Mother Jones marched her "children's army" to President Theodore Roosevelt's summer home, from Philadelphia to Long Island, feeding them with donations from people along the way. Although the president refused to see them, the nation became aware of the "crime of child labor" and shortly thereafter Pennsylvania passed a child labor law setting a minimum age of 14 for child employment. Often beaten and jailed, Mother Jones continued until her death to "fight like hell" for children and the rights of labor.[52] National intervention in child labor was prohibited by the Constitution, so reforms were fought out state by state. Although thirty-four states eventually passed child labor laws, they had so many loopholes that they were, for the most part, ineffective. The paradox is clear. Labor would benefit from the restriction of child labor, giving more jobs to men. However, labor standards for children would raise wages and reduce profit; therefore, although altruism won the day in law, exceptions nullified the victory in favor of factory owners.

*Child Labor and Social Reform.* In 1902 Lillian Wald and Florence Kelley called a meeting of representatives of thirty-two settlement houses in New York City to discuss child labor, and in 1903 the group secured passage of a law regulating street trades. A national child labor committee was formed in 1904 as a clearinghouse against child labor, with such members as Edgar Gardner Murphy, Lillian Wald, Felix Adler—a crusader for housing reform—New York COS director Edward Devine, New York COS president Robert DeForest, and Jane Addams.[53] This committee influenced President T. Roosevelt to call the 1909 White House Conference on Child Dependency, which was attended by two hundred prominent men and women. The Conference went on record as favoring home care for children rather than institutionalization; and recommended the creation of a public bureau to collect and disseminate information on children and child care.

In 1912, that bureau, called the Children's Bureau, was established by William Howard Taft as a permanent part of the Department of Commerce and Labor. Its primary purpose was to protect children from early employment, dangerous occupations, and diseases. It advocated a minimum work age of 14 in manufacturing and 16 in mining, with documented proof of age, and an 8-hour workday and prohibition of night work. The first fifteen social workers employed by the federal government were hired to staff it, with Julia Lathrop as its director.[54] The bureau investigated and reported on all matters pertaining to child welfare and child life: infant mortality, birth rates, children's institutions, juvenile courts, desertion, dangerous occupations, accidents and diseases, child labor, and children's legislation. Its initial appropriation of about $25,000 was doubled, but was still far less than money spent for animal research—a million and a quarter dollars.[55] The mortality rate for young animals at that time was lower than that of children.

All child labor reforms were called Bolshevik plots to "nationalize" children and families and were consistently declared unconstitutional. The Keating-Owens bill to control child labor came to Congress in 1916 but failed to pass the courts; then an attempt to place a 10 percent tax on interstate commerce using child labor was outlawed. Finally, in 1924, a constitutional amendment was proposed, but was defeated by a lobby of manufacturers and Catholics, who believed it was a threat to family life. Nevertheless, by 1930, all states and Washington, D.C., had enacted child protection laws.

*Mothers' Pensions.* The most important social welfare reform of the Progressive Era was the granting of mothers' pensions—outdoor relief—to poverty-stricken widows. Social workers consistently opposed this, claiming that outdoor relief would spread the contagion of pauperism to the next generation. They favored institutionalization: A study in New York found that COS workers had committed 2,716 children to orphanages solely because their mothers were poor, and almost another thousand whose mothers were ill.[56] However, this practice was increasingly questioned by settlement workers and judges in the juvenile courts for, as Grace Abbott noted, mothers' child-caring contributions far exceeded their earning power in the marketplace.[57] Florence Kelley, speaking in favor of mothers' pensions, said that

> No money earned in the United States costs so dear, dollar for dollar, as the money earned by the mothers of young children.[58]

State after state chose to give mothers' pensions without consulting social workers. Faced with *faits accomplis,* they demanded the right to investigate and administer the pensions with social casework, to prevent recipients from "expecting relief as their right," and to "redeem" recipient families. They claimed that casework would ensure moral homes and proper upbringing for poor children. Convinced by their arguments as professionals and by the omnipresent public hatred of outdoor relief, social workers were given the tasks they asked for. Their investigations were

> thorough if not humiliating. If accepted for aid—and the rejection rate was very high—the mother was assumed to be in need of "supervision." . . . Why was a mother presumed to be competent to rear her children without case-worker supervision as long as the breadwinner was in the home but presumed to be incompetent when deprived of the breadwinner's support? . . . The growing profession of social work would doubtless have considered such a question impertinent.[59]

By 1911, twenty states provided mothers' pensions, and within ten years forty states allowed them. The first statewide law began in Illinois, also in 1911, as an addendum to the Juvenile Delinquency Code called the "Funds to Parents Act." Wisconsin was next. The bills aimed both at providing for destitute children and establishing moral homes for children, via a contract between the mother and the courts. If the agreement was violated by the mother, her children could be placed either in foster homes or in institutions. The programs were selective in the families they would serve, for there was still a strong reluctance to give outdoor relief. Recipients, therefore, were required to be of good moral character, widows, and white. Bell notes that

> Blacks were rarely admitted to this elite program for fatherless families, and as late as 1922 social workers reported that "low-type" families . . . Mexicans, Italians, and Czechoslovakians were seldom helped. If they were they usually received lower grants than "high-type" Anglo-Saxons.[60]

Most early laws confined aid to widows in the belief that assisting deserted mothers would encourage more desertion. By 1926, however, only five states still limited aid to widows. Also included, at local discretion, were divorced mothers and those with husbands totally incapacitated, physically or mentally impaired, imprisoned, epileptic, or in an institution for the insane. Six states had no mothers' pensions—Alabama, Georgia, Kentucky, Mississippi, New Mexico, and South Carolina. Coll says that

> In all states mothers' aid was not mandatory but at the option of county or municipality. So they were maintained only in a few towns. Ratios of children aided per 100,000 . . . ranged from 1.4 to 331 in 1926. A few—Arkansas, Indiana, Texas, Tennessee, Virginia—aided less than 20 per 100,000 . . . .By 1934, about half the aid to mothers . . . [went] to cities of 50,000 or more.[61]

In 1926, maximum grants ranged from $70.00 a month in states such as California, Michigan, Indiana, and Ohio to $30.00 in Illinois, Iowa, Louisiana, Missouri, Montana, and Nebraska. In others, grants were made individually by administrative decision and according to need but could not exceed the cost of institutional care.[62] In California, women receiving mothers' pensions were called "gilt-edged widows," but in reality the payments were so low that welfare mothers still had to work—as domestics, laundresses, and so on. In Chicago, where mothers' pensions began, Judge Pinckney's average award to mothers was $262 per year, and he was one of the most liberal of judges.

*Child and Maternal Health.* The health of women and children was a primary concern of the Children's Bureau. Findings in 1909 indicated an unusually high infant and maternal mortality rate, higher for women than any cause except tuberculosis. The maternal death rate was 6.7 per 1,000 live births and more than 250,000 infants died before the age of 1 (10 percent). Poor clinical and obstetrical training were blamed, for at least half of all maternal deaths were considered preventable. Nearly 40 percent were caused by puerperal sepsis, toxemia, pelvic disproportion, and hemorrhage. As head of the Children's Bureau, Julia Lathrop drew up a bill to establish public health clinics and hospitals, later called the Sheppard-Towner Act (1918). Her bill was labeled a Bolshevik plot and an infringement on physicians' privileges, and opponents ridiculed its writer as an unmarried nonmother who presumed to instruct mothers on child care. Missouri Democrat James Reed went so far as to ask Julia Lathrop if she had ever been a mother, to give her the right to talk about children. She replied, "No, sir, have you?"[63]

In 1921, after three years of lobbying, the Sheppard-Towner Act passed. Lathrop retired immediately before its passage, and Grace Abbott, newly appointed to direct the Children's Bureau, was given a five-year $1,252,000 grant to administer it. The program served nearly three thousand child and maternal health centers in forty-five states, and infant and maternal mortality dropped so significantly that it was extended for another two years. After the 1929 crash, a congressional committee ruled it too expensive, and though Congress dropped it, the program was reconstituted as part of the Social Security Act of 1935.

One of the most important new health programs was the Kentucky Committee for Mothers and Babies (renamed the Frontier Nursing Society in 1928). Mary Breckinridge, a nurse, developed the program in 1925 to train nurse midwives, in order to cut the alarming infant and maternal mortality rates in doctorless rural areas. Breckinridge hoped to gain federal Sheppard-Towner funds, but the director of Kentucky's Bureau of Maternal and Child Health Care stonewalled federal grant application on the grounds that Kentucky's twenty-five hundred practicing midwives, rather than outside nurses, should be trained. Breckinridge withdrew her federal proposal and raised money through women's committees to carry out her program.[64]

### Medical and Psychiatric Social Work

As early as 1879 the National Conference on Charities and Corrections discussed mental illness and organized the National Association for the Protection of the Insane and the Prevention of Insanity. Its goals were research and education for better hospital policies and conditions, but it was opposed by hospital administrators and so failed after seven years. Psychiatric social work began on an organized basis in 1895 when New York State Hospital Services established its Pathological Institute, and in Albany, New York, in 1902 with a treatment program for the mentally ill. In 1905, Dr. Adolf Meyer was named chief of the New York State Hospital's Pathological Institute and moved it to Manhattan State Hospital. Meyer and his wife, a social worker, saw mental illness as maladjustment, and as Mrs. Meyer began to collect case histories, social workers became part of the mental health team. By 1906, the New York COS had established privately supported aftercare programs in each state hospital, and medical social work began to proliferate.

In 1905, the first social service department in a hospital was organized in Massachusetts General Hospital in Boston. Social workers went into the community to see patients in their homes and to investigate social conditions that had sent them to hospitals or to which they had to return. Belle-vue in New York City was established soon thereafter, and in 1907 Johns Hopkins established a social work outpatient section. In 1921 Johns Hopkins began a two-year program to train medical social workers. Between 1905 and 1917 more than a hundred hospitals in thirty-five cities hired hospital social workers, and in 1918 the American Association of Hospital Social Workers formed.

The mental hygiene movement itself began when a former mental patient, Clifford Beers, voiced his distress at his treatment in three years in mental hospitals in the book *The Mind That Found Itself.* He founded the National Committee for Mental Hygiene and supported it himself, going deeply into debt, until in 1912 Henry Phipps donated $50,000 to the asso-ciation. The Rockefeller Foundation also helped to support the NCMH, and with added funding from the Russell Sage Foundation, it began to look at broader concerns than mental hospital reform—over Beers's objections. The broadened mental hygiene movement focused on

1. Issues of the role of mental hygiene in education, criminology, and economic dependence
2. Programs of "preventive" mental health and mental health treatment
3. Research to define the "normal" personality (especially through improved child-rearing and education and the early detection and treatment of "abnor-mality"
4. Training a new generation of mental health professionals[65]

This latter meant especially professional social workers, whose schools, professional associations, and journals were funded by the Russell Sage Foundation, the Commonwealth Fund, and the Laura Spelman Rockefeller Memorial Fund. Soon hospitals, private mental hospitals, and universities were establishing their own psychiatric care units. The mental hygiene movement led to the development of an alternate method to explain psychological problems, which had before been considered almost genetic in nature. This meant that mental disorder or deviance became a disease that could be prevented, detected, and treated. New diagnoses included the "maladjusted," the "psychopathic personality," the "bor-derline patient." People with personality disorders, according to a text in use in the 1920s, included paupers, prostitutes, misfits, criminals, drug users, bashful people, gypsies, old maids (by choice), unskilled laborers, dreamers and artists, deep thinkers, radicals and agitators, chronic grouches, peace-loving pacifists, and the over-studious.[66]

Veterans' services also had impact on the new mental hygiene move-ment. Battle fatigue, a problem of soldiers returning from World War I, presented a different problem to the helping professions. No longer were the poor or deviant the only appropriate subjects for mental health care. The National Committee on Mental Hygiene and the Boston State Hospital collaborated to set up an intensive training program for social workers, at Smith College in 1918. This program later became the Smith College School for Social Work, a model for psychiatric training for social work professionals.[67]

As early as 1896 Lightner Witmer had developed the first psychological clinic in the United States (at the University of Pennsylvania) to introduce scientific knowledge about children and to train teachers, social workers, and psychiatrists. In 1907 he opened a hospital school for residential treatment of children with learning disabilities, and in 1909 Jane Addams and Julia Lathrop served on the advisory committee that established the Institute of Juvenile Research in Chicago. From these beginnings, Child Guidance Clinics began to open, funded in 1921 by the Commonwealth Fund for Prevention of Juvenile Delinquency. The Commonwealth Fund provided monies for many offshoots of the mental health movement: research on the causes and prevention of delinquency; establishment of an experimental system of school social workers; programs of direct public education; and the Child Guidance Clinics, which were actually demonstration projects.

The clinic personnel set up the first clinic in St. Louis and, when it became self-supporting, moved on to other cities throughout the nation. The clinics were oriented to providing "proper" child-rearing practices; that is, they stressed giving advice to parents and working with them, along with schools and courts, to prevent juvenile delinquency. Such clinics gave a tremendous impetus to the social work profession by stressing the need for trained caseworkers; they also set new standards for child care, based on new mental health knowledge and middle-class standards. A particular kind of conformity in child-rearing was intimated across class lines, and once again social welfare practices legitimated *parens patriae,* this time through mental health rather than poor relief.

### Veterans' Welfare

Prior to the outbreak of war in 1914, veterans' pensions cost $174 million annually.[68] However, the war's terrible devastation made the nation eager to expand benefits for its survivors. In 1917, Wilson appointed a Council of National Defense to review and recommend veterans' benefits, and a new benefit—the offer of readjustment and rehabilitation services for psychiatric problems such as shellshock—was added. Compulsory allotments were voted for families, at first paid by soldiers but later by the government. The War Risk Insurance Act was expanded to include voluntary insurance against death and total disability, medical and surgical hospital care, prostheses for those injured in service, and vocational rehabilitation.

By 1918, of the 4,744,000 in service, 116,000 died and 204,000 were wounded. By the mid-1920s the Public Health Service had to increase its beds to 11,639 in fifty-two hospitals to accommodate veterans. Congress also authorized the use of beds in army and navy hospitals and in sixty national homes for disabled veterans. Because veterans' benefits were fragmented among the Bureau of War Risk Insurance, the Rehabilitative Division of the Federal Board for Vocational Rehabilitation, the Public Health Service, and the Armed Services, President Harding appointed a board (the Dawes Commission) in 1921 to establish the Veterans' Bureau. Benefits were further expanded in 1925, including the use of veterans' hospitals for veterans whose disabilities were not service connected.[69]

During the war, the Red Cross provided canteens and clubs for ser-vicemen, gave social services to men in military hospitals, and provided services to servicemen's families to help them cope with wartime separa-tion. Although social work services had been previously provided for the nonpoor, they had been in special categories, such as the mentally ill. The use of social work services for problems of "normal" (though stressed) people who were not poor gave a new impetus to casework as the profes-sional social work method.

### Aid to the Blind

Social workers objected to giving home relief to the blind because, they argued, flat grants did not take into account the degrees of need, discouraged industry among the blind, and made no provision for their rehabilitation.[70] However, aid to the blind was approved by most people, and this was the first group to receive outdoor relief as a right, in Ohio in 1898. In 1915 Illinois required counties to grant $365 annually to blind persons with incomes of less than $465 a year, and by 1925, twenty-seven states had Aid to the Blind. Some also had Aid to the Disabled programs such as the employment bureau opened by the New York COS to place the physically, mentally, and socially handicapped in employment where their disabilities would not interfere with their work. After two years, the number of applicants averaged a hundred a month, and placements aver-aged eighty a month.[71] Vocational rehabilitation to help all categories of handicapped people was established in 1920 in the Department of Educa-tion. The need continually outpaced the available federal funding, so not all in need were served.

### Old Age Assistance

Pensions for the aged were one of the last reforms to be made, proba-bly because society believed people should save for their old age or that relatives should support their aged parents. However, with new medical technologies and better nutrition people lived longer. To support them often went beyond the ability of their children, and their small savings could not stretch through their longer old age. Many groups, including social workers, demanded that industry provide pensions, but they refused to do so voluntarily. Even had they been willing, many aged persons would have fallen outside their pension plans—women who had not worked, those in domestic service, farm workers, and day laborers, for example.

By 1905, the Massachusetts Bureau of Statistics had noted the prob-lems of the aged poor and recommended pensions as the only humane way of dealing with them (though Massachusetts decided against pensions in 1910). Both the National Conference on Charities and Corrections and the Progressive Party endorsed social insurance in 1912, including old age insurance. However, by 1914, only Arizona and Alaska had even limited plans, and fewer than 1 percent of workers were covered by private plans. After the war, pensions for the aged were tied to health insurance by such groups as the Consumers League, Women's Trade Union League, and American Association for Labor Legislation. This was fought both by employers and the American Medical Association, and old age pensions were lost in the battle.

As increasing numbers of the aged sank into poverty, dependence on public assistance grew, and beginning in 1923 some states moved toward old age pensions. They helped "only persons of good character," however, and excluded persons who deserted wives or husbands, and those who had been tramps or beggars. Some states required fifteen years of residency and had limits on earned income and assets. Many also placed liens on recipients' property, to be claimed after death.[72] Montana, Nevada, and Pennsylvania passed limited voluntary bills in 1923, and the first mandatory bill was passed by California in 1929.[73] By 1929, eleven states had bills to provide pensions for the aged, and between 1929 and 1933, nineteen more enacted them.[74] Laws passed after 1929 were compulsory for the entire state, and states contributed to the fund. However,

> In 1929 only a little over 1,000 elderly persons received assistance, at a total cost of $222,000; by 1932 more than 100,000 persons were receiving OAA at a total cost of $22 million a year.[75]

Most states set age eligibility for assistance at 65, required that relatives support the aged if possible, set residency requirements, required recipients to be U.S. citizens, and ordered recipients to exhaust their savings before application.

Powerful lobbies for the aged grew up during the 1920s. One of the major ones was the Townsend Plan, proposed by Francis E. Townsend, a retired California doctor. It asked for a pension of $200 per month for every person over age 60. The money would be financed by a sales tax and had to be spent within each thirty-day period or returned. The plan gained an estimated ten million adherents, and soon there were Townsend Clubs all over the country, presenting a major challenge to setting up the Social Security Acts of 1935.

### Unemployment Insurance

John R. Commons and John B. Adams of the University of Wisconsin led the fight for unemployment insurance, public employment offices, and regulation of industry. Although bills were introduced in a number of states, none passed until Wisconsin in 1932 made unemployment insurance voluntary in January and compulsory in June of the same year. On the federal level, a bill was proposed to be administered by the Children's Bureau under a Federal Board of Unemployment Relief. It would have provided $125 million for the first six months with another $250 million for the second. This bill also failed to pass, and not until the Social Security Act of 1935 was unemployment dealt with.

### Worker's Compensation

Worker's compensation, to help those injured on the job or the survivors of those killed at work, was first discussed at the American Sociological Association Conference in 1902 and again in 1905 and 1906.

Despite the horrendous rate of industrial accidents at the time, Samuel Gompers and unions vehemently opposed worker's compensation, for they wanted welfare to be a union function and feared state intervention in union affairs.[76] However, the nation moved inevitably toward worker's compensation. Every year, half a million workers were injured in industrial accidents and fifteen thousand were killed. Employers blamed this on workers, saying that they knew the risks of the jobs when they took them. Courts generally supported this claim, although some states, including Massachusetts and Illinois, recommended industrial insurance to factory owners during this period.

In 1906, under Theodore Roosevelt, the Federal Employment Act was passed, providing a minimum worker's insurance for federal employees, and in the same year the National Conference on Charities and Corrections appointed a committee on the issue. A National Conference on Worker's Compensation was called in 1909, and shortly thereafter a major study was undertaken in Pittsburgh. This study, a comprehensive survey of all labor conditions in the entire city, was one of the most important of social research efforts of the era. It was funded by the Russell Sage Foundation, and members of its committee included Paul Kellogg, a social worker; William H. Matthews, head of the Pittsburgh Settlement House; Robert Woods, a settlement house worker; Florence Kelley, the director of the National Consumers' League; and John R. Commons, a well-known economist. The study looked at wages, hours, conditions of labor, housing, schooling, health, taxation, fire and police protection, recreation, and land values. In 1910, Crystal Eastman published its final report, "Work Accidents and the Law," arguing that the high rate of industrial accidents would continue as long as employers were not held responsible. After the Eastman report, thirty states investigated safety conditions in industry.[77] Ten states enacted worker's compensation laws in 1911, and by 1920 forty-two states had adopted her suggestions into law. Generally, they included compensation for workers and their survivors based on economic loss due to industrial accidents; employer responsibility for all accidents regardless of fault; and a voluntary insurance pool under public administration. Although many people were not covered and benefits were limited, it was a beginning.

### Health Insurance

Reformers tried to include health insurance in the worker's compensation package, but heavy opposition came from the medical profession, insurance companies, employers, Christian Socialists, superpatriots who saw all 'social insurance as "made in Germany," and, strangely enough, labor unions. Because of this, health coverage was dropped from consideration (except in some maternal and child health cases) until the major 1960 reforms in Medicare and Medicaid. Supporters of health insurance during the Progressive Era believed that illness was a more important cause of poverty than industrial accidents. They claimed it would not increase costs of medical care in the long run and that it would prevent poverty as it prevented illness. However, once more came the cry of bolshevism, and progress toward health insurance ceased. Katz says

In their struggle against social insurance measures opponents deployed the old American ideology of voluntarism, condemning the interference of the state, praising the efforts of private philanthropy, and stressing the importance of individual achievement. In place of voluntarism they held out the menace of social and racial degeneration, the destruction of the moral basis of American society, and the victory of other social systems, that is, socialism and Bolshevism.[78]

### Juvenile and Criminal Justice

By the Progressive Era, the juvenile justice system had significantly changed the lives of poor children. *Parens patriae* influenced juvenile laws, new children's codes, the control of child labor, and mothers' pensions. Foster care, adoption, and protection for the abused child were instituted by this time, as were separate facilities for delinquent children or probation under local courts for children committing federal crimes. The Federal Bureau of Prisons, organized in 1930, set up a national training school for boys, two detention centers, and federal prison camps.

For adults, the criminal justice system was making much more use of probation, parole, and rehabilitation. In 1910 the New York COS led the way to a system of probation and fines for drunks so that they would not be incarcerated. For long-term offenders, commitment to a farm colony and hospitals for care and cure was recommended.[79] Federal prisons were established in 1890, and after riots in 1919 were considerably improved. The Department of Justice introduced parole services and began probation investigations in 1925. In 1930 the Federal Bureau of Prisons expanded its services to include vocational training, recreation, and educational facilities, medical and dental care, and religious and cultural activities; and set up reformatories and correctional facilities for minor crimes and short-term sentences. For the physically and mentally ill, a medical center was established.

## WOMEN'S MOVEMENTS AND PEACE PROTESTS

Women continued their reform movements in the Progressive Era, encompassing labor reform and children's welfare, the suffrage movement, the peace movement, and reforms related to sexuality. The areas of struggle, though often carried out by different groups, were related both by content and by interlocking memberships.

### Suffrage

The suffrage groups that split after the Civil War coalesced in the 1900s into the National American Women's Suffrage Association (NAWSA). After a brief presidency by Carrie Chapman Catt (1849–1947), who succeeded Susan B. Anthony in 1900, Dr. Anna Howard Shaw (1847–1919), a Methodist minister and physician, became president. Although Shaw was an eloquent orator, she had almost no administrative skills and little tact. She consistently alienated men in power by attacking their politics, thus undermining their political support for women, and left NAWSA's administration in a shambles, with many of its staunchest supporters, such as Florence Kelley, resigning. Shaw resigned in favor of Jane Addams in 1911, and in 1915 the presidency was resumed by Carrie Chapman Catt.[80]

Catt, a tireless lobbyist, built NAWSA into a strong organization at both state and federal levels. She developed a "Winning Plan" of support and influence for legislative leaders in return for their favorable votes on women's issues such as voting rights in party primaries and federal elections. During World War I, though Catt joined Jane Addams in forming the Woman's Peace Party, she supported Wilson's war policies. As reward, he threw his weight behind both suffrage and temperance movements, and the prohibition amendment was passed in 1919 and suffrage ratified in 1920. Its major goal attained, NAWSA became the League of Women Voters. In 1925, Catt founded the National Committee on the Cause and Cure of War and served as chairman until 1932. She was also active in support of the League of Nations, for relief of Jewish refugees from Germany, and on behalf of the child labor amendment.

Politicians, unsure of the effect of the new women's vote, established the Women's Bureau in the Department of Labor in 1920 and passed the Sheppard-Towner Act for maternal and child health in 1921. Changes were also made in the civil service system, making it fairer to women, and in consumers' rights systems for pure food. However, women continued either not to vote or to vote with their husbands, and soon their effect on the national structure was discounted. After 1924, with the election of Warren G. Harding, the nation reverted to conservatism in terms of women's issues.

A more radical suffrage movement existed alongside that of NAWSA, merging into a peace movement that opposed Wilson's war policies. Among its leaders were Alice Paul, Lucy Burns, Rose Winslow, Crystal Eastman, and Mary Ritter Beard. Alice Paul (1885–1977), a devout Quaker, studied at the New York School of Social Work and lived at the New York College Settlement. She became disillusioned as a social worker and in 1906 went to England to work in settlements there. She joined the British suffrage movement led by Emmeline and Christabel Pankhurst, a radical group that practiced nonviolent resistance, including blocking roads and picketing homes and government buildings, and was jailed three times. Returning to the United States in 1910, she joined NAWSA but became impatient with its timid policies.

In 1913 Paul and her radical cohort formed the Congressional Union for Women's Suffrage.[81] The Union adopted a stance of active interference, including a spectacular suffrage parade in Washington, D.C., on the day of Wilson's inauguration (1913). The parade became a riot, and troops were brought in to put down the crowd that was beating the women. The sympathy they aroused, however, was short-lived, and in 1914 NAWSA withdrew its support of Paul. Although the suffragists never committed acts of violence, violence on a new scale was committed upon them. Uniformed soldiers attacked women pickets blocking the White House, and by June 1917, they were being arrested. At first, the charges were dropped, but gradually the courts began to convict and jail them for up to six months. More than two hundred women from twenty-six states were arrested for blocking the streets, and ninety-seven were sent to the District of Columbia jail or the infamous Occoquan workhouse, where "the rats were so big dogs were afraid."[82] They were beaten at random, Alice Paul was tortured by being kept awake, and the authorities responded to hunger strikes by force-feeding the women by tube until their noses bled. Rose Winslow writes

> Yesterday was a bad day for me in feeding . . . vomiting continually. . . . The tube has developed an irritation somewhere that is painful. Never was there a sentence like ours for such an offense as ours, even in England. . . . Don't let them tell you we take this well. Miss Paul vomits much. I do too, except when I'm not nervous . . . we are making this hunger strike that women fighting for liberty may be considered political prisoners. . . . God knows we don't want other women ever to have to do this over again.[83]

The Union joined with the Woman's Party in 1917 to become the National Woman's Party, and Paul became its major spokesperson and organizer. After passage of the Suffrage Amendment in 1920, she drafted the first equal rights amendment in 1923. When it failed, she turned crusader for the League of Nations and founded and represented the World Women's Party at its meetings in Geneva. She continued as chairman of the National Woman's party from 1942 until her death in 1977, still seeking an equal rights amendment to end a societal sexism nearly untouched by the suffrage amendment of 1920.

### Women and Health

The public health movement came at a time when women were still mostly excluded from regular medical practice. In 1920, for example, only 40 of 482 general hospitals accepted women as interns, and from 1925 to 1945 there was a 5 percent quota on women admitted to medical schools.[84] It was also a middle-class women's movement perceived as "cleaning society" as women cleaned their homes. Its financing was often justified with classist arguments about costs to the middle class of sickness among workers, absenteeism due to illness, and relief for orphans. Public health was closely related to the police: in fact, in earlier years it had been a police function, and public health workers continued to call on the police to enforce their mandates. Raids on tenements were commonplace, as police sought out disease-carriers, including prostitutes, and such problems as typhoid were looked upon as visitations from God against sin.

*Prostitution and Venereal Disease.* One major goal of the public health movement was to conquer venereal disease, and the method was to control prostitutes. Their own health was not the issue, despite their high mortality rate after entering the field. Rather, control aimed at keeping "clean" middle-class wives from infection. The fault of men who used prostitutes and spread the disease went unnoticed: prostitutes were blamed. Both men and women in the movement agreed on fighting prostitution, especially when "fallen sisters" obviously preferred prostitution to the back-breaking, low-paying jobs available to them.

A small minority of immigrant women prostitutes first caught the public eye, confirming Social Darwinist, sexist, and nativist stereotypes. Women immigrants outnumbered men by the early 1900s, and many were young single women without family or friends trying to survive in a new culture. The Immigration Bureau entered the battle to deport such "immoral" persons as part of its venereal disease control program. Its commission found prostitution in virtually all ethnic communities but failed to note the power of poverty and the double standard in perpetuating it. Grace Abbott, then director of the Immigrants Protective League of Chicago, believed that poverty, loneliness, ignorance, and a desire for romance made immigrant women particularly vulnerable to sexual exploitation.[85] She condemned America's moral "double standard" and advocated that the Immigration Service pay less attention to keeping "immoral" women from immigrating and more to helping them to survive in America.[86]

Men transmitted venereal diseases across all class lines. In 1904, Prince Morrow, the chair of a committee investigating venereal disease, estimated that 60 percent of the adult male population would have either syphilis or gonorrhea within their lives (an estimated 450,000 new infections per year).[87] In 1910, a new estimate stated that 80 percent of urban males had venereal disease and 60 to 75 percent of "marriageable" men had gonorrhea.[88] Syphilis caused sterility—for both men and their wives (as well as the prostitutes)—and general paresis, a deterioration of the brain. Eight to 20 percent of insanity cases were linked to venereal diseases.

Children also suffered: In 1905 research showed that between 25 and 40 percent of all congenital blindness in infants was caused by gonorrhea from infected mothers,[89] and one of every four babies was blind. Wives were infected because often doctors colluded with husbands to keep venereal diseases secret even after they became detectable (for syphilis, with the Wasserman blood test in 1906) and curable (a 1910 arsenate compound destroyed the syphilis spirochete). Alexander Fleming's discovery of penicillin dropped the infection rate dramatically. Medical control was possible, but social ideologies prevented it. Many physicians would not discuss venereal disease, especially in public, for "by its nature it besmirched them." Although as early as 1903 the AMA formed a standing committee on venereal disease, because of its "dirty" nature, many hospitals would not admit sufferers as patients.

A study in 1914 estimated that between 28 and 100 percent of prostitutes had venereal disease [90] and that infection of men was in most cases directly traceable to prostitutes. A later study by Dr. Howard Woolson, of the Bureau of Social Hygiene, estimated that there were at least 200,000 prostitutes in "a regular army of vice" and that 60 to 75 percent carried venereal diseases. An estimated 25 to 35 percent of the adult population was infected. He also noted that there was considerable shuffling back and forth between prostitution and low-paid jobs.

Legislatures took action to protect innocent wives: In Washington in 1909 and Wisconsin in 1913, laws required men to have physical exams, and by 1921 twenty states had similar laws. Venereal disease control was added to the U.S. Public Health Service in 1918, and by 1922 all forty-eight states had some kind of legislation requiring the reporting of VD.[91] However, hiding the disease made the laws ineffective. Also, since wives were perceived as victims, they were not examined, so clandestine affairs or previous sexual liaisons continued to spread the disease. Finally, exams were not given carefully or the results examined because of doctors' belief in the morality of their clients, and therefore much VD simply escaped notice.

Police efforts cut severely into prostitution, and its regulation became a major issue. Since prostitution was considered "essential" for men, they could not be regulated—but women could. One camp advocated moving all prostitutes to a particular "red light" district under medical control. A wide variety of people opposed this, some feeling that medical regulation would give moral legitimation to the trade and others believing it was an infringe-ment on the rights of freedom of women. Such eminent people as Theodore Roosevelt opposed the opening of a "tenderloin" district, calling for a war on commercialized vice rather than its regulation. Feminists and social workers such as Jane Addams and Maude E. Minier opposed regulations because it controlled the lives of women but not the men that used them. Antiregulationists could also point to a study of European regulation by Dr. Abraham Flexner, who reported in 1914 that such containment and supervision was simply ineffective.[92]

In addition to wage-earning prostitution, there was a worldwide active "white slave trade"—women kidnapped and sold into prostitution. In 1873 Congress had passed an act aimed at breaking up this "trade," and the Immigration Law of 1903 particularly excluded "prostitutes and persons who procure or attempt to bring in prostitutes or women for the purpose of prostitution." The law was strengthened in 1907 so that women immigrants who became prostitutes within three years could be deported. In 1904, a worldwide conference was held on white slavery, and following its mandate the United States in 1910 made procurement of immigrant women for immoral purposes a felony. In addition, alien women living in a house of prostitution or employed in a place frequented by prostitutes could be deported.[93]

*Abortion and Contraception.* Abortion and contraception were also public health issues. Both were looked upon as vice, and this closed the only avenues open to women who feared death in childbirth or the added burden of more and more children. Poor women still frequented abortionists, paying in pain and death, but middle-class women could arrange for "legal" abortions because of their "delicate conditions." In 1904, a symposium on abortion in Chicago, along with the Chicago Medical Society, came out against abortion. For a short time this influenced newspapers to drop their thinly disguised abortion ads and doctors to cut back on the number of abortions they performed. However, by 1908 the ads were back, producing an estimated $50,000 a year in revenue, and doctors resumed their profitable illegal practice on which city officials took protection payoffs.[94] It is estimated that after 1900 between five and ten thousand women died every year from botched abortions,[95] and by the mid-1930s, there was one abortion for every four pregnancies,[96] with about a million illegal abortions a year.

The fight for contraception was a fight against abortion, death in childbirth, and poverty. Pioneers included the socialist Emma Goldman (1869–1940), who as a midwife saw the desperate need for birth control and believed that women's control of their own reproduction was among their most important rights. Goldman gave the first public lecture on contraception, for which she was jailed. (Goldman also spent two years in jail for speaking out against the draft, and when the red scare hit the nation after the War, she was among 248 leftists deported to Russia, in 1919.)[97]

Another leader was Margaret Sanger (1883–1966), one of Goldman's students and founder of Planned Parenthood. A nurse among New York's immigrants, she saw her own mother die young from bearing too many children and like Goldman believed that women's emancipation began with control of their own bodies. She saw the terrible problems rising from lack of such control: too many children and the effects of illegal or homemade abortions. She wrote

> I heard over and over again of their desperate efforts at bringing themselves "around"—drinking various herb teas, taking drops of turpentine on sugar, steaming over a chamber of boiling coffee or even turpentine water, rolling down stairs, and finally inserting slippery-elm sticks, or knitting needles, or shoe hooks, into the uterus. . . . Life for them had but one choice: either to abandon themselves to incessant child-bearing, or to terminate their pregnancies through abortions.[98]

Attending a woman who nearly died from an abortion and whom another pregnancy would kill, she heard her beg the doctor for contraceptive information. The doctor replied "Tell Jake to sleep on the roof." Three months later the woman was dead.

Sanger began her campaign for contraception by distributing handbills, some through the mails. She was arrested under the Comstock Act for sending out "obscene materials" and fled with her family to Europe. In Holland, she found that state-dispensed diaphragms had reduced maternal mortality by half. She returned to the United States in 1916 with more knowledge of contraception and opened the Brownsville Clinic in New York, conducting a house-to-house canvass to inform possible clients. Police closed her clinic and arrested Sanger and her sister Ethel Byrne. Byrne was sentenced to thirty days in jail and began a hunger strike. After 103 hours without food, Commissioner of Corrections Lewis ordered her force fed. Dangerously ill from the effects of the forcefeeding, she was released on the promise she would not speak again of contraception.[99]

In Sanger's next clinic, opening in 1917, physicians dispensed diaphragms smuggled in from Europe only to those women whose medical history indicated that another pregnancy would be a health hazard. Other women were referred to sympathetic doctors.[100] Unable to get a license,

Sanger turned over her Birth Control Research Bureau to physician Robert Layton Dixon, but he was also unsuccessful at obtaining a license. By 1927, Dr. Hannah Stone, the clinic's medical director, could demonstrate and prescribe diaphragms, but not until 1936 were doctors allowed to distribute contraceptives. The Depression, with its skyrocketing welfare costs, made contraception less socially offensive.[101] Although the American Medical Association in 1937 recognized that contraception was an important medical topic, it remained illegal until 1938, when a court ruling allowed physicians to import, mail, and prescribe devices. Even so, the "under-the-counter" racket in contraception remained a $250-million-a-year business because doctors were still unwilling to prescribe contraceptives.

## THE PROFESSIONALIZATION OF SOCIAL WORK

A professional association for social workers developed from community social work clubs affiliated with the Conference on Charities and Corrections, and the Intercollegiate Bureau of Occupations organized a separate social work bureau in 1913. In 1917, a National Social Work Exchange was organized—anyone who believed she or he was eligible was accepted as a member. By the end of World War I, there were seventeen schools of social work, and in 1919, under the leadership of Porter Lee, school representatives agreed on a standardized curriculum with casework as the major method. This group evolved first to the Association of Professional Schools of Social Work and then into the Council on Social Work Education. In 1921, the Conference on Charities and Corrections became the American Association of Social Workers—later the National Association of Social Workers—and members were required to have four years of experience or academic and professional training.

Professionalization also came through the fund-raising community chests of charity organization societies. The first of these came in 1900, when the Cleveland Chamber of Commerce organized a Committee on Benevolent Institutions to accredit charities and evaluate methods for collecting and accounting for money. Altruism was only part of the goal, for the Hollis Amendment to the income tax law just before World War I provided tax loopholes for donors up to 15 percent of their income. In addition, those who supported community chests could decide which agencies would live and which would fail, and community chest boards, made up of locally prominent people, achieved great power over budgets and programs for member agencies.

Community chests became today's United Fund or United Way, while the service portion of charity organization societies evolved first into the name of the American Association of Charities and then the Family Welfare Association of America. In 1946 these organizations confederated into the Family Services Association of America. Settlement houses also became member agencies of United Way, losing their autonomy by accepting funds from community chests and losing their impetus for reform in the bureaucratization and professionalization of social work. During the same period, public welfare workers went from being overseers of the poor to county level government bureaucrats in charge of investigating and doling out money to the "worthy poor." Thus the two historic themes of welfare—public and private charity—merged in the early decades of the century and parted in the 1930s to become public welfare and family casework services. Social reform movements that stressed that poverty was caused by economic and social issues solidified into the settlement house movement; this movement lost its voice for reform in the newly prosperous nation.

By 1929, there were forty-six hundred social workers belonging to forty-three chapters of the American Association of Social Workers (founded in 1921). Almost as many belonged to the American Association of Hospital Social Workers and the American Association of Psychiatric Social Workers. Twenty-five masters' degree programs led to MSW degrees and a new professionalism that would legitimate social work and gain support from state legislatures, foundations, and philanthropists. Psychoanalytic casework was the method of choice, and social workers could now come to the profession equipped with learnable skills as well as good will. New human behavioral theories became the knowledge base of the profession, which subsequently moved away from its historic mission of care for the poor. Veterans' services, the mental health movement, child guidance clinics, the growth of an organized theory of social development, the growing interest in psychology, and Freudian psychoanalysis became the threads that bound the profession together. At the Milford Conference of 1929, social casework was proclaimed as the generic method of social work in both purpose and methodology regardless of practice setting.

## CONCLUSION: NEW FREEDOMS AND OLD CONSTRAINTS

From the Progressive Era and World War I to the stagnation and depression of the 1920s, social reform and social work took separate paths. Social reform had virtually ended by 1920, and social work had become a middle-class profession. The government's reform legislation had bureaucratized county and state departments of public welfare, with more regularized funding and more accountability. The move away from institutionalization of the poor was almost complete, while pensions, though far from adequate, were the trend of the future.

Although we often think of this era as one of increasing equality, in reality America had lost little of its classism, racism, and sexism. The gains unions had made were primarily for men, and now by law women's secondary status in the job market was confirmed in most states. The polarization of classes had increased, and the great wealth of the few insulated and isolated them from the problems of the poor. By 1929, 5 percent of the population owned half the nation's wealth, and 42 percent of all families earned less that the $1,500 required for minimum health and decency for a family of five.[102] Racism based on economic problems and exacerbated by attitudes of Social Darwinism existed as though the Civil War and Emancipation had never been.

In this era, each social movement contributed to the new definitions of deprivation, dependency, and public and private social welfare responsibilities. Social reform also set forth *ideals* of equality for workers, people of color, and women and laid the bases for future civil rights action. Finally, the era clearly crystallized the scope and method of professional social work and set it apart from social reform. Concern with poverty, whether for the benefit of the needy or to maintain a low-wage work force for business, became the domain of government bureaucrats. The new domain of social work became casework—mental health, psychiatric casework, school social work, medical social work, and so on—for people who could afford such services or were entitled to them as members of society.

As the government under Herbert Hoover continued to support big business as a right, unemployment began to push the economy into its downward spiral toward the stockmarket crash of 1929. Despite the many warning signals, the nation continued to operate as if economic realities did not exist: the "invisible hand" of the marketplace would set everything right, and the new profession of social work would, through casework, set to rights the growing number of the unemployed and poor. Suddenly, however, the bubble burst, and the United States faced a crisis that might destroy it.

## STUDY QUESTIONS

1. What were the major targets of social welfare in the Progressive Era?
2. Who were the powerful women in that era, and what did they do?
3. What were the common treatments for children, the aged, and the poor, and how did they change during the Progressive Era?
4. What roles did the emerging profession of social work play in the changes in Question 3?
5. What were the major women's movements, and what were their outcomes?
6. What other reforms and new knowledge set the bases for today's social welfare? Today's social work profession?
7. What were the factors leading to the Great Depression?

## FOOTNOTES

[1]June Axinn and Herman Levin, *Social Welfare: A History of the American Response to Need*, 2nd ed., (New York: Harper & Row, 1982), p. 134.

[2]Beulah Compton, *Introduction to Social Welfare and Social Work*, (Homewood, Ill.: The Dorsey Press, 1980), pp. 350–52.

[3]John Ehrenreich, *The Altruistic Imagination: A History of Social Work and Social Policy in the United States*, (Ithaca: Cornell University Press, 1985), p. 37.

[4]Axinn and Levin, *Social Welfare*, p. 135.

[5]Blanche Coll, *Perspectives in Public Welfare: A History*, U.S. Department of Health, Education, and Welfare, Social Rehabilitation Service 1969, (Washington, D.C.: U.S. Government Printing Office, 1971), p. 63.

[6]Axinn and Levin, *Social Welfare*, p. 129.

[7]Ibid., p. 128.

[8]Angela Davis, *Women, Race, and Class,* (New York: Random House, 1981), p. 212.

[9]Joseph Hraba, *Racial and Ethnic Minorities,* (Itasca, Ill.: F. E. Peacock Publishers, 1979), p. 18.

[10]Davis, *Women, Race, and Class,* p. 214.

[11]Stephen Kern, *The Culture of Time and Space: 1880–1918,* (Cambridge: Harvard University Press, 1983), p. 260.

[12]Ehrenreich, *Altruistic Imagination,* pp. 45–47.

[13]Axinn and Levin, *Social Welfare,* pp. 128–129.

[14]Coll, *Perspectives in Public Welfare,* p. 63.

[15]Compton, *Introduction to Social Welfare,* pp. 322–23.

[16]Coll, *Perspectives in Public Welfare,* p. 66.

[17]Compton, *Introduction to Social Welfare,* p. 322.

[18]Hraba, *Racial and Ethnic Minorities,* p. 321.

[19]Compton, *Introduction to Social Welfare,* p. 349.

[20]Axinn and Levin, *Social Welfare,* pp. 128–129.

[21]Lerone Bennett, Jr., *Before the Mayflower: A History of the Negro in America,* (Chicago: Johnson Publishing Co., Penguin Ed., 1966), p. 287.

[22]Ibid., pp. 292–293.

[23]Ibid., an account by Walter White, p. 294.

[24]Ibid., p. 277.

[25]Ibid., pp. 296–97.

[26]Linda K. Kerber and Jane DeHart Mathews, eds., *Women's America,* (New York: Oxford University Press, 1982), pp. 261–262.

[27]Bennett, *Before the Mayflower,* p. 284; and Robert McHenry, ed., *Famous American Women: A Biographical Dictionary from Colonial Times to the Present,* (New York: Dover Publications, 1980), pp. 434–435.

[28]Angela Dorenkamp, John McClymer, Mary Moynihan, and Arlene Vadum, *Images of Women in American Popular Culture,* (New York: Harcourt Brace Jovanovich, 1985), p. 343.

[29]Samuel Mencher, *From Poor Law to Poverty Programs,* (Pittsburgh: University of Pittsburgh Press, 1967), p. 382.

[30]Ibid., p. 385.

[31]Ehrenreich, *Altruistic Imagination,* p. 45.

[32]Alice Kessler-Harris, "Where Are the Organized Women Workers?" in Kerber and Mathews, eds., *Women's America,* pp. 226–241.

[33]William J. Jacobs, *Women in American History,* (Encino, Calif.: Glencoe Publishing, 1976), p. 140.

[34]Axinn and Levin, *Social Welfare,* p. 141.

[35]Compton, *Introduction to Social Welfare,* p. 337.

[36]Alice Kessler-Harris. *Out to Work: A History of Wage-Earning Women in the United States,* (New York: Oxford University Press, 1982), p. 238.

[37]Ibid.

[38]Carole Hymowitz and Michaele Weissman, *A History of Women in America,* (New York: Bantam Books, 1980), pp. 254–259.

[39]Ibid., p. 259.

[40]Pauline Newman, "Triangle Shirt Waist Fire," in Kerber and Mathews, eds., *Women's America,* p. 224.

[41]Maxine Schwartz Seller, *Immigrant Women,* (Philadelphia: Temple University Press, 1984).

[42]Newman, "Triangle Shirt Waist Fire," in Kerber and Mathews, eds., *Women's America,* p. 224.

[43]McHenry, ed., *Famous American Women,* p. 136.

[44]Michael B. Katz, *Poverty and Policy in American History*, (New York: Academic Press, 1983), pp. 226–227.

[45]Coll, *Perspectives in Public Welfare*, p. 74.

[46]Axinn and Levin, *Social Welfare*, p. 127.

[47]Seller, *Immigrant Women*, p. 198.

[48]Compton, *Introduction to Social Welfare*, pp. 331–332.

[49]Hymowitz and Weissman, *History of Women*, p. 239.

[50]Compton, *Introduction to Social Welfare*, p. 332.

[51]*The Autobiography of Mother Jones*, 3rd rev. ed., (Chicago: Charles H. Kerr, Publisher, 1977).

[52]Jacobs, *Women in American History*, p. 124.

[53]Compton, *Introduction to Social Welfare*, p. 332.

[54]Ibid., p. 364.

[55]Ibid., p. 360.

[56]Coll, *Perspectives In Public Welfare*, p. 77.

[57]Winifred Bell, *Aid to Dependent Children*, (New York: Columbia University Press, 1968), p. 6.

[58]Axinn and Levin, *Social Welfare*, p. 160.

[59]Coll, *Perspectives in Public Welfare*, p. 79.

[60]Bell, *Aid to Dependent Children*, p. 21.

[61]Coll, *Perspectives in Public Welfare*, p. 80.

[62]Ibid., p. 79.

[63]Compton, *Introduction to Social Welfare*, p. 364, quoted from *Social Service Review*, 1951, p. 384.

[64]Nancy Schrom Dye, "Mary Breckinridge, The Frontier Nursing Service, and the Introduction of Nurse-Midwifery in the United States," in Judith Walzer Leavitt, ed., *Women and Health in America*, (Madison: The University of Wisconsin Press, 1984), pp. 327–344.

[65]Ehrenreich, *Altruistic Imagination*, pp. 65–67.

[66]From William Sadler, *Theory and Practice of Psychiatry*, discussed in Mary Shea, "The Ideology of Mental Health and the Emergence of the Therapeutic Liberal State: The American Mental Hygiene Movement, 1900-1930," Ph. D. diss., University of Illinois at Champaign-Urbana, 1980; in Ehrenreich, *Altruistic Imagination*, pp. 65–67.

[67]Ehrenreich, *Altruistic Imagination*, p. 67.

[68]Axinn and Levin, *Social Welfare*, p. 155.

[69]Ibid.

[70]Gerald Handel, *Social Welfare in Western History*, (New York: Random House, 1982), p. 131.

[71]Frank Dekker Watson, *The Charity Organization Movement in the United States*, (New York: Arno Press and *The New York Times*, 1971), p. 369.

[72]Handel, *Western History*, p. 131.

[73]Axinn and Levin, *Social Welfare*, p. 145.

[74]Coll, *Perspectives in Public Welfare*, p. 81.

[75]Ibid.

[76]Katz, *Poverty and Policy*, p. 225.

[77]Axinn and Levin, *Social Welfare*, p. 137.

[78]Katz, *Poverty and Policy*, p. 222.

[79]Watson, *Charity Organization Movement*, p. 372.

[80]Jacobs, *Women in American History*, p. 213.

[81]Dale Spender, *There's Always Been a Women's Movement This Century*, (Boston: Pandora Press, 1983), p. 16.

[82]Ibid., p. 22.

[83]Doris Stevens, *Jailed for Freedom*, (New York: Boni and Liveright, 1920), pp. 187–189, referenced in Seller, ed., *Immigrant Women*, pp.269 ff.

[84]Seller, *Immigrant Women*, p. 117

[85]Ibid., p. 130.

[86]Compton, *Introduction to Social Welfare*, p. 338.

[87]Mark Thomas Connelly, "Prostitution, Venereal Disease, and American Medicine," in Leavitt, ed., *Women and Health*, pp. 196–221.

[88]Ibid., p. 200.

[89]Ibid., p. 201.

[90]Ibid., p. 197.

[91]Ibid., p. 203.

[92]Bettina Berch, *The Endless Day: The Political Economy of Women and Work*, (New York: Harcourt Brace Jovanovich, 1982), p. 45.

[93]Seller, ed., *Immigrant Women*, pp. 130 ff.

[94]James C. Mohr, "Patterns of Abortion and the Response of American Physicians, 1790-1930," in Leavitt, ed., *Women and Health*, pp. 117–123, esp. p. 119.

[95]Ibid.

[96]Hymowitz and Weissman, *History of Women*, p. 293.

[97]Jacobs, *Women in American History*, p. 191.

[98]Kerber and Mathews, eds., *Women's America*, p. 312.

[99]Ibid., p. 318.

[100]Hymowitz and Weissman, *History of Women*, p. 296.

[101]James Reed, "Doctors, Birth Control, and Social Values, 1830- 1970," in Leavitt, ed., *Women and Health*, p. 131.

[102]John Ehrenreich, *Altruistic Imagination*, p. 49.

# 9

# THE GREAT DEPRESSION AND SOCIAL SECURITY FOR AMERICANS

## OVERVIEW OF THE PERIOD

The years between the complacency of the 1920s and the social revolt of the 1960s taught us many lessons. First, though society clung to work ethic traditions, the Depression of the 1930s made it clear that social and economic forces rather than individual fault could create poverty, making new paupers of those who, throughout their lives, had worked. The Depression hit not only the poor and laboring classes but the rich, though their losses were modest in comparison.

The Social Security Act of 1935 was undoubtedly the most important social legislation in American history, but it retained ideals and traces of legislation predating the Elizabethan Poor Laws of 1601. Among these were definitions of worthy and unworthy poor, the maintenance of a low-wage work force kept in line by social programs, the influence of the elite in the programs to prepare future workers, and the dedication to work as the moral way of American life.

As the federal government assumed care of the poor, private agencies and the social work profession, inspired by psychoanalytic theory, new social research, and new theories of human development, moved to a focus on mental health. The social welfare system effectively split into two sections: The private sector, staffed by professionals, treating middle-class clients with emotional problems, and the public sector providing income maintenance assistance to the poor. The public sector was further split in two: local public relief offices, usually staffed by people hired by political appointees, and the state/federal bureaucracies, staffed with more highly educated civil servants and often administered by professional social workers. The latter included

1. State Employment Security Commissions
2. The Social Security Offices, which administered social security pensions
3. Bureaus of Social Aid, which were co-financed by state and federal governments and administered in local counties to give "categories" of persons public relief: the aged, blind, disabled, and dependent children

Although the Social Security Act provided a safety net for many of the poor, some still fell through. The racist attitudes of welfare workers discouraged people of color from public assistance programs even though they might qualify. People who headed intact families but did not work or worked at marginal jobs qualified neither for Social Security nor for unemployment insurance, and they were ineligible for the major categories of public assistance. Restrictive county programs of poor relief and general assistance were their only recourse. Mothers with dependent children, already suspect because they were disattached from a male breadwinner, became increasingly devalued as increasing divorce and desertion rates led them to seek public relief. While war efforts and unionization lifted most white male laborers out of poverty, these other groups remained stigmatized and needy.

World War II, with its new demands for war production, brought prosperity once again. The war economy became the staple support of government and the military-industrial complex from that time on. In addition, the places of women and people of color in society changed radically—they learned about equal pay for equal work during the war. More important, they taught their children that equality might be within their grasp. Both women and men picked up the threads of traditional marriage and family roles after the war, but their expectations and awareness were changed.

The war changed the economic system of the United States from consumer to military production. The latter was immensely profitable because it was ultimately consumable—as fast as weapons were produced they became outdated, and if used were destroyed. Moreover, war production was capital intensive rather than labor intensive so that as more sophisticated automation developed, workers and their demands became less important in profit making. Hard-won unionization became increasingly oriented to management's needs once basic rights were secured.

Women working in factories were displaced by returning war veterans and went back to child-bearing with a vengeance, producing the generation of children known as the "baby boom." Remembering the lessons of World War I, the nation kept many veterans out of the labor market by giving them opportunities for education and financing for homes and new consumer goods such as automobiles. This latter changed the demographic face of America as the new middle class took their families to the suburbs, leaving inner cities to people of color and the poor. After World War II, the economy began its upward swing once more.

## THE GREAT DEPRESSION

The Great Depression did not crash full blown on the economy in 1929. There were many warnings—high unemployment, lack of consumer buying, the loss of homes and farms as people could not meet their mortgage payments, and strikes and riots as workers found themselves unable to support their families. However, the business boom of the early 1920s led to faith in the economy to "right" itself. In fact, President Herbert Hoover urged companies to high production and high prices in a "supply-side" economics: provide the goods people want, they will buy, and once more the economy will rise.

However, this essentially conservative, wait-and-see philosophy could not deal with the deepening depression. This was different from former depressions: It was based on "paper money," stocks and bonds for the rich and easy credit for the poor, with little real wealth—gold or silver—to back it up. Workers—the vast underpinnings of any economy—had scant real money to purchase goods. A 1929 study by Brookings Institution showed that although $2,000 per year was needed for basic necessities, almost 12 million families, or about 40 percent of the population, had annual incomes of less than $1,500, and another 30 percent made less than $3,100 per year.[1] Although credit lent a sense of security as payments could be delayed "till things got better," when consumers lost their jobs, creditors foreclosed.

The whole structure of the economy collapsed in October 1929. A spiral began of falling sales, rising unemployment, declining income, further production cuts, and more unemployment, which in some cities reached 40 percent and in some counties 90 percent. The gross national product, at an all-time high of $103 billion in 1929, fell to $55.6 billion in 1933 (down 25 percent) and did not reach pre-Depression levels until 1941.[2] By 1933, manufacturing was 20 percent below its 1929 level. Average weekly wages were down 35 percent, and aggregate corporate profits, which had hit a record $8.7 billion in 1929, dropped to minus $2.7 billion in 1933.[3] Unemployment increased in nine months from nearly 3 million to over 4 million; three months later, in May 1930, it was at 4.6 million, and by September 1930 over 5 million were unemployed. By the spring of 1931 over 8 million were jobless, and by 1932, one of every four persons in the labor force was unemployed and one of every five was on welfare.[4]

The first people laid off were Hispanic and Afro-American men. By 1932, 56 percent of all Afro-Americans were unemployed, and by 1933 nearly 18 percent of Afro-American family heads were certified for relief.[5] Next to go were Afro-American women as white women displaced them in domestic labor. White blue-collar men lost their jobs next, and finally white women working in food and garment industries. White-collar workers and people in sales managed to hold on into the 1930s.[6]

By 1935, 30 percent of Afro-Americans were on relief rolls,[7] twice the relief rate for whites. In the South it was worse: in Atlanta 65 percent were on relief and in Norfolk, Virginia, 81 percent. In some areas, a de facto slavery returned; in others, communists began to organize Afro-Americans into cells by offering to help them deal with white employers, renters, and welfare agencies. People of color were less likely to be given relief than were white people, and the grants were lower. Lynchings nearly doubled in the South as white unemployment worsened, and Afro-Americans in the North lived in absolute squalor. Men rarely found work, and women worked at any jobs they could find. Domestics made an average $6.17 per week and did a white family's weekly wash for 50 cents.[8]

Wage-earning women in 1930 numbered more than ten million, working primarily at "women's jobs" rather than in heavy industry because of previously mandated protective legislation. Those already employed kept their jobs longer than did men because owners could pay them less. As husbands lost jobs, wives went to work in the expanding clerical and human services sector—jobs men refused to take because of low pay.[9] Minimum wage levels for women rose dramatically—in New York, for example, they climbed 16.6 percent in eighteen months by November 1934 (while men's rose only 3.4 percent). However, their wages were still so low that employers preferred to hire women over men.[10] Women's Bureau surveys in the 1920s and 1930s showed that 90 percent of women who worked did so for economic reasons and that 25 percent were the family's principal wage-earners. In 1920, only 23 percent of married women worked; in 1930, 28.9 percent worked; and by 1940, 36.7 percent had entered the labor force.[11] Fewer than a third of all employed women were married.[12] The Depression destabilized the family: The marriage rate per 1,000 unmarried women declined from 92 in 1920 to 68 in 1930, and the birthrate went from 27.7 in 1920 to 21.3 in 1930 and 18.4 in 1933.[13] While divorce rates showed no appreciable change, suicides and desertions increased.

Problems of the Depression were compounded by a massive drought all the way from Virginia to Arkansas and new farm and manufacture technologies that threw tens of thousands off the farm. They migrated to cities in search of work, adding to unemployment and dependency there. The Depression was worldwide, and the market for farm exports dropped to $2.5 billion in 1932, less than half that of 1919. Individual farm incomes dropped from $945 in 1929 to $379 per farm in 1933, although farm production fell less than 5 percent.[14]

Not until 1931 did Congress enact the Wagner-Rainey bill over Hoover's veto. It authorized the Reconstruction Finance Corporation to make loans to tide companies over this "self-limiting" crisis. Although the RFC permitted both direct and work relief, no such efforts were undertaken. Believing in the power of the private sector and its charities, Hoover instituted a voluntary fund-raising drive at the national level to help the unemployed: The Emergency Committee on Employment's directive was to ensure cooperation among private and public charities so that no one would be cold or hungry. However, the committee became merely a clearinghouse for correspondence, advice, and encouragement and gave little real aid.[15]

Public expenditures for relief had skyrocketed by 1931 to $54 million. The Russell Sage Foundation reported that 74 percent of relief expenditures ($31 million) came from public funds during 1929. In 1930, all relief expenditures doubled, with 75 percent ($51 million) coming from public funds. States tried to meet the demand: in 1931 New York, under the governorship of Franklin D. Roosevelt, disbursed funds to cities and counties for outdoor relief and work projects, and seven more states followed suit before 1932.[16]

Charities struggled valiantly to turn the tide of poverty and incidentally prove the value of private casework methods by counseling people out of poverty, but by 1931 both the Russell Sage Foundation and the National Conference of Social Welfare placed responsibility for relief on the federal government. Family welfare associations (formerly COSs) and the National Federation of Settlements argued that poverty, at this point in history, was a societal rather than a personal failure, and for all practical purposes the social work profession gave the job of disbursing poor relief to public welfare. Between 1929 and 1932, public relief expanded eightfold, but still provided less than an average of $30 per recipient a year.[17]

### Social Revolt and Temporary Relief

Demonstrations, strikes, and riots occurred nationwide as the Depression worsened. In March 1930, more than a million people demonstrated in dozens of cities, demanding relief. Some forty workers were killed in strike-related incidents, and in 1933–34 troops were called out in sixteen states.[18] Petition drives, at least three with more than a million signatures each, demanded government action. Unemployment councils fought against evictions, protested cutbacks in what little welfare there was, and demanded a massive program of relief. The New York Unemployment Council, for example, claimed to have prevented 77,000 evictions between 1930 and 1934. Across the nation, two million people were involved in unemployment movement actions, with thousands jailed or hurt and fourteen killed.[19]

In 1932, between fifteen and twenty thousand World War I veterans marched on Washington, demanding early the bonuses they had been promised by 1945. They and their families erected shacks across from the White House, but after a month Hoover dispatched soldiers to burn the "Hoovervilles." Although he vetoed the early bonus bill, Congress overrode the veto, granting half their "adjustment compensation certificates" to be paid in 1937. When the Federal Economy Act cut veterans' pensions and benefits, veterans marched again in 1933 and 1934, and the protest became so severe that in 1934 Congress rescinded the Economy Act. More than ten thousand veterans stranded in Washington were assigned to work camps in the Civilian Conservation Corps, and another seven thousand were sent either to special work camps if they were disabled or to the Works Progress Administration. The bonus payment, made in 1937, put nearly $3.5 billion into the hands of veterans.[20]

Workers turned to the left: Communists played a major role in San Francisco's longshoremen's strike; in Toledo independent radical socialists demonstrated; and in Minneapolis the Trotskyite Social Workers party led a general strike.[21] Six million workers organized in three years. Other citizens took political action. A retired California physician named Townsend started a movement to have pensions for every worker over age 65— $200 per month, returnable to the government if unspent. By 1935 he had

25 million signatures and 3 million persons in Townsend clubs across the nation.[22] During Franklin D. Roosevelt's campaign for presidency in 1936, Huey Long, the reform governor of Louisiana, established a Share the Wealth political organization, with 27,000 clubs around the nation and seven million mailing names. The movement challenged the Roosevelt candidacy, but the threat ended when Long was assassinated in 1935.[23]

Roosevelt, with social worker Harry Hopkins, had led New York in providing benefits and work projects for the unemployed. He knew that only emergency measures could quell the growing social unrest and rioting, and he sent Labor Secretary Frances Perkins to Europe to study social programs that had staved off revolt there. The 1934 landslide victory of Democrats in Congress mandated a restructuring of the economy, and Roosevelt's subsequent actions strengthened the executive branch of the government enormously in the area of economic security. He expanded the cabinet and doubled the number of civilian government employees during the Depression years.[24]

### Roosevelt's Emergency Measures

Roosevelt was convinced that Keynesian economics—demand-side consumerism—was the key to economic health. The demand-side Keynesian economics meant, briefly, that if consumers had money, they would buy, and the economy would begin its upward spiral. His goal was to put money in the hands of consumers through saving their farms and homes, reducing farm production, hiring out the unemployed in public works, and supporting manufacturers so that they could hire the unemployed. His temporary measures were successful in reducing unemployment; using fiscal and monetary policy to control savings, investment, and consumption; and developing mechanisms to keep people out of the labor market.[25]

According to Dye and Zeigler, Roosevelt's wealth predated the Civil War and he did not have Social Darwinistic "training." He believed in social justice and felt that the government was obligated to help the distressed.[26] His Federal Emergency Relief Act, administered by Harry Hopkins, was based on the belief that relief from unemployment was a right, and that any work, even digging holes and refilling them, was preferable to direct relief.[27] They determined to give the estimated 70 percent of those without work jobs until they could be reabsorbed into private employment.[28]

Roosevelt's major temporary programs, both passed in 1933, were the Federal Emergency Relief Act (FERA) and the National Industrial Redevelopment Act (NIRA). Both were declared unconstitutional and were replaced, respectively, with the Social Security Act of 1935 and the Works Progress Administration. However, they were successful during the time they were in operation.

*Federal Emergency Relief Act.* Roosevelt appointed Harry Hopkins to direct FERA and gave him almost unlimited authority to disburse $500 million in grants for direct relief. Hopkins took office in May 1933, and by the end of the next month had paid out $51 million to forty-five states, Washington D.C., and Hawaii, putting about twenty million people on the relief rolls. By the end of the year $324.5 million had been distributed with the rest gone soon after. Half went to states on a matching basis ($250 million)—one federal dollar for every three state dollars— and another $250 million was distributed on need. No more than 15 percent could go to any one state, and states were to bear part of the cost of relief, though no formal plan for determining "shares" was provided. States that raised the most would get the most.

To qualify for FERA funds, each state had to establish an emergency relief authority to receive and disburse federal monies. States and political subdivisions estimated how much their people needed for food, shelter, medical needs, and necessities—and used means testing to find how many people fell below those standards.[29] Rents and medical care expenses were paid directly to landlords and health providers. FERA provided direct relief to both individuals and families, but work relief was encouraged. Discrimination against people of color was to be avoided but was not forbidden. This last was appropriate because of Southern racism, for a disproportionate amount of FERA money went to rural areas in the South.

One of FERA's most far-reaching effects was that relief monies could be distributed only through public agencies. This legally ended the participation of voluntary/private agencies in poor relief and added impetus in the move of social work from public relief work. Aubrey Williams, a social worker and deputy administrator of the Works Progress Administration, said that

> the sooner social work as a profession can turn its back on direct relief as a valid form of social treatment, the better off will be the nation and the higher the standing of social work.[30]

There were no set guidelines for relief giving except for means testing to determine need, and workers' discretion determined eligibility and amount of grant. Trained social workers were required in supervisory positions, and family caseworkers conducted investigations for both direct and work relief according to a family policy that allowed intact families assistance. Applicants registered at a central agency and investigators checked real property and bank accounts; conducted interviews with a recent employer; canvassed families, relatives, friends, and churches for other support; and visited recipient families once a month. Work relief was supposed to be paid in cash but was often in kind.[31] In the three years of its existence, FERA spent over $3 billion.

*National Industrial Recovery Act.*    The National Industrial Recovery Act instituted federal control of production, prices, and the rights of workers in industry. Its codes were intended to end cutthroat competition, raise prices, limit output, and provide for reasonable wages. It also reaffirmed the 1932 Norris-LaGuardia Act restricting federal courts from issuing injunctions against unions engaged in peaceful strikes, thereby legitimating unions and collective bargaining. For the first time, the courts came out on the side of workers rather than employers. Unionization, which had been in a decline since 1920, began to pick up, and by 1935 unions had 3.7 million members.

Within half a year the ten largest industries in the nation had signed the codes and came under the National Recovery Administration.[32] Although the NIRA was declared unconstitutional in 1935, it set standards in the two years of its existence for 2.5 million employers and 16 million workers. In that time, employment rose by 2 million, production rose from 62 percent to 79 percent of 1929 levels, and the gross national product increased from $55.6 billion to 72.2 billion.[33] Yet in 1935, 20 percent of the labor force was still unemployed.

Title II of NIRA gave industry $3.3 billion for public improvement investment through the newly created Public Works Administration (PWA). Part of its $400 million was allotted to the Civil Works Administration (CWA), but neither the PWA nor the CWA used the money primarily to increase employment. The Works Progress Administration, successor to both, hired the unemployed directly, putting money in the hands of workers and setting a precedent for government as employer of last resort.

NIRA set up a National Labor Board to mediate labor disputes and to hear complaints of unfair labor practices. It was successfully fought by the large corporations whose power it limited and was replaced by the National Labor Relations Act of 1938 (the Wagner Act).[34] The excesses of industries vis-à-vis workers aided in the passing of the Wagner Act. Congressional investigations found that in 1934 General Motors spent a million dollars spying on workers, and in that year a business executive approached an army general, offering to finance an army of 500,000 men to overthrow the government.[35] In 1936–37 a Senate investigating committee chaired by Robert LaFollette found that Republic Steel had an arsenal to be used against strikers that included 352 pistols, 64 rifles, 245 shotguns, 143 gas guns, and 2,707 gas grenades. Other companies had spent $9.4 million on strikebreakers, labor spies, and munitions between 1933 and 1936.

The Wagner Act outlawed company-dominated unions, heard unfair labor practices, and gave the Labor Relations Board power to determine bargaining units and petition courts to enforce its decisions.[36] It also set a minimum wage of 25 cents an hour to be increased to 40 cents in seven years, a 44-hour workweek to diminish to 40 hours in three years, and a minimum age of 16 for child labor in industries of interstate commerce.[37] The Wagner Act led to massive unionization of unskilled workers, whose unions joined in 1937 to become the Congress of Industrial Organizations (CIO). By 1939 there were 10.6 million members in organized labor: 5 million in the CIO and 4.6 million in the AFL. Afro-American workers were welcomed into the CIO, although most other unions continued their discrimination against them until the early 1940s.

Unfortunately, the Wagner Act discriminated against women workers. Although NIRA administrator Hugh Johnson, Secretary of Labor Frances Perkins, and Eleanor Roosevelt all opposed differential wages for men and women, about a quarter of the codes, covering nearly 17 percent of all workers, allowed lower wages to women.[38] The Walsh-Healy Act of 1936 abolished child labor and set standards for workers in industries with sizable federal contracts. In 1939 twenty-one states still had no minimum wage laws for women, while thirty states still lacked 8-hour workday laws.

*Other New Deal Programs.*    Between 1930 and 1934, more than four thousand banks failed because unemployed mortgage holders could no longer make their payments on homes and farms. Although they foreclosed, banks could not recoup their investments or pay their investors because they could not resell the homes. This caused "runs" on the bank of depositors trying to get back their savings before the banks closed. Roosevelt took immediate steps to protect the banks and their clients by declaring a "bank holiday," forbidding gold payments and exports, and establishing penalties against banks that hoarded gold. Roosevelt's emergency banking bill led to Federal Reserve banks and enabled the Treasury Department to regulate the banking industry.[39] The Federal Deposit Insurance Corporation (FDIC) was instituted to provide federal insurance against loss of depositors' savings. It also led to nationwide banking systems.

More than 250,000 families lost their homes in 1932, with another 1,000 a month in 1933. To combat this, Roosevelt set up the Home Owners Loan Corporation, through a Federal Housing Authority, to give insured loans for home repair, to refinance mortgages in danger of failing, and to grant new mortgages for prospective home purchasers.[40] A later bill, the 1937 Housing Act, provided for federally subsidized housing, under which, for example, the New York Housing Authority planned, built, and managed housing for 500,000 people.[41]

As farm income fell, farmers threatened a nationwide strike. In response, Roosevelt authorized the Agricultural Adjustment Act in 1933 to provide money for new farm technology and limit farm production by paying farmers to slaughter their animals and leave their fields empty. However, only large farmers could afford the new technology, and marginal farmers and tenant farmers, particularly Afro-Americans, lost their footholds in the land. The number of tenant farmers decreased by 303,000, and Afro-American farmers constituted 56 percent of this total decrease. Not until 1935 were farmers required to keep the same number of tenants when they received federal help, and by then most had gone to cities, where they added to unemployment problems. The AAA also bought surplus food under the Federal Surplus Commodities Corporation, which it then distributed to the poor.

By 1935, Roosevelt had ordered all federal agricultural agencies, including the AAA, into the Farm Credit Administration (FCA), and farm income was raised from $2.5 billion in 1932 to more than $5.9 billion in 1935. By 1940, there were about 6 million farms but this was a loss of almost 200,000, almost entirely in farms of Afro-Americans.[42]

*Youth Programs.*    Roosevelt established programs with the dual purposes of removing young people from the job market and giving them work training. The National Youth Authority (NYA) kept young people in high schools or colleges by giving them jobs to support them during their education. The Civilian Conservation Corps (CCC) employed young people to work in the preservation of natural resources in conservation camps.

Young men age 18-25 from relief families worked on reforestation, soil conservation, and flood control. They were given board and room and $30 a month, of which $25 was sent to their families. More than 2.75 million participated during the life of CCC, which was terminated in 1942.

*The Works Progress Administration.*   Roosevelt's first job program was the Civil Works Administration, established in 1933 under the direction of Harry Hopkins. Workers were paid at regular rates for civil works already in progress, but the program lost money, and along with PWA, the CWA became the Emergency Work Relief Program under FERA. Roosevelt's Grand Design, however, envisioned a better program, one that paid money directly to the employee, and on this basis he instituted the Works Progress Administration in 1935 to hire workers until the economy revived or until the Social Security Act became operative. WPA was funded at $4.9 billion, but in its short lifetime spent $10 billion. While WPA paid less than did regular employment, it was higher than poor relief, and by 1936 WPA employed one-third of all unemployed Americans at minimum security wages in nearly 8 million jobs. From 1935 to 1941, more than 2 million men per month were on WPA payrolls, with a peak of 3.25 million in November 1938. WPA financed more than 250,000 projects and spent $11 billion in the construction of roads, bridges, libraries; in painting of murals; for unemployed artists, actors, writers, and musicians for projects to continue the uplifting of American culture; and in myriad other works.[43]

Through WPA, the government became employer of last resort when vast unemployment threatened the nation's security. Its still obvious results, in roads, bridges, dams, and artwork demonstrate a constructive use of humanpower even though it was more costly than a comparable program of poor relief would have been. Macarov notes that

> work relief during the depression was more expensive than direct relief would have been . . . whether the work accomplished was worth the extra cost is debatable, but that it would have been cheaper to give out checks is hardly questionable.[44]

### Eleanor Roosevelt and Women in the New Deal

Eleanor Roosevelt (1884–1962) was a settlement house worker in the early decades of the twentieth century, and at age 18 she joined the National Consumers' League and worked in the labor movement. She married her cousin Franklin in 1905 and provided constant support to him in his political career, particularly after his crippling attack of polio in 1921. While rearing six children, she continued her interest and activities in social causes and public affairs. She worked at Red Cross canteens for soldiers during World War I, encouraged the appointment of Frances Perkins first as New York's state industrial commissioner and then as U.S. secretary of labor, and was instrumental in such forward-looking social legislation as the National Youth Authority. She worked to improve conditions for the mentally ill, coordinated the League of Women Voters' legislative plans, and was an active member of the Women's Trade Union League and the Democratic Party. In addition, she worked with her husband to establish the national polio center at Warm Springs, Georgia. She also taught sociology, economics, and government at the Todhunter School in New York City, of which she was part owner.

After Roosevelt's election, Eleanor brought an unprecedented number of women into his administration to work in WPA and FERA. Among them were Ellen Woodward, Hilda Worthington Smith, and Florence Kerr, all of whom held WPA appointments, and Lorena Hickok, a social worker who became the eyes and ears of Harry Hopkins, observing the impact of his New Deal programs. Eleanor also encouraged the rejuvenation of the women's division of the Democratic party under the leadership of Molly Dawson.[45]

Because of the president's disability, Eleanor did much of the ceremonial and public relations work of the presidency, including the inspection of government works projects. She actively supported civil rights, insisting that discrimination had no place in American life. She publicly resigned from the Daughters of the American Revolution after it denied the Afro-American operatic contralto Marian Anderson permission to sing at Constitution Hall and arranged an Anderson concert at the Lincoln Memorial that was attended by 75,000 people. She lobbied for civil rights legislation, fought to make lynching a federal crime, and was a financial patron of the NAACP. She argued for the elimination of discrimination in the armed services and defense employment, supported student socialist groups, provided a forum for women's causes, defended social welfare programs, and served as advocate for Jewish refugees—especially when the President refused admission of Jewish children to the United States during Hitler's pogroms. She brought the poor and disenfranchised to dinner at the White House so her husband could hear them, though he seldom acted on their issues. Among them were poor southern textile workers, northern garment workers, Afro-Americans civil rights workers, and student activists.

After her husband's death, Eleanor continued to be the most effective woman in American politics. She implored Truman to push forward with civil rights and to maintain the temporary Fair Employment Practices Commission. She became the American delegate to the United Nations in 1945 and was the fundamental author of the Universal Declaration of Human Rights passed by the General Assembly in December 1948. As a commissioner of the U.S. Commission on Human Rights in 1953, she was outspoken against the McCarthy communist hunts. Retiring in 1953, after Dwight D. Eisenhower became president, she continued to work in the American Association for the United Nations. Her last official position was a chair of President Kennedy's Commission on the Status of Women, to which she was appointed in December 1961 and which she held until her death in 1962.[46]

## SOCIAL INSURANCE IN THE UNITED STATES

Roosevelt became president with a clear knowledge of European social insurance programs, the first of which was developed by Chancellor Otto von Bismarck in Germany in 1879 to subvert growing socialist influences.

Between 1881 and 1887, Bismarck's plan provided compulsory insurance against illness, job accidents, and old age and disability insurance for workers in mines and factories who earned less than 2,000 marks a year (1881). In 1889 he regularized financial support for social insurance, requiring contributions from workers, employers, and the government. However, he refused to legislate working hours, the employment of women and children, factory inspection, or control of labor unions.

By 1900 all the countries of continental Europe had some form of social insurance. For example, Great Britain established workmen's compensation in 1897 and health and employment insurance in 1911. However, the European philosophy on social insurance was by now different from programs developing in the United States. Bell says

> As European nations adopted comprehensive social welfare programs, they also made a commitment to maintain full employment. In doing so, they reflected a conviction that everyone should have the right and opportunity to work . . . it was expected that the workplace would be adapted to workers rather than forcing workers to adapt to the workplace.
>
> Nowhere is the difference in values between other industrialized nations and the U.S. more striking than around the issue of full employment.[47]

The American social insurance movement officially began in 1906 with the founding of the American Association for Labor Legislation among economists and political scientists investigating labor conditions. Its main tenet was that

> social insurance was not charity but a basic human right, and that problems arising from poverty, age, sickness and accident ought to be guaranteed by the state rather than relying on either private charity or the benevolence of employers.[48]

Support for social insurance was based on evidence collected by social welfarists that demonstrated clearly the structural rather than personal nature of poverty. Factory safety conditions were so bad that hundreds of workers were mangled or died every year, and their deaths and disabilities meant that mothers and children, even those who worked full time, became public dependents. In 1912 delegates to the National Conference on Social Welfare endorsed social insurance, and it became a part of Theodore Roosevelt's 1912 presidential platform. In 1913, Isaac M. Rubinow published a book that showed that between 80 and 90 percent of all wage-earners earned less than they needed to support families. The first state law was passed in Arizona, in 1915, but was declared unconstitutional. Massachusetts passed the first state worker's compensation law in 1916, but the first unemployment insurance law was not passed until 1932. By the time the Social Security Act was passed, thirty states already had their own Old Age Assistance Programs, twenty-seven had Aid to the Blind programs, and a few had Aid to the Disabled. Vocational Rehabilitation was a federal rather than state program, set into the Department of Education in 1920.

In the private sector, corporations began to expand social insurance, realizing that social insurance was, overall, a good investment. It kept people on the job and loyal, and decreased their tendency to strike. Since loss of jobs meant loss of future pensions, it also led to more satisfactory job performance. A pension plan also made possible the retiring of elderly workers and the hiring of young, quicker workers at lower wages.[49]

### Worker's Compensation: State Social Insurance

Worker's compensation came state by state rather than through national legislation. Most states set up their programs under state Departments of Labor or independent Worker's Compensation boards through private insurance agencies. Employers almost always fund such programs, though some states contribute funds and some employees may contribute to medical care. The state may also impose a penalty against employers who do not have insurance. Premiums are based on the size of the firm and the nature of the risk, and many states still exclude agricultural workers, domestic workers, and workers in casual employment.

Worker's compensation provides benefits to victims of work-related accidents and illnesses regardless of fault, although workers must prove their injuries were not from gross negligence, willful misconduct, or intoxication. Benefits for disabled workers or the survivors of dead workers are based on wages at the time of injury or onset of illness. They are given in cash and without means testing to spouses until remarriage and to state-set ages for children. Benefits can be limited by time, amount, or extent of disability—temporary or permanent. Many states pay for the total length of the disability, including life, and some pay medical benefits. Some have a maximum number of weeks for temporary disability. Medical services, rehabilitation, and job training may be provided though some states limit this liability.

In 1970, the National Occupational Safety and Health Act set standards for safe and healthy work conditions and authorized a National Commission on Workers' Compensation Laws to evaluate situations. The commission recommended compulsory coverage, no exemptions for small firms and government employees, coverage for all types of workers, coverage of all work-related diseases, and weekly cash payments at two-thirds of the gross wage up to a weekly benefit equal to 100 percent of the average weekly wage in the state. Also it recommended no limits for permanent total disability benefits or for medical services and physical rehabilitation. The interest of the federal government as indicated in the Occupational Act of 1970 shows that more federal intervention may be forthcoming in the future.[50]

### Roosevelt's Social Security Act of 1935

In June 1934, Roosevelt appointed the Committee on Economic Security: the secretaries of labor, the treasury, and agriculture; the attorney general; and Harry Hopkins, administrator of FERA. Frances Perkins, secretary of labor, was named chair. The committee's charge was to build a "Grand Design" of social insurance for workers and public assistance for unemployables, so that no citizen would go "ill-housed, ill-clothed, or ill-fed." In defense of his proposal, Roosevelt said to Congress in 1934

> People want decent homes to live in; they want to locate them where they can engage in productive work; and they want some safeguard against misfortunes which cannot be wholly eliminated in this man-made world of ours. . . . The complexities of great communities and of organized industry . . . [compel us] to employ the active interest of the nation as a whole through government in order to encourage a greater security for each individual who composes it.[51]

To avoid the charge that it had no basis in constitutionality, Frances Perkins suggested that the Social Security Act (SSA) be financed through the taxing powers of the federal government, a ploy upheld in court despite arguments against it.[52]

Although a health insurance plan was considered before the Social Security Act was passed, it was so strongly opposed by the American Medical Association that it was dropped so that the entire Social Security Act would not be threatened. The program for Aid to Dependent Children, originally intended to be placed under the Children's Bureau with provisions for all poor children including those in intact families was given at the last minute to the Department of Labor. This took the focus off the child, placing it on mothers' morality and work ethic considerations, and reinstituted discrimination against single mothers.

Submitted in 1935, the Social Security Act passed with many amendments and became law in August 1936. It demonstrated clearly the final federal responsibility for the well-being of its citizens and set a precedent not seriously questioned until the presidency of Ronald Reagan. A revolutionary act in itself, SSA borrowed heavily from the past, expecting many of the Depression needs to "wither away" as the "invisible hand" of the market revived. It continued categorizing the poor as worthy—those who had been connected with the labor market—and unworthy—those peripheral to it.

> Frances Perkins . . . and Edwin Witte . . . who guided the 1935 law through . . . believed that open-ended government handouts to citizens must be avoided. In their view temporary "relief" payments to unemployed people, and minimal "public assistance" programs for dependent children and old people, had to be kept separate from "social insurance" programs that workers would earn as a matter of right through regular tax contributions from themselves or their employers.[53]

The SSA left many gaps: It provided nothing for the unemployed able-bodied worker; had no health insurance provision; gave unemployment benefits only for a short time; neglected permanent disability; excluded millions of people because laws covered only regular employment of certain types; and made benefit levels extremely low.[54]

As a political document, SSA filled the immediate needs of those needing help—both poor and rich. Galper says it was an extension of state activity into the social welfare arena to meet corporate needs. He believes it was used to socialize the costs of production so that the government, rather than the elite, would have to support the working poor. These costs included

Preparing (through job training) and maintaining the labor force

Subsidizing low and/or irregular wages

Stimulating consumer purchasing power by an influx of cash benefits during periods of high unemployment and/or recession[55]

The Social Security Act provided for the general welfare through two primary systems: federal social insurance for people connected in some way with the labor force, and federal/state categorical public assistance. The former provided direct payments to retirees and their survivors or dependents from the federal government, and the latter gave grants-in-aid partly financed by the federal government but administered on the state and local levels. Each state had to submit a proposal to get Social Security coverage, and the proposal had to include merit hiring, sound administrative procedures, fair hearings, and adequate records on which to compile annual reports. The categories eligible for aid were aged persons, blind persons, and dependent children. Under separate titles, the Social Security Act made provisions for crippled children and their vocational education, maternal and child welfare, and the administration of the unemployment compensation laws.

The act was actually passed in two separate pieces of legislation, the first as a payroll tax and the second a pension plan. Harry Hopkins was appointed director of Social Security and said

I have never liked poverty. I have never believed that with our capitalistic system people have to be poor. I think it is an outrage that we should permit hundreds and hundreds of thousands of people to be ill clad, to live in miserable homes, not to have enough to eat; not to be able to send their children to school for the only reason that they are poor.[56]

Now he had the power to do something about poverty.

### Social Insurance through the Social Security Act

Social insurance, generally, was for the deserving poor—those who had worked or were working. Two categories were included in the Social Security Act: Old Age and Survivors Insurance (OASI) (Title II) and Unemployment Compensation (Title III).

### OLD AGE AND SURVIVORS INSURANCE

This title provided for pensions for retirees and their spouses at age 65. It gave equal pensions for people across the nation and was not means tested. No social work services were required, and therefore OASI was outside the purview of the profession of social work. Monies were collected from both employer and employee and paid into a reserve fund, from which come the pensions. The amount of contribution was based on actuarial tables developed by the secretary of the treasury. In 1937, employers and employees paid 1 percent of the first $3,000 earned, but both percentages and grants have risen. In no case was the benefit to be over $85.00 (changed later), and if there was overpayment, it had to be paid back dollar for dollar. A death benefit was also set up.

Most workers were "covered" by working forty quarters (three-month periods), except for farm and domestic workers, casual day laborers, and officers or crew of sailing vessels; federal or state employees; and charity employees.[57] Survivors insurance was added in 1939, providing pensions for widows and children of deceased workers (OASI). Disability coverage was not added until the 1950s (OASDI), and health insurance (Medicare) was added in 1961 (OASDHI). Most worker categories, including the self-employed, were added in the 1950s, and now coverage is nearly universal. While at first workers could not earn income and still collect their pensions, this was relaxed and retirees allowed to earn a small amount. At age 72 retirees can earn any amount and still receive total benefits.

The OASDHI program is administered by the Social Security Administration of the Department of Health and Human Services, through about 1,250 offices located across the country and with a central record office in Baltimore. The Treasury Department collects taxes, prepares checks, and maintains the trust fund. Disability determinations are made by state agencies and reviewed by the Social Security Administration. Although it was set up as a trust fund to receive monies, the fund has become basically a bookkeeping function, and monies have flowed more or less freely between the trust fund and federal general revenues since Truman's time. Thus, fears that the Social Security system will "go bankrupt" are unfounded.

To gain support, OASI was presented to the nation as an insurance program, on the quasi-myth that benefits would be based on actuarial models of contributions. However, benefits have never been statistically related to contribution; rather than an insurance it is a tax, bearing most heavily on the poor because the rate takes an equal percentage of a set amount from all employees. Although participants are viewed as "investors" who must receive a reasonable return, in fact the relation of benefit to monies paid in is tenuous at best. OASI pensions have both a minimum and maximum grant level, and because people are taxed on an upper limit of income, the tax is regressive—those making over the maximum taxable amount pay nothing more.

The system is inequitable in many ways. Families with two wage-earners get two benefits, yet the work of wives in the home is ignored: when the wife stays at home, social insurance entitles the family to only one and a half benefits. Housewives, though they contribute to workers' earning ability, receive only the lower dependents' benefits. Women divorced after less than twenty years of marriage (now ten) have no claim on survivor's insurance, though their children do. If the mother remarries she loses her survivor's benefit, and when the children reach majority (now age 17), the mother loses survivor's benefits until she reaches age 62. Those who cannot earn good wages because of institutional discrimination—people of color and women—will always have inadequate social insurance. Finally, workers today are paying for the Social Security of the already retired rather than investing in their own retirement, and the children of today will pay Social Security for present workers.

### UNEMPLOYMENT COMPENSATION: TITLE III

Four million dollars was appropriated for this title for 1936 and $49 million for each fiscal year thereafter. The costs of unemployment grants are not paid by the federal government—it pays only for states' administration of their programs. The amounts paid to states are based on state estimates of the labor force, and if a state denies a substantial number of claims, it could lose funding. Although the Social Security Act requires that employers pay a tax to provide unemployment compensation, employers may offset the federal tax by paying an equal amount (up to 90 percent) into a state unemployment fund. Within a short period, all states established such funds, along with agencies to administer the state programs and provide employment services (now called state Employment Security Commissions). One of the purposes of the program was to prevent layoffs, and so employers with stable employment records were charged reduced taxes. Employers hiring eight or more persons for twenty months or more pay a 3 percent tax on their payrolls. Excluded from this tax originally were farm and domestic employers, the government, railroads, and nonprofit organizations, although most are now included. Railroad employees were covered in 1938 by a special railroad retirement plan, and federal government employees were brought into the program in 1954. In 1956 the program was amended to cover four, rather than eight or more, employees.

Unemployment insurance provides regular cash benefits for a limited time to people who have worked a "base" period and then been let go from regular employment. At first the base period for coverage was "forty quarters" or the equivalent of ten years, but more recently earning $250 is considered to constitute a quarter of covered employment. The unemployed worker must file for benefits and must be willing, able, and available for work, but benefits cannot be denied for refusal to accept work where conditions are below those prevailing in the community, or if the job requires or prohibits joining a union. Unemployment payments vary by state but are around 50 percent of the worker's normal wages. There is no means tests, and benefits are determined on previous wage and number of children, making this program half-way between OASDI and public assistance. The programs usually provide benefits for up to twenty-six weeks, and while the federal-state extended benefits program provided up to thirteen additional weeks of benefits in some states, this has been cut by the Reagan administration. Almost 88 percent of wage and salaried employees were covered in 1982.

The unemployment insurance program is based in the Employment Security Administration of the U.S. Department of Labor, and taxes are collected by the U.S. Department of the Treasury. However, states administer their own programs, and these vary state to state.

### Public Assistance under the Social Security Act

The public assistance provisions were Old Age Assistance (OAA, Title I), Aid to the Blind (AB, Title C), and Aid to Dependent Children (ADC, Title IV). They were instituted as temporary measures that would "wither away" as the market provided jobs and income or as social insurance benefits took over. Recipient grants were based on federal/state sharing, and states determined both their needs and grant levels on which the federal government's share is based. Needs and grants for the aged, blind, and disabled were set low, while those for children were set even lower. Coll says

> All the statistics now available show that most recipients of public assistance were elderly persons, dependent children, or the temporarily or permanently sick or disabled. . . . But . . . the public, often led by the opinions of leaders of voluntary charities, spoke and acted as if the majority of recipients . . . were able-bodied loafers and good-for-nothings. Hence in part, the continued emphasis on the work ethic, the common agreement to keep grants at a bare subsistence level, the assumption that each and every dependent person is in need of reform.[58]

While social insurance is considered entitlement, public assistance was generally for the undeserving poor—undeserving because they had not made the most of opportunities to work or save. Eligibility, based on means testing and home investigations, was at the discretion of workers, which meant that workers could use their value judgments as to who deserved help. Blaming the poor for their poverty was still a keynote of assistance, even among the most forward looking of reformers. Harry Hopkins said

> The means test is our one way of keeping panhandlers off the rolls. It calls for the most detailed prying into the lives and habits of every applicant for relief.[59]

Public assistance categories came under the Social Security Administration, placed later by Truman in the Department of Health, Education, and Welfare (DHEW). During the Reagan administration, the Department of Education was made a separate office and DHEW became the Department of Health and Human Services (HHS).

*Old Age Assistance.*  For this category, the federal government paid half the grant amount in any quarter up to $30.00 per month, along with 2.5 percent of the costs of administration. Eligible persons were all those over 65 who fell below state grant levels and were ineligible for OASI. Although federal eligibility was set at age 65, until 1940 states could set it as high as age 70. No citizens could be excluded, and states could not demand that persons reside in the state for more than five of the preceding nine years. OAA was a partial answer to the Townsend movement, but was not as ubiquitous or generous. Along with Aid to the Blind and Aid to the Disabled, the category became an entitlement program under the Social Security Administration in 1971.

*Aid to the Blind.*    Aid to the Blind was for those persons judged legally blind by medical authorities. Again, the federal government paid half the grant up to $30.00 and for 5 percent of administrative costs.

*Aid to the Disabled.*    This title was added to the Social Security Act in 1956. People had to have medical determination of permanent and total disability to qualify for the program and not qualify for such programs as worker's compensation. At first, disability meant only physical disability, but it now includes mental or emotional disablement. When this program moved to Social Security in 1971, recipients under the new program actually lost income, for states had been more generous than was Social Security. This discrepancy was the major force behind the establishment of Supplemental Security Income, since the disabled had to be brought up to state standards of need.

*Aid to Dependent Children.*    This was the most controversial categorical program of the Social Security Act of 1935. Originally, the Children's Bureau was expected to administer it, and provision was to be made for all needy children, including those in intact families. However, at the last minute it was placed in the Labor Department and restricted to families where the father had died or deserted. Dependent children were defined as "children under age sixteen who have been deprived of parental support or care by reason of the death, continued absence from the home, or physical or mental incapacity of a parent, and who are living with father, mother, grandfather, grandmother, brother, sister, stepfather, stepmother, stepbrother, stepsister, uncle or aunt, in a place of residence maintained by one or more of such relatives as their own home."[60]

The wording of the bill designates a dependent child as one who has been deprived of "parental support" rather than one in need. This allowed for worker discretion in deciding the definition of "support," and in some states it came to mean whether or not a father figure was available for "emotional support" rather than financial need. Thus, if welfare workers suspected that a woman was involved with a man, whether or not he contributed financial aid, the family could be put off the ADC program. This gave rise to "suitable home" and "substitute parent" policies in which workers can take away funds if they consider the home immoral. Moreover, since "unsuitability" was often equated with neglect, it gave workers power to remove children from mothers they considered unworthy. Eligibility determinations often excluded out-of-wedlock children; those from divorced parents, because the mothers were considered sexually immoral; and Afro-American children, because of the racism of workers who believe Afro-Americans "always manage to get along."

Appropriations for 1936 were $24,750,000 and as much as needed thereafter, with the federal government paying up to one-third of the first $18.00 for the first child and up to one-third of $12.00 for each succeeding child per month. (Contrast this with the federal input of half of $30.00 for the aged and blind.) ADC had to be given across each state at the same grant level, and a one-year residence requirement was allowed (later struck out as unconstitutional). An allowance for the adult caretaker was not granted until 1950, when the program became Aid to Families of Dependent Children (AFDC). Although ADC would allow the mother to stay home caring for her children, ADC was not granted for this purpose. Those mothers judged "fit and proper" by investigators might remain in the home, but the rest had to work, find alternative means of support, give up their children, or have them taken away under neglect statutes. Local administrators could require eligible mothers to work as a condition for the grant.

Federal financing for ADC was probably enacted only because it was tied to other, more popular, bills. Although some believe that disinterest led to ADC's meager provisions, intentional neglect because of institutional sexism and racism were more likely causes. By November 1936, while forty-two states were receiving money for Old Age Assistance, only twenty-six were receiving ADC monies, though it had been legislated in all but three states—Alabama, Georgia, and South Carolina—by the end of 1935.[61] In 1936, 162,000 families received $49.7 million in benefits, or about $307 per family.[62] The basic eligibility requirement for ADC was need, set by state standards and determined by needs testing. Although now fewer children were placed in orphanages, and to that extent ADC was a positive step, grants were always low and the threat of removal of children always present.

Today, AFDC is a federal-state program, with 75 percent federal and 25 percent state funding. Need levels are still determined by each state and, generally, intact families (with both parents at home) are not eligible. The benefits are available until the youngest child is 17 years of age, although before the Reagan administration states had the option of providing for school children up to 21 years old if still in school. In some states, intact families may qualify if the major wage-earner is incapacitated (AFDC-I) or unemployed (AFDC-UP).

### Maternal and Child Welfare

Another major part of the Social Security Act of 1935, neither social insurance nor public assistance, was the provision of preventative and remedial care for children under Title V, the Maternal and Child Welfare Act. It provided funding for several kinds of programs:

1.  Child welfare services for the care of homeless, dependent, and neglected children, and those in danger of becoming delinquent. Money would be given to states on plans developed jointly by state departments of public welfare and the Children's Bureau.

2. Vocational training and rehabilitation for crippled and physically handicapped children.
3. Funding for programs to promote the health of children and mothers. This also included prenatal and birthing care for mothers, and eventually some programs of contraception. School districts used this section to fund school nurses, and some public health programs were established through this title.

In 1936, $3,800,000 was approved, with grants to be given under the authority of the chief of the Children's Bureau—the secretary of labor. Each state was allotted $20,000 plus part of $1,800,000, depending on the proportion of state to national live birthrate. Another $980,000 was available for grants according to financial need of the states. State health agencies were required to administer these programs, with states contributing funds on a matching basis.

## PROFESSIONALIZATION OF SOCIAL WORK

Because private agencies could not distribute relief, and most professional social workers were with private agencies, the split between professional social workers and public welfare was nearly complete. Public relief was delegated to two parallel agencies: county relief—in local welfare offices—and bureaus of social aid. Workers in the first were hired by local directors who often were political appointees. Bureaus of Social Aid were also established at the county level under a central state administration and provided Old Age Assistance, Aid to the Blind, Aid to Dependent Children, and later Aid to the Permanently and Totally Disabled.

A new breed of activists arose to champion the cause of the poor—the workers in bureaus of social aid. Typically, young, unemployed college graduates staffed the new federal offices—teachers, salesmen, engineers—unsocialized to "professionalism" and deeply critical of it as a defense of status and a tool of oppression. They became the rank and file of new social services unions, which gained 15,000 workers in the 1930s. As early as 1931 workers of the Jewish Federation in New York City organized the New York Association of Federation Workers, and a little later the first strike in social work history occurred. This laid the groundwork for social work trade unions in the public sector, the first of which was the Home Relief Employees Association (December 1933). By 1938, 14,500 people belonged to social work locals, while the American Association of Social Workers had an estimated 10,560 of the 60,000 social workers in the nation. Eighty-three percent of those unionized were in public agencies.[63] While they were concerned with their own job issues, they were also aware of the needs of their clients. Within a year, their successes had encouraged new unions in Chicago, Cincinnati, Cleveland, Detroit, Minneapolis, Newark, Philadelphia, and Pittsburgh.[64]

However, "red-baiting" campaigns in the late 1930s and after World War II, during the McCarthy witchhunts of the 1950s, brought the downfall of social work unions. Many social workers were in fact communists or socialists, for example, Mary Van Kleeck, who attacked the New Deal because of its commitment to the needs of the elite rather than the needs of the poor at the May 1934 meeting of the National Conference of Social Workers. Bertha Reynolds, a graduate of Smith in 1918, identified with both communism and the rank and file movement, saying that "caseworkers were employed to see that society was not troubled by [the economically unsuccessful]."[65] Although she was deeply respected in the profession, she never worked again as a social worker after the McCarthy red scare.

"Professional" social workers turned to social casework, usually based on psychoanalytic models or the new developments in family-child relationships. By 1937, child services and family agencies were developing mergers and cooperative structures because of the similarity of their practice base and clientele. Freud's theories of psychosexual development and the emphasis on inner self created a ripe field for social work practice and gave "scientific" support to blaming those who were having problems with life adjustment. The theories "prescribed" psychoanalytic treatment as the "cure"—rationalizing the medical model of social work above that of the social or structural model. Ehrenreich says

> As social workers more and more became psychotherapists . . . concerned with the life cycle problems of the middle class, their theoretical base widened . . . behavior modification and learning theory, existentialism and humanist therapy, transactional analysis and gestalt therapy, systems theory and "social ecology" and a dozen varieties of family therapy and group work joined . . . Freudian psychodynamic theories as part of many social workers armamentorium of approaches and techniques. What was "social" about these techniques few ever asked.[66]

From this perspective, the *presenting* problem was, then, not the *real* problem. Requests for help, such as paying bills or dealing with authorities, either masked emotional problems or was indicative of psychological inability to cope with such problems. Disposing of the immediate problem, such as heat turnoff or need for food, was seen as

> unprofessional, potentially destructive, and [creative of] even further dependency. All casework services have to be . . . "constructive" parts of a "plan." . . . the coercive aspects of the casework relationship . . . stemmed from the structural position of the agencies which gave them enormous power over clients. . . . They were extensions of other authoritative agencies—the police, the schools, the health agencies—or the key to desperately needed benefits.[67]

Freud's dictum "happiness is to love and to work" reinforced work as therapy for troubled souls. Moreover, Freud's differential psychosexual development theories for men and women reinforced women's secondary status in work and in the home. It also gave society scapegoats for the perceived growth of juvenile delinquency—mothers who put their own needs over those of their children by remaining in the labor market.

## WORLD WAR II

Although the Social Security Act alleviated some basic subsistence problems, war was the real reason for the end of the Depression. It came to Europe when Germany invaded Poland in 1939, but its gestation was much earlier. Germany was brought to its knees by World War I, and a "democratic" government imposed by its victors—the Weimar Republic—could not keep its people from starving. As the worldwide depression intensified, the German economic situation worsened. By 1923, the German mark had fallen to four million per one U.S. dollar.

As early as 1920, Adolf Hitler announced his National Socialist (Nazi) program, and in 1921 his personal storm troopers began to terrorize political opponents. Although his 1923 coup d'état in Munich failed, Hitler served only eight months of the four-year prison term to which he was sentenced. Mussolini's successful formation of his Fascist regime in Italy provided both example and potential ally to Hitler, and by 1925 Hitler's Nazi party had 27,000 members. The interallied military control of Germany ended in 1927 and Germany's economic system collapsed. In 1930, the Nazis gained 107 seats in parliament, and by 1931, with all German banks bankrupt, the Nazi party had 800,000 members. In the next election, Hitler won 11 million votes against Hindenburg's 18 million, and in 1933, with 96 percent of the vote, became chancellor. Granted dictatorial powers, he established the first concentration camps in Germany where, little more than a decade later, eight to ten million prisoners were detained and six million killed. In 1935, Hitler and Mussolini declared the Rome-Berlin Axis, and a bloodbath of political opponents in Germany left Hitler, now Fuehrer, arming for war. In 1936 Germany and Japan, under Emperor Hirohito, signed the Anti-Comintern Pact, and Japan declared war against China.

Although the United States was an ally of Britain and Poland, it had signed a Neutrality Act in 1937 and was, furthermore, involved in its own program development and a new recession with strikes by half a million workers. In 1939 Roosevelt finally acknowledged the possibility of war, asking for $552 million for defense, but by this time Germany was bold enough to invade Poland, precipitating war in Europe. Not until Japan attacked Pearl Harbor, on December 7, 1941, did the United States finally enter the war as an uneasy ally with China and its communist ally, Russia.

### Internment of Japanese Americans

As the United States went to war, its selective racism showed on many fronts. One of the most crucial was the internment of Japanese Americans as a threat to national security. The first action against the Japanese took place on state and local levels: The legislature of California passed a bill reducing elections of Japanese Americans to state government; state and federal police raids intensified; and more than two thousand people of Japanese descent were arrested.[68] Most such cases were thrown out for lack of evidence, but this, according to California Attorney Earl Warren, merely "reflected the cunning of the Japanese." Japanese businesses were forced to close and citizens illegally detained, evicted, and fired. At least three dozen violent attacks were documented.

In 1942, Roosevelt proclaimed Western California, Oregon, Washington, and Southern Arizona as areas where no Japanese, German, or Italian aliens could reside. A War Relocation Board moved a small number of Japanese, German, and Italian aliens from "sensitive" military areas and restricted their movements. However, only the Japanese were pressured to resettle: 200,000 Italians and Germans were not. The Federal Reserve Bank was ordered to protect their property, but most sold it at low prices, and businesses and farms went at losses.

The Japanese were detained and then transported, without any semblance of trial or due process, to barb-wired concentration camps. By fall 1942, more than 112,000 Japanese Americans, two-thirds of them citizens, were interned in ten concentration camps under guard by the military. They were allowed few personal possessions and were housed in partitioned-off barracks with inadequate supplies. Small monthly wages were paid to those who would work. Local camp governments were established under the direction of the War Relocation Authority, with a council selected from the prisoners. The internees underwent constant political screening to ferret out disloyalties, and their demonstrations and riots were generally without result. A few thousand students and workers in special agricultural assignments were released, and many joined the army, in which their segregated unit was the most decorated in World War II. Some six thousand renounced their U.S. citizenship. In 1943 more than ten thousand relocated to the East.

In 1944, one-third of the prisoners were allowed to leave the concentration camps, and in late 1944 the order to hold them was rescinded. Most returned to the West coast and in the next two years eight hundred returned to Japan.[69] The cost to the United States for the evacuation was about $250 million, and Japanese American losses have been estimated at at least $400 million. The internees formed the Japanese American Citizens' League to protest the evacuation and its losses to them formally, and by 1946 it was pressing for compensation. By 1950 nearly twenty-four thousand claims were filed, totaling $132 million, but the government paid only $38 million, less than 10 percent of the estimated losses. In 1980, the Commission on Wartime Relocation and Internment of Civilians recommended that sixty thousand survivors should receive $1–2 million,[70] but this was still minimal in the face of Japanese American losses from the internment.

### The War Years

The federal government had refused since 1932 to hire married women whose husbands were already employed (Federal Economy Act, married person's clause) and fired 1600 of those whose husbands held federal jobs. At the same time, 77 percent of the nation's school systems refused to hire married women as teachers and half dismissed those who married. In Texas, women who worked in railroad companies were fired if their husbands earned over $50.00 per month. As late as 1939, when twenty-one states still had no minimum wage laws for women and thirty lacked 8-hour workday laws, legislatures in twenty-six states were considering bills to bar married women from all employment. A live-in domestic in New York, at the nation's highest salary, earned $34 per month, and the Women's Bureau thought $6.00 per week was an adequate salary for a 72-hour workweek.[71] Because of the recession, both government and private employers began to fire women. Norman Cousins, echoing the public sentiment of the day, said in 1939,

> There are approximately 10 million people out of work in the United States today. . . . There are also 10 million or more women, married or single, who are jobholders. Simply fire the women, who shouldn't be working anyway, and hire the men. Presto. No unemployment. No relief rolls. No depression.[72]

When the Japanese attacked Pearl Harbor, the United States had already been gearing up for war for two years. More and more people were being recruited to factory work: Afro-American men from the South, Puerto Ricans from their island, Mexicans and Mexican Americans from the Southwest, women, and even young people. Factory recruiters paid high school principals to send them students, and the minimum age for employment was reduced from 18 to 16 so that they could be employed. Military and civilian demand pushed the economy upward. In 1940 the gross national product was $99.7 billion, and in a total population of 132.1 million, the number of workers in the labor force was 55.6 million, with 540,000 persons in the armed services and civilian employment at 47.5 million. The unemployment rate was 14.6 percent, or 8 million workers. Sixty-four percent of the working population made annual wages of under $2,000 and 84 percent were under $3,000.

With the Selective Service Act of 1942, factories were left inadequately staffed to produce sufficient amounts of goods and war materiel. More than 16 million men were transported for military reasons; women, wives, and family followed them. Another 16 million moved for job reasons.[73] When war employment soaked up the residue of unemployed men, employers turned to women. They were recruited not only into the "women's" labor market, but into war production plants. The War Manpower Commission estimated, in fact, that only 29 percent of America's 52 million adult women had jobs and told them they were shirking their patriotic duties if they did not work. During the first two years of war, twenty states and Washington, D.C., enacted emergency laws to extend maximum daily or weekly working hours for women. Laws against night work were modified in eight states, and in four states various occupations previously covered by protective legislation were exempted. By February 1943, *Fortune* magazine suggested drafting women if they did not come forward to work.[74]

Nearly 11 million women had jobs before 1940, and 3 million were looking for work.[75] By 1940, nearly 16 million women of a total female population of 50.1 million were working full time despite discrimination, lower pay, and segregated job classifications. Of the female work force before the war, 48.4 percent were single, 36.4 percent were married, and widows and divorcees comprised 15.1 percent. Labor force participation of women over age 14 increased from 25 to 36 percent.[76] During the war, the percentage of single women workers decreased to 40.9 percent, while those married rose to 45.7 percent. Two million women went to work in offices, half in the federal government. By 1945, the wartime peak, 19.5 million women were employed, excluding those in the Red Cross and military service. By 1950, women were 32 percent of the labor force.[77] Three-fourths of new women workers were over age 35, 60 percent were married, and the majority had children of school or preschool age.[78]

Forty percent of black women—1.5 million—worked (compared with 25 percent of white women) before the war. More than half were in service occupations such as domestic employees (72 percent) and 20 percent were farm workers. By war's end in 1945, 2 million black women were working, with 18 percent in factories and the greatest increase in manufacture of metals, chemicals, and rubber. Their numbers as factory workers quadrupled, and there was a noticeable and permanent decrease in their employment as domestic workers.

Pay for women changed with war employment as the federal government endorsed equal pay for equal work in government and war-connected jobs, and unions fought for equal pay so that men's pay would not be reduced. Union membership for women, which had been 500,000 in 1937, reached 3,500,000 by 1940. By 1944 more than 3 million women constituted 22 percent of trade union members.[79] Still, in many jobs women received lower pay even when equal pay clauses were written into labor contracts. The National War Labor Board defended employers against women on the grounds that they would leave the labor force with the end of the war. Although some 700,000 workers received industrial training in the last half of 1941, only 1 percent of these were women.

The presence of women in factories led to improved working conditions in many ways, including company cafeterias, a few day care centers, transportation facilities, rest breaks, and some shopping and banking facilities on plant sites. In 1942 the federal government allotted $400,000 to assist local communities in funding child care, and the 1943 Lanham Act authorized money for day care centers, though few communities came up with matching funds to build them. Day care centers were expensive (up to $6 per child) and inconveniently located, and their hours open did not consider the travel needs of working women. Thus they operated at only a quarter of capacity and were cost ineffective to continue. With the end of the war, the issue of day care centers as needed facilities faded away, to be replaced by the feeling that, at best, day care centers made it easy for mothers to be neglectful and, at worst, they were part of a leftist plot to destroy the American family. A 1945 bill asking for $30 million to continue day care centers failed, with some congressmen arguing that "women should be driven back to their homes." While a bill for $20 million to continue centers through 1946 did succeed, it included no money for expansion and soon all federal support for day care ended.[80]

By 1943, unemployment was virtually ended, with a rate of 1.2 percent—about 1 million unemployed. Twenty-four percent of all women of working age were in the labor force. By 1945, with a population of 105.5 million, the gross national product was $211.9 billion, and civilian employment rose 11.1 percent, reaching 52.8 million.[81] Total employment in 1946 was 56.7 million, of whom 15.8 million were women.

### The War and People of Color

While many people of color shared in the benefits of the Roosevelt years, the country still maintained a racist bias. For example, the Civilian Conservation Corps had a racial quota that limited participation; Federal Emergency Relief, National Industrial Recovery, and Agricultural Adjustment Act monies were given discretionarily according to race; the National Labor Administration had codes with discriminatory pay rates; and government employment was discriminatory and offices were segregated. Roosevelt, in political debt to the Southern aristocracy, refused to support antilynch laws and would not endorse a broad civil rights program.[82] Although he appointed more than one hundred Afro-Americans to federal positions between 1933 and 1940, it was always at lower levels. William Hastie was appointed to the third U.S. Circuit Court, the highest Afro-American judicial appointment up to that time; Robert C. Weaver was given a post in the Department of the Interior; and E. K. Jones took a post in the Commerce Department, Laurence Oxley in the Labor Department, Ira D. Reed in the Social Security Administration, and Mary Bethune in the National Youth Authority.[83]

The 1928 Merriam Survey had given impetus to major changes in Native American affairs under Commissioner Charles J. Rhoads. In 1933, Roosevelt appointed John Collier as commissioner (a post he held until 1946). Collier, who had been active in supporting Native Americans since the 1920s, instituted major changes under the Indian Reorganization Act of 1934 (Wheeler-Howard Act), and most Native Americans had the right to decide whether or not they would participate in the changes. The act stopped allotment of Native American lands to white people and ended the forced assimilation of their cultures; allowed Native Americans to develop their own constitutions and elect tribal councils; created a fund to provide credit for agriculture and industrial projects so that Native Americans could develop tribal business corporations; and gave them over a million acres of new land. Health and school services were improved. The act also allowed for preferential hiring in the Bureau of Indian Affairs to Native Americans. The secretary of the interior, however, could still veto constitutions and make rules for tribal elections, and he also continued to supervise expenditures and regulate land management. Almost twenty-five thousand Native Americans entered the armed services, mostly as draftees, and almost twice as many left reservations to work in war industries.[84] They came back as veterans entitled to such services as rehabilitation, education, housing, and jobs, and became the fathers of the generation that rebelled in the 1960s.

Before the war, partly in response to Roosevelt's New Deal, Afro-Americans began to become Democrats. (He received about one- fourth of their vote in 1932, but in 1940 gained 53 percent.) In 1944 the Supreme

Court ruled that they could not be barred from primaries in southern states, and by the late 1940s an estimated 600,000 Afro-American voters were registered. By the time of World War II, Afro-Americans had become more vocal in their demands for equality. They had migrated to urban areas, become educated, and participated in the Works Progress Administration, the National Youth Administration, and vocational training. Their victories were few but steady: By 1940, 73 percent of Afro-American men in the labor force had blue-collar jobs, despite tremendous resistance to their employment, and despite resistance to their induction, more than a million men and women of African descent served in the armed forces, although in segregated units. For the first time they entered combat units rather than those assigned to menial chores, and they could now enter the Army Air Corps and the Marines. Although Afro-American officers were commissioned and sent to integrated officers' training schools, segregation continued for the regular soldier in living quarters and in training and recreation.

On the home front, their activism continued. The Urban League in 1940 had a membership of 26,000 in 46 branches, and the NAACP had 481 branch offices and 85,000 members nationwide. The latter's attention focused on the South, pushing for antilynching laws and laws to end the quasi-peonage and debt slavery there; for educational and employment opportunities; equitable treatment in courts; equal pay for work equal to that done by white workers and access to labor unions; and the fair distribution of public education funds and the end of segregated facilities.

In 1943 the Congress of Racial Equality (CORE) began to challenge segregation in restaurants, swimming pools, and municipal facilities in northern and border states and staged its first sit-in in a restaurant in the Chicago Loop. CORE was inspired by the Gandhian tactics of nonviolence, and by the militancy of a new leader, A. Phillip Randolph. Randolph, son of an African Methodist minister, had won recognition for the Brotherhood of Pullman Car Porters after twelve years as a labor organizer. Protesting unfair labor practices, he threatened Roosevelt with a march on Washington by 50,000 to 100,000 black workers. In efforts to dissuade him, Roosevelt asked him, Walter White of the NAACP, and T. Arnold Hill, acting executive of the Urban League to end plans for the march, but Randolph was adamant. In response to the threat, Roosevelt wrote an executive order barring discrimination in war industries and the armed services on June 25, 1941, and Randolph called off the march.[85]

This first Fair Employment Practices Committee met widespread defiance and was ineffective because it lacked power to punish offenders. Its institution touched off, in 1943, the worst series of riots by white workers since 1919. In a Mobile, Alabama, shipyard Afro-American workers were promoted and white workers rioted until troops were called in to quiet them. There were riots in Harlem, and in Detroit thirty-four persons died in a riot over jobs. Because Afro-American labor was necessary to the war effort, both the National Defense Advisory Committee and President Roosevelt spoke out against discrimination. This, along with the growing protest movements, fostered a second Fair Employment Practices Commission (FEPC) in 1943. Soon Afro-American workers held 1 million factory jobs, union membership increased to 500,000, and their number in government increased from 50,000 in 1939 to 200,000 in 1944. The proportion of Afro-Americans in war-related industries increased from 3 to 8 percent during war years, but layoffs at the end hit them much harder than whites. Their unemployment has since then remained consistently double that of whites.

Not until the war ended did President Truman abolish segregation in army units, and at the same time ended discrimination in firms doing business with the federal government. As the war ended, however, racism once more took its toll. White people mobbed and attacked neighborhoods where Afro-Americans lived and lynched returning veterans. Truman refused to recant his civil rights stand, however, and set forth a civil rights platform for the 1948 presidential election. Although he won the election on the Afro-American city vote, it cost him the Southern vote and his proposed civil rights bill failed in Congress, which continued to refuse legislation to protect voting rights. Not until 1951 was lynching finally made a federal offense.

### Social Welfare Services: The War and After

During the war, Roosevelt turned to problems of dislocation and distress related to the war itself. In November 1940 he named the administrator of the Federal Security Agency as coordinator of the Office of Health, Welfare, and Related Defense Activities. This office provided services for training camps and their civilian communities. In 1941, he placed the Office of Civilian Defense in the Office of War Management to integrate servicemen's health, welfare, and recreation services with defense activities. By 1943, these had been integrated into the Office of Community War Services under the Federal Security Agency, serving both armed forces and the civilian population.

The Community Facilities Act 1941 (Lanham Act) provided federal funds for defense-impacted communities for construction of houses, schools, day care centers, hospitals, water and sanitation plants, and recreational facilities. Routine physical health care was encouraged: During the war years, the Emergency Maternal and Infant Care program (1943) served more than 1.2 million military wives with 230,000 infants. Inoculation programs for all children were undertaken through public health services.

Education became a major service goal when Army examinations showed an illiteracy rate of one in five among inductees. The U.S. Office of Education was expanded to make federal aid available for elementary and secondary education and for agricultural extension services in rural areas. In addition, it awarded enormous government contracts for research in engineering, science, and civil aeronautics; education in defense industries; management; and the Reserve Officers Training Corps (ROTC).[86]

More than 16,535,000 servicemen went to war: The death toll for Americans was 292,000 while in action and 114,000 for other causes. Nearly 700,000 were wounded. While the servicemen were gone, some never to return, the government concerned itself with helping the families who had given up fathers, sons, and husbands to the national need. The Servicemen's Dependent Allowance Act of 1942, under the War Department, provided family allotments. At first paid half and half by the serviceman and the government—by 1943, $797 million—by 1945 allotments totaled $3 billion, with the government paying $2 billion.[87]

After the war, major social legislation centered on veterans, both because the nation believed they deserved reward for services to their country and to avert a major economic catastrophe. We had learned from World War I: The release of millions of soldiers into the employment market when millions were laid off as the war economy declined would have produced a massive depression. Although the Selective Training and Service Act of 1940 provided that inductees be reemployed at the end of service in positions of like seniority, status, and pay, the government took steps to keep veterans out of the labor market. The first was the "52–20 Plan," which provided veterans $20 each week for a year whether or not they were disabled or involved in battle.

The second was the Servicemen's Readjustment Act of 1944, called the G.I. Bill of Rights. Its only eligibility requirement was that the veteran have served during a specific time. It provided stipends to support veterans and their families while the veterans went to school for vocational education or higher education; paid for tuition; and paid for home loans, business and farm loans, unemployment insurance payments, and veterans' employment services. G.I. Bill expenditures were $3.4 billion in 1946 and $9.3 billion in 1950—23 percent of that year's federal expenditures.[88] In addition to averting a depression, the G.I. Bill upgraded the quality and earning power of American work force for a generation. Third, the National Mental Health Act of 1946, in response to the mental health needs of veterans, began to fund research and training in mental health and to establish community mental health services. This led to even more programs and agencies for social work professionals.

### Women after the War

The nation made a radical turnabout regarding women's work at the end of the war. Within two years, fourteen million veterans returned to civilian work. The number of women working as operatives and craftsmen dropped by over a million. Where they had been recruited and had won many gains for all workers because of the manpower shortage, now it became their patriotic duty to leave the factory and return to marriage and family roles in the home. The Selective Service Act of 1942 contained a tacit assumption, since it guaranteed veterans the jobs they had held before the war, that women would want to go home. Frances Perkins, secretary of labor, insisted that their war effort was only temporary and they would return to the home when men came back. However, this did not acknowledge that many women had to work and that, for the first time, they had been paid reasonable wages. Many did not want to give this up. In a UAW poll asking if women would work after the war if jobs were available, 98.5 percent of single women, 100 percent of widows, and 68.7 of married women said yes.[89]

Unions helped little in retention of women's jobs after the war: In Detroit, for example, the AFL-CIO had between 300,000 and 350,000 women members by war's end. Yet when layoffs occurred, 41 percent of men laid off were offered new jobs at 8.5 cents lower per hour (the average wage of Willow Run workers was $1.23 an hour), but less than 3 percent of women were offered other jobs, and those who were lost more than 48 cents per hour. Layoffs for women were always higher than for men, with the old excuses of "heavy work," late hours, and women needed at home. A clause in a contract between United Steel and Wire and local 704 said

> When a man is the youngest employee in a classification involved in a reduction of force . . . he shall be permitted to bump any woman filling a job designated as a man's job . . . in case of plant-wide layoffs, women employees holding duly designated men's jobs will be laid off before any man employee. . . . A woman employee is not permitted to bump a man employee off a man's job.[90]

Women protested and picketed but in general to no avail. In the two months following VJ Day (Victory over Japan), women were laid off at rates of 75 per 1,000, twice that of men. By the end of 1946 2 million women had been fired from heavy industry, and some companies reinstated old policies of not hiring women.[91]

In 1946, the Women's Bureau held a conference on union contract provisions affecting women. The majority of the recommendations were for equal treatment rather than protection of women because of their "frailty." The bureau held that pregnancy should not be grounds for dismissal and that women returning after maternity leave be given their former jobs at current salary. Job classification and wage rates should be set by job and not by sex, and no new employees should be hired if women were available for upgrading.[92] A 1947 bureau report showed that one million fewer women were employed, and that though half were actively seeking work, there was an obvious shift to unemployment insurance and later to the welfare rolls. By 1953, one million women were seeking jobs, of whom Afro-Americans were the largest percent.[93]

Women as workers faced increasing hostility after the war, fired by the growth of the social sciences and the casework emphasis of the profession of social work. The new information on child development, the Freudian interpretation of the roles of women and psychosexual development, and an intense concentration on the problem of juvenile delinquency blamed absent mothers for all kinds of problems. "Latch-key children"— given keys to get into their homes by working mothers—were investigated by welfare departments, juvenile justice systems, and the growing number of family and children's agencies. These last, though they were unlikely to serve poor children whose mothers had to work, researched the problems of juvenile delinquents in terms of parent-child relationships and the "mental illness" of women who worked (that is, took on male roles). They came to conclusions, very useful to a government trying to reduce the labor force and to men returning from war to their previous roles, indicating that the working mother was an affront to the rights of children for "good parenting" and the American way of life.

Although it is likely that the concentration on juvenile delinquency came from new reporting, new casework theories, and the fact that young people could not get jobs because veterans were returning to employment in a time of economic downswing, the whole issue was used to influence women to return home and participate in the baby boom. Women who entered male fields after the war—law, mathematics, physics, business, industry, technology—faced a consensus that they "should" be discriminated against,[94] because the psychic maladjustment that made them want to leave home made them poor business risks. Fewer than half of both men and women believed that women should have equal chance at jobs, even if they were sole breadwinners.[95] It was said that

> feminism represented a neurotic reaction to male dominance and a deep illness which encouraged women to reject their natural sex-based instincts.[96]

On moral, political, and economic grounds the case against women in the work force was made.

Three million fewer women were employed in 1946 than at wartime peak, and between 1945 and 1947, 2.7 million women were removed from industrial employment.[97] However, by 1950 female employment neared its top wartime level. Need for money was still the main reason women worked: In 1947, 31 percent of all families still had incomes below $2,000 and 50 percent earned less than $3,000.

## THE RESURGENCE OF SOCIAL WORK

Shortly after the war, the economy began to pick up because of the massive backlog of demands for consumer goods. The return of veterans, the almost forceable reduction in the female labor force, and the ideology—partly enforced by social welfare/social work—that women "ought to be" in the home, with babies and under the support of a husband, led to an increase in marriages and a "baby boom" that meant a new market. Soon after the war ended, the birthrate reached a high of 26.6 births per 1,000.[98] As people could afford to move into the suburbs because of the availability of home loans and the growing number of educated people finding better jobs, the isolation of women from one another began, contributing to their loneliness and depression. Moreover, as they moved far from their mothers, the normal channels for learning about homemaking and child care were closed off. Once more, social work professionals took over, and all "failures"—misbehaving or unhappy children—were blamed on the mother.

Treatment in all forms of social welfare continued to be skewed by the idea of woman as dependent, nonassertive, and emotionally immature. Women who wanted to work were judged to be mentally ill, and worse, to be destroying their families and their children. Although social workers believed deviance arose from the environment, the environment in question was not social and economic conditions but home, early training, and how children dealt with authority, especially around the learning of toilet training and eating. These produced different disorders that could be "cured" by social work treatment.

The fear of juvenile delinquency began to alter the national consciousness as well as that of the profession. Between 1940 and 1960 the number of cases rose from 200,000 to 813,000, and Cloward and Ohlin's idea of a "deviant subculture," in which children learned criminal behavior from their peers, began to obfuscate the structural and economic reasons for delinquency. The profession of social work expanded and grew on this new emphasis of mental illness—called an epidemic—and by 1955, some 558,000 persons resided in psychiatric hospitals, and new admissions were about 200,000 a year.[99] Mental health clinics had 300,000 more clients, and the community mental health program began.

In addition to juvenile delinquency, drug abuse became a major interest for social work. During the first two decades of the century, alcohol consumption had been the "morality issue" of social welfare. This ended with Prohibition, but Prohibition itself created two massive organizations devoted to crime management: organized crime, which provided alcohol to those who wanted it, and enforcers of the Prohibition amendment, the bulk of whom were in the Treasury Department as "revenuers." When Prohibition was rescinded in 1933, both organizations turned to the business of drugs that now became illegal—marijuana, cocaine, heroin. Where previously drug abuse had been a medical problem, with relatively low costs for society, now it was a legal problem and a mental health problem, and the costs skyrocketed.

The number of social workers expanded in the 1930s from thirty-one thousand to seventy thousand. The number of professional organizations also expanded: By 1930 they included the American Association of Medical Social Workers, the National Association of School Social Workers, the American Association of Psychiatric Social Workers, and the American Association of Social Workers. Members of these organizations comprised less than 25 percent of the social work force: The remainder were not affiliated or were in public assistance jobs and organizations.[100] By 1939 the American Association of Schools of Social Work had required two year Master of Social Work programs. In 1946, the National Council on Social Work Education was formed, and in 1952 it became the accrediting body for American and Canadian schools of social work until 1970, when Canada set up its own council.

Fees for service and private practice began: In 1943, Jewish Family Services in New York began fee charging, and other family agencies followed suit with sliding fee scales. Now community centers, or organizations for young people—Girl Scouts or YWCAs, for example—set up paid "memberships" for participation. The profession moved away from service and into support by middle- and upper-class clientele. Now parents could learn about child development and the skills of parenting from experts, but lower-class clientele were not welcome, for they were not "treatable." By 1960, 9 percent of social work clients were in the upper socioeconomic class, and 48 percent were in the middle class.

Group work practice was professionally recognized in the 1930s also. Early settlement work led the way to its development, but group work developed primarily from the work of Mary Follett (1868–1933). Follett, a theorist in the field of organization and bureaucracy, adapted Frederick Taylor's scientific management to humanistic management. From 1908 to 1920, she developed community centers within neighborhood schools and worked for minimum wage legislation. Her 1924 book *Creative Experience* detailed her theory of humanistic management and posited a new form of democracy based on spontaneous organization, or grass-roots development through the creative interaction of people and groups. Group work was legitimated with the Association of Group Workers and the Social Work Research Association (1949). Near the same time, the Association for the Study of Community Organization was also formed, based on Follett's theories and settlement house experiences.[101]

While social work continued on its course, a split arose within it. On one side were the proponents of psychosocial casework, defended by such eminent social workers as Gordon Hamilton and Florence Hollis. On the other side were "functionalists," who believed that while psychosocial investigation might be interesting, social work practice belonged in the here and now and psychosocial practice's demand for long-term relationship, differential diagnosis, and setting of long- and short-term goals did not serve clients but controlled them. Among its proponents, Jessie Taft argued for a process model of helping, and Ruth Smalley argued against control of the client. Virginia Robinson's "A Changing Psychology in Social Work," written in 1930, was heavily influenced by Otto Rank and challenged Freud's paternalistic models. Robinson said that casework should focus on the relationship between client and environment, the client should be central, and the worker-client relationship was to strengthen clients rather than control them. John Ehrenreich says

> The functional school sustained a serious and coherent effort at dealing with the welfare state and its implications for social work theory, practice, and professional status. . . . It sought to rethink radically the relationship between the social environment and the individual. But it never convinced more than a minority.[102]

The debate between the functional school and psychosocial casework grew bitter and threatened to end all the professional gains made. Although the debate has never really ended, Helen Perlman's eclectic problem-solving model, which focused on systems and could incorporate either type of casework, helped to bridge the gap and reunited, however uneasily, the casework profession.

### Reorganizing Federal Social Welfare Efforts

After the war, President Truman asked former President Hoover to head a commission to study the federal bureaucracy and make recommendations. From this study, the Federal Security Agency and several other domestic agencies were formed into a single cabinet-level department, the Department of Health, Education, and Welfare,[103] which then housed the Social Security Administration. Some new legislation was passed—the national school lunch program of 1946, the Housing Act of 1949, a special milk program for the poor in 1954. The Housing Act authorized 135,000 public housing units per year, but only 25,000 to 40,000 per year were built in the following decade. The houses that were built under this act, the public housing act, and the G.I. bill promoted the movement of middle-class whites to the suburbs, while people of color and poor people moved into the central cities. Most social legislation other than for veterans took the form of incrementing existent programs after the war—new provisions added to laws, eligibility expanded, or increased payments in both public assistance and social insurance.

## CONCLUSION: MOVING TOWARD THE FUTURE

As the nation moved into the 1950s, a new configuration to life and to social welfare began. The social legislation of the 1930s and the nation's adaptation to the war had created a welfare state, however minimal its provisions, for most the needy groups in society. Poverty was changing: Now the working force had some power to demand living wages, but groups without the capability for unionization were little better off than before. People of color, inspired by their earning power during the war and the advances they had achieved with little if any help from social institutions, were also demanding rights.

However, backlash soon emerged—in race riots, in the communist hunting of the McCarthy era, and in the recalcitrance of both county relief and the Bureaus of Social Aid to extend benefits to those who were eligible but who were not "morally correct." During the next decade, the profession of social work would have little to do with issues of reform but would continue to firm up its psychological intervention techniques. While researchers were well aware of the problems of people oppressed because of poverty, race, and sex, their work had little impact on society's orientation to the poor—still to blame for their poverty—or the distressed, now mentally ill rather than disadvantaged.

The children who reached adulthood during the 1950s have been called the "Silent Generation." Yet this may be only in comparison to the eruption of mass social movements in the 1960s. Surely the problems were there, and recognized, throughout the 1940s and 1950s—the unrest of people of color, the baby boom, the white flight to the suburbs, and growing urban unrest. Perhaps this generation taught its children that life did not have to be unfair. People of color and women for the first time had been treated equally, and though after the war attempts were made to suppress them they had learned. They had money and could earn more, protected by fair employment laws. They became educated and vocal, and taught their children that their oppression was not only immoral but illegal. Automobiles gave them physical mobility and television widened their perceptions to the world rather than the neighborhood. The accent on education helped them to question not only local political situations but those of the world.

The causes of gender and civil rights were nurtured during World War II, and many of the changes in social welfare sprang from changes in the War and its aftermath. The G.I. Bill made money available to a great number of people and created a new middle class. In addition, new technologies made the world smaller in both physical and mental senses, adding to the immediacy of new social welfare programs. The profession of social work had altered nearly completely from the provision of income maintenance for the poor to an accent on mental health for the middle class, and social workers had become professionals rather than reform voices crying in the wilderness. New services to children, to veterans, to the middle class; new research into developmental theories and the knowledge bases of sociology, education, psychology; and an elaboration of skills and techniques via social casework and group work legitimated the profession as a part of American society.

## STUDY QUESTIONS

1. What were the causes of the Depression, and what effect did the Depression have on the rich? On the poor? On women? On people of color?
2. What were the underlying values of Roosevelt's Grand Design?
3. What effect did the Depression and the Grand Design have on the provision of social welfare? Explain the split between public and private agencies.
4. How did the profession of social work react to the onset of World War II? What were the changes it made in services?
5. What was the status of women before, during, and after the war? How did this reflect on the provision of social welfare services?
6. What happened to people of color before, during, and after the war, and what consequences did this have for civil rights?
7. Explain how the G.I. Bill changed the face of the middle class.
8. How did the new technologies in communication change the social welfare world?

## FOOTNOTES

[1]June Axinn and Herman Levin, *Social Welfare: A History of the American Response to Need,* 2nd ed. (New York: Harper & Row, 1982), p. 175.

[2]Ibid., p. 176.

[3]John Ehrenreich, *The Altruistic Imagination,* (Ithaca: Cornell University Press, 1985), p. 86.

[4]Thomas R. Dye and L. Harmon Zeigler, *The Irony of Democracy,* (Belmont, Calif.: Wadsworth Publishing Co., 1970), p. 83.

[5]Axinn and Levin, *Social Welfare,* p. 192.

[6]Carole Hymowitz and Michaele Weissman, *A History of Women in America,* (New York: Bantam Books, 1980), p. 303.

[7]Frances Fox Piven and Richard Cloward, *Regulating the Poor,* (New York: Random House, 1971).

[8]Hymowitz and Weissman, *A History of Women,* p. 307.

[9]Alice Kessler-Harris, *Out to Work: A History of Wage-Earning Women in the United States,* (New York: Oxford University Press, 1982), pp. 257–60.

[10]Ibid., p. 264.

[11]Axinn and Levin, *Social Welfare,* p. 187.

[12]Ibid., p. 202.

[13]Kessler-Harris, *Out to Work,* p. 256.

[14]Axinn and Levin, *Social Welfare,* p. 181.

[15]From Albert U. Romasco, *The Poverty of Abundance—Hoover, the Nation, and Depression,* (New York: Oxford University Press, 1965), p. 147, in Gerald Handel, *Social Welfare in Western Society,* (New York: Random House, 1982), p. 134.

[16]Axinn and Levin, *Social Welfare,* p. 190.

[17]J. Ehrenreich, *Altruistic Imagination,* p. 87.

[18]Joe R. Feagin, *Racial and Ethnic Relations,* (Englewood Cliffs, N.J.: Prentice Hall, 1985), p. 280.

[19]Ehrenreich, *The Altruistic Imagination,* p. 88.

[20]Axinn and Levin, *Social Welfare,* p. 189.

[21]Ehrenreich, *The Altruistic Imagination,* p. 89.

[22]Ibid., p. 93.

[23]Ibid., p. 95.

[24]Ibid., p. 97.

[25]Ibid., p. 96.

[26]Dye and Zeigler, *The Irony of Democracy,* p. 83.

[27]Joseph Heffernan, *Introduction to Social Welfare Policy,* (Itasca, Ill.: F. E. Peacock Publishers, 1979), p. 194.

[28]Axinn and Levin, *Social Welfare,* p. 194.

[29]Ibid., p. 214.

[30]Ibid., p. 204.

[31]While Heffernan, *Introduction to Policy,* p. 199, says that all benefits were to be paid in cash, Axinn and Levin, *Social Welfare,* p. 214, say that most often benefits had to be worked off on public property.

[32]Axinn and Levin, *Social Welfare,* p. 184.

[33]Ibid.

[34]Ibid., p. 185.

[35]Ehrenreich, *Altruistic Imagination,* p. 93.

[36]Axinn and Levin, *Social Welfare,* p. 186.

[37]Ibid.

[38]Kessler-Harris, *Out to Work,* p. 270.

[39]Axinn and Levin, *Social Welfare,* p. 181.

[40]Beulah Compton, *Introduction to Social Welfare and Social Work,* (Homewood, Ill.: Dorsey Press, 1980), p. 414.

[41]Axinn and Levin, *Social Welfare,* p. 180.

[42]Ibid., p. 182.

[43]Gerald Handel, *Social Welfare in Western Society,* (New York: Random House, 1982), p. 136.

[44]David Macarov, *Work and Welfare: the Unholy Alliance,* (Beverly Hills, Calif.: Sage Publications, 1980), p. 209.

[45]William Jay Jacobs, *Women in American History,* (Encino, Calif.: Glencoe Publishing, 1976), p. 238.

[46]William H. Chafe, "Eleanor Roosevelt," in Linda K. Kerber and Jane DeHart Mathews, eds., *Women's America,* (New York: Oxford University Press, 1982), pp. 344–353; and in Robert McHenry, *Famous American Women: A Biographical Dictionary from Colonial Times to the Present,* (New York: Dover Publications, 1980), p. 354.

47Winifred Bell, *Contemporary Social Welfare*, (New York: Macmillan Publishing Co., 1983), p. 7.

48Michael B. Katz, *Poverty and Policy in American History*, (New York: Academic Press, 1983), p. 221.

49Samuel Mencher, *From Poor Laws to Poverty Program*, (Pittsburgh: University of Pittsburgh Press, 1967), p. 306.

50Ralph Dolgoff and Donald Feldstein, *Understanding Social Welfare*, 2nd ed., (New York: Longman Press, 1984), pp. 180–181.

51Mencher, *Poor Law to Poverty Programs*, p. 333. F. D. Roosevelt, "Message to Congress," June 8, 1934, 73rd Cong., 2d Session (Washington, D.C.: United States Government Printing Office, 1934), pp. 10, 770.

52Andrew Dobelstein, *Politics, Economics, and Public Welfare*, (Englewood Cliffs, N.J.: Prentice Hall, 1980), p. 29.

53*New York Review of Books*, February 28, 1986, p. 7., reviewing Gosta Esping-Anderson, Martin Rein, and Lee Rainwater, eds., *Stagnation and Renewal in Social Policy*, (New York: M. E. Sharpe, 1986).

54Ehrenreich, *Altruistic Imagination*, p. 99.

55Jeffrey Galper, *Social Work Practice: A Radical Perspective*, (Englewood Cliffs, N.J.: Prentice Hall, 1980), p. 77.

56Harry Hopkins, quoted in Robert E. Sherwood, *Roosevelt and Hopkins*, (New York: Harper & Row, 1948), p. 297.

57Axinn and Levin, *Social Welfare*, p. 220.

58Blanche Coll, *Perspectives in Public Welfare: A History*, U.S. Department of Health, Education, and Welfare, Social Rehabilitation Service 1969, (Washington, D.C.: U.S. Government Printing Office, 1971), p. 63.

59Handel, *Western Society*, p. 138, quoted from Harry L. Hopkins, in Josephine Chapman Brown, *Public Relief, 1929–39*, (New York: Henry Holt, 1940), p. 396.

60Axinn and Levin, *Social Welfare*, p. 225.

61Ibid., p. 202.

62Macarov, *Work and Welfare*, p. 52.

63Ehrenreich, *The Altruistic Imagination*, p. 111.

64Galper, *Social Work Practice*, p. 169.

65Ehrenreich, *The Altruistic Imagination*, p. 118.

66Ibid., p. 207.

67Peter Day, *Social Work and Social Control*, (London: Tavistock Publications, 1981), p. 86.

68Joe R. Feagin, *Racial and Ethnic Relations*, p. 329.

69Ibid., pp. 329—330.

70Axinn and Levin, *Social Welfare*, p. 231.

71Ibid., p. 135.

72Norman Cousins, "Will Women Lose Their Jobs?" *Current History and Forum*, Vol. 41 (September, 1939), p. 14, quoted in Kessler-Harris, *Out to Work*, p. 246.

73Kessler-Harris, *Out to Work*, p. 276.

74*Fortune* poll, cited by Sheila Tobias and Lisa Anderson, "Rosie the Riveter: Demobilization and the Female Labor Force," in Kerber and Mathews, eds., *Women's America*, p. 299.

75Ibid., p. 357.

76Ibid., pp. 354 ff.

77Kessler-Harris, *Out to Work*, p. 278.

78Hymowitz and Weissman, *History of Women*, p. 313.

79Kessler-Harris, *Out to Work*, p. 291.

80Tobias and Anderson, "Rosie the Riveter," in Kerber and Mathews, eds. *Women's America*, p. 369.

81Axinn and Levin, *Social Welfare*, p. 230.

[82]Ehrenreich, *The Altruistic Imagination,* p. 99.

[83]Compton, *Introduction to Social Welfare,* p. 438.

[84]Ibid., p. 440.

[85]Discussed in Feagin, *Ethnic Relations,* p. 229, and Lerone Bennett, Jr., *Before the Mayflower: A History of the Negro in America 1916–1964,* rev. ed., (Chicago: Johnson Publishing Co., Penguin ed., 1966), p. 304.

[86]Axinn and Levin, *Social Welfare,* , p. 242.

[87]Ibid.

[88]Ibid., p. 243.

[89]Ibid., p. 244.

[90]Tobias and Anderson, "Rosie the Riveter," in Kerber and Mathews, eds., *Women's America,* p. 361.

[91]Ibid., p. 364.

[92]Hymowitz and Weissman, *History of Women,* p. 313.

[93]Tobias and Anderson, "Rosie the Riveter," in Kerber and Mathews, eds., *Women's America,* p. 371.

[94]Ibid.

[95]Kessler-Harris, *Out to Work,* p. 297.

[96]Compton, *Introduction to Social Welfare,* quoting Chafe, 1971, p. 443.

[97]Ehrenreich, *The Altruistic Imagination,* p. 147.

[98]Axinn and Levin, *Social Welfare,* p. 233.

[99]Ehrenreich, *The Altruistic Imagination,* p. 153.

[100]Compton, *Introduction to Social Welfare,* p. 143.

[101]McHenry, *Famous American Women,* p. 136.

[102]Ehrenreich, *The Altruistic Imagination,* p. 135.

[103]Dobelstein, *Politics and Welfare,* pp. 84–85.

# 10

## CIVIL AND WELFARE RIGHTS IN THE NEW REFORM ERA

**THE BEGINNINGS OF UNREST**

After the upheavals of the 1930s and 1940s, the nation entered the next decade almost with a sigh of relief. War hero Dwight D. Eisenhower was elected president in 1952, and his administration was competent and benign. On the surface, prosperity reigned, but there were troublesome undercurrents. First was the fear that the Soviets would obtain the secret of the atomic bomb and threaten the peace of the world. Next came a backlash against the Social Security Act as a "communist plot," and a new red scare exacerbated by the Korean conflict. Finally, there was an increasing ideological frustration that the promises of equality of the 1930s and 1940s went still unfulfilled in the 1950s.

The atomic bomb had eliminated Hiroshima and Nagasaki on Truman's order, even though surrender talks were in progress. The Chinese Communists under Mao Tsetung flexed their muscles in Korea and defeated U.S. forces at the 38th parallel. Renewed fear of communism led to the establishment of the House Un-American Activities Committee and the Federal Employee Loyalty Program (1947). Under the leadership of Senator Joseph McCarthy of Wisconsin (who charged the Roosevelt and Truman administrations with "twenty years of treason" because of their social programs), the committee launched a hunt for communists and the Internal Security Act (McCarran Act) passed Congress. It established six concentration camps to house political prisoners and allowed imprisonment without trial for those suspected of treason. Kennedy, Nixon, and Johnson, all senators who would become presidents, supported the McCarran Act.

By 1953, a great number of dissidents were in jail or in hiding, for anyone might be suspect. Thousands of teachers, social workers, newspapermen, screenwriters, government workers—guilty of usually nothing more than organizing unions, belonging to the Communist party during the wartime alliance of the United States and Russia, attending a radical meeting, or supporting liberal causes—lost their jobs for refusal to cooperate with investigatory committees. Under pressure of investigation, the labor movement pulled back from radical action; liberals renounced their social programs; libraries removed controversial books; and books teaching communism or socialism were barred. Ethel and Julius Rosenberg were executed for giving the secret of the atomic bomb to Russia, a charge never proved. Schools, universities, and many public organizations required oaths of loyalty as a criterion for employment. In New York City, a loyalty oath was even required for a driver's license. As welfare workers resisted the label of "soft" or "pink," eligibility regulations tightened and benefits were withdrawn from recipients.[1]

By 1954, McCarthy's accusations were so outrageous that he was censured by the Senate and removed from the committee. However, Federal Bureau of Investigation procedures were firmly in place. Anyone voicing differing opinions might be investigated. Great numbers of dossiers went into F.B.I. files, including those of civil rights activists such as Dr. Martin Luther King, Jr.

Roosevelt's emergency relief measures during the Depression, new educational opportunities, unionization, and veterans' benefits opened up new resources to people of color. During the war, they earned wages competitive with white people and could support their families, and they were unwilling to give up their gains. New political channels opened to them through voting, their presence in unions, and through legislation and court cases that supported their citizenship. The frustration of people of color and the poor was invisible, for it did not impact on the lives of the upwardly mobile middle class. However, in the "Silent Generation" tension grew as those who had shared however briefly in economic equality in unions, labor, and the war effort taught their children to expect equality.

The struggle was no longer primarily economic, though many were still hungry. Unionization and veterans' benefits had empowered white laborers in the 1930s: Now those winnowed out of success—women, the aging, and people of color—began to fight. Television added a new dimension to awareness: "Around the world" became next door as Americans watched famines, wars, riots, oppression, and death over the evening meal. We saw people dying in Korea; the justice system manhandling peaceful demonstrators; poverty in a society of affluence. We saw war becoming the basis for economic prosperity: From 1945 to 1970 the federal government spent 69 percent of its total budget on defense ($1 trillion). In the Kennedy-Johnson era, the defense budget increased dramatically, and by the end of the 1960s, 10 percent of all jobs were tied to the defense budget.[2] We saw young people's lives traded for monetary profit and foreign countries were invaded in the name of economic prosperity. And we began to ask why.

As we found answers, social revolution erupted. Students rioted against their schools and people of color staged demonstrations demanding equality. Women, joining civil rights groups, saw class and race hatred compounded for them by sexism. Welfare and economic rights became intimately related with civil rights in the new ideological struggle for human rights. To counter the unrest, idealists and pragmatic politicians developed new social programs and expanded civil rights. Presidents John F. Kennedy and Lyndon B. Johnson joined the battle claiming that the United States, having the power to create a great society, should do so. But the bubble of idealism lasted less than a decade. The internal political stresses of the war on poverty and the disastrous and expensive war in Vietnam led to a renewed backlash of conservatism that undermined the 1960s-inspired movements, and all too soon welfare cutbacks and civil repression returned.

## THE STATE OF THE NATION UNDER EISENHOWER

Dwight D. Eisenhower became president in 1952, a respected war hero in a time of reasonable prosperity for middle and upper classes. While the gross national product in 1940 was $100 billion, it rose to $286.5. billion by 1950, and by 1960 it was $400 billion.[3] Unemployment reached only 4.5 percent in the early 1950s, and though it rose to nearly 7 percent in 1958, it returned to 5.7 percent in the next decade.[4] A series of mild recessions occurred in 1961–63, and nearly 2 million people were added to the unemployment rolls. By 1960 almost 40 million people, or 22.4 percent of the population, lived below the poverty line of $3,022 for a family of four.[5] Unemployment was exacerbated as the displaced farm population, including many of African descent, moved to the cities. Between 1940 and 1969, the number of farms owned and operated by Afro-Americans decreased by 87 percent, from 680,000 to 90,000.[6] Within three decades 16 million white people and 4 million Afro-Americans moved to the cities, and by 1950, 64 percent of the U.S. population was urban.[7]

With the population changes, patterns of family life altered as drastically as during the Industrial Revolution. New middle-class families began to move to the suburbs, leaving the inner cities to the in-migration of people of color and poor people. Consumerism boomed as more people could afford a "home in the country," and the baby boom meant even more buying. By 1960 the U.S. birthrate nearly equaled that of India. The age of marriage lowered: 14 million were engaged by the time they were 17 (1960) and the average age at marriage for women was below 20. Sixty percent of all college women dropped out to marry before they earned their degrees.[8]

Although consumerism and mobility increased material goods, "personal good" suffered. The community bonds of family and friends ruptured, and the separation of poor from wealthy, white from people of color, grew. Young white mothers, in the suburbs far from their older women relatives, became isolated and depressed. Mental health and parenting programs were overtly aimed at helping women find happiness as wives and mothers. Poor women were increasingly defined as mentally ill or deviant on two counts: poverty and "unwomanliness" because they worked. "Pockets of mental illness" were found in low-income areas, especially after the Joint Commission on Mental Illness and Health reported in 1960 that stress-creating situations such as poor health, poor housing, unemployment, and poverty should be considered in planning for mental health.

After World War II, emotional problems took on new meaning. Where *mental illness* had been stigmatized and hidden, now *mental health* became the right of every American. The social work profession argued that all social problems could be solved with casework treatment and psychoanalytic techniques, and the power of the profession increased synergistically with new mental health funding. Two innovations moved the focus of treatment from mental hospitals to the community: The use of tranquilizers became widespread after 1954, and the federal government declared mental illness a disability, making patients eligible for up to half their community care under OASDI. A study by Alfred Stanton and Morris Schwartz (1954) demonstrated that the mental hospital itself made people sicker, and the exodus to community care began. Despite more people being admitted to mental hospitals, their population showed a definite decrease by 1957.[9]

The availability of tranquilizers was particularly problematic for women. Any doctor could prescribe them for any reason, and women were particularly vulnerable as they became more isolated and depressed. Sex roles expected them to be happy with their suburban homes and families, and those who were not were often defined as "mentally ill" and in need of medication. Tranquilizers, rather than action, became the panacea for unhappiness, and their misuse often resulted in emotional dependency, addiction, or ongoing and irreversible physical or emotional damage. The mental health movement and the excessive use of tranquilizers also put a great number of people under surveillance and paved the way for a more subtle behavioral control.

## SOCIAL PROGRAMS IN THE 1950s

Few new social programs were instituted under Eisenhower, though eligibility and benefit levels of public assistance were expanded. Theorists and researchers concluded that, except for some "pockets of poverty" and personal "case poverty," America's poverty problem was solved. Concern for the aged provided a constant pressure, and conferences on aging in 1950 and 1951 kept the nation aware of their need for services. Private benefit plans expanded under pressure from unions—by 1962 their expenditures were more than 11 percent of the total expended for workers' pensions and health care ($9.8 billion).

## Social Insurance

More people became covered under social insurance until, by 1961, 90 percent of the potential population was covered.[10] By 1950, wives or divorced mothers with entitled children—to age 18 or 21 if still in school—were included in survivors' grants. In 1956 disability insurance was added to OASI (now OASDI), and mentally ill persons were included in the classification of disabled. In 1957, persons disabled before the age of 18 became entitled to their own, rather than survivor's, benefits.[11] The age of eligibility was reduced to 62 for retiring and 60 for dependent spouses (age 50 if disabled).

Dependent spouse survivors' benefits were increased to 82.5 percent of the deceased worker's entitlement at age 62, or for young spouses caring for children to 75 percent of the entitlement plus an equal amount for the children.[12] In 1940 the average pension was $22.71 per month (maximum $40.00); by 1950 it was $31.00 (maximum $80.00); by 1960, $82.00 (maximum $105.00); and by 1970, $124.00. By the end of the 1970s it had tripled to $363.00 per month. The income subject to social insurance taxes reached $3,600 in 1951 and was $7,800 by 1967, with a tax increase from 2 percent to 6.65 percent.[13]

## The AFDC Program

During this same period, while costs for social insurance increased from $47.0 billion in 1950 to $123.9 billion in 1960,[14] public assistance expenditures increased from $2.3 billion in 1950 to $3.3 billion ten years later. Although the number of *aged* recipients decreased from 2.8 million in 1950 to 2.2 million in 1965,[15] numbers of recipients on the whole increased by 800,000, or 13 percent. The AFDC population boomed along with the baby boom. By 1960, AFDC rolls had increased to more than 3 million persons, and expenditures by 92 percent to more than $1 billion. During 1961, the first year under Kennedy, the number of AFDC recipients rose another half million, and expenditures rose another $2 million.[16] There were, however, structural rather than personal reasons for the increase in numbers of women seeking AFDC:

1. Simple *population growth*, especially with the baby boom, accounted for many of the new cases. Between 1940 and 1970 population increased over 50 percent and the number of children under age 14 increased by 80 percent.

2. The *number of divorces* doubled between 1935 and 1970. While in the 1940s 60 to 70 percent of families were eligible because of death or incapacitation of the father, by 1971 nearly three-fourths of all applicants were separated, divorced, or unmarried, and 5 percent of fathers had deserted.[17]

3. The *out-of-wedlock birth rate* tripled between the beginning of World War II and 1968, from one out-of-wedlock birth per twenty-five births to one in ten. Of the fathers absent from home, 28 percent were not married to mothers of children being served.

4. *Legislation* and *court decisions* extended coverage to needy children without regard to the marital status of their parents. In addition to adult caretakers of

dependent children (1950), states could also choose to include incapacitated breadwinners in grants (AFDC-I). In 1961 states could choose to add unemployed parents to the rolls (AFDC-UP), although only half did so (the family was dropped when the breadwinner worked more than 100 hours per month).[18] Thus parents and nonworking adults became part of the AFDC population. To society, this meant that women were "rewarded" for not having a husband's support and men were "rewarded" for not having jobs. Two of the strongest values in society were violated.

5.   *Ideas about employability* changed. One reason for the Social Security Act's AFDC program was to remove women from labor force competition with men. Another was the rationale that a mother could care for her children more cheaply and more competently than could day care or institutionalization. But wives and mothers worked during the war and after, so justification of mothers' pensions became increasingly difficult on those grounds.[19]

6.   The great *displacement of agricultural workers* to the cities added thousands of women, many of them Afro-American, to AFDC rolls and racist hostility toward the program increased.

To "contain" AFDC, states restricted eligibility, reduced need levels, restricted residency requirements, and tried to embarrass recipients and new applicants by publishing their names or closing entire caseloads, forcing the needy to reapply. Fewer applications were accepted: While in 1948, 66 percent were accepted, in 1958 only 54 percent were.[20] Especially in the South, families might be put off public assistance when it was assumed they could find work in the fields. Mandell says

> The welfare system has been used as an instrument of economic exploitation by communities and states that needed cheap labor. This has been especially true in the southern states. For example, the farm policy adopted by Arkansas in 1953 required able-bodied mothers and older children to accept employment whenever it was available. This policy was responsible for 38.6 to 58.6 percent of all closings between [19]53 and [19]60.[21]

A classic example occurred when the city manager of Newburgh, New York (1961), closed all cases and allowed them to reopen only under grossly stigmatizing conditions: Applicants had to prove they had applied for city jobs and had not left other jobs voluntarily, and they had to reapply at police offices. All new cases had to be reviewed by the city manager and active ones by the city attorney. All able-bodied men had to work and vouchers rather than cash were given. Upon appeal, the state welfare board would not allow the new regulations, but the months they were in effect were painful for many.[22]

The greatest hostility was directed against women because of their "sexual immorality," their "great numbers" of illegitimate children, and, again, the implication of mothers in causing juvenile delinquency. Part was a racist attack against the burgeoning nonwhite welfare population (in 1948, 31 percent of the recipients were nonwhite, while by 1974, 48 percent were nonwhite).[23] States gave their workers wide discretion in defining the "suitability" of the home, and the higher the rolls, the more stringent became the requirements. "Suitable homes" meant homes where no illegitimate children lived and women had no men friends—no "men in the house." In further refinement of dependency, "need" became lacking a "father substitute" rather than needing money. Thus, children of women with men friends were not "needy" even if the friends contributed nothing economically. Violation of either suitable home or substitute parent policies, or even the accusation of such violation, could mean loss of grants.

In 1960, twenty-three states had "suitable home" rules, and such policies allowed Louisiana, in 1960, to remove twenty-two thousand illegitimate children from the rolls, 95 percent of them Afro-American, though only two-thirds of the caseload was Afro-American.[24] In Arkansas, Governor Faubus proudly asserted that "8000 illegitimate children were taken off the welfare roles during my term of office." In Florida, AFDC applicants with unsuitable homes were told to place their children in foster care or institutions or else face court action to have them taken away. Only 186 of 2,908 families complied: the rest withdrew their welfare applications[25]— what the department really wanted anyway. Handler says

> Sexual promiscuity, men in the house, divorce, remarriage, and so forth . . . patterns of sexual behavior outside of conventional moral standards are tolerated by the public as long as the public is not called upon to support those who engage in such activities. The poor must stay married or become celibate. . . . As the price of survival, the poor are required to engage in certain behavior not required of the rest of society or to forego amenities and pleasures enjoyed by others.[26]

AFDC workers were "investigators" whose purpose was to find ways to reduce rolls. They investigated

> employers, banks, credit agencies . . . [and often neighbors]. . . . This . . . assumes dishonesty . . . and applicants . . . [must prove their] statements. The punitive administration of intake is, ostensibly, to protect the public by excluding applicants who do not qualify. It also protects the welfare rolls by using stigma as a rationing device.[27]

Investigations could take place at any time of the day or night, often with the cooperation of police. Workers "raided" women's homes looking for evidence—men's shoes under the bed, clothes in the closet, or assets that would not be purchasable on AFDC grants. These "midnight raids" continued even after they were declared unconstitutional by the Supreme Court in 1967. Investigators also kept information from recipients: amounts of grants, rights to fair hearings, other programs. Clients asking for their rights were perceived as "challenging" and might lose their grants or their children—risks they could not afford. Although every kind of documentation was needed to qualify for AFDC, disqualification required very little—perhaps only an anonymous report from a neighbor.

Suitable home rules, farm work provisions, and residency requirements were disproportionately applied to Afro-American families moving north.[28] The removal of grants from homes where there were out-of-wedlock children halted in 1961 when Arthur Fleming, the secretary of the

Department of Health, Education, and Welfare under Kennedy, ruled that support could not be removed unless the welfare department found new "suitable homes" for the children. "Substitute parent"/man in the house requirements were eliminated in 1968, under the *King* v. *King* decision, and residence requirements ended in 1969 with the *Shapiro* v. *Thompson* decision.

## CIVIL RIGHTS BEFORE KENNEDY

In 1948, the Dixiecrats in Congress—Southern Democrats led by Strom Thurmond—successfully challenged the Democratic party's support of civil rights when it defeated Truman's bill to reestablish the Fair Employment Practices Commission, eliminate segregation in public transportation, and outlaw poll taxes. This hostility to civil rights continued throughout Eisenhower's administration (though a federal antilynching law was passed in 1951). Segregation was deeply ingrained in both North and South: Seventeen states and Washington, D.C., required it, and four states—Arizona, Kansas, New Mexico, and Wyoming—authorized it at local option.

This economic and political oppression meant that the nonwhite median income in 1947 was 51 percent that of white families. In 1952 it was 60 percent that of whites, decreasing by 1962 to 56 percent. In 1952, 5.4 percent of Afro-Americans were unemployed, compared to 3.1 percent of white workers; in 1960, 10.2 percent versus 4.9 percent; and in 1964, Afro-American workers had 11 percent unemployment versus 4.6 percent white unemployment.[29] Generally, Afro-American unemployment remained double that of white unemployment even through the poverty programs of the late 1960s: In 1970, 4.5 percent of white workers were unemployed as compared to 8.2 percent of nonwhite workers.[30]

The NAACP's policy of taking grievances to court increased the legal rights of people of color. Thurgood Marshall, Walter White, and William Hastie led the battles against segregation, along with Charles Hamilton Houston, vice dean of Howard University Law School.[31] In three court cases in 1950, the Court struck down segregation in schools and dining cars, saying unequal rights were more than physical facilities, and in 1954, it ruled in *Brown* v. *Topeka Board of Education* that separate educational facilities were inherently unequal. This overturned the separate-but-equal doctrine of *Plessy* v. *Ferguson* but revitalized the white backlash—the Ku Klux Klan, White Citizen's councils, and vigilante groups.[32]

Elected police and justice officials refused to reinforce the federal rulings, and Afro-Americans realized that legal victories were not enough. In Little Rock, young people tried to enter Central High School, and as white adults attacked them, Governor Orbal Faubus proclaimed that they would never enter white schools. His resistance finally provoked President Eisenhower to send federal troops to enforce the ruling. Still, ten years after the *Brown* decision, only about 2 percent of segregated schools had been integrated, and fifteen years later almost 80 percent of Afro-American youth were still in separated facilities.[33] Dye and Zeigler say that the *Brown* decision meant nothing to the overwhelming majority of Negroes, whose frustrations were intensified by the discrepancy between the declarations of the Supreme Court and the behavior of the local officials. Legally they were victorious, but politically they were impotent, since the South stubbornly refused to abide by the decisions of the court.[34]

Segregationists renewed Social Darwinist arguments against school integration with new "scientific" proof from researchers Arthur Jensen and Richard Hernstein, among others. They argued that inherited intelligence differences among racial groups required different educational techniques and that the national IQ would be lowered by higher Afro-American birthrates. However, the tests they used showed a white cultural bias. New tests indicate that better economic and learning environments improve test scores; for example, Afro-American children in the North may have higher scores than white children in the South.

Militancy increased with the evidence of the ineffectiveness of court action. The Congress of Racial Equality (CORE), founded in 1942, began a series of sit-ins in the North in 1955. Black Muslims, a religious group advocating separatism, became more vocal under the charismatic Malcolm X, who led Afro-Americans to reexamine their oppression by whites and be proud of their African heritage. However, the key to mass civil rights activity came in December 1955, in Montgomery, Alabama, when Rosa Parks, a woman tired from her day's work, refused to give up her bus seat to a white man and was jailed. This triggered a decade of protests and demonstrations, beginning with a year-long municipal bus boycott led by the young minister Martin Luther King, Jr. Although King and the people who worked with him were subject to threats, violence, false arrest and imprisonment, they persevered, and after thirteen months the buses were desegregated.

King was a student of the nonviolent tactics of Indian leader Mahatma Gandhi. Educated at Morehouse College, Howard University, and Boston University, he preached a new social gospel. Adding religion to resistance, he gave spiritual and civil leadership to people of color and the white liberals who fought alongside them. After the Montgomery boycott, he helped to organize the Southern Christian Leadership Conference (SCLC) in Atlanta, which became the central organizing body for passive resistance. During one of his imprisonments, King won the Nobel Peace Prize, accepting it in the name of all those working for equality.

Young people in the South became increasingly active in demonstrations and sit-ins, but there was little organization among these student groups until 1957, when Ella Baker, a graduate of Shaw University and long-time civil rights activist, organized a SCLC youth conference. Attended by about two hundred delegates from southern communities in twelve states, the group subsequently met monthly to coordinate student demonstrations across the South. In 1960, it became the Student Non-Violent Coordinating Committee (SNCC) and organized demonstrations across all color, age, and income lines, with the ideals of nonviolence and passive resistance.

SNCC organized "freedom rides"—busloads of activists going to southern communities to register voters and support civil rights activities.

In 1961, at Anniston, Alabama, the first freedom bus was burned. Later, riders in Birmingham were attacked by white mobs. By September of that year, freedom riders had worked in more than one hundred cities in twenty states. At least 70,000 students of all colors participated, with 3,600 students arrested and 141 students and 58 faculty members expelled from their universities for political action.

Television brought an immediacy to civil rights as, for the first time, people far removed from such problems viewed firsthand the paradox of freedom denied in a free country, police brutalizing the innocent, and the efforts of elected officials and the police in defense of, often the cause of, violence. Through television, citizens observed the gentleness and firm resolve of Martin Luther King, Jr., and the pacifism of young people as they were beaten, set upon by police dogs, and even murdered without official response. The image of the police became police chief Eugene "Bull" Connor directing firehoses and police dogs against children, women, and old men. For some, this was the end of innocence and belief in the American system. Civil rights was no longer "somewhere and someone else": It was a national awareness and shame.

Other protests began: among Native Americans, Hispanics, the young, welfare activists, and women. Most protests were modeled at first on King's nonviolent example. Social workers were far from the forefront in this movement: Generally, they argued caution rather than activism.

### Native Americans

Congress, in 1949, began to turn Native American programs over to state governments to rid itself of the "Indian problem." In 1953 it began the process of "termination," ending federal supervision of the tribes and freeing Native Americans from government wardship. Termination gave certain states the right to overturn or replace laws of the 1934 Reorganization Act. Supporters of termination, according to Feagin, included land-hungry whites and members of Congress seeking to cut costs, along with some tribal members. Between 1954 and 1960, several dozen tribes were terminated from federal guardianship.[35]

Ostensibly, termination gave Native Americans the same privileges and responsibilities as other citizens. In fact, many necessary support programs were abandoned through termination. The problems Native Americans had are exemplified in the case of Wisconsin's Menominee tribe: The state created a county from the former reservation and immediately billed Native Americans for property taxes. They were unable to pay, and lost sanitation services, police and fire protection, and highway maintenance. Their tax base was too small to support adequate schools and health services, and their sawmill and forest holdings were endangered. Many lost their homes and life savings.

Some tribes, such as the Klamath in Oregon, were not treated so harshly—they were given interim financing, transportation and moving costs, and help with jobs and housing. However, from the Native American perspective termination was another kind of oppression. Native American groups such as the National Congress of American Indians (founded 1944) worked vigorously against it. Nevertheless, between 1954 and 1960, several dozen groups were terminated.

Although President Kennedy ended termination, it had become a rallying point for activism. In 1961 the National Indian Youth Council was created, with a Red Power ideology, and in the next decade 194 instances of protest or civil disobedience occurred. Of these, 141 were legal suits and formal complaints; the rest were protests such as delaying dam construction, occupying government facilities, picketing, and sit-ins.[36] The economic status of Native Americans grew increasingly worse. By 1960 unemployment had risen to 38 percent compared to 5 percent of all males.[37]

### Mexican Americans

Traditionally, Hispanics in the United States have been agricultural workers. In the general social unrest after World War II, when the average annual income of Hispanic Americans was $2,600 (1956), Chicanos (Mexican Americans) began to organize for political action. During the next decade, when Hispanic income had increased about a third—still less than half that of white people[38]—more organizations were formed: the Mexican American Political Association, the Association of Mexican American Educators, the Mexican American Legal Defense and Educational Fund, and the Political Association of Spanish Speaking Organizations, a coordination council. However, they were all relatively ineffective.

More militant groups formed in the civil rights years: the paramilitary Brown Berets and the Chicano Moratorium Committee, La Raza Unida (California, South Texas, Colorado), the United Mexican American Students, and finally, a more violent group, the Chicano Liberation Front in Los Angeles, which claimed credit for a number of bombings of Anglo institutions. Under La Raza Unida in Denver, "Corky" Gonzales organized school strikes and action against police brutality. La Raza ran as a third party, undercutting Democratic strength in the area, and though it was unsuccessful in the elections, it helped Hispanics to become recognized as a united political force.[39]

Excluded from labor unions, Hispanic agricultural workers were continually denied economic advancement until Cesar Chavez organized the National Farm Workers Association. Some small strikes brought victories, but in 1965 police began harassment and brutality in California, while the hated Texas Rangers were brought in to enforce the growers' demands in Texas. Strikers and their leaders were imprisoned. Despite Anglo violence, Chavez kept the movement nonviolent and joined in 1966 with the Agricultural Workers Organizing Committee to form the United Farm Workers Organizing Committee.

The most militant of the Chicano groups was the Alianza Federal de Mercedes, formed in 1963 by Reies Tijerina, who in 1966 took his grievances concerning old Mexican land grants to the New Mexico government at Santa Fe. At the same time, another group of Chicanos made citizens arrests of Forest Rangers for violating old land boundaries, but Tijerina's group was arrested and tried for civil disobedience. In 1967, Tijerina was arrested at an Alianza meeting and taken to the courthouse at Tierra Amarilla, where later a group of armed Chicanos tried to arrest the district attorney. Some officials were wounded, and in retaliation a number of Hispanics camping at a nearby picnic ground were detained without adequate shelter or water, by armed police and national guards who claimed that Tijerina planned to take over northern New Mexico. Tijerina was charged with insurrection but acquitted for lack of evidence. However, he was jailed in 1969 because his wife had burned two national forest signs (government property).[40]

### Puerto Ricans

Until the 1930s, Puerto Rico was an agricultural colony based on sugar production, with the amount of land natives could own determined by the U.S. government. Massive strikes against U.S. dominated business led to the Independence Party, under the leadership of Harvard-educated Pedro Albizu Campos. In March 1937, government officials massacred marchers in Ponce, and police raids led to armed revolt in five cities, with hundreds killed and two thousand arrested for advocating independence. In 1948, Puerto Rico was given permission to elect its own government, and it became a Commonwealth in 1952. Soon after, "Operation Bootstrap" began—to industrialize the island and help it pull itself out of the poverty U.S. ownership had created. Possible investors were promised cheap labor and no taxes, and soon U.S. agribusiness had taken over so much land that Puerto Rico had to import food. By 1970, 80 percent of all industry in Puerto Rico was owned by U.S. corporations.[41]

Increasingly, Puerto Ricans were moving to the mainland, especially along the East Coast. By 1940, there were 70,000 Puerto Ricans in the continental United States, and from 1946 to 1955, 406,000 entered. In the next decade, immigration dropped drastically, but in 1966 alone, 121,000 Puerto Ricans came to the Midwest and West.[42] During the 1950s, one-fifth of the Puerto Rican population left the island, encouraged by the government to migrate both to relieve unemployment on the island and to work on the mainland as cheap labor. In the United States, when they could find work, they became concentrated in blue-collar jobs, with women in sales and clerical jobs.[43] During the civil rights years, the Puerto Rican average income decreased from 71 percent to 59 percent of the national average.

While the civil rights demonstrations of Puerto Rican Hispanics were less noted than were others, they did occur, particularly under the leftist-leaning Young Lords in Chicago. During the Johnson years, such groups were active in organizing programs for school breakfasts and lunches and providing protection against police brutality and advocacy assistance against social welfare agencies.

### Chinese Americans

During World War II, China became an ally of the United States, and in 1943 Congress repealed the Chinese Exclusion Act. After the war, in addition, Chinese war brides were taken out of the regular immigration quota, and Chinese began to immigrate, about 90 percent of them women. Thirteen thousand Chinese Americans had served in the armed forces, 17 percent of the Chinese American population. On their return as veterans, they took advantage of such benefits as the G.I. Bill. Barred from laboring jobs by the anti-Chinese attitudes of unions, they became educators, researchers, doctors, lawyers, accountants, nurses, ministers, white-collar workers, and social workers. By 1970, 24 percent of all Chinese American men had college degrees—double the U.S. average and higher than any other ethnic group.

However, the McCarthy red scare soon lit the fires of anti-Chinese racism again, especially after the Chinese Revolution that in 1949 made China a communist state. The political situation of Chinese Americans worsened during the Korean conflict (1950–1953), when China supported the North Koreans against U.S. forces. McCarthy and his ilk urged that Chinese Americans be incarcerated as had been the Japanese, because they were a danger to the U.S. war effort. Although this did not occur, Chinese in the United States were once more discriminated against.

Many, especially the elderly, lived in poverty. Because of Chinese traditions of family and benevolent associations, only about 25 percent of those eligible for public assistance actually received it—whenever possible, the Chinese took care of their own. As the nation entered the War on Poverty, some civil rights agitation did occur, especially in the great Chinatowns of California and New York. Mostly this centered on housing needs, for 60 percent of Chinese dwellings were substandard. In the past, the Chinese Consolidated Benevolent Associations (CCBA) had served as the Chinese voice for civil rights and welfare, but now they were joined by more activist groups: the Chinatown Park and Recreation Committee, Chinatown Coalition for Better Housing, and the Chinatown Neighborhood Improvement Resource Center, a coalition of several activist groups.[44]

## CIVIL RIGHTS IN THE KENNEDY YEARS

When John F. Kennedy won the presidency in 1960, people took his victory as a sign of a new era of liberalism. His Democratic Party had lost power in the South, where white Dixiecrats opposed social programs that would benefit people of color, and among white urban workers, who had traditionally been Democrats because of Roosevelt's social insurance programs. Now Afro-American urban Democrats were competing for jobs with white erstwhile Democrats, and the balance of power was shifting. If the Democrats helped the Afro-American urban poor, they would alienate both the white urban workers and the Southern aristocracy.[45]

Because Kennedy needed Southern support, it was politically difficult for him to respond to the needs of people of color. For two years he temporized, but by the summer of 1963 he could not ignore the facts his own investigators brought him: Poverty was widespread in America, and people of color were being systematically discriminated against in all facets of American life. Although he urged people to ask what they could do for their country rather than what the country could do for them, he began to understand the responsibilities a country had to its people—particularly a country that had the power to end poverty and discrimination. He began to seek redress for the ills of the nation.

In 1963, there were prolonged demonstrations and riots throughout the South. In Mississippi, Air Force veteran James H. Meredith tried to enroll at the University of Mississippi but was stopped by Governor Ross R. Barnett himself. Twelve thousand federal troops, marshals, and national guardsmen were rushed to campus to put down the riots.[46] However, the key demonstrations were in Birmingham, Alabama, where in a massive voter campaign Afro-Americans marched to the registrar's office to demand registration. An escalation of white violence there brought Martin Luther King, Jr., to lead the demonstration, and he was arrested and jailed by "Bull" Connor. Eight white church leaders of all faiths—Catholic, Jewish, and Protestants—denounced King and chided the Afro-American community for following him. President Kennedy alerted Attorney General Robert Kennedy that intervention might be needed, and upon King's release April 20 violence began again.

By May 1, nearly a thousand people had been imprisoned. King called on Afro-American children to march on May 2, and though "Bull" Connor held off for a day he finally attacked them, some no more than 6 years old, with firehoses, clubs, and dogs.[47] More than two thousand people participated in subsequent demonstrations. Kennedy sent a mediator to intervene, and after six days of rioting, on May 10, Birmingham agreed to desegregation of lunch counters, restrooms, fitting rooms, and drinking fountains. The city officials acted in good faith over the next three months, setting up a biracial committee, desegregating public facilities, and releasing twenty-four hundred demonstrators from jail. However, on May 11—the day after the agreement—the Ku Klux Klan retaliated, bombing King's brother's home and the motel housing King's temporary headquarters, and a counterriot ensued.

More riots broke out in Virginia, Maryland, and Georgia. Cambridge, Maryland, was under limited martial law for more than a year. In Mississippi, Medgar Evers, a World War II veteran, led a demonstration of seven hundred persons. He was assassinated on June 12.[48] Until then, Kennedy had pursued a "sophisticated tokenism," but on the eve of Evers's death he began to compile a civil rights bill that guaranteed equal accommodations and gave the attorney general power to file suits to enforce the Fourteenth and Fifteenth amendments. It remained bottled in Congress, and unrest grew worse—an estimated 1,412 demonstrations in the summer of 1963.

On August 28, King led a march of 250,000 people—including 60,000 white people—on Washington, where, before the Lincoln Memorial, he spoke of his dream of peace and civil rights. Eighteen days after the march, a church was bombed in Birmingham, and four children were killed and twenty-one injured. This was the twenty-first bombing of establishments or homes of Afro-Americans and the twenty-first time the bombers were not apprehended. Over the year, there were more than ten thousand racial demonstrations, and more than five thousand Afro-Americans were arrested for political activities.[49]

Kennedy was assassinated on November 22, and although they mourned, Afro-Americans continued their demonstrations—among them a school boycott in Chicago involving 220,000 children. White resistance escalated, and demonstrators were arrested and confined for "insurrection" under Truman's McCarran Act. However, Kennedy's death gave the nation and Congress the moral thrust to attend to his civil rights bill that, along with the new president Johnson's War on Poverty, became the legacy of democratic action in the 1960s.

## JOHNSON AND THE GREAT SOCIETY

Johnson assumed the presidency with a belief that the people had mandated a new day, one in which social welfare and civil rights were intimately connected. He called for a War on Poverty, and with his advisors—a liberal intellectual elite—drew up a coordinated attack on the many fronts of discrimination. Social workers argued that social treatment could end the apathy of the poor and break the cycle of poverty, and claimed that by opening opportunity structures more "normal" families would evolve, further solving the problems of delinquency and poverty.

Johnson's philosophy was "not a hand out but a hand up" and linked personal change with social reform. Although the poor were still considered "unmotivated," new theories pointed out the structural reasons for their lack of employment, and both personal rehabilitation and change in opportunity structures became the cornerstones of the War on Poverty. The job-related poverty programs focused on men; the poverty strategy for women was to secure their right to welfare, not to get them into the labor force.[50] The many-pronged attack on poverty began with the passage of the Civil Rights Act in July 1964. In November Johnson was reelected by a landslide, and Congress passed his Economic Opportunity Act the same year and the Voting Rights Act in 1965.

### The Civil Rights Act and Continued Protest

*Black Protest.*    The Civil Rights Act of 1964 was the first significant entry by Congress into the Civil Rights field since the Civil War. The bill was still opposed by the Dixiecrats, and as a joke or as a last-ditch effort to defeat it, Howard V. Smith, a Virginian congressman, attached an amendment to the bill outlawing sex discrimination. In the following discussion, Representative Martha Griffiths and Senator Margaret Chase Smith fought to have it retained.[51] The bill passed both houses by more than a two-thirds vote, with the amendment intact. By its provisions

1. It became unlawful to apply unequal standards in voter registration or to deny registration for irrelevant errors or omissions on records or application.

2. Discrimination and segregation became illegal in places of public accommodation and in all establishments whose operation affected interstate commerce or whose discriminatory practices were supported by the state.
3. The attorney general was authorized to undertake civil action on behalf of persons so denied. Those who refused to abide by the law were considered in contempt of court and subject to fines or confinement without trial by jury [thus circumventing local politics].
4. The orderly desegregation of schools was called for.
5. Congress was to study deprivation of the right to vote and inform the president and Congress for their actions.
6. All federal agencies and departments were required to end discrimination to receive federal funds. [The withdrawal of federal grant money was an innovation in enforcement.]
7. Discrimination in employment or labor unions with twenty-five or more people was forbidden.[52]

The Civil Rights Act made all discrimination illegal on a federal, and therefore nationwide, basis. It forbade discriminatory employment practices based on race, color, religion, sex, or national origin and created the Equal Employment Opportunity Commission (EEOC) to enforce civil rights.

Racial demonstrations became, if anything, more violent after the act passed in July, perhaps because

> masses do not revolt until they perceive the possibility of actually bettering their lot in life, while at the same time perceiving that their attempts to do so are being thwarted.[53]

White resistance was overwhelming. The summer of 1964, when the bill was passed, was a Red Summer equal to that of 1919, and the summer of 1965 was known as the "long hot summer," with riots in Watts (in Los Angeles), in Newark, New Jersey, and in Detroit. As late as 1970–71, there were 250 race riots of various sizes in the nation.[54] The murder of white civil rights workers shocked the nation—Viola Liuzzo, Michael Schwerner, Andrew Goodman, and James Chaney, among others. Although an FBI agent witnessed Liuzzo's murder, the Southern jury failed to convict the murderer, who was finally convicted in federal court of depriving her of civil rights and was imprisoned but released after ten years. It is significant that Liuzzo's murderers were not prosecuted for depriving the Afro-American with her of his civil rights.

Because Afro-Americans could not participate in the Democratic party's delegate selection in Mississippi, the Student Non-Violent Coordinating Committee sponsored its own election of delegates to the National Democratic Party Convention in 1964, under the name of the Mississippi Freedom Democratic party. Their delegates were denied seats and SNCC lost faith in the whole process of peaceful demonstration. In 1965 it removed white people from its leadership and in 1966 from its membership. Stokely Carmichael became its chairman, and "Black Power" became the password. Its leaders—including Carmichael, H. Rap Brown, and John Lewis—defined Black Power as

> political and economic power and cultural independence of black people to determine their destiny individually and collectively, in and out of their own communities.[55]

Much of the theoretical underpinning of Black Power came from Malcolm X, of the Black Muslims. After having visited Moslem countries in Africa, he determined that liberation required political organization and involvement. Early in 1965 he founded the Organization of Afro-American Unity (OAAU) in Harlem, a united front organization to encompass all liberation groups and organizations (though no white groups). Malcolm X was assassinated in February 1965, but his teachings were passed on to other separatist/nationalist organizations.

James Farmer charted the new direction for the Congress of Racial Equality on Malcolm X's insights. His major target was Afro-American economics, and he urged the development of cooperatives in the South and community programs for self-help in Northern ghettos. Farmer could not support Black Power within CORE and so stepped down, leaving the directorship to Floyd B. McKissick. In 1968, Roy Innis succeeded McKissick, with policies of self-help, government aid to Afro-American capitalists, and private business involvement.

Huey Newton and Bobby Seale organized the Black Panthers in Oakland, California, in 1966, rallying around Malcolm X's statement that self-defense and freedom by any means were the ways to equality:

> We should be peaceful, law-abiding, but the time has come to fight back in self-defense whenever and wherever the black man is being unjustly and unlawfully attacked. If the government thinks I am wrong for saying this, then let the government do its job.[56]

Armed Black Panthers monitored police who used unnecessary force, protested rent evictions, informed welfare recipients of their legal rights, taught classes in Afro-American history, and demanded school traffic lights in a street where several Afro-American children had been killed.

Eldridge Cleaver, author of *Soul on Ice,* became their minister of information, and the Black Power movement took another turn. Cleaver believed that destruction of capitalist imperialism was necessary to gain power for people of color. Under his leadership, Marxist-Leninism became the new ideology, and Black Panthers formed alliances with communists, the Student Democratic Society (SDS), and the Young Lords—a Chicago-based Puerto Rican militant group—and shifted its emphasis to internationalism.

***Women's Protest.*** By 1960, 40 percent of all American women were working in full- or part-time jobs and made up about a third of the labor force. Sixty-eight percent were in blue-collar or traditional female professions. Nearly half were mothers of school-age children, and many were middle class. Their individual freedom was still secondary to the needs of their husbands, however. In 1962 a Connecticut court ruled (*Rucci* v. *Rucci)* that

> a wife must both be a solicitous helpmeet and perform her household and domestic duties . . . without compensation therefore. A husband is entitled to the benefit of his wife's industry and economy.[57]

Kennedy appointed the first Presidential Commission on the Status of Women in 1961, chaired by Eleanor Roosevelt. The commission worked actively against the trend to blame women for juvenile delinquency and in 1966 demanded that the Equal Employment Opportunity Commission (EEOC) take action against sex discrimination.[58]

Women had worked actively for civil rights and against the war in Vietnam. In those battles they learned the rhetoric of equality and methods of political action, and also that men did not consider them equal partners even in those activities. In both the Student Democratic Society (SDS) and SNCC, for example, they were rarely allowed to speak and continued to perform "women's work"— making coffee, taking notes, and doing secretarial labor. A famous quote from Stokely Carmichael was that "the only position women had in the movement was prone." Realizing that their issues were a part of the larger struggle, women argued that patriarchy was the oldest and most basic form of oppression. When their voices went unheard, many split off from men-dominated groups to form protest movements of their own.[59]

Betty Friedan's systematic look at women's oppression added support to women's struggle. She talked of the romanticization of domesticity, the infantilization of women, and the transformation of the suburban home into a comfortable concentration camp. In 1966, three hundred women and men organized the National Organization of Women (NOW), and Friedan was named its president. Its goal was to bring women into full participation as equals in American society. In 1967, NOW adopted a Bill of Rights urging the Equal Rights Amendment, joined the Women's Commission in calling on the EEOC to enforce antidiscrimination legislation, and worked for equal and unsegregated education, maternity leaves that preserved job security and seniority, tax deductions for child care, inexpensive day care centers, reform of the welfare system, and equality of benefits.[60]

Discussion of abortion as a woman's right began in the early 1960s, and NOW picked up the issue, advocating the right to contraceptive information and devices and safe legal abortions. Health care organizations also advocated legalized abortion as a medical issue, and laws were passed to permit it in certain instances. The War on Poverty established family planning programs and clinics and Medicaid began to pay for abortions for poor women.

*Youth Protest.*   The youth movement was one of disenchantment from the "establishment"—groups and institutions that made the rules and laws many young people considered immoral. Young people demonstrated against colleges and universities, against the Vietnam war, and against the draft. Their protests were often brutally repressed by police, and university authorities denied the right of students to speak out. Demonstrations against the invasion of Cambodia in May 1970, and the killing of student protestors at Kent State and Jackson State (Mississippi) Universities virtually closed down the country's college and university system.[61] Youth became heavily involved in Senator Eugene McCarthy's bid for the Democratic presidential nomination in 1968. He made the war in Vietnam and the Youth Movement his causes and hundreds rallied to him. During the Chicago nomination convention in August 1968, confrontations between the police and the thousands of young people there became violent. Many were arrested and jailed, and for some the imprisonment, in both prisons and mental hospitals, continued for years.

The Youth Movement was, in essence, a protest by middle-class young people against the materialism of their elders. Its concerns were the nation's continued injustices against the poor and people of color and the government's involvement in the internal affairs of other nations for profit. Young people turned from materialism and sought new ways of life offering freedom and creativity in such forms as communal living and, later, involvement in drugs as a way to heightened awareness. By 1973, the youth movement had crumbled. No longer looking outward to change the world, young people turned increasingly inward. However, their search for new awareness and freedom was far from selfish in the beginning. That what they sought could not be found in an unresponsive government is, perhaps, one of the shames of our society. Other than some success in their protests against the war in Vietnam and the lowering of the voting age, few real benefits emerged from their struggle. However, Nixon's administration did end the draft in response to their protests.

## CIVIL RIGHTS IN THE KENNEDY-JOHNSON YEARS

### The Voting Rights Act

The Voting Rights Act of 1965, along with Johnson's Affirmative Action Order in 1968, effectively ended *legalized* segregation. Almost a million southern Afro-Americans registered to vote within three years, and by 1970 nearly 70 percent of eligible voters were registered.[62] Local sheriffs and judges who had been instrumental in denying civil rights to Afro-Americans became vulnerable to the new voting blocks. While in 1964 there were only about 100 elected officials in the nation who were of African descent, in 1965 approximately 70 more were elected and by 1968 there were 248. By 1980, there were more than 4,900 elected Afro-American officials in offices ranging from county clerks to mayors and judges.

The first to serve in a presidential cabinet was Robert Weaver, in 1967 named the secretary of Housing and Urban Development (HUD), and Andrew Brimner became the first to serve on the Federal Reserve Bank Board. Thurgood Marshall was appointed to the Supreme Court, and Patricia Harris became the first Afro-American ambassador.[63]

### New Legal Rights

One of the most important legal decisions during the Kennedy administration was the *Gault* decision. Before then, because of the tradition of *parens patriae* in juvenile justice, children had no real legal rights. Even minor offenses such as shoplifting or status offenses could mean years of detention in children's institutions—often to age of majority. The *Gault* decision secured due process for juveniles and gave young people the same rights as adults in the justice system, including adequate notice of charges and rights to counsel, to confront accusers, to avoid self-incrimination under the Fifth amendment, and to cross-examination. Although *Gault* decision rights are still overlooked in many instances, they are now at least available.

Under Johnson, new legal rights included the assignment of counsel to those unable to afford attorneys and, in 1966, the *Miranda* decision that mandated clarifying a suspect's rights before his or her arrest. The *Miranda* decision began to be circumvented immediately with the 1972 decision denying right to counsel in line-ups. Judicial and administrative decisions also strengthened the rights of the retarded, aged, mentally ill, prisoners, and juveniles.

### Work Training and Industrial Development Programs

Several programs led the way to or enhanced the programs of the War on Poverty. One was Kennedy's Manpower Development Training Act (MDTA) in 1962, designed to deal with institutional causes of unemployment by training people for better jobs. Johnson incorporated both the funding and the ideals of MDTA into the Title I and IV programs of the Economic Opportunity Act. Another Kennedy program, the Area Redevelopment Act of 1961, gave financial and technical aid to depressed regions by luring new industries to areas of regional unemployment and expanding industries already there. Johnson built on this program with Titles III and V of the Economic Opportunity Act of 1964 and the Economic Development Act of 1965, funding industries in depressed areas in Appalachia, New England, the Coastal Plains, the Ozarks, the Upper Great Lakes region, and a poverty-stricken sector in the Southwest.[64]

### The Economic Opportunity Act of 1964

The Economic Opportunity Act of 1964 (EOA) overtly aimed at calming riots and providing job training and employment for the poor and people of color—those most likely to rebel. Title I included Job Corps training centers for out-of-school and unemployed youths; Work Training programs to help young people stay in school; and Work Study programs to enable them to go to colleges. Unfortunately, job training programs were often run by white middle-class people who believed that lack of motivation, rather than unavailability of jobs, caused unemployment. Participants came because they were paid for their attendance, but many perceived the programs themselves as childish and inauthentic: teaching people to use alarm clocks and public transportation, for example, or filling out job applications when there were no real jobs available.

Unlike Roosevelt with his WPA, Johnson did not attempt to create new jobs. According to Ehrenreich, this would have implied

> a direct government role in corporate investment decisions, a step that Johnson-era America was not ready to take and that the poor never gained enough power to demand.[65]

Although jobs became increasingly available at the same time as the training programs,

> it was the war in Vietnam, not the War on Poverty . . . that both stimulated the economy and provided "jobs" (although often fatal ones) for many of the poor.[66]

Title III provided grants and loans to buy or improve real estate, reduce debts, or construct buildings; to operate family farms; and to participate in cooperative associations, particularly in rural areas. Title IV targeted black-owned businesses and investment opportunities by providing small business loans for Afro-American entrepreneurs.

Title V, Work Experience Programs, permitted businessmen to use funds from the Manpower Development Training Act (MDTA, 1962) and Vocational Education Act (1963) to hire low-income and minority people, including AFDC recipients—money was channeled to the workers through the businesses. WEP also established Volunteers in Service to America (VISTA) to work in programs for Native Americans, migrant workers, or people in need in Washington, D.C., Puerto Rico, Guam, American Samoa, the Virgin Islands, and the Trust Territory of the Pacific Islands. Vista volunteers also worked in agencies for the care and rehabilitation of the mentally ill or retarded.

Title II, for Community Action Agencies, was the most controversial Title. It gave money directly to grass-roots public or nonprofit agencies established by the poor, bypassing the traditional channels of state and local governments, United Ways and social agencies, and political parties, though many traditional agencies also shared in the funding. A key term was *maximum feasible participation* of the poor. There were very different interpretations of how much "maximum participation" was feasible. To liberals and the poor, it meant that they had to be represented in developing goals and policies, and in maintaining the programs receiving federal funds by administering and working in them. To mayors, governors, and traditional social agencies, it meant that people whom they had previously controlled now had massive funds and needed neither their advice nor control. The Office of Economic Opportunity (OEO), which administered the programs, was under attack from the first by mayors and political machines, and legal suits were filed against its programs.

Community Action Programs (CAPs) were the local arms of OEO. Their services included advocacy against public or federally funded private agencies that discriminated or withheld services; job training and employment services; Head Start, a nursery school for deprived children; Upward Bound, giving remedial educational skills so that young people might enter college; day care centers for employed parents; neighborhood recreation centers to enhance the lives of children in poverty; and neighborhood health and family planning centers. The New Careers Program trained tens of thousands of indigenous paraprofessionals to work in social agencies, increasing social work person power but threatening the profession's argument that only highly trained social workers could give services. It provided career ladders, increased on-the-job experience, and gave inservice training and release time for college. Legal Services Organizations provided class actions against established agencies: By 1968 there were approximately 250 LSOs, with 1,800 lawyers initiating more than 25,000 cases per year against schools, welfare departments, mental hospitals, police, city administrations, and courts. Other programs included mental health family-centered care, adult basic education, information and referral centers, police relations programs, and volunteer programs.

Although a manifest purpose of the Economic Opportunity Act was to enable social agencies who qualified for OEO funds to be innovative and responsive to the needs of their clients, this rarely happened. Rather, agencies took the federal money and used it to expand their clientele in poverty areas while they maintained the same attitudes and intervention modalities—belief in personal fault and the efficacy of casework. For example, community mental health centers, expected to pioneer new services, remained attached to their entirely conventional outpatient services, though they now offered them in poor communities.[67] Funds intended to create neighborhood health centers were captured by hospitals for institutional expansion. School systems took the funds but did not use them to innovate. Ehrenreich says

> in the end, despite the successful reorganization of many agency practices and attitudes, the poverty program failed to reform the service delivery system, much less to eliminate poverty.[68]

The fight against OEO at state and local levels was effective. In late 1966, Congress cut back and restricted the scope of the CAPs, and legislation in 1967 required OEO funds to be channeled through the offices of mayors. The fight went out of the OEO movement. Many mayors already had political control, or the agencies were so innocuous as not to matter anyway.[69] President Johnson, sensing the failure of the War on Poverty and concerned about his loss of support, abandoned OEO to throw the nation's resources behind the war in Vietnam.

The most important immediate reason for the failure of OEO was the false assumption that "no one had a vested interest in maintaining poverty"[70] when in fact many people found it functional. Moreover, indigenous leaders of the civil and welfare rights battles were coopted by the good government pay, and this loss of leaders devastated both movements. Further, a major tenet of OEO was to train the disadvantaged to take jobs in society. As with other such programs, this whole "work ethic" basis was inauthentic, for the jobs simply did not materialize no matter how effective the training. Finally, OEO did in fact fulfill its latent purposes and so was no longer needed: It quelled the rebellious by giving them some benefits, coopted the leaders, and put control back in the hands of those who needed a cooperative low-wage work force.

## SOCIAL PROGRAMS IN THE KENNEDY-JOHNSON YEARS

Poverty was easier to deal with than was the civil rights issue. The Social Security Administration's reports on poverty from 1959 census data, Attorney General Robert Kennedy's firsthand reports, and books such as Michael Harrington's *Other America* (1962) and Dwight MacDonald's *Our Invisible Poor* (1963) pointed out the hidden pockets of poverty in the cities, among the aged or disadvantaged, or in rural areas such as Appalachia that existed even in this time of affluence. President Kennedy's 1962 plans were modest: some advances in public assistance; the extension of unemployment insurance and liberalized OASI benefits; an increased minimum wage and an increase in AFDC benefits; a new housing act to create more jobs in construction; some training bills; and financial and technical aid for depressed regions. To stimulate consumer buying and corporate investment, he also cut personal and corporate income taxes.[71] He sought prevention rather than cure when possible: In 1963 alone the Department of Health, Education, and Welfare (DHEW) spent $130 million for basic support services, personnel training, research, construction of residential facilities, and income maintenance; and for strengthening maternity and infant care programs, including health screening programs, especially in high-risk populations.

### Kennedy's Social Security Amendments (1962)

The most important changes for social welfare by far were those of the Social Security Amendments of 1962, called the Service Amendments. In 1961, Kennedy appointed a twenty-five-member Ad Hoc Committee on Public Welfare with members from both public welfare and private social work. They were charged to recommend methods leading to adequate financial assistance, efficient administration and organization of public assistance offices, research into the causes of dependency and family breakdown, and provision of rehabilitation services by trained personnel. The guiding ideals were still that

1. People would not work if they could get welfare.
2. Rehabilitative services by social workers could return recipients to the work force.

The committee gave full support to social work's claim that casework and psychoanalytic intervention could "cure" the problem of motivation and strengthen the family and that this would cause a drop in welfare rolls. Its major recommendation was that schools of social work receive enough funding to train new workers to "rehabilitate" AFDC families. Other recommendations included

Support for unemployed and incapacitated parents

Research and demonstration projects on illegitimacy, dependency and family breakdown

The removal of residence requirements for public assistance

New funding for day care

Vouchers rather than cash for recipients who could not manage money

Money earned by children be exempted when figuring family eligibility or grant levels.

Kennedy's message to Congress in 1962 dealt solely with public dependency, reiterating the "blaming the victim" and work ethic stances of most public assistance rhetoric. He called for a "new" approach to dependency:

a return to seeking causes within the individual, buttressed by job training and employment services for the dependent and those who might become dependent.[72]

To carry out this new approach, the Social and Rehabilitative Service (SRS) was established in the Department of Health, Education, and Welfare.

Massive funding was provided to schools of social work, and new standards were set to ensure that workers could provide adequate services. They were to have caseloads of no more than sixty—patently impossible as rolls continued to rise—with one supervisor for each five caseworkers. Home visits were to be made as often as "necessary" to improve family functioning, and homemaker services, which had been increasing rapidly in the 1950s, became available to the poor. Every child was to have a "service plan," and workers had discretion to manage families where parents did not (or could not) provide "appropriate" services for them, including establishing guardians when AFDC funds were misused. The concept of group homes grew rapidly in this period, and many children were removed to such homes or to foster care. Institutionalization was also an option: there were approximately 306,000 children in institutions at the time. Of these, 23 percent were labeled neglected and dependent, a third were adjudged juvenile delinquents, and a little over a third were in homes and schools for the mentally and physically disabled.[73]

Employment was the most important goal, and those AFDC recipients who refused training without good cause were removed from the grant (though their children remained recipients). Success of the amendments was to be measured in terms of the new financial independence of former recipients. Unfortunately, the rolls continued to expand, now faster than unemployment rates, and "services" became increasingly suspect.[74] While in 1955, 3 percent of all children were receiving AFDC, in 1970, 8.5 percent were on the rolls.[75] Although the numbers of people in poverty dropped by nearly half from 1960 to 1969, AFDC rolls increased more than twice, from 2.9 million to 7.3 million. Expenditures tripled in the same period, from $1 billion to $3 billion, and by 1972 had increased tenfold, to $10.3 billion.[76] In 1961, in real dollars the average monthly AFDC payment was $117 per family. A decade later, it was $183, or about $49 per person (compared with per capita income of $307 in the general population).[77] Levitan says

> There is no evidence that the provision of social services for welfare recipients has induced labor force participation. . . . The failure of social services to "rehabilitate" welfare recipients led to a new emphasis on concrete programs related to employability. The emphasis shifted to day care, family planning, manpower training, and compensatory education.[78]

Under Johnson, the Social Security Act was further amended, first with the massive health programs of Medicare and Medicaid in 1964 (operationalized in 1965) and then with further AFDC amendments in 1967.

*Medicare.*   Medicare was added to social insurance (OASDI), making it OASDHI—Old Age, Survivors, Disability, and Health Insurance. Medicare is an insurancelike system with two programs (Part A and Part B) to provide health care for people over age 65. As a social insurance program, it is not means tested. Part A is compulsory, and a "premium" is automatically deducted for it from monthly OASDHI checks. People may choose to participate in Part B, paying a higher premium (also deducted from their checks) for expanded services. General revenues, rather than the premiums, pay most of the cost. The program is operated through private mediaries such as Blue Cross/Blue Shield, to which the government pays a 2 percent administrative fee.

Part A pays for part of the costs of hospitalization (ninety days, with $40.00 deductible for the first sixty and $10.00 a day for the remaining thirty); skilled nursing home care for up to one hundred days ($5.00 per day for last eighty days); 80 percent of outpatient diagnostic tests; and up to one hundred home nursing visits following hospitalization (in one year).[79]

Part B has a $50.00-per-year deductible and a monthly premium (in 1982 $12.20 per month). It pays 80 percent of "reasonable" expenses for physicians' and surgeons' services, more home nursing visits, up to $250.00 for mental health care, and for a number of medical appliances and diagnostic tests. For hospital stays of more than 90 days, a patient can draw on a 60-day lifetime reserve, and hospice care for the terminally ill was available until 1986.

Medicare does not pay for such needs as eyeglasses, dentures, hearing aids and batteries, prescription drugs not given by health professionals, and home care for fragile, nonambulatory, or senile people when other adults in the family work.[80] Recipients get no money: Vouchers go directly to the health services. Because Medicare pays only "reasonable" costs, patients must pay all unreasonable or overcosts. When Medicare is exhausted, the recipients must pay their own way, rely on private insurance plans, or, having sold all their assets, turn to public assistance (Medicaid).

(Under the Reagan administration, in an attempt to limit Medicare costs, "diagnostic related group" categories (DRGs) were established. Under DRGs, health care providers are paid a set amount for all patients admitted with a certain category of ailment. Additional ailments at the time of admission are not paid for, and when the "reasonable costs" for the category have been paid, the patient must be released. Often, seriously ill patients are sent home, where they must provide their own care, or to nursing homes not set up to provide intensive medical care.)

*Medicaid.*    Medicaid's forerunner was the Kerr-Mills Bill of 1958. It is a means tested public assistance program rather than social insurance, and is administered through state departments of public welfare or public health. As with Medicare, Medicaid is a voucher program, with payment going directly to health care providers. It is funded through general revenues and is given on an open-ended basis to the participating states depending on per capita income, giving grants-in-aid of from 50 to 83 percent of Medicaid costs. The federal administrative agency is the Health Care Financing Administration (HCFA), under the Department of Health and Human Services (formerly Department of Health, Education, and Welfare).

Medicaid's primary target is people on public assistance, although others below the poverty line may be covered if states so choose. States also must give Medicaid for people in other selected categories, such as children under 21 in foster homes or institutions for whom public agencies provide some financial support. In general, Medicaid pays for all costs of hospitalization, doctor's services and calls, prescriptions, diagnostic testing, emergency services, doctor's visits, and extended nursing home care for the aged or those with long-term disabilities who have exhausted other payment alternatives (including Medicare). Also, depending on different state guidelines, Medicaid may or may not pay for eyeglasses, hearing aids, dental care, false teeth, prostheses, appliances, and so on. According to Bell, most Medicaid money goes for nursing home care, and this has caused the elaboration of for-profit systems. About forty-five hundred new nursing homes have appeared since 1964, and

> the bulk of the 18,000 plus now operating are private, profit-making institutions relying chiefly on government for their support. . . . The current cost of nursing home care averages about $10,000 yearly.[81]

Medicaid funds are also paid to train professional medical personnel and facility inspectors, and for administrative needs such as information systems. By the end of 1964, thirty-nine states had Medicaid programs, five were establishing them, and six had decided not to. In 1982, thirty-four states chose to provide for the medically needy (in addition to public assistance recipients), but still only about three-fifths of poor households are covered.

Because health care providers understand that Medicaid is guaranteed payment by the government, one result has been highly inflated medical costs not only for Medicaid recipients but for the general public. Ironically, many health care services and physicians will no longer take Medicaid clients, leaving them to rely on a limited number of physicians and hospital emergency rooms rather than the preventative health care envisioned by those who developed the Medicaid program.

*Social Security Amendments of 1967.*    During 1967, the Department of Health, Education, and Welfare underwent reorganization. One of the most interesting changes was the creation, in AFDC, of an Assistance Payments Administration, which divorced income maintenance functions from social services functions and split public welfare departments into two sections: social services, whose workers provide counseling services and services to neglected, abused, or dependent children and older people; and assistance payments, whose workers determine eligibility and set amounts of grants based on state levels of need, number in family, and their own discretion. Purchase of services from the private sector, for such treatment as mental health care, drug abuse, or family services, was also authorized.

The social work community had been for some time arguing that services to the poor should not be connected with whether or not they received financial aid. The National Association of Social Workers supported the "split in services" as clients' right to self-determination, acknowledging that need did not necessarily call for services.[82] However, the split in services caused some unfortunate consequences. Services personnel were required to have bachelors' degrees (in any field), but assistance payments (AP) workers needed no more, generally, than a high school education. Therefore, less educated workers, often with harsh values regarding work and sexual morality, were AFDC's gatekeepers and had real power over subsistence issues. Services workers could only suggest to AP workers that clients' financial needs (beyond grants) be filled—more food, for example, or the purchase of a refrigerator or bedding. In effect, the split in services made the more educated workers powerless except in an advisory capacity, and caused dissension within departments of public welfare.

Social services for children included protective services for the abused and neglected; licensing of foster homes, day care centers, and institutions; and placement services (foster care, institutionalization, or adoption) for children who could not remain with their natural parents. Workers were required to maintain contact with both natural and foster parents for the duration of need, and they could also request permanent termination of parental rights. In 1968, state and local departments provided services for 656,000 children, or 80 of every 10,000. Of these, half lived with parents or relatives, a third more in foster homes, 10 percent in institutions, and 7 percent in adoptive homes. Private agencies served another 219,000 children: 27 percent in their homes, 21 percent in foster care placements, 1 percent in group homes, and a third in institutions. Eighteen percent more who were served were adopted. In fiscal year 1968, child care cost $499.7 million, a 13 percent increase over 1967. Of the money, only 9 percent was federal money, with over half coming from the state and the rest from the local level. Day care took the most—more than 60 percent.[83]

The sexual morality of single mothers remained an intense issue among AFDC policymakers. One result was a freeze on the number of illegitimate or deserted children who could receive aid; however, this was overturned in 1969 because it punished needy children.[84] In 1970, there were 5.6 million children on AFDC, an increase of 900,000 from 1969, and family planning programs services under Medicaid began to be offered to AFDC clients. Some people of color, especially Afro-American men, perceived this as race genocide, but in general women hailed it. Workers, whether services or AP, continued to believe society's sex and race stereotypes of their clients: that "most welfare mothers are promiscuous" and that "black women are worse (in sexual immorality) than are white women."[85]

Some states also chose to provide protective services to dependent aged or disabled adults, for many were subject to "granny beating" or mistreatment from those with whom they resided. Also, services workers in some states licensed nursing homes for the elderly or disabled and day care or group homes for developmentally disabled adults. Guardians were assigned as needed for either child or adult dependents.

The 1967 amendments made employment and training top priorities. The major AFDC work program was the Work Incentive Program, first called WIP, an appropriate name soon changed to WIN. It required AFDC parents with no children under the age of 6 to register for work training and job placement. Any adult who refused to enroll, unless incapacitated or needed at home, was disqualified for benefits (though the children still received their portion of the grant). Children out of school and over age 16 also had to register or be disqualified. WIN was a joint Public Welfare and Labor Department program that in the long run cost more with fewer long-term benefits than would have simple grants.

New work incentives developed under the new amendments. Day care monies became reasonably generous, though in many cases day care providers made more money than did AFDC mothers. Providing the same amount to mothers to care for their children at home would probably have resulted in happier families. Work expenses, such as payment for uniforms and transportation, were also paid by the Departments of Public Welfare. Very important, the "$30.00 and a third" disregard was instituted; that is, working parents could keep the first $30.00 they earned, along with a third of the remainder of their income, without a reduction in AFDC benefits.

### Other Kennedy-Johnson Social Programs

*Food Programs.*   On his first day in office, Kennedy doubled the Surplus Commodity Program (reactivated by Eisenhower in 1957) by which the Department of Agriculture bought surplus food from farmers and distributed it to the poor. Concerned that this was a "white" diet—white flour, white rice, white lard—without nutrition, he instituted in selected counties a Food Stamp Program through the Department of Agriculture (aimed also at supporting farm prices).

Under the Food Stamp Program, people purchased "vouchers" including a "bonus" amount, determined on family size and assets, beyond the dollar value of the stamps. Stamps were redeemable for any U.S. grown foodstuffs, but no alcohol, tobacco products, or cleaning or paper products were allowed. Since the whole amount had to be purchased at one time (later twice a month), poor families could not afford to buy it out of their meager AFDC or general assistance allowances. Johnson formalized the Food Stamp Program, extending it to all states that wished it (though at first only twenty-two elected to have it). Over the next two decades, the benefit levels rose and coverage was increased from only those on public assistance to those qualifying as needy under state guidelines. In addition, food stamps became free rather than having to be purchased, increasing their use among eligible persons.

Other food programs also began: the National School Lunch Program and the Special Milk Program, which paid for an extra half pint of milk sold to children for their school lunches. After Johnson took office, War on Poverty Programs made money available to Community Action Agencies, schools, and groups such as the Young Lords or CORE to provide nutritional school breakfasts and lunches to children in deprived areas.

*Mental Health and Mental Retardation.* Concerned very personally with the lack of services for his sister, who was developmentally disabled, Kennedy in 1962 appointed a mental health panel. It proposed a national program presented to Congress in 1963. The Mental Health Act, not passed until after Kennedy's death because of resistance from the American Medical Association, provided for construction of mental retardation facilities and community mental health centers, comprehensive services, and education and consultation to upgrade the nation's services. It also provided funding for the training of more social workers. While Johnson's administration aimed at more practical aid, such as job training and housing, he did agree on the training of new social workers and continued their educational funding under the Social Security Amendments of 1967.

Another Kennedy program, the Juvenile Delinquency and Youth Offenses Control Act, was funded at $10 million a year for three years. It researched the social causes of delinquency and developed innovative method empowerment programs such as Mobilization for Youth (MFY), on the Lower East Side of New York City. MFY offered comprehensive services to youth gangs to break the cycle of delinquency and crime and organized the groups themselves to search out and provide services to young people. Under Johnson's Economic Opportunity Act, such innovative programs continued. One of the best known was Haryou—Harlem Youth Opportunity program—which offered supportive services and self-help and training classes for the youth of Harlem.

*Housing.*  In the 1940s and 1950s, federal grants for housing averaged $2 billion a year, increasing in the 1960s to $7 billion. In 1961 Kennedy proposed to desegregate all federally funded housing, and in 1962, the government spent $820 million for housing for the poor (though it allowed $2.9 billion in subsidies for middle- and upper-income levels). An array of agencies administered the programs directed primarily at middle- and upper-income families on the assumption that the poor would take over housing vacated by them. In 1966, the many agencies dealing with housing were consolidated into a superagency, Housing and Urban Development (HUD), and expenditures reached $16 billion for construction guarantees and another $12 billion for mortgage guarantees. HUD administered

1. Urban Renewal, to construct middle-class housing and tear down slums
2. Mortgage guarantees for all income classes
3. Public housing
4. Housing for special groups, such as the aged and disabled

HUD also brought housing programs up to date. The 1949 Federal Housing Administration was modified to help lower-income families, and new public housing and housing for special groups was constructed. Urban Renewal was a mixed blessing, giving money to rid cities of slums but displacing many of the poor those slums had sheltered. So many Afro-Americans were left homeless that Urban Renewal was often called "Negro Removal." In the period between 1949 and 1964, an estimated 177,000 family dwelling units and 66,000 individual family units were razed by Urban Renewal, which replaced only 68,000, of which only 20,000 were for low-income people.

In 1966 the Model Cities Program began under HUD, its goal to provide assistance to cities to coordinate their welfare activities: in "a massive and comprehensive effort to rebuild or restore entire sections and neighborhoods of slum and blighted areas. In 1968 HUD was authorized to provide 6 million new dwellings for low- and moderate-income groups. Its budget was $2.6 billion, of which $412 million was earmarked for Urban Renewal. By 1971, it approached $10 billion, excluding loan insurance and guarantees, while Model Cities was budgeted at about $390 million a year.[86]

*Specialized Programs.*  The Older Americans Act of 1965 developed from the National Conference on Aging (1950), the Committee on Geriatrics (1951–56), and the 1961 White House Conference on Aging. These conferences created the Administration on Aging to fund community planning services and training, establish state agencies on aging, support research and demonstration projects to study the status of the elderly, and provide grants for community service programs. Amendments in 1967 extended the provisions and increased funding for community planning and innovative demonstration projects. It gave State Aging Offices the responsibility for statewide coordination and planning. Under Nixon, in

1973, the Older Americans Comprehensive Amendments established a National Clearinghouse on Aging; increased grants for State and Area Agencies on Aging; gave training and research money for multidisciplinary centers of gerontology; and established multipurpose senior centers. It also provided for community service employment for the elderly, administered by the Department of Labor. The Retired Senior Citizens' Program and Foster Grandparents program were created, and nutrition programs were authorized in senior citizens' centers.[87]

The Elementary and Secondary Education Act of 1965 offered grants and services to schools serving low income areas, including inner cities, bilingual communities, and Native American schools. Before the act, such schools had a low property tax base and therefore lacked new and high-quality educational materials and facilities. Because of this, they were very often staffed by teachers fresh out of college (since older, more experienced teachers often had the right to fill vacancies in newer suburban schools), who were unable to provide new and innovative teaching materials or could not cope with the needs of these children. ESEA money was used to compensate for the low tax base and helped to provide better buildings, better teaching materials, and more experienced teachers attracted by the chance of creating innovative educational experiences. For Spanish-speaking children, ESEA provided bilingual classes.

## WELFARE, CIVIL RIGHTS, AND THE SOCIAL WORK PROFESSION

Only after 1964 did social work interest turn to social action and civil rights, especially in schools of social work. With an influx of activist students often supported by government grants, schools became more flexible and varied, offering tracks in community organization, administration, and policy. Courses on ethnic minorities were established, and enrollments of people of color soared. By the early 1970s, almost 25 percent were minority students, and many civil activists had joined the schools as students.[88] This new generation worked for empowerment rather than to change their clients. At the same time, in Community Action Programs, paraprofessionals who served clients with great skill and care overturned the professional social work belief that only highly trained social workers could deliver human services.

In 1967, a new challenge rose to traditional service orientation. Under the leadership of Dr. George Wiley, a dentist turned advocate, welfare workers, welfare recipients, civil rights workers, members of the Student Democratic Society, poverty program workers, and a large number of VISTA volunteers met to establish a National Coordinating Committee of Welfare Rights Groups to plan welfare demonstrations. In the summer of 1967 they formed the National Welfare Rights Organization (NWRO). By 1969, NWRO had more than 22,000 dues-paying members in 523 local groups—the most members it ever had, which was around 2 percent of adult recipients of public assistance.[89]

NRWO's members militantly demanded publicity about welfare rights and benefits, information heretofore kept classified, and after extended struggles prepared and distributed handbooks on client rights to welfare mothers. They continued to demonstrate: In Philadelphia, when the welfare department refused requests for school shoes for their children, welfare mothers went en masse to a blood bank to sell their blood and purchase shoes. Of the twenty-seven who came, twenty-five were rejected because of anemia resulting from poor nutrition.[90]

In 1969, NWRO, the Association of Black Social Workers, the radical student-based Social Welfare Workers Movement, and a newly formed women's organization—Women of the American Revolution—took over the National Conference on Social Welfare. Doors were barred and they demanded that the conference donate $35,000 to NWRO and the conference attendees another $25,000. Those demands went unmet, but negotiators agreed to seek an increase in minority membership and to focus the following annual conference on poverty and racism. At the 1970 National Conference on Social Welfare, Mrs. Johnnie Tillmon, an AFDC mother from Watts and 1970 NWRO chair, told the assembled social workers

> If it hadn't been for you people who administer social services, we would have no organization. We organized because we were tired of being beat around by social workers.[91]

NWRO lobbied for a minimum guaranteed income of $6,500 for a family of four, the poverty level at the time, but was generally ignored. The idea of single mothers supporting families on welfare was an important challenge to key values of marriage and the work ethic, but NWRO argued that

> work in the home is a valuable aspect of the nation's productive efforts and that women have a right to be paid wages for caring for children in their homes.[92]

In the long run, NWRO was unsuccessful in lobbying either for increased benefits or increased coverage. Although the idea of a guaranteed annual wage was seriously considered by President Nixon, Congress refused the Family Assistance Plan that would have instituted it.

Although some welfare workers organized in support of welfare clients and the new young activists took their part, mainline social workers remained conservative and casework-oriented in their approach. They cautioned the National Welfare Rights Organization, felt threatened by proposals to use paraprofessionals in their agencies and to train bachelors' level people in social work, and feared the new people they now had to deal with, in their communities and often in their agencies—Hispanic- and Afro-Americans, welfare department staffs, community action agency personnel, and poverty agencies.

## CONCLUSION: LOOKING BACK ON THE 1960s

Near the end of his second term, Johnson, worn down by the demands of the War on Poverty and the failure of the war in Vietnam, decided not to seek reelection. White backlash, protests of people of color, and failure in Vietnam meant his defeat on both international and domestic fronts. However, his dedication to the Vietnam War (1964–1968) was much higher than to the War on Poverty: Vietnam cost the federal government $120 billion, while the Economic Opportunity Act of 1964, from 1965 to 1973, spent only $15.5 billion, less than a tenth.

The civil rights movement splintered: Militancy and Black Power movements, along with Red Power movements among Native Americans and Brown Power movements among Hispanics, were the rule of the day. In 1966 there were riots in forty-four cities, and in the 1966 elections, Republicans gained forty-seven seats in the House of Representatives. Reagan became governor of California.[93]

> The angry mood of the public was also reflected in Congress, where President Johnson's proposal of a federal open housing law was killed by a Senate filibuster. In the same session, limits were imposed upon the authority of DHEW to divert funds from schools failing to desegregate . . . a trend toward repressive legislation directed against those who were responsible . . . for the urban violence.[94]

Although the Open Housing Law passed in 1968, it was probably in response to the slaying of Martin Luther King, Jr. rather than a liberal action.[95] The backlash against civil rights and welfare rights continued throughout the election year of 1968. Both Democratic Hubert Humphrey and Republican Richard Nixon moved their rhetoric closer to the conservative side. Status quo and law and order were the keynotes of this election year.

Neither the Social Service Amendments of 1962 nor the Economic Opportunity Act of 1964 reduced welfare rolls, nor did they quell civil unrest. However, social justice prevailed more during that time than since the 1930s, and perhaps since before the 1300s. The idea of services as a right, even though translated through the work ethic ideology, brought more people into programs and helped more than ever before. Relief programs came under federal standards which shared their costs even though "need levels" were determined by the states. In addition, thousands of new social workers were trained and thousands of "paraprofessionals" were given jobs in the social service system.

Looking back, we find lasting benefits in the increased level of social insurance through OASDI and Medicare. Coverage was extended to over 90 percent of the population, though it still excluded federal government employees; railroad employees, irregularly employed farm and domestic workers who did not have minimum income for coverage; and self-employed persons earning less than $400 annually. Benefit levels came under indexing; that is, they rose with the cost of living. Medicaid underlaid social health insurance for the nation. Civil rights legislation is now a permanent part of the polity, although its enforcement may depend on the willingness of repressed people to fight for their rights. Nevertheless, these rights are more elaborated and more legitimated than ever before. Perhaps the greatest benefit has been the emphasis on education and the movement of people of color, however slowly, into better and higher-status jobs.

Gains from the War on Poverty are few. Although community action agencies still exist, their major efforts are tied very securely into local governments. Head Start and Upward Bound programs continue, but at lower funding levels and with far less autonomy and innovation. Maximum feasible participation is now, apparently, either tokenism or a thing of the past. Other programs such as Legal Services have been severely cut back.

Benefits provided by the Social Security Amendments of 1962 and 1967 have been increasingly cut back, and the era of social rights for the disadvantaged seems to have disappeared. Programs that were to provide an adequate living, such as AFDC and Food Stamps, still stigmatize their recipients and are still minimal in comparison with need. The poor remain in the secondary labor market and in the secondary welfare system: marginal jobs and public assistance.

We learned many things from the decades of the 1950s and 1960s. Perhaps the most enduring lesson is that when rebellion threatens, the response is first accommodation and then, when the force of the movement is dissipated, renewed denial. As we moved into the Nixon years, control of the poor and other minorities tightened. Even during the Carter administration gains for social justice were few. During the Reagan years repression seemed once more to become the goal of society. However, the Decade of the Dream—of freedom and social justice—did happen. The shame is that, unless repression becomes severe enough to cause rebellion, it may not happen again.

## STUDY QUESTIONS

1. What were the trends that led to the civil unrest of the 1960s? Who were the important leaders of the times?
2. Why was Kennedy unable to achieve civil rights and social reforms during his tenure? Why was Johnson able to do so?
3. What were the civil rights achieved under Johnson?
4. What social reforms were achieved during the Kennedy-Johnson years?
5. How did the 1960s change the social work profession?
6. What were the latent reasons behind the gains made in civil rights and public welfare during the 1960s?
7. Did the War on Poverty succeed in reaching its manifest goals? Its latent goals?

## FOOTNOTES

[1]John Ehrenreich, *The Altruistic Imagination,* (Ithaca: Cornell University Press, 1985), p. 140.

[2]Beulah Compton, *Introduction to Social Welfare and Social Work,* (Homewood, Ill.: The Dorsey Press, 1980), p. 437.

[3]*Social Security Bulletin,* Vol. 46, no. 7 (July 1983), p. 95.

[4]June Axinn and Herman Levin, *Social Welfare: A History of the American Response to Need,* 2nd ed., (New York: Harper & Row Publishers, 1972), p. 230.

[5]The "poverty line" was developed early in the 1960s by Mollie Orshansky. It was the amount of the budget that constituted a short-term emergency diet times a factor of 3, since it was estimated that a family should not have to spend more than one-third of its budget on food.

[6]Ehrenreich, *The Altruistic Imagination,* pp. 148–149.

[7]Axinn and Levin, *Social Welfare,* p. 235.

[8]Carole Hymowitz and Michaele Weissman, *A History of Women in America,* (New York: Bantam Books, 1980), p. 326.

[9]Compton, *Introduction to Social Welfare,* p. 479.

[10]Ibid., p. 253.

[11]*Social Security Bulletin,* Vol. 49, no. 2, (February 1986), p. 38.

[12]Compton, *Introduction to Social Welfare,* p. 446.

[13]*Social Security Bulletin,* (July 1983), p. 13.

[14]Ibid.

[15]Gerald Handel, *Social Welfare in Western Society,* (New York: Random House, 1982), p. 139.

[16]Axinn and Levin, *Social Welfare,* p. 245.

[17]Sar Levitan, Martin Rein, and David Marwick, *Work and Welfare Go Together,* (Baltimore: Johns Hopkins University Press, 1972), p. 6.

[18]Compton, *Introduction to Social Welfare,* p. 454.

[19]Martin Rein, "The Welfare Crisis," in Lee Rainwater, ed., *Social Problems and Public Policy,* (Chicago: Aldine, 1974), p. 50.

[20]Levitan, Rein, and Marwick, *Work and Welfare,* p. 12.

[21]Betty Reid Mandell, "Welfare and Totalitarianism: Part I. Theoretical Issues," *Social Work* (January 1971), p. 24.

[22]Axinn and Levin, *Social Welfare,* p. 246.

[23]Levitan, Rein, and Marwick, *Work and Welfare,* 1972; Rein, in Rainwater, ed., *Social Problems,* 1974.

[24]Winifred Bell, *Aid to Dependent Children,* (New York: Columbia University Press, 1965), pp. v and 137.

[25]Ibid., p. 121.

[26]Joel Handler, *Reforming the Poor,* (New York: Basic Books, 1972), p. 139.

[27]Ibid., p. 26.

[28]Dorothy C. Miller, "AFDC: Mapping a Strategy for Tomorrow," *Social Service Review* (December 1983), pp. 599–613, esp. p. 601.

[29]Thomas R. Dye and L. Harmon Zeigler, *The Irony of Democracy,* (Belmont, Calif.: Wadsworth Publishing Co., 1970), p. 297.

[30]Axinn and Levin, *Social Welfare,* pp. 231–232.

[31]Lerone Bennett, Jr., *Before the Mayflower: A History of the Negro in America 1619–1964,* rev. ed. (Chicago: Johnson Publishing Co., Penguin ed., 1966), p. 303.

[32]Ibid., p. 313.

[33]Compton, *Introduction to Social Welfare*, p. 482.

[34]Dye and Zeigler, *The Irony of Democracy*, pp. 296–297.

[35]Joe R. Feagin, *Ethnic and Cultural Relations*, 2nd ed. (Englewood Cliffs, N.J.: Prentice Hall, 1984), p. 515.

[36]Ibid., p. 190.

[37]Joseph Hraba, *American Ethnicity*, (Itasca, Ill.: F. E. Peacock Publishers, 1979), p. 227.

[38]Feagin, *Ethnic Relations*, p. 274.

[39]M. Barrera, C. Munoz, and C. Ornelas, "The Barrio as an Internal Colony," in Harlan Hahn, ed., *Urban Affairs Annual Review*, Vol. 6. (Beverly Hills: Sage Publications, 1972), pp. 465–498.

[40]Feagin, *Ethnic Relations*, p. 188.

[41]Ibid., p. 299.

[42]Ibid., p. 303.

[43]Ehrenreich, *The Altruistic Imagination*, p. 152.

[44]Joe Chen, *The Chinese in America*, (San Francisco: Harper & Row Publishers, 1980), pp. 201–260.

[45]Bennett, *Before the Mayflower*, p. 323.

[46]Ibid., p. 338.

[47]Ibid., p. 344.

[48]Dye and Zeigler, *The Irony of Democracy*, p. 299.

[49]Bennett, *Before the Mayflower*, p. 327.

[50]Miller, "AFDC: Mapping A Strategy," p. 602.

[51]Hymowitz and Weissman, *History of Women*, p. 343.

[52]Dye and Zeigler, *The Irony of Democracy*, p. 300.

[53]James C. Davies, "Toward a Theory of Revolution," *American Sociological Review*, Vol. 27 (February 1962), p. 318, cited in Dye and Zeigler, *The Irony of Democracy*, p. 309.

[54]Feagin, *Ethnic Relations*, p. 226.

[55]Raymond Hall, *Black Separatism and Social Reality: Rhetoric and Reason*, (New York: Pergamon Press, 1978), pp. 165–167.

[56]Ibid.

[57]Lisa Peattie and Martin Rein, *Women's Claims: A Study in Political Economy*, (New York: Oxford University Press, 1983), p. 42, quoting Leonore J. Wietzman, "Legal Regulation of Marriage: Tradition and Change," *California Law Review*,Vol. 62, 1974, p. 1187.

[58]Alice Kessler-Harris, *Out to Work: A History of Wage-Earning Women in the United States*, (New York: Oxford University Press, 1982), p. 305.

[59]Hymowitz and Weissman, *History of Women*, p. 327.

[60]Jane DeHart Mathews, "The New Feminism and the Dynamics of Social Change," in Linda K. Kerber and Jane DeHart Matthews, eds., *Women's America*, (New York: Oxford University Press, 1982), pp. 397–425, 408.

[61]Ehrenreich, *The Altruistic Imagination*, p. 182.

[62]Compton, *Introduction to Social Welfare*, p. 439.

[63]Feagin, *Ethnic Relations*, p. 238.

[64]Axinn and Levin, *Social Welfare*, p. 246.

[65]Ehrenreich, *The Altruistic Imagination*, p. 178.

[66]Ibid.

[67]Ibid.

[68]Ibid., p. 177.

[69]Ibid., p. 179.

[70]Ibid., p. 161.

[71]Ibid., p. 179.

[72]Ibid.

[73]Compton, *Introduction to Social Welfare,* p. 473.

[74]Axinn and Levin, *Social Welfare,* p. 255.

[75]Frances Fox Piven and Richard Cloward, *The New Class War: Reagan's Attack on the Welfare State and Its Consequences,* (New York: Pantheon Books, 1982), p. 14.

[76]Levitan, *Work and Welfare,* p. 8.

[77]John E. Tropman, Alan Gordon, and Phyllis J. Day, "Welfare Codebook," unpublished manuscript developed 1971, based on data from *Statistical Abstracts of the United States 1971,* (Washington, D.C.: U.S. Government Printing Office, 1972), p. 312; and *County and City Data Book 1964,* (Washington, D.C.: U.S. Government Printing Office, 1960), p. 4.

[78]Levitan, *Work and Welfare,* p. 46.

[79]Compton, *Introduction to Social Welfare,* p. 448, and Bell, *Aid to Dependent Children,* p. 195.

[80]Bell, *Aid to Dependent Children,* p. 195.

[81]Ibid., p. 196.

[82]Axinn and Levin, *Social Welfare,* p. 261.

[83]Compton, *Introduction to Social Welfare,* p. 134.

[84]Axinn and Levin, *Social Welfare,* p. 260.

[85]Phyllis J. Day, "Sex Role Stereotypes and Public Assistance," *Social Service Review* (March 1979), pp. 106–115.

[86]Robert Morris, *Social Policy of the American Welfare State,* (New York: Harper & Row Publishers, 1979), pp. 101–104.

[87]Wilma Doyle, Leonard Z. Breen, and Robert Eichhorn, *Synopsis of the Older Americans Act,* Revised, (W. Lafayette, Indiana: Department of Sociology and Anthropology, Purdue University, 1976).

[88]Ehrenreich, *The Altruistic Imagination,* p. 198.

[89]Michael B. Katz, *Poverty and Policy in American History,* (New York: Academic Press, 1983), p. 231.

[90]Ehrenreich, *The Altruistic Imagination,* p. 195.

[91]Hall, *Black Separatism,* p. 164.

[92]Jan Mason, John S. Wodarski, T.M. Jim Parham, "Work and Welfare: A Reevaluation of AFDC," *Social Work,* (May–June 1985), pp. 197–202.

[93]Dye and Zeigler, *The Irony of Democracy,* p. 304.

[94]Ibid., p. 302.

[95]Ibid., p. 303.

# 11

## THE RETURN TO THE PAST

**A RETREAT FROM THE WELFARE STATE**

The 1960s was a time of flower children, psychedelics, free love, rock and roll—when everything was touched with beauty, and love was the key word, when dreams grew into possibilities and possibilities could come true. We did not know how precious this time was until we lost it, but we knew with finality it was over when our children, demonstrating against U.S. involvement in Cambodia in 1970, were shot at Kent State University. That the killings were accidental is unimportant. The government was there with its show of force in the National Guard, and the guns were there to back up their power. Death by our own hands was the result. Others had died in the 1960s, but they died for the dream. With Kent State, the dream died.

As Johnson withdrew from his failures at home and abroad, the conservative backlash that plagued him in his second term of office accelerated. Nixon's election began the retreat into conservatism. Increasingly severe recessions racked the economy during the 1970s, with that of 1975 equal to the Great Depression, though softened by the Roosevelt social programs, and an even more severe economic crisis in 1981–82. Unemployment averaged 5.4 percent until 1975, when it jumped to 8.5 percent, returning by 1979 to 5.8 percent. By 1970, manufacturing had declined to 25 percent of all employment, 17 percent of employment was in service occupations, and the government employed 18 percent of all workers.[1] The gross national product grew during the 1970s from $982 billion to $2,369 billion, but because of inflation, real median family income grew only 5 percent. In May 1980 the overall unemployment rate stood at 7.8 percent, with twice that for Afro-Americans and three times for teenagers.

Despite its failure to end poverty, the Kennedy-Johnson legislation had a significant effect in reducing it. Although the Office of Economic Opportunity received less than $6 billion in all—not even 1 percent of the federal budget—from 1965 to 1968, twenty million people rose above poverty levels by 1969. Yet as OEO programs ended, poverty began to climb and by 1982 had jumped to 15 percent of the population.

Social Security (OASDI) increases were tied to cost of living in the 1970s, and poverty among the elderly fell by about one-third, from 35.2 percent to 24.5 percent. By 1980, there had been a reduction of more than another third among the aged.[2]

Nixon and his conservative Congress set about "welfare reform." Their first task was to dismantle OEO, the next to respond to cries for law and order by pouring funds into law enforcement (Law Enforcement Assistance Administration, LEAA). Part of the push for law and order was against civil dissidents, who were even more subject to political control as Nixon's COINTELPRO (counterintelligence program) stepped up surveillance and harassment of militant and radical community and student groups.[3] By the time of Nixon's reelection, in 1972, most civil and human rights movements had ended, though the women's movement remained strong.

The war in Vietnam ended in 1968, but pressures from the military-industrial complex—corporations with interlocking memberships in the government and the military—involved the United States almost immediately in Cambodia. War production is self-sustaining and always profitable: its products are either destroyed (bombs, missiles, etc.) or grow rapidly obsolete. U.S. foreign policies supported war by intervening in other countries to overturn governments—the Dominican Republic, Brazil, Chile, and more recently El Salvador and Nicaragua—consequently providing markets for war materiel.

The oil crisis of the 1970s provided a political/economic impetus to reunite the nation "against the world." The world, however, was the new market for multinational corporations that owe no allegiance to any country or government. During the 1950s, massive industrial conglomerations began, and between 1965 and 1974, just under 13,000 companies merged. In 1977 alone $40 billion was spent on mergers, including those of 133 banks. The effects of multinationals on the U.S. economy was drastic, since they could hire cheap labor outside unionized America and because Congress voted them massive tax breaks, thereby taking money away from the general revenues. Multinationals in 1973 invested more than $165 billion in foreign companies, and the share of taxes they paid to the United States declined rapidly, from 30 percent of federal revenues in the 1950s to 16 percent by 1978.

Nixon's New Federalism revenue sharing actually channeled more money to cities than had the Johnson programs, but it made social agencies compete with one another and with other urban programs for a share of the federal pie. Most programs other than social insurance suffered cutbacks, although Nixon expanded the Food Stamp Program and provided funds for child nutrition and rent subsidy programs. Food stamp expenditures rose from $550 million in 1970 to $4.4 billion in 1975—an eightfold increase—and more than doubled again by 1981, to $10 billion. Public assistance became increasingly restrictive about work and training even though jobs were growing scarcer. As the middle class became more vulnerable to runaway inflation and as jobs closed down, the outcry against the poor led to taxpayers' revolts, most notably Proposition 13 in California, which set an upper limit on the amount that could be used for social spending (including even police and fire departments).

Nixon continued to support civil rights, though not with Johnson's fervor. Three important changes were enacted: The Equal Employment Opportunity Commission (EEOC) was given power to sue firms that discriminated; the Office of Federal Contract Compliance Programs (OFCCP) could impose sanctions against federal contractors for not hiring people of color; and the Fair Housing Act was amended to prohibit sex discrimination. The EEOC, OFCCP, and the Justice Department increased their activities against institutional discrimination. The nation's political climate deteriorated in Nixon's second term, partly because his use of power as an executive right led to the illegal activities at Watergate. Several of Nixon's top advisors were implicated and sent to prison, and Nixon, with impeachment seemingly inevitable, resigned. Congress then appointed Gerald Ford to serve out the Nixon term.

Democrat Jimmy Carter was elected in 1976. Both Ford and Carter maintained a holding pattern on conservatism, though Carter tried to move the nation toward social progress with a new welfare reform bill aimed at a guaranteed annual income, inflation reduction, and more jobs. Carter's federal appointments reflected his civil rights stance: Of the 298 federal judges appointed by him, 23 percent were minorities, 15 percent were women, and many had records of sympathy toward civil rights and equal opportunity.

After the 1960s, the social work profession began a retreat to conservatism, with social work activists becoming fewer and staid professionals thoroughly ensconced in the mental health movement. With the defeat of the War on Poverty, there was a growing mood of indifference, passivity, and resignation. Social action programs in schools of social work suffered declining enrollments, and in many were quickly forgotten.[4] In 1970, the National Association of Social Workers added an action network: the Educational Legislative Action Network (ELAN) to lobby in Congress, and in 1976 the Political Action for Candidate Selection lobby was added (PACE). Also, NASW began to admit baccalaureate social workers to membership, and in 1971 CSWE began to accredit undergraduate programs of social work education (BSW degrees). By 1976 NASW membership was 70,046, or 17,000 more than in 1970, and in 1975 schools of social work granted more than 43,000 MSW degrees. Between 1970 and 1976, social work jobs increased by 79,000. Caucuses also formed to represent minority interests: in 1968, the National Association of Black Social Workers and the Association of Puerto Rican Social Service Workers, and in California the Asian American Social Workers; in 1971, the Association of American Indian Social Workers.[5] By 1982, there were 384,000 social work jobs, with 88,000 in professional associations. Two-thirds of these were women and 19 percent were nonwhite.[6]

## SOCIAL PROGRAMS IN THE 1970s

Although President Ford did not tackle welfare reform, both Presidents Nixon and Carter proposed basic guaranteed annual income plans to provide a minimum income through benefits and tax credits. Nixon's plan provided only for families with children, but Carter's plan would have set an income floor for all Americans. Both plans were securely tied to work for the able-bodied, but provisions were made for those who could not work. Under both presidents social insurance benefits were incrementally expanded.

Nixon's Family Assistance Plan (FAP) proposed to replace AFDC and unemployment insurance with a guaranteed minimum income to every family with at least one child under the age of 18, or 21 if in school. Mothers with children 3 and under—6 in the first proposal—could have remained in the home, although a bonus of $30 per month would have been given for work or training. Both single-parent and intact families were to be covered, conditional on the agreement of at least one adult to become employed or enter training. Obviously inadequate grants—$500 per year per couple, with $300 for each additional family member—were the incentive to work rather than remain on welfare.[7] The first $60 earned would be disregarded in figuring benefits, as well as one-half of the remaining earnings. Day care facilities were to be greatly expanded, and 150,000 new training slots were to be developed.[8]

FAP passed the House but failed in the Senate by eight votes (1969). Reintroduced in 1971, it seemed likely to pass despite the opposition of liberals who, ignoring the revolutionary change to a guaranteed annual income, opposed its low benefit levels. However, Nixon requested a year's moratorium on welfare reform, and the bill died. FAP would have aided all those making less than 80 percent of the national median income, with states required to supplement to current state levels of need. More than 14 million people would have been added to the welfare rolls, and a good share of the populations of particularly poor states would have been included. In Mississippi, for example, 35 percent of the population would have qualified. It would have cost $9.1 billion, more than $4.1 billion over the then current cost of public assistance.[9]

President Carter's Better Jobs and Income Proposal was a negative income tax plan for all poor people, including singles, people without children, and the employed poor. It would have been administered by the Internal Revenue Service and would have consolidated all public assistance programs—AFDC, SSI, and Food Stamps—under one cash benefit plan. Carter's plan was similar to Nixon's proposal in its provision for a federal minimum income guarantee, benefits with work incentives, job training, and child care. Under the program, those "expected to work" included adults in two-parent families; single parents with the youngest child over age 13; and single persons and childless couples. Those "not expected to work" included the aged, blind, and disabled; single parents with children under age 7; single parents with children ages 7 to 13 if work and day care were not available; and parents in two-parent families where one was incapacitated.

The "expected to work" were offered a basic minimum income of $2,300 a year, increased if the wage-earner could not find a job after eight weeks and reduced when a job was refused. To provide work incentives, the first $3,800 and one-half the remaining income per year would be disregarded in determining eligibility and grant level, and cash assistance would be given until earned income reached $8,400 for a family of four. Thus the basic yearly income could be $6,100 before any disregard went into effect. For the "not expected to work," the plan offered an assured minimum of $4,200 for a family of four—a level lower than that of thirty-eight states. Individuals would receive $2,500 and couples $3,750. Earnings disregards were offered for those unexpected to work who chose to work anyway.

The Carter program would have given federal money to state and local governments to create 1.4 million public services jobs and training slots, paying minimum federal wages. These jobs had to provide skills and training that would be useful in the private sector. To be eligible for a public service job, persons would first have a five-week job search, receiving unemployment compensation during that time. If no job could be found, the head of household would be eligible. After one year in the public job, the process would be repeated.[10] Benefits for the job search were set at $44 per week for a family of four, though if the job was not found, the benefits increased. However, Carter's proposal failed in Congress.

### Social Insurance

*Old Age, Survivors, Disability, and Health Insurance (OASDHI).* There were two major policy changes in social insurance in the 1970s. The first was the legislation in 1972 that granted cost-of-living adjustments (COLAs) to recipients of social insurance according to the Consumer Price Index, which rose 27 percent from 1970 to 1974 and another 15 percent to 1976. Thus, with every rise in cost of living, additional benefits were paid to recipients. The second major change was the transfer of all adult public assistance categories from public assistance to social insurance in 1971. This meant that recipients of Old Age Assistance, Aid to the Blind, and Aid to the Permanently and Totally Disabled were placed under the OASDI programs, with the effects of drastically increasing the number of "entitled persons," whether they had worked in "covered" insurance or not, and enabling them to have a guaranteed nationwide minimum income without the stigma of public assistance.

The Social Security Amendments of 1978 changed the method by which coverage was determined so that rather than counting "quarters of the year" for coverage, workers were credited with a quarter year of employment for each $250 of earned income. Fully covered workers could now retire at age 62, although with reduced benefits, and could receive full benefits at retirement age of 65. Surviving spouses could collect benefits at age 62 or, if disabled, at age 50, and benefits were provided a spouse of any age caring for children under age 16 or disabled. Surviving unmarried children would collect benefits until age 18 or 19 if still in school. Legitimate children or those born out of wedlock still qualified as survivor dependents, and a continuously disabled child would qualify to age 22, when OASDI benefits would begin. For disability coverage, persons had to be permanently unable to work and not yet 65 years old, and to have worked for a certain period before disablement.

Social welfare expenses boomed during the 1970s because of new entitlements and inflation. In 1970 expenditures reached nearly $146 billion, about 17 percent of the gross national product, and then almost doubled, to $290 billion, in 1975. With private expenditures included, 28 percent of the GNP went to social welfare in 1970. By 1976, social insurance accounted for 44 percent of welfare expenditures, increasing to 52 percent by 1983.[11] More than $55 billion a year went for retirement, with another $28 billion in benefits to disabled workers, dependents, and survivors.[12]

The federal share of expenditures for social programs increased: By 1970 it was somewhat more than 50 percent, but by 1978 it was 61 percent.[13] By 1978, expenditures were $394.5 billion, and by 1983, nearly $642 billion, hovering at about 19 percent of the GNP. Wildavsky suggests that inflation caused between 35 and 45 percent of the increase—from $77,175.3 million to $245,855.7 million between 1965 and 1975.[14] Food stamp benefits were also tied to the Consumer Price Index and, therefore, increased proportionately with inflation.[15] (See Figure 11.1.)

Income maintenance varied widely both by geographic area and by type of program. In 1979 benefits varied from $101 monthly in Mississippi for an AFDC family of four to an average of $580 for widowed mothers with three children on Social Security. Retired couples on Social Security averaged about $431 a month, while couples with no other income except Supplemental Security Income received between $189 and $284, depending on living arrangements. Unemployment benefits averaged about $350 monthly, including dependent allowances in the few states that paid them. In a number of states, maximum benefits payable to survivors or workers killed on the job were lower than those for temporary disabilities.[17] In 1978, widows with two children received benefits averaging $592 monthly, but with three or more children $583. Aged couples received an average of $438.00.[18] As of 1980, no family could receive more than 150 to 180 percent of the former worker's benefit, so the greater the number of children, the less per capita was received.

One reason for the generosity of Congress vis-a-vis OASDI payments was that, early in the 1970s, the program had surpluses not since matched. In 1970 OASDI collected $35 billion in taxes and paid out $32 billion. However, the worsening economy changed the surplus situation by 1975, and in 1979 benefits of $104.3 billion exceeded contributions of $103 billion. The deficit increased in the early 1980s, and prices increased faster than wages. OASDI benefits, however, because they were COLA-indexed, rose faster on the average than workers' take-home pay—by 1980 by 19 percent more. In 1981, OASDI paid out $145 billion while collecting only $140 billion.[19]

Most people receive much more than they put into the Social Security system, and pensions depend on current legislation rather than on legislation at the time the person becomes eligible. Benefits are paid from current

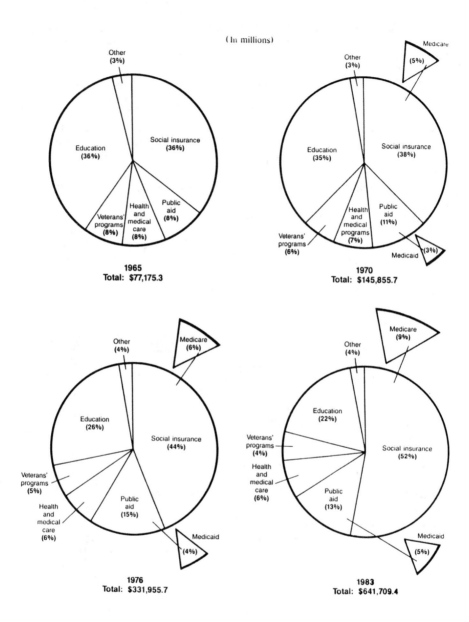

**FIGURE 11.1**   Distribution of Social Welfare Expenditures, Selected Fiscal Years 1965–1983 (in millions).[16]   *Source*: U.S. Department of Health and Human Services, Social Security Administrations Office of Policy, *Social Security Bulletin*, February 1986, vol. 49, no. 2, p. 20.

funds rather than the so-called trust or reserve fund, and funds collected from people now being paid are in actuality those being contributed by workers today.

> The Social Security system in America made its first payment on January 31, 1940, to a retired unmarried woman who died 35 years later at the age of one hundred . . . for a total tax contribution of about $22.00 she received more than $20,000 over the 35-year period. Her payment in 1940 was $22.54, and in 1974 was $109.20.[20]

*Unemployment Insurance.* The recessions of 1969–71 and 1974–75 were moderated by the expansion of unemployment benefits. The period of eligibility was extended and offices were kept open nights and weekends. People are eligible for unemployment insurance if they have worked for a "base" period depending on the state. Most states restrict benefits for students, pregnant women, and people unemployed because of marital or family obligations. Also, people fired from jobs for misconduct or refusing suitable work are treated differently: the waiting period for unemployment insurance is delayed. Most states figure benefits on base pay, with minimum and maximum levels, and a few states add extra for dependent children. In 1980, without public attention, $26 million was funneled into the program, up $6.8 billion from 1972.[21]

Approximately 20 percent of the population is not covered by unemployment insurance, although more than 90 percent of jobs are covered. Employers with fewer than four employees are not covered, and people looking for first jobs or having only brief employment do not qualify. Moreover, many employers will not hire full time, or will let employees go before the "base" period is covered so they need not pay unemployment insurance taxes. This "secondary labor market," providing neither social insurance nor company fringe benefits, is a prime employer of young people, women, and people of color.

### Public Assistance Programs

Public assistance after the Johnson years had several themes: the promiscuity of welfare mothers, the laziness of recipients, and fraud—secret jobs, use of money to support communes, lying, and cheating. Heffernan says

> The personal fault theme was supplemented by a belief that current welfare programs . . . encouraged withdrawal from the labor force, family splitting, and migration . . . for the purpose of receiving aid.[22]

Social Darwinism was still active in the public idiom, for example, in 1974 William Shockley, a Nobel Laureate in physics, advocated paying the "unfit poor"—those who did not pay income taxes—for eugenic sterilization at the rate of $1000 for each point they fell below IQ 100. The bonuses, placed in a trust fund, would be doled out over the individual's life span. He noted that

> $30,000 put in a trust for a 70 IQ moron potentially capable of producing twenty children might return $250,000 to taxpayers in reduced costs of mental retardation care.

Obviously, his greatest interest was in control of women, for men can father many more children than twenty. He also established a "sperm bank" for contributions from men of genetic superiority.[23]

The move of adult categories—the blind, aged, and disabled—out of public assistance and into OASDI meant that these groups were finally recognized as "deserving poor." The change had two major results. On the one hand, it channeled even more hostility toward "undeserving" AFDC recipients. On the other, it finally gave the nation a guaranteed annual minimum income for most other needy people. It soon became obvious that OASDI income was less in some states than recipients had received on public assistance, particularly for the disabled. To remedy this, a new federal public assistance program, Supplemental Security Income (SSI) was legislated in 1972 and put into effect in 1974. Funded through general revenue, it was located in the Department of Health, Education and Welfare (DHEW) with state-level administration and means testing and social services through local departments of public welfare.

*Supplemental Security Income (SSI).* In this program, people falling under the states' standard of needs receive an additional cash pension beyond their OASDI grants, indexed with cost of living. Recipients qualify for food stamps in most states, and for Medicaid when their Medicare eligibility is exhausted. Social services, including protective services, are available. Some assets and income are exempt from eligibility or grant determination: Recipients can have no more than $1,500 in liquid assets, or $2,250 for a couple. Their homes must be worth less than $25,000 and their cars worth less than $1,200.

To receive SSI, blind and disabled people under the age of 65 must be referred to vocational rehabilitation. Income from spouses or children living with them is counted as a resource. SSI recipients may keep the first $65 they earn in the year and an additional $20 per month of income from any source without benefit reduction. States that had been granting more than the federal SSI grant allowed in 1972 were required to provide further supplements, up to state levels of need, until that amount exceeded the total spent on former OAA, APTD, and AB, when the federal government picked up the extra costs.

In 1975, SSI pensions were set at $158 per month, and SSI still has a higher benefit for two than is the AFDC benefit for two. Moreover, it is higher than a four-person AFDC household in twenty-two states.[24]

*Aid to Families with Dependent Children: The Work Incentive and Absent Fathers Programs.* Despite the social protest movements of the 1960s, gains for AFDC families were soon lost. The National Welfare Rights Organization had made two proposals that were given serious consideration by the legislature. The first, cost-of-living increases, was a joint legislative-welfare reform effort in 1967. Although it was approved in a federal legislative committee, states refused to give up their rights to set levels of need as they chose, and particularly to raise benefit levels to 100 percent of need. The Department of Health, Education, and Welfare took the position that it had no power to coerce the states and the Supreme Court upheld the position of the thirty-nine states that refused to comply.[25]

The second proposal (1969), eligibility by declaration, allowed welfare departments to rely solely on applicants' statements without in-depth verifications. The system was supposed to be in effect in twenty-two states by early 1971, but the General Administration Office (GAO) found that it had been so modified on the local level that it was ineffective. Yet New York City used it with apparent success for some time, effecting quick determinations of eligibility and savings in administrative money.[26]

In the 1970s, AFDC recipients came under even more hostile scrutiny by the public, the legislatures, and public assistance workers. Slippage of civil rights—the right to privacy, to equal protection under the law, and to due process—continued apace. Searches under false pretenses for "men in the house" and midnight raids continued even against Supreme Court decisions,[27] and other regulations were ignored or finessed; for example, although residence requirements for AFDC were unconstitutional, New York refused AFDC to newcomers who could not find "appropriate" housing. Workers again had free discretion, and those not meeting their standards were removed from AFDC rolls. AFDC grants continued to be minimal: in constant dollars, between 1970 and 1981, average benefits declined by almost 20 percent. Average monthly grants as of 1981 ranged from a low in Mississippi of $96.00 to California's $463.00. Even with food stamps, benefits dropped by 9 percent.[28]

The Talmadge amendments of 1971 made participation in the Work Incentive Program (WIN) mandatory for all adult recipients with children age 6 or over, where previously it had been voluntary. Because there were not sufficient spaces in the WIN training programs, "creaming" became a problem, since program administrators wanted good success records. In 1971, more than half of those in WIN programs were white, and 40 percent were men.[29] That WIN did not work seemed beside the point: it was required not for its effectiveness but because of the desire to punish those who did not work. Senator Russell Long said

> Of 250,000 welfare referrals found appropriate and referred to the Work Incentive Program during its first 21 months, less than 60 percent were enrolled in the program . . . and out of the 145,000 who were enrolled, one-third subsequently dropped out. Only 13,000 welfare cases have been closed following participation in the . . . program.[30]

This was called the "WIN Funnel":

> of 2,664,000 assessed (through 1971),
>   627,000 were found appropriate,
>     493,000 were referred to WIN,
>       286,000 were enrolled,
>         170,000 left, and
>           36,000 completed successfully.

The total appropriation was $500 million, an exorbitant cost per person.[31]

WIN and other such work programs were based on the myth of the "culture of poverty," which assumes that the poor hold values that do not emphasize work. Generally speaking, this assumption is wrong. In 1979, nearly 30 percent of AFDC recipients remained on the program for less than one year, and the majority less than four years. Fewer than 8 percent were on AFDC without interruption for more than ten years.[32]

In 1972, Title IV.D. of the Social Security Act was enacted. This was the child support enforcement law—called the "absent pappy" law which required AFDC mothers to file suit against the putative fathers of their children so that the state could collect back support. As early as 1960, Kaplan concluded that

> absent fathers of needy children, like their families, tend to be poor, and even the most vigorous law enforcement does not create income. Collections from fathers are grossly inadequate to meet their families' needs. The unemployment and underemployment of men, particularly . . . [Afro-American men], appear to be the most pressing problem.[33]

Nevertheless, Notice to Law Enforcement Officials (NOLEO) went into effect. Mothers, often against their wills, became instruments of the law in compelling support from the fathers, under threat of the loss of their AFDC benefits for noncompliance. Some had to sign warrants or complaints with the district attorney, others had to swear out paternity suits, and some had to submit to lie detector tests.[34] The law also opened Social Security and income tax records to help the new Offices of Child Support locate absent parents and permitted garnishment of federal wages and stipends to pay delinquent support orders.

Although in 1978 there were five times more mothers above the poverty level than below whose court-ordered payments were absent or in arrears, most attention focused on poor fathers who did not pay support. In 1979, 34.6 percent (2.5 million) of 7.1 million children under 21 received child support payments. However, over one-third of all fathers are not required to pay anything because of limited earning ability, and the amounts ordered bear little relationship to the man's income. After a year or two, in most cases, noncompliance is the rule rather than the exception. Of men ordered to support, two-fifths rarely pay anything, and one-tenth only pay sporadically. On the average, Afro-American fathers are more conscientious about child support payments, and the poor are at least as conscientious as are middle- or upper-class fathers.[35]

*Social Services (Title XX).*   The Services Amendments of 1962 had provided an open-ended authorization by which the federal government would reimburse states for social services up to 75 percent of their costs. Social work professionals persuaded legislators that such services would cut costs in the long run, but state welfare departments saw Title XX as an opportunity to gain more federal dollars and expand the domain of their services. In many states, welfare departments began to charge the federal government for services they had traditionally provided, rather than developing new services. Grants for the purchase of services from private agencies were unusually generous, stimulating the growth of the "personal social service" industry—casework treatment—and encouraging social workers to enter private practice or organize private consultant firms.[36] States were reimbursed 50 percent of the cost in 1956, 75 percent in 1962, and up to 90 percent in 1975.

By 1972, costs to the federal government had increased enormously, with no real end in sight. To control these flyaway costs, in September 1972, Congress "capped" the program at $2.2 billion through the Revenue Sharing Act. Although the cost of social services incremented every few years, its "open invitation" policy ended. Ninety percent of social services money had to be spent for people on public assistance, with the remaining amount to be used for child care and family planning services, and for services to the mentally retarded, drug addicts, alcoholics, and children in foster care.

With federal money limited, newly developed services began to deteriorate. Purchase of services from private agencies—for mental health counseling, drug abuse, child care—dropped abruptly. Therefore, in 1974, legislators created a new title to the Social Security Act for block grants for which agencies competed. The title "capped" expenses at a permanent ceiling of $2.5 billion (raised to $3 billion for 1982), with a requirement that at least half the funds be spent for low income people. Block grants were allocated to states on the basis of population, with state matching required, usually at a 75:25 ratio. Some services qualified for a 90:10 ratio, especially administrative and staff development and social work education.

One effect of the new block grant system was that states had to plan comprehensively to develop social services. Each service had to have at least one of the following goals:

1. Reduce the dependency of clients.
2. Help them gain economic independence (get off the welfare rolls).
3. Prevent or remedy the neglect, abuse, or exploitation of children and adults unable to protect their own interests, including the preservation, reuniting, or rehabilitation of the family system.
4. Provide for the least intrusive care—usually community-based or home care rather than institutional care.
5. Secure institutional care when other kinds are inappropriate, and provide services to those so placed.

About 10.6 million persons received social services in 1978, of which about 30 percent were AFDC clients, 37 percent other people in poverty, and 13 percent persons receiving services not related to income level. Child day care was the most costly item, totaling $732.3 million, and $324.8 million went for homemaker services, though only 11 percent of homemaker services went to AFDC families.

Because of the Nixon cutbacks, by 1972 mental health centers were in serious trouble. Even with increased funding, services were targeted to AFDC and SSI groups, though people with incomes of up to 115 percent of the state median income could qualify for free services. The most frequently provided services were counseling, child day care, child protective services, health related services, homemaker services, transportation, and family planning. While community mental health services might have reasonably begun to deal with the great numbers of mentally ill being released from hospitals, they neglected to do so. Compton says

> The staff of such centers accustomed to providing clinical counseling services, had neither skill nor interest in giving the social care services which were . . . needed by the former patients.[37]

The result has been a national shame: homeless men and women wandering the streets of large cities, without food, clothing, or shelter, living and often dying with nobody to care.

Concern for children once again came to the fore in the 1970s, especially for out-of-wedlock children. According to the National Center for Health Statistics, there were 418,000 births to unwed mothers in 1974—13.2 percent of all live births—and ages of mothers decreased. Child abuse and neglect continued to receive increased funding, and in 1975 the Office of Child Development initiated a number of research projects. In 1971 Congress passed the Comprehensive Child Development Act, which would have provided funds for comprehensive high-quality day care, but it was vetoed by President Nixon on the grounds that it would destroy the family, duplicate already existing services, and establish communal child-rearing against American values.

One unanticipated consequence of block grants was the move toward taking children from parents not considered "adequate." New institutions, foster care, and group home situations proliferated, with higher funding than for in-home preventative services. Thus, rather than giving support to intact but unstable families, millions were spent for child placement after families had disintegrated or deteriorated. Looking at yearly costs per child for types of care, homemaker services, family day care, and day care centers cost between $2,000 and $3,000 per child. For remedial care, $5,200 per child is spent yearly for foster home care; $15,400 per child for group home care; $18,600 for each child in group residences; $34,000 per child in general institutions; and $42,100 for each child placed in secure detention facilities.[38] Currently, about 700,000 children have been placed away from their parents: about 400,000 in various types of foster care and another 300,000 in institutions. One-third of these last are in corrections facilities.[39] Institutional classism, sexism, and racism are all evident in such placements: there are more poor children and children of color placed in institutions, and boy and girl children are placed differentially, girls more often for status offenses and boys for offenses that would be criminal if committed by an adult.[40] Nearly half are locked up because of running away from home, being truant, or not being wanted at home.

One reason Congress amended the Juvenile Justice and Delinquency Prevention Act in 1974 was the overuse of secure institutions and jails that became "schools of crime" for children institutionalized for noncriminal and minor delinquencies. There were almost no rehabilitative programs, and children in such institutions were often subject to physical abuse while there.[41] Another reason for the legislation was the increasing estimates of child abuse—between sixty thousand and two million cases per year. Estimates indicated that half of the approximately two million children who ran away from home annually were physically and sexually abused by relatives and other adults, and that at least six children were beaten to death by adults on an average day.[42] The Child Abuse and Treatment Act (1974) accelerated the development of state programs to aid the mistreated child; established the National Center for Prevention and Treatment of Child Abuse and Neglect at the University of Colorado Medical Center; authorized runaway shelters and hot lines; and promoted research and professional training in the areas of child abuse and protection, though funds were not allocated until Carter's administration. The Child Welfare Act of 1980 provided funds and federal regulations to alter the pattern by which children were removed to foster care, of whom in 1980 there were 500,000.

*Food Stamps.* In 1965, food stamp expenditures were $35 million; in 1970 $550 million; by 1975 more than $4.4 billion; and in 1981 they were $10 billion.[43] In 1977, recipients were no longer required to buy food stamps, and "bonuses" figured on income level and number in household were simply given to eligible recipients. Still, many eligible people did not receive food stamps because, among other problems, they were not informed about the program or their eligibility, certification requirements were too difficult, offices were inaccessible, and using stamps was embarrassing to proud people. During the late 1970s, income levels were changed several times, resulting in a 2.5 million drop in users between 1976 and 1978. Worsening economic conditions still pushed the number of food stamp users to new heights before the 1980s began.[44] In 1979, the average monthly bonus per person was $34, so that $1,638 would be added to the purchasing power of a family of four over a year, still about $960 below the poverty threshold.[45]

### Other Social Welfare Programs

*Comprehensive Education and Training Act (CETA).* CETA arose from the Manpower Development and Training Act of 1962, the Economic Opportunity Act of 1964, and the Emergency Employment Act of 1970. Nixon's administration established the program in 1973 to provide entry-level jobs in the private sector for young urban minority people and the chronically unemployed. In 1977, for example, five-sixths of CETA employees were school drop-outs averaging below-sixth-grade reading ability. One-half were from single-parent families, their family sizes were nearly twice the national average, and their family's per capita income was less than one-third of the total population's average. Eighty percent had previous arrests and 75 percent prior convictions. More than one-third had never held a 20-hour a week job for longer than one month.[46]

State and local governments determined the extent of the program by how much matching funds they were willing to put up. In 1974, however, a severe recession added millions to the unemployment rolls in the private sector and eliminated the competition for jobs there. In response, CETA became an employment agency for temporary public service jobs, in government and social agencies, that were to be picked up with local funding when CETA subsidies ended. However, almost two-thirds of the six million CETA jobs, which cost the federal government nearly $24 billion, ended when subsidies were terminated. From 1974 to 1979 CETA was one of the largest governmental agencies, and spent $55 billion during the eight years of its operation.[47]

*Education and Youth Programs.* The remnants of OEO, including Head Start, Upward Bound, Talent Search, and Job Corps, were moved to other agencies and continued with varying success. There is substantial evidence that Head Start, one of the few remaining OEO programs, has a positive effect on nearly every aspect of early childhood development, including the inhibition of serious educational and behavioral problems. According to Levitan,

> The Children's Defense Fund estimated that Head Start's benefits outweigh its costs by reducing costs of special education services often associated with disadvantaged children.[48]

Such children are less likely to be in special education classes, more likely to be in their regular grade at school, and more likely to graduate from high school, enroll in college, and obtain a self-supporting job. They are also less likely to be arrested or on welfare when adults. In 1983, Head Start served 400,000 children at a cost of $907 million, and reached about 20 percent of 4- and 5-year-olds from disadvantaged homes.[49]

Upward Bound and Talent Search programs, which encourage continuation of education for young people, also have reasonable success rates. Nearly 60 percent of Upward Bound students enter college and remain at least two years, and Talent Search in 1976 placed between 75 and 90 percent of its students in postsecondary institutions. Job Corps was not quite so successful, with only 30 percent completing vocational training from the Corps. Nevertheless, in 1977 those who did earned $1,250 more annually ($1,500 for women) than young people in the same life situations who were not in Job Corps, and generally obtained jobs with higher status and better working conditions. Trainees also attended college more frequently and were less likely to engage in criminal activities by 35 percent.[50]

In 1965, the Education for All Handicapped Children Act was added to the Elementary and Secondary Education Act (ESEA). It mandated that school districts provide appropriate educational opportunities for educationally impaired children. The act aimed for basic skills improvement,

consumer education, bilingual education, and the acquisition of instruc-
tional materials and equipment. It was revised and extended in 1975
(Developmentally Disabled Bill of Rights Act), before which students with
physical or mental handicaps could be taught in classrooms separated from
the conventional classroom. With the revision, every child was required to
have an individualized program in the least restricted feasible environment—the regular classroom where possible—with teachers specifically
trained in special education. The federal government paid a substantial
portion of the added costs of school districts. Since the federal government
has no direct legal authority over public schools, the law was passed to
protect the constitutional rights of handicapped students.

Five-sixths of all ESEA funds were designated for educationally
deprived and disadvantaged children, and grants were allotted according
to the number of children from low-income families served by the school
district. Special grants were also given for migrant, neglected, and delinquent children. ESEA has been credited with eliminating over 40 percent
of the difference in reading achievement between 9-year-old white and
Afro-American children since 1965. In 1982, 10 percent of monies for
bilingual programs were cut from ESEA by the Reagan administration,
with another 50 percent to follow in 1983. For remedial instruction and
related services, however, $3.5 billion was provided in 1984.[51]

*Housing.*    Nixon, Ford, and Carter did little in the area of housing.
The Model Cities Program, along with public housing and Urban Renewal,
was deemphasized by the Nixon administration in 1973 and effectively
terminated by the Housing Act of 1974, which shifted federal resources to
revenue sharing strategies. Low-rent public housing, home loans for low-
income families, and rent supplement programs were made available to the
poor, along with special Department of Housing and Urban Development
programs for the aged (HUD Title 8). The U.S. Department of Agriculture
also gives home loans to farmers, and the Office of Indian Housing is
administered by HUD. Most such programs are means tested, with the
exceptions of Veteran's Housing Assistance and guaranteed mortgage
loans from the Federal Housing Administration and HUD.[52]

*Corrections.*    Attention to crimes of violence led Congress to establish
the Law Enforcement Assistance Administration (LEAA) in the Department of Justice in 1968. It was designed to conduct and fund research,
promote efforts to improve personnel in the field of corrections, and to
encourage demonstration projects. Between 1969 and 1972, its budget rose
from $60 million to $700 million,[53] providing impetus to the training of
people to work in criminal justice.

While society has great faith in the justice system, the fact is that it
perpetuates institutional racism and classism. A study of the legal and social
characteristics of 2,419 consecutive felony probation cases found most
likely to be labeled as felons were defendants who were older, non-white,
poorly educated; had a prior record; and were defended by a court-
appointed attorney. These groups also are more likely to receive severe

punishments such as imprisonment or death for rape and murder. Former Attorney General Ramsey Clark says

> Racial discrimination is manifest from the bare statistics of capital punishment. Since we began keeping records in 1930, there have been 2,066 Negroes and only 1,751 white persons put to death. Hundreds of thousands of rapes have occurred in America since 1930, yet only 455 men have been executed for rape—and 405 of them were Negroes. There can be no rationalization or justification of such clear discrimination. It is outrageous public murder, illuminating our darkest racism.[54]

Lesser punishments also show bias: Parole often depends on the value judgments of parole board members, corrections officers, and others in power. The safest risks, according to their biases, are middle-class white educated men, with white-collar rather than skilled or unskilled job training. Afro-Americans have about one- half the chance of early release versus whites at the same educational level.[55] While the growing numbers in prison validate our beliefs in the growing crime rate, research shows that the reporting of crimes rather than the actual number of crimes is increasing exponentially. Because of racist and classist bias, there is a winnowing out of white, middle-class, white-collar men, and those left are generally people of color, especially Afro-American men, and the poor. The national incarceration rate for Afro-Americans is 600 per 100,000 as compared to 70.8 for whites.[56]

Currently, there are about five thousand city and county jails, four hundred state and federal prisons, and a variety of other detention centers. In some states, the cost of imprisonment for one inmate is above $20,000 per year, not including the cost of his family's support if they must go on AFDC. On an average day, about 1.3 million persons are confined. Spending for prisons and jails rose 50.9 percent during the first half of the 1980s, and in 1983 $10.4 billion was spent on corrections, up from $6.9 billion in 1980. Spending for police, courts, and prisons came to $39.7 billion in 1983.[57] The number of correctional officers has more than doubled in the ten years before 1986, to nearly 100,000.[58]

## CIVIL RIGHTS IN THE 1970s

While the 1964 Civil Rights Act brought some lasting benefits to people of color and to women, the Equal Employment Opportunity Commission was unable to keep up with complaints in the 1970s. In 1974 nearly 57,000 persons filed complaints that took more than two and a half years to resolve, leaving a backlog of 100,000 cases by 1980. By 1982, the backlog was 5,000 to 10,000 cases.[59]

### Native Americans

Native American protests became more radical after the Civil Rights Act of 1964, for though the War on Poverty brought some benefits in temporary jobs and training, systematic discrimination continued. Literacy tests and the gerrymandering of district lines, especially in Western states, continued to deprive Native Americans of their civil rights. Nevertheless, increased voter turnout elected Navahos to the New Mexican legislature for the first time in 1964, and by 1967 an estimated fifteen native Americans served in legislatures of six Western states. Only two dozen have served in state legislatures since 1900, and only a handful in the U.S. Congress, although Charles Curtis, born in 1869 on the Kaw Reservation, served as representative for fourteen years, senator for twenty, and vice president under Hoover.

During the 1960s and 1970s, tens of thousands of Native Americans were encouraged to leave reservations for the cities. Half to three-fourths of urban relocatees returned to reservations after a few years because of continued poverty and discrimination in jobs and housing, but by 1980 half of all Native Americans lived in metropolitan areas. In 1968, the government attracted industry to some reservations, and by 1972 there were two hundred factories there. However, only half the jobs went to Native Americans, and even in agriculture, where by the late 1960s the industry's gross income was $300 million, Native Americans received only about $100 million.[60]

With the beginning of the Indian Health Service in 1955, the status of health for Native Americans improved markedly. Mortality rates declined and life expectancy increased: Between 1955 and 1971, the infant death rate decreased by 56 percent and the maternal death rate by 54 percent. Deaths from tuberculosis, gastritis, and influenza pneumonia declined by 86, 88, and 57 percent, respectively. Still, Native Americans die younger than any other group, and infant mortality on some reservations is comparable to that of Third World countries.[61] In 1970, two-thirds of all the U.S. population aged 16 to 24 years old had finished high school, compared to 50 percent of Native Americans in urban areas and 25 percent in rural areas.

The American land grab of Native American lands is still in progress. A case in point is the treaty that only recently took Alaskan land to build an oil pipeline. Custom has it in the United States that, whenever Native Americans abandon actual use and occupancy of their land, they lose aboriginal title to it. As recently as 1971 Alaskan Natives held aboriginal title to nine-tenths of Alaska, and in 1970 a judge held that an oil pipeline could not be laid across the Yukon until permission was obtained. However, "On December 14, 1971, Congress took note of the Alaskan Natives' aboriginal title and extinguished it."[62] In return, Congress gave them a business corporation for each of their 220 villages to manage land they will be allowed to take back from selected areas and agreed to pay them something less than a billion dollars from North Slope Oil revenues, though there is no deadline for payment. Since there are 80,000 Native Americans affected by the act, each will get 1/80,000th of a share in the corporation, but this cannot be sold until 1991. The only tangible benefit is a cash dividend, which in 1974 amounted to about $181.[63]

In 1973, the American Indian Policy Review Commission—the first top-level investigative commission in Indian affairs since the Merriam Report in 1928—was formed. Its members were five Native Americans and seven senators and congressmen, the majority from states with large Native

American populations. In 1975, they ruled that tribes are sovereign political bodies with power to enact and enforce their own laws, and that a special trust relationship still exists between them and the U.S. government.[64]

In 1977 their full report was issued: it noted that

> From the standpoint of personal well-being, the Indian of America ranks at the bottom of virtually every social statistical indicator . . . the highest infant mortality rate, the lowest longevity rate, the lowest level of educational attainment, the lowest per capita income, and the poorest housing and transportation in the land.[65]

Of all men in the United States in 1977, 74 percent were employed, but only 56 percent of all Native American men worked, and women averaged less than $400 a year for their employment. Rural residents lived in greater poverty than did those in cities, but 34 percent of Native Americans had an annual income of $4,000 or less, compared with 15 percent of the total population; only 22 percent earned $10,000 or more, compared with 47 percent of the general population.[66] Forced assimilation of Native Americans still exists. A prime example is the taking of Native American children from their families as part of the general discretionary trend of welfare and mental health workers,

> and placing these children in white foster homes or institutions. In some areas 25 to 40 percent of all children are taken from their homes. Social workers argue the homes of poor Native Americans are not "fit" places for children . . . . the poverty and "dirt" in the lives of Native Americans are fundamentally the result of the destruction of Native American resources . . . over hundreds of years of colonial oppression.[67]

Among Native American protest groups, the most radical was the American Indian Movement (AIM). In 1969, after student protesters occupied the no longer used prison island of Alcatraz, a hundred AIM members replaced them, arguing that their treaty rights guaranteed them unused federal lands. They were forcibly removed in 1971. In 1973, AIM led an armed occupation at Wounded Knee on Pine Ridge Reservation, arguing that the tribal government was dominated by whites. Federal agents and disguised army units occupied the reservation with an armed struggle that lasted seventy-one days, with two Native Americans killed and two federal officials wounded. Up to three hundred Native Americans were involved. Illegal wiretapping and paid witnesses led to the defeat of the suit against AIM, but a dozen suspicious murders and accidents later happened to AIM members, with few arrests or convictions for the crimes. Recently, the 8th Circuit Court of Appeals reversed a lower court's dismissal of complaints that their constitutional rights had been violated because the military had intervened in a domestic problem with Air Force planes for surveillance and high-ranking military officers on hand, under the direction of Alexander Haig, vice chief of staff under Nixon. The court decided that

> the use of military forces to seize civilians can expose civilian government to the threat of military rule and the suspension of constitutional liberties.[68]

In 1974 a band of Mohawks occupied a forest preserve in New York's Adirondack State Park, claiming its six hundred acres along with nine million additional acres in New York and Vermont. In September the state went to federal court seeking to evict the Mohawks, and the Mohawks countered with a suit charging that the land had been usurped by fraud. On appeal, the Mohawks were granted rights to considerable land in the state. Further, in 1975 armed Menominees occupied the Alexian Brothers' novitiate building, and as a consequence a committee, formed to supervise contacts between Native Americans and police, has been successful in improving police behavior. In 1979 the Supreme Court upheld a 1974 decision that treaties reserved fishing rights for Native Americans differently than for whites and recognized tribal rights to fishing resources. However, this led to a significant backlash of congressional bills aimed at breaking treaties, overturning court decisions, and exterminating land claims.[69]

In the 1970s, three dozen tribes created the Council of Energy Resources (CERT) to protect their interests and hired a former Iranian oil minister to help them with contracts because in dealing with white Americans for the development of coal, oil, and other resources they rarely received the correct royalties. CERT obtained several millions of dollars of grants for technical assistance and reservation industrialization. Throughout this time, however, the government tried to coopt CERT, because Native American lands included one-third of the strip coal mining resources of the West and half the uranium outside public lands.[70]

Feagin says

> Native American lands have been taken for dams, reservoir projects, national parks, and right of ways for roads. The sale of lands to private lumbering and mineral interests—200,000 acres in 1970—continues. . . . Large proportions of the usable land in reservations have been leased to whites.[71]

By 1973 some three hundred land claims had been heard and over $300 million awarded to Native American societies. However, this represents less than 4 percent of the amount claimed. In New York and Maine, the Oneida society's claims against the government have returned some illegally taken land. An agreement providing for the acquisition of 300,000 acres to be held in trust for Native Americans was developed, and a $27 million trust fund was signed by Jimmy Carter in 1980.[72] In 1984, appropriations included $254 million to the Bureau of Indian Affairs for the operation of Indian-controlled boarding and day schools, and an additional $69 million went to the Department of Education to support the education of Native American children in public schools.[73]

However, Reaganomics has hit hard on Native Americans. Since 1980, average unemployment on reservations has jumped from 40 percent to a devastating 80 percent, and in some tribes average income has fallen to $900 per year for a family of four. Because Native Americans receive no state or local aid, they have had to rely on the federal government for help. Programs that have assisted them since the War on Poverty include CETA, the Economic Development Administration, Housing and Urban Development, and Health and Human Services. However, these are the agencies that have been cut most heavily, virtually eliminating the "safety net" for these poorest of the poor in the United States.

### Japanese Americans

Although Japanese Americans suffered personally and economically from their internment during World War II, they soon began to recoup their losses. In 1950 Japanese American activities in Hawaii led to statehood, and Daniel Inouye, a war hero, became the first Japanese American in the House of Representatives. Spark Matsunaga was second in 1962, and Inouye then became the first Japanese American senator in 1964. Patsy Takemoto Mink became the first Japanese woman in Congress. While these congresspersons came from Hawaii, in 1976 Samuel Hayakawa was the first Japanese American senator from the mainland, reelected in 1982.[74]

In 1970, there were 591,000 Japanese Americans in the United States, with the heaviest concentrations in Hawaii (217,307) and California (213,280). Their median family income was $12,500 (all incomes median, $9,600), though Japanese American women earned much less than men, at $5,880 compared with $5,122 for white women. Only 7.5 percent lived below the poverty level. By this time their education level was higher than any other population group: Nearly all had finished high school and over half the men and one-third of the women were college graduates. By 1980, Japanese American median family income was $22,025.[75]

Japanese Americans have continued to press against their illegal internment. In January 1983, Gordon Hirabayashi, who was jailed in 1943 for arguing against internment, sought to have his conviction set aside (along with that of Fred Koromatsu in 1944) on grounds that government lawyers had concealed important evidence at his trial—a Naval Intelligence report contradicting the Army's claim that widespread disloyalty among Japanese Americans required their evacuation and internment. The "proof " that convicted them was a decoded intelligence statement suggesting that Japanese Americans working in aircraft plants had sent production figures to Tokyo—figures printed ten days before in the *Los Angeles Times*. A star witness could not connect those cables to a single American citizen of Japanese ancestry.

The U.S. Court of Appeals for the District of Columbia recently heard a $12 billion damage suit brought on behalf of all surviving internees. A federal district court judge dismissed the suit on statute of limitations grounds, but the Circuit Court reversed the dismissal. Nevertheless, a resurgence of racism against Asians across the country is evident in the 1980s recessions. Peter Irons says

From California to Boston, violence against Asians has spread, as the "Rambo syndrome" and "Japan-bashing" have become respectable. The murder of Vincent Chin in Detroit and the wave of attacks on Vietnamese and other Indochinese refugees testify to the ugly strain of racism the Reagan Administration has done little to counter.[76]

### Other Asian-American Minorities

In 1970, there were 435,000 Chinese and 343,000 Filipinos in the United States. During 1973, immigration brought in approximately 21,700 Chinese, 30,000 Filipinos, and 5,500 Japanese. There were from 1.5 to 3.5 million Asian immigrants from 1970 to 1980, and by 1980, Chinese had surpassed Japanese as the nation's largest Asian group. One-half million Indo-Chinese immigrated to the United States in 1970, of which two-thirds were from Vietnam. This last group was particularly threatened when they settled around the Gulf of Mexico, with incidences of burning in effigy and harassment of fishermen by the Ku Klux Klan.[77]

### Mexican Americans

In 1970, the population of Mexican Americans numbered more than 4.5 million, with almost 80 percent living in Arizona, California, Colorado, New Mexico, and Texas. Their median family income was $6,972 (though substantially lower in Texas), while that of all families was $9,600.[78] One quarter of the Mexican American population (Chicanos) lived below the poverty level. Approximately 17 percent of all children in the Southwest were Mexican Americans, though only 4 percent of the 325,000 teachers in the Southwest were Mexican Americans. These children were overrepresented in classes for the retarded, evidencing that testing was done in English. Although significant provisions were made for bilingual education under the Elementary and Secondary Education Act of 1968, and in 1974 the *Law v. Nichols* decision determined that schools could not ignore the language problems of non-English speakers, most schools still have only weak bilingual programs. In 1979, more than 50 percent of Mexican American children did not finish high school, and one quarter had less than an elementary school education. In 1982, the Supreme Court ruled that all children, including illegal aliens, had to be provided schooling without tuition in U.S. schools.[79]

Little real progress has been made in assuring equality for Chicanos. Part of the problem is the lack of differentiation between Chicanos and immigrant Mexicans, both in the public mind and in the way they are treated economically. Officially, legal immigration has been limited: There were new restrictions in 1960, and in 1965 the Immigration Act limited immigration from the Western Hemisphere to 120,000. In 1976, an immigration cap of 20,000 was placed on Mexico. However, throughout this time, whenever more labor was needed, illegal immigration has been supported by growers. Between four and seven million Mexican undocumented laborers—*braceros*—entered the United States between 1920 and 1980. Many return to Mexico, but many more stay because of their extreme poverty in Mexico. Labor smugglers go into Mexico to bring in workers when growers need their labor and charge $300 to $1,100 per person to bring them to the U.S.

Whole families come to America, where they have no legal protections. Despite abuses amounting even to death—for example, a truckload was left in a locked truck to die in the desert early in the 1980s—they are afraid to go to authorities for help. Since workers picking crops are often paid by the basket, their children work in the fields too, without adequate shelter, food, or health care. Although hiring of American children is prohibited by law, Hispanic children—whether illegal immigrants, legal immigrants, or Hispanic Americans—rarely have such protection. Major canneries and food producers do not bother to ask who has picked the baskets of food turned in for pay.[80]

In the mid-1970s, nearly all employers of Hispanics refused government help in finding American workers to replace Mexican workers who had been caught. There are no legal penalties against employers who knowingly hire undocumented workers, and though a 1982 Senate bill would have imposed fines as high as $10,000 and jail, it failed in the House. It was widely condemned by supporters of agribusiness based on Hispanic labor: A Heritage Foundation report said that imposing sanctions on employers who hire illegal aliens would cause significant economic disruption, and that immigrants, both legal and illegal, have been "net contributors to the nation's economy." It recommended increased enforcement efforts by the U.S. Border Patrol, an increased quota for immigrants, and the establishment of a legal guest program rather than fines for growers. Only between 1 and 2 percent of Hispanic workers are illegal aliens, considerably lower than the five to ten million official estimate.[81]

Because of the outcry against illegal Hispanic aliens a new immigration law passed in 1987 that allows 350,000 "guest workers" into the United States at any one time and grants amnesty to those who entered the country before January 1, 1980. They will eventually be eligible for citizenship. Although the amnesty bill is, in reality, a means to allow growers to keep their low-income workers, it will prove beneficial for the many aliens who have entered the United States for a better life. It will also lead to an increased demand for false documents as more recent arrivals seek to come under the amnesty provisions.

### Puerto Ricans and Cubans

The 1974–75 recession that brought cutbacks in the petrochemical industry left the island of Puerto Rico in permanent recession. *Puertoriqueños*, pushed out by the recession and encouraged to migrate to the mainland, came in great numbers. However, life was little better for them: In 1976 over 16 percent of Puerto Rican men and 22 percent of Puerto Rican women were unemployed. Except for Native Americans, Puerto Ricans are the poorest of all people of color in the United States. In 1980, when there were two million *Puertoriqueños* on the mainland, their median income was $9,900, one-half the national average.[82]

Puerto Ricans in the United States are discriminated against in more than employment and housing. A federally funded survey by the Hispanic

Health Council found that of 153 women in Hartford, Connecticut, fully half have been sterilized. Women told interviewers they had signed consent forms without understanding them. The rate of sterilization in Puerto Rico has been between 30 and 35 percent for many years, encouraged by the government as a means of controlling population and welfare costs.[83] Sterilization for poor women of all ethnicities is a pervasive though usually undocumented reality of welfare life.

Among Puerto Rican activist groups are ASPIRA, which tries to provide educational opportunities for young people, the Puerto Rican Legal Project, the Puerto Rican Defense Fund, the League of Puerto Rican Women, the Puerto Rican Teachers Association, the Puerto Rican Forum, and the Puerto Rican Family Institute.

### Cuban Immigrants

A more recent group of Hispanic peoples came to the United States from Cuba, after Castro's revolution. In the first wave, those who came were the professional and monied classes fleeing from the nationalization of their wealth. They were, therefore, extremely conservative. In 1980, a new influx began of people poorer and less well educated.[84] Unable to find work, they have swelled the welfare rolls and competed with Miami's Afro-American low-wage workers. The tensions between the two groups are severe, sometimes resulting in riots: In 1980 a major riot broke out in Miami, with three days of extensive burning and looting. It left sixteen dead, four hundred injured, and caused $100 million in property damage.[85] In Miami alone, by 1982 Cubans constituted 39 percent of the population as compared to 44 percent white and 17 percent Afro-American. Despite the needs of this most recent wave of immigration, the government has taken few steps to deal with the pressures beyond increasing law and order forces.

### Afro-Americans

Although significant gains were won for people of color in the 1960s, there have been real problems in enforcing civil rights. A major issue during the 1970s was school busing to enforce desegregated education. In 1971, in the *Swann v. Charlotte-Mecklenburg Board of Education* decision, the Supreme Court upheld busing. However, white people continued to oppose it as being against the "neighborhood school"—a thin veil for racism, since at least 44 percent of all children regardless of color ride buses to school and fewer than 4 percent of all children are bused for the purposes of desegregation.[86] While some school districts quietly and effectively integrated their schools, many continued the battle into the 1980s. Currently, the issue has all but disappeared not because schools are integrated but because there is little enforcement. In the same way, equal housing opportunities and fair employment practices get little attention today.

Afro-Americans, despite educational gains, remain unemployed and underemployed at far greater rates than do white people—consistently double the unemployment. In 1970, 56 percent of young Afro-Americans 25 to 29 years of age were high school graduates, and 10 percent had college degrees. In 1979, 75 percent had high school diplomas and 21 percent had at least some college. By 1980, the Afro/Caucasian differential in years of school had effectively ended. However, this has not significantly increased the chances of employment for Afro-Americans.[87] In recessions, they lose jobs at twice the rate of white workers—last hired, first fired. Official estimates of unemployment seriously underestimate real joblessness, subemployment, and underemployment. Those not counted, according to a nationwide study in 1980, were discouraged workers—off the official unemployment rolls because they stopped trying (3.5 percent); part-time workers (5.4 percent); and full-time workers at poverty wages (9.5 percent). This brings the real unemployment rate significantly above official levels. In the 1981–83 recession, Afro-American unemployment generally went above 20 percent and, in some areas, for young men between ages 17 and 25, it soared to over 50 percent.[88]

While few Afro-Americans have reached political eminence, a few have become leaders—among them Barbara Jordan, congresswoman from Texas; Shirley Chisholm who in 1972 declared her candidacy for presidency; Andrew Young, formerly an aide to Martin Luther King, Jr., the U.S. representative to the United Nations and then Democratic mayor of Atlanta; and Reverend Jesse Jackson, who launched a powerful but unsuccessful bid for presidency in 1984 under the banner of the Rainbow Coalition. Afro-American mayors include Marion Berry, Washington, D.C.; Tom Bradley, of Los Angeles; and Richard Hatcher of Gary, Indiana.

Violence against people of color continues, triggered by economic recessions. There is now a resurgence of the Ku Klux Klan, in media coverage if not in numbers. By 1970, Klan membership was down to an estimated two thousand, but by spring of 1976 it was reinvigorated, growing, and engaged in activities

> such as infiltrating the Marine Corps, protesting busing in Boston and Louisville, joining the textbook fight in Charlestown, West Virginia, creating a scandal in the New York state prison system, burning crosses from California to Maryland, going to court to sue and be sued, and appearing on national talk shows.[89]

Estimates of Klan membership in the late 1970s ranged from 2,000 to 10,000 members, with from 30,000 to 100,000 sympathizers. There are many "klans" today, each with their own point of view but all united in their race hatred.

Among the major reasons the Klan exists are a belief in white supremacy; fear of loss of jobs to people they believe to be inherently inferior; belief that large numbers of nonwhite immigrants will pollute the national "gene pool"; and hatred of Jews as both a religious ideology (alleged to be the murderers of Jesus) and an economic one (alleged control of banks and money). Their most potent belief is their fundamentalist Christianity, though they espouse no particular denomination. They do espouse traditional values for women, the importance of home and family life, and male supremacy, though they began to admit women (and Catholics) to their membership in the 1970s.[90]

Klans and other white supremacy groups have begun to prepare for a race war. Paramilitary camps span the country, and include significant numbers of neo-Nazis as participants or as trainers. Some have "security forces," run national Klan book services, distribute paramilitary training manuals, and publish books on making bombs, explosives, and so on. The United Racist Front, formed in 1979, is a coalition of the National Socialist Party of America, the National States Rights Party, and the Federated Knights of the Ku Klux Klan. It was implicated in the 1979 Greensboro, North Carolina, incident at which American Communist party members and union officials were slain at an anti-Klan rally.[91]

Right-wing extremists include the Klan, the Aryan Nation, and neo-Nazis, among others. While some authorities believe that such groups are essentially harmless, others feel that violence by the ultraright is a real danger in the United States and point out that one group of the Aryan Nations—the Order, the Sword, and the Arm of the Lord—have robbed banks to support their efforts and killed Jewish talk show host Alan Berg in Denver. Raphael Ezekial, a professor of psychology, says

> they have very dangerous things to tell us: . . . that racism has deep roots, that terror is widespread in this country, and that more people than we like to think can be moved by unsophisticated ideas.[92]

### Women

The women's movement during the 1970s became more politically aware if more fragmented, its values based on a deep-seated conviction that personal problems of women, such as poverty or low-wage work, spring from political causes. The National Organization for Women remained the strongest group. By the late 1970s, membership was nearly a quarter of a million. NOW worked for two major goals: passage of the Equal Rights Amendment (ERA) and the rights of women to control their reproduction through birth control and abortion. ERA was the overt issue, and though there has been much controversy over it, the amendment states simply that

> Equality of rights under the law shall not be denied or abridged by the United States or by any State on account of sex.

In the 1960s, ERA was endorsed by both Presidents Johnson and Nixon. In 1972, the Senate joined the House in approving ERA, and sent it to the states for ratification. Twenty-one ratified it quickly, but by the spring of 1973, a significant counterattack had begun, stalling it three short of the needed three-fourths approval. In response to the backlash, some states even began rescinsion processes. ERA is, for all practical purposes, a dead issue in the 1980s.

Perhaps the strongest foe of ERA was Phyllis Schlafly, a woman attorney, who insisted that ERA would bring such horrors as a military draft for women, unisex toilets, and enforced lesbianism, and force women who were dependent on men into the labor market. Her charismatic leadership mobilized women to fight against ERA and convinced politicians in Nebraska to rescind their earlier vote for ERA and to defeat it in Alabama. By the late 1970s, she was leading all the anti-ERA campaigns in the fifteen unratified states.[93]

To counteract women's liberation movements, antifeminist organizations began. For example, Happiness for Women (HOW) was created in 1971. Within a year it boasted ten thousand members and by 1981 had fifteen thousand. It is "dedicated to the preservation of the family, preservation of the masculine role as provider, and preservation of the feminine role as wife, mother, and homemaker." Members support

> God's divine plan, the family structure, removal of Communist and Socialist teachings from the schools, removal of radical elements of Women's Liberation Movement teachings from the schools, teaching the joys of womanhood to young girls, preservation of femininity, restoration of morality, elimination of drug abuse, return to patriotism, and the election to government of men and women dedicated to God, Family, and the Country.[94]

Perhaps the most influential among antifeminist groups, however, have been the New Right and the Moral Majority, who believe that feminism is the primary cause of the present breakdown in family and marriage patterns because it takes away women's "right" to stay in the home. Moreover, they believe feminism to be anti-god and that, because it rejects male supremacy, it must be eliminated so that traditional values can be restored. The groups are particularly concerned with freedom of reproductive choice, sex education, and abortion, for they believe these are the province of church and family. Abortion, of course, concerns the sacredness of life, and although many of these people support both the death penalty and massive arms buildups, this has become the transcendant moral issue in the fight against feminism. Ironically, the groups also oppose public assistance that might support unwanted children. Some claim these groups have as members fifty million conservative Protestants, thirty million Catholics, and millions of allies among Mormons, Orthodox Jews, and members of fringe sects.[95]

Although our society has voiced great concern over the growing number of teenagers who become pregnant without being married, the moral issue of religious control seems to outweigh worry about unwed pregnancies. In fact, out-of-wedlock pregnancy supports moral control in the home, because it provides a long-lasting punishment for those who disobey and keeps young women either out of the job market or on call in the secondary job market. The situation for women of color is slightly different, because parents of unwed pregnant teenagers seem more supportive of their children and less moralistic, but the results in terms of keeping them and their children under economic control is the same.

About 35 percent, or almost five million, girls age 13 to 19 are sexually active, as are 75 percent of young men ages 15 to 21. About 80 percent of these sexually active teens use some kind of birth control, although only about half are prescribed and physician-supervised.

Between 1963 and 1978, premaritally conceived births increased 25 percent for white teenagers and 50 percent for Afro-American teenagers. Between 1975 and 1978, 6 of 10 children born to white teenagers and 9 of 10 born to Afro-American teenagers were premaritally conceived.[96] Between 1970 and 1978, out-of-wedlock births rose from 399,000 to 515,000, representing nearly 11 percent of all live births in 1970 and 15.5 percent in 1978. (Of 1 million pregnant teens in 1978, 270,000 induced abortions and 140,000 had miscarriages.) By 1979, there were 597,800 premaritally conceived births. Although rates for Afro-Americans declined, they remained about six times that for whites. By the mid-1970s, girls aged 15 to 19 years had about half of all out-of-wedlock births. Bell notes that

> if current trends continue, four of every ten girls will be pregnant sometime during their teen years; one out of every eight will have an abortion; and one out of every four will become a mother . . .[97]

During the 1960s, white unwed teenagers began to keep their babies rather than giving them up for adoption. Bell notes that white illegitimate babies were the major source of supply for the adoption market: As many as 76 percent of white unwed teens kept their babies in 1976, increasing to 93 percent by 1978. At present, only about 10 percent give up babies for adoption, creating a real shortage for white adoptive parents.[98]

Despite the religious backlash against birth control programs, many have been funded: The Bureau of Indian Affairs made family planning available in 1965; in 1966 the Children's Bureau began to support family planning through state health departments; the 1967 OEO amendments included family planning funds for the parents division of Head Start; and in 1975 the Office of Child Development initiated research and demonstration projects. Under Medicaid and through family planning clinics such as Planned Parenthood, funds came from Title XX or Title X of the Public Health Act. Sixty-three new fertility-related laws were passed in 1981, the largest number since 1973.[99] In 1983, influenced by pressures from far-right groups, the Department of Health and Human Services proposed that family planning clinics receiving Title X funds should be required to notify parents before prescribing contraceptives for teenagers. This "squeal rule" triggered some sixty-five thousand protests, four to one against the regulation, but was passed and implemented in many states.

The abortion issue strikes at the heart of the reactionary religio-political system of the United States. Despite the fact that abortions are less dangerous than is carrying a fetus to term, especially for teenagers, legal abortions are increasingly restricted. In the 1950s and 1960s, many states had reformed abortion laws to permit it in certain instances. In 1970 New York passed laws to allow it for any reason in the first trimester. Still, laws restricted abortion until the *Roe v. Wade* decision in 1973 upheld women's rights to decision over abortion in the first two trimesters of pregnancy, declaring that the interest of the woman was paramount in the first three months. The court explicitly rejected the idea that life begins at conception and the fetus is a person protected by the Fourteenth Amendment.

After *Roe v. Wade,* legal abortions approached one-third of all pregnancies. New programs developed to help women with their abortion decisions, the most useful of which was probably that Medicaid would pay for abortions for poor women. However, the conservative backlash increased, and in 1976 the Hyde Amendment, or Human Life Amendment, was proposed—a constitutional amendment against abortion. It was defeated, but Congress imposed increasingly strict limits on the use of federal funds for abortions. Finally, in the 1980 *Harris v. McRae* decision, the Supreme Court ruled that states were no longer required to use Medicaid funds for abortions for otherwise eligible women except for rape or unless the pregnancy endangered the woman's life. The number of Medicaid-funded abortions dropped from 300,000 in 1977 to 17,983 in 1981.[100]

### Gay Liberation

Gay Liberation began in the late 1940s and early 1950s with the founding of the Mattachine Society in Los Angeles and the Daughters of Bilitis in New York and San Francisco. These organizations remained generally hidden from public awareness because homosexuality itself is, in many areas, illegal, and homosexuals are almost always subject to persecution. The organizations dedicated themselves to research and education rather than to the active repeal of antihomosexual laws. In the 1960s and 1970s, gay liberation emerged as a political issue.

Homosexual men and women comprise about 15 percent of the nation's population. As a group, they have been systematically deprived of rights to jobs and other personal freedoms without regard to their capabilities or needs, simply because of their sexual preference. Frank Kameny, who led the fight for gay liberation, stated in 1964

> I do not see the NAACP and CORE worrying about which chromosome and gene produced black skin or about the possibility of bleaching the Negro. I do not see any great interest on the part of B'nai B'rith Anti-Defamation League in the possibility of solving the problems of anti-semitism by converting Jews to Christians. In all of these minority groups, we are interested in obtaining rights for our respective minorities as Negroes, as Jews, and as homosexuals. Why we are Negroes, Jews, and homosexuals is totally irrelevant, and whether we can be changed to white Christians or heterosexuals is equally irrelevant.[101]

Active resistance began when, in New York, police raided a gay bar and patrons fought back. This incident is widely accepted as the beginning of Gay Liberation, the major group of which is the Gay Activist Alliance, which uses a nonviolent strategy to persuade gays to perceive themselves as an oppressed minority.

The gay movement took on greater national significance with the formation first of the Lambda Defense and Educational Fund in 1972 and then the National Gay Task Force in 1973. The Lambda Fund defended civil rights of homosexuals in employment, housing, education, child custody, and the administration of justice, working solely through the court systems. It paid for legal representation on behalf of homosexual clients and maintained a national network of attorneys willing to take cases pertaining to homosexual rights. In 1986, Lambda counted over seven thousand people as regular contributors. The National Gay Task Force, a clearinghouse for federal legislation affecting gays, claims ten thousand members. It coordinates the activities of local gay groups, works with the media to facilitate a more accurate portrayal of homosexuality, and assists foundations and associations working with the homosexual community. It was the prime organizer of the October 1979 March on Washington for Lesbian and Gay Rights attended by just under a quarter of a million people.[102] Although few gains have been made for homosexuals, since 1983 Wisconsin and most of the larger U.S. cities have enacted gay rights laws and more than half the states have repealed sodomy statutes.[103]

Since the Reagan administration, there has been little progress toward gay liberation. As the Moral Majority grows in strength, so does heterosexism and hostility. The epidemic of Acquired Immune Deficiency syndrome (AIDS) is a case in point. Despite the fact that its consequences are always fatal, not until it began to infect heterosexuals did the national government begin to fund research adequately. In fact, AIDS among homosexuals has been labeled as God's curse against their sins and trivialized with jokes reaching as high as the presidential level.[104] Since it is a sexually transmitted disease, the new religious right and many persons in the political right have become outspoken against measures considered necessary to contain the disease such as condoms and sex education. They preach abstinence and assert that AIDS is God's punishment for the promiscuous.

## CONCLUSION: TIGHTENING THE REINS

Throughout the 1970s, conservativism increased. Where legislation could not be denied, as in the case of civil rights, it was supported. However, in dealing with women, children, people of color, and the poor, programs became increasingly more restrictive and even hostile. The hostility was augmented with the upsurge of groups devoted to male supremacy and their own brands of morality, ranging from such physically violent groups as the Ku Klux Klan and neo-Nazism to ideologically violent groups such as the Far Right or the Moral Majority. The election of Ronald Reagan in 1980, and his reelection in 1984, should have been no surprise to those watching the reactionary trends so evident in politics. With the overt backing of both Far Right and Moral Majority, his election became a mandate to enforce certain ideological beliefs, among them the Christianization of American politics, the return to marriage and family norms, the breakup of social programs that supported people outside marriage and outside the work ethic, and the retreat from civil rights. In addition, his adherence to a war ethic—a "refusal to blink"—is "reasonable" given the reactionary trends of the 1970s. To intervene in sovereign nations for the sake of the economy, or to end the world in defense of a principle are not beyond the pale of such beliefs.

## STUDY QUESTIONS

1. What does OASDHI mean? SSI? AFDC? Explain who the programs are for and what kinds of income maintenance they provide.
2. What was Title XX of the Social Services Act? How did it provide for the poor? What were some unanticipated consequences in terms of the social work profession?
3. What happened to the civil rights gained in the 1960s under President Nixon and later under Ford? Carter? Reagan?
4. How did the status of women evolve from World War II into the 1980s? What is the present status of women?
5. How did the status of people of color change during the 1960s and 1970s? Is it better now or worse than in the 1970s?
6. What changes occurred in the social work profession in the Nixon, Ford, and Carter years? What effect did the social work profession have on social welfare? How did it affect AFDC?

## FOOTNOTES

[1] June Axinn and Herman Levin, *Social Welfare: A History of the American Response to Need*, 2nd ed., (New York: Harper and Row, 1982), p. 236.

[2] Ibid., p. 289.

[3] John Ehrenreich, *The Altruistic Imagination*, (Ithaca: Cornell University Press, 1985), p. 202.

[4] Ibid., p. 203.

[5] Beulah Compton, *Introduction to Social Welfare and Social Work: Structure, Function, and Process*, (Homewood, Ill: Dorsey Press, 1980), p. 496.

[6] Ralph Dolgoff and Donald Feldstein, *Understanding Social Welfare*, 2nd ed., (New York: Longman Press, 1984), p. 272.

[7] Axinn and Levin, *Social Welfare*, p. 292.

[8] Andrew W. Dobelstein, *Politics, Economics, and Public Welfare*, (Englewood Cliffs, N.J.: Prentice Hall, 1980), pp. 150–151.

[9] Joseph Heffernan, *Introduction to Social Welfare Policy*, (Itasca, Ill.: F. E. Peacock Publishers, 1979), p. 247.

[10] Gerald Handel, *Social Welfare in Western Society*, (New York: Random House, 1982), pp. 152–153.

[11] Axinn and Levin, *Social Welfare*, p. 289.

[12] "Current Operating Statistics," *Social Security Bulletin*, Vol. 46, no. 7, (Washington, D.C.: U.S. Government Printing Office, July 1983), p. 20.

[13] Ibid.

[14] Aaron Wildavsky, *Speaking Truth to Power: The Art and Craft of Policy Analysis*, (Boston: Little, Brown, and Co., 1979), p. 106.

[15] Francis X. Russo and George Willis, *Human Services in America*, (Englewood Cliffs, N.J.: Prentice Hall, 1986), p. 242.

[16] "Social Welfare Expenditures 1963-1983," *Social Security Bulletin*, Vol. 49, no. 2, (February 1986), p. 20.

[17] Winifred Bell, *Contemporary Social Welfare*, (New York: Macmillan Publishing Co., 1983), pp. 170–171.

[18] Ibid., p. 130.

[19] Russo and Willis, *Human Services*, p. 244.

20Handel, *Western Society*, p. 194.

21Frances Fox Piven and Richard Cloward, *The New Class War: Reagan's Attack on the Welfare State and Its Consequences*, (New York: Pantheon Books, 1982), p. 122.

22Heffernan, *Introduction to Social Welfare Policy*, p. 238.

23Bell, *Contemporary Welfare*, p. 157.

24Compton, *Introduction to Social Welfare*, p. 502.

25Joel P. Handler, *Reforming the Poor*, (New York: Basic Books, 1972), p. 58.

26Robert Morris, *Rethinking Social Welfare*, (New York: Longman Press, 1986), p. 246.

27Bell, *Contemporary Welfare*, p. 130.

28Sar A. Levitan and Clifford M. Johnson, *Beyond the Safety Net*, (Cambridge, Mass.: Ballinger Publishing Co., 1984), p. 78.

29Ibid., pp. 36–37.

30Senator Russell Long, quoted in Dobelstein, *Politics, Economics, and Public Welfare*, p. 129.

31Levitan and Johnson, *Beyond the Safety Net*, pp. 36–37.

32Ibid.

33 Quoting Saul Kaplan, "Support from Absent Fathers of Children Receiving ADC," Public Assistance Report #41, (Washington D.C.: U.S. Government Printing Office, 1969), in Bell, *Contemporary Welfare*, p. 214 footnote.

34Handler, *Reforming the Poor*, (New York: Basic Books, 1972), p. 32.

35Bell, *Contemporary Welfare*, pp. 133–135.

36Ibid., p. 22.

37Compton, *Introduction to Social Welfare*, p. 513.

38Bell, *Contemporary Welfare*, p. 224.

39Ibid.

40Rosemary Sarri, *Under Lock and Key*, (Ann Arbor: National Assessment of Juvenile Delinquency, 1974).

41Kenneth Wooden, *Crying in the Playtime of Others*, (New York: McGraw-Hill Book Co., 1976).

42Russo and Willis, *Human Services*, p. 65.

43Axinn and Levin, *Social Welfare*, p. 289.

44Bell, *Contemporary Welfare*, p. 169.

45Ibid., p. 105.

46Levitan and Johnson, *Safety Net*, p. 124.

47Piven and Cloward, *New Class War*, p. 31.

48Levitan and Johnson, *Safety Net*, p. 118.

49Ibid.

50Ibid., p. 125.

51Joe R. Feagin, *Racial and Ethnic Relations*, (Englewood Cliffs, N.J.: Prentice Hall, 1985), p. 303.

52Dolgoff and Feldstein, *Understanding Social Welfare*, pp. 201–202.

53Compton, *Introduction to Social Welfare*, p. 513.

54Ramsey Clark, *Crime in America: Observations on its Nature, Causes, Prevention, and Control*, (New York: Simon and Schuster, 1970), p. 335.

55D. Stanley Eitzen, *In Conflict and Order: Understanding Society*, 3rd ed., (Boston: Allyn and Bacon, 1985), p. 213.

56Joseph E. Palinski, "Race Relationships in Prison: A Critical Social Work Concern," in Albert R. Roberts, ed., *Social Work in Juvenile and Criminal Justice Settings*, (Springfield, Ill.: Charles C. Thomas Publishers, 1983), p. 364.

57From the Justice Department's Bureau of Justice Statistics, reported in the *Lafayette (Indiana) Journal and Courier*, July 26, 1986, p. A4.

[58]From the American Correctional Association, reported in the *Lafayette (Indiana) Journal and Courier*, September 12, 1986, p. A7.

[59]Feagin, *Racial Relations*, p. 234.

[60]Ibid., p. 195.

[61]Ibid., p. 199.

[62]Eric Treisman, "The Last Treaty," *Harper's Magazine*, February 1975, pp. 37–39.

[63]Ibid., pp. 37–38.

[64]Feagin, *Racial Relations*, p. 193.

[65]Ibid.

[66]Ibid., p. 198.

[67]Ibid., p. 205.

[68]*Lafayette (Indiana) Journal and Courier*, AP report, September 17, 1986, p. A1.

[69]Feagin, *Ethnic Relations*, pp. 190–193.

[70]Ibid., p. 196.

[71]Ibid.

[72]Ibid., p. 191.

[73]Levitan and Johnson, *Safety Net*, p. 119.

[74]Feagin, *Ethnic Relations*, p. 333.

[75]Ibid., p. 340.

[76]Peter Irons, "The Return of the 'Yellow Peril,' " *The Nation*, October 19, 1985, p. 316.

[77]Feagin, *Ethnic Relations*, p. 362.

[78]Ibid., p. 275.

[79]Ibid., p. 265.

[80]Ibid., p. 264.

[81]Ibid., p. 265, and *Lafayette (Indiana) Journal and Courier*, August 22, 1985, p. B3.

[82]Feagin, *Ethnic Relations*, p. 303.

[83]Carol Giacomo, "Sterilization Count Higher than Expected," *Hartford (Connecticut) Courant*, October 13, 1980, pp. A10 and A12.

[84]Feagin, *Ethnic Relations*, p. 351.

[85]Ibid.

[86]Ibid., p. 245.

[87]Ibid., p. 243.

[88]Ibid., p. 232.

[89]Lisa Langenbach, "Modernist and Traditionalist Issue Groups in the American Party System: An Examination of the Realigning Potential of Cultural Issues in Changing Cleavage Structures," unpublished doctoral dissertation, Purdue University, West Lafayette, Indiana, August 1986, p. 128.

[90]Ibid., pp. 138–140.

[91]Ibid., quoting the Anti-Defamation League report, 1981, p. 66.

[92]Kate Kellogg, "The Far-Right Fringe," *Michigan Today*, June 1987, p. 6.

[93]Langenbach, "Issue Groups," p. 167.

[94]Ibid., p. 164, citing Katherine Gruber, *Encyclopedia of Associations*, (Detroit: Gale Research Co., 1981).

[95]Ibid., p. 186, citing Michael Lienesh, "Right Wing Religion: Christian Conservatism as a Political Movement," *Political Science Quarterly*, Vol. 97, 1982, pp. 403–425, esp. p. 404.

[96]Russo and Willis, *Human Services*, pp. 91–92, citing Phipps-Yonas, 1980.

[97]Bell, *Contemporary Welfare*, pp. 121–122.

[98]Ibid., p. 124.

[99]All figures are from ibid., pp. 123–124.

[100]Ibid., p. 123, and Axinn and Levin, *Social Welfare*, pp. 287–288.

[101]Langenbach, "Issue Groups," pp. 75–76, quoting Toby Marotta, *The Politics of Homosexuality*, (Boston: Houghton Mifflin, 1981).

[102]Langenbach, "Issue Groups," pp. 75–81.

[103]Eitzen, *Conflict and Order*, pp. 222–223.

[104]Reagan alluded to gays when he jokingly remarked that Moammar Khadafy should be sent to San Francisco because he wears robes, and an assistant trivialized both gays and AIDS by suggesting that Khadafy be infected with AIDS.

# 12

# THE REACTIONARY VISION

## BITING THE CONSERVATIVE BULLET

The election of President Ronald Reagan in 1980, and his reelection in 1984, was only the tip of a reactionary iceberg affecting every area of American life. Faced with a downward-spiraling economy, Reagan promised to eliminate the proliferation of government regulations that "strangled private enterprise" and to balance the budget, regardless of who had to "bite the bullet." These ideas were not new: Nixon's election in 1968 began to limit the nation's responsibility to the distressed and disadvantaged and to institute new fiscal responsibility. However, although the administrations of the preceding decade deemphasized social spending, they did not advocate the end of the welfare state and in fact increased social funding through revenue sharing.

Reagan's policies constituted a return to the pre-Civil War ideology demonstrated by the Pierce veto (in 1851) of Dix's plan for federal care for the indigent mentally disabled and reversed the trend toward a guaranteed annual income. His goals: to balance the budget without cutting military preparedness and to eliminate social programs except for a "safety net" for the "truly needy." Reagan's basic "safety net program" follows the two-tiered welfare system: those covered by social insurance would generally keep their benefits, though some programs would be cut; but those on public assistance, and the young and the poor, would see programs substantially cut, encouraging their return to work or workfare—working off public assistance.

### Reaganomics

Reaganomics is, basically, a belief in supply-side economics; that is, keeping production and prices high. High production will keep a large supply of goods on the market, people will continue to buy, and this buying will keep the economy going while taxes on the goods will keep the government going. Investment by the government in business via tax breaks, subsidies, and government contracts will add to high productivity, producing new jobs and enabling more buying. What is wrong with the theory is, primarily, that the number of people who can buy high-cost products is very limited, while the great majority who buy the most goods can no longer afford them. The national policy of keeping some unemployment, the Reagan policy of trading unemployment to cut down inflation, and a capital-intensive economy that does not need high employment to begin with means that even higher numbers of people cannot buy.

This bears great similarity to the period before 1929, when businesses were urged to high productivity even though unemployment spiraled. The saving grace today, keeping people from actually starving and therefore rioting, are bank insurances and social programs. Now, even though food may be cans of cat food or dog food, or an endless diet of rice, social insurance and public assistance do provide food. The other factor that operates to keep calm is that, although there are many *men* who are poor, the greatest number in poverty are women and children, who are less likely to rebel violently.

### The New Reagan Morality

According to Bell, Reagan's election heralded a return to

> the old-fashioned virtues of economic individualism, unfettered private enterprise, and a very limited role for government. The social security system, unemployment compensation, public welfare, government intercession in the health care system, food stamps, public education, and the explosion of new community services are vigorously attacked for their overwhelming cost, depressing effect on savings and private investments, and as ill-conceived liberal efforts.[1]

The administration has far-reaching support among conservatives, the elite, and fundamentalist religious groups. The New (Far) Right supports the return to less federal government, free enterprise, and a return to traditional sex roles—men as the economic supporters of the family and women in homemaking and child-rearing roles. The so-called Moral Majority supports political action to enforce morality: Internationally they advocate saving the world from "Godless communism" through U.S. intervention, while domestically they advise legislation against pornography, abortion, and education for birth control, and for prayer in schools and a return to traditional male/female roles in marriage. Both the New Right and the Moral Majority call for the control of women (control of reproduction along with male-dominated marriage), of the poor (especially the working poor), and of those who are "different," whether at home (people of color) or abroad (intervention in foreign governments).

Three morality-based issues permeate Reagan's policies. First is the sanctity of the nuclear family and the maintenance of its traditional male/female roles and statuses. This ideology ignores the fact that two adults working full time at minimum wages remain in poverty in today's economy, or that the number of female-headed families is growing exponentially. Second is the moral value of income-producing labor at any wage. The often-realized threat of taking jobs to other countries for cheaper labor keeps American workers quiet and destroys unions. For women, although their work is encouraged in rhetoric, it only rarely provides a path to earnings sufficient to support their families.

Reagan's third morality stance is less precise—a superpatriotism and religious belief in the God-ordained future of America. Protection of the "American way of life" and "making the world safe for democracy" underlie it and rationalize American hostility toward other countries, belief in an increase in war and war technologies, and a "dare you to cross this line" attitude on the international level. This leads to ever-increasing defense preparation that profits the wealthy while devaluing labor (since it is capital rather than labor intensive). Moreover, it legitimates the increased production of war materiel while cutbacks in social programs and jobs at marginal income encourage citizens to enter the armed forces.

## ECONOMIC AND POLITICAL STATUS IN THE 1980s

In the 1980s, U.S. population is about 235 million, of whom 11 percent are Afro-Americans, less than 1 percent are Native Americans, 6 percent are Hispanics, and 1.5 percent are Asian/Pacific Americans. More than 24 million people are over age 65, and there are nearly 63 million children under age 18. The gross national product for the nation in 1980 was $2,631.7 billion, increasing by September 1985 to $3,915.9 billion. The nation's wealth remains at the top: the top 2 percent earning $100,000 or more a year control

30 percent of all financial assets
50 percent of all stocks in private hands
71 percent of all tax-free bonds
20 percent of all real estate
39 percent of taxable bonds

The wealthiest 6 percent of families own 57 percent of all the nation's wealth while the top 16 percent own 75 percent.[2] Reagan's tax policies virtually abolished corporate income taxes and drastically reduced personal income taxes for the rich. According to Piven and Cloward,

The federal tax structure has been reorganized to promote a massive upward redistribution of income. New investment and depreciation write-offs favor large corporations over small businesses; 80 percent of the benefits go to the 1700 largest corporations (which have generated only 4 percent of all new employment over the past 20 years). . . . An estimated $750 billion in federal revenue over the next five years has been forfeited.[3]

During his first year in office, Reagan slashed business taxes by an estimated $169 billion and reduced individual taxes by $500 billion over six years. Families earning over $100,000 received a tax cut of nearly $9,000.[4] In 1973 the nation's largest corporations paid about $20 billion to foreign governments, double what they paid to the U.S. Treasury, and by 1982 such taxes comprised only about 10 percent of federal revenues. Multinationals can defer U.S. taxes until money is brought into the country (so why bring it in?) and receive dollar for dollar tax credits for foreign taxes.[5]

On the other hand, the average taxes of the poorest one-fifth of Americans rose by 22.7 percent from 1980 to 1984, and a family of four at the poverty line in 1982 paid an average $956 in federal income and payroll taxes.[6] Families below incomes of $10,000 had a net loss of $240 in 1985, while those earning over $80,000 had a net gain exceeding $20,000.[7] Although Reaganomics has attempted to "balance the budget on the backs of the poor" through social program cuts, the real and unrecoverable expenses are patently elsewhere.

The poverty level for a family of four was $7,450 in 1980, and by 1987 was $11,000. By the end of 1982, over 9 million more people were officially in poverty than in 1979, with 5.5 million new people just since 1980. By 1983, 35.5 million people, or 7.3 million families, lived below the poverty line, an increase from 1978 of 38 percent.[8] The poverty rate among white people is from 12 to 14 percent, while among people of color it is about three times that, at 35 to 42 percent. The number of white people in poverty grew 41 percent between 1978 and 1984, probably due to mass layoffs from factories—jobs that were later replaced by automation. Poverty among Afro-Americans rose 25 percent in the same time.[9] The typical Afro-American family, with a median income of $3,397, had less than 10 percent of the assets of the average white family (median income $39,135) and the average Hispanic family's income was $4,913 (1986 figures).[10] Though between 1968 and 1982 the average income of two-earner Afro-American families rose from 73.2 percent to 84.8 percent of white income, their 1982 median income has returned to 55.3 percent that of white, virtually the same as in 1960. Afro-American families headed by women are four and a half times as likely to be poor: Their poverty rate is 67 percent while for white women-headed families it is 40 percent and for Hispanics 43 percent.[11]

In 1982, almost half the income of the bottom half of the population came from public social benefits—Social Security, Supplemental Security Income, veterans' benefits, AFDC, unemployment insurance, or food stamps.[12] Of families in poverty, only one-third receive public assistance and only about 60 percent receive such vendor benefits as food stamps, free lunches, or Medicaid. Two-thirds of these families are white, more than half have at least one worker, and one-fifth has two or more workers. Of poor adults not working, 2.7 million were ill or disabled, 2.3 million were teenagers going to school, and 2.1 million were retired. In 1984, 14.6

million poor people lived in married-couple or male-headed families, and 11.8 million lived in female-headed families. The remainder, 7.2 million, lived alone or with nonrelatives.[13]

## REAGANOMICS AND THE NEW FEDERALISM

Reagan's New Federalism had two facets: reprivatization, in which private charities and churches would take over care of the poor on a local "neighborly" basis; and the assumption by state governments of all costs for Aid to Families of Dependent Children, Supplemental Security Income, and food stamps, while the federal government would take full responsibility for Medicaid. However, it was demonstrated in the Depression that private charities cannot command the resources needed to provide for the poor, and states, particularly in the South, do not have an adequate tax base to provide sufficiently. Unequal levels of care across the nation, now tempered by the influx of federal funds, would have been exacerbated as each state set lower levels for assistance and set eligibility depending on particular local stereotypes and prejudices. Civil rights that were gained just through more money being placed in the hands of the poor would have been lost as state and local governments used their discretion unmodified by federal guidelines, and the move toward a nationwide standard of support through Supplemental Security Income would have ceased. The New Federalism would have eliminated most federal grants for education, training, health, and social services. To replace them, states would have been required to increase their own taxes, a most unlikely situation.

Although Congress refused the proposed state/federal trade of Medicaid for AFDC, SSI, and food stamps, it did allow new interest penalties on states borrowing to cover unemployment insurance deficits; supported lower state shares for Medicaid, thereby reducing federal costs; and placed new eligibility and income limits on many social programs. It did not oppose the withdrawals of support for civil rights actions or policies to deregulate wage rates and occupational health and safety conditions. It supported Reagan cutbacks in social services and income maintenance, allowing about half the cuts he proposed.

In the social service area, Title XX was capped in 1980 at $2.7 billion, which states or localities are required to match at a 25 percent rate. In 1981, under Reagan's Omnibus Reconciliation Act (OBRA), the Social Services Block Grant replaced Title XX, removing the matching requirement and most federal regulations that required services to the poor. The Block Grant consolidated more than ninety categorical programs into four blocks, with a 20 to 25 percent reduction in federal funding for each. Since states no longer had to match funds, this meant a real reduction of 50 percent from the programs, in most cases. It also fostered competition among agencies for scarcer resources—a "divide and conquer" strategy that left social agencies fighting for existence rather than combining their strength for better services. Finally, because private enterprise could compete for the grants, the for-profit service industry began to burgeon, particularly in child care, nursing homes, and for-profit hospitals. Palmer and Sawhill say that:

> The dismantling of the public sector social service delivery system has been defended as a way to obtain cheaper, more effective, more flexible and efficient, and more innovative services. In practice . . . few of these benefits have been realized . . . the more services are contracted out, the less citizen participation found, the less oriented services were to overall service goals, and the more oriented the agencies were toward institutional maintenance goals. Contracted out services were no cheaper than those performed by the public service agency . . . and were more difficult . . . to monitor.[14]

Naturally, states cut their own programs. A study in 1982 of fourteen states and forty local governments showed that only about a fourth of the federal cuts were replaced in employment, job training, compensatory education, health, and social services programs. In fact, some states reaped savings on the cutbacks because of the eliminated 25 percent matching costs.[15] States reported significant increases in mental health problems as programs were reduced at the same time unemployment increased: more than thirty-eight states detailed increases in severe child abuse and molestation, in suicides, and in broken marriages. In 1983, thirty-two states reported less child care than in 1981, with the total expenses for such programs dropping by 14 percent.[16]

However, the worst cuts came in income maintenance, particularly for the AFDC program. They were authorized by the Omnibus Reconciliation Act of 1981 (OBRA), the Tax Equity and Fiscal Responsibility Act of 1982, the Deficit Reduction Act of 1984, and the Gramm Rudman Hollings Bill, in 1986. Cuts were compounded upon one another with each new reduction bill, in the guise that money was being retargeted from the less to the more needy:

> In fact . . . in no entitlement programs were real (inflation-adjusted) benefits increased . . . when eligibility levels were reduced. . . . for the typical AFDC family, combined AFDC, Food Stamps, and Low Income Energy benefits declined nearly a fifth, from 88 percent of the official poverty threshold in 1970 to 71 percent in 1981. . . . State supplements for SSI fell nearly 20 percent.[17]

All social welfare programs were cut back an average of 7 percent during Reagan's first three years, but

> cutbacks totaled 29 percent in child nutrition; 13 percent in welfare and food stamps; 17 percent in compensatory education; and 60 percent in employment and training programs. Spending for means-tested programs [where the poor truly are] dropped from 13.3 percent of total federal expenses in 1980 to 11.1 percent in 1983, though universal programs [social insurance] rose from 40.8 to 42.9 percent.[18]

In 1980, $5.3 billion was cut from social programs, and from 68 to 85 percent of all poor lost income. Legal Services Organizations, gadflies to the administration for bringing class action suits, lost most of their funding. The CETA program was eliminated and less heating assistance was available. Approximately 400,000 to 500,000 families whose adult members worked were put off AFDC, losing extra benefits such as food stamps and Medicaid in the process, and another 300,000 families suffered severe cuts in benefits. States were no longer required to give cost-of-living increases for Supplemental Security Income, sustaining a real money loss for the poorest recipients. Approximately half the disabled on OASDI were cut from the program because of presumed "malingering" or faked disabilities. Planned construction of subsidized public housing and veterans hospitals was reduced, the Vietnam veteran counseling centers were eliminated, and Veterans Administration personnel was cut.

The Reagan cuts have been particularly devastating for children. The average number of children on AFDC per 100 children in poverty dropped dramatically from 71.8 percent in 1979 to only 52.5 percent in 1982, despite the increase of about one million children in poverty.[20] (See Table 12.1.) Low birth weight, prenatal death, and prematurity have increased, especially among children of color, so that now the United States ranks eleventh in infant mortality. According to the Children's Defense Fund,

> In 1984, the Reagan cuts imposed on poor children will save the federal government a million dollars an hour. This must offset new Reagan increases: $9 million an hour on defense, $1 million more on tax breaks for corporations; $10 million more an hour on tax breaks for the wealthy; $2 million more an hour on interest on the national debt, to which we add $23 million an hour.[21]

More than 34 million Americans today are poor—one in seven—and one in five children lives in poverty. Half of all Afro-American children are poor, as are four of every ten Hispanic, Native American, or Asian American children. More than 50 percent of all women-headed households are poor, and in those headed by Afro-American and Hispanic women more than 70 percent are poor. In two-parent homes, one in nine children lives in poverty.[23] In 1982, 2.4 million children lived in families with incomes less than one-third of the poverty level.

The latest cutting bill, Gramm-Rudman-Hollings (GRH) of 1986, was intended to make "fair" across-the-board cuts to end the federal deficit by 1991 if Congress and the President cannot agree on a deficit-reducing budget. It took effect immediately, and for fiscal year 1986 required auto-

**TABLE 12.1    Children below the poverty line 1984**[22]

| | ALL HOUSEHOLDS | | WOMEN-HEADED HOUSEHOLDS | |
|---|---|---|---|---|
| | UNDER 18 | SIX AND UNDER | UNDER 18 | SIX AND UNDER |
| White | 14.7% | 16.8% | 42.7% | 59.1% |
| Black | 44.9 | 48.6 | 67.7 | 74.2 |
| Hispanic | 35.4 | 36.3 | 67.3 | 74.5 |

Source: *American Children in Poverty*, copyright 1984, Children's Defense Fund, 122 C St., NW, Washington, DC 20001, p. x.

matic budget cuts totaling $11.7 million. GRH exempted some key health and income maintenance programs and made modified cuts in others (that is, not across-the-board cuts), but these were already massively cut by earlier bills. Among these were Social Security; AFDC; Child Nutrition; Food Stamps; Medicaid; SSI; Veterans Compensation and Veterans Pensions; the Women, Infants, and Children Nutrition program (WIC); Medicare; federal input into state unemployment benefits; the Social Services Block Grant; and health programs for migrants, veterans, Native Americans, and communities.

Unprotected programs will suffer cuts every year until 1991. They include Head Start; general revenue sharing; rural development; elementary, secondary, and higher education grants; training, employment, and rehabilitation services; low-income energy assistance; special services to elderly and other groups; health research; housing assistance; and consumer/occupational health and safety programs. Most administrative costs (for example, for Medicare) are not exempt, and while these benefits remain intact, administrative cuts ensure long delays and cutbacks in services that require worker-intensive care. In 1987, federal spending for education, employment and training, and social services was reduced by $827 million; Medicare administration by $74 million; low-income energy assistance by $81 million (29 percent); and a $104 million reduction in nonexempt programs such as child support enforcement. New units of housing were reduced between 2,500 and 4,000 from the 97,000 authorized in 1986; and Legal Services, already drastically cut, lost another $13 million.[19]

Although ostensibly half the GRH cuts are from defense and half from nondefense programs, the *percentage amount* for nondefense programs is greater because of a higher base for defense. Also, at least in 1986, President Reagan had wide discretion to exempt some programs and reallocate funds for others. For example, he exempted virtually all military personnel accounts and the entire Strategic Defense Initiative (Star Wars). In addition, the Defense Department has nearly $50 billion in previously appropriated but unobligated funds (therefore nonprogram funds) that are exempt from GRH. Defense authorization is still roughly double 1980 levels, totaling an estimated $268 billion in 1986 (about 6 percent in 1985). Finally, in a clever sleight-of-hand, half the savings from cost-of-living adjustments and pensions were credited toward meeting the defense target. The rationale is that many of those affected are government employees—retired military and civilian defense department personnel and civil service retirees, for example. However, many pensions undergoing cost-of-living cuts are only governmental by a stretch of the imagination—longshoremen's and harborworkers' compensation benefits or black lung disability benefits, for example.[24]

Despite its intent to end the deficit willy-nilly, GRH is another example of voodoo economics. Sixty percent of the present deficit ($131 billion out of $217 billion) stems from tax policies that grant more tax breaks than the budget can afford, and GRH neither broadens the tax base nor brings in more revenues. Supporting a triple-failsafe defense system, with enormous cost overrides and without increased taxes, is another unrecoverable waste. Finally, the enormous tax breaks given to the rich and allowed to multinational corporations, with little if any reinvestment in the government, continue to drain revenue from the nation.

### Reaganomics and Income Maintenance

*Aid to Families with Dependent Children.* Before the Reagan cuts, federal, state, and local governments spent about $14 billion to provide for 3.7 million AFDC families with more than 11 million recipients: 7 million children, 3 million under age 6. Twenty-seven percent of the families were on AFDC less than a year, and 55 percent were recipients for fewer than three years.[25] Only 51.7 percent of poor white and 43.9 percent of poor Afro-American families were on AFDC rolls, and of these, 88 percent were headed by women. As of January 1983, in thirty-six states the combined AFDC and Food Stamp benefit level was less than 75 percent of the poverty level—only eleven states had benefits of more than $400 a month, and many paid less than $200 per month. Mississippi, Texas, Alabama, and South Carolina averaged grants from $96 to $138. In 1983, the average benefit across the nation was $100.20 per person a month—about $3.47 per day for all costs.[26] The average grant for in-home care, therefore, was $1,264.40 per year (compared with foster care at $3,753.69 per child per year and $16,712.55 per year for institutionalization).[27] Cash benefits to over 10.3 million people were cut by 15 percent.[28]

The Reagan restrictions and cutbacks were based on the following: assumed income, windfall income, retrospective budgeting, assets tests, subsidy considerations, support, eligibility caps, age limits, and new work regulations.

#### ASSUMED INCOME

The regulations allowed welfare eligibility workers to assume that recipients had income whether or not they actually received it. This restricted eligibility for many and reduced grant levels for all. Among the sources assumed were

*Stepfathers' income.* While previously stepparent income was not counted against the grant if stepparents were not legally responsible for children in the home, now it must be considered.

*Support from absent parents.* Court-ordered or voluntary support had not been counted unless actually received. Now, it is assumed received. New regulations are in force to collect from absent parents, but in fact poor families often have poor fathers, and taking them to court for support is not likely to work. Even reciprocal state arrangements to return absent fathers are ineffective, since the harboring state reaps little benefit in return for the work. With increasing unemployment nonsupport becomes worse, and the courts are flooded with nonsupport cases brought by welfare departments. The Internal Revenue Service has been given authority to take overdue support payments—at least $150 and three months in arrears—and states can deduct child support from unemployment insurance. For many families, either is too low to matter. Nevertheless, all support is counted against AFDC grants whether received or not.

*Tax credits.*  AFDC mothers are assumed to file income tax returns, whether or not they do; they are assumed to gain tax credits for their child dependents; and those credits are assumed to come on a monthly basis even though they do not. Therefore, future assumed returns are prorated and removed from grants monthly.

*Windfalls.*  One-time large windfalls, such as gifts, insurance benefits, or inheritances are prorated against future AFDC payments and removed from future grants on a monthly basis. Therefore, recipients realize no benefits from them at all.

### ASSETS TESTS

New regulations reduced allowable assets to $1,000, except for home and reasonably priced car. Recipients are required to make monthly reports showing any kind of change, and once more workers may investigate homes and place discretionary values on belongings and resources—this makes refusal of eligibility for noneconomic reasons (such as racism) extremely easy. States must exclude one burial plot and one funeral agreement per family and exempt for six months any real estate the family is trying to sell if they agree to use the proceeds to repay AFDC. Income of parents or guardians of a minor parent must be counted if the minor parent is living in their house.[29]

### ELIGIBILITY CAPS

While OBRA capped eligibility at 150 percent of state needs levels, the Deficit Reduction Act of 1984 increased the gross income limitation from 150 to 185 percent of need. States set the level of need, always lower than poverty levels and particularly low in Southern states, and have the option not to increase it. Those with incomes above the cap are not eligible for AFDC.

### AGE LIMITS FOR CHILDREN

Reagan has lowered age limits at which children can be included in both OASDI and AFDC grants. Previously, children of 18 and those in school of age 21 qualified for grants. Now children over age 16 no longer qualify (for either grant) even if they remain in school. As children are disqualified by age, even if they remain at home under their mother's care, the grant is reduced. This is a tacit expectation that they will join the labor force, even if that means quitting school. Many will join the armed services. Another consequence is that the remaining children in the family sustain a loss in total income, and, as the last child is dropped from the grant, so is the mother, who may have neither the skills nor the ability for self-support and must then rely on either low-wage work or general assistance.

### RETROSPECTIVE BUDGETING

Rather than basing grants on current month's income for mothers who work, grant levels are based on previous months' incomes. Since women usually apply for welfare after they no longer have jobs or money, this effectively causes a waiting period of one or several months. Past wages are prorated at welfare levels; that is, income earned for one or two months in the past, even at minimum wage, is assumed to last much longer at AFDC rates. Of course, the applicants may have no actual money at all, but that is not considered.

### NEW WORK PROVISIONS

*$30 and a third disregard.* The most devastating cut for welfare mothers was probably the elimination of the rule allowing AFDC to disregard the first $30 and one-third of earned income in determining grant levels. Under new regulations, the $30 is taken from their grants after four months and the third of earned income after another eight months—a 100 percent tax rate on earned income. For the year the abbreviated incentives are allowed, reductions apply to net rather than gross income, further reducing the value of the disregard. If they lose their jobs, recipients must wait for twelve months without receiving AFDC before disregards begin again. This cut immediately eliminated many working women from the AFDC program with less than a month's notice. Also, depending on state regulations, they lost Medicaid and food stamp benefits (although states must continue Medicaid for a year following loss of AFDC eligibility and may extend it at option for another six months). This regulation hit particularly hard at the 27 percent of working welfare women and the 13 percent more who are actively seeking work.

Forty percent of all AFDC recipients who leave the program have incomes below poverty levels for at least the following year.[30] A quarter of the respondents in a study by Zinn and Sarri said they had run out of food at least seven times in the year after having lost benefits, and half at least once. A major problem was the loss of Medicaid: one in seven had serious chronic illnesses—cancer, diabetes, epilepsy, hypertension, sickle cell anemia, and arthritis/rheumatism. The problems of loss of income led to further behavior problems for their children: More than a third of the mothers were called in to schools to discuss their children in 1982.[31]

*Standardization of work expenses.*   Now a flat $75 for full-time and $50 for part-time work is allowed before AFDC benefits are reduced, rather than allowing real expenses for tax deductions, health insurance, meals, transportation, and union dues. Child care costs were also capped, at $160 a month for each child regardless of the real costs for child care. As a result, many mothers cannot afford adequate care for their children. For many, it is more responsible to stay on AFDC and remain with their children, even at reduced benefits, than to try to deal with the new Reagan restrictions on the program.

## OTHER REGULATIONS

*Casual and incidental income.*   In the past, such income was not counted against grants, but now AFDC workers have no discretion in allowing tips, small gifts, and so on. Final regulations published in March 1986 denied even the right to sell blood for extra money. The Department of Health and Human Services regulation states that

> Historically, AFDC and adult assistance programs have considered money from the sale of blood as casual and inconsequential income. Most states elected to disregard this type of income . . . [now,] only gifts can be disregarded as casual and inconsequential income. Consequently, it is no longer permissible to disregard money from the sale of blood. . . . In order to promote consistency and uniformity in federal assistance programs, money resulting from the sale of whole blood or blood plasma is to be considered as earned income from employment.[32]

Many blood banks are required to report sales of blood, and in at least some areas, that money is retroactively counted against public assistance grants (both AFDC and SSI).

*Alien regulations.*   Although aliens could previously become welfare recipients if their sponsors were public or nonprofit agencies, now they are deemed to have the income and assets of their sponsors for three years.

*Vendor payments.*   States may now deduct from AFDC grants the value of food stamps and housing subsidies if they exceed the AFDC allowables for these costs. This reduces AFDC benefits by as much as a third in states with low needs standards (principally Southern states).

*Protective payments.*   Under prior law, states provided protective payments to a payee when a caretaking parent was removed from the grant (for failure to register for WIN, employment search programs, or work projects). Now the sanctioned caretaker continues to receive grants if no reasonable protective substitute can be found.

*Pregnancy.*   Previously, pregnant women without children on AFDC were entitled to become covered in their first trimester. That has been moved to the third trimester, eliminating both nutritional and health care through subsistance money and Medicaid. Pregnant women already on AFDC are exempted from work registration and training as of their sixth month of pregnancy.

*Two other AFDC programs are available at state option.*  The first is Emergency AFDC, providing for the time between application for AFDC, when a family has no income, and that of the first regular AFDC check. As of June 1984, twenty-three states, the District of Columbia, Puerto Rico, and the Virgin Islands participated in this program, serving 29,519 families. The second is *AFDC for the Unemployed Parent* (AFDC-UP), in which by June of 1984 twenty-three states, the District of Columbia, and Guam participated. A total of 1,202,556 recipients in intact families were served by AFDC-UP, and of the recipients, 667,540 were children.[33]

Welfare recipients, generally speaking, have work ethics similar to members of the general society. How much they work is not a question of motivation but of the need for child care, the state of their health, and jobs available.[34] The welfare system is like a "revolving door" used by the poor to fall back on when they lose their marginal jobs. The average length of stay on welfare is about twenty-seven months. The majority of welfare families are on AFDC less than four years, and fewer than 8 percent stay on AFDC without interruption for more than ten years. In addition, longitudinal studies have found that children in four of five poverty-stricken families will escape the poverty of their parents. Less than 2 percent live always in poverty, although a quarter are poor at any given time because of random events: business conditions, personal difficulties, structural economic changes.[35]

About eight of ten female-headed households receive public cash transfers, compared with four of ten male-headed households. Although tranfers to women are lower, they are one-third of women's total income as compared to one-tenth the total income in male-headed households. Bell says

> No other western nation has such an expensive assistance program as our AFDC, partly because with lower unemployment rates more women can be self-supporting, and partly because European nations have done more to facilitate paid employment for mothers. But being equally committed to protecting the mother-child bond and the health and adequate care of children, European nations have planned policies and programs with the unique risks and needs of mothers with children in mind.[36]

In countries such as France, East Germany, West Germany, Hungary, and Sweden, there are paid maternity leaves for three, six, or nine months and, in Hungary, up to three years. In Sweden both mother and father are eligible for full- or part-time leaves. All-day preschools for children ages 3 to 6 are part of the regular educational system and are available whether mothers work or not. Family allowances, day care, and relatively extensive programs for toddlers also keep families and children from poverty.[37]

## Supplemental Security Income, General Assistance, and Poor Relief

*Supplemental Security Income.*  In 1985, over four million people received *Supplemental Security Income* (SSI). More than 60 percent were disabled, over 33 percent were aged, and the remaining were blind. SSI grants totaled $929.5 million, including both state and federal shares, and the average yearly grant was $2,709. SSI for the blind was relatively higher, at $3,300 per year, while the grant for the disabled was $3,117 and for the aged $1,960. The average monthly payment was $225.09.[38] The new procedures for SSI were the same as for AFDC, including retroactive and windfall payments, workfare, and loss of casual or inconsequential earnings such as blood donations.

*General Assistance.*  General Assistance, the state supplementary program for those not qualifying for other income maintenance programs, had 1,386,043 recipients in June 1984. Grant amounts vary by states in this program, but they are all well below AFDC and SSI grant levels. The program primarily serves intact families with incomes below AFDC standards of need and childless indigent single men and women who are socially disabled—unable to find or hold jobs, transients, the homeless, those with substance abuse problems—and do not qualify for OASDI. Displaced homemakers who cannot find sufficient work, often because of age and sex discrimination, are thrown onto General Assistance when their children leave home, disqualifying them for AFDC or OASDI.

*Poor Relief.*  Only Indiana has Poor Relief, the extremely discretionary substitute for general assistance. It is administered without real accountability or state controls by 1,008 elected township officials.

### Old Age Survivors and Disability Insurance

Because of the deficit in the OASDI account in 1981, new regulations postponed cost-of-living adjustments (COLAs) for six months; increased the voluntary premiums of Medicare; placed a tax on one-half of all Social Security benefits that, when added to tax-exempt earnings, exceeded $25,000 for one person or $32,000 for couples; raised the amount subject to withholding taxes for the years 1984, 1988, and 1989; raised the retirement age to 66 by 2009 and 67 by 2027; and decreased future benefit levels to 70 percent for retirement before age 67.[39] Taxes were increased for both employers and employees, and federal workers, other governmental workers, and the President became covered. States or local governments within the OASDI system were forbidden to leave. Higher bonuses for delayed retirement will start in 1990, raising from 3 percent to 8 percent in the year 2008.[40]

Over 37 million people were receiving OASDI benefits in December 1986. Most—more than 30 million—were aged. Average monthly benefits for retired workers and their dependents were $488.44. For the disabled, grants averaged $487.86; for aged widows and widowers, $444.09; and for children of deceased workers, $366.41.[41] Administration rulings delayed COLAs for these groups for six months, money that is nonrecoverable for the beneficiaries. Also, COLAs will be set for the future to either price or wage increases, whichever are lower (rather than actual cost of living increases).[42]

Taxes for Social Security have been raised, from $7.05 of the first $37,800 of all earnings (previously just income) in 1985 to $7.65 in 1986.[43] To prevent failure to report earnings, the Social Security Administration now identifies categories likely to be overpaid (primarily disability grants) and monitors them more closely. New rules make resident aliens subject to the same withholding taxes as U.S. citizens, while nonresidents pay a 30 percent tax on half of all earnings.[44]

The disabled have suffered disproportionately under presumptions that the reason for high disability rolls was malingering or poor management rather than true disability. Disability reviews, beginning in 1980, increased termination from the programs fourfold. Sixty percent of those cut off won reinstatement, demonstrating their disqualifications were in error. Many were severely hurt by their inabilities to support themselves during the disqualified time, although the government saved 10 percent on grant monies paid out. However, new medical screening costs are estimated at between $27 million and $69 million. Claimants were required to use federally appointed doctors, who overbilled and marked up lab fees by 300 to 400 percent. A small number of the thousands of doctors hired— 108—did 22 percent of all the exams and earned an average of $348,672. Six doctors earned more than $1 million each, and one received $3 million for one year.[45] Congress has recently enacted legislation that is more cautious in disqualifying disabled beneficiaries.

### Unemployment Insurance and the "New Poor"

Beginning in 1979, the unemployment rate began to climb, from 5.7 percent to 10.8 percent by December 1982. By May 1980, with national unemployment at 7.8 percent, white unemployment was 5.8 percent, Afro-American unemployment was 11.8 percent, and Hispanic unemployment was 8.9 percent. For teenagers, the unemployment rate was 19.2 percent, but the rate for minority youth was nearly 60 percent. A total of 12 million people lost their jobs, but actual unemployment went far beyond those statistics: 6.6 million workers could find only part-time employment and 1.8 million were "discouraged workers," people no longer on the official unemployment rolls.[46] According to Ehrenreich, the actual number of unemployed reached more than 35 million, or 23.9 percent of the working population.[47]

In 1976, with 7.6 million persons unemployed, unemployment insurance benefits were $31 billion. However, in 1982, with 10 million unemployed, less than $24 billion was paid out.[48] In 1983, $30 billion was paid in unemployment insurance.[49] The weekly average unemployment benefit was $128.98 in 1983, and 50 percent of all families experiencing unemployment received no federal assistance. Because the Reagan administration reduced the number of weeks of unemployment insurance available by thirteen (in most states), the unemployed received less in benefits and were more quickly forced into marginal jobs. Sixty percent did not receive unemployment benefits, and 82.8 percent received no food stamps. Of the officially unemployed—those registered with unemployment insurance offices—only 42 percent received unemployment benefits, and those payments averaged only 46 percent of before-tax earnings.[50] In addition, claimants owing child support had amounts deducted by local offices and forwarded to the appropriate state or local child support enforcement agency.[51] Benefits are subject to tax if they, along with other earnings, exceed certain levels. In 1982 these levels were $12,000 a year for individuals and $18,000 for couples.

The 1981-83 recession was not solely a "natural" economic cycle but a Reagan administration decision to trade unemployment for a reduction in inflation. Economists say that an unemployment increase of at least a million for two years will reduce inflation by a single percentage point. According to Levitan,

> Making a conscious decision to battle inflation with longer unemployment lines, President Reagan precipitated a deep recession which brought the highest jobless rates since the 1930s and transformed the marginal income losses of rising prices into the total income losses of forced idleness. His sweeping tax and spending reductions further skewed income distribution in favor of the wealthy, slashing federal benefits for low income Americans while significantly reducing the tax liability of the rich.[52]

Since many of the poor already worked to their physical and social capacities, real employment increased less than 1 percent.[53]

The primary labor force is that which employs people permanently, at reasonable wages and with fringe benefits, and entitles them to Social Security programs. The secondary labor force includes people working at marginal jobs, or in part-time or low-paying jobs. Businesses employing people from the secondary labor force are usually small and highly competitive (such as fast-food chains) and hire for less than full time at low wages, firing their employees before they qualify for fringe benefits or for Social Security programs. Earning $4.74 per hour, a worker is at the poverty threshold. A worker earning minimum wage has a yearly income of $6,968, well below the poverty line. Over one-third of all jobs are now in the secondary sector and are predominantly held by women, youths, and people of color.[54] In addition to forcing many regular workers into the marginal labor market, these economic policies also threw thousands more into it through cuts in AFDC, SSI, and OASDI, and by ending CETA, which had employed 400,000 workers.

Even in full-time covered work, workers' control over their employment is rapidly waning. During the Reagan recession, many in the age group 40–60 found themselves unemployed after years on the job, at a time when their earnings should have been highest, leading to future high Social Security benefits. Companies took that time to "retool" and roboticize their factories, and the jobs disappeared. Many of the unemployed found new jobs, but at salaries significantly lower than former earnings. For example, in electronics the wage is typically 61 percent of that for factory jobs. Such "job skidding" produces not only current low income but will produce poverty among the aged in the future. Between 1979 and 1984, an estimated 11.5 million people lost their jobs through plant closings, job relocations, and technical innovations.[55]

Another group of the "new poor" are farmers. While small farms were dying, the Senate nevertheless supported large agribusiness by killing amendments to put a $500,000 lid per farmer on government subsidies, where some operations collected as much as $20 million in government support (1986).[56] As in the past, the support of agribusiness and new technology forced small farmers off their farms, out of ownership positions, and into whatever labor they were able to find.

## REAGANOMICS AND NUTRITION

According to Raymond Wheeler,

> We can document decreases in illness, in infant and maternal deaths, in premature births, and in the incidence of iron deficiency anemia and retarded growth among children of the poor . . . these reductions in illness and death have accrued most significantly by women, blacks, and American Indians, and in the ten states with the highest incidence of poverty and malnutrition.[57]

The AFDC program itself provided more food on a regular basis than most poor people would otherwise have had, and cutting it threw millions into hunger. Beyond that, a major target of Reaganomic cuts were programs of nutrition: Food stamps, school meals, nutrition for women and children.

*Food Stamps.* By 1982, almost eight million persons of the twenty-two million receiving food stamps lost their eligibility, of whom 54 percent were children under age 18 and 78 percent were unable to work because of age, disability, or dependent care. New eligibility regulations totally excluded strikers and temporarily unemployed workers from the food stamp rolls and eliminated more than 200,000 students, leaving an estimated 50,000 students still eligible. These cuts "saved" the government an estimated $7 billion but took their toll in human well-being. Households receiving food stamps have an average income of $3,900, and 90 percent of food stamp recipients are below the official poverty line. With food stamps, households buy 50 percent more food than they would otherwise.

Almost 70 percent of food stamp families are headed by women. In 1980 the average monthly food stamps per person was $34.34, or about 44 cents a meal. Even if this amount—an average of $1,638—were added to a family's income, it would still fall about $960 below the poverty threshold.[58] Half of food stamp spending goes to retail food markets and 36 percent to the American farmer, probably over $2 billion in 1981.[59] Income eligibility for food stamps and other programs of child nutrition, such as school lunches, has been set by the Reagan administration at 130 percent of AFDC need.

*The School Lunch Program.*  This, the government's largest child nutrition effort, suffered cuts of 30 percent, dropping 3 million children. In 1982, despite the cuts, it still served 23.6 million children at a cost of $2.9 billion. However, prices were raised, thereby eliminating many children marginally able to buy lunches, and the quantity and quality of the lunches was lowered dramatically. One example of taking food from the mouths of children was the redefinition of catsup and relish as "vegetables" that would provide children a "balanced meal." Until 1981 the goal of this program was to provide one-third of a child's nutritional needs, and the Department of Agriculture concluded that poor children got one-third to one-half of their daily nutrition from school lunches. Lekachman says

> In the new order, pickle relish and catsup count as vegetables, jam masquerades as a serving of fruit, cookies and cakes define themselves as bread, and the egg in the cake substitutes for meat. A hearty lunch for an adolescent might be two slices of cheese, one-fourth of a cup of grape juice, one cupcake, a cup of whole milk (four, not eight ounces), and a quarter cup of canned peaches.[60]

In response to public outrage, the administration withdrew the changes in school lunch standards, but they have crept back as school lunch sizes decrease and their costs increase. The school breakfast program, a supplemental program usually carried out by community groups or agencies with surplus commodities, some federal funding, and private donations, now reaches only about one-third of eligible children, while the summer lunch program reaches only 16 percent.

*The Women, Infants, and Children Nutrition Program.*  The Women, Infants, and Children Nutrition Program (WIC) also suffered a 30 percent reduction. It had been available, at the option of state departments of public welfare and local charitable agencies, to provide supplementary food grants for women during pregnancy and children to age 4. All monies except for administration costs came from the federal government, and the only regulation, aside from means-tested eligibility, was that a local agency administer the program. There were numerous counties throughout the nation that refused to include WIC programs in their social offerings, thereby limiting the use of WIC in any case. Nationally, only 2.4 million—fewer than half of those eligible—received WIC food (valued at an average of $378) in 1983. Yet even that small amount markedly reduced the incidence of low birth weight, with results in savings for long-term care estimated at three dollars for every dollar spent. The cost of WIC is about a dollar a day per recipient. The Center for Disease Control found that WIC reduced anemia in infants and helped to prevent retarded physical growth, susceptibility to contagious diseases, and mental retardation. The nutrition WIC provides saves $20,000 to $40,000 in remedial care for low-birth-weight infants, $1,400 a week for hospitalization for undernourished children, and between $.5 million and $1 million over a lifetime for children requiring institutional care for retardation.[61]

Hunger is an ever-present problem for millions in the United States today. And it is not only a statistic: it is real and painful. In a recent book, a woman confides

> I keep praying I can have the will to save some of my food so I can divide it up and make it last. . . . On Friday, I held over two peas from the lunch. I ate one pea on Saturday morning. Then I got into bed with the taste of food in my mouth and I waited as long as I could. Later on in the day I ate the other pea.

> When there are bones I keep them . . . I am almost ashamed to tell you, but these days I boil the bones till they're soft and then I eat them. Today there were no bones.[62]

## REAGANOMICS AND HEALTH CARE

All public health care programs—including Medicare, Medicaid, temporary disability insurance, worker's compensation, general hospital and medical care, armed forces and dependents care, school health, other public health activities, veterans' hospital and medical care, medical vocational rehabilitation, and OEO health and medical care—cost $144,204,000 in 1983. Private costs beyond that were $202,921,000.[63] By 1986, reductions under Gramm-Rudman-Hollings for community health centers, migrant health centers, and the Indian Health service costs totaled $10 million.

*Medicaid.*    Medicaid is the major health program for the poor. Since Reagan took office, every state has cut back on its matching funds, thus allowing massive federal cutbacks. In addition, eligibility for Medicaid was cut with AFDC and SSI eligibility, and 700,000 children were thrown off. State options were reduced: Children in poor two-parent families covered before the Reagan administration until age 18 (21 if still in school) are now covered only to age 5. Medicaid and AFDC throughout a child's first year of life costs about $5,378, but only 73 children of every 100 on AFDC receive Medicaid. Total cost for Medicaid in 1983 was $36,327,000, and, according to the Congressional Budget Office, the estimated costs for Medicaid for three years are $520 million—about half what we estimate the Defense Department wastes annually through inefficient spare parts procurement.[64]

*Maternal and Child Health Program.*    Title V of the Social Security Acts has suffered a 47 percent cutback. Maternal and Infant Care (MIC) programs are especially hard hit, at a time when there is an 84 percent increase in demand related to high unemployment. A survey of ten states found that about 90 percent of MIC clinics either had funds frozen (a real money cut due to inflation of about 20 percent) or had budgets reduced. In Kentucky and Maine, budget reductions were at 50 percent, and in several states staff were cut by 50 percent. Only two of twenty clinics were still able to cover hospitalization for a majority of clients. In Florida, only 38 percent of 65,000 pregnant low-income women got comprehensive prenatal care after the cuts, and in Michigan 10,000 of 140,000 delivering mothers had fewer than five of twelve recommended prenatal visits. Total outlay for Maternal and Child Health in 1983 was $1,009,000.[65] The U.S. infant mortality rank fell from sixth place to a tie for last place among the twenty industrialized nations as nearly 40,000 of the 3.6 million babies born in 1984 died before their first birthday. Afro-Americans are nearly twice as likely as whites to die before age 1. Babies whose mothers receive no prenatal care are three times more likely to suffer low birth weight and greater risks of birth defects and death, and at the current rate of funding for such aid the nation will fail to meet nearly all the Surgeon General's 1990 objectives for reducing infant mortality, the number of low birth weights, and the number of women who receive late or no prenatal care. That failure will result in more than 300,000 children of low birth weight before 1990, at a cost of $2.1 billion for medical care during the first year of life.[66]

*Block Grant Programs.*    Block Grant Programs for health served seventeen million pregnant women and children in 1981, and the Early Screening and Diagnosis Program through AFDC, along with Medicaid payment for early treatment, served more than ten million poor children. Since the Reagan cuts, a study has demonstrated that of thirty-three states reporting, twenty-six showed an increased percentage of women receiving late or no prenatal care, especially nonwhite women. Between 1981 and 1982, death rates for all infants increased in eleven states, and the death rate of infants in Washington, D.C., exceeds that in Cuba and Jamaica. Some cities are even worse—two census tracts in Baltimore show infant death rates as high as 56.4 per 1,000. This is more than double USSR rates.[67]

States have studied the cost-benefit ratio of health maintenance programs and have generally found that, in the long run, they save money. A Texas study found, for example, that the state saved eight dollars in avoided medical costs for every dollar spent on preventive services, and a North Dakota analysis demonstrated a drop of one-third in Medicaid costs for children who received preventive health care.[68] While the cost for prenatal care is $1,500, the remedial care for a premature infant can run from $20,000 to $40,000. A $10 cost to immunize against all childhood diseases can save $500,000 to $1 million for children left retarded by measles. The Center for Disease Control showed that $180 million for measles vaccination saved $1.3 billion in medical and long-term deafness, blind, and retarded care. While $325 can purchase full preventive health care for a year, a one-day stay in the hospital may cost $325.[69] All children up to one year, along with poor pregnant women, could be covered for about $120 million—roughly the costs of 100 MX missiles and a third of what the federal government spent in 1982 for inspection of animal care facilities to ensure humane treatment.[70]

*Medicare.*    Medicare has also come under attack. In 1984, at the same time Social Security costs of living increases were cut, the Medicare deductible rose to $400 from $356, and recipients now pay everything over $100 per from the sixty-first to ninetieth day (was $89) and everything above $200 a day, up from $178, for lifetime reserve days. The basic premium rose from $14.60 to $17.90 per month (an increase of 15.5 percent) as of January 1, 1987, and Part B coverage rose to $146 per year. Medicare payments to hospitals were frozen for all of 1986, and physicians' payments were frozen through March 1986. As a result, the elderly got less care or had to pay more from their own income for medical services.[71] Reductions in Medicare administrative costs were $74 million in 1987, further reducing services. In the future, people will work longer before they are eligible for Medicare: the age of eligibility will increase to age 66 in 2001 and 67 in 2007. At present, about 30.5 million persons are covered, and costs are expected to increase from $63.1 billion in fiscal year 1984 to $73.3 billion in fiscal year 1985.

## HOUSING UNDER REAGANOMICS

Although Reagan officially endorsed housing allowances, federal subsidy programs for rent have been reduced, funds for the maintenance of public housing has been cut, and housing grants have become close ended. Under Gramm-Rudman-Hollings, the Farmers Home Administration reduced direct loans for rural housing in 1987 to $2 billion, or $91 million less than in 1986 and $1.2 billion (37 percent) less than 1985.[72]

For many there is no housing, and the homeless among us have become a national scandal. While a Housing and Urban Development report sets the number at from 250,000 to 300,000, the Community for Creative Non-Violence (CCNV) estimates the number at a third of a million to two million Americans.[73] Many are former mental patients with little awareness of their rights, though a great number also are those pushed out of work, off the farms, and into the cities by unemployment and consequent loss of their homes. CCNV has noted a 20–25 percent increase in the number of homeless in 1986, with families—mostly children—representing the fastest-growing group. Given no change in present policy, CCNV estimates that by 2003 there will be 18.7 million homeless in America.

The Community for Creative Non-Violence has erected tent cities across from the White House, and its leader, Mitch Snyder, has periodically fasted to bring attention to the plight of the estimated five thousand to ten thousand homeless in Washington, D.C. Because of one such fast, President Reagan agreed to renovate a deserted government building to a model home for the homeless, at a cost of from $5 to $10 million from the Federal Emergency Management Agency. Reneging on the plan, the General Services Administration developed a lower-cost shelter—four huge barrackslike rooms—grossly unlike the model shelter promised, and upon the objection of CCNV ordered the homeless once more into the streets.[74] The CCNV experience demonstrates clearly—in ways that statistics hidden in charts and books cannot—the reluctance of today's government to provide for those obviously unable to provide for themselves. Congress in 1987 authorized an emergency homeless bill, the Urgent Relief for the Homeless Act, of $500 million, but this is far from enough to deal with the problem of why people are homeless, how to care for them on the streets, and how to ensure that Americans will have food and shelter despite their lack of money to pay for them.

## EDUCATION AND TRAINING PROGRAMS

One of Reagan's first acts in office, in 1981, was to rescind $440 million in funding for Title I of the Elementary and Secondary Education Act. This program, developed especially to serve disadvantaged and handicapped children, had provided compensatory education to minorities and the poor, funding for bilingual education for Hispanic children, and extra services for Native American and Afro-American children. More than half the children ESEA served before 1981 were children of color: 29 percent Afro-American, 21 percent Hispanic, and 4 percent other. New policies subsumed the Emergency School Assistance Act, intended to help schools desegregate, into the new Block Grant system, which was then cut by 35.3 percent—about $269 million—and desegregation funds were virtually eliminated. Head Start, the model OEO program, continues but now reaches only 18 percent of eligible preschoolers.[75]

In *higher education*, basic education opportunity grants, legislated in 1972, became the major source of financing for college education for disadvantaged youth. Among those it served, 70 percent were from low-income (below $12,000 annual income) households, and 57 percent were minority students. BEOGs, renamed Pell grants, became less available under the new regulations. All grants, loans, and work-study support became more difficult to get and more costly—loan interest rose sharply. Financial aid offices now had to assume that parents would contribute $750 whether or not that money was actually available. Despite the cuts, Pell grants in 1983 provided $2.8 billion to needy students, and for 1984, for all student aid programs, $4 billion was appropriated.[76] According to a study by the College Board, federal aid to postsecondary students has dropped from $22.2 billion to $20.7 billion in constant dollars since 1980, and the 1988 budget calls for cutting another $2 billion.

Federally guaranteed loans and work-study employment reached nine million students in 1983, attesting to the level of need even with reductions in funding. However, a great many young people have been shunted away from higher education. Bell says that keeping certain people—the poor and minorities—out of school will create an educationally segregated elite and make more people available for the labor market. She adds that

> This is a good illustration of how selective programs can be manipulated to keep poor people poor and to nip aspirations in the bud.[77]

In addition, many young people formerly supported will remain out of school to help their families.

Enrollment of Afro-American students is dropping rapidly: in 1980 about 11 percent of college graduates were Afro-Americans, but for the first time in two decades, their number is decreasing. In the 1984-85 school year it declined by 20 percent, to 8.8 percent of the undergraduate population. Although a few top-ranked Afro-American colleges are graduating record numbers, drop-out rates at predominantly white schools are abysmal. In graduate and professional schools Afro-American enrollment declined by 11.9 percent (between 1980 and 1984), and the percent of Afro-American faculty and administration, never very large, has decreased by 4.3 percent.[78]

The Comprehensive Education and Training Act (CETA) was one of the first victims of Reagan's budget cutting, in 1983. Its termination threw almost 400,000 new unemployed into the labor market. CETA had paid public and private nonprofit agencies for salaries with which to employ poverty-level workers. Reagan replaced it with the Job Training Partnership Act (JPTA), which subsidizes private sector organizations to retrain experienced but unemployed adult workers and to train disadvantaged youths with marketable skills. The money was to "trickle down" through the private employers. JTPA serves both fewer people and people who are less disadvantaged (because private employers "cream"—take the best candidates). It provides a subsidy to businesses without targeting particular groups in need, since wages and numbers of employees are no longer specified.

While Reagan wanted to cut the AFDC Work Incentive Program altogether, Congress only reduced its funding. In some areas, it was replaced by the Community Work Experience Program (CWEP), a workfare program enabling states to subsidize private sector jobs. CWEP also offers Medicaid and earned income disregards up to nine months, with AFDC grants diverted to wages. Although CWEP workers can work in federal offices or agencies, they are not considered federal employees and do not qualify for fringe benefits. People already employed but at low wages, incapacitated recipients, parents with children younger than age 3, and children between 13 and 16 (18 if attending school) are exempted.

Several states have instituted workfare programs. In California, it is called Greater Avenues for Independence (GAIN). GAIN offers training opportunities, including college, and three months of child care services for recipients who find jobs. All able-bodied welfare recipients without children or with children older than 6 must have a job, register for job training—which includes English classes if needed—or work at assigned jobs in the public sector. After training, recipients have three months to

find work, and those who do not must enroll in a "preemployment program" that in fact places them in low-level work, such as cleaning parks, to
work off their welfare grants. Recipients sign a contract listing the responsibilities of their workfare.

The National Association of Social Workers in California approved
the GAIN program after gaining amendments guaranteeing that clients
will not have to work off child support or overpayments. They are also
guaranteed grievance procedures and fair hearings. GAIN will coordinate
many training and development programs, and will infuse $178 million
into the child care industry. However, it is seen as a serious threat to
government employees because they will be laid off to be replaced by wage-
subsidized recipients. Other workfare programs are in operation in Massachusetts, New York, and other states, with minor variations.

According to many, workfare is morally justified because it causes an
upward economic push by the poor, who need what George Gilder terms
"the spur of their poverty." However, work in the secondary market or on
workfare cannot lead to an end to poverty. People in poverty are over-
whelmingly children—70 to 80 percent—and

> of the remaining . . . a majority cannot work because of mental handicaps,
> physical disabilities, or childrearing responsibilities. In 1982, more than 9
> million Americans worked during some part of the year yet lived in poverty.
> Almost a third—nearly 3 million—worked full time.[79]

## COSTS OF SOCIAL WELFARE

### Estimating Poverty

Some people believe that vendor payments—food stamps, housing
subsidies, and Medicaid—should be counted when estimating the poverty
rate. However, such calculations are an illusion: Payments actually go to the
service provider, not the poor.

> Thus, at market value, an AFDC mother with two children . . . "received" an
> additional $1287 in 1979 because she was covered by Medicaid . . . of course
> . . . she did not receive a dime. . . . Poor people receive medical services, not
> income; the latter goes to providers.[80]

Thus in 1982 the poverty rate was "reduced" from 11 percent to 9.4 percent because a family of four receiving Medicaid coverage had $547
"released" (or available) to spend on goods other than medical care—an
extra $45.58 per month. However, without the vendor payments the per-
son would either not get the services or take the money needed to pay for
them out of food money. It is not really "received" money. Besides, as
Ehrenreich says,

> the question of whether 20 million or 34 million or 50 million Americans are
> "poor" is surely an indecent one; the lowest of these figures is a national

scandal. . . . No matter how poverty is measured, the decline in poverty that began in the sixties slowed and then stopped in the seventies; since 1978, the numbers below the poverty level have steadily risen.[81]

### How Much Does It Cost?

Despite our concern for social welfare costs, in 1980 all programs constituted only 18.5 percent of the gross national product. All means-tested cash transfers came to $30.1 billion, increasing to $39.9 billion in October 1985, while OASDI payments were $252.7 billion in 1980 and $388.6 billion in 1985. Health and medical care cost $3.9 billion, veterans' benefits $2.6 billion, and education $141.2 billion.[82] The federal share of social welfare costs were about 48 percent in 1970 and 56.5 percent in 1980, but reversed to 54.8 percent in 1984.[83] As is evident in Table 12.2, the percentage of GNP spent for social welfare programs was fairly constant in the early 1980s. The increase in 1983 came primarily in OASDI and in health (Medicare and Medicaid, primarily). While public assistance (AFDC and SSI) comprised only 2.7 percent of the total GNP in 1980, it actually decreased in 1983.

Although dollar spending rose in public assistance, its percentage of the cost of social welfare declined from about 11 percent of $36,515.2 million in 1976 to about 9 percent of $57,753.9 million in 1983. Even with Medicaid added ($13,278.2 million in 1976 to $32,085.5 million in 1983), the total declined by two percentage points. By 1983, OASDI and Medicare constituted 35 percent of all social welfare expenditures, at about $220 billion, while all costs of public assistance totaled $80 billion. As a comparison, AFDC cost about $8 billion while the interest on the national debt cost $111 billion.[85]

While individual taxpayers are misled into thinking social welfare programs, particularly public assistance, take the biggest bite from our tax dollars, in fact the per capita tax cost for each of us to pay for public assistance is about $30.16 per month (see Table 12.3). True, we pay more than in earlier years—in 1960, per capita cost was about $1.87 per month, in 1970 about $6.60, and in 1980 $26.01. The outcry against social welfare programs has little to do with whether the nation can afford to provide for its poor. John Ehrenreich says

> The argument that we can't afford such programs is specious. Merely returning to the tax rate structure of 1980 would generate enough revenue to allow

**TABLE 12.2   Gross National Product and Costs of Selected Programs (in billions)[84]**

| | | $ | % | % | % | % | % | % | % | % | % |
| Date | GNP | Total All Programs | Federal | State | OASDI | Public Assistance | Health | Veterans' Benefit | Education | Other |
| --- | --- | --- | --- | --- | --- | --- | --- | --- | --- | --- |
| 1980 | 2,631.7 | 18.7 | 11.5 | 7.2 | 8.0 | 2.7 | 3.8 | .8 | 4.6 | .5 |
| 1983 | 3,304.8 | 19.4 | 12.1 | 7.3 | 10.0 | 2.6 | 4.4 | .8 | 4.3 | .4 |

*Source*: U.S. Department of Health and Human Services, Social Security Administration, Office of Policy. *Social Security Bulletin*, vol. 49, no. 2, February 1986, p. 17. Table 3. Gross National Product and Costs of Selected Programs as Percent of GNP.

**TABLE 12.3    Total and per capita social welfare expenditures (1983 dollars)[86]**

| | TOTAL (MILLIONS) | PER CAPITA | | | |
|---|---|---|---|---|---|
| | | TOTAL | SOCIAL INSURANCE | PUBLIC ASSISTANCE | HEALTH |
| 1960 | $ 52,106.3 | $ 265.42 | $ 105.35 | $ 22.46 | $ 35.03 |
| 1970 | 145,483.9 | 689.90 | 261.75 | 79.26 | 121.32 |
| 1980 | 492,070.1 | 2,139.38 | 995.06 | 312.91 | 438.92 |
| 1983 | 640,026.3 | 2,698.72 | 1,387.79 | 361.91 | 608.05 |

Source: U.S. Department of Health and Human Services, Social Security Administration, Office of Policy. "Monthly Benefit Statistics, February 1986," p. 18.

lifting every family in the United States above the official poverty level, without the need to make cuts in other programs.[87]

## REAGANOMICS AND PRIORITIES

### Supporting Big Business

We know how to end poverty. Our greatest welfare success was Supplemental Security Income, a negative income tax primarily benefiting the elderly. By 1982, older Americans were less likely to live in poverty, at a 14.3 percent poverty rate, than were children. Yet we seem unwilling to invest money for the future generations—the number of children in poverty is the same now as in 1965.[88] The antipoverty work and training programs of the 1960s worked, but programs aimed at an unemployed work force of 3 percent do not have chances against unemployment rates of 7, 8, and 10 percent or 55 percent (for young Afro-American men).

Our social aim today is not to end poverty but to make profits, and the targets of society's largesse are not the poor but the rich. Moreover, the decision making that controls our economic policies, including those aimed at social programs, are controlled by those who will reap the benefits. Most of America's capital is owned "not by individuals but by corporations, banks, insurance companies, and pension trusts."[89]

> Formal control over the economic life of the nation is concentrated in the hands of a very few men: the presidents, vice presidents, and boards of directors of the nation's corporate institutions . . . in a small number of giant corporations.[90]

The top 2 percent of the shareholders (in three thousand top companies) own nearly 58 percent of the common stock.[91] Economist Gabriel Kolko says

> The concentration of economic power in a very small elite is an indisputable fact . . . a democratized economic system . . . is quite obviously not in accord with social reality . . . even if . . . these men act benevolently toward their workers and the larger community, their actions still would not be the result

of . . . a formal democratic structure and group participation, which are the essentials for democracy.[92]

Another kind of investment to benefit the wealthy is investment in the military-industrial complex—the interlocking relationships of the armed forces, defense department, military contractors, and congressmen representing defense-oriented constituencies. Dye and Zeigler say

> Whether or not the military-industrial complex is conspiring to keep us perpetually armed, the fact remains that each year the U.S. government spends more of its resources on national defense.[93]

American military spending has doubled since 1980 and is well on its way to tripling by 1988. It now costs about 50 cents of every income tax dollar. High levels of military expenditures redistribute wealth and income upward. According to a recent study, the billions of dollars spent for SDI is going to a handful of defense contractors—more than 90 percent to five states with senators on the Armed Services Committee and the Defense Subcommittee of the Senate Appropriations Committee. The top twenty contractors and laboratories were given contracts totaling $5.7 billion since 1983, or 75 percent of the total $7.7 billion spent.[94] Meanwhile, the Pentagon's share of the budget rose from 24 cents of each federal dollar in 1981 to 37 cents by 1986.

### Civil Rights

The attack on social programs since 1980 is paired with the rejection of civil rights for people of color and women. Administration policies clearly show that programs for empowerment or human rights have been consistently underfunded or withdrawn.

To recapitulate, the civil rights gained in the 1960s were

> The Civil Rights Act of 1957 established the Justice Department's Civil Rights Division to sue for voting rights.
>
> The Civil Rights Act of 1964 barred discrimination in public schools, facilities, employment, federally financed activities.
>
> The Voting Rights Act of 1965 broadened guarantees of the right to vote.
>
> The Civil Rights Act of 1968 forbade housing discrimination.
>
> The Educational Amendment of 1972 made illegal discrimination on the basis of sex in schools receiving federal support.
>
> The Rehabilitation Act of 1973 barred discrimination against the handicapped.
>
> The Civil Rights for Institutionalized Persons Act of 1980 gave civil rights protection to prisoners, the mentally ill, and other institutionalized people.[95]

Attacks on civil rights through the courts were part of the backlash of the 1970s. One of best-known was *Bakke v. Regents of the University of California* in 1978. Bakke had been denied admission to medical school because a percentage of slots were reserved for people of color, some of whom had grade point averages below his. The Supreme Court ruled in favor of Bakke, though it upheld the right of the University to have quotas to ensure places for people of color. This decision accelerated the trend away from compensation for institutional discrimination on the basis of race. One evidence of Reagan's personal support for institutional discrimination came when the Supreme Court in 1983 upheld Boston's firing of seven hundred white workers rather than more recently hired black and Hispanic workers (more recently hired because of past discrimination in hiring). Reagan filed a "friend of the court" brief in favor of the white firemen, arguing against "reverse discrimination."

According to the Civil Rights Commission, Reagan's own record of employment evidenced sexism and racism:

> through the first two years of the Reagan administration, appointments were 8 percent female and 8 percent minority (4 percent black); Carter's appointments were 12 percent female and 17 percent minority (12 percent black).[96]

Because of the commission's criticism, Reagan fired three of its six members and tried to fire two others. Finally, a new eight-member commission was created with members whose civil rights views were more in accord with his.[97]

In two recent decisions, the Supreme Court rejected the administration's argument that affirmative action should be limited to actual victims of past bias to avoid reverse discrimination against the innocent, primarily white, people. It approved by a 6-3 vote a plan to reserve one-half the promotions in the Cleveland fire department for qualified minority candidates, and by 5 to 4 that a sheet metal workers union in New York and New Jersey had to double nonwhite membership to 29.3 percent by August 1987.

Reagan has encouraged voluntary compliance with fair employment and antidiscriminatory rules but tried to reduce federal enforcement against violations. In all, he has required plaintiffs to show personal intent to discriminate, rather than acknowledging past institutional discrimination, before requiring businesses to take remedial action. He has taken the position that only identifiable victims should be compensated, rejecting class action suits or compensation for past discrimination, and has rejected quotas, numerical goals, and timetables to redress past discrimination. Of particular import, he has spoken out against busing to end school desegregation, an action recently upheld (October 1986) by the Supreme Court.

Funding for civil rights action declined 9 percent from 1981 to 1983, and the budgets for the Economic Employment Opportunity Commission and the Office of Federal Contract Compliance Programs (OFCCP) were reduced 10 and 24 percent, respectively. Staff reductions for EEOC were 12 percent, while OFCCP was cut by 34 percent.[98] As a result, the number of employment discrimination cases brought by the EEOC and the Justice Department have declined by half from 1980, though the number of complaints has increased by nearly 50 percent. Cases with "no cause" findings (not guilty of discrimination) increased by a third. The number of complaints against government contractors for discrimination in hiring filed by

OFCCP dropped from fifty-three in 1980 to eighteen in 1983—and there were only five in 1982 (see Table 12.4).

**TABLE 12.4    OFCCP Enforcement Activities.[99]**

| ACTIVITY | 1980 | 1981 | 1982 | 1983 |
|---|---|---|---|---|
| Complaint investigations | 1,726 | 2,136 | 2,589 | 2,375 |
| Compliance reviews | 2,627 | 3,135 | 3,081 | 4,295 |
| Complaints filed | 53 | 15 | 5 | 18 |
| Debarments | 5 | 1 | 0 | 0 |
| Back pay awarded (millions) | $9.3 | 5.1 | 2.1 | 3.6 |
| Recipients | 4,336 | 4,754 | 1,133 | 1,758 |

Source: John L. Palmer and Isabel V. Sawhill, eds., *Reagan Record: An Assessment of America's Changing Domestic Priorities*. Ballinger Publishing, 1985, p. 205; OFCCP Enforcement Activities FY 1980—FY 1983, table 6.5.; Lynn C. Burbridge, "The Impact of Changes in Policy on the Federal Equal Employment Opportunity Effort." Washington, D.C.: Urban Institute, Nov. 1983, Table 3.

The Justice Department has filed only one school desegregation case and has not required systemwide remedies for desegregation, while the number of investigations of segregation by the U.S. Department of Education dropped from 10.4 percent in February 1981 to 4.4 percent in January 1982. Moreover, it has failed to release findings of eighty-six completed investigations. In Washington state, when citizens filed a referendum against busing, the Justice Department held that it was racially motivated and therefore unconstitutional, but when Reagan took office this stance was reversed.[100]

In the Department of Health and Human Services, thirty violations by recipients of federal funds were put on hold rather than pursued.[101] Between 1980 and 1983, there was a 25 percent drop in support for enforcement activities such as class action suits against employers and government contractors.[102] There has been little action taken against civil rights violations in prisons and mental hospitals, such as allowing Central Prison in Raleigh, North Carolina, to remain segregated.[103] In housing, only six fair-housing suits were filed during Reagan's first thirty months in office, compared to forty-six for Carter in the same time period.

In addition to stonewalling efforts *for* civil rights, Reagan has supported actions *against* such rights. For example, his administration has exempted three hundred small colleges from laws barring sex and race discrimination and has tried to grant tax exemptions to larger schools practicing discrimination. In one such instance, the Justice Department tried to withdraw a suit from the Supreme Court that would have denied tax-exempt status to the Goldsboro Christian Schools for racial discrimination, and Bob Jones University, which forbade interracial dating and housing. The Supreme Court ruled against the Justice Department in these instances.

Some gains have been made despite the administration's tacit approval of institutional racism, primarily because of the increased education and political action of people of color in earlier decades. The number of elected officials of African descent at all levels of government rose from

1,472 in 1970 to 5,606 in 1983, and 248 cities have Afro-American mayors while 47 cities have Hispanic mayors.[104] Nevertheless, the move toward civil rights has been considerably slowed by the whole move to conservatism as well as the personal involvement of the president in such discriminatory actions.

## THE "NEW MORALITY" OF SEX ROLE SOCIALIZATION

As the world turns toward the twenty-first century and the nation turns toward the past, the dynamics of the new "morality" have become seriously intertwined with the political economy of oppression. While the New Right and the Moral Majority call for less government on the economic level, the demand increases for government intervention on private and personal levels. This demand is focused on a return to two elements of past traditions of the family. One is the right or obligation of men to support their families, the converse of which is that women should not enter the labor market. The second is the right or obligation of women to remain in marriages, to bear and rear children, and to provide a home where men can find surcease from the problems of life. This old "new morality" directly strengthens "traditional" sex roles: work and support roles for men and dependency roles for women.

The most vital intrusion of these ideas in personal and private lives are the cutbacks in basic maintenance social programs, and the control of both work and family behavior that such cutbacks mean. If the necessities of life are controlled, then behavior is controlled. When sustenance is threatened, people become what is expected of them in return for sustenance. At this time in our society, when women and children are at their most vulnerable in terms of dependence, men and women workers are finding that their labor is not needed except in low-paying and marginal jobs. The confluence of these factors creates an increasingly polarized nation economically, though it is hidden in the rhetoric of work and the morality of marriage.

The withdrawal of freedoms hard-won over the years, from civil rights to reproductive freedom for women, is another aspect of the same force. Empowerment of any kind creates unruliness and possible rebellion, and therefore must be controlled. Thus such "moral" issues as the restriction of birth control and abortion; pornography; sexual activity among teenagers or among consenting adults; prayer in schools; or the definition of AIDS as a homosexual disease that should not receive research funds are government definitions that result in the control of personal "rebellions." Such new programs as urine testing for drug use[105]—who would refuse, given that they would lose their jobs?—or the new "moral" battle against drugs[106] only obfuscate bread and butter issues in the economy and power issues in the polity.

The call to traditional roles strengthens divisions among people that had been waning. Classes polarize as fewer opportunities for adequate income are available to the middle class while the profits of a small elite increase. White workers are divided from workers of color as competition for scarce jobs becomes more fierce, unions fail, and government support for civil rights ends. Finally, it divides men from women as particular fundamentalist moralities—Protestant work ethic and Puritan moralities—are reinfused into roles and relationships. Where society was approaching a more egalitarian stance, now conflict is fomented.

### Women and the New Morality

Our attitude toward the "place of women" has not touched the basic problems of institutional sexism: Women still earn only 60 percent of men's wages for the same work. According to the National Advisory Commission on Economic Opportunity,

> All other things being equal, if the proportion of the poor in female households . . . were to . . . increase at the same rate as it did from 1967 to 1978, the poverty population would be composed solely of women and their children before the year 2000.[107]

Women constitute well over half the users of most major social programs. They are 64.8 percent of recipients of Medicare, and 70 percent of housing subsidies go to households headed by women or women living alone. Because of the two-tiered welfare system, in which work-related social programs provide more financial benefits because they are consciously structured to respond to the needs of the white male worker, women receive only 41.1 percent of unemployment insurance benefits but are 81.1 percent of adult AFDC recipients, a program structured precisely because of their "mother" roles.[108]

There are two primary "moral" problems for women today: the control of reproduction and women's status in marriage.

### 1. Control of Reproduction

Attitudes toward sexual behavior are becoming increasingly constricted, particularly in the areas of sex education in the schools, teenage pregnancy, contraception, and abortion. Movements to delete "humanist" education and "values clarification"—which is, in many instances, a euphemism for sex education—from school curricula are ostensibly based on the religious rights of parents to teach morality for their children.

The result of this, however, is that sex education and access to contraception may be denied young people at the time teenage pregnancies are booming. Withdrawal of money from family planning clinics and "squeal rules" that require notification of parents before birth control is prescribed are some results. Effects include early pregnancies, often described as "punishment" for immoral behavior; early marriages that prevent young women (and often young men) from gaining better education or training for more gainful employment; greater financial difficulty either for the new mother or the new family; and often public dependency with little hope of becoming independent.

In the abortion issue, at question is when a fetus becomes a human being: Pro-lifers believe that the moment of conception is the beginning of human life—the joining of ovum and sperm, and even, for some, in the prevention of that joining through birth control. It is significant, however, that with all the outcry against abortion, more than half the population of the United States believes women should have the right to control their reproduction. The withdrawal of Medicaid funding for abortion, reaffirmed by the Supreme Court in 1980, was perhaps one of the most significant cuts in social programs, because it made abortion an issue for the poor and for working people. Women of other classes can afford either to maintain their pregnancies or to end them, but the lack of this choice for poor women must either bear children or go to back-alley abortionists. Langenbach says

> If a woman cannot effectively control her fertility, she will be unpredictably and frequently pregnant, thus effectively barred from the labor market and tied to home and children. This perpetuates the traditional family. . . . Thus, the major reason New Right groups oppose abortion is not so much an abhorrence of state sanctioned killing (because they favor the death penalty by large margins) but because abortion allows a woman to control when and if she has children.[109]

### 2. Women's Status in Marriage

According to the new morality, women should remain in marriage. If they do not, they "deserve" the stigmatization and lack of financial support that institutional sexism dictates. There is a triple thrust against adequate finances for women outside marriage. We have already discussed the first two: lack of good jobs and terribly inadequate public programs such as AFDC. The third is lack of child support from the fathers of their children. No-fault divorce, once thought a boon to women, has boomeranged in its effect on their support. While before the 1960s women had some protection and support, now many are financially worse off than in traditional divorces. Their standard of living drops 73 percent in the first year, while that of men rises by 42 percent. About 90 percent of women get custody of their children, contributing to their lowered standard of living, and more than half get no court-ordered support. About 85 percent are not awarded alimony.[110] Leonore Weitzman, in a study of no-fault divorce, concluded that women lose bargaining positions with no-fault:

> in attempting to divide the assets of the marriage "equally" the law . . . virtually compels [the sale of the family home] in order to let the man "cash out." At the same time, the husband's less tangible assets—good will in business, a professional degree or license (often gained with the wife's income)—are either undervalued by judges or neglected altogether.[111]

Because most judges (mostly men) do not want to limit the former husbands' initiative to work, they are rarely required to pay more than 25 percent of after-tax income in child support or more than 32 percent in child support and alimony combined. Women, however, regardless of their training or earning ability, are supposed to go to work because they have the real responsibility for the children. Frequently, joint custody is established, thereby also reducing child support. Weitzman believes that

> [a] custody fight leaves women more vulnerable both economically and in their emotional need to retain custody, so often they trade away financial benefits for fear of losing their children.[112]

To remain married, regardless of the personal or emotional cost, would solve the problem. Barring that, the low AFDC grants and low-wage work perform the same purpose in keeping women "in their place"—economically dependent.

The emphasis for men on jobs and job training, despite the decreasing number of jobs except at low-paying service levels, is coupled with a cry for women to return to their homes, produce babies, and become once more dependent on men. Besides curtailing women's freedom, this places double burdens on men to support families at lessened wages and without their wives' incomes. Some supporters of this "moral" battle are straightforward; for example, George Gilder decries the fact that women are entering the job market in greater than ever numbers, taking away the "right" of men to support their families. Other efforts, however, seem more removed, for example, the emotionally infused abortion issue. With more children, women will not be able to work, and without that work, many more families will drop into poverty. Men will be forced to take any jobs, as jobs continue to disappear with automation. Thus, once more, a greater number than ever of both men and women will be under the control of those who command the economy.

Social work and social programs contribute to the regression of women's status—it would be strange indeed if it did not, given the conservative trends of society. It has begun to ignore techniques to empower women and has returned to the "safer" encouragement of marriage and family roles. Peter Day says

> Stereotyping the client as [dependent and] child-like enables social workers to adopt the role of parent, but it may make it necessary to deny or invalidate aspects of the clients' behavior which do not fit in with the stereotype . . . social work diminishe[s] the client's status as an adult and citizen . . . reminiscent of, though more subtle than, the ways the person receiving poor relief in the nineteenth century was stigmatized and diminished.[113]

Decisions about their lives *must* be taken, because society has the right and the responsibility to "cure" them through the good offices of social welfare "even against their will and even if the cure is both painful and uncertain."[114]

According to D'Vera Cohn, therapists still lump women into traditional categories and ignore their real mental health needs. Therapists are still more likely to prescribe drugs for women, who get 73 percent of psychotropic drug prescriptions, 71 percent of antidepressants, and 80 percent of amphetamines. Moreover, the practice of trying to get women to adjust to roles that do not fit them is still common.[115] In addition, there are three new mental illness categories that may be particularly devastating to women's empowerment. The first, premenstrual dysphoric disorder, defines women as pathological because of reactions to menstrual periods. The second refers to low self-esteem after being battered (masochistic personality disorder). Finally, rape is no longer considered an act of aggression or violence but a sexual disorder, and therefore is treatable and excusable (paraphilic rapism) regardless of its effect on women as victims.[116]

### The "New" Work Morality

The insistence on work in a society where routine tasks have become automated and production is enhanced by technology is a strange paradox. Output per-person hour, which now, for example, allows one farmer to produce food for more than sixty people, demonstrates a society potentially capable of creating wealth with only half its current labor force.[117] Gartner et al. say

> We stand on the verge of an era in which more people can be engaged in more creative and fulfilling activity than ever before; in which the process of production of the necessities and pleasures of material life can be less taxing of people's labor than ever before; in which the ability to communicate with others, to have access to education and entertainment and to participate in the society is greater than ever before.[118]

The idealization of work, according to Macarov, rests upon four assumptions:

> That society needs all the work its members can produce.
> That only work is the moral, desirable, and practical means of supporting life.
> That work offers spiritual, emotional, and self-actualizing satisfactions beyond monetary ones.
> That working is a measure of normalcy and self-identification.[119]

> to say that society needs all the work of which everyone is capable, or even that there is a need for more human labor, is to reiterate a belief, not to state a fact. . . . [A] world which cannot provide paid work for everyone ready, willing, and able to work, which legally limits the hours that people are permitted to work in a constantly decreasing fashion, which legislates more and more holidays/vacations, and which requires people to retire at a given age cannot be seriously viewed as a world short of workers or one desirous of needing more work.[120]

We have, apparently, forgotten that until about the onset of mercantilism, work had little value beyond subsistence and was looked upon by the elite as degrading and demoralizing.

As we look at the future of work—the reduction of work hours, continued growth of the aged population, and structural unemployment—the maintenance of a low wage exploitable work force becomes anachronistic. Yet we continue to demand workfare for the poor even though their work is unneeded and may take jobs away from the marginally employed. We retrain and retool even though in terms of nonwelfare income, education explains only between 25 and 36 percent of variance in incomes.[121] (The differences in income are more likely to be explained by institutional discrimination against people of color and women which bar their upward economic mobility.)

The jobs of the future will be in the secondary employment market, in the service area. An estimated 29 percent of net growth in the work force during the next fifteen years will be in minority groups, where institutional discrimination has meant high drop-out rates—up to 40 or 50 percent in some inner-city areas—and no real job training. Women will comprise about 63 percent of new entrants into the labor force by the year 2000. High-technology industries, which can afford to pay for training, pick workers from other groups and in any case account for only 4 to 5 percent of the new positions created each year. In the next decade about six million more jobs are projected in the high-technology segment compared to only about one million in the less skilled and laborer categories.[122]

With multinational corporations where profit is the bottom line, it makes economic sense to take labor from unionized areas, such as those in the United States, to countries where labor can be purchased for a few dollars a week. Between 1966 and 1974, the net American job loss due to corporate movement abroad was estimated at about 1.6 million jobs. In the Dominican Republic branch of Gulf + Western, the average wage in 1978 was 34 cents an hour. In Nicaragua, a computer assembly job paid 25 cents an hour. In South Korea, 44 percent of unionized textile workers earn less than $62 monthly, $30 below their country's poverty level. Container Corporation of American and B. F. Goodrich have used prison labor at substantially less than prevailing wage rates in Colombia, a practice outlawed in the United States for decades.[123]

Because of the international character of jobs, automation, and robotization, unionism in the United States is failing. Only about 17 percent of American workers are now unionized. The declining political influence of the unions is clearly interrelated with conservative victories in American life. Basic middle-income jobs are disappearing, leaving low-paying dead-end jobs at the bottom and technical and managerial skills at the top.[124]

Clearly, although the need *for* work is diminishing in the increasingly international economic system, the demand *to* work continues to grow. This painful paradox is exacerbated by human service workers caught in the rhetoric of conservatism and the aura of the past. Macarov says

> Social workers participate in and support the work-welfare structure not only because they believe the work to be needed and the jobs to be required, but because work is a normative activity, and in order to be normal, one must work . . .[125]

and

the manner in which poverty is viewed as deviance, and refusal to work is considered the cause, dates back to the Puritan's dictum that those who will not work should not be permitted to eat . . . an attitude not conspicuously absent from the public mind today.[126]

The profession of social work could make a difference. Social welfare contributes vastly to the economy: It provides jobs for fifteen million people, or 14 percent of the American labor force. These jobs consume the products of other industries; for example, hospitals spend $30 billion a year for supplies. Finally, social welfare provides money to consume even more: It supervises the transfer of $78 billion a year to all varieties of recipients, who then spend the money in all kinds of markets.[127] As such, it could exert a power over the political economy and the definitions of work. Galper says that

> The value of work and of being a good worker is a cornerstone of the value system of this country, and it has been adopted all too uncritically by the social services. . . . Because the services do not understand or address the radical possibility of encouraging different kinds of work—a personally and socially useful work—they have been left in the position of encouraging the typical patterns of work as we have known them.[128]

## CONCLUSION: PAST IDEOLOGY IN A POSTINDUSTRIAL WORLD

Social welfare depends on the political economy of the society, one now infused with a religious morality not truly conducive to help for the distressed, and social work as a profession is paying too little attention to the wider social issues of the time, even though it helps individuals in many ways. These ways, unfortunately, are often aimed at adjusting and fitting clients in rather than at empowerment and social action. Thus the historic mission of social work is lost in this shuffle of this "more professional" therapeutic orientation.

The emphasis on work when jobs are becoming less and less available, the reemphasis on women's home and family roles, and the withdrawal of support for social programs and for civil rights together reenforce the ever-present problems of institutional racism, sexism, and classism in the nation. Multinational corporation and military-industrial complex policies head us toward disaster on both a national and a worldwide scale. Yet, with the threat of the world burning, the general populace and the social welfare professionals fiddle, immersed in inauthentic problems such as workfare when there is no work, training when there are no jobs, and therapy for victims when it is society that is sick.

There is no doubt that the Reagan administration has made deep inroads on social welfare in the United States. With a few strokes of a pen,

Reagan has set back human and civil rights decades, or four centuries, depending on one's perspective:

> The president clearly did seek to turn back the social policy clock. . . . Given his way, the president would have eradicated most of the hallmarks of the Great Society and would have shrunk the social insurance programs to a scope more nearly approximating their New Deal origins. On the civil rights front the president would have scrapped the federal government's role as a "commanding general" in the war for equal opportunity, in favor of something more like a reluctant sergeant; broad goals, quotas, and timetables would have been replaced by individual disciplinary action according to rather narrowly interpreted rules.[129]

What this reactionary administration has done is to redefine those who disagree with traditionalism as malcontents, deviants, and the un-American. Levitan and Johnson say

> The inequities and hardships imposed by the Reagan administration's economic and social policies cannot be construed as merely a response to the demands of an angry public. Reagan social welfare policies, founded on right-wing ideology, have never been ratified by the voting public, and they deviate sharply from the American commitment to opportunity and compassion.[130]

Reagan's ostensible attack on big government, Ehrenreich argues, was

> an attack on the idea that government can or should protect people against the power of corporations, landlords, and merchants. The attack on "entitlement" programs is an assault on the idea that economic well-being is a political right. The attack on the . . . legal services program, on affirmative action programs, on laws regulating corporate behavior is an attack on the laws and institutions that enable people to express their rights.[131]

That Reagan only led this attack, and that millions of Americans followed in this battle against justice, is an even more terrifying statement about the state of our society.

The legacy of the Reagan administration will be three generations of deprivation: those now being deprived; their children, who will suffer from the lack of adequate programs such as health, income maintenance, and nutrition; and their children's children, whose parents, deprived by the Reagan cutbacks, will not be able to provide for them adequately. If Reagan's foreign policies of war give us time, perhaps we will recognize the extent to which our society has fallen, and perhaps we can begin a new spiral into humanity.

## STUDY QUESTIONS

1. What is the new Reagan morality: What impact has it had on women? On the poor?

2. What is Reaganomics: What effect has Reagonomics had on the poor? The aged and disabled? Women and their children?

3. What were the AFDC cutbacks under the Reagan administration?

4. Who are the "new poor," and what are the social and economic reasons for their poverty?

5. What has happened to Civil Rights under Reagan?

6. What kinds of productive behavior, aside from money-earning work, should be considered worthwhile? Name five kinds, and tell why you think they are as valuable as earning money.

## FOOTNOTES

[1] Winifred Bell, *Contemporary Social Welfare*, (New York: Macmillan Publishing Co., 1983), pp. 42–43.

[2] Ralph Dolgoff and Donald Feldstein, *Understanding Social Welfare*, 2nd ed., (New York: Longman Press, 1984), p. 144; and *Chicago Tribune*, July 19, 1986, pp. 1-2. Taken from U.S. Bureau of Census Reports.

[3] Frances Fox Piven and Richard Cloward, *New Class War: Reagan's Attack on the Welfare State and Its Consequences*, (New York: Pantheon Books, 1982), p. 7.

[4] Sar A. Levitan and Clifford M. Johnson, *Beyond the Safety Net*, (Cambridge, Mass., 1984), p. 151.

[5] Bell, *Contemporary Social Welfare*, pp. 81–84.

[6] Levitan and Johnson, *Beyond the Safety Net*, p. 151.

[7] Ibid.

[8] John L. Palmer and Isabel V. Sawhill, eds., *Reagan Record: An Assessment of America's Changing Domestic Priorities*, (Cambridge, Mass.: Ballinger Publishing Co., 1985).

[9] Jule M. Sugarman, Gary D. Bass, Nancy Amidei, David Plocher, Shannon Ferguson, and Julie Quiroz, *OMB Watch: A Citizen's Guide to Gramm-Rudman-Hollings*, (Washington, D.C.: Focus Project, Inc., 1986); and from "Capital Steps," (Indianapolis: United Way of Indiana, n.d).

[10] *Chicago Tribune*, July 19, 1986, pp. 1-2, from U.S. Bureau of Census Reports.

[11] Rosemary C. Sarri, Elizabeth Cramer, and Virginia du Rivage, "A Look at the Socioeconomic Status of Women in Michigan and the United States—1984," (Ann Arbor, Michigan: University of Michigan Institute for Social Research and the School of Social Work, 1985).

[12] Barbara J. Nelson, "Women's Poverty and Women's Citizenship: Some Political Consequences of Economic Marginality," *Signs: Journal of Women in Culture and Society*, Vol. 10, no. 2. (Winter 1984), pp. 209–231, esp. p. 216.

[13] Ibid.

[14] Palmer and Sawhill, *Reagan Record*.

[15] Levitan and Johnson, *Beyond the Safety Net*, p. 83.

[16] Palmer and Sawhill, *Reagan Record*.

[17] Ibid., p. 193 and footnote p. 193.

[18] Levitan and Johnson, *Beyond the Safety Net*, p. 152.

[19] From the Democratic Study Group, U.S. House of Representatives, James L. Oberstar, chairman, "Special Report: Gramm Rudman—the Cutting Begins." (Washington, D. C.: U.S. House of Representatives, January 1986) no. 99-26.

[20] Children's Defense Fund, "American Children in Poverty," (Washington, D.C.: CDF, 1984), p. 3.

[21] Ibid., p. x.

[22] Ibid.

[23] Palmer and Sawhill, *Reagan Record*, p. 222.

24Sugarman et al., "Citizen's Guide to GRH," p. 4.

25Piven and Cloward, *New Class War*, pp. 3–4.

26Children's Defense Fund, "American Children in Poverty," pp. 27–28.

27Ibid., p. 33.

28Tom Joe, "The Case for Income Support," in Alan Gartner, Colin Greer, and Frank Reismann, eds., *Beyond Reagan: Alternatives for the Eighties*, (New York: Harper and Row, 1984), pp. 81–90.

29"Current Operating Statistics," *Social Security Bulletin*, Vol. 47, no. 12, December 1984, p. 43.

30Deborah K. Zinn and Rosemary Sarri, "Turning Back the Clock on Public Welfare," *Signs: Journal of Women in Culture and Society*, Vol. 10, no. 2, (Winter 1984), pp. 355–370, esp. p. 357.

31Ibid.

32Mike Royko, "Welfare Recipients Blood Money Can No Longer Be Ignored," *Purdue Exponent*, October 1, 1986, p. 6.

33"Current Operating Statistics," *Social Security Bulletin*, Vol. 49, no. 2, (February 1986), p. 50.

34Marlene Sonju Chrissinger, "Factors Affecting Employment of Welfare Mothers," *Social Work*, Vol. 25, (January 1980), pp. 52–56.

35Levitan and Johnson, *Beyond the Safety Net*, p. 35.

36Bell, *Contemporary Social Welfare*, p. 128.

37Ibid.

38"Current Operating Statistics," *Social Security Bulletin*, February 1986, Table M-20, p. 42, and Table M-23, p. 44.

39Francis X. Russo and George Willis, *Human Services in America*, (Englewood Cliffs, N.J.: Prentice-Hall, 1986), p. 245.

40Dolgoff and Feldstein, *Understanding Social Welfare*, pp. 167–168.

41"Current Operating Statistics," *Social Security Bulletin*, February 1986, p. 3; and December 1986, p. 1.

42Ibid.

43Neil Gilbert and Harry Specht, *Dimensions of Social Welfare Policy*, (Englewood Cliffs, N.J.: Prentice Hall, 1974), pp. 171–172.

44"Current Operating Statistics," *Social Security Bulletin*, September 1984, p. 3.

45"Panel: Welfare Exams Wasted Millions," *Lafayette (Indiana) Journal and Courier*, October 30, 1986, p. 1.

46Levitan and Johnson, *Beyond the Safety Net*, p. 40.

47John Ehrenreich, *The Altruistic Imagination: A History of Social Work and Social Policy in the United States*, (Ithaca, N.Y.: Cornell University Press, 1985), p. 217.

48Children's Defense Fund, "America's Children," pp. 27–28.

49Levitan and Johnson, *Beyond the Safety Net*, p. 132.

50Michael Harrington. *The New American Poverty*, (New York: Holt, Rinehart, and Winston), 1984.

51Dolgoff and Feldstein, *Understanding Social Welfare*, pp. 173–174.

52Levitan and Johnson, *Beyond the Safety Net*, p. 150.

53Palmer and Sawhill, *Reagan Record*, p. 199.

54Howard Stanback, "Attacking Poverty with Economic Policy," in Gartner et al., *Beyond Reagan*, pp. 57–73, esp. p. 62.

55"Change in America," *Chronicle of Higher Education*, Vol. 32, no. 3, (September 17, 1986), p. 1.

56*Lafayette (Indiana) Journal and Courier*, October 2, 1986, p. 37.

[57]Barbara Howell and Leon Howell, "Food Stamps: Stories and Statistics," *Christian Century*, January 23–30, 1983, p. 730.

[58]Bell, *Contemporary Social Welfare*, p. 105.

[59]Howell and Howell, "Food Stamps: Stories and Statistics," p. 728.

[60]Robert Lekachman, *Greed is Not Enough: Reaganomics*, (New York: Pantheon Books, 1982), p. 85.

[61]Children's Defense Fund, "American Children," p. 33.

[62]Loretta Schwartz-Nobel, *Starving in the Shadow of Plenty*, (New York: G.P. Putnam's Sons, 1983). A review in *Lafayette (Indiana) Journal and Courier*.

[63]"Current Operating Statistics," *Social Security Bulletin*, February 1986, p. 21.

[64]Children's Defense Fund, "American Children," p. viii.

[65]Ibid., p. 6.

[66]"Reducing the Infant Mortality Rate," *Lafayette (Indiana) Journal and Courier*, February 4, 1987, p. C-4.

[67]Children's Defense Fund, "American Children," pp. 1–4.

[68]Levitan and Johnson, *Beyond the Safety Net*, p. 115.

[69]Children's Defense Fund, "American Children," p. 33.

[70]Ibid.

[71]"Current Operating Statistics," *Social Security Bulletin*, April 1983, p. 70.

[72]Oberstar et al., "Gramm Rudman—The Cutting Begins."

[73]"HUD Defends Accuracy of Count: Group Rebuts Report on Homeless," *Kansas City Times*, August 16, 1984, p. 5.

[74]Jack Anderson and Dale van Atta, "Model Shelter or Workhouse?" *Washington Post*, July 21, 1985, p. 2.

[75]Children's Defense Fund, "American Children," pp. 17–19.

[76]Levitan and Johnson, *Beyond the Safety Net*, p. 128.

[77]Bell, *Contemporary Social Welfare*, p. 131.

[78]"Education," *Newsweek on Campus*, February 1987," pp. 10–18.

[79]Levitan and Johnson, *Safety Net*, pp. 43–44.

[80]Leonard Beeghley, "Illusion and Reality in the Measurement of Poverty," *Social Problems*, Vol. 31, no. 3, (February 1984), pp. 324–333, esp. p. 329.

[81]Ehrenreich, *The Altruistic Imagination*, p. 222.

[82]"Current Operating Statistics," *Social Security Bulletin*, February 1986, p. 20.

[83]Ibid., p. 55.

[84]Ibid., Table 3., p. 17.

[85]United Way of Indiana, "Capital Steps," Indianapolis, 1986.

[86]"Current Operating Statistics," *Social Security Bulletin*, February 1986, p. 18.

[87]Ehrenreich, *The Altruistic Imagination*, p. 221.

[88]Levitan and Johnson, *Beyond the Safety Net*, p. 132.

[89]Dye and Zeigler, *Irony of Democracy*, p. 98.

[90]Ibid., p. 100.

[91]Ibid.

[92]Gabriel Kolko, *Wealth and Poverty in America*, (New York: Praeger Publishers, 1962), pp. 68, 69, in Dye and Zeigler, *Irony*, p. 106.

[93]Dye and Zeigler, *Irony*, p. 113.

[94]*Lafayette (Indiana) Journal and Courier*, October 27, 1986, p. A4.

[95]Michael Wines, "At Issue: Civil Rights," *National Journal*, March 27, 1982, p. 539.

[96]Palmer and Sawhill, *Reagan Record*, p. 208.

[97]Ibid.

[98]Ibid., p. 204.

[99]Palmer and Sawhill, in *Reagan Record*, p. 205. Source: Lynn C. Burbridge, "The Impact of Changes in Policy on the Federal Equal Employment Opportunity Effort," Washington, D.C.: The Urban Institute, November 1983, table 3. From Table 6.5. "OFCCP Enforcement Activities, FY 1980–FY 1983."

[100]Wines, "At Issue," pp. 536–541.

[101]Ibid., p. 539.

[102]Joe R. Feagin, *Racial and Ethnic Relations*, 2nd ed., (Englewood Cliffs, N.J.: Prentice Hall, 1984), p. 240.

[103]Wines, "At Issue," pp. 536–541.

[104]Levitan and Johnson, *Beyond the Safety Net*, p. 129.

[105]A black market in clean urine samples is developing to evade the problems of job drug testing. In addition, urine testing, particularly when a witness must watch the sample being taken, seems a real invasion of the Constitution's Fourth Amendment protection against unreasonable search and seizure. The General Accounting Office says that drug testing of federal employees is vague and potentially unconstitutional, and that the potential benefits are unmeasurable while the estimated costs are significant.

[106]In October 1986, Reagan launched a massive new war on drugs, after having taken away 46 percent of drug funding, according to the National Association of State Alcohol and Drug Abuse Directors. Reagan has proposed that $100 million be distributed to state-run alcohol and drug abuse treatment centers. This does not come close to replacing the cumulative loss of funds over the last several years. The Reagan administration cut spending for state drug and alcohol treatment by 25 percent in the 1982 fiscal year, and what was left was further undermined by inflation.

[107]Gartner, Greer, and Reissman, *Beyond Reagan: Alternatives for the Eighties*, p. 59.

[108]Barbara J. Nelson, "Women's Poverty and Women's Citizenship: Some Political Consequences of Economic Marginality," *Signs: Journal of Women in Culture and Society*, Vol. 10, no. 2, (Winter 1984, pp. 209–231, esp. p. 230.

[109]Lisa Langenbach, "Modernist and Traditionalist Issue Groups in the American Party System," unpublished doctoral dissertation, Purdue University, West Lafayette, Ind., August 1986, p. 174.

[110]Leonore Weitzman, "Give Women a Break in Settling Divorces," a review in *USA Today*, August 22, 1986, p. 10A.

[111]Ibid.

[112]Peter Shrag, "Review" of *The Divorce Revolution*, by Leonore J. Weitzman, (Free Press), in *The Nation*, December 7, 1985.

[113]Peter Day, *Social Work and Social Control*, (London: Tavistock Publications, 1981), p. 74.

[114]David Macarov, *Work and Welfare: the Unholy Alliance*, (Beverly Hills, Calif.: Sage Publications, 1980, p. 205.

[115]D'Vera Cohn, "Women's Mental Health Studied," *Chicago Tribune*, January 13, 1985, Section 6, p. 11.

[116]From the *NCASA News*, Spring 1986, *Premenstrual dysphoric disorder*: Symptoms are "persistent irritability or anger, tension, depression with a pessimistic attitude toward the future or markedly negative evaluation of self; emotional swings; marked fatigue, decrease or increase in appetite, food craving or binge eating; difficulty concentrating; decrease or increase in sexual interest; loss of interest in usual activities, insomnia, or hypersomnia. Ellen Goodman says that

> this could be read as another message that women go crazy that time of the month. It is still by and large men who define normal, even while committing 90 percent of the crimes and waging nearly all the wars. *Lafayette (Indiana) Journal and Courier*, May 14, 1986, p. A4.

*Masochistic personality disorder:* Symptoms are feelings of martyrdom and self-defeating behavior with at least six of the following: remains in relationships in which other exploit, abuse or take advantage of him or her, despite opportunities to alter the situation; sacrifices own interest for those of others; rejects help so as not to be a burden; complains about being unappreciated . . . feeling undeserving and pessimistic about the future. . . .

*Paraphilic rapism.* Symptoms include a persistent association, lasting a total of six months, between intense sexual arousal or desire, and acts, fantasies, or other stimuli involving coercing or forcing a non-consenting person to engage in vaginal, anal or oral intercourse . . . also sexual sadism if the individual is sexually aroused by the person's suffering, (e.g., more force is used than necessary to achieve the sexual acts desired).

[117]Macarov, *Work and Welfare,* p. 105.

[118]Gartner, *Beyond Reagan,* pp. 33–34.

[119]Macarov, *Work and Welfare,* pp. 160–161.

[120]Ibid., pp. 105–106.

[121]John Tropman, "Image of Public Welfare: Reality or Projection," *Public Welfare,* Vol. 35 (1977), pp. 17–83, esp. p. 71.

[122]"Change in America," *Chronicle of Higher Education,* Vol. 32, no. 3, (September 17, 1986), p. 1.

[123]Bell, *Contemporary Social Welfare,* pp. 81–84.

[124]Gartner et al., *Beyond Reagan,* p. 33, p. 34.

[125]Macarov, *Work and Welfare,* pp. 117–123.

[126]Ibid., p. 201.

[127]Ehrenreich, *The Altruistic Imagination,* p. 215.

[128]Galper, *Social Work Practice,* p. 51.

[129]Palmer and Sawhill, *Reagan Record,* pp. 214–215.

[130]Levitan and Johnson, *Beyond the Safety Net,* p. 157.

[131]Ehrenreich, *The Altruistic Imagination,* p. 185.

# 13

## FUTUREWORD

Social welfare does not exist in a vacuum. It is a product of the "moral state," influenced by and dependent upon the political economy of the nation. Therefore, its policies are fundamentally political and responsive to the requirements of those few who hold economic power in the United States. While altruism and the connection with spirituality have existed in the practice of social welfare from earliest times, rarely has altruism—or love—been enough to institute or maintain policies and programs that did not offer advantages to the elite. Where social welfare policies could help to control economic production, they have been instituted. Where they were primarily for the benefit of the recipients, they have been refused until such time as civil activism has threatened production. Even in our times of greatest humanitarian progress this has been true—the Social Security Act, the War on Poverty, and the civil rights movements of the 1960s would not have brought change without their threats of civil unrest.

On the other hand, the presence of social reformers and, since the middle 1800s, of the growing social work profession has given answers to civil unrest in a way that helped the distressed and disadvantaged. Their constant altruistic pressure, combined with an awareness of what the political traffic would bear, has produced many new programs and benefits. Although in the implementation of programs the social work profession has maintained a more or less conservative ambiance, the beginnings of movements have often been radical, innovative, and dedicated to the needs of those discriminated against by the structures of society. The double purposes of social welfare—social treatment and social control—have worked themselves out in as humanitarian a manner as the societal context would allow.

The retrenchment to conservatism in social welfare during the 1970s and 1980s represents a real change in the welfare state. Although the demand for social services has been growing, the resources for them—including social workers to staff programs—is drastically reduced. Demographic changes are having major implications for social welfare: For example, better medical care has prolonged the life of the elderly, meaning they will require long-term support and care. Other changes include the greater risk of poverty for children because of the effects of institutional racism and sexism on single-parent families; continued high unemployment and poverty of people of color because of their higher fertility rates combined with institutional racism; problems of child care as women enter the labor market in greater numbers than ever; and the continued failure of unions and lowering of wages throughout the United States and the world as multinational corporations continue to take work out of the nation and exploit workers in other countries.

The social work profession itself is following this conservative turn as workers become private practitioners more attuned to middle-class business than to social reform. Poor and high-risk populations, already falling through the "safety net" as government monies for programs are ripped away, are also denied access to private social work services for which they cannot pay. Social workers appear to be hiding from the realities of class polarization, ignoring new discrimination against women and people of color, and taking no stands on such horrendous problems as our growing numbers of homeless or the AIDS pandemic. For right now, we have taken the low road, turning away from the broader political problems that impact on the distressed and disadvantaged and leaving the leadership of social welfare to politicians who have little interest in altruism.

Perhaps the truth is too frightening to face, or perhaps we are settling for the little problems we can solve rather than the larger ones over which we have no power. Nevertheless, if we are to solve any problems, we must understand where they come from and why they persist, and this understanding requires that we look to the social context of social welfare, including the political and economic arenas of the nation and the world, along with the underlying values that spur on whatever activities taking place. The first step is knowledge: without it, we cannot begin. The second step is to rid ourselves of the obfuscations that confuse and limit us—among them that social welfare is solely benevolent, that society will protect the helpless, that our economic system is fair. The third step is to reassess our belief in income-producing work. We need to find a new definition of work as *socially* productive, one that values such occupations as mothering or fathering, homemaking, artistry, the writing of literature and music, social innovations, and technical inventions even if they do not produce income. Perhaps, given a new attitude toward ourselves and our technology, we can produce a society of well-being and beauty rather than one where money is the only standard of value.

## UNDERSTANDING SOCIAL POLICY

To be able to solve social problems requires an understanding of how policy is formulated and implemented. Any social welfare program begins with the *recognition that there is a social problem* that impacts on the well-being of individual, group, and community life and that other institutions no longer effectively handle it. For example, day care was not identified as a social problem to any great extent until World War II, when women were needed for factory work. Day care changed from a family problem to a social one and it became the province of social welfare. After World War II, day care in great part reverted from social problem to family problem, not to emerge again as a social concern until the 1960s.

The *history of the problem* also impacts on development of a social policy, as is illustrated by mothers' pensions. Single mothers, regardless of the reasons they were without husbands, have been suspect as sexually immoral or economically incapable almost literally from the beginning of the patriarchal system of property ownership. For this reason, despite the social evidence that children, families, and society as a whole would probably be better served with pensions than with institutionalization, national attempts to develop mothers' pensions failed until the Social Security Act of 1935. Even then the Aid to Dependent Children program was bound up with regulations to ensure that families receiving pensions would abide by strict "morality" rules or lose the pensions.

The *historic time* at which a new program is possible must also be considered: its success requires the serendipitous occurrence of political, economic, and spiritual or religious recognition of need. For AFDC, earlier reform efforts, increased need during the Depression, a growing awareness that "moral" widows could take care of their families (though state surveillance had to insure it was still needed), and altruistic ideals about the place of mother in the family converged. Mothers' pensions became possible in the 1900s, whereas in the 1800s they were still seen as abetting pauperism in children.

Figure 13.1 illustrates that society's values at any particular time will elicit awareness of certain social problems. Policies are created and are shaped by the social context. The programs that develop are never simply in response to needs but at every step are influenced by the social values of the time (see Figure 13.1).

The *question of values* is particularly important in analyzing a policy. Any social program is underlaid with societal values as well as humanitarian ones, and these may not always agree. For example, Medicare was set up on the basis that older people deserve medical care, yet our private enterprise values declare that the private sector should provide competitive medical care so that clients can choose what they want. This is a major reason that national health coverage took so long to evolve. Moreover, economic and political values often overwhelm humanitarian ones. Our national unemployment policy of 5 percent unemployed is a good example of this: By maintaining such an unemployment standard, a low-wage work force is always available. This profits producers in several ways: they make more profits with more sales, and they need not pay their marginal workers at full pay or full time, saving costs of fringe benefits.

The *making of policy* is a political process—formulating, developing, making concessions to values and to other needs, planning the goals and means of policy, and implementing the policy in a social program. Any policy is a *political artifact* and is seldom a product of straightforward altruism and action. The highest ideals of service must bend to political necessity and compromise to be implemented, and policy makes strange bedfellows—for example, the abortion issue has made political teammates of far-right Christian fundamentalists and conservative Jews and Catholics—people who may not agree on any other issue.

Policies may be written—in legislation, court decisions, manuals of organizational procedure, or bylaws. However, unwritten policies—things that happen by default, unwritten "laws" of procedure in an agency, or "custom"—are just as important as are written policies. For example, it is a written policy in many prisons or jails that education be provided for inmates. However, since many policies do not specify *how* education be provided, officials set their own procedures. For some, real schooling in classes is provided and may lead to a degree. In others, "education" may be

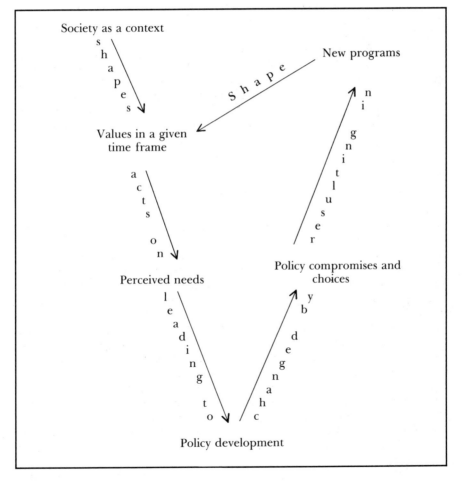

**FIGURE 13.1**  The Context of Policy

the provision of television or writing paper. These "ways of procedure" are in fact policies by omission.

New social welfare policies are almost never "new." Rather, existing policies are expanded upon or "incremented." Once a base policy is established, adding new details is easier. Our history abounds with examples of "policy by increment"—for example, the addition of the Aid to the Disabled program to the Social Security Act of 1935; changing the surplus foods program incrementally first to food stamps purchased by recipients, then free food stamps; the additions over the past two decades to the Medicare program; "price indexing" added to Social Security benefits; the addition of the Supplemental Security Income (SSI) to public assistance; and the increments in cash benefits to all categories of social insurance and public assistance.

Once a policy is agreed upon, subpolicies as to how it will be carried out must be decided, and again each choice is subject to politics and to compromise. For example, the most basic political compromise of Medicaid was to use private health care-givers rather than setting up a system of socialized medicine. Although policymakers realized the need for nationalized health care, it had important foes—the American Medical Association, health care providers such as hospitals and nursing homes, and the private health insurance industry. They were successful in limiting medical care to the means tested poor through private care-givers. Only the process of means testing was to be a public program: Medicaid claims are authorized by public welfare departments but handled through private medical insurance companies.

## DYNAMICS OF SOCIAL POLICY FORMULATION

To help us understand some of the problems of policy formulation, let us take a current problem—the AIDS pandemic, one of the most overwhelming social issues today. There are real questions as to whether American society considers AIDS a social problem. To begin with, it is ostensibly a medical problem; like venereal disease or abortions as medical problems, however, AIDS is so ringed around with values that its medical effects appear secondary to morality. Many members of society consider AIDS either a personal problem (not one potentially affecting all of society) or a moral problem (a punishment from God for homosexual, promiscuous, or criminal behavior such as drug use). Powerful people and groups are arguing that the federal government should stay out of the AIDS fight. Thus at at time when other nations are arming themselves, the United States is caught up in debates about sexual morality: people would not get AIDS if they were "decent." This perspective has prevented research into the causes and cures of AIDS, delayed help for AIDS victims and their families, and denied education about AIDS to many of the most vulnerable people—sexually active teenagers.

There is no doubt that other nations consider AIDS a social and medical problem, and an extremely dangerous one. In May 1986, the

World Health Organization (WHO) hired an American, Dr. Jonathan Mann, to lead its team of AIDS researchers. Their 1987 budget is $34 million, with a projected budget for 1988 of $63 million. In five years WHO expects to be spending $200 million a year in research and service delivery for AIDS. WHO estimates that half a million Europeans are infected, as are more than forty thousand Americans, and some nations in West Africa are in such dire straits that WHO believes nothing can be done for them.

The United States needs a national policy on AIDS, and soon, for it can strike anyone and causes catastrophic effects on physical health, mental health, medical care, economic care, and the humanitarian aspects of our society. According to the National Academy of Sciences, only a massive research campaign can avert a national tragedy. It asks that funding be quadrupled from the 1986 level—$1 billion in new funds. In addition, it recommends another $1 billion a year be spent on sex education, public health programs, efforts to help high risk people to change their sexual habits, blood screening, and rehabilitation for drug abusers, including providing disposable syringes. They estimate that the cost of caring for persons with AIDS will rise to between $8 billion and $16 billion by 1991.[1]

Of persons testing positive for carrying the AIDS virus, it is believed that about one third will actually get the disease. By late October 1986, 26,875 Americans had developed AIDS and 15,070 had died. As of spring 1987, it was estimated that one of every thirty men in the United States carries the AIDS virus, or 1.5 million between the ages of 20 and 50. Reports of heterosexually transmitted AIDS has increased by over 200 percent in the United States, while cases among gay men and intravenous drug users grew by 80 percent. The total heterosexual caseload in December 1986, was 1,079 persons, or 4 percent of the 28,532 cases.[2] Among other high risk groups are prostitutes, though they are more likely to pick up AIDS from intravenous drug use than from sexual contact; Catholic priests, of whom it is estimated that about one third under the age of 45 are sexually active; members of the Armed Forces (in 1986, 1.5 per thousand tested positive)[3]; and people needing blood transfusions. Infants born to AIDS carriers may also develop the disease.

Given the scope and possible consequences of AIDS, only a national program of funding would be adequate, and this means national standards for service. Such a policy would lead to programs on health care, AIDS research, mental health care, educational policies, blood bank policies, the care of children with AIDS, the distribution of sterile needles to drug addicts or perhaps new policies on the treatment of drug addicts, and massive informational campaigns.

Let us assume that value issues will be overcome by the sheer number of problems associated with AIDS. Although it is first and foremost a health problem, many of its ramifications will fall into the province of social welfare. They include social help and counseling for AIDS victims and their families; birth control clinics that now offer counseling and help for sexually transmitted diseases; care of indigent AIDS victims through public assistance, Medicaid, and Medicare; and the care of the children of AIDS victims and children who are themselves AIDS victims, to name only a few.

As social workers we have always stepped into the breach when no one else would help, and AIDS is a problem that will call on social workers in many ways. Not all social workers can do all things: Some may be able to work with individuals, and some others must lobby, teach, and do research on the problems associated with AIDS. Now, however, is the time to plan, for the problems will come as surely as the AIDS virus spreads throughout the world.

Incrementalism may help in the development of programs to deal with AIDS, though it is a very slow process. We already have Medicaid, and possibly some AIDS victims are already using it. AIDS could also be seen as a kind of total disability and its victims qualify for Social Security, SSI, and Medicare, particularly if a catastrophic health bill is passed. Child welfare might also be incrementalized within the Crippled Children's program or programs for protective services in both Departments of Public Welfare and the Juvenile Justice system. Mental health counseling must be made available to AIDS victims and their families regardless of their ability to pay. Public assistance must be prepared to deal with a new kind of poverty as the cost of AIDS wipes out families' financial resources.

National policies and programs on AIDS will change the face of all our social welfare care and, very likely, of society itself. They will incrementalize to other kinds of care as we move to an institutional perspective on health care. In addition, AIDS will undoubtedly change the way we look at sexual morality, for education for AIDS recognizes the fact that teenagers are sexually active despite religious and family teachings. Bringing AIDS education into the open will bring sex education into the open with more than a focus on biology. Children will learn methods of birth control as well as AIDS control, and sexual choice—especially the choice to say no—will become a part of our teenage culture. It is likely also that the age of sexual liberation is past, because now free sexuality may mean death.

In any event, AIDS will change our society. Great numbers of people will probably die before a cure is found, causing repercussions in both polity and economy. Marriages and child-bearing may be delayed or put off altogether, and people will be much more careful about sexual promiscuity. However, these are long-range changes in our culture. In the short run, we must change our attitudes about AIDS or we will have no long run.

It is time for the social work profession to become more involved in public social policy, not just for AIDS victims but in every area of care for the distressed and disadvantaged. The course of events that have pushed social welfare back to the 1930s, and the AIDS pandemic as an outside spur to action, require action by the group of people who have traditionally answered calls for help. Being consciences for society is never easy, but the times call for conscience. Hopefully, the social work profession will answer.

## CONCLUSION

We began this journey through the history of social welfare by talking about love. Yet, through much of the book, our topics have seemed far from the idea of love and very much about social control, because the story of social welfare is as much one of control as of help. Since before the time of Jesus welfare reform has meant giving women only barely enough to eke out their lives if they had no man to support them. For the poor, welfare has meant providing benefits to quell their revolt against inequities in their labor for other people. For people who are "different," whether in appearance, religion, or place of origin, it has meant depriving them of equality in human rights so that they might be exploited even more. While poor men have been used as the cogs in the grinding mill of production, women have been used both in this manner and as reproducers of children for future work. Racism has complicated and augmented exploitation of women and workers alike.

Life is never "fair," but as social welfarists, we must be particularly aware that our immediate "band-aid" efforts may only perpetuate an inequitable system; for some, we help to make life even more unfair. We must understand that we serve the rich and powerful as well as the distressed and disadvantaged. In the "welfare reform" of the Reagan 1980s we are repeating the past: of pre-Christian times for women; pre-Civil War times for people of color; and pre-mercantilist times for the poor. The Moral Majority, the New Right, and Reaganomics are undermining gains won by women over the past two decades (and two centuries and two millenia), gains that were not antimale or antifamily or anti-American but pro-equality, pro-choice, pro-humankind, in relationships of respect and honor with men.

We must also be concerned, in this era, about the nation's retreat from civil rights. There is no good or logical reason why people of color, or those who depart from the "American ideal" because of mental, physical, or social differences, should be denied rights and opportunities. Civil inequalities are written into our political and economic structures, but we must not allow civil rights to be eroded by newly legitimated prejudices as businesses refuse to hire, courts refuse to hear, and those whose sworn duty it is to enforce antidiscriminatory laws and procedures turn to facile excuses of "reverse discrimination."

It is the unconditional love for humanity in all its colors, forms, and features that inspires the best part of social welfare. We must not permit any shadows to blind us from that vision. Love is not enough to change the world, but it is surely the best place to begin.

## STUDY QUESTIONS

1. In specifically behavioral terms, state a national policy for the homeless deriving from the value stance that every citizen should have a permanent home (rather than homeless shelters).

2. Taking the problem of overpopulation in the world, list groups and persons that might be opposed to abortion and those who would support it, and explain where the values of each set comes from.

3. Explain where the values for and against wife battering come from in our society.

4. Take any program that might come from a national policy on AIDS and discuss eligibility for it, the services to be provided, and how the services will get from the organization to the client.

5. If one policy that comes from the AIDS pandemic is that all AIDS victims must be quarantined in federal institutions, that would mean that the federal government would have to pay for their medical care until their deaths. What are the negative consequences of this? What are the positive consequences?

## FOOTNOTES

[1]*Lafayette Journal and Courier*, (Lafayette, Indiana), June 2, 1987, p. 1.

[2]Katie Lieshman, "Heterosexuals and AIDS," *Atlantic Monthly* February 1987, pp. 39–58, esp. p. 40.

[3]Ibid., reporting the results of a study by Dr. Joyce Wallace, president of the Foundation for Research on Sexually Transmitted Disease in New York, p. 46.

# BIBLIOGRAPHY

ABBOTT, EDITH. *Some American Pioneers in Social Welfare*. Chicago: University of Chicago Press, 1937.

ABRAMOVITZ, MIMI. "The Conservative Program is a Women's Issue." *Journal of Sociology and Social Welfare*. Vol. 9, no. 3, (September 1982), pp. 399–424.

ADAMS, GORDON. "Restructuring the National Defense Policy." In Gartner et al., *Beyond Reagan*, pp. 167–192.

ADDAMS, JANE. *A Centennial Reader*. New York: Macmillan Publishing Co., 1960, pp. 10–14.

AGUIRRE, LYDIA R. "The Meaning of the Chicano Movement," *Social Casework*, Vol. 55 (1971), p. 259.

ANDERSON, CHARLES. *Toward a New Sociology*, 2nd ed. Homewood, Illinois: Dorsey Press, 1974.

ANDERSON, JACK, and DALE VAN ATTA. "Model Shelter or Workhouse?" *Washington Post*, July 21, 1985.

ANDERSON, JOSEPH. *Social Work Methods and Processes*. Belmont, Calif.: Wadsworth Publishing Co., Inc., 1981.

ARONOWITZ, STANLEY. "Labor Is the Key." In Gartner et al., eds., *Beyond Reagan*, pp. 256–263.

"AVOIDING A MEDICAL CATASTROPHE." *Lafayette (Indiana) Journal and Courier*, October 30, 1986, p. A7.

AXINN, JUNE, and HERMAN LEVIN. *Social Welfare: A History of the American Response to Need*, 2nd ed. New York: Harper & Row, 1982.

BAIGENT, MICHAEL, RICHARD LEIGH, and HENRY LINCOLN. *Holy Blood, Holy Grail*. New York: A Dell Book, 1982.

BARON, SALO W. *A Social and Religious History of the Jews:* Vol. I. *To the Beginnning of the Christian Era*. New York: Columbia University Press, 1962.

BARRERA, M., C. MUNOZ, and C. ORNELAS. "The Barrio as an Internal Colony." In Harlan Hahn, ed. *Urban Affairs Annual Review*, Vol. 6. Beverly Hills: Sage Publications, 1972, pp. 465–498.

BECKER, EARNEST. *The Denial of Death*. New York: Free Press, 1973.

BEEGHLEY, LEONARD. "Illusion and Reality in the Measurement of Poverty." *Social Problems*, Vol. 31, no. 3. (February 1984), pp. 324–337.

BEERS, CLIFFORD. *A Mind That Found Itself*. Garden City, New York: Doubleday & Co., 1935.

BEL, LEACHMAN, and ALVIN SCHORR. *Public Policy and Income Distribution.* New York: New York University Center for Studies in Income Maintenance Policy, 1974.

BELL, WINIFRED. *Aid to Dependent Children.* New York: Columbia University Press, 1965.

BELL, WINIFRED. *Contemporary Social Welfare.* New York: Macmillan Publishing Co., 1983.

BENNETT, LERONE, JR. *Before the Mayflower: A History of the Negro in America,* rev. ed. Chicago: Johnson Publishing Co., 1966.

BERCH, BETTINA. *The Endless Day: The Political Economy of Women and Work.* New York: Harcourt Brace Jovanivich, Inc., 1982.

BERRY, BENJAMIN D. "Black Power and Straight White Males," in Glenn R. Bucher, ed. *Straight/White/Male.* Philadelphia: Fortress Press, 1976, quoting Franz Fanon, *Black Skin, White Masks,* trans. Charles L. Markmann. New York: Grove Press, 1967.

BIANCHI, EUGENE C., and ROSEMARY RADFORD RUETHER, eds. *From Machismo to Mutuality: Essays on Sexism and Woman-Man Liberation.* New York: Paulist Press, 1976.

BIANCHI, EUGENE C. "Psychic Celibacy and the Quest for Mutuality" In Eugene C. Bianchi and Rosemary Radford Ruether, eds. *From Machismo to Mutuality.*

BIANCHI, EUGENE C. "The Super-Bowl Culture of Male Violence." In Bianchi and Ruether, eds. *From Machismo to Mutuality.*

BLACKER, C. P., ed. *Problem Families.* London: Eugenics Society, 1947.

BREMMER, ROBERT H. *From the Depths.* New York: New York University Press.

BRILL, NAOMI. *Teamwork: Working Together in the Human Services.* New York: J.B. Lippincott Company, 1976.

BROVERMAN, I.K., D.M. BROVERMAN, F.E. CLARKSON, P. S. ROSENKRANTZ, and S.R. VOGEL. "Sex Role Stereotypes and Clinical Judgments of Mental Health," *Journal of Counseling and Clinical Psychology,* Vol. 34 (1975), pp. 1–7.

BROWN, PRUDENCE. *Women, Children, and Poverty in America.* New York: Ford Foundation, January 1985.

BRUERE, ROBERT W. "The Good Samaritan, Inc." *Harper's Monthly Magazine,* Vol. 120, 1910.

BUCHER, GLENN R. "The Oppressor Dehumanized," in Bucher, ed., *Straight/White/Male.*

BUCHER, GLENN R., ed. *Straight/White/Male.* Philadelphia: Fortress Press, 1976.

BURBRIDGE, LYNN C. "The Impact of Changes in Policy on the Federal Equal Employment Opportunity Effort." Washington, D.C.: The Urban Institute, November 1983, Table 3.

CAPRA, FRITJOF. *The Tao of Physics: An Exploration of the Parallels between Modern Physics and Eastern Mysticism.* Berkeley, Calif.: Shambhala Publications, 1975.

CHAFE, WILLIAM H. "Eleanor Roosevelt." In Linda K. Kerber and Jane DeHart Mathews, eds. *Women's America.* New York: Oxford University Press, 1982, pp. 344–353.

CHEN, JACK. *The Chinese of America.* San Francisco: Harper & Row, Publishers, 1980.

CHILDREN'S DEFENSE FUND. "American Children in Poverty." Washington, D.C.: CDF, 1984.

"CHOICES," Vol. 3. (Forest Hills, New York: Women's Medical Center, Summer/Fall 1984). From "Feminization of Poverty," a series of hearings held in New York in June, 1984, by Gail S. Shaffer, secretary of state, New York State, and Ronnie Eldridge, director, New York State Women's Division.

CHRISSINGER, MARLENE SONJU. "Factors Affecting Employment of Welfare Mothers." *Social Work,* Vol. 25 (January 1980), pp. 52–56.

*CHRONICLE OF HIGHER EDUCATION.* "Change in America," Vol. 23. no. 3 (September 17, 1986).

COHN, D'VERA. "Women's Mental Health Studied," *Chicago Tribune,* January 13, 1986.

COLL, BLANCHE. "Public Assistance in the United States: Colonial to 1860." In In E. W. Martin, ed. *Comparative Development in Social Welfare.* London: Allen and Unwin, 1972, pp. 128–158.

COLL, BLANCHE D. *Perspectives in Public Welfare: A History.* U.S. Department of Health, Education, and Welfare Social Rehabilitation Service 91969, Washington, D.C.: U.S. Government Printing Office, 1971.

COMPTON, BEULAH R. *Introduction to Social Welfare and Social Work: Structure, Function, and Process.* Homewood, Illinois: The Dorsey Press, 1980.

CONGRESSIONAL RECORD S6180, May 23, 1968.

CONNELLY, MARK THOMAS. "Prostitution, Veneral Disease, and American Medicine." In Judith Walzer Leavitt, ed. *Women and Health in America.* Madison: Univesity of Wisconsin Press, 1984, pp. 327–344.

CONOVER, PAMELA JOHNSON, and VIRGINIA GRAY. *Feminism and the New Right: Conflict over the American Family.* New York: Praeger Publishers, 1983.

CONSTANATELOS, D. *Byzantine Philanthropy and Social Welfare.* New Brunswick, N.J.: Rutgers University Press, 1968.

CORNING, PETER. *The Synergistic Hypothesis.* New York: McGraw Hill Book Co., 1983.

COUNCIL ON SOCIAL WORK EDUCATION. *Statistics on Social Work Education in the United States: 1983.* New York: Council on Social Work Education, 1984.

COWARD, ROSALIND. *Patriarchal Precedents: Sexuality and Social Relations.* London: Routledge and Kegan Paul, 1983.

CRAMPTON, HELEN M., and KENNETH KAISER. *Social Welfare: Institution and Process.* New York: Random House, 1970.

DALY, MARY. *Gyn/Ecology: The MetaEthics of Feminism.* Boston: Beacon Press, 1978.

DANZIGER, SHELDON. A speech at Ball State University, Muncie, Indiana. October 6, 1986.

DARENKAMP, ANGELA, JOHN McCLYMER, MARY MOYNIHAN, and ARLENE VADUM. *Images of Women in American Popular Culture.* New York: Harcourt Brace Jovanovich, 1985.

DAVIES, JAMES C. "Toward a Theory of Revolution," *American Sociological Review,* Vol. 27 (February 1962).

DAVIS, ANGELA. *Women, Race, and Class.* New York: Vintage Press, February 1983.

DAVIS, KINGSLEY, and WILBERT E. MOORE. "Some Principles of Stratification." *American Sociological Review,* Vol. 10, (1945).

DAY, PETER. *Social Work and Social Control.* London: Tavistock Publications, 1981.

DAY, PHYLLIS J. "Social Welfare: Context for Social Control." *Journal of Sociology and Social Welfare,* Vol. 8, no. 1 (March, 1981).

DAY, PHYLLIS J. "Values Clarification Through Science Fiction." *Journal of Sociology and Social Welfare.* Vol. 7, no. 6 (November, 1980).

DAY, PHYLLIS J., HARRY J. MACY, and EUGENE JACKSON. "A Simultaneity Model of Social Work Practice." *Journal of Social Work Education,* Vol. 20, no. 2 (Spring, 1984), pp. 17–24.

DAY, PHYLLIS J. "Sex Role Sterotypes and Public Assistance." *Social Service Review,* (March, 1979), pp. 106–115.

DAY, PHYLLIS J., HARRY J. MACY, and EUGENE JACKSON. *Social Working: Exercises in Generalist Practice.* Englewood Cliffs, N.J.: Prentice Hall, 1985.

DEGLER, CARL N. "What Ought to Be and What Was: Women's Sexuality in the Nineteenth Century." In Judith Walzer Leavitt, ed. *Women and Health in America.* Madison: University of Wisconsin Press, 1984.

DE RIENCOURT, AMAURY. *Sex and Power in History.* New York: Dell Publishing, 1974.

DOBELSTEIN, ANDREW W. *Politics, Economics, and Public Welfare.* Englewood Cliffs, N.J.: Prentice Hall, 1980.

DOLGOFF, RALPH, and DONALD FELDSTEIN. *Understanding Social Welfare,* 2nd ed. New York: Longman Press, 1984.

DOYLE, WILMA, LEONARD Z. BREEN, and ROBERT EICHHORN. *Synopsis of the Older Americans Act, Revised.* West Lafayette, Ind.: Department of Sociology and Anthropology, Purdue University, 1976.

DROUT, JOHN A., and DIXON R. FOX. *The Completion of Independence.* New York: Macmillan Publishing Co., 1944, pp. 373–374.

DUNN, FINLEY PETER. "The Carnegie Libraries." In *Democracy and the Gospel of Wealth.* Gail Kennedy, ed. Boston: D.C. Heath and Co., 1949.

DYE, MARY SCHROM. "Mary Breckinridge, The Frontier Nursing Service, and the Introduction of Nurse-Midwifery in the United States." In Judith Walzer Leavitt, ed. *Women and Health in America.* Madison: University of Wisconsin Press, 1984, pp. 327–344.

DYE, THOMAS R., and L. HARMON ZEIGLER. *The Irony of Democracy.* Belmont, Calif.: Wadsworth Publishing Co., 1970.

EELLS, KENNETH et al., *Intelligence and Cultural Differences.* Chicago: University of Chicago Press, 1951.

EHRENREICH, BARBARA, and DEIRDRE ENGLISH. *Complaints and Disorders: The Sexual Politics of Sickness.* Old Westbury, N.Y.: The Feminist Press, Glass Mountain Pamphlet no. 2, 1973.

EHRENREICH, JOHN. *The Altruistic Imagination: A History of Social Work and Social Policy in the United States.* New York: Cornell University Press, 1985.

EISENSTEIN, ZILLAH R. "The Patriarchal Relations of the Reagan State." *Signs: Journal of Women in Culture and Society.* Vol. 10, no. 2 (Winter 1984), pp. 329–338.

EITZEN, STANLEY. *In Conflict and Order: Understanding Society,* 3rd ed. Boston: Allyn and Bacon, 1985.

ESPING-ANDERS, GOSTA, MARTIN REIN, and LEE RAINWATER, EDS. *Stagnation and Renewal in Social Policy.* New York: M. E. Sharpe, 1986.

FASTEAU, MARC FEIGEN. *The Male Machine.* New York: McGraw-Hill Book Co., 1974.

FEAGIN, JOE R. *Racial and Ethnic Relations.* Englewood Cliffs, N.J.: Prentice Hall, 1985.

FEDERICO, RONALD C. *The Social Welfare Institution: An Introduction.* Lexington, Mass: D. C. Heath and Company, 1976.

FONER, PHILIP S. *History of the Labor Movement in the U.S.* New York: International Publishers, 1947.

FRIEDLANDER, WALTER A., and ROBERT Z. APTE. *Introduction to Social Welfare.* Englewood Cliffs, N.J.: Prentice Hall, 1974.

GALBRAITH, JOHN KENNETH. *The Affluent Society.* Boston: Houghton Mifflin, 1960.

GALPER, JEFFREY. *Social Work Practice: A Radical Perspective.* Englewood Cliffs, N.J.: Prentice Hall, 1980.

GARTNER, ALAN, COLIN GREER, and FRANK REISSMAN, EDS. *Beyond Reagan: Alternatives for the Eighties.* New York: Harper & Row, 1984.

GIACOMO, CAROLE. "Sterilization Count Higher than Expected." *Hartford (Connecticut) Courant,* October 13, 1980.

GIES, FRANCES, and JOSEPH GIES. *Women in the Middle Ages.* New York: Barnes and Noble, 1978.

GILBERT, NEIL, and HARRY SPECHT. *Dimensions of Social Welfare Policy.* Englewood Cliffs, N.J.: Prentice Hall, 1974.

GILBERT, NEIL, and HARRY SPECHT. *Emergence of Social Welfare and Social Work,* 2nd ed. Itasca, Ill., F. E. Peacock Publishers, 1981.

GIMBUTAS, MARIJA. *The Goddesses and Gods of Old Europe.* Berkeley and Los Angeles: University of California Press, 1982.

GINGER, RAY. "The Women at Hull-House." In Linda K. Kerber and Jane DeHart Mathews, eds. *Women's America.* New York: Oxford University Press, 1982, pp. 263–272.

GLASS, JUSTINE. *Witchcraft: The Sixth Sense.* North Hollywood: Wilshire Book Co., 1973.

GOROFF, NORMAN. "Humanism and Social Work: Paradoxes, Problems, and Promises" (mimeographed). West Hartford, Conn.: University of Connecticut School of Social Work, 1977.

GOUGH, KATHLEEN. "The Origin of the Family." In Rayna Reiter, ed. *Toward an Anthropology of Women.* New York: Monthly Review Press, 1975, pp. 51–76.

GRAY, ELIZABETH DODSON. *Green Paradise Lost.* Wellesley, Mass.: Roundtable Press, 1981.

GREEN, COLIN, and JOHN DE WIND. "A Labor-Oriented Perspective on Immigration Policy." In Gartner, Greer, and Reissman, eds. *Beyond Reagan: Alternatives for the Eighties.* New York: Harper & Row, 1984.

GREENWOOD, ERNEST. " 'Attributes of a Profession." In Neil Gilbert and Harry Specht, eds. *The Emergence of Social Welfare and Social Work,* 2nd ed. Itasca, Ill., F. E. Peacock Publishers, 1981, pp. 241–254.

GREENWOOD, ERNEST. "Attributes of a Profession' Revisited." In Neil Gilbert and Harry Specht, eds. *The Emergence of Social Welfare and Social Work,* 2nd ed. Itasca, Ill., F. E. Peacock, Publishers, 1981, pp. 255–275.

GROB, GERALD N., advisory editor. *The State and Public Welfare in Nineteenth Century America.* New York: Arno Press, 1976.

HALBERSTRAM, DAVID. *The Best and the Brightest.* New York: Random House, 1972, cited by Gray, *Green Paradise Lost.* Hall, Raymond, ed. *Black Separatism and Social Reality: Rhetoric and Reason.* New York: Pergamon Press, 1976.

HALL, RAYMOND, ed. *Black Separatism and Social Reality: Rhetoric and Reason.* New York: Pergamon Press, 1976.

HANDEL, GERALD. *Social Welfare in Western Society.* New York: Random House, 1982.

HANDLER, JOEL. *Reforming the Poor.* New York: Basic Books, 1972.

HANDLER, JOEL, and ELLEN J. HOLLINGSWORTH. *The Deserving Poor: A Study of Welfare Administration.* Chicago: Markham Publishing, 1971.

HANDS, A. R. *Charities and Social Aid in Greece and Rome.* Ithaca, N. Y.: Cornell University Press, 1968.

HARRINGTON, MICHAEL. *The New American Poverty.* New York: Holt, Rinehart and Winston, 1984.

HARRIS, JAY T. "2 Americas, black, white, move to bigger divisions." *Lafayette (Indiana) Journal and Courier,* November 4, 1984, p. B-3.

HEFFERNAN, W. JOSEPH. *Introduction to Social Welfare Policy: Power, Scarcity, and Human Needs.* Itasca, Ill.: F. E. Peacock Publishers, 1979.

HILL, FLORENCE. *Children of the State.* London: Macmillan, 1868.

HOLLINGSHEAD, AUGUST B. *Elmtown's Youth.* New York: Science Editions, 1961.

HOWELL, BARBARA, and LEON HOWELL. "Food Stamps: Stories and Statistics." *Christian Century,* June 23–30, 1982.

HRABA, JOSEPH. *American Ethnicity.* Itasca, Ill.: F. E. Peacock, 1979.

"HUD DEFENDS ACCURACY OF COUNT: GROUP REBUTS REPORT ON HOMELESS." *Kansas City Times,* August 16, 1984.

HUNTER, MARY SKI, and DENNIS SALEEBY. "Spirit and Substance: Beginnings in the Education of Radical Social Workers." *Journal of Education for Social Work,* Vol. 13, no. 2, (Spring 1977), pp. 60–70.

HUNTER, ROBERT. *Poverty.* New York: Grosset and Dunlap, 1904.

HUTTMAN, ELIZABETH D. *Introduction to Social Policy.* New York: McGraw-Hill Book Company, 1981.

HYMOWITZ, CAROLE, and MICHAELE WEISSMAN. *A History of Women in America.* New York: Bantam Books, 1980.

IFFERT, ROBERT E. "Retention and Withdrawal of College Students." *Office of Education Bulletin No. 1.* Washington, D.C.: U.S. Government Printing Office, 1958.

IRONS, PETER. "The Return of the 'Yellow Peril'." *The Nation,* October 19, 1985.

JACOBS, WILLIAM JAY. *Women in American History.* Encino, Calif.: Glencoe Publishing, 1976.

JANSSON, BRUCE S. *Theory and Practicie of Social Welfare Policy.* Belmont, Calif.: Wadsworth Publishing Co., 1984.

JOE, TOM. "The Case for Income Support." In Gartner, Greer, and Reissman, eds. *Beyond Reagan: Alternatives for the Eighties.* New York: Harper & Row, 1984.

JOHNSON, E. A. J. *American Economic Thought in the Seventeenth Century.* London: P. S. King, 1932. 31.

JOHNSON, MICHAEL P. "Smothered Slave Infants: Were Slave Mothers at Fault?" In Linda K. Kerber and Jane DeHart Mathews, eds. *Women's America.* New York: Oxford University Press, 1982, pp. 102–110.

JONES, MARY GLADYS. *Hannah More.* Cambridge: Cambridge University Press, 1952.

KAHN, ALFRED J. *Social Policy and Social Services.* New York: Random House, 1973.

KATZ, MICHAEL B. *Poverty and Policy in American History.* New York: Academic Press, 1983.

KELLOGG, KATE. "The Far-Right Fringe." *Michigan Today,* June 1987, pp. 6–9.

KERBER, LINDA K., and JANE DEHART MATHEWS, eds. *Women's America.* New York: Oxford University Press, 1982.

KESSLER-HARRIS, ALICE. *Out to Work: A History of Wage-Earning Women in the United States.* New York: Oxford University Press, 1982.

KESSLER-HARRIS, ALICE. "Where are the Organized Women Workers?" In Kerber and Mathews, eds. *Women's America.* New York: Oxford University Press, 1982, pp. 225–240.

KOLKO, GABRIEL. *Wealth and Poverty in America.* New York: Praeger Press, 1962.

LAFAYETTE (INDIANA) JOURNAL AND COURIER. February 4, 1987; June 21, 1987; July 23, 1987.

LAING, R. D., and A. ESTERSON. *Sanity, Madness, and the Family.* Harmondsworth: Penguin, 1971.

LANGENBACH, LISA. "Modernist and Traditionalist Issue Groups in the American Party System: An Examination of the Realigning Potential of Cultural Issues in Changing Cleavage Structures." Unpublished dissertation. Purdue University, West Lafayette, Ind., August 1986.

LANSING, J. B., T. LORIMER, and C. MORIGUCHI. *How People Pay for College.* Ann Arbor: University of Michigan Press, 1960.

LEAVITT, JUDITH WALZER, ed. *Women and Health in America.* Madison: University of Wisconsin Press, 1984.

LEISHMAN, KATIE. "Heterosexuals and AIDS." *Atlantic Monthly, February 1987, pp. 39–58.*

LEKACHMAN, ROBERT. *Greed Is Not Enough: Reaganomics.* New York: Pantheon Books, 1982.

LEONARD, P. "Towards a Paradigm for Radical Practice." In R. Bailey and M. Brake, eds. *Radical Social Work.* London: Edward Arnold, 1973.

LEOPOLD, ALDO. *A Sand County Almanac with Essays on Conservation from Round River.* New York: Sierra Club/Ballantine Books, 1970.

LEVITAN, SAR A., MARTIN REIN, and DAVID MARWICK. *Work and Welfare Go Together.* Baltimore: Johns Hopkins University Press, 1972.

LEVITAN, SAR A. and CLIFFORD M. JOHNSON. *Beyond the Safety Net.* Cambridge, Mass.: Ballinger Publishing Co., 1984.

LEWIS, OSCAR. *La Vida.* New York: Random House, 1966.

LIGHT, IVAN. *Ethnic Enterprise in America.* Berkeley: University of California Press, 1972.

LOEWE, MICHAEL. *Everyday Life in Early Imperial China.* New York: Harper & Row Perennial Library, 1968.

LONDON, JOAN, and HENRY ANDERSON. *So Shall You Reap.* New York: Crowell, 1970.

LOWELL, JOSEPHINE SHAW. "One Means of Preventing Pauperism." In *Proceedings of the National Conference of Charities and Corrections [NCCC] Chicago, 1879.* Boston: G. Ellis, 1879.

LUBOVE, ROY. *The Professional Altruist.* Cambridge, Mass.: Harvard University Press, 1965.

MACAROV, DAVID. *The Design of Social Welfare.* New York: Holt, Rinehart and Winston, 1978.

MACAROV, DAVID. *Work and Welfare: The Unholy Alliance.* Beverly Hills, Calif.: Sage Publications, 1980.

MALTHUS, T.R. *Essay on Population,* Vol. II. London: J. M. Dent, 1914.

MANDELL, BETTY. "Welfare and Totalitarianism: Part I. Theoretical Issues." *Social Work,* January, 1971.

MARDEN, CHARLES F., and GLADYS MEYER. *Minorities in American Society.* New York: American Book, 1962.

MARSHALL, ALFRED. *Principles of Economics,* 8th ed. New York: Macmillan Publishing Co., 1920.

MASON, JAN, JOHN S. WODARSKI, T.M. JIM PARHAM. "Work and Welfare: A Reevaluation of AFDC." *Social Work,* May–June 1985.

MATHEWS, JANE DeHART. "The New Feminism and the Dynamics of Social Change." In Kerber and Mathews, eds. *Women's America.* New York: Oxford University Press, 1982, pp. 397–425.

McHENRY, ROBERT, ed. *Famous American Women: A Biographical Dictionary from Colonial Times to the Present.* New York: Dover Publications, 1980.

McMASTER, JOHN B. *A History of the People of the United States.* New York: D. Appleton, 1895.

MENCHER, SAMUEL. *From Poor Law to Poverty Programs.* Pittsburgh: University of Pittsburgh Press, 1967.

MERCHANT, CAROLYN. *The Death of Nature: Women, Ecology, and the Scientific Revolution.* San Francisco: Harper & Row, 1980.

MILLER, DOROTHY C. "AFDC: Mapping a Strategy for Tomorrow." *Social Service Review,* December 1983, pp. 599–613.

MIRINGOFF, MARC L., and SANDRA OPDYCKE. *American Social Welfare: Reassessment and Reform.* Englewood Cliffs, N.J.: Prentice Hall, 1986.

MOHR, JAMES C. "Patterns of Abortion and the Response of American Physicians." In Judith Walzer Leavitt, ed. *Women and Health in America.* Madison: University of Wisconsin Press, 1984.

MORGAN, JAMES N., with the assistance of NORMA MEYERS and BARBARA BALDWIN. *Income and Welfare in the United States.* University of Michigan Survey Research Study. New York: McGraw-Hill Book Co., 1962.

MORRIS, RICHARD B. *Government and Labor in Early America.* New York: Columbia University Press, 1946.

MORRIS, ROBERT. *Social Policy of the American Welfare State.* New York: Harper & Row, 1979.

NATIONAL ASSOCIATION OF SOCIAL WORKERS. *Encyclopedia of Social Work,* Vol. II. New York: NASW, 1977.

NELSON, BARBARA J. "Women's Poverty and Women's Citizenship: Some Political Consequences of Economic Marginality." *Signs: Journal of Women in Culture and Society,* Vol. 10, no. 2. (Winter 1984), pp. 209–231.

NEWMAN, PAULINE. "Triangle Shirt Waist Fire." In Kerber and Mathews, eds. *Women's America.* New York: Oxford University Press, 1982, pp. 222–224.

*NEWSWEEK ON CAMPUS.* February 1987, pp. 10–18.

NICHOLLS, SIR GEORGE. *History of the English Poor Law.* New York: G. P. Putnam's Sons, 1898.

OBERSTAR, JAMES L., Chairman. "Special Report no. 99–26: Gramm-Rudman—The Cutting Begins" (mimeographed). Washington, D.C.: Democratic Study Group, U.S. House of Representatives, January 22, 1986.

OFFICE OF MANAGEMENT and BUDGET. *Tax Expenditures: Special Analysis G of the Budget: U.S. Government 1983.* Washington D.C.: U.S. Government Printing Office, February 1982.

OGREN, EVELYN H. "Public Opinion About Public Welfare." *Social Work,* January, 1973.

PALENSKI, JOSEPH E. "Race Relationships in Prison: A Critical Social Work Concern." In Roberts, ed. *Social Work in Juvenile and Criminal Justice Settings,* pp. 363–372.

PALMER, JOHN L., and ISABEL V. SAWHILL, eds. *Reagan Record: An Assessment of America's Changing Domestic Priorities.* Cambridge, Mass.: Ballinger Publishing Co., 1985.

"*Panel: Welfare Exams Wasted Millions.*" *Lafayette (Indiana) Journal and Courier,* October 30, 1986, p. 1.

PARRINGTON, VERNON L. *Main Currents in American Thought, Vol. II.* New York: Harcourt Brace, 1930.

PARVEY, CONSTANCE T. "The Theology and Leadership of Women in the New Testament," in Rosemary Ruether, ed. *Religion and Sexism.* New York: Simon and Schuster, 1974, pp. 117–148.

PEARCE, DIANA M. "Farewell to Alms: Women and Welfare Policy in the Eighties." Paper presented at the American Sociological Association Annual Meeting, San Francisco, September 1982.

PEATTIE, LISA, and MARTIN REIN. *Women's Claims: A Study in Political Economy.* New York: Oxford University Press, 1983.

PERLMAN, HELEN HARIS. *Relationship: The Heart of Helping.* Chicago: University of Chicago Press, 1979.

PICCARD, BETTY J. *An Introduction to Social Work: A Primer.* rev. ed. Homewood, Ill.: The Dorsey Press, 1979.

PIERCE, DEAN. *Policy for the Social Work Practitioner.* New York: Longman Press, 1984.

PIVEN, FRANCES FOX, and RICHARD CLOWARD. *The New Class War: Reagan's Attack on the Welfare State and Its Consequences.* New York: Pantheon Books, 1982.

PIVEN, FRANCES FOX, AND RICHARD CLOWARD. *Regulating the Poor.* New York: Random House, 1971.

PLATT, ANTHONY M. *The Child Savers: The Invention of Delinquency.* 2nd ed. Chicago: The University of Chicago Press, 1977.

POMEROY, SARAH B. *Goddesses, Whores, Wives, and Slaves: Women in Classical Antiquity.* New York: Schlocken Books, 1975.

*PROCEEDINGS, NATIONAL CONFERENCE ON CHARITIES AND CORRECTIONS.* Boston, 1881; Indianapolis, 1891; Cincinnati, 1899.

REED, JAMES. "Doctors, Birth Control, and Social Values, 1831- 1970." In Leavitt, ed. *Women and Health in America.* Madison: University of Wisconsin Press, 1985, pp. 124–140.

RAINWATER, LEE, ed. *Social Problems and Public Policy: Inequality and Justice.* Chicago: Aldine Publishing Co., 1974.

REIN, MARTIN. "The Welfare Crisis." In Rainwater, ed. *Social Problems and Public Policy.* Chicago: Aldine Publishing Co., 1974, pp. 89–102.

REITER, RAYNA R., ED. *Toward an Anthropology of Women.* New York and London: Monthly Review Press, 1975.

RICHMOND, MARY. *Social Diagnosis.* New York: Russell Sage Foundation, 1917.

RICHTER, M. *The Politics of Conscience: T. H. Green and His Age.* London: Weidenfeld and Nicolson, 1964.

RITZ, JOSEPH. *The Despised Poor.* Boston: Beacon Press, 1966.

ROBERTS, ALBERT R., ed. *Social Work in Juvenile and Criminal Justice Settings.* Springfield, Ill.: Charles C. Thomas, Publisher, 1983.

ROBY, PATRICIA, ed. *The Poverty Establishment.* Englewood Cliffs, N.J.: Prentice Hall, 1974.

ROYKO, MIKE. "Welfare Recipients Blood Money Can No Longer Be Ignored." *Purdue Exponent,* Lafayette, Ind., October 1, 1986, p. 6.

RUBINOW, I. M. "Poverty," *Encyclopedia of the Social Sciences.* New York: Macmillan Publishing, 1934, pp. xii, 285.

RUETHER, ROSEMARY RADFORD. *Sexism and God-Talk.* New York: Orbis Press, 1981.

RUETHER, ROSEMARY RADFORD. "Sexism and the Liberation of Women." In Bianchi and Ruether, eds. *From Machismo to Mutuality: Essays on Sexism and Woman-Man Liberation.* New York: Paulist Press, 1976.

RUETHER, ROSEMARY, "Misogynism and Virginal Feminism in the Fathers of the Church," in Ruether, ed. *Religion and Sexism.* New York: Simon & Schuster, 1974.

RUETHER, ROSEMARY RADFORD. *Religion and Sexism.* New York: Simon & Schuster, 1974.

RULE, JAMES. *Insight and Social Betterment: Applied Social Science.* New York: Oxford Press, 1978.

RUSSO, FRANCIS X., and GEORGE WILLIS. *Human Services in America.* Englewood Cliffs, N.J.: Prentice Hall, 1986.

RYAN, WILLIAM O. *Blaming the Victim.* New York: Pantheon Books, 1971.

SAFILIOS-ROTHSCHILD, CONSTANTINA. "The Study of Family Power Structure: A Review 1960–1969." *Journal of Marriage and the Family,* Vol. 32, no. 4. (November, 1970), pp. 539–551.

SAGGS. H. W. F. *Everyday Life in Babylonia and Assyria,* 2nd ed. New York: G. P. Putnam's Sons, 1967.

SANDS, ROBERTA. "The DSM-III and Psychiatric Nosology: A Critique from the Labelling Perspective." *California Sociologist,* Vol. 6, no. 1 (Winter 1983), pp. 77–87.

SARRI, ROSEMARY. *Under Lock and Key.* Ann Arbor, Mich.: National Assessment of Juvenile Delinquency, 1974.

SARRI, ROSEMARY C., ELIZABETH CRAMER, and VIRGINIA duRIVAGE. "A Look at the Socioeconomic Status of Women in Michigan and the United States—1984." Ann Arbor, Mich.: University of Michigan Institute for Social Research and the School of Social Work, 1985.

SAUER, CARL O. *Seventeenth Century in North America.* Berkeley, Calif.: Turtle Island Foundation, 1980.

SCHEIDER, DAVID, and ALBERT DEUTSCH. *The History of Public Welfare in New York State.* Chicago: University of Chicago Press, 1938.

SCHNEIDER, HERBERT W., ed. *Adam Smith's Moral and Political Philosophy.* New York: Hafner, 1948.

SCOTT, ANNE F., and ANDREW M. SCOTT. "One Half the People: The Fight for Woman Suffrage." In Kerber and Mathews, eds. *Women's America.* New York: Oxford University Press, 1982, pp. 295–309.

SELLER, MAXINE SCHWARTZ. "Education of Immigrant Women, 1900–1935." In Kerber and Mathews, eds. *Women's America.* New York: Oxford University Press, 1982, pp. 244–256.

SELLER, MAXINE SCHWARTZ. *Immigrant Women.* Philadelphia: Temple University Press, 1984.

SERVICE, ELMAN R. *The Hunters.* Englewood Cliffs, N.J.: Prentice Hall, 1966.

SEXTON, PATRICIA CAYO. *Education and Income.* New York: Viking Press, 1961.

SCHWARTZ-NOBEL, LORETTA. *Starving in the Shadow of Plenty.* New York: G.P. Putnam's Sons, 1983.

SHAFFER, GAIL S., and RONNIE ELDRIDGE. "Choices," Vol. 3. Report on a series of hearings held in New York in June 1984 on the feminization of poverty, chaired by Gail S. Shaffer, secretary of state of New york State and Ronnie Eldreidge, director New York State Women's Division.

SHERWOOD, ROBERT E. *Roosevelt and Hopkins.* New York: Harper, 1948.

SLOCUM, SALLY. "Woman the Gatherer: Male Bias in Anthropology," in Reiter, ed. *Toward an Anthropology of Women.* New York: Monthly Review Press, 1975, pp. 36–50.

SINCLAIR, A. *The Emancipation of the American Woman.* New York: 1966.

SMITH, VERNON K. *Welfare Work Incentives.* Lansing: Michigan State Department of Social Services, 1974.

*SOCIAL SECURITY BULLETIN.* Washington, D.C.: U.S. Government Printing Office, April 1983, July 1983, September 1984, February 1986, and November 1986.

*SOCIETY TODAY.* Del Mar, Calif.: Communications Research Machines, 1971.

SPENDER, DALE. *There's Always Been a Women's Movement This Century.* London: Pandora Press, 1983.

STANBACK, HOWARD. "Attacking Poverty with Economic Policy." In Gartner Greer, and Reissman, eds., *Beyond Reagan.*

STIVERS, RICHARD. "Social Control in the Technological Society." In James F. Davis and Richard Stivers, *The Collective Definition of Deviance.* New York: Free Press, 1975.

STONE, MERLIN. *Paradise Papers.* London: Virago Press, 1976.

STONE, MERLIN. *When God Was a Woman.* New York: Harcourt Brace Jovanovich, 1976.

SUGARMAN, JULE M., GARY D. BASS, NANCY AMIDEI, DAVID PLOCHER, SHANNON FERGUSON, and JULIE QUIREZ. *OMB Watch. A Citizen's Guide to Gramm-Rudman-Hollings.* Washington, D.C.: Focus Project, 1986.

TAWNEY, R. H., and EILEEN POWER, EDS. *Tudor Economic Documents.* London: Routledge and Kegan Paul, 1930.

TEISMAN, ERIC. "The Last Treaty." *Harper's Magazine,* February 1975, pp. 37–39.

TIMMS, NOEL. *Social Work.* London: Routledge and Kegan Paul, 1973.

TOBIAS, SHEILA, and LOIS ANDERSON. "What Really Happened to Rosie the Riveter: Demobilization and the Female Labor Force, 1944–47." In Kerber and Mathews, eds. *Women's America.* New York: Oxford University Press, 1984, pp. 354–373.

TORREY, E. FULLER, and SIDNEY M. WOLFE. *Care of the Seriously Mentally Ill: A Rating of State Programs.* Washington, D.C.: Public Citizen Health Research Group, 1986.

TROPMAN, JOHN. "The Constant Crisis," mimeographed. Ann Arbor, Mich.: University of Michigan School of Social Work, 1974.

TROPMAN, JOHN. "Image of Public Welfare: Reality or Projection." *Public Welfare,* Vol. 35 (1977), pp. 17–83.

TROPMAN, JOHN, PHYLLIS J. DAY, and ALAN GORDON. "Welfare Codebook," unpublished manuscript developed 1971. Based on data from *Statistical Abstracts of the United States 1971,* Washington, D.C.: U.S. Government Printing Office, 1971, p. 312; and *County and City Data Book 1960,* Washington, D.C.: U.S. Government Printing Office, 1964, p. 4.

TUMIN, MELVIN. "Some Principles of Stratification: A Critical Analysis." *American Sociological Review,* Vol. 10, no. 4, (1953).

U.S. CONGRESS JOINT ECONOMIC COMMITTEE, SUBCOMMITTEE ON FISCAL POLICY. *Studies in Public Welfare.* Washington, D.C.: U.S. Goverment Printing Office, 1972–1975.

U.S. DEPARTMENT OF LABOR. *Proceedings of Conference on Mothers' Pensions.* Providence, Rhode Island, June 28, 1922. Children's Bureau Publication #109. Washington, D.C.: U.S. Government Printing Office, 1922.

UNITED WAY OF INDIANA. "Capital Steps." Indianapolis, 1986.

UNIVERSITY OF MICHIGAN SCHOOL OF SOCIAL WORK WORKING PAPER I, FOR INTERDISCIPLINARY SEMINAR. "The Future of Social Work: Implications for Social Work Education." Fall 1986.

WARNER, AMOS G., STUART A. QUEEN, and ERNEST B. HARPER. *American Charities and Social Work,* 4th ed. New York: T. Y. Crowell, 1930.

WATSON, FRANK DEKKER. *The Charity Organization Movement in the United States.* New York: Arno Press and *The New York Times,* 1971. Originally printed by Macmillan, 1922.

WAXMAN, CHAIM. *The Stigma of Poverty,* 2nd ed. New York: Pergamon Press, 1983.

WEBER, MAX. *Ancient Judaism.* New York: Macmillan Co, 1952.

WEBER, MAX. *The Protestant Ethic and the Spirit of Capitalism.* New York: Scribner, 1976.

WEBSTER, PAULA. "Matriarchy: A Vision of Power." In Reiter, ed. *Toward an Anthropology of Women.* New York: Monthly Review Press, 1975, pp. 141–147.

*WEBSTER'S NEW COLLEGIATE DICTIONARY.* Springfield, Mass.: G. & C. Merriam Company, 1980.

WEITZMAN, LENORE. *The Divorce Revolution,* a review by Peter Shrag in *The Nation,* December 7, 1985.

WEITZMAN, LENORE. "Give Women a Break in Settlement Divorces," a review in *USA Today,* August 22, 1984, p. 10A.

"WHAT DO RICH HAVE: MOST OF U.S. MONEY." *Lafayette (Indiana) Journal and Courier,* July 15, 1986, p. A1.

WILDAVSKY, AARON. *Speaking Truth to Power: The Art and Craft of Policy Analysis.* Boston: Little, Brown, and Co., 1979.

WILENSKY, HAROLD L. *The Welfare State and Equality: Structural and Ideological Roots of Public Expenditures.* Berkeley: University of California Press, 1975.

WILENSKY, HAROLD L., and CHARLES LEBEAUX. *Industrial Society and Social Welfare.* New York: Russell Sage Foundation, 1958.

WILSON, ELIZABETH. *Women and the Welfare State.* London: Tavistock Publications, 1977.

WINES, MICHAEL. "At Issue: Civil Rights." *National Journal,* March 27, 1982.

WOODEN, KENNETH. *Weeping in the Playtime of Others.* New York: McGraw-Hill Book Co., 1976.

WOODROOFE, K. *From Charity to Social Work.* London: Routledge and Kegan Paul, 1962.

YANG, MARTIN M. C. *Chinese Social Structure.* Taipei, Taiwan: National Book Co., 1969.

YATES, J. V. N. "Report of the Secretary of State in 1824 on the Relief and Settlement of the Poor," reprinted in the 34th Annual Report of the State Board of Charities of the State of New York (1900), Vol. I., pp. 939–963.

ZASTROW, CHARLES. *Introduction to Social Welfare Institutions,* rev. ed. Homewood, Ill.: The Dorsey Press, 1982.

ZASTROW, CHARLES. *The Practice of Social Work,* 2nd ed. Homewood, Ill.: The Dorsey Press, 1985.

ZINN, DEBORAH K., and ROSEMARY SARRI. "Turning Back the Clock on Public Welfare." *Signs: Journal of Women in Culture and Society.* Vol. 10, no. 2. (Winter 1984), pp. 355–370.

# INDEX

Freedom rides, 321–22
*Freedom's Journal*, 189
Freud, Sigmund, 216
Friedan, Betty, 330
Friedlander, Walter A., 35
*Friendly Visiting Among the Poor* (Richmond), 232
Functionalism, 38–39
Funds to Parents Act, 255
Future, 426–34

Gadsden Purchase, 191
Gallaudet, Thomas H., 179
Galper, Jeffrey, 119, 198, 288, 419
Gannett, Deborah Sampson, 153
Garment industry, 206
Garrison, William Lloyd, 189, 192
Gartner, Alan, 417
Garvey, Amy Jacques, 246
Garvey, Marcus Moziah, 242, 246
*Gault* decision, 332
Gay Liberation, 378–79
Geary Act of 1892, 209
General Assistance, 397
General Federation of Women's Clubs, 215
Generalist social workers, 56
Genocide, 182–84, 211
Gentlemen's Agreement, 243
Ghost Dance, 210–11
G. I. Bill of Rights, 303
Gilbert, Neil, 32, 37, 57
Gilbert, Thomas, 116
Gilder, George, 407, 416
Golden Triangle, 150–52
Gompers, Samuel, 207, 208, 249, 261
Gonzales, Corky, 323
Goroff, Norman, 27
Gramm-Rudman-Hollings (GRH), 390–91
Grandfather clause, 214
Granny beating, 340
Great Awakening, 149
Greater Avenues for Independence (GAIN), 406–7
Great Society, 327–31
Greece, 76–80
Greeley, Horace, 194
Greenhow, Rose O'Neal, 201
Greenwood, Ernest, 51, 55
Gregory of Nyssa, 84
Grimke, Angelina, 192
Grimke, Sarah, 192
Griscom, John, 180
Grob, Gerald, 157
Group work, 57, 306–7
Guilds, 101
Gurteen, Rev. S. Humphreys, 220

Haig, Alexander, 369
Hale, Nathan, Jr., 216
Hamburg, Germany, 111
Hamilton, Alice, 225
Handel, Gerald, 97, 111, 113, 139
Happiness for Women (HOW), 376
Harding, Warren G., 263
Harrington, Michael, 335
Harris, Patricia, 332
*Harris* v. *McRae*, 378
Harrison, William Henry, 183
Hartley, Robert, 167
Hatcher, Richard, 374
Hathaway, Jonas, 115, 116
Hayakawa, Samuel, 370
Hayes, Mary Ludwig, 153
Hayes, Rutherford B., 208, 213
Haynes, George Edmund, 247
Head Start, 334, 364
Health care, 24
  post-Civil War, 230
  Progressive Era, 255–56, 264–68
  Reaganomics and, 402–4

Health Care Financing Administration (HCFA), 338
Health insurance, 261–62
Heffernan, W. Joseph, 357
Henry, Patrick, 154
Henry VII, 112
Henry VIII, 108, 112
Heterosexism, 25
Hickok, Lorena, 284
Higher education, 405–6
Hill, Octavia, 123
Hirabayashi, Gordon, 370
Hispanic Americans, 19, 190–91, 243–44
Hitler, Adolph, 296
Holistic nature, 59
Hollis Amendment, 268
Holy Roman Empire, 86
Home, suitable, 319, 320
Home Owners Loan Corporation, 282
Home rule, 213
Homestead Acts, 177, 184, 191, 193–94
Homophobia, 25
Homosexuality, 25, 78, 378–79
Hoover, Herbert, 270, 276
Hopewell Culture, 129–30
Hopis, 135
Hopkins, Harry, 279, 286, 288, 291
Hopper, Isaac, 182
Hospitals, 101, 173, 175–78
Housing, 162, 308, 342, 365, 404–5
Housing and Urban Development (HUD), 342
Houston, Sam, 191
Howard, John, 117
Howe, Samuel Gridley, 177, 179, 194, 230
Hull House, 224
Human Life Amendment, 378
Hunger, 402
Hunt, Harriet, 175
Hunter, Mary Ski, 3
Hutchinson, Anne, 142
Hyde Amendment, 378
Hymowitz, Carole, 162

ILGWU (*see* International Ladies' Garment Workers Union)
Illegitimacy, 115
Immigration
  1970s, 272, 371, 373
  post-Civil War, 207, 209
  pre-Civil War, 160–61
  Progressive Era, 242, 265
Impotent poor, 114–15, 146
Income, 13–14, 20
  Reaganomics and, 389, 392–96
  Social Security and, 355
Incrementalism, 430, 432
Indenture, 137–39
Indian Health Service, 367
Indian Trade and Intercourse Act, 184
Indirect practice, 57
Individualism, 5–6
Indo-Chinese, 371
Industrial development programs, 332
Industrial revolution, 55, 120–23
Industrial Workers of the World (IWW), 249
Infants, 187–88
Inflation, 399
Inheritance, 72
Innis, Roy, 329
Inouye, Daniel, 370
Institution, 31–37
  interstitial, 31
  perspective of, 40–42
  social welfare, 35–51 (*see also* Social welfare)
Institutional discrimination, 18–26
Institutionalization, 169, 220, 229
Insurance
  health, 261–62
  property, 151

social, 46–47 (*see also* Social insurance)
unemployment, 260, 290–91, 357, 398–99
International Ladies' Garment Workers Union (ILGWU), 248, 249
International Society for World Peace, 224
Internment, 296–97, 370
Interstate Commerce Act, 205
Interstitial institution, 31
Interventive techniques, 58
Invasion, 69–72
Investigations, 319
Involuntary poverty, 100
Iron Age, 73
Islam, 94
Israel, 70–72

Jackson, Andrew, 183
Jackson, Jesse, 374
Jacobs, William Jay, 140
Jamestown, 140
Japanese Americans, 242–43, 296–97, 370–71
Jeanne d'Arc, 104
Jeremiah, 73
Jesus, 6, 83–85
Jewish Book of Law, 72
Jews, 103, 165
Jim Crow laws, 214
Job Corps, 364
Job training, 332–33, 363–64, 406–7
Job Training Partnership Act (JTPA), 406
Johnson, Andrew, 203, 212
Johnson, Clifford M., 420
Johnson, Henry, 244
Johnson, Lyndon B., 327
Johnson-O'Malley Act, 247
Joint funding, 149
Jones, Eugene K., 247
Jones, Mary Harris, 252–53
Jones Act, 244
Jordan, Barbara, 374
Judaeo-Christian values, 6
Judaism, 73–74
Junior League, 223
Justice, 179, 228, 262, 363, 365–66
Justinian Code of Laws, 94
Juvenile delinquency, 305, 306, 341
Juvenile justice, 179, 228, 262, 363

Kahn, Alfred J., 50
Kameny, Frank, 378
Kansas-Nebraska Act of 1854, 184
Kaplan, Saul, 360
Katz, Michael B., 164, 170, 233, 261
Keating-Owens bill, 254
Kelley, Florence, 224, 254
Kennedy, John F., 325–27
Kennedy, Robert, 326, 335–43
Kennedy-Johnson years, 325–43
  civil rights in, 325–27, 331–35
  Great Society in, 327–31
  social programs in, 335–43
King, Martin Luther, Jr., 321, 326
*King* v. *King*, 320
Klaits, Joseph, 104, 108
Kleeck, Mary Van, 295
Knights of Labor, 207
Knowlton, Charles, 217
Knox, John, 110
Kolko, Gabriel, 409
Koromatsu, Fred, 370
Ku Klux Klan, 212, 245, 374–75

Labor, 105–7
  child, 147, 226, 252–54
  colonial, 137, 147
  contract, 98, 121
  Hispanic, 372
  post-Civil War, 205–7, 226

Progressive Era, 247–50, 252–54
Reaganomics and, 399–400
Ladies of Charity, 110
LaFollette, Robert, 281
Lambda Defense and Educational Fund, 378–79
Langenbach, Lisa, 415
Langston, John Mercer, 189
Lanham Act, 299
La Raza Unida, 323
Latch-key children, 304
Latent functions, 38
Lathrop, Julia, 224, 225, 232, 254, 256
Laughlin, Harry, 240
Law of charitable trusts, 113
Law Enforcement Assistance Administration (LEAA), 365
*Law* v. *Nichols*, 371
LEAA (*see* Law Enforcement Assistance Administration)
League of Women Voters, 263
Lee, Porter, 268
Lee, Richard Henry, 154
Lee, Robert E., 190, 191
Legal Services Organization (LSO), 334
Lekachman, Robert, 401
Levin, Herman, 157
Levitan, Sar A., 364, 399, 420
Life necessity services, 46–48
Lincoln, Abraham, 200–201, 203, 204, 212
Liuzzo, Viola, 328
Local responsibility, 144–45
Locke, John, 120
Long, Huey, 279
Long, Russell, 359
Louisiana Territory, 189
L'Ouverture, Toussaint, 188
Lowell, Francis Cabot, 163
Lowell, Josephine Shaw, 220, 221, 231
LSO (*see* Legal Services Organization)
Luther, Martin, 7, 108, 109–110

Macarov, David, 35, 90, 160, 417, 418
McCarthy, Eugene, 331
McCreary Amendment, 209
MacDonald, Dwight, 335
Macfarlane, Alan, 104
McKissick, Floyd B., 329
Madison, James, 154
Magna Carta, 96
Malcolm X, 321, 329
Malthus, Thomas, 8, 120
Mandell, Betty, 318
Manifest destiny, 183
Manifest functions, 38
Mann, Horace, 177
Mann, Jonathan, 431
Manors, 86
Manpower Development Training Act (MDTA), 332
*Manus*, 81
Marine Hospitals Service, 230
Marriage, 10–11, 415–17
  colonial, 140
  Green, 80
  Protestant, 109
  Roman, 83
  slave, 187
Marshall, John, 160
Marshall, Thurgood, 332
Marx, Karl, 120, 218
Marxist perspective, 43
*Mary Ellen* case, 226
Mary Magdalene, 84
Massachusetts State Charities Board, 171
Maternal and Child Welfare Act, 293–94
Maternal and Infant Care (MIC), 402–3
Matsunaga, Spark, 370
Maximum feasible participation, 333
MDTA (*see* Manpower Development Training Act)